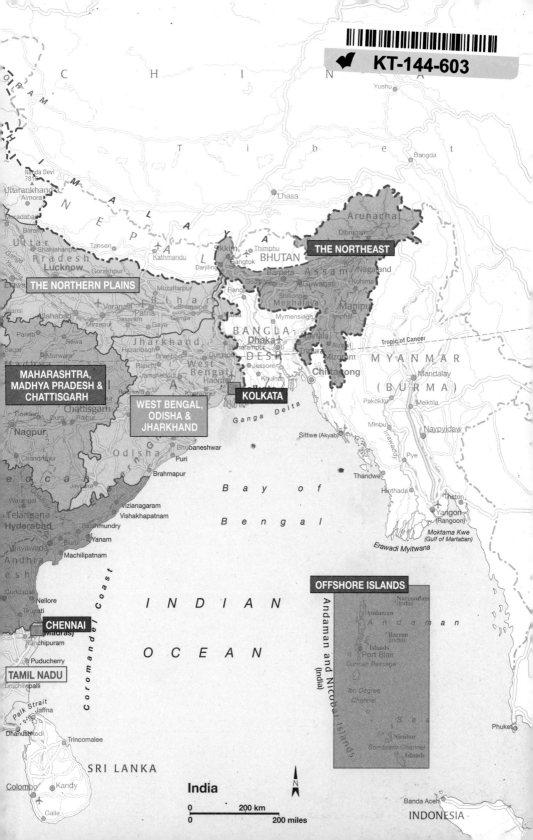

C H I N A

Yushu

GIRAM

Yushu

T i b e t

Bangda

Nanda Devi
7816
Uttarankhand
Almora

H I M A L A Y A

Lhasa

Bangda

Moradabad

Bareli

Tansen

N E P A L

Sikkim

Thimphu

Arunachal

Dibrugarh

Shahjahanpur

Uttar

Lucknow

Pradesh

Gorakhpur

Kathmandu

Darjiling

Gangtok

BHUTAN

THE NORTHEAST

Barpeta

Assam

Nagaland

Ganga
Yamuna

THE NORTHERN PLAINS

Muzaffarpur

Bihar

Ranga

Goalpara

Guwahati

Shillong

Kohima

Patna

Ganga

Bhagalpur

Maldah

Meghalaya

Manipur

Allahabad

Mirzapur

Sasaram

Varanasi

Gaya

Mymensingh

Imphal

Panna

Rewa

Jharkhand

Hazaribagh

Dhanbad

B A N G L A

Bhairampur

D E S H

Dhaka

Agartala

Tripura

Aizawl

Mizoram

M Y A N M A R

Mandalay

Sagar

Madhya

Murwara

Ranchi

Jamshedpur

Durgapur

West

Jessore

(B U R M A)

**MAHARASHTRA,
MADHYA PRADESH &
CHATTISGARH**

Chattisgarh

Raipur

Rourkela

Kharagpur

Bengal

Haora

Khulna

Chittagong

Pakokku

Meiktila

Tropic of Cancer

Gondia

Duru

**WEST BENGAL,
ODISHA &
JHARKHAND**

Ganga Delta

Sittwe (Akyab)

Minbu

Naypyidaw

Pye

Irrawady

Nagpur

Bilaspur

Odisha

KOLKATA

Chandrapur

Bhubaneshwar

Puri

Brahmapur

Bay   of

Bengal

Thandwe

Hinthada

Thaton

Warangal

Telangana

Hyderabad

Vizianagaram

Vishakhapatnam

Yangon
(Rangoon)

Vijayawada

Eluru

Yanam

Machilipatnam

*Moktama Kwe
(Gulf of Martaban)*

Andhra
Desh

Erawadi Myitwana

I N D I A N

Cuddapah

Nellore

Tirupati

OFFSHORE ISLANDS

Narcondam
(India)

O C E A N

Andaman
Islands

A n d a m a n

Coromandel Coast

CHENNAI
(Madras)

Kanchipuram

Barren
(India)

Port Blair

Duncan Passage

TAMIL NADU

Tiruchirapalli

Puducherry

Ten Degree
Channel

Palk Strait

Jaffna

Andaman and Nicobar Islands
(India)

S e a

Dhanushkodi

Trincomalee

Nicobar

Sombrero Channel
Islands

Phuket

SRI LANKA

Colombo

Kandy

India

N

Galle

Banda Aceh

0   200 km

0   200 miles

INDONESIA

INSIGHT ◉ GUIDES

INDIA

⦿ Walking Eye App

Your Insight Guide now includes a free app and eBook, dedicated to your chosen destination, all included for the same great price as before. They are available to download from the free Walking Eye container app in the App Store and Google Play. Simply download the Walking Eye container app to access the eBook and app dedicated to your purchased book. The app features an up-to-date A to Z of travel tips, information on events, activities and destination highlights, as well as hotel, restaurant and bar listings. See below for more information and how to download.

MULTIPLE DESTINATIONS AVAILABLE

Now that you've bought this book you can download the accompanying destination app and eBook for free. Inside the Walking Eye container app, you'll also find a whole range of other Insight Guides destination apps and eBooks, all available for purchase.

DEDICATED SEARCH OPTIONS

Use the different sections to browse the places of interest by category or region, or simply use the 'Around me' function to find places of interest nearby. You can then save your selected restaurants, bars and activities to your Favourites or share them with friends using email, Twitter and Facebook.

FREQUENTLY UPDATED LISTINGS

Restaurants, bars and hotels change all the time. To ensure you get the most out of your guide, the app features all of our favourites, as well as the latest openings, and is updated regularly. Simply update your app when you receive a notification to access the most current listings available.

TRAVEL TIPS & DESTINATION OVERVIEWS

The app also includes a complete A to Z of handy travel tips on everything from visa regulations to local etiquette. Plus, you'll find destination overviews on shopping, sport, the arts, local events, health, activities and more.

Shopping in Oman still revolves around the traditional souks that can be found. in every town in the country – most famously at Mutrah in Muscat, Salalah and Nizwa, which serve as showcases of traditional Omani craftsmanship and produce ranging from antique khanjars and Bedu jewellery to halwa, rose-water and frankincense. Muscat also boasts a number of modern malls, although these are rare elsewhere in the country.

HOW TO DOWNLOAD THE WALKING EYE

Available on purchase of this guide only.
1. Visit our website: www.insightguides.com/walkingeye
2. Download the Walking Eye container app to your smartphone (this will give you access to both the destination app and the eBook)
3. Select the scanning module in the Walking Eye container app
4. Scan the QR code on this page – you will be asked to enter a verification word from the book as proof of purchase
5. Download your free destination app* and eBook for travel information on the go

* Other destination apps and eBooks are available for purchase separately or are free with the purchase of the Insight Guide book

Contents

Introduction

The Best of India...................... 6
The Allure of India................. 19
Land and Climate 21
Wildlife 24
Society and Religion............... 31

History

Decisive Dates........................ 44
Beginnings............................. 48
Europeans in India 57
Independent India 67

Features

Contemporary Issues 77
Food and Drink 87
Performing Arts...................... 94
Cinema.................................. 98
Art and Architecture 103

Insights

MINI FEATURES

Conservation 26
The Adivasis........................... 34
Hill Stations 178
Gujarati Textiles 228
The Parsis 248
Indian Tea 328
Yoga, Spas and Retreats....... 386

PHOTO FEATURES

Festivals................................. 92
Hindu Deities........................ 112

The Taj Mahal 170
Indian Railways 222
Ajanta and Ellora 258
Khajuraho 276
Hampi................................... 362
Cruising Kerala's Green
    Backwaters...................... 406

Places

Introduction 121
The North 125
Delhi..................................... 129
The Northern Plains 145
The Himalayas 173
The Desert States 197
Rajasthan 199
Gujarat 225
West-Central India 241
Mumbai (Bombay) 243
Maharashtra, Madhya Pradesh
    and Chattisgarh 261
Goa...................................... 279
East and Northeast India 289
Kolkata (Calcutta)................. 291
West Bengal, Odisha and
    Jharkhand......................... 305
The Northeast....................... 323
The South........................... 341
Karnataka, Andhra Pradesh
    and Telangana 343
Chennai (Madras)................. 365
Tamil Nadu........................... 373

Kerala...................................**393**
Offshore Islands **409**

Travel Tips

TRANSPORT
Getting There **418**
  By Air **418**
  Overland **418**
Getting Around......................**418**
  Air Travel within India **418**
  Boats...................................**419**
  Buses..................................**419**
  Cars and Taxis **420**
  Driving in India..................**420**
  Railways.............................**420**
  Rickshaws and Tongas......**423**

A – Z
Accommodation **424**
Admission Charges **424**
Begging **425**
Budgeting for Your Trip **425**
Children.................................**425**
Climate..................................**425**
Crime and Safety..................**425**
Customs **426**
Disabled Travellers **426**
Electricity **426**
Embassies and
  Consulates........................**426**
Etiquette **427**
Gay and Lesbian Travellers ...**427**

Health and Medical Care **428**
Insurance..............................**430**
Internet **430**
Maps **430**
Media **430**
Money Matters **430**
Nightlife.................................**431**
Opening Hours......................**431**
Outdoor Activities **431**
Photography **431**
Postal/Courier Services........**431**
Public Holidays **432**
Restricted/Protected
  Areas **432**
Shopping...............................**432**
Telephones **432**
Time Zone **433**
Tipping..................................**433**
Toilets...................................**433**
Tourist Information **433**
Visas and Passports.............**434**
Water.....................................**434**
What to Bring **434**
Women Travellers **434**

LANGUAGE
Traveller's Hindi....................**435**
Traveller's Tamil **437**
Glossary of Commonly
  Used Terms........................**438**

FURTHER READING 439

Maps
India **122**
Delhi......................................**126**
The Northern Plains **146**
The Himalayas......................**174**
Rajasthan **200**
Gujarat **226**
Mumbai (Bombay)................**246**
Maharashtra, Madhya Pradesh
  and Chattisgarh................**262**
Goa.......................................**281**
Old Goa **285**
Kolkata (Calcutta)................**292**
West Bengal, Odisha and
  Jharkhand..........................**309**
The Northeast.......................**326**
Karnataka, Andhra Pradesh
  and Telangana **344**
Bengaluru (Bangalore) **347**
Hyderabad **357**
Hampi....................................**363**
Chenai (Madras) **368**
Tamil Nadu and Kerala.........**374**
Lakshadweep **410**
Andaman and
  Nicobar Islands **412**
Inside front cover India
Inside back cover Delhi

THE BEST OF INDIA: TOP ATTRACTIONS

Discover the very best that India has to offer, from the bright lights of Mumbai and colourful Rajasthani cities to ancient ruins and the cool heights of the Himalayas.

△ **Kerala.** The intense greens of the Kerala backwaters, overhung by innumerable coconut palms, encapsulate tropical India like nowhere else. See page 406.

▽ **Udaipur.** One of India's most romantic locations, Udaipur is centred on its famous lake and overlooked by one of the most resplendent Rajput forts in Rajasthan. See page 214.

▽ **Jaisalmer.** The desert citadel of Jaisalmer, with its golden sandstone fort and wonderful havelis, is the oldest Rajput capital. It also has some beautiful and ornate Jain temples, and is the base for excursions into the Thar Desert. See page 220.

▽ **The Taj Mahal.** It is India's most recognisable sight. This truly stunning monument in white marble is seductive in its perfect proportions and fine details. See page 170.

△ **Varanasi.** This is the most sacred place on India's most sacred river – the bathing ghats present a spectacle that covers the panoply of human existence. See page 162.

△ **Hampi.** The ruined Vijayanagar capital is perhaps India's most evocative archeological site, set amidst a wonderful boulder landscape in the heart of India. A World Heritage Monument, the Vittala Temple has a wealth of sculptural detail. See page 362.

◁ **Kullu Valley.** Set in the beautiful lush green foothills of the Himalayas, the valley is a relaxing and picturesque place to unwind. See page 180.

▷ **Darjeeling.** A summer-time retreat for the British Raj, the city has extra-ordinary views over the eastern Himalayas. It is reached by a "Toy Train", itself a World Heritage Monument. See page 311.

▽ **Ajanta.** Dating back to the 2nd century BC, these carved rock temples lie in a beautiful, forested ravine. The stunning frescoes are some of the greatest works of ancient Buddhist art. See page 258.

△ **Mumbai.** It is the heartbeat of modern India, brash and vibrant, sometimes frustrating, always fascinating. See page 243.

THE BEST OF INDIA: EDITOR'S CHOICE

From the essential experiences that make a visit to India live long in the memory, to temples, festivals, food, fascinating cities, beautiful beaches and tiger-spotting in the national parks... here are our recommendations on what to prioritise to make the most of your trip.

MOST MEMORABLE INDIA EXPERIENCES

Tiger-watching at Corbett, Ranthambore or Kanha National Parks. Ranthambore offers the best chance of seeing a wild tiger in India, although Bandhavgarh and Kanha give a more complete experience. See page 176, 211 and 274.

Riding the rails. There is nothing quite like an overnight journey on an Indian train. It's a great way to meet locals, the rail network is extensive and trains, on the whole, comfortable and reliable. See page 222.

Mumbai at night. The vibrant megalopolis is at its best in the evening. Bars, cafés and clubs are here in abundance, with a dash of Bollywood glam. Begin the evening with a sunset stroll along the seafront. See page 253.

Khajuraho at dawn. These temples, famed for their erotic sculpture, are best seen in the early morning before the tour groups arrive. See page 276.

A Rajasthan fort. To capture the romance of India visit one of Rajasthan's flamboyant forts – the best are at Jodhpur, Amber, Bikaner, Udaipur and Jaisalmer. See page 199.

Hindu festivals. There is no better way to experience India's vivid colour than by seeing a Hindu festival in full swing. See page 92.

Camel safari. Setting out from Jaisalmer for a desert safari is for many people the most long-lasting memory of India. See page 221.

Sleep in a palace. Many of India's old royal palaces have been converted into luxury heritage hotels. See page 201.

Indian food. The cuisine in India is quite different from that found abroad, and varies a great deal. Street food can be very good, too. See page 87.

Mumbai at night.

URBAN HIGHLIGHTS

Delhi. India's dusty capital is full of interest, from the shops of Connaught Place to major sights such as the Red Fort and Qutb Minar. See page 129.

Jaipur. Close to Delhi and Agra, the pink city is an intoxicating introduction to the splendour of Rajasthan. See page 201.

Kolkata (Calcutta). Centre of British power, this dynamic city lies off the main tourist trail. See page 291.

Bengaluru (Bangalore). At the forefront of India's brave new 21st-century world. See page 346.

Chennai (Madras). This steamy southern metropolis has great food, colonial relics and vibrant culture. See page 365.

Varanasi. Arguably the most intense, atmospheric place anywhere in India. See page 162.

Hyderabad. Historic Muslim hub of the south. See page 354.

Mysore. The old sandalwood city is one of India's most pleasant urban centres; don't miss its incredible palace. See page 348.

Madurai. Towering temple *gopurams* dominate the skyline of this ancient Tamil city. See page 383.

Kochi-Ernakulum (Cochin). Reached by ferry from modern Ernakulam on the mainland, the historic Fort quarter's red-tiled merchant's mansions and godown warehouses recall the hey day of the region's colonial trade. See page 403.

Holi festival celebrations.

TEMPLES AND ANCIENT SITES

Ellora Caves. The Ellora site is remarkable for its scale, notably at the Kailasa Temple. See page 267.

Mamallapuram. The wind-eroded shore temple, a World Heritage Monument, is a mini masterpiece of Tamil (Dravidian) religious art. See page 375.

Bhubaneshwar. A stunning array of temples on the Orissan coast featuring some of the finest stonework anywhere in India. See page 315.

Golden Temple, Amritsar. Shimmering in the Punjabi heat, the magnificent Golden Temple is the centre of the Sikh universe. See page 150.

Bodhgaya/Mahabodhi. The founding place of Buddhism is a tad commercial but still fascinating. See page 168.

Orcha. An ancient treasure trove combining Hindu and Mughal architecture to stunning effect. See page 271.

Fatehpur Sikri. Within easy reach of Agra, this ruined Mughal city is a magnificent ensemble, and very well preserved. Visit in the early morning if you can. See page 156.

Tibetan monasteries in Ladak. Dozens of medieval Buddhist monasteries nestle amid the spectacular Himalayan side valleys around the Ladakhi capital, Leh. See page 190.

The train to Shimla.

BEST HILL STATIONS

Simla. The summer capital of the British Raj, the town retains a handful of evocative British vestiges, among them some delightfully stiff-upper-lipped hotels. See page 177.

Kodaikanal. A cool retreat, high above the Tamil plains on the rim of the Palani hills. See page 390.

Matheran. Perched at a refreshing 800 metres (2,600ft) in the forests of the Western Ghats, this former British hill station offers a welcome escape from the heat and fumes of nearby Mumbai. See page 264.

Ootacamund (Udhagamandalam). 'Snooty Ooty' was once a fixture on the British social calendar. The surrounding hills offer almost limitless opportunities for walkers. See page 388.

Dharamsala. Home to the exiled Dalai Lama and a large Tibetan community in the upper town. The surrounding mountains form an exquisite backdrop. See page 183.

Mount Abu. Rajasthan's only hill station is also a sacred Jain pilgrimage site, renowned for its elaborately carved white-marble temples. See page 217.

UNIQUE EXPERIENCES

Yoga. It originated here in India and a wealth of schools, ashrams and spas offer the chance to practise your poses. See page 386.

Houseboat cruises, Kerala. There's no better way to experience the special atmosphere of Kerala's Kuttinad backwater region than from a converted rice barge. See page 406.

Elephant safari, Kaziranga. India's benchmark wildlife park offers tiger- and rhino-spotting safaris on elephant back, allowing you to get closer to the big fauna than you can in Jeeps. See page 330.

Bollywood movie, Mumbai. Catch the latest Hindi blockbuster at one of Mumbai's lavishly restored Art Deco cinemas. See page 98.

Saree shopping. Kanchipuram and Varanasi are the two most illustrious sources of luxury, hand-woven, brocaded silk sarees, but you can admire their output at emporia in towns and cities across the country. See page 432.

Tiger at Ranthambore.

Kanheri Caves, Mumbai.

BEST BEACH AREAS

Goa. Mile after mile of palm-fringed sands and tourist facilities well ahead of those elsewhere in the country, plus the enduring Portuguese influence, make Goa unique. The most congenial, low-key resorts are Benaulim, Agonda, Palolem, Aswem and Arambol. See page 279.
Lakshadweep. This remote and rarely visited archipelago in the Arabian Sea has wonderfully pristine beaches and some of the world's best scuba-diving. See page 409.
Puri. A combination of a Hindu pilgrimage centre and one of India's finest beaches – though the currents can be treach-erous. See page 317.
Kovalam/Varkala. Kovalam is the best-known beach in India's deep south, and a fully-fledged resort. A little further up the coast, Varkala is much quieter. See page 397.

BEST NATIONAL PARKS AND SCENERY

Kanha. In the heart of the Deccan Plateau of central India, the Kanha area provided the inspiration for Rudyard Kipling's *Jungle Book*. The beautiful forests and grasslands of the park are some of the best places in India to see tigers, and a wealth of other wildlife. See page 274.
Kaziranga. Last stronghold on the Indian one-horned rhino, this world-famous park on the floodplains of the Brahmaputra in Assam is one of the few places in the subcontinent where you can track tigers on elephant back. See page 330.
Corbett. Another prime tiger-spotting location, this time in the beautiful Himalayan foothills. Named after Jim Corbett, tiger hunter turned conservationist. See page 176.

Periyar. High in the Western Ghats of Kerala, Periyar has a superb setting and is one of the best places to sight wild elephants. See page 402.
Kullu Valley to Leh. The spectacular road route from the lush Kullu Valley up to the arid heights of Leh is one of India's great journeys. See page 180.
Sikkim. With the gleaming snowfields of Kanchenjunga on the horizon, this remote Himalayan region has some of the most magnificent scenery anywhere in the world. See page 323.
Ranthambore. Aside from its relative high tiger density, this reserve in Rajasthan is dotted with pretty lakeside ruins that make an irresistibly photogenic backdrop for photographing wildlife. See page 211.

Well-preserved ruins at Fatehpur Sikri.

Goa is famous for its beaches.

OFF THE BEATEN TRACK

Gujarat. Most travellers skip Gujarat en route between Mumbai and Rajasthan. This is a mistake – the state has a great deal to offer from other-worldly salt flats to superb hilltop temples. See page 225.

The Northeast. Almost cut off from the rest of India by Bangladesh, the northeastern hill states are a fascinating mosaic of different ethnic groups and landscapes, ranging from ice peaks to jungles. See page 323.

Andaman Islands. A two-hour flight east of Chennai (Madras), the Andamans are home to a fascinating minority culture, wild forests and pristine, coral-fringed beaches. See page 411.

Madhya Pradesh. The best known sights are Khajuraho and Kanha National Park, but other parts of this large central state are of interest, too, with a significant proportion of India's remaining forest cover surviving in the rural backwaters. The hill station of Pachmarhi, Gwalior Fort, Orcha's riverside cenotaphs and ancient Buddhist remains at Sanchi are other highlights. See page 268.

Andhra Pradesh. Another large, seldom-visited part of India, Andhra has a distinctive culture and some stunningly beautiful rocky landscapes. See page 360.

The hennaed hands of an Indian girl.

BEST FESTIVALS AND EVENTS

Kumbha Mela. These huge Hindu festivals take place every three years, culminating in the Maha Kumbha Mela at Allahabad every 12 years, the world's largest religious gathering. See page 162.

Holi. The North Indian harvest festival, taking place in March, is celebrated with brightly coloured powder – bystanders are not excluded! See page 92.

Divali. A celebration of Rama's return from exile, the festival of lights is a magical spectacle. See page 92.

Pushkar. Over the full moon of November (Karthik Purima), the holy Hindu lakeside town of Pushkar hosts a spectacular bathing festival, with a vibrant camel fair amid the adjacent dunes, where desert villagers trade and socialize dressed in their traditional finery. See page 210.

Navaratri. The 'nine nights' festival takes place in September or October, and is a major event celebrating Kali and Durga in various fearsome manifestations. See page 92.

Shatrunjaya Temple, Gujarat.

TIPS FOR TRAVELLERS

India can be a daunting place for the uninitiated, but by following simple rules you can minimise the chances of being ripped off or robbed.

It's best to use a pre-paid **taxi** from airports. Black city taxis should be metered, but get an estimation of the fare before you set off.

When travelling by **rickshaw**, always agree a fare beforehand to avoid arguments later on.

Don't let rickshaw or taxi drivers take you to a hotel you don't want to go to – insist that you have a reservation at your specified hotel.

Beware of **credit card fraud**, and don't let your credit card out of your sight when paying by plastic.

Carry **valuables** on your person at all times if possible, or leave them in your hotel safe, rather than unsecured in your room. When travelling on overnight trains, padlock your bags to the frame of the bunk to avoid midnight pilferers.

Make sure you have comprehensive **travel insurance**, and that it covers you if you're doing any adventure activities such as trekking, climbing or whitewater rafting.

A busy intersection, Chandni Chowk, Delhi.

The Sun Temple, Modhera, Gujarat.

The annual Holi festival, where brightly coloured paint powder is thrown.

Fatehpur Sikhri, Uttar Pradesh.

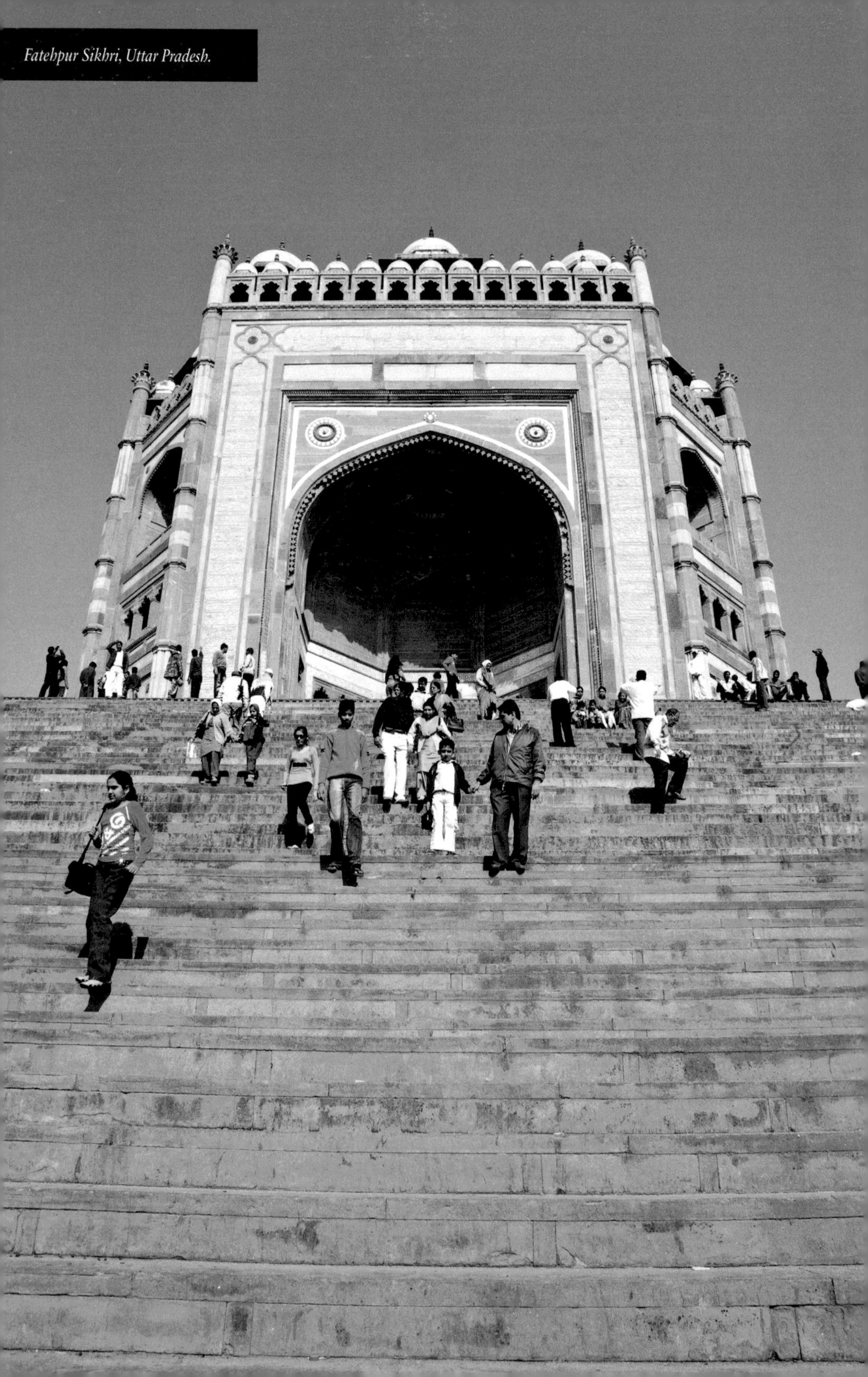

THE ALLURE OF INDIA

India is like nowhere else on earth – thrilling, frustrating, inspiring and, most of all, incredibly diverse. With around 850 different languages in daily use, the sheer profusion of its peoples and landscapes is unparalleled.

An Indian woman in traditional dress.

India's long history of accepting and absorbing new-comers, and of changing over time to express their ideas, is reflected in its open-minded and welcoming attitude, and fascinating range of cultures and beliefs. With landscapes that vary from the world's highest mountain ranges to tropical beaches, India has an almost endless variety of peoples and places to explore; the sights and sounds of this enormous country have a spellbinding effect, and live long in the memory. Despite the advances brought by 21st-century globalisation, with rising prosperity, high-tech industries and burgeoning car ownership, India largely retains its mesmeric otherness, a kind of old-fashioned handmade, homespun quality that sets it apart from everywhere else.

There is evidence, from the earliest times, of great movements of peoples across South Asia, sometimes replacing existing populations, sometimes integrating with them. They came from West and Central Asia in massive sweeps through the lofty passes in the north-west, bringing with them the rudiments of the Hindu faith, later to be developed on Indian soil into a subtle and highly complex religion. Other religions, such as Buddhism, Islam, Christianity and Zoroastrianism, have developed and been absorbed into India's pro-

A family on a bike in Kerala.

verbial sponge. With these peoples and religions have come a variety of ethnicities, art, architecture, culture, philosophy, science and technology that have all influenced India's intricate mosaic.

While it is India's variety and complexity that make it so appealing, negotiating the turmoil can be a challenge. But if you are prepared to delve deeper than the first, chaotic impression, the rewards can be substantial. Be ready to take things as they come: for things that shouldn't work at all to work perfectly, and for the simplest things to go wrong. Everyone's perception is different. The prominent, 20th-century British journalist James Cameron summed up its appeal when he wrote: 'I like the evening in India, the one magic moment when the sun balances on the rim of the world, and the hush descends, and 10,000 civil servants drift homeward on a river of bicycles, brooding on the Lord Krishna and the cost of living.'

*View of the Western Ghats from
Eravikulam National Park.*

LAND AND CLIMATE

Few countries encompass as richly varied topography, or as extreme swings in climate, as India. From the world's highest mountains in the north to the tropical south via plains and plateaux, the land is watered by the monsoon and burnished by the sun.

From snow-clad Himalayan peaks to sun-baked plains, deserts and rocky plateaux, lush jungles and mangrove swamps, India is a vast and varied land. Extending through 30 degrees of latitude, it is the world's seventh-largest and second-most populous country – home to more than one sixth of the world's people.

Mountains and plains

The Himalayas form an unbroken chain along India's northern frontier, a forbidding 2,500km (1,600-mile) barrier that emphatically separates the tropical climes of the subcontinent from the cold, arid Tibetan Plateau to the north. One small corner of India – Ladakh – lies beyond this great divide, its camel-coloured high-altitude landscapes in complete contrast with the rest of the Indian far north. The country's highest peak is Kanchenjunga in Sikkim, towering 8,598 metres (28,209ft) over the tea plantations of Darjeeling.

The great Ganges and Brahmaputra rivers surge southwards from the frozen wastes, tumbling down to vast, fertile plains in which cluster some of the world's greatest concentrations of humanity. The Ganges plain is home to almost 40 percent of India's 1.3 billion people, its farmland producing almost four-fifths of the country's food with intensive cultivation of wheat (mainly in the drier west), rice (in the wetter east), maize and sugarcane. Far to the east, the Brahmaputra cuts its way south from Tibet through the Assam-Burma range, running across its wide valley in an immense rocky corridor.

The Brahmaputra and Ganges rivers merge to the east of Kolkata, forming an enormous, and ever-growing, delta. This swampy region is

The Keralan backwaters region.

INDIA'S FRUIT BOWL

Due to the extreme variation in elevation, Himachal Pradesh in the western Himalayas offers a wide range of landscapes. Numerous rivers feed the Indus and Ganges basins, and the area is rich in agriculture. In the southern part of the state, forests of Chir pine and deodar (Himalayan cedar) enclose the steeply sloping terraces of the Sutlej River, covered with potato and rice fields. Orchards are plentiful, with apples the most popular crop. Flowers such as lilies and roses are cultivated, while the higher slopes and meadows above the Kullu and Parvati valleys, in the north of the state, are one of the world's main centres of cannabis cultivation.

criss-crossed by tributaries and home to some of the world's most extensive mangrove forests – preserved in the Sunderbans National Park, which is also a refuge for tigers.

In contrast to the rest of the country, India's southeast has not one, but two monsoons: the first from June to September, as is usual elsewhere, but then again from October to December; the second is generally less severe.

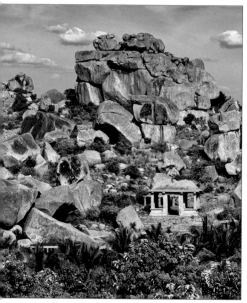

Boulder-strewn hills mark the backdrop to the dramatic ruins at Hampi in the southern Deccan.

The desert states

To the west of the Gangetic plain the land becomes ever drier and dustier. The plains of the Punjab receive moderate amounts of rainfall – although the reliability of the rains is more of an issue than further east. Rajasthan is drier still, and towards the Pakistan border the true desert, the Thar, takes over, extending southwards to the Rann (saline marshlands) of Kutch in Gujarat.

Elsewhere, Rajasthan is open scrub country, with rocky hills often capped by the forts of the Rajput kings and populated by wandering herds of sheep, goats and camels. Separating these lands from the Gangetic plain and the

Deccan lava tableland are rugged plateaux and badlands, interspersed with fields of mustard and wheat.

Deccan plateau

It was on the "table-tops" hills of the black lava-covered Deccan plateau, India's dry and stony heartland, that the Marathas built a series of impregnable fortresses. For much of its extent the Deccan, which averages 600 metres (3,000ft) in altitude, is separated from the coast by the lush, forested heights of the Western and Eastern ghats, the latter being lower and more broken. The north of the plateau is edged by the relatively low Aravali, Satpura, Sahyadri and Vindhya ranges.

To the east, forming a large part of the states of Odisha, Jharkand and parts of Bihar and Chattisgarh, is the Chota Nagpur plateau, heavily forested and populated by Adivasi tribal peoples. The plateau is also home to extensive mineral and coal deposits, which have been the source of increasing conflict between mining companies eager to exploit these natural resources, and tribal peoples determined to preserve their hereditary land. Significant areas of forest remain in the state of Madhya Pradesh.

In the southern Deccan, the relatively wet Karnataka plateau is home to dense sandal, teak and sissoo forests, where elephants roam wild. The Telengana plateau, largely within the state of Telangana further east, has only a thin cover of red lateritic soils, where thorny scrub and wild Indian date palms grow.

The coastlands and the deep south

India's east coast, the Coromandel, is characterised by long, exposed beaches scattered with aloes and palm trees, and swampy alluvial shores, merging northwards into the fertile deltaic lowlands of the Krishna, Godavari and Mahanadi rivers. Fields of sugar cane and tobacco give way to forested areas as the land rises inland to the Eastern Ghats and the Deccan plateau.

Luxuriant rainforests blanket the hills along the southwest coast (the Malabar) in Kerala, where the lowland lagoons are canopied by coconut trees. A narrow coastal strip extends north to the estuarine plains of Goa, where wide sunny beaches are lapped by the gentle waves of the Arabian Sea. The rest of the littoral is mostly rocky, rising to the forest-covered slopes of the Western Ghats, reaching 2,695 metres (8,842ft) in Kerala. North of Mumbai the coastal plain becomes salt-encrusted, with marshy lowlands rich in birdlife.

India's deep south is predominantly Tamil. The Western Ghats reach their highest point in the blue Nilgiri Hills, home to coffee and tea plantations, and wildlife sanctuaries. Just to the east are the cloud-covered Palani Hills, reaching over 2,500 metres (8,200ft). In the rain shadow of these heights is the Coimbatore plateau, which extends east to the coast near Chennai.

end of September, and continuing as late as December in the southeast.

In November, with the strength of the sun diminishing, the winter season starts in the northern plain. Until February the weather remains cold in the Himalayas and their foothills, and pleasantly warm in the plains. Central and southern India remains warm to hot throughout the year. The Deccan and the northern plains start to warm up from late February, and from March until the end of May and into June the heat steadily builds, the land becomes sunburnt and dusty, a shimmering heat haze under the blue-white sky.

Palolem Beach, Goa.

The Kaveri River, which rises here, flows east into the Tamil Nadu plains. Its fertile delta is the rice bowl of the south.

Strung out across the warm waters of the Indian Ocean, the archipelago of Lakshadweep is comprised of coral atolls, while the Andaman and Nicobar islands in the Bay of Bengal, part of India but actually much closer to Thailand, are protrusions from an undersea mountain range. There are few significant islands immediately offshore from the Indian mainland.

Weather patterns

Indian life has always followed the rhythm of the monsoon, with the life-giving rains dominating the whole country from late June to the

The intense heat of the northern plain eventually forms an area of low pressure, which draws the monsoon winds across the entire country. Starting from the southwestern coast in early May, the rains extend inexorably eastwards and northwards, typically reaching the Ganges plain in torrential cloudbursts by early or mid-June, although the timing does vary from year to year, and in some years the rains can fail catastrophically.

As these winds retreat in October, the land dries out. Southeastern areas, however, have rainy weather until January. India's Bay of Bengal coastlands are vulnerable to tropical cyclones from September to December and March to May.

For more on India's climate, see page 425.

WILDLIFE

Habitats are diminishing and poachers are flouting the laws, but the astonishing variety of animal, reptile, bird, insect and plant life in India is there for all to see.

Animals are never far away in India. Even common house pests could include such exotic creatures as a red-rumped monkey or a mongoose, besides the geckoes flexing on the wall or a scorpion hiding inside a shoe. Mynah birds and an occasional cobra in the garden come as no surprise. Camels and elephants wander in the street traffic, and humped cattle sometimes outnumber the vehicles on the road. Water buffalo loll beside the dhobi ghats, where laundry is done, while huge birds of prey – vultures or pariah kites – spiral overhead.

Big cats and bears

Lions, tigers and bears – savage and shy – inhabit South Asia from Himalayan cloud forests to desert scrub. Land-clearance has encroached on much of the former hunting grounds, and without the game reserves and sanctuaries many more might disappear. There's no chance of spotting a cheetah now; the last of these died in 1994. The government of India continues to permit the destruction of big cats that are proven man-eaters, and so-called 'cattle-lifters' are often gunned down for revenge as well. These can be leopards or tigers, though snow leopards and the daintier clouded leopard are often spared.

Hundreds of stocky Asiatic lions prowl the Gir Forest Reserve in Gujarat, the only place in the world where they thrive. Unlike African lions, these cats don't have much mane, but carry most of their shaggy hair on the tip of their tails and elbows. In the 1990s some young males strayed outside the park and were neutered by rangers, who were anxious that local cattle-herders shouldn't start shooting the lions if they dared put a paw outside their sanctuary. Striped hyenas feed on the lions' leftovers, and

A one-horned Indian rhinoceros.

there are more leopards visible in the Gir – pronounced 'gear', not 'grrrr' – than in any other Indian park.

Bears are more aloof. Himalayan brown bears are heavy-set and larger than their black cousins, who live below the tree line on Himalayan slopes. Sloth bears, found over much of India, are mostly nocturnal. All three varieties can climb trees and swim if put to the test. The sloth bear grunts with pleasure or anger, and digs for termites and other grubs. It gobbles bees, but prefers honeycomb or sweet fruits and berries. The bears are hunted for their gall bladders, sold for Chinese fertility medicine. Miserable-looking sloth bears used to be a feature in the most touristy cities, shuffling along in chains and a muzzle, and earning a few rupees for their captors, but this loathsome tradition has now largely died out. In the forests of the northeast red pandas, resembling slim, auburn raccoons, are found.

Tigers

Tiger sightings are rare these days. A census conducted in 2015 by the National Tiger Conservation Authority estimated 2,226 adult tigers in existence in India, down from 3,300 in the 1990s (but an increase from the previous count of 2011, when the total tiger population was estimated at only 1,706).

Whatever the true extent of the country's big cat population, the threat to the Indian tiger remains critical; its habitat has been drastically reduced by a rapidly growing human population, and lack of food makes it virtually impossible for tigers to survive outside protected areas. Poaching is still widespread, fuelled by an international demand for tiger parts used in Chinese medicine. Poorly paid game wardens are no match for the organised poachers working in remote game parks (see page 26).

A formidable hunter, the tiger usually takes its quarry from behind, laying its chest on the back of the animal, grabbing the neck in its canines, sometimes bracing a forearm on the forelimb of the quarry and trying to pull it down by their combined weight. The tiger's sharp retractile claws also play a significant role in capturing and holding on to its quarry. A swipe of the forearm is sometimes used to stop a fleeing animal or to kill very small prey like monkey or peafowl. Depending on the size of its kill, a tiger may feed on it for four to five days. By the end, it will have eaten all the flesh, small bones, the skin and hair.

The tiger's choice of quarry is not chosen by species. It is, rather, by size; the bigger the better. With very large prey, such as the gaur or the buffalo, a tiger will generally go for the sub-adults. When a tigress is training her cubs, many monkeys and langur are killed, regardless of size: this is the only form of communal hunting seen among tigers.

The best bet for glimpsing a tiger in the wild is to visit an Indian sanctuary. At Kaziranga (Assam), Bandhavgarh or Kanha (Madhya Pradesh), Dudhwa or Corbett (Uttar Pradesh), Ranthambore (Rajasthan) or Bandipur (Karnataka), odds are more favourable than at parks where poachers penetrate. Even during the dry season, when thirsty animals slow down and are visible against the parched leaves, luck is still a key ingredient. Dusk or dawn is a likely hour. Jeeps, elephants, and even dugout canoes carry visitors deep into the bush, and few will be disappointed by the experience, even if they only see the pug marks of big predators.

Rhinos and elephants

The one-horned Indian rhinoceros keeps mainly to the northeastern woods around Kaziranga in Assam, though a number have been reintroduced to Dudhwa park in Uttar

The sloth bear is an endangered species.

ELEPHANTS

Elephants have voracious appetites: an adult consumes around 200kg (450lbs) of green fodder a day. The elephant has few natural enemies; calves are jealously guarded by their mothers and tigers seldom get the chance to take them. The elephant, therefore, is an apex species and an excellent indicator of the health of its habitat; where elephants thrive, so do their associate species, such as deer, which in their turn support predators like the tiger or the leopard. Poaching represents the main threat to elephant populations in India, but dozens of deaths each year are also caused by train and road accidents, and by electrocution.

Conservation

Despite some honest endeavours, conservation in India has been dogged by corruption and poaching, although there are recent signs that things are improving.

Animal conservation in India has had something of a chequered history. Many of the country's game reserves were created from hunting grounds estab-

Efforts are now being made to protect Indian elephants.

lished by the British, and the transition from shooting for sport to protecting from poachers has not always been easy. One of the most renowned practitioners was Jim Corbett, an avid hunter who vowed to kill only big cats that had turned man-eaters, and later kick-started the conservation movement in India; a national park was named after him in 1957. With so much of the human population living in poverty, attempts to prioritise the welfare of India's wildlife are sometimes ignored. Corruption has also seen several well-meaning projects end in scandal.

Project Tiger

The best-known animal conservation project in India is the government-run Project Tiger. Established in 1973 in response to the alarming demise of national

tiger populations, the project has overseen a period of further decline in tiger numbers, as well as a number of unfortunate controversies. Directors have been accused of manipulating tiger census numbers in order to encourage more funding from international agencies such as the World Wildlife Fund. In 2008 the Indian government set up the Tiger Protection Force to combat poachers, and has relocated more than 200,000 villages to minimise human–tiger interaction. More controversially, in 2012 the Indian government banned all tourism in core areas of the country's national parks. Opponents of the new laws pointed out that banning visitors would do little to protect the tigers, and nothing to deter the poachers. However, following an outcry from businesses and communities dependent on wildlife tourism in and around the sanctuaries, the government capitulated.

Elephants, crocodiles and rhinos

While tigers tend to grab the headlines, there are numerous other species under threat in India; Project Elephant, for example, was established in 1992 both to protect the wild tusker and to ensure humane treatment of captive animals, many of which are employed in the logging or tourism trades. More recently the plight of the owl, sacrificed during taboo traditional rituals, has been brought to light by TRAFFIC India. Over half of the 29 species in India are thought to be endangered by this practice. One example of an animal-conservation project gone right is the Madras Crocodile Bank, 40km (25 miles) south of Chennai in Tamil Nadu. Founded in 1976 to protect the mugger, gharial and saltwater crocodiles from extinction, the park has since bred over 6,000 crocodiles, which are now supplied to zoos and wildlife parks around the world. While the initial aim was to re-stock natural populations, the dwindling habitat in India has forced this action to be curtailed after significant early success. They also undertake interesting work in the extraction of snake venom.

Another success story has been the one-horned rhino. The majority of the world's population of these formidable beasts now live in Assam's Khaziranga National Park. From 10 to 20 rhinos at the park's creation in 1905, the population during its centenary year was at least 2,050, a remarkable turnaround given the high value of rhino horns to Chinese medical practitioners. But concerns have been raised over the fact that this success has not been replicated elsewhere in India despite many attempts to do so, and that the concentration of such a large proportion of the world's rhinos in one place leaves them vulnerable to natural calamities.

Pradesh, nudging India's total of rhinos to around 2,200. They stand about 1.6 metres (5.5ft) at the shoulder and weigh around 1,820kg (4,000lbs). Adult males are larger than females, with horns that are usually thicker at the base and often broken or split at the tip (the horn of the female is usually slender and unbroken). Adult females may also be accompanied by calves. Floodplain grassland interspersed with marsh, swamp and lake, and the adjoining riverine forest, are their favoured habitat. Rhinos prefer to feed on short grasses and seek shelter in thick stands of tall grass, sometimes 6–8 metres (20–5ft) high.

Rhinos are usually viewed from the back of domestic elephants. Wild tuskers found in the jungles are feared, with good reason. Some may roam close to villages, developing a taste for alcohol after drinking the contents of a still. Others stampede through villages, mowing down everything in their path – usually after being provoked by villagers defending their crops. Yet spying a herd of wild elephants tearing calmly through the shrubbery is a definite thrill. Such enormous beasts can move with surprising silence.

There are an estimated 27,700–31,300 wild elephants in India (2012 census), with thousands more working at temples, logging camps, game parks, or hired out for weddings. Wayanad, in Kerala, is the best place to view elephants in the wild. Parks in West Bengal and Assam are also good bets.

Other creatures

A wide range of animals can be seen inside all of the wildlife parks. Look out for the pangolin, a scaly anteater that resembles an armadillo but lives high in the treetops. This nocturnal creature, found mainly in dense eastern rainforest, hisses and rolls up into an armoured ball when agitated. The rare slow loris curls into a fuzzy ball by day, then moves hand over hand through the trees, hunting in slow motion.

Mugger crocodiles are extremely adaptable and live in any freshwater (sometimes even brackish water) habitats, from large reservoirs to small streams. During extreme dry months or drought they make deep tunnels or even trek miles overland throughout India but, again because of hunting pressure, are now confined to a few protected reservoirs and rivers. Narrow-nosed gharial live well on fish, growing up to 5

metres (16ft) long in Indian rivers. In winter, they emerge to sun themselves and are more easily spotted. The huge saltwater crocodiles (the biggest in the world) are confined to the Andaman Islands, the Sunderbans in West Bengal and Bhitar Kanika in Odisha.

Of the 238 snake species in India, the four most common poisonous snakes are the cobra, krait, Russell's viper and the saw-scaled viper. Together, they cause 10,000 snakebite deaths every year in India alone. There are several species of non-venomous 'garden snakes' common throughout the region. The large rat snake

Tiger stripes are as unique as human fingerprints.

SAVING THE TIGER

Tiger numbers have sunk to catastrophic levels. In 2005 the Sariska Reserve in Rajasthan was found to have been emptied by poachers. This discovery led the Indian government to work with conservation agencies to try to save the tiger from extinction. Two were airlifted from Ranthambore National Park to Sariska in 2010 and appear to be thriving, meaning that more animals will be moved in to re-establish a viable community. Meanwhile, tiger deaths from poaching continue to spiral elsewhere. In 2012, the government of the western state of Maharasthra gave permission for forest guards to shoot on sight any poachers encountered on patrol.

is often mistaken for a cobra but has a more pointed head, large eyes and, of course, does not spread a hood. The biggest snake in India is the reticulated python, which grows up to 10 metres (30ft) in length.

Elsewhere on the plains, groups of black-buck, recognisable by their elegant antlers, cluster together. Other antelopes, such as the large nilgai (or blue cow), prefer open forest. The widespread sambar deer can be found from the Himalayas to Kanniyakumari; and on the higher slopes of the Himalayas ibex clamber freely. Brow-antlered deer, one of the

symbol. Many rare birds stop over in India, joining the beauties that reside year-round. Heavy-headed hornbills fly in pairs over north-eastern and southern jungles. Apart from the ubiquitous crows and kites, raucous flocks of rose-ringed parakeets wheel over the trees in city parks, while in rural areas keep an eye out for the bright-blue flash of the common king-fisher. Other water birds to be found in India include herons, spoonbills, flamingos, egrets and teal ducks.

The Keoladeo Ghana National Park at Bharatpur, near Agra, is renowned for the

The nilgai, an antelope species most commonly seen in northern India.

Rhesus macaques are comfortable around humans.

country's rarest creatures, hide in the dense northeastern forests.

Himalayan flowers seem to hover above the meadows, until closer inspection reveals that they are in reality butterflies evaporating dew from their iridescent wings. Many species take sanctuary in game reserves around the country, including gazelles, wild boar, leatherback tur-tles, blind river dolphins (often spotted playing in the Ganges), porcupines and flying squirrels.

Bird life

Perhaps the most iconic of India's huge variety of birds is the peacock, found predominantly in Rajasthan but widely used as a national

number and spectacular variety of its visiting species. However, in most recent years the Sibe-rian cranes that usually spend winter at the park have failed to show up. Scientists blame fighting in Afghanistan, which lies beneath their migratory flight path, for the disruption of their journey, but the drying up of the lake on which the birds depend, a consequence of local water management policy, has doubtless played its part.

Another major problem is the near extinc-tion of the once widespread vulture, whose numbers have declined by 98 percent in the last 10 years or so. At first it was thought that an unknown virus was to blame, but research-ers have now discovered a link between the

One of the major nesting sites for Olive Ridley marine turtles, a threatened species, is the Bhitar Kanika National Park in Odisha. More than 200,000 turtles come ashore at Gahirmatha beach over just three or four days in January.

drug diclofenac (widely used as a veterinary painkiller in South Asia) and kidney failure in vultures. Vultures perform the vital function of scavenging rotting carcasses (from which they absorb the diclofenac). This helps prevent the spread of disease and keeps down the population of feral dogs. The Parsis of Mumbai are also facing problems because it is the vultures who dispose of the corpses from their Towers of Silence.

Game tourism

Indian game-viewing began on a grand scale in the 1950s, and even today the arrangements sometimes resemble gentlemen's shooting parties of that era. Creature comforts are not ignored in the wild, and some tents are amazingly luxurious, though many forest houses are rustic, and safari suits are now worn mostly by chauffeurs for the middle class.

Wild animal watching in India takes patience. Many of the most spectacular beasts hide in the shadows, lone predators waiting for their opportunity. Game reserves are not easily accessible (except for Ranthambore in Rajasthan, near a railway connection). A few parks require special permits in advance, usually for a minimum group of four. In the northeast, where shy pandas and macaques hide, militants and Adivasis often do, too. The government limits visits near strategic borders or guerrilla areas. It is always wise to check before setting out, since situations change without warning. At any sanctuary, dress in sensible camouflage and keep quiet; the creatures are easily frightened. Yet with almost 350 species of mammal, a couple of thousand types of bird, and at least 30,000 kinds of insect (more than you want to know personally), India provides an unmatched range that justifies several trips.

The peacock is the subcontinent's most iconic bird.

FLORA

You will frequently spot huge versions of familiar houseplants growing wild in India. There are some 15,000 different species, including rare ladyslipper orchids, groves of precious sandalwood or pines interwoven with scarlet rhododendrons. Tangled mangrove swamps compete with casuarina trees. Thickets of bamboo thrive in the northeastern states, where it is used for papermaking. Wild flowers carpet high Himalayan meadows in the summer and salt breezes toss the fronds of several types of palm. Although the mixed deciduous forests have been severely depleted, fire-resistant stands of sal trees or teak are still found. Banyan trees with multiple trunks, sacred pipal figs and Ashoka trees with spear-shaped leaves remain quintessentially Indian. What often fascinate visitors are the flowering trees that shade city parks: jacarandas unfurl blooms like lavender-blue fans, while white magnolia flowers gleam against glossy leaves. Feathery gulmohar trees suddenly blaze bright crimson. The Flame of the Forest's large orange flowers are used to make yellow dye. Blossoms of the frangipani (temple tree) can be cream, pink or deep fuschia. Most fragrant of all are jamun plum trees, the blossoms of which emit a scent to rival tuberose or jasmine. Tamarind is another beautiful flowering tree commonly seen in Indian towns and cities. Its leaves have many uses in traditional medicine.

SOCIETY AND RELIGION

India's greatest resource is the number and variety of its people, but the social order is hugely intricate, with myriad religious traditions and institutions such as the caste system spinning a formidable web for the outsider to untangle.

With over 1.3 billion people – around 17 percent of the world's total – and a hugely diverse range of cultures, languages and belief systems, it's impossible to identify just one representative "Indian" society, let alone a representative 'Indian'. For every example of what is typical there will be another group of people whose ideas and social practices operate in an entirely different way.

The caste system

Traditionally the overarching form of social organisation in South Asia is the caste system. While this is now complicated by the emerging issue of class, caste is still the primary way in which people identify and group themselves. The concept has proved so enduring that even religious communities that are theoretically outside the system have retained caste structures. In the case of Muslim, Sikh and Christian groups this is often a hangover from their families' pre-conversion days.

Bathing in the sacred Ganges river.

DALITS AND DISCRIMINATION

Although banned by the Indian constitution for 50 years, discrimination against the lowest castes is still a daily occurrence. In the early 20th century, Mahatma Gandhi took some of the first steps in combating this prejudice and insisted that everyone must take turns cleaning the toilet. He renamed outcastes (then known as 'Untouchables') the Harijans ('Children of God'). The low castes now prefer the less patronising term Dalit (literally 'the oppressed'), which is more forthright than the bureaucratic acronyms SC and ST (Scheduled Castes and Scheduled Tribes). This terminology comes from the Indian constitution, written by B.K. Ambedkar, an early Dalit campaigner and brilliant lawyer, who

converted to Buddhism in protest at what he saw as the Hindu veneration of caste.

A verse in the *Upanishads* (800–400 BC) vividly illustrates the despicable religious discrimination faced by Dalits. Only through a life of virtue could they expect to improve their lot in their next life. In no way, however, could they aspire to boosting their current status:

'Those whose conduct on earth has given pleasure can hope to enter a pleasant womb, that is the womb of a Brahmin, or a woman of the princely class.

But those whose conduct on earth has been foul can expect to enter a foul and stinking womb, that is, the womb of a bitch, or a pig, or an outcaste.'

There are a vast number of castes, most relating to a traditional profession, although the structure is more flexible than it might at first appear. New castes can sometimes be created to accommodate new arrivals, and castes can reposition themselves within the overall structure, usually by adopting names associated with higher castes or achieving hegemony in certain economic activities, thereby gaining more power and status. Such adjustments take time, however, and it is far more difficult for those at the bottom, or the Dalits who are positioned below the lowest stratum of the system,

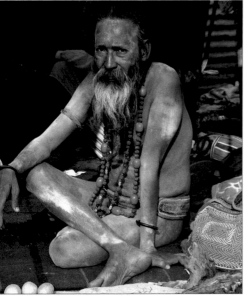

Sadhus (holy men) are dedicated to achieving moksa (liberation) through meditation and contemplation.

to improve their lot, even if they convert away from Hinduism.

India's caste system is based on the twin concepts of *dharma* and *karma* – the duties one must fulfil in this life and the effects one's actions will have on any future lives. These, coupled with the principle of hereditary occupation and strong concepts of 'pollution', have produced a highly stratified society, which, due to its flexibility, is one that can absorb new peoples without much difficultly.

The Laws of Manu (*c.* AD 150) spell out codes for life in a multiracial society. Each individual is born into a particular *jati* or caste that predetermines both profession and status, regardless

of the wealth of the parents. These castes are said to fall into four basic divisions, or *varna*.

The Brahmins are intellectuals and priests – the link between mortals and millions of Hindu deities. Kshatriyas are rulers and warriors, in charge of justice and administration. Both Brahmins and Kshatriyas are considered "twice-born" and display their status with a sacred thread worn over the shoulder. Below them are the Vaishyas, merchants or traders, and the Shudras, agriculturalists. However, the most menial tasks are reserved for the outcastes, in practice the peoples conquered by

> Two concepts govern many aspects of South Asian society; they are 'auspiciousness' and 'pollution'. Not necessarily mutually exclusive, they lie at the heart of the workings of the caste system.

higher castes and considered unworthy to be part of the system. Their jobs include cleaning latrines, sweeping the streets, scavenging, burning corpses and gathering dead animals (which extends to working with leather, making shoes and playing drums at funerals or weddings).

In the social division imposed by the Laws of Manu there was an implicit racism based on skin colour (*varna* derives from the Sanskrit for 'colour'). Within the new hierarchy the lighter-skinned arrivals from the northwest were at the top of the heap, with the darker Dravidian and indigenous peoples pushed to the bottom and into menial positions, a distinction that exists to this day.

Rites of passage and family life

The concept of caste has a great impact on the life-cycle rituals of birth, coming of age, marriage and death. Midwives have traditionally been from the low castes, as blood and afterbirth are seen as polluting. In the past, and even now among some very strict adherents to the caste system, if a high-caste person was to come into physical contact with an item or person who was considered polluting then they would have to go through elaborate rituals of cleansing and purification.

On coming of age (essentially reaching puberty), high-caste males go through a ritual whereby they receive their 'sacred thread'

– a string worn across the body over one shoulder that is a marker of their high-caste status. This practice has now been adopted by some lower castes in an attempt to raise their status and profile.

Marriage is traditionally the most important event in anyone's life in India. Fraught with complications, from caste and the negotiation of a dowry, the vast majority of marriages in India are still arranged by the couple's parents. In the past a marriage broker would have been employed to find a suitable match for a son or daughter, but now newspapers are full of 'matrimonials', and the internet has greatly expanded the family's potential for finding a spouse. For high-caste matches the demands are often very specific, demanding and tinged with an underlying racism; women are advertised as having 'wheatish complexions', and there are requests for Green Cards, higher degrees and high potential earning power. Nowadays, these kinds of ruthless demand are not only restricted to the upper castes as a pan-Indian 'Sanskritisation' encourages the low castes to ape the behaviour of those more rich and powerful.

Extended family life in a densely populated country can be fraught with problems of privacy. Most societies in India are patriarchal, and a daughter must leave her parents to set up a household with the groom's family. There are a bewildering number of terms for family relationships. It can sometimes seem that everyone in a room is distantly related in some fashion. '*Bahu*', the daughter-in-law, and '*Sas*', the mother-in-law, are notorious adversaries in the Indian family and a focus for conflicts over duty, obedience and respect.

Brother, '*Bhai*', and older sister, '*Didi*', are affectionate and respectful terms of address, even for people outside the nuclear family. It is common to call a visitor 'Aunty' or 'Uncle', and older people may call you son, '*Beta*', or daughter, '*Beti*.' '*Mata*' and '*Pita*' are terms for mother and father (often with the respectful tag, *ji*, added), and there are many other names for relatives that indicate the birth order and branch of the family.

A deeply religious country

In many ways India's multiplicity of peoples and forms of social organisation are best seen through the prism of its numerous religions. These are not only the repository of many of its subtle philosophical traditions, but have also proved flexible enough to absorb influences from newly arrived traditions, such as Islam and Christianity (the third most-followed religion in India today, with nearly 28 million adherants), as well as influencing the new arrivals in turn. While, in general, the interaction between different religious groups has been positive, at times there has also been considerable friction.

Hinduism

There is no one set of beliefs that might sum up India's dominant belief system, Hinduism.

Hindu temple offerings.

No other religious tradition, or group of devotees, is so eclectic; it is not traced to a specific founder and does not have a single holy book as its scriptural authority. There are a plethora of deities, some only local, that can be worshipped through a tradition of direct devotion (*bhakti*) or by elaborate temple rituals. The land and landscape of India is intimately entwined with Hindu beliefs, from holy rivers such as the Ganges, to Mount Kailash in Tibet – the holy mountain of Shiva – and sacred groves of trees.

Hinduism thrives on contrasts. At one end is the most abstruse metaphysical speculation about Ultimate Reality; at the other there are popular practices based on the worship of local deities. Absolute monism goes hand in hand

The Adivasis

Adivasis, literally 'original inhabitants', comprise a substantial indigenous minority of the Indian population, though their way of life is under threat.

Also known as 'tribals', the Adivasis are found from the Nilgiris to the Himalayas, and from Rajasthan to Arunachal Pradesh. This blanket

A Lamani woman in Goa.

term refers to a hugely diverse selection of societies and cultures, and is commonly used as a catch-all for peoples who are not easily categorised in terms of India's dominant groups or ideologies.

Origins

Many Adivasi groups, particularly those living in Odisha, Bihar, and Madhya Pradesh, may be descendants of the very first inhabitants of South Asia. Linguistically and culturally distinct from other contemporary Indian peoples, it's thought that their presence in the region predates the two waves of immigration from the north and west that brought the now dominant groups of the north and south.

As these new peoples moved in, they displaced the existing inhabitants, forcing them into the hills and forests where there was less pressure for land. Over time there was interaction between these groups, but due to their relative isolation, many Adivasis have retained highly individual identities.

The northeastern states have, after Madhya Pradesh, Chattisgarh, Jharkand and Odisha, the highest concentration of Adivasis. The groups who live here have more in common culturally and linguistically with peoples living in Burma (Myanmar) to the east than they do with, say, the Todas or Kotas of Kerala and Tamil Nadu.

What does unite these peoples, however, is the degree of discrimination they have suffered. Where Adivasis have had close contact with Hindus, their place within the caste system has been considered extremely low, working as agricultural labourers or undertaking menial tasks (often those believed to be "polluting" by high-caste Hindus).

Adivasi land

Traditionally, landownership patterns among Adivasi groups are not governed by individual ownership laws, making it easy for unscrupulous politicians and landowners to appropriate Adivasi lands.

Some of the worst offences have been committed by the state. Many large dams have flooded areas populated by Adivasis, providing power and drinking water to urban areas while handing out pitiful, or no, compensation to the people they displace. Land-reform programmes in states such as Kerala have redistributed land that had traditionally supported Adivasi groups. Logging has decimated many of the forests previously inhabited by Adivasi groups, and areas such as Jharkand, which are rich in mineral wealth, have seen the displacement of many people, as well as widespread pollution of their lands.

However, a potential breakthrough in this otherwise downward trend came in August 2010, when the Union Environment Ministry withdrew permission that had earlier been granted to the Vedanta mining company to extract bauxite, the main ore of aluminium, from the Niyamgiri Hills in Odisha, traditional home and hunting ground of the 8,000-strong Dongria Kondh tribal community. The Supreme Court upheld the decision in May 2016 in the face of continued challenges by Vedanta.

with extreme pluralism. On the one side, Hinduism accepts the validity of many paths leading to the same goal, and is willing to recognise the divinity of the prophets of other religions. But along with this tolerance, at present under threat, go rigid adherence to caste distinctions and custom-ridden practices. Defying attempts to define it, this multiplicity is perhaps Hinduism's most defining characteristic.

The Vedas and early texts

It is thought that peoples arriving from Central Asia in around 1500 BC brought the prototypes for the body of Sanskrit hymns and prayers recorded in the four *Vedas* (from the Sanskrit root *vid*, to know). These form, in essence, the founding texts of Hinduism, of which the most important is the *Rig Veda*. The hymns and rituals were transmitted orally for centuries, but were not written down until the beginning of the first millennium AD.

Composed between 1600 and 1000 BC, the Vedic hymns were addressed to gods and goddesses who were regarded as personifications of the powers of nature: Indra, god of

Riverside ghats are used for bathing, laundry and performing rituals.

CANONICAL HINDUISM

In the ancient Sanskrit texts, it is asserted that Brahman, the Creator, is the sole reality and everything else is a mere 'appearance'. However, the values and distinctions of human life must be accepted. The fundamentals of canonical Hinduism might be summarised as:

Goal and paths: the ultimate goal is *moksa*, liberation from the cycle of existence.

Karma and rebirth: until *moksa* is attained, all human beings are subject to rebirth. The conditions of life in each birth are determined by the cumulative results of *karma* (deeds) in previous lifetimes.

Four objectives: in addition to attaining *moksa*, three proximate ends are recognised as legitimate: *kama*

(pleasure, including sex), *artha* (prosperity and fame) and *dharma* (truth or correct behaviour).

Four stages in life: these are the stage of the learner, demanding self-control and abstinence; the stage of the householder, when *kama* and *artha* are valid ends; the stage of detachment; and the stage of renunciation, when one leads a spiritual life, preparing for *moksa*.

Four *varnas*: differences in aptitudes and temperaments are reflected in four social divisions: Brahmins (priests and teachers); Kshatriyas (warriors and rulers); Vaishyas (traders/merchants); and Sudras (farmers).

Yoga: through yoga one can proceed from physical to mental control.

rain and thunder; Prajapati, lord of the crea- tures; Agni, god of the sacred fire; the Maruts, gods of winds and storms; Savitr, the sun god; Ushas, goddess of dawn; and Varuna, god of the sea and upholder of the moral law. The hymns are believed to have been composed by *rishis* (sages) who were divinely inspired.

The *Vedas* contain ideas and suggestions that have shaped the entire Hindu tradition and show a tendency to move from plural- ism to monism. Although different gods were, and continue to be, worshipped, they were increasingly seen as manifestations of a single divine principle. The Vedic concept of *rita* (cosmic law) points to a single rhythmic force animating the entire universe.

Vedic religion consisted mainly of sacrifi- cial rituals. A sacred flame was kindled in the

> By combining religion with philosophy and poetry, the Vedas initiated a typical Hindu concept of perfection – that wisdom must combine the intellectual clarity of the philosopher with the faith of the sage and the aesthetic of the artist.

centre of a raised platform, and the sacrificer gave offerings to the flame while the priest chanted hymns and invocations. In the cen- turies that followed, the mystical and sym- bolic meaning of the *yajna* (sacrifice) receded into the background as the ritual became all-important. Every detail had to be meticu- lously followed: the kindling of the fuel, the shape of the vessel containing the holy water, the intonation of the words. The Brahmins, who performed this ritual, became the domi- nant class of society.

The *Upanishads*, written between 800 and 400 BC, represent a reaction against a perceived decline in values and seek to impose a more sys- tematic form of the religion. They are dialogues between teachers and disciples and are regarded as a continuation of the *Vedas*. The Hindu epics (the *Mahabharata* and the *Ramayana*) were probably composed in the 1st century AD. Sto- ries from these epics were later elaborated in a literature known as the *Puranas*, which were completed by AD 500.

The basic principles of Hinduism received fresh support from the *Vedanta* philosophy. Based on the *Upanishads*, *Vedanta* was brilliantly put together by the Hindu pandit Shankaracha- rya in the 8th century. This Sanskritised ortho- doxy has attained the status of what might be described as a 'Hindu canon'.

The Hindu epics

Perhaps the most popular philosophical Hindu text is the *Bhagavad Gita*, the final sec- tion of the *Mahabharata*. Krishna's discourse, with occasional questions from Arjuna, cov- ers almost every aspect of human life. The *Gita*'s tremendous appeal derives from its

A scene from the Bhagavad Gita, a section of the Mahabharata.

THE MAHABHARATA

The *Mahabharata* revolves around the conflict between the five Pandava brothers, their joint wife Draupadi, and the Pandavas' cousins, the Kauravas, who have wrongly laid claim to the kingdom. Krishna becomes the charioteer of Arjuna, the com- mander of the Pandava army. But on the eve of battle, Arjuna refuses to fight against his relatives whereupon Krishna gives him a discourse on the immortality of the soul and his obligation to fulfil his *dharma* (sacred duty). Roughly ten times the length of Homer's *Odyssey* and the *Iliad* combined, the *Mahabharata* is often likened in terms of its cultural significance to the Bible and Qu'ran.

earnestness, optimism and tolerance. As with many popular religious texts, there is something in it for everyone. The *Gita* accepts the validity of three different paths leading to the common goal of self-realisation: the path of *jnana* (knowledge), the path of *bhakti* (devotion and love) and the path of *karma* (work). These are said to equate with the intellectual, emotional and practical sides of human nature. In addition, the special path, the path of *yoga*, is also recognised. The central message of the *Gita* is sometimes said to be: work without attachment, dedicating the fruit of your work to the divine.

The *Ramayana*, whose author, Valmiki, is a legendary figure, has exerted a deep influence on the religious and cultural life of India. A different message comes from this text. The hero Rama, an incarnation of Vishnu, emerges from the narrative as Purushottama (Perfect Man). He is the ideal king, the ideal brother and the ideal son. Stories of Rama's devotion to his parents and teachers and his courage and compassion are woven into the poem, and there are vivid descriptions of the regions through which he passes.

Mythology and local deities

In India, mythology has always been close to the actual life of the people. There are hundreds of stories about gods, goddesses, heroes, sages, demons, and natural phenomena like the sun and the moon, lakes, rivers, mountains, trees, flowers and animals. They are kept alive through fairs and festivals, in traditional songs, dramas and dances, and provide the main motifs in court and stage performances, as well as hugely popular TV 'dramas, or 'mythologicals'.

As the Vedic deities (such as Brahma and Surya) lost some of their importance, other gods, particularly Rama and Krishna, probably local hero-gods that were absorbed into Hindu mythology, became popular. Vishnu and Shiva, who were minor deities in the *Vedas*, became predominant in the later Hindu pantheon.

The *Mahabharata* and the *Ramayana* are a treasure house of mythology, as are the *Puranas*. Of these, the *Shiva Purana*, the *Vishnu Purana* and the *Bhagavata* are especially important since they contain myths of Shiva, Vishnu and Krishna respectively.

However, it is not necessarily these canonical deities that are closest to the lives of many, particularly rural, Indians. It is their pantheon of local village gods and, more often, goddesses that claim the greatest attention. These local deities perform vital functions in delineating and protecting the village. Goddesses, in particular, are associated with disease – most commonly smallpox, as with the powerful South Indian goddess Yellama – and their appeasement is an essential yearly ritual.

The shrines of the more powerful, and hence most dangerous, deities are often to be found

A Hindu shrine in Mumbai.

THE RAMAYANA

The story of the *Ramayana* is known by almost all Indians. Rama, the eldest son of King Dasharatha of Ayodhya, is banished for 14 years following a plot by the mother of one of Rama's brothers (the king has three queens). He goes into the forest, accompanied by his wife, Sita, and his younger brother, Laksmana. Sita is then kidnapped and taken to Sri Lanka on the orders of the demon-king, Ravana. Rama is helped in his mission to rescue his wife by an army of monkeys led by Hanuman, who assumes a giant form to strike across the straits to Lanka, where they defeats Ravana before returning triumphantly to Ayodhya.

outside the village boundaries, where they are not only at a safe distance, but form a protective ring around the dwellings, warding off disaster such as famine or disease. The *pujaris*, or priests, of these local deities are generally not the Brahmins of the village temple, but are drawn from the lower castes.

Not only does this caste division emphasise the divergence of the Sanskritised pan-Indian Hindu tradition from local religion, but also points out differences in ritual. The local goddesses often demand blood sacrifices, of a buffalo, goat or chicken, thought of as "polluting"

The mosque at Kodungallur, Kerala, is believed to be the oldest in India, dating back to the 7th century.

by the higher castes, and the rituals are often accompanied by drumming, an activity also associated with the lower castes as animal skins also carry the stigma of "pollution".

Hinduism and Islam

The coming of Islam to India in the 12th century was a turning point in the evolution of Hinduism. The Sikh religion, founded by Guru Nanak in the 15th century, played an important part in bringing the two faiths (Islam and Hinduism) together. In orthodox terms, no two religions in the world appear on the surface to be as dissimilar as Hinduism and Islam. Islam was founded by a historical person and has a specific scripture, the *Qur'an*; Hinduism's origins lie in a speculative distant past. Hinduism is eclectic and pluralistic; Islam is homogeneous and has a definite concept of God. The Hindu temple is enclosed on three sides, and there is mystery in the dark inner sanctum; the Muslim mosque is open on all sides, exposed to light and air. Hindus worship sculptured images of deities; to the Muslim, worship of images is a sin. Hinduism has traditionally shunned proselytising; Islam welcomes converts.

Yet these two faiths met in India, influenced each other and, after initial conflict, enriched each other. Within a few decades of their arrival in India, Muslims began to consider the Subcontinent as their home. Between the 13th and 18th centuries, northern India witnessed a synthesis of Hindu and Islamic elements in almost every sphere of life. This unique Indo-Islamic culture gave rise to a huge flowering of cultural endeavour in poetry, painting, architecture and music. Indeed, India is unimaginable without Islam; its influence is everywhere, from music and architecture to food.

Islam in India

Arab traders came to India as early as the 7th century, and the first Muslim invaders came as far as Daibul, close to present-day Karachi, and Multan (both now in Pakistan), in 712. Islam gradually spread north through missionary activity, and in 977 Mahmud of Ghazni, a Turkish ruler from Central Asia, invaded India as far as the Ganges. His descendants consolidated their hold over the Punjab and, when the Ghaznivad dynasty was replaced by Muhammad Ghauri at the end of the 12th century, Islamic influence reached Delhi and Ajmer. By the beginning of the 13th century the Delhi Sultanate was established and Muslim rule gradually extended eastwards and southwards.

When the Sultanate's power declined, the Mughal Empire, founded by Babur in 1506, replaced it as the ruler of North India. One of the greatest Mughal emperors was Akbar (1556–1605), whose policy of religious tolerance brought Hindus and Muslims together. Subsequently, Emperor Aurangzeb (1658–1707) gained notoriety for destroying many temples and thereby alienating his Hindu population.

In its first phase, Islamic rule in India was aggressive, but it was not through the temporal power of the Islamic armies that the vast majority of converts were made; the mystics of Islam, known as Sufis, played an important part in spreading the message of universal love. The Sufi saints, or *pirs*, taught their disciples through *zikr*, or the repetition of religious formulas. The message of Islamic mysticism was also conveyed effectively by the classical Persian poets, particularly by Rumi, who expressed the spirit of Sufism through beautiful symbols and images. Persian, not Arabic, was the court language during Muslim rule.

Among the *pirs* who settled in India, Mu'inuddin Chishti of Ajmer and Nizamud-

by Kabir and Nanak. Born into a Brahmin family, Kabir was brought up by Muslim foster parents. He was a disciple of Ramananda, a famous Hindu saint, but he was also deeply influenced by Sufism.

Nanak came from the Punjab, a region where Hindus and Muslims had come into close contact. A Hindu by birth and training, Nanak was attracted from his childhood towards both Hindu and Muslim saints and poets. He visited the sacred places of Hinduism and also made the pilgrimage to Mecca. He saw the essential teachings of both reli-

Buddhist monks in a monastery near Darjeeling.

din Aulia of Delhi were the most influential. Annual festivals held in their honour are celebrated to this day. Amir Khusrau was a disciple of Nizamuddin and was famous as a poet in the classical Persian tradition, but he also wrote religious poetry in Urdu. The prevalent spirit of Hindu-Muslim integration was reflected admirably in Khusrau's work. The tombs of these poet-saints are still places of pilgrimage for both Muslims and Hindus, particularly at the time of the saints' *urs* (anniversary of their death).

Sikhism

This process of bringing the religions of Hinduism and Islam close to each other was continued

gions as being the same and began to preach a message of unity. He attracted many followers and soon came to be known as Guru Nanak. His disciples came together, and a new religious tradition was born. The term Sikh is derived from the Sanskrit *shishya* (disciple).

Angad succeeded Nanak as the Guru of the Sikhs, and started compiling Nanak's writings. He also used a script that was used by some Punjabis, called *Gurmukhi*, and it became the official script of the Sikhs. Guru Arjun, the fifth in succession, started building the temple at Amritsar, which later became the holiest Sikh shrine. Arjun also systematised the collection of sacred hymns and poems by Nanak, Kabir and other saints. This collection became the holy scripture of the Sikhs, known as Adi *Granth Sahib* (Book of the Lord).

The spread of Sikhism alarmed orthodox Muslims, which led to the persecution of the faith. Guru Arjun was put to death on a charge of sedition in 1606. Arjun's martyrdom convinced his successors that Sikhs must have military training to defend themselves. The 10th Guru, Govind Singh, transformed the pacifist Sikh sect into a martial community and introduced rites of initiation into a well-organised Sikh army known

Buddha statue in Andhra Pradesh.

as the *Khalsa*. Govind Singh also decided to terminate the succession of gurus. He asked his followers to look upon the Adi *Granth Sahib* as the sole object of veneration. The holy book became the symbol of God.

Buddhism

The teachings and stories of the life of the Buddha have influenced the lives and thoughts of millions of people in Asia. The Buddha was born in India in *c.*563 BC, and until his death in *c.*483 BC he travelled extensively, disseminating his teaching to disciples. His life forms the backdrop to many Buddhist teachings, from his disillusionment with the material world, to the sermons he

preached as he travelled, to his meditations through which he gained enlightenment.

While Hindu thought was preoccupied with the essential nature of absolute reality, the Buddha avoided metaphysical controversies. 'The arising of sorrow, the termination of sorrow, that is all I teach,' he said. Two philosophical principles are implicit in the Buddha's teaching. First, there is the Law of Impermanence. Everything in the phenomenal world is subject to change. The second assumption is the Law of Causation; nothing happens by chance. Apart from natural causes, we are subject to the operation of our *karma*. It follows that the popular notion of a soul that somehow survives the body is illusory. The Buddha urges us to discard this illusion.

The Buddha's first sermon is called the Sermon of the Middle Way and steers between two sets of extremes: on the ethical plane, the extremes of self-indulgence and asceticism; on the philosophical plane, the extremes of naive acceptance of everything as real and the total rejection of everything as unreal. He described the Eightfold Path of the good life, consisting of right conduct, right motive, right resolve, right speech, right livelihood, right attention, right effort and right meditation. By following this path of restraint and self-perfection, Buddha claimed one could conquer craving. Having achieved that, one is within sight of *nirvana*, the transcendental state of complete emancipation.

Shortly after the Buddha's death, his oldest disciple, Kashyapa, convened a council at Rajagriha. The Buddhas's teachings were classified

Guru Nanak (1469–1539) founded the Sikh religion with the avowed purpose of synthesising Hinduism and Islam. Islam's spirit of brotherhood helped in loosening the rigidity of the caste system.

into three sections, known as *Tripitaka* ('three baskets'). These, along with later commentaries, became the scriptures of Buddhism.

In the 3rd century BC the Mauryan emperor Ashoka, shocked by the destruction wrought by a battle at Kalinga (modern-day Odisha), became a Buddhist. Ashoka's conversion marked the beginning of a period of Buddhist expansion. Ashoka set up inscriptions throughout South Asia exhorting his subjects to follow the Buddha's message of compassion and tolerance.

In modern India, there has been a revival of interest in Buddhism, particularly among outcaste Dalits following Dr Ambedkar's public conversion. Buddhists constitute a very small proportion of the Indian population, but refugee communities of Tibetan Buddhists and Dalit converts have significantly boosted their numbers since the 1960s.

Jainism

About the same time as the Buddha was preaching his *dharma*, and in the same region, another religious tradition was being established. Vardhamana, better known by his title Mahavira ('great hero'), was an elder contemporary of the Buddha. The two teachers had much in common: both were Kshatriyas of royal descent but renounced the worldly life; both rejected caste barriers and questioned the sacredness of the *Vedas*. Unlike the teachings of the Buddha, Jainism, the religion preached by Mahavira, did not travel beyond South Asia, but it established a significant presence within India.

The concept of a deity has little or no place in Jain doctrine. The popular deities of Hinduism are accepted, but they are given less significance than the *jinas*, who are regarded as the true focus of devotion. Mahavira, though usually accepted as the founder of the faith in the context of history, is said to be the last of a line of 24 *jinas*. All of them are said to have attained perfect wisdom (*kaivalya*) through different penances, to vanquish desire and break their bonds with the material world. The *jinas* are also known as *Tirthankaras* ('crossing-makers'), referring to the passage from the material world to the realm of enlightenment.

Jainism not only rejects the notion of a personal deity, but also the idea of a single impersonal absolute reality. It regards each living being as an independent *jiva* (soul). In its mundane condition, the soul is permeated by material particles through the working of *karma*. To attain liberation, a double process is necessary: the incursion of new *karma*-particles must be stopped; and those that have already tainted the soul must be

expelled. This is possible only through right faith, right knowledge and right conduct: the *tri-ratna* ('three jewels') of Jainism.

Right conduct is seen as the rejection of falsehood, theft, lust, greed and violence. Of these

> The theme of self-conquest is supremely important to the Jains. The word Jain is derived from jina ('conqueror'). Carrying the idea to its extreme, Jainism has become the world's most rigorously ascetic faith.

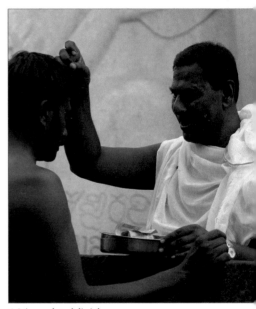

A Jain monk and disciple.

five sins violence is the most heinous. The highest virtue is the total abjuration of any thought or action that can hurt a living being. Sometimes the Jains carry their non-violence, like their asceticism, to extreme limits. For instance, Jain monks and nuns can be seen with their nose and mouth covered by a fine cloth mask to ensure that they do not involuntarily kill insects while breathing, and may use a broom to sweep their path clear.

Jains have made valuable contributions in many areas of Indian culture, including philosophy, literature, painting, sculpture and commerce. However, the greatest glory of Jain religious art lies in its temple architecture, particularly at Girnar, Palitana and Mount Abu.

Holy cow on the Vishram Ghat at Mathura.

DECISIVE DATES

Early history

c.2500–1600 BC
Urban settlements of Harappa and Mohenjodaro established in the Indus Valley.

A statue at the Indian Museum in Kolkata.

c.1500 BC
Peoples from Central Asia invade northern India. Sacred Sanskrit texts of the *Vedas* are composed.

521–486 BC
The Persian king, Darius, occupies Punjab and Sind. Buddhism and Jainism develop.

321–184 BC
Northern India is ruled by the Mauryan emperors; the most notable ruler is Ashoka (269–232 BC).

AD 319–606
Gupta Empire is established in the north. Science (especially astronomy and maths), literature and the arts flourish. Brahmanical Hinduism reasserts itself.

550–1190
The Chalukya and Rashtraka dynasties rule central India from Karnataka. The Pallava and Chola dynasties rule the South and establish trading links with Indonesia.

The Rajput Period: 900–1200

c.850
Anangpal builds Lal Kot, Delhi's first city.

1000–1300
Hoysala Empire rules the South.

1192
Muhammed of Ghor invades the north and makes Qutb-ud-Din Aibak Delhi's first ruler.

The Delhi Sultanate

1206
Qutb-ud-Din becomes sultan of Delhi. His dynasty is overthrown in 1296 by Feroz Shah, a Turk, who builds Delhi's second city east of Lal Kot.

1321
Ghias-ud-Din Tughlaq is proclaimed sultan. He starts building Tughlaqabad, the third city of Delhi.

1325
Muhammad-bin Tughlaq becomes sultan and builds Jahanpanah, the fourth city of Delhi. In 1351 Feroz Shah Tughlaq builds Ferozabad, the fifth city.

1414
Power passes to the Sayyids.

1451
Buhlbal Lodi, an Afghan noble, captures the throne and founds the Lodhi dynasty.

14th–16th century
Islam is established throughout the North. The South remains independent under the Hindu Vijayanagar dynasty.

Hampi (Vijayanagar Dynasty).

1498
Vasco da Gama completes the first ever sea voyage from Europe and India via the Cape of Good Hope. Portugal quickly establishes trade links with kingdoms on the Malabar Coast (Kerala), importing spices and cotton for vast profits. Rival powers Holland, France and England follow suit.

The Mughal Dynasty: 1526–1857

1526
Babur, from Samarkand, defeats the Sultan of Delhi at the Battle of Panipat, and

Purana Qila, Delhi.

proclaims himself the first Mughal emperor.

1540
Humayan succeeds his father, Babur, and starts to build Purana Qila, Delhi's sixth city.

1556
Akbar is enthroned, aged 13. Considered the greatest of the Mughal emperors, he pushes the borders of the empire three-quarters of the way across South Asia.

1565
Akbar starts to build the Red Fort in his capital city, Agra. Meanwhile, a coalition of forces led by the Muslim Bahmani dynasty bring down the Vijayanagars in the South.

1569–74
Akbar moves his capital to Fatehpur Sikri, near Agra, but the court returns to Agra ten years later. Akbar then starts to build his tomb at Sikandra.

1600
Queen Elizabeth I grants a trading charter to the British East India Company; English

merchants set up a trading base at Surat (Gujarat) in 1608.

1605
Akbar is succeeded by his son, Jahangir.

1627
Shah Jahan, Akbar's grandson, becomes emperor. In 1632 he starts to build the Taj Mahal in memory of his wife. In 1638 he moves the capital from Agra to Delhi and lays the foundations for Shahjahanabad, the seventh city. He begins work on Lal Qila (the Red Fort) in 1639.

1659–1707
Aurangzeb becomes emperor by imprisoning his father, Shah Jahan, in the Red Fort, Agra, and killing his brothers. Following his death the Mughal empire declines. Calcutta begins to expand as a trading post of the East India Company.

1739
Persian king Nadir Shah invades Delhi and slaughters 30,000 residents of Shahjahanabad before returning to Persia with the Peacock Throne and the Koh-i-noor Diamond.

1756–63
In the Seven Years War the British East India Company ousts the French from Bengal.

1857
Uprising against British rule breaks out in Meerut. The campaign spreads across India, causing much bloodshed. The British defeat the insurgents. Bahaudur Shah, last of the Mughal emperors, is exiled to Burma. The reign of the East India Company comes to an end.

The British Raj: 1858–1947

1858
The British Crown imposes direct rule and appoints a viceroy as the sovereign's representative.

1877
Queen Victoria is proclaimed Empress of India.

1885
The first political party, the Indian National Congress, is founded.

1911
George V, king and emperor, announces that the capital

Procession of the last Mughal Shah, exiled to Rangoon after the Uprising.

will be transferred from Calcutta to Delhi.

1908
The Muslim League is set up.

1915
Mohandas Gandhi, dubbed "Mahatma" (great soul) by Rabindranath Tagore, returns from South Africa and starts to campaign against British rule.

1919
General Dyer orders his Gurkha troops to open fire on a peaceful anti-British protest meeting in Amritsar, killing at least 379 and wounding 1,200.

Prince of Wales and Maharajah, 1922.

1930
Gandhi's non-cooperation movement gains momentum with his Dandi Salt March from Ahmedabad to protest against taxes on Indian-produced salt.

1931
New Delhi inaugurated as the capital of India.

1935
Mohammed Ali Jinnah, head of the Muslim League, calls for a

new Muslim nation of Pakistan.

Independence (1947–present)

1947
India gains independence at midnight on 15 August. Jawaharlal Nehru becomes first prime minister. India is divided in two: the mainly Hindu nation of India and the Muslim nation of Pakistan. Pakistan is divided into West and East Pakistan. During Partition more than 10 million migrate in each direction across the divided Punjab. Communal violence between Hindus, Sikhs and Muslims claims between 200,000 and 1 million lives.

1948
Mahatma Gandhi is assassinated on 30 January, shot at point-blank range by a Hindu nationalist.

1950
The constitution of India comes into force.

1964
Nehru dies. In 1965 his successor, Lal Bahadur Shastri, defeats Pakistan in a war over Kashmir.

1966
Indira Gandhi, Nehru's daughter (no relation to Mahatma Gandhi) becomes prime minister.

1971
War with East Pakistan leads to the creation of the new independent nation of Bangladesh.

1975–77
Indira Gandhi imposes a state of emergency, suspends civil

liberties and imprisons her political opponents. She is defeated in the 1977 elections.

1977–79
Janata Party in power under Morarji Desai.

1980
Indira Gandhi returns as prime minister.

1984
Sikhs demand independence for Punjab; 1,000 people die when the army storms the Golden Temple in Amritsar. Indira Gandhi is assassinated on 31 October by Sikh militants. Her son, Rajiv Gandhi, becomes prime minister, and immediately sets about liberalising the Indian economy, opening it to foreign investment.

Rajiv Gandhi.

1990
Communal and civil disturbances in Jammu and Kashmir and Assam. Religious violence in Punjab.

1991
Rajiv Gandhi is assassinated. Congress forms a minority government led by Narasimha

Rao, who continues Rajiv's programme of economic reform.

1996
A leftist coalition under Deve Gowda, later succeeded by I.K. Gujral, takes office.

1998
BJP-led coalition; Atal Bihari Vajpayee becomes prime minister. India carries out nuclear tests in the Thar Desert.

1999
A BJP-led coalition (the NDA) under Atal Bihari Vajpayee wins a general election. Fighting breaks out in the Kargil Valley between India and Pakistan.

2000
India's population surpasses 1 billion.

2001
Huge earthquake hits western Gujarat.

2002
Communal violence between Hindus and Muslims kills over 1,000 in Gujarat.

2004
India and Pakistan begin talks to resolve 'all outstanding issues'. Congress-led coalition wins general election, Manmohan Singh is prime minister. A tsunami devastates the Andaman and Nicobar Islands and parts of the Tamil coast.

2005
The first bus service starts between Indian-administered and Pakistan-occupied Kashmir.

2006
More than 200 people die and over 700 are injured from bombs placed in Mumbai's transport network.

2008
Islamist terrorist attacks in Mumbai kill 173 and bring the city centre to a standstill for 3 days.

2009
Tata launch the Nano, the world's cheapest car. The Congress Party unexpectedly records a sweeping victory in the national elections.

2010
India hosts the Commonwealth Games amid allegations that $4bn (£2.7bn) were embezzled by officials. September sees the long anticipated court verdict in the Ayodhya temple dispute, with a third of the site going to each of the three parties involved.

2011
Anti-corruption campaigner, Ana Hazare, begins a series of high-profile hunger strikes which form the focus of a mass movement against India's culture of corrupt officialdom.

2012
Hundreds of thousands of landless poor march on New Delhi, and a massive electricity black out leaves 700 million people without power.

2013
The year begins with mass demonstrations in Delhi after the victim of a violent rape on a city bus dies from her injuries. Five men are convicted of the with the murder, with some sentenced to death.

2014
Narendra Modi of the BJP is elected prime minister.

2015
India is ranked 7th among the world's largest economies.

2016
Jat community protests spread across the state of Haryana and reach Delhi, with 16 people dead and over 150 injured in the clashes. The protests end with a government-Jat deal.

The devastation caused by the tsunami on the Andaman Islands.

BEGINNINGS

India's history is epic, going back to the first traces of human culture and punctuated by invasions, the birth of religions and the rise and fall of great civilisations.

The Indian Subcontinent has many rivers, fertile soils and a benevolent climate. Cultivation and settlement have a long history here: there is a Neolithic site, with the remains of mud-brick buildings, at Mehrgarh, now in western Pakistan, that dates back to around 6500 BC.

A much more highly developed Harappan civilisation was well established by 2500 BC, with settlements in the Indus Valley of Pakistan, and over a wide area of northern and western India. Among the Indian sites are the ones at Ropar in Punjab, and Lothal and Kalibangan in Gujarat and Rajasthan, whose towns housed tens of thousands. They were built of baked bricks and well laid out on a grid system. Pottery was made on the wheel, furnaces were used to produce bronze, copper, lead and tin, and wheeled wagons were drawn by oxen. Thousands of seals have been found with elaborate depictions of humans and animals, some with the symbols of a script. Unfortunately, this has yet to be deciphered. In the second millennium BC the Harappan civilisation went into decline and eventually expired. The reasons are not known, but they were possibly flooding, salination and desertification.

The court of Akbar.

Aryan invasion

Much controversy surrounds the origin of the successors to the people of Harappa, the Aryans. At one time it was suggested that the Aryans were a race rather than a linguistic group. This view was vigorously propagated by the Nazis and also by some Indians. It is now agreed by most experts that there is no genetic evidence for this theory. The language of the Aryans in India was Sanskrit, and this is closely related to a large number of languages in Europe, including Latin, Greek, English, French, German, Russian, Polish and Spanish.

In about 1500 BC, Aryan tribes from Central Asia invaded Northwest India. Their horses and chariots, and the fact that they were semi-nomadic, gave them considerable advantage in warfare. Although there is virtually no archaeological evidence from this early period, the Aryans composed a series of orally transmitted Sanskrit religious and secular verses, the Rig Veda, which have been dated to around 1400 BC, and give some idea of their life. They originally invaded the Punjab and then spread east to the plain of the Ganges river, bringing with them a new set of gods and a new social structure.

The Vedic age

The Vedic gods included Indra, the god of war, Agni, the god of fire, and Varuna, the god of the cosmic order. A hereditary priestly caste, the Brahmins, supervised the placation of these gods with prayers and sacrifices, while the Aryan tribes each had an elected chief from among the warriors. Society was divided into three groups – the priests, the warriors and the common people. When the indigenous people where subjugated, they became a fourth class of low labourers, the Shudra. Later, another class was added who, because of their occupation or

> *Around the time of Stonehenge, complex urban settlements existed in India, with fortifications, public buildings, granaries, baths, and separate areas for housing the better-off and the artisans.*

strange habits, even the Shudra despised; these were the "untouchables". Within the Aryan family there was a strict hierarchy too. The father was all-powerful over his wife and children, boys were prized over girls, and property was inherited only by men. The Aryans were fond of singing and dancing, gambling with dice and drinking. Apart from alcohol they also drank *soma* at religious ceremonies, the composition of which is disputed, but it seems to have been a herbal concoction that was both narcotic and psychedelic.

As the Aryans became more settled and more powerful they began to set up kingdoms based on territory rather than on roving bands of warriors. Agriculture flourished on the rich lands under the plough; the population grew rapidly and sizeable towns were established. Chiefs who previously had been elected were replaced by hereditary kings. Religious sacrifices became more elaborate, with hundreds of bulls being killed as well as horses. The most important kingdoms in North India were those of Kosal on the plain north of the Ganges, and Magadha, south of the river and further east. Deposits of iron ore were found at Magadha, which the people learnt to smelt. The religion of the Vedas was supplemented by the sophisticated ideas of *karma* and rebirth in the 8th century BC.

In 326 BC, Alexander the Great invaded India. His army, consisting of 25,000 or more

cavalry, crossed the Indus river, took Taxila without opposition and defeated some Aryan armies. Moving east across the Punjab, Alexander learnt of the wealth of Magadha and contemplated an assault. His army, however, was exhausted and forced him to return home. This enabled Magadha to expand into the areas Alexander had conquered.

Mauryan India

Chandragupta Maurya became king of Magadha around 324 BC. His armies moved west and defeated the garrisons left by Alex-

Buddha, Archaeological Museum, Mathura.

ander. Even further west they took control of Gujarat, in the east they took Bengal, and in the north, Chandragupta acquired the Greek conquests. He established an empire that reached the ocean to both the east and west, stretching from Afghanistan southwards all the way to Karnataka, where it is said he passed his final days as a Jain monk.

The Mauryan Empire under Chandragupta and his successors was vastly different to anything that had gone before. The capital at Pataliputra (now Patna, the capital of Bihar) on the banks of the Ganges was 13km (8 miles) long, and surrounded by a wall with 570 towers. During this period, weights and measures were standardised, coins were minted, wages were fixed – from the highest officials to the lowest labourers – and remissions were given to those who opened up new land. The empire established and managed mines, shipbuilding yards and factories for arms. Visitors reported that it had an army of 600,000, with 30,000 cavalry and 9,000 elephants.

Emperor Ashoka

Chandragupta abdicated in 301 BC and was succeeded by his son, who in turn was followed by his son, Ashoka, the most famous ruler of ancient India. He inherited an empire

At the Indian Museum, Kolkata.

BUDDHISM AND JAINISM

As society grew, the division between rich and poor became more and more marked. In the 6th century BC, the stark contrast between the abject poverty of the masses and luxurious decadence of the few led two men, Buddha and Mahavira, the founder of Jainism, to seek answers to the question of why people suffer. Both men came upon the same ideas as answers; a moderate, balanced life would free one of greed and suffering. The philosophies of the Buddhists and Jains, preached in commonly spoken languages, won popular acceptance owing to their immediacy and practicality, and would profoundly affect the future history of India.

that covered most of northern India, with the exception of Kalinga (modern-day Odisha), and ruled from 269 to 232 BC. This Ashoka conquered, but the sight of battlefields littered with dead bodies so shocked him that he renounced worldly ambition and became a convert to Buddhism. He had edicts, written in Brahmi, the first Indian script, carved on pillars throughout the empire, calling for wise government and a moral lifestyle, in accordance with the Buddha's teachings. However, Ashoka did sometimes resort to force to impose order, and his empire expanded; eventually he ruled from Kashmir to southern Karnataka, from what is now Bangladesh to Afghanistan. Pataliputra became what was probably the biggest city in the world at the time.

Ashoka travelled widely across his empire, ensuring that roads were lined with shady trees, wells dug, and that rest-houses for travellers were established. He forged contacts with many foreign countries, exchanging diplomatic missions with Syria, Egypt and the Greek kings. This period also saw the development of Buddhism, with missionaries despatched across the Subcontinent, and a flourishing of the arts, especially sculpture. Ashoka's mark on the country is best represented by his standard, surmounting one of his pillars at Sarnath – the four lions and the Wheel of Law that are now the symbols of India.

Such were Ashoka's powers of leadership that on his death in 232 BC, the Mauryan Empire went into a rapid decline. It was confined to Magadha, which it managed to rule until about 184 BC, when the last ruler was assassinated. However, the idea of an India united under enlightened rule would echo down to modern times.

The Gupta Empire

The second vast empire in Indian history emerged in the 4th century AD. It too covered a large part of South Asia, though not as large as the Mauryan Empire. This was the Gupta Empire, which ruled northern India from about AD 320 to AD 700. Orthodox Hinduism reasserted itself against the heretical sects that had sprung up, but Buddhists and Brahmins lived in peaceful coexistence. This was a time of considerable achievements in literature, science and the arts, during which exquisite sculptures, particularly of the Buddha, were carved. The playwright Kalidasa produced his great Sanskrit plays, including the masterpiece *Shakuntala*.

The Guptas opened up commerce with China and Southeast Asia, with ships sailing through the Straits of Malacca to Indonesia. It was not only Indian goods which were exported at this time; Hinduism and Buddhism

> The Iron Pillar, erected in Delhi in the 4th century, still stands today, upright and without trace of rust, evidence of the Gupta's considerable knowledge of metallurgy.

spread east to places where they can be found today, like in Bali, and the large number of Buddhists who went to China were so successful that in 397 Buddhism became the state religion.

Feudal society

The Gupta era was a period of high cultural achievement, but there were also defects. The Guptas had a much less centralised administration than the Mauryans, and many decisions were taken locally. It became common to assign land, and the tax revenue from it, to Hindu priests, the Brahmins, or to provincial officials, which tended to put them outside central control; the owners had the right to as much as one-third or even half of the crop produced by the cultivators. These changes marked the beginnings of a feudal society. The position of women deteriorated, early and child marriages were advocated, while widows were urged to remain celibate. It was during this time that the religious self-immolation of widows, known as *sati*, began. The position of those at the bottom of society also deteriorated as laws were increasingly biased against the Shudras. The "untouchables" had to announce their arrival at the market in advance so that others could avoid them.

In the 5th century the now weakened Gupta Empire was attacked from the northwest by nomadic tribes from Central Asia, the Huns.

The South

The people of South India were Dravidians, speaking languages that bore no relationship to those of the north. It is presumed that they predate the arrival of the Aryans; little is known of their early history, but they were

helped by the opening up of trade routes, by land and sea, to distant markets. They were fortunate in having produce, such as pearls and pepper, which was in great demand, bringing Romans to their ports, as well as traders from Southeast Asia and China. Although the region lacked the great flood plains of the north, the Dravidians developed sophisticated irrigation systems that boosted agricultural productivity, and with their wealth they developed advanced kingdoms.

The early trade links of southern India brought Christianity in to the 1st century. It

Sculpture and Buddhist stupa.

THE GOLDEN AGE

The time of the Gupta Empire (from around AD 320 to 700) is referred to by some scholars as the Golden Age of India, akin to the Han and Tang dynasties and the Roman Empire. It was during the Gupta's reign that the classical Hindu temple emerged. Some of the finest examples still survive at Deogarh and Aihole. Temples were dedicated to the increasingly popular deities of Shiva and Vishnu; the goddesses Durga, Parvati and Lakshmi became generally worshipped. Animal sacrifice was largely discontinued, and meat-eating gave way to vegetarianism. It was at this time that the Buddhist caves at Ajanta were painted.

is believed that St Thomas the Apostle arrived on the Kerala coast in AD 52 and on a second visit died in Tamil Nadu. In the 6th century, Christian missionaries from the Middle East made further conversions. The mechanism of how Vedic traditions and later Hindu rituals reached the south is disputed, but one theory is that they came on the trade routes. It is known that both Buddhism and Jainism had many adherents until the 7th century, but when the Pallava king transferred his patronage to Shavism, the worship of the Hindu god Shiva, the Hindus gained ground. The

had established itself at Ghazni in Afghanistan in the 10th century, and in 997, Mahmud of Ghazni started making annual raids into India. His own kingdom was a centre of culture, but his armies looted, killed and raped without mercy. They made a point of attacking Hindu temples, taking their treasures and smashing their idols. Mahmud took possession of the Punjab, and further raids by other Muslim rulers followed. In the 12th century, Muhammad of Ghur took Lahore and Delhi, although the Rajput dynasties of north India never completely surrendered.

The caves at Ajanta (2nd century BC).

priestly caste of Brahmins became politically and culturally dominant, and the position of the lower castes, who were excluded from the temples, deteriorated further. In opposition, a separate Tamil cult of the Hindu gods arose that was followed by large numbers of the lower castes.

Arab traders brought Islam to what is now Kerala, and the first of many mosques were built in the 7th century. There was no conflict with the Hindus or Christians – a pattern of peaceful coexistence that was to continue.

The Sultanates

In the north the arrival of Islam was extremely violent. A Turkish Islamic dynasty

Buddhist monasteries were attacked by the Muslims with such fervour that Buddhism was almost extinguished in India, the land of its birth. The first mosque in North India, the "Might of Islam" at the Qutb Minar in Delhi, was completed in 1198 and still stands. It was constructed from the remains of 27 Hindu and Jain temples, whose decorations can still be seen. A new state was established in 1206 which came to be known as the Delhi Sultanate; it would pass down through five dynasties and last for 320 years.

During the Sultanate the main tax was on the cultivators of the land, who usually had to give up half their crop. There was also a poll tax, the *jizya*, levied on non-Muslims, which meant that many people converted to Islam. In addition, thousands of those who were captured in the wars were enslaved and forcibly converted.

A series of rebellions led to the break-up of the Delhi Sultanate during the rule of Muhammad bin Tughlaq (from 1325–51). Bengal

The Sultanates introduced new styles of architecture: minarets, as at Qutb Minar; the perfect round dome on a square or rectangular base; and the true arch.

The arrival of the Mughals

The collapse of the Delhi Sultanate opened the way for a new force from the north. In 1398 a Mongol army under the command of Timur (Tamburlaine) crossed the Indus river. Having already taken Baghdad and plundered much of Russia, he marched towards Delhi, destroying towns and taking 50,000 prisoners as slaves. At the battle for Delhi, Timur stampeded the enemy's elephants with burning bundles of grass tied to the backs of camels and buffaloes, and a rout ensued. Delhi was looted and burnt, while

The Qutb Minar, Delhi, built in the 13th century and still the tallest free-standing minaret in the world.

declared independence, and two new kingdoms were established in the south. A Muslim official set up an independent Bahmani kingdom, with its capital at Gulbarga, and the other kingdom was Vija yanagar.

The founder of Vijayanagar was Harihara I, who ruled from 1336–57. He had converted to Islam so as to serve as a governor for the Delhi Sultanate. Sensing its weakness, he reconverted to Hinduism and set up a new empire with the help of Hindu warriors who had been forced south by the Sultanate. The empire expanded and was to last for 200 years. Proceeds from spices and cotton financed the construction of a spectacular capital at Hampi, whose ruins can still be seen today.

MUGHAL EMPIRE

The time of the great Mughals was a time of great art, poetry and architecture. Akbar managed to establish religious tolerance, although other Mughals were not so benign. The central fault of the empire was in its administration of the land. Many officials took everything they could from the peasants, and when they died their wealth reverted to the emperor. While technology was transforming the outside world, the Indian economy stagnated, drained by Aurangzeb's endless military campaigns in the Deccan, and by the inexorable rise of the British East India Company in the eighteenth century.

neighbouring rulers bought off invasion by sending tributes. Craftsmen were rounded up and packed off to embellish Timur's capital at Samarkand. A few days later, laden with booty, Timur began the journey home, leaving behind him devastation and famine. It would be more than 100 years before the Mongols, or the Mughals as they became known, would return to Delhi.

Babur, the first of the Mughal emperors of India, was born in 1483. On his father's side he was descended from Timur, on his mother's from Jenghiz Khan. He was a petty prince in

Vijayanagar ruins at Hampi.

the empire assembled by Timur. Based in Kabul in Afghanistan, he acquired artillery and Turkish gunners and then marched into India with 12,000 men. They defeated the Sultan of Delhi's army at Panipat in 1526, and within a few days he occupied Delhi and Agra. The following year he defeated an army of Hindu princes from Rajasthan. He died at Agra in 1530 and was eventually buried at Kabul.

Akbar

It was during the reign of Babur's grandson Akbar (1556–1605) that the basic institutions and policies of the empire were framed. A series of campaigns against the Hindu rulers of Rajasthan brought most of that province under Akbar's control, and despite all the bitter fighting, Akbar proved pragmatic in victory. He allowed the Hindu rulers to continue in power provided that they recognised his supremacy. To cement these ties he took several of their daughters as wives, and, unlike previous Muslim rulers, he allowed them to continue to practise Hinduism.

There were two categories of land in Akbar's empire. Some land was under the crown, which collected the tax on the peasants, while the rest was assigned to the empire's military and civil officials, for them to take the revenue in lieu of salary. The cultivator normally had to give one-third of his harvest, which was collected in cash at local prices. This system had been much abused in the past, but Akbar ensured that the official assessment was rarely exceeded. He also gave tax concessions to those who opened up new land, which considerably expanded production and the amount of revenue collected.

Despite having 300 wives, Akbar had produced no children. He visited a Sufi mystic at Fatehpur Sikri, 32km (20 miles) southwest of Agra, who predicted he would have three sons. When this was fulfilled, Akbar moved his capital there, building a magnificent palace.

Akbar used religion to consolidate his position, realising that any dynasty that wanted to rule India needed support from both Hindus and Muslims. In his numerous buildings at Fatehpur Sikri and Agra, there is an exquisite assimilation of Islamic and Hindu architectural styles. He abolished the *jizya*, the tax on non-Muslims, and he introduced

MUGHAL EMPEROR AKBAR

The greatest Mughal is said to have been Akbar, who inherited the throne in 1556 when barely in his teens and went on to rule for 49 years and build an empire that lasted two centuries more. He controlled virtually all of North and Central India and most of Afghanistan. Akbar became a patron of literature and the arts, even though he was illiterate. He had 300 wives and 5,000 concubines. Rajputs were permitted to keep their kingdoms and in turn they happily supplied soldiers to this Mughal overlord. Akbar received ambassadors from Elizabethan England and Jesuit priests from Portugal, and synthesised a new religion with himself as God King.

Hindu festivals, such as Divali, to his court. In order to liberate himself from the Muslim clerics, Akbar made himself the arbiter of their disputes, and he began to move away from orthodox Islam. Searching for enlightenment, he discussed religion with Hindus, Jains, Zoroastrians and Jews, and even with Portuguese priests.

Although only semi-literate, Akbar was fascinated by books. He commissioned a comprehensive history of his reign, and everything that occurred in his court was recorded in minute detail. He had works in Sanskrit

by birth he was three-quarters Hindu, he took no Hindu wives, he ordered the destruction of all new Hindu temples, and demolished Christian churches at Lahore and Agra.

Aurangzeb

Aurangzeb, an ultra-orthodox Muslim and the third of Shah Jahan's four surviving sons, came to the throne after imprisoning his father and killing his brothers. The deposed Shah Jahan remained confined until his death eight years later, and was buried next to his wife in the Taj Mahal.

The Taj Mahal, the finest example of Mughal architecture.

and Latin translated, and many books were finely illustrated. A synthesis of Persian and Hindu painting produced exquisite illuminated manuscripts.

A keen interest in the arts was characteristic of the Mughal Empire. Akbar's son and grandson, Jahangir and Shah Jahan, are notable for their extensive patronage of the arts and architecture. Shah Jahan's fame rests on the creation of the Taj Mahal, built in memory of his queen who had died giving birth to their 14th child. Other monuments left by Shah Jahan include the Red Fort and Jama Masjid in Delhi, which became his capital.

Shah Jahan did not share his grandfather Akbar's liberal religious policies. Although

Aurangzeb ruled India for 48 years, imposing an austere regime. He banned music, took no interest in literature, and imposed orthodox restrictions on the building of new Hindu temples. He reversed the policy of Akbar and reimposed the *jizya*. The last 26 years of Aurangzeb's long reign were largely spent on the battlefield. He invaded Rajasthan and destroyed the alliance with its Hindu rulers, and then fought a series of wars further south, trying to put down the Marathas led by Shivaji.

Aurangzeb died in 1707. His long absence from the bulk of his empire in the north led to serious administrative failure, and the Mughal Empire collapsed. The emperors that succeeded Aurangzeb became little more than ciphers.

EUROPEANS IN INDIA

Of all the Europeans who came to trade in India, it was the British who ruled, making the Subcontinent the 'jewel in the crown' of their empire. Successive campaigns finally led to Indian independence in 1947.

By the time the last great Mughal leader Aurangzeb died in 1707, the Europeans were well established in India. It was the Portuguese who were the first to begin trading when, in 1498, the explorer Vasco da Gama landed at Calicut, having sailed via the Cape of Good Hope. He arrived in Malabar (Kerala) looking for a mythical Christian empire and for spices, particularly pepper, which were in great demand in Europe.

Knowing that the island of Goa had an excellent harbour, the Portuguese set about conquering it, the first annexation of Indian territory by a European power since that of Alexander the Great. Throughout the 16th century the Portuguese managed to send valuable cargoes back to Europe and to construct impressive buildings in India. There were at least 50 major Portuguese forts in India and many minor fortifications.

It wasn't long before other European countries followed Portugal's lead and took advantage of India's commerce; in the 17th century,

Vasco de Gama.

The Portuguese introduced many plants to India from the New World, including pineapples, papaya, prickly pears, passion fruit, cashew nuts, cassava, maize and even chillies. The first known reference to them in India is in 1604.

England, France, the Netherlands and Denmark floated East India Companies. Chartered as trading companies by their respective governments, they sought chiefly Indian textiles – silk, cotton and indigo.

The Dutch and English soon emerged as the dominant European powers, however, as both

countries had developed navies which could outfight the clumsy Portuguese galleons.

English merchants

The East India Company established by English merchants in 1600 was to be strictly for peaceful trade; having obtained a royal charter to pursue their ambitions in the East, the merchants had guns on their ships only for defence against European and other rivals. A major reason for the company's success was its policy of religious tolerance, attracting skilled artisans and merchants from all communities. Slowly but surely the English company expanded, and many Indian rulers allowed it to establish trading posts, including those at Chennai and

Kolkata. In 1662 the English king Charles II married a Portuguese princess and, as part of her dowry, received the islands of Mumbai, which were transferred to the company. Indian textiles became the fashion in England, and by

> The beginning of the 19th century saw a huge increase in British control over India. The East India Company gradually became an organisation that governed much of India for Britain.

Watching an elephant fight.

the end of the century they had far overtaken spices as the company's main source of income.

The Portuguese were defeated in the Far East by the Dutch and constantly attacked by them on the high seas. This pushed the Portuguese into a decline in India, which was accelerated by their attempts to maintain too many forts and garrisons. The Dutch then returned to India and captured the Portuguese bases in the south, including that at Kochi. The Portuguese holed up in Goa, which fell into decay. The Dutch themselves became involved in wars with Indian rulers, and the expense of these forced them to scale down their operations. With the Portuguese and Dutch both being eclipsed it seemed that, at the dawn of the 18th century, England (or

Britain as it would become after the Union with Scotland of 1707) was in the ascendant.

British conquest

The Dutch soon shifted their focus to Indonesia, and the Portuguese were no longer a significant threat; the real contest was between the English and the French. It was in Bengal that the English made the first successful bid for rule in India. In 1757 and again in 1765 they defeated the Bengal ruler. This was made easier by the vacuum left after the disintegration of the Mughal Empire that followed the death of Aurangzeb.

There were successful wars against the Marathas and the Sikhs, and the Punjab and a number of other states were annexed. In other places, particularly in Rajasthan and Hyderabad, treaties with local rulers took away many of their powers. A huge army, comprised mostly of Indians, facilitated this expansion, and by 1850 most of India was either directly or indirectly under British rule.

A new system of administration was put into place, which has remained largely unaltered to this day. Each district was put under the charge of a 'collector' (of taxes), who was answerable to the governor of the province. There was a separate police service and an independent judicial system was created.

The British made fundamental changes to the ownership of land. Previously, although the right to part of the revenue from crops had been asserted by the state or its assignees, the owner of the land had been the peasant cultivator. The British, seeing similarities between those who took the tax revenue and large landlords in Britain, changed the system. The person who had collected the tax became the legal owner of the land, and was responsible for paying the tax to the government. The peasant became a tenant who paid part of his crop to the landlord. This new system left the peasant at the mercy of the landlord, and resulted in many of the new landlords defaulting on their tax, and being forced to sell. Much land passed from the control of local families to merchants and bankers in the cities, who were only interested in extracting the maximum return from their investment. The new landlords became enthusiastic supporters of British rule. Slavery was abolished in India in 1843, but many of the peasants were little more than serfs, bought and sold with the land. Unscrupulous moneylenders also reduced many to debt-bondage.

Anglo-Indian culture

Kolkata (Calcutta) was the British capital in India. It also became the centre of what came to be known as the Hindu Renaissance, where an Anglo-Indian synthesis of culture grew up. Hindu College, where the Kolkata intelligentsia sent their sons, was founded in 1816, and two years later the city boasted India's first public library. There was a keen desire among many of India's elite, in the south as well as the north, to learn more about Western science and culture, and to learn English. In 1835 the Company decided to make English the medium for the

The economy

Under British rule there was considerable development of the Indian economy. Large-scale irrigation was used to great effect, particularly in the Punjab, and raw cotton and jute became major exports. But the most profitable crop was opium. The East India Company needed something to export to China to pay for the tea it was exporting from there to Britain, and opium, although illegal, was much in demand. The Company encouraged the planting of the poppy in India, and the crop was bought by the East India Company for auction in Calcutta and onward transmission

Depiction of hunting tigers, circa1800.

Many blamed the East India Company for the Uprising, and the administration of India passed directly to the British crown. The Governor-General became the British Queen's Viceroy.

to China. By 1838 India was exporting 4 million pounds of opium a year; it had become the world's most valuable trade commodity.

The Uprising

In the 1850s a series of events in North India came together to cause an uprising against the British. A new rifle was issued to the army which required the soldiers to bite off the end of the cartridges before loading. A rumour spread that the cartridges had been coated with fat from cows and pigs, which alienated both the Hindu and the Muslim soldiers. When they refused to load their rifles with the new cartridges they were expelled from the army, without pay or pension, and left to walk back to their faraway villages. On 10 May

education it financed; English replaced Persian as the official language of the administration and higher courts. Ambitious Indians, who wanted jobs in the civil service or in the British companies that were coming to India, realised that English was the key to advancement. In 1857 the universities of Delhi, Chennai and Kolkata were founded.

1857 soldiers at Meerut, near Delhi, mutinied; they freed their comrades who had been shackled for disobedience, and killed several British officers. Then they headed for Delhi.

At Delhi, the Indian soldiers threw open the gates for their comrades and then joined the revolt, which spread quickly through northern and central India. It was a bitter fight, with bloodshed and violence on both sides, and the outcome did not favour India. The mutiny failed, and peace was declared on 8 July 1858.

In victory the British showed no mercy. The roads were lined with gallows, from which hung some mutineers but many innocents, and whole villages were destroyed. In some respects the Uprising was not too serious; it had been confined to a relatively small area of North India, and southern India was completely unaffected. Many rulers in the north, who had no love for the Mughals, had stayed loyal to the British, and some had even fought for them. Nevertheless, it had profound and long-lasting repercussions. Parliament in Britain was appalled at the events.

The psychological legacy of the Uprising was lasting. The mutiny produced a sense of unity

East India Company cavalry at Queen Victoria's Golden Jubilee, 1887.

INDIA'S RAILWAYS

In order to capture the vast Indian market, the British recognised that transport and communications had to be developed. Steamships started navigating Indian rivers, roads were repaired and improved, but it was the railways that really boosted the economy. The first few miles of railway line were laid before the Uprising, and by the end of the 19th century there were 40,000km (25,000 miles) of track. Industries like coal mining could take advantage of cheap and efficient transport to expand. What really spurred the expansion of the rail network, however, was the cotton crisis in America following the Civil War, which fuelled a boom in Indian exports.

between the Hindus and the Muslims, and the British never really trusted the Indians again. They made sure that, in future, large numbers of troops from Britain were always on hand. Many Indians, too, were scarred by the events; defeat and retribution had stirred resentment.

The British Raj

The British policy of gradually absorbing the independent states came to a halt. The rajas and nawabs had their treaties confirmed, and became, in most cases, fervent supporters of British rule. In 1876 Queen Victoria was proclaimed Empress of India, and the following year an Imperial Assemblage was staged at Delhi, where India's hereditary rulers came to pay homage to the British viceroy. In all, 84,000 Indians guests came to pay their respects.

This pageant coincided with a famine that claimed at least 5 million lives. There had been famines in India before the British arrived, but the supposedly superior British rule did nothing to check them, and there had never been a shortage of food across the whole country. The problem was that those whose crops had been ruined by drought no longer had money to purchase anything to eat. Camps were set up for some victims, who received food in exchange for work on public projects, but huge numbers died. Well-meaning British officials at local level often did their best to alleviate hardship, but they were powerless against the ruthless indifference of the hierarchy.

Improved communications

Better roads, river steamers, railways, the telegraph and the post produced great changes, and the opening of the Suez Canal in 1869 put India closer to the markets of the West. Mumbai became one of the world's busiest ports. The first telegraph line and postal service opened in 1854, and prices were kept low. Those who had gone off to the expanding cities could now afford to keep in touch with their families. The villages, where the vast majority of Indians resided, became significantly less isolated.

From the great Uprising to the end of the 19th century the British tightened their hold on India. Revenue that came from agricultural and commercial expansion was used to expand the army and civil service. One hugely successful crop planted around this time was tea. When the East India Company's monopoly of trade between Britain and China came to an end it planted up experimental tea plantations in India. The success of these led to British companies planting up vast acreages, mostly in Assam and Bengal. By the 1890s India was exporting more tea than China.

Political activity

In 1883 a bill was introduced that would have made it possible for a European to be tried by one of the few Indian magistrates or judges. This provoked uproar among the British community, who held meetings and ran newspaper advertisements proclaiming that 'niger natives were' not the equal of Britons. As a result

of this, they managed to have the bill watered down. Educated Indians, and some supporters among the British, had united in the battle to save the bill. One of these, Allan Octavian Hume, a retired member of the Indian Civil Service, wrote to Kolkata University graduates proposing that an umbrella organisation be set up to protect Indian interests, and the Indian National Congress had its first meeting in Mumbai in 1885. This organisation became the vehicle for the new middle class to make their grievances felt. Congress urged that 'the basis of the Government should be widened and that

Queen Victoria, "Empress of India".

the people should have the proper and legitimate share in it.'

A quarter of India's revenue was used to cover the 'home charges' – the money that was sent back to Britain to pay for recruitment costs, pensions and the interest on loans. A sharp rise in home charges coincided with a series of poor monsoons and famine. Grain had been exported to meet the cost of the home charges, which left insufficient for famine relief. Millions died.

The Independence movement

In 1905 the government implemented a measure that galvanised Indian public opinion. Without any consultation, it decided to partition Bengal. Supposedly this was to improve the administration, but Indians did not believe this. The division of Bengal would create an eastern half, merged with Assam, where Muslims would be in a majority. The western half of Bengal would be Hindu but would have a majority of non-Bengali-speakers. The Bengali-speakers from Kolkata, who were proponents of Indian nationalism, would lose their power. It was seen as a part of a deliberate British policy of divide and rule.

There were mass protests all over Bengal, and Congress took up the cause across India. Petitions attracted innumerable signatures, but the government refused to give way. In demonstrations in Kolkata, bonfires were made of imported British cloth. The government broke

> At the beginning of the 20th century, 90 percent of India's cloth came from Britain. Cheap imports from Lancashire, boosted when the Indian government removed import duty, had largely destroyed the livelihood of India's weavers.

Many Indian soldiers fought in World War I. This image is of a training exercise in southern England.

M.K. GANDHI

Mohandas Karamchand Gandhi (1869–1948) was a British-trained lawyer and a radical proponent of non-violence, pioneering mass civil disobedience as a form of protest. He was the spiritual leader of the Indian Independence movement,

Born in Porbander, Gujarat, 1869, he left Mumbai in 1893 for South Africa to work as a lawyer, where he became involved in the struggle for workers' rights. In 1915 he returned to his homeland and became involved in the movement for Indian self-rule, assuming leadership of the Indian Congress Party in 1921. Gandhi revived the hunger strike as a potent political protest, and his passive resistance tactics inspired freedom movements worldwide. While arch enemy Winston Churchill dubbed him 'that half-naked fakir', his followers called him 'Mahatma' (Great Soul), though many preferred 'Bapu' (Little Father). An ascetic, he preferred village to urban life and adopted the villagers' dress of dhoti and shawl. Gandhi led a Salt March in 1930 in defiance of British tax demands. In 1947 he negotiated an end to 190 years of British colonial rule. The following year he was assassinated at the age of 78 by a Hindu nationalist who objected to his continued religious tolerance, following the savage communal violence that accompanied Partition. Gandhi's birthday, 2 October, is a national holiday in India.

up demonstrations using excessive force, but the movement spread across the country, and Congress became a major political force.

The division of Bengal had other political consequences. The Muslims in eastern Bengal were happy to be running their affairs free from the politicians of Kolkata, and a new capital was established at Dacca. A university for Muslims had already been established in 1875 at Aligarh, between Agra and Delhi. The Muslims of eastern Bengal combined with those at Aligarh and others from further south to ask the viceroy for Muslim representation on any official council. The viceroy was sympathetic to this, and in 1906, only a year after the partition of Bengal, Muslim delegates from across India met in Dacca to found the All-India Muslim League. Initially, the League was largely composed of nobility and landowners, and was generally pro-British. Many other Muslims still supported Congress.

To appease Bengalis for Kolkata's loss of status, Bengal was reunited, and the success in reversing government policy on Bengal boosted Congress. The Muslim League became less conservative. Both organisations were now calling for self-government within the British Empire.

World War I

When war broke out in 1914, the viceroy told India that it, too, was at war. Somewhat surprisingly, all factions in India offered their loyalty. Congress imagined that their support, followed by victory for the British, would bring self-government. The Indian contribution to Britain's war effort was very substantial, with 1 million going overseas and Indian troops fighting in many battles. The British exported large quantities of wheat out of India, which inflated the price within the country and caused much hardship.

The end of World War I did not bring the benefits hoped for by Congress. There was a small increase in democratic representation, but this was more than counterbalanced by the extension of the wartime state of emergency and press censorship. A flu epidemic that claimed 12 million lives strengthened disillusionment with British rule.

The Gandhi era

During the war two Indian lawyers had come to prominence in Indian politics, Jinnah and Gandhi. Muhammad Ali Jinnah (known officially as Quaid-e-Azam in Pakistan) was born into a wealthy Gujarati family in 1875. He went to London to study law and, aged only 19, qualified as a barrister. Returning to India, he became a successful lawyer, joined

> No Indian was allowed to rise to an officer's position in the army until after 1910. Indians could compete for high civil service jobs, but few were successful.

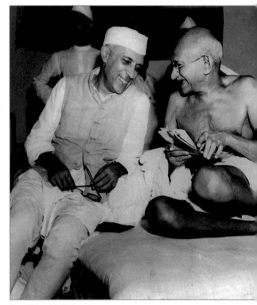

Gandhi with Nehru in 1946.

Congress and was a member of the government's legislative council, expounding ideas of Muslim-Hindu unity. He joined the Muslim League, was elected its president in 1916 and masterminded a pact to act jointly with Congress. Jinnah believed in a constitutional approach to achieving self-rule, putting him at odds with Gandhi.

Mohandas Karamchand Gandhi was born in Gujarat in 1869. He had travelled to Britain, been called to the Bar, and then gone to South Africa, where he championed equality. When he returned to live in India in 1915 he was given an enthusiastic reception, and in 1917 won his first victory when he defended the peasants of Bihar against their oppression by European indigo-planters. The following year he led a successful campaign for higher wages in the cotton mills at Ahmadabad. Gandhi believed that non-violent protest would achieve self-government.

In 1919 Gandhi urged Indians to protest against the post-war restrictions on political action. Defying laws frequently led him into prison, but Gandhi always imposed one inviolable condition – that civil disobedience must be completely peaceful. In a march in 1919 in the Punjab, British troops opened fire and killed several marchers, after which

Gandhi's salt protest.

General Dyer banned all public gatherings. When 100,000 people gathered to celebrate a Hindu holiday in Jallianwala Bagh, General Dyer marched his troops in, closed off the exit, and without giving a warning ordered them to open fire. Four hundred Indians were killed and 1,200 wounded.

The government of India eventually decided that there had been "an error of judgment". Dyer was sent back to Britain, where he received a hero's welcome. The repercussions in India were enormous; millions of Indians who had backed British rule now became committed nationalists, and Congress abandoned cooperation with the government to adopt Gandhi's policy of

non-violent protest. Jinnah opposed Gandhi and resigned from Congress.

Salt protest

The Prince of Wales's visit to India in 1921 was met with protests and black flags, and subsequently, 20,000 activists were imprisoned. In 1930 Gandhi embarked on a new crusade that captured the imagination of the country and the world. The British had enforced a monopoly on the manufacture of salt, which they taxed. Gandhi led his followers from his ashram in Ahmedabad to

> Gandhi put much effort into trying to abolish untouchability. An Act in 1933 to support this was only partly successful, and great prejudice against the Untouchables continues to the present day.

Dandi on the coast in order symbolically to make salt from the sea. The government took no action. However, similar defiance of the salt laws across India brought thousands of arrests. Gandhi himself was arrested and imprisoned, as was the entire working committee of Congress.

In 1931 Gandhi was released from jail and invited to talks with the viceroy. Gandhi suspended non-cooperation, and was invited to a conference in London to discuss India's future. Immediately after his return to India, however, he was rearrested. Under a new viceroy, the government had decided to toughen its stance, and 80,000 Indians were jailed. Boycotts, protests and terrorism spread across India.

Success for Congress

In 1937 the government granted some provincial autonomy. All members of the legislative assemblies were to be elected, a property qualification gave 35 million men and women the vote, and there would be special representation for Muslims, Sikhs, Anglo-Indians, Europeans and the lowest castes. In the election Congress was victorious and formed ministries in most provinces. Jinnah proposed that the Muslim League and Congress should join forces. However, he stipulated that Congress must accept the League as the only voice of the Muslim community.

As Congress had many Muslim members, his proposal was rejected. Some of the new Congress ministers seemed to favour their own Hindu community and this caused resentment among Muslims, who started to look towards the League for protection. There were voices calling for a separate Muslim province in northeastern India.

India at war

When World War II broke out in 1939, the viceroy declared that India was at war with Germany. Congress was appalled at the

in the war, and the Indian army grew ten-fold to around 2 million.

One of the worst episodes of British rule occurred during the war when, in 1943, there was a famine in Bengal. The war had cut off rice supplies from Burma and the military were stockpiling in case of invasion. These events caused a rumour that there was a shortage of food, which led to hoarding and price rises. The government was very slow to act, allowing the export of food from Bengal for some time and not providing sufficient food aid. At least 2 million died.

Quit India movement march, Mumbai, 1947.

absence of any consultation and its provincial ministers all resigned. The Muslim League offered up thanks for deliverance from Congress 'oppression'. This marked the end of the dream of a united independent India.

Congress decided to oppose the war effort with non-violent protest, and Gandhi and 14,000 others were jailed. When Japan entered the war and captured Malaya and Singapore, the threat of India being invaded led the British to release Congress dissidents for talks. These came to nothing. In 1942, Gandhi launched the Quit India campaign in which he urged the British to leave India immediately. Demonstrations and violence led to 60,000 arrests. Many Indians, however, supported the British

INDIAN NATIONAL ARMY

Subhas Chandra Bose had originally been in Congress but, as he believed in violent resistance to the British, broke away to lead his own party in Bengal. Bose escaped arrest in 1941 and managed to reach Berlin, where he received help from Hitler to beam anti-British broadcasts to India. He then went to Singapore by submarine. The Japanese helped him form an Indian National Army from the prisoners of war in order to liberate India; they reached northeast India but were repulsed. Most surrendered in Burma. Bose escaped and was probably killed in a plane crash in Taipei on 18 August 1945.

The Mountbattens on their way to the Constituent Assembly, August 1947.

INDEPENDENT INDIA

From independence to a burgeoning economy now competing
on the world stage, India's democracy is a triumph in a land of
multiple ethnic, religious and secessionist interests.

At the end of the war a Labour government came into power in Britain that was sympathetic to Indian Independence. New elections were held, and although Congress did well, the Muslim League took all the reserved Muslim seats. A trial of the captured Indian National Army officers, who had fought alongside Japan in the war, made them heroes and they received suspended sentences. Further anti-British sentiment was expressed in mutinies carried out by the Indian Navy and Air Force.

In 1946 more talks to devise a constitution ended in stalemate. Jinnah felt the Muslims were being marginalised by the British and Congress. He decided to abandon constitutional methods and resort to direct action. Muslim demonstrations in Kolkata degenerated into attacks on Hindus, and the Hindus retaliated. In three days 5,000 died, and the violence spread to other cities. The viceroy asked the Congress leader, Jawaharlal Nehru, to form an interim government. Nehru was born to a wealthy family in Allahabad and, after graduating from Cambridge University, he qualified as a barrister and rose to be president of Congress. Despite being a protégé of Gandhi, he was an atheist, and a pragmatic, capable administrator.

The new state of Pakistan

In February 1947 the British government announced that it would hand over power no later than June 1948. Lord Mountbatten, a man of great charm who was related to the British royal family, became Viceroy of India.

Mountbatten formed a close friendship with Nehru, but did not see eye to eye with Jinnah. The date of Independence was brought forward, and the end of empire was accelerated with disastrous consequences. On 15 July 1947

Lord Mountbatten announces Independence.

it was announced that one month later Partition would create two independent countries, India and Pakistan. There was a frantic scramble to divide up all of the government's assets in proportion to the populations of the new countries – 82.5 percent to India, 17.5 percent to Pakistan. It was already clear that Pakistan would be itself divided into two provinces, West Pakistan and East Pakistan, separated by a thousand miles of Indian territory.

A British lawyer, Sir Cyril Radcliffe, who had never been to India, was charged with dividing the country – those areas with a Hindu majority to India, those with a Muslim majority to Pakistan. On the borders of these zones there was terrible bloodshed as those of the majority religion tried to remove any possible ambiguity. Following Independence, a massive migration across the new border – of Muslims to Pakistan, Hindus and Sikhs to India created terrible violence on both sides, resulting in many deaths, estimated to be at least half a million, if not a million. At least 10 million people changed countries.

Independent India

At midnight on 14 August 1947, Jawaharlal Nehru, India's first prime minister, had proclaimed independence. One of the first tasks for the new government was to force accession on

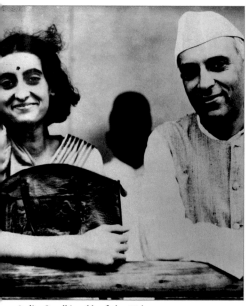

Indira Gandhi and her father, Nehru.

THE NEW CONSTITUTION

India became a republic on 26 January 1950, with a new constitution that stressed the secular nature of India and the equality of all its citizens. Although untouchability had been outlawed in the constitution, the position of the Dalit community was, after many centuries of discrimination, still notably inferior. Penalties were introduced to stop oppression, and a quota was established to give the Dalits representation in the legislatures and government service. Measures were also introduced to emancipate women. Child marriage was banned and Hindu women gained the right to initiate divorce proceedings and have the same inheritance rights as men.

a number of undecided Princely States. Most acceded peacefully. Hyderabad and Junagadh had Muslim rulers, but their populations were mostly Hindu. Both were eventually taken over by force. Kashmir was a largely Muslim state ruled by a Hindu. Hoping that he might retain an independent status, the maharaja prevaricated. Some Muslim peasants revolted against their Hindu landlords, and Muslims from Pakistan crossed into Kashmir to give them help. The maharaja then acceded to India and asked for assistance. Mountbatten stipulated that once order was re-established there should be a plebiscite to establish what the people of Kashmir wanted. Fighting continued until Kashmir was split in two. A ceasefire in 1949 left Kashmir divided, as it still is.

Gandhi assassinated

Gandhi was appalled by the Hindu attacks on Muslims and the callous treatment by Congress of the refugees. To force a change of policy, he went on hunger strike. Hindu nationalists opposed Gandhi for his liberal views, and as Gandhi walked to his prayer platform, one of them opened fire and killed him. The shock brought the nation to its senses. Nehru was able to act against the extremists and impose order.

The new India was broadly Socialist during Nehru's many years as prime minister. The economy was directed from the centre through a series of five-year plans. Nehru managed to negotiate a non-aligned foreign policy, which enabled India to profit from the Cold War rivalry; both Western and Russian finance and technical assistance enabled India to industrialise. Major facilities were installed to manufacture steel, fertilisers and cement, and to build the power stations India needed. The increases in food production, however, were largely offset by large increases in the population. Although malnutrition was (and still is) common, there were none of the famines of the British period or its predecessors.

Jawaharlal Nehru died, while still prime minister, in 1964. Millions attended his funeral and mourned the loss of probably the most powerful and most loved ruler India had ever had. After his death there was a more collective rule by Congress, but this new leadership was almost immediately challenged by Pakistan.

Un-neighbourly relations

The civilian government here had been toppled in a military coup in 1958, and General Ayub

Khan had become president. America saw him as a bulwark against Communism and gave Pakistan much military hardware. Pakistan had tried to reopen negotiations on Kashmir with India, but India had insisted that Pakistan vacate Kashmir first. Ill feeling between the two countries was exacerbated by Pakistan allying itself with China after India's defeat in the Indo-Chinese War.

Following Pakistan's foray into Gujarat in early 1965, a ceasefire brokered by the UN forced Pakistan's withdrawal. When Pakistani-trained guerrillas crossed into Indian Kashmir, India sent its troops across the demarcation line and so did Pakistan. The Indians, who had been receiving help from America since the war with China, were stronger, and their army almost reached Lahore. The Soviets arranged a summit meeting and a ceasefire, and both countries withdrew their armies.

Indira Gandhi

Nehru's daughter, Indira Gandhi (not related to Mahatma Gandhi), was a close companion and confidante of her father. She travelled widely with him, and her international connections were to prove useful later in her political career. After his death, she became Minister for Information and Broadcasting, which would prove to be beneficial experience. When she became prime minister in 1966, the monsoon had failed and the country was facing starvation. She flew to Washington and was able to secure from a sympathetic American government millions of tons of wheat and financial assistance.

Mrs Gandhi devalued the rupee to help exports. This, however, was interpreted as a manifestation of Congress's economic mismanagement. Faced with militant demands by Sikhs for a separate state, she split the old Punjab into a smaller Sikh-dominated Punjab and a Hindi-speaking Haryana. Many saw this as weakness and to add to these difficulties, there were strikes and food riots.

Indira Gandhi fought the old guard of the party to move to increasingly socialist policies. She nationalised the banks and started the redistribution of agricultural land. She took away the privileges of the former rulers of the Princely States. In the election of 1971, with the slogan 'Eliminate Poverty', she won a sweeping victory.

India opposed American policy in Vietnam. The Americans resumed arms shipments to Pakistan and backed the new military ruler, Yahya Khan. India had refused to sign the Treaty on Nuclear Non-Proliferation and was producing plutonium. Meanwhile, the relationship between West and East Pakistan was deteriorating. The Bengali-speaking East was ruled by the army and bureaucrats of the Urdu-speaking West. A clampdown on politicians and dissent in the East was supported by the Americans. In March 1971, the people in the East took to the streets to demand freedom. The West Pakistan army then killed thousands of East Pakistanis as it restored control. By the end of the year 10 million refugees had fled to India.

Muslim refugees cram onto a train bound for Pakistan from New Delhi in 1947 following Partition.

New challenges for Mrs Gandhi

The centralised economy was hugely bureaucratic and corrupt. Rampant inflation, which destroyed people's savings, also fuelled discontent. In Bihar, J.P. Narayan led a coalition against the government; in Gujarat, Morarji Desai led the attack on the corrupt state government of Congress. Mrs Gandhi was dealt a severe blow when the High Court ruled that she had been guilty of electoral malpractice. Next day it was announced that Morarji Desai had defeated Congress in the Gujarat elections. He and J.P. Narayan joined forces to urge anti-government protests and disobedience. Mrs Gandhi then declared a state of emergency. Desai, Narayan and many thousands of politicians, student activists, lawyers and journalists were arrested and jailed.

Mrs Gandhi initiated a drive against corruption and inefficiency. A good monsoon helped bring down the price of food. The banning of strikes raised industrial production. Business leaders were sympathetic to the authoritarian regime and boosted investment. In 1977 Mrs Gandhi felt confident enough to release her opponents and call an election. But Morarji Desai and J.P. Narayan revived their Janata Party and won a resounding victory. Desai became prime minister.

The Janata government was plagued with dissent and was ineffectual. Inflation rose again. Indira Gandhi fought a by-election and won. In January 1980, Mrs Gandhi became prime minister again, with a large majority.

Problems in Punjab

Indira Gandhi's administration was plagued by separatist insurrections. In the northeast seven tribally dominated states were engaged in violent protests against an influx of Bengalis. After many of the migrants were killed, Mrs Gandhi imposed martial law. The biggest threat to the central government, however, came from the Punjab, India's most affluent state. Jarnail Singh Bhindranwale, a fundamentalist who wanted a Sikh nation, became the Punjab's leader. In 1984, he and his armed followers took over the tower of the Golden Temple at Amritsar and resolved to stay until the state was given autonomy. Mrs Gandhi ordered in the army. In a two-day battle, Bhindranwale and thousands of Sikhs were killed. The Sikhs' holiest temple was badly damaged. Eighteen months later two of Indira Gandhi's Sikh bodyguards gunned her down. As news of Mrs Gandhi's death spread, Hindus took to the streets of Delhi, and thousands of Sikhs were killed.

Gandhi's successor

Mrs Gandhi had groomed her son, Sanjay, to follow her, but he had died four years earlier. The other son, Rajiv, had originally chosen to avoid politics, but he became politically active on his brother's demise. He was only 40 when he became prime minister. He called an immediate election, which he won by a huge majority. Rajiv Gandhi was a champion of new technology and modern management. He moved away from the Socialist policies of his mother, removing many of the restrictions on business and relaxing the controls

on imports. Rajiv Gandhi also became involved in the efforts to stabilise the conflict in Sri Lanka.

Rajiv Gandhi came in on a promise to curb corruption. This was taken seriously by his Finance Minister, V.P. Singh, who was moved to defence when he began to probe too deeply. Singh uncovered signs of corruption at the highest level of Congress in the award of a massive contract to the Swedish company Bofors. He resigned to form the National Front party.

The election of 1989 brought the National Front to power in a coalition with a small majority, with V.P. Singh as prime minister. This admin-

Harvest, Punjab, 1970. India benefited from the so-called "Green Revolution", bringing high-yield crops.

istration had a short but important tenure. Singh went to the Golden Temple and apologised for the attack in 1984, which led to an easing of the confrontation with the Sikhs, and also withdrew the peacekeeping force in Sri Lanka. In Kashmir, however, heavy-handed interventions escalated the conflict. Singh also introduced legislation to reserve a proportion of government jobs for the lower-caste Hindus who had been historically disadvantaged, and this had a considerable long-term effect on social mobility.

Rajiv Gandhi was assassinated by a Tamil woman suicide bomber in 1991. Elections then brought Congress back to power under Prime Minister P.V. Narasimha Rao. The Indian stock exchange was opened to foreigners and foreign capital poured in; industrial production and exports grew rapidly, although the benefits did not percolate down to the poor. Meanwhile, Rao's government was perceived to be engaged in widespread corruption.

Ayodhya and the rise of the BJP

In 1992 a group of Hindu zealots destroyed a 16th-century mosque at Ayodhya, which they claimed had been built on the site of an important Hindu temple. Riots and curfews spread across India. Next year a series of bombs were set off in Mumbai that killed 250 people. This attack was widely seen as a reprisal for Ayodhya. Reprisals were, in turn, made against Muslims.

The BJP (Bharatiya Janata Party), was able to take advantage of the sectarian unrest. Founded in 1980, the party was the political arm of a group of Hindu right-wing organisations that championed the idea of Hindutva, a Hindu homeland. In the 1996 elections, no party had an overall majority, but the BJP secured the most seats. The BJP leader Atal Bihari Vajpayee put together a coalition, but it lasted barely two weeks, and was replaced by a Socialist-led coalition under H.D. Deve Gowda and, later, Inder Kumar Gujural. Gujural was able and honest, but the warring factions in his coalition made decisive government impossible.

In 1998 the BJP did well in the elections and Vajpayee became prime minister again. The opening up of the economy to foreign companies proceeded apace, but the BJP's rather extreme form of Hindu nationalism meant that national scientific and cultural institutions were purged of those who did not follow the Hindutva line, and school textbooks were rewritten to promote their interpretation of history. Meanwhile, violence against Hindus led to anti-Muslim riots across Gujarat. About 2,000 Muslims were killed and 150,000 fled to refugee camps.

Relations with Pakistan were growing more strained. After the Indian government authorised nuclear tests in the Thar Desert, Pakistan detonated its own bomb. Pakistan had managed to infiltrate remote areas of Kashmir for several months before India noticed, and it required the loss of 1,000 Indian soldiers to eject them. In 2001 an attack by terrorists on the Indian parliament, thought to have been backed by Pakistan, brought the two countries close to nuclear war.

The return of Congress

The press assumed that the election of 2004 would return the BJP to power. The party campaigned on the slogan 'India Shining'. It was true that the upper segments of society had never had it so good, but the poor had seen very little improvement in their lives, and voted accordingly. A Congress-led alliance won power. The leader of the Congress was the widow of Rajiv Gandhi, Sonia Gandhi. Italian-born and Catholic, she would have been unacceptable to many. She therefore decided to exercise her influence from behind the scenes and nominated the ex-Finance

Indira Gandhi, during her election campaign in 1971.

CREATION OF BANGLADESH

Hostilities between India and Pakistan began in December 1971. To counteract pressure from the Americans, who supported West Pakistan, India entered into a mutual defence treaty with the Soviet Union. India trained East Pakistani guerrillas to return to their country and disrupt government. India then invaded. The Pakistan air force attacked Indian airfields, after which India attacked West Pakistan as well as East Pakistan. Within a few days the Indians crushed the Pakistan army in the East and forced their surrender. East Pakistan then became independent Bangladesh. The new, smaller Pakistan was no longer a serious threat to India.

Minister, Manmohan Singh, to lead the country – India's first Sikh prime minister. There was a swift improvement in relations with Pakistan.

The economy continued to grow strongly. By 2007 India had the fourth-largest number of dollar billionaires in the world, although the global economic slowdown of 2007–10, while affecting India less than other countries, took its toll, with GDP down 1 percent at the lowest point. The economy has since recovered and is predicted to maintain its meteoric growth rate of at least 7 percent for some time (almost 8 percent in 2015–16); it is now ranked as the 7th-biggest economy in the world. Crucially, and almost uniquely in Asia, this growth is largely fuelled by domestic consumption, whereas Japan, China and the 'Asian tigers' have all largely relied on export-based growth. India is expected to overtake China as the world's most populous country within two decades.

The Left parties in the ruling coalition have been able to modify the neo-liberal economic policies of Congress, and allocate more money for the poor, although economic inequality is still a major cause for concern. In 2008, around 300 million of the population of 1.3 billion was living in abject poverty, although this represents a decline in percentage terms, and the figure has remained at 25 percent since then. In truth, as the largely urban middle class continues to expand, the rural poor are being left ever further behind. A champion of this cause is Rahul Gandhi, son of Congress premier Sonia Gandhi and a scion of this famous political family.

Terrorist attacks

The relative calm that had prevailed since the attacks on the parliament building in Delhi was shattered at the end of 2008 when a series of bombings by Islamist militants took place across northern India, including several at Delhi markets.

This new wave of violence was to break even more dramatically into the news across the world when a group of ten Islamic suicide attackers arrived by hijacked trawler in Mumbai and started randomly shooting people in the streets, railway stations and hospitals. Two luxury hotels, including the famous Taj Mahal Palace, were besieged and set on fire. 'Black Cat' commandos eventually liberated the buildings and killed the Islamists, but not before the eventual death toll had reached 173. India was left reeling from these attacks on such high-profile targets, and security was stepped up across the country.

Meanwhile, in the wake of 104 civilian deaths in a period of two months in Kashmir, concerted attempts were made to calm a population on the brink of full-scale uprising. The much-loathed shoot-to-kill powers granted the Indian army were repealed, and for a while the political situation was calmer.

At the time of writing in early 2016, however, the British Foreign and Commonwealth Office (FCO) was once again advising against any travel to Jammu and Kashmir (with the exception of travel to and within the cities of Jammu and

The Golden Temple siege, 1984.

STATE OF THE PARTIES

The political kaleidoscope of India is forever changing, creating unlikely patterns and alliances. Parties include the Congress (Indira), which still plays on the Nehru legacy; the Bharatiya Janata Party (BJP), Hindu nationalists; the Left Front, a coalition of parties, including the Communist Party of India and the Communist Party of India (Marxist); and the Samajwadi Party, representing the low castes and Muslims. Regional parties include the Sikh activists, Akali Dal; two Dravidian parties in Tamil Nadu, the AIADMK and DMK; the Telugu Desam Party active in Andhra Pradesh and Telangana; and the Hindu and Maratha extremist Shiv Sena, based in Mumbai.

Srinagar), where terrorist incidents had become more frequent. This goes with warnings against travel to the state of Manipur and the immediate vicinity of the border with Pakistan.

The problem of corruption

In 2010, Delhi hosted the Commonwealth Games – an event marred by the failure of the Indian government to complete the sporting facilities on schedule. The red faces got even redder when it emerged the reason for the debacle was that an estimated $4billion of public money had been embezzled during the run up to the games – a revelation that surprised no one in a country whose population has grown increasingly frustrated and angry at the ineptitude and dishonesty of its politicians.

The following year, a 74-year-old anti-corruption activist named Ana Hazare became a rallying point for the nation's fury when he staged a series of hunger strikes in New Delhi to protest at the abuses of power perpetrated by India's elected representatives.

In 2012, the anti-corruption lobby was momentarily upstaged by a march involving hundreds of thousands of landless poor aimed at drawing attention to rural poverty. A report published shortly after highlighted the scale of the problem: despite boasting 5–9 percent growth in annual GDP, an estimated 40 percent of Indian children suffer from malnutrition. The country may be on the rise economically, but it holds a gradually increasing number of the world's poor.

Attitudes to women

Another source of concern in modern India is the generally poor status of women, and in particularly the country's poor record with sexual crime – a fact highlighted in December 2012 when a young medical student was gang raped on a night bus in Delhi. She subsequently died of injuries sustained in the attack, which prompted an international outcry against the lack of seriousness and vigour with which rape cases are prosecuted by the Indian police. Mass demonstrations were organized in the capital as the country once again found itself in the international spotlight – for all the wrong reasons.

In the last few years, there have been several further reports of horrific gang rapes on both foreign nationals and locals, whose numbers have included children and elderly women. The government, aware of the damage the international spotlight on these cases is doing to India's profile, has sought to impose harsher punishments on rapists. Crucially, there is a realisation that more emphasis needs to be placed on changing the cultural mindset about women. See page 85.

Caste struggles

In February 2016, large-scale violence erupted as members of the Jat caste, a traditionally agricultural community who are considered high-caste, demanded the lowering of their caste status in order to access the quotas of gov-

Narendra Modi, the 15th and current Prime Minister of India.

ernment jobs and educational opportunities reserved for members of 'backward', or lower castes. This inversion of the usual attitude to caste status emerged as the politically-influential Jats, who are mainly based in northern India states such as Haryana, have struggled with a drying up of private sector jobs and reduction in farming incomes. Protests across India, mainly in Haryana and Delhi, grew violent, disrupting transport and the water supply system, among other services, while 16 people have been reported dead and over 150 injured in clashes with the police. At time of writing, the Jat community had reached a deal with the BJP government, promising more access to government jobs.

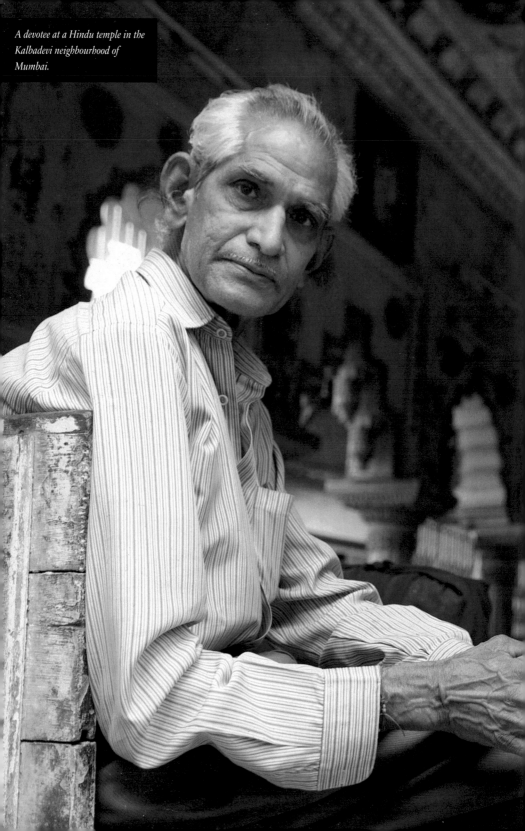

CONTEMPORARY ISSUES

Although India has seen record rates of growth in the past few years, it still faces huge problems of illiteracy, poverty and vast disparities in wealth.

Contemporary India can be bewildering, a place of extremes shot through with contradictions and seemingly changing from week to week. Visitors seeking to negotiate this phenomenally complex country may well find much of what they see makes them uneasy. The juxtapositions of extreme wealth and appalling poverty alongside a liberated young middle class and levels of social repression rarely encountered in the West make a visit to India at once fascinating, challenging, frustrating and disturbing.

Money and power

Full-blown capitalism is a recent arrival in India. While the country has always had strong mercantile instincts – the Gujaratis in particular are famed for their trading prowess – for many years after Independence the economy followed a nominally state-controlled pattern of development. This was put in place by the socially minded Nehru, whose dream was to see state ownership, industrialisation and an 'India first' policy – indigenous production and consumption coupled with protectionist import policies. He also pushed for universal literacy and education, as well as land reform and a redistribution of wealth. In these he was far less successful, and subsequent governments have done little to improve India's record on human development and sanitation.

Recent commentators have tended to denigrate the industrial legacy of Nehru, but they often fail to take into account that at the time of Independence India was in a less than flourishing state; there was hardly any indigenous industry, and literacy rates were exceptionally low. As part of a move towards an increasingly service-based economy, much effort has been expended since the 1990s undoing the

Dehusking rice, a highly labour-intensive process.

GOING FOR GROWTH

One of the reasons that India has fared better than most during the recent global economic meltdown was that as businesses in the West looked to tighten their belts, India's highly qualified, but low-salaried workforce became difficult to ignore. Initially seen as a call-centre-based industry, today, from medical reports to pharmaceutical research to IT, India has emerged as a leading player for back office work/outsourcing. Even so, falls in agricultural and manufacturing output challenged India's seemingly unstoppable growth, which fell by half from 2010 to 2012. But by 2016 it had increased again to 7.6 percent, with further growth predicted in 2017.

structures put in place by post-Independence Congress governments.

Nonetheless, Nehru's radical solutions to the economic difficulties and fragmented nature of India's post-colonial society created the very industrial base that many are now so keen to see privatised. The literate workforce from India's universities that is supposed to take over more service-industry jobs from the West (examples are software industries, some legal positions and call centre work) is, in part, the product of Nehru's progressive education policies.

A commuter in Chennai.

At a governmental level, a huge programme of 'disinvestment' (privatisation) has recently been put in place, and inward investment has greatly increased, largely to the benefit of the much-lauded Indian middle class. At the same time, attitudes to social welfare have hardened among policy-makers, with large tax breaks given to the well-off, while the nation's poor become increasingly marginalised in both the political and economic debate. So far the 'trickle down' of wealth has not materialised, and the disparity in income between rich and poor has widened.

> *It was Nehru who was largely responsible for pushing through the post-Independence programme of industrialisation, famously claiming that large dams were the 'temples of modern India'.*

One of the most significant problems that stand in the way of Indian development goals is corruption, which is well entrenched at all levels of society. Despite the high profile of campaigns led by hunger striker Ana Hazare in 2011–12, it is hard to see this disappearing in a country where so much depends on favours and connections, and where members of parliament can continue to hold their seat even if they are convicted of a crime and sent to prison.

The middle class and the poor

While caste has traditionally been the dominant organising principle of Indian society, as the country begins to go through what appears to be a period of considerable change, other structures of social organisation are emerging that run both in parallel with and across caste boundaries. At the heart of this change lies the much-vaunted Indian middle class.

This hard-to-quantify group continues to receive a huge amount of attention in the Western press, blamed for, amongst other things – due to its increasing consumption of material goods – world food shortages and the increase in the demand for oil. Untangling the myth from the reality can be difficult. While there is no absolute measure of who exactly comprise the Indian middle class (a very broad category that covers a wide range of people, including larger rural landowners, civil servants, managers

LITERACY

One in three of the world's illiterate people live in India; a staggering number, and a trend that looks set to continue. Only around 48 percent of girls are enrolled in primary education, and for these there is a 10 percent drop-out rate. According to the government, overall literacy is at about 74 percent. However, the government measure is set very low, with many people being functionally illiterate. Kerala has the highest literacy rate at around 94 percent, Bihar the lowest at 63. Investment in education and campaigns to promote literacy by the Keralan government, as against widespread corruption in Bihar, account for the disparity.

and the super-rich), the best guesses seem to be around 250 million people, or just over 20 percent of the population. From this is it possible to calculate a breakdown by class for the rest of the India's many people.

Around one third of India's 1.3 billion people live below the country's official poverty line. This equates to more impoverished people in absolute terms than exist in all of sub-Saharan Africa.

It is not surprising, then, that many – especially children – still suffer from malnutrition, while the country as a whole is a net exporter of

in recent years, economic liberalisation and the expansion of a consuming class.

Many of those living below the World Bank definition of a poverty line might be classed as 'employed', but underemployment remains a serious issue. These include railway workers, factory workers, small landowners and tenant farmers amongst others; while their lives are not as desperate as those who can barely survive, they too have yet to see any real improvement in their lives from India's recent economic progress. Indeed, in rural areas many small-scale famers have been facing ruin through crop failures and debt.

The new India: Hyderabad's 'Cyber City'.

While India's super-rich indulge themselves in buying teams in the flashy Indian Premier League cricket competition, many of their compatriots are still sleeping on the streets or dying of malnutrition.

food. In addition, India has a comparable infant mortality rate to neighbouring – and much poorer – Bangladesh. Sanitation is an ongoing concern, with much of the rural population still not having access to potable water supplies. Little has been done for this desperate group, as economic policies have tended to concentrate on either large-scale state-owned enterprises or,

Other indicators of public well-being do nothing to brighten the gloomy picture. According to the UN, less than 50 percent of the population have access to essential drugs and there is a chronic shortage of health facilities (in rural India there are only 50 hospital beds per 100,000 people; in the UK there are around 390).

Only 30 percent of people have access to adequate sanitation, and according to the UN, as many as 2.1 million children die before the age of 5 every year – that's one every four minutes – because of malnutrition.

Child labour also continues. While the government figures asserts that there are around 20 million child labourers in India, NGOs, including the International Labour Organization, insist the true figure is probably closer to 60 million (with some estimates ranging upwards of 100 million. A huge amount of these are 'bonded', effectively a form of slavery.

The government has embarked on creating a series of 'special economic zones' (SEZs) as an incentive for investment. This has entailed a huge land grab, with millions being displaced with little or no compensation. In 2007, in supposedly communist-run West Bengal, villagers in Nandigram protested against the allocation of their lands to form a SEZ for a chemical

This is projected to rise sharply over the next few years, especially following the launch of the world's cheapest new car, the Nano, in 2008.

The 'creamy layer'

Those who are left at the top of the pile are the middle class, known in India as the 'creamy layer'. By no means a homogeneous grouping, they are best identified by their ability to consume, and this increasingly means desirable Western consumer goods. The bulk of the Indian middle class is made up of those who have traditionally occupied the role. These

Pupils at a prestigious school.

company. The ruling Communist Party of India (Marxist) sent in the police and cadres from the party to break up the demonstration, resulting in the deaths of up to 50 villagers. There were reports of rape and torture to break the resistance, and at least 3,500 people were forcibly displaced. In this case the state government came under intense scrutiny and pressure and the project was moved to another area. However, people continue to lose their lands and homes as the policy is followed across the country.

As elsewhere, cars are a sign of wealth and status in India, but although it might not seem so from the polluted and congested roads, only 15 per thousand people actually own one (as opposed to 526 in the UK, or 809 in the US).

All statistics relating to India should be seen as rough estimates; the concept of a national census in a country of this size and complexity is mind-boggling at best.

include lower-level civil servants, shop owners and larger farmers. They might have a small car, or almost certainly a 'two-wheeler' (motorbike or scooter), and basic consumer items such as a fridge and a TV. This group has tended to retain traditional ways of thinking and dressing but has seen its capacity to consume increase.

Those most visible on the streets of the large cities are the aspiring young. It is these educated

20- and 30-year-olds who present the glamorous face of contemporary India. They work in service industries such as IT, PR or in call centres, earning around 10,000 rupees upwards per month. They dress fashionably, shopping in new air-conditioned malls, own cars and two-wheelers and drink and smoke in chic bars.

However, not all is what it seems: for all their apparent modern worldliness, the vast majority of this group follow traditional paths: they are likely to live at home with their parents, and follow their wishes in whom they will marry, and much of their consumption is based on credit (now easily available in India). Most people in this income bracket who own a car or other expensive items calculate their monthly salary as a system of units, a certain number of which are already spent (through paying off loans on items or for cash) before they actually get the cash in their hands. This represents a large social shift, with the middle class traditionally having been wary of debt and now, to a certain extent, selling off the family silver to finance their new lifestyles.

At the very top of the heap are the policy-makers: top managers, politicians and civil servants, who can comfortably afford their large houses and cars. These are eclipsed by an even more select few, the super-rich. These industrialists and film stars are some of the wealthiest people on the planet, such as the chairman of Reliance Industries, Mukesh Ambani, pharmaceuticals mogul Dilip Shanghvi and Azim Premiji, chairman of software giant Wipro.

The political challenge

The greatest challenge facing India's politicians is to reduce the gap between rich and poor, and in so doing, stave off social unrest (already rife in some parts of the country, particularly the 'Naxalite belt' of Central India) in the face of such startling inequalities.

On current showing, this is not something with which they are having much success. The UPA government's rural job-guarantee scheme (promising 100 days' paid work to all workers in rural areas) was lauded as a huge step forward when launched in 2006, but has been beset with problems – not the least of which is corruption.

The major parties, however, may be facing the results of their decades of inaction as regional low-caste parties continue to gather

support. Currently the most prominent of these is the Bahujan Samaj Party (BSP), whose former leader, the charismatic Dalit spokeswoman, Mayawati, served as chief minister of India's most populous state, Uttar Pradesh until 2012. Her coalition of the low castes, Muslims

> A sign of India's recent advance into the ranks of technologically advanced nations can be seen in its space program. An unmanned moon mission launched in 2008.

At the Taj Hotel Club in Hyderabad.

and impoverished Brahman families remains a potent force in Indian politics, with a power base spreading across neighbouring states. Currently sitting in the Upper House of the Indian parliament, the Rajya Sabha, Mayawati is hotly tipped to be India's first Dalit prime minister.

The temple and the bomb

Alongside the socialist policies put forward after Independence by leaders such as Nehru, secularisation and, to borrow a government slogan of the time, 'unity through diversity' were also encouraged. These liberal ideas, however, have been under attack since the inception of modern India. While a disturbing political phenomenon of recent years has been the rise of the chauvinistic religious right, the movement's roots lie much further back in the country's political history.

This rise of the religious right has been dubbed 'saffronisation' after the colour associated with high-caste Hinduism, and its moment of arrival, and defining point in modern Indian history, was seen by many as the destruction of the Babri Masjid (mosque) in Ayodhya in 1992. This was the culmination of a process leading back to the Independence struggle.

Anti-Muslim riots at Partition saw the prominent Congressmen Sardar Vallabhai

Worshippers at a Kolkata mosque.

Patel, India's first Home Minister, and Rajendra Prasad call for the withdrawal of protection for Muslim citizens and the sacking of Muslim civil servants. However, the cause of Hindu nationalism suffered a severe setback when Gandhi, who preached tolerance, was assassinated by Nathuram Ghose, a Marathi Brahman with links to the RSS (Rashtriya Swayamsevak Sangh, a hard-line Hindu nationalist organisation). This gave Nehru the chance to outlaw communalist organisations, thus burying the ambitions of the Hindu right for the next two decades.

It was Nehru's daughter, Indira Gandhi, who next indulged in communal politics. Although she declared allegiance to the secular ideals of

her father, she actively courted Hindu support by surrounding herself with Hindu holy men and being seen to participate in Hindu rituals, particularly after her defeat in 1977 by a coalition government, which included a fledgling BJP (Bharatiya Janata Party).

The flirtation of Congress with communal politics (not only Hindu but also, with more immediately disastrous consequences, Sikh separatism in the Punjab) broke the taboo that had existed since Mahatma Gandhi's assassination, and the 1980s saw a steady rise in support for overtly communal parties, aided by disillusionment with the corruption-ridden Congress.

The main challenger was the BJP, led by veteran politician L.K. Advani (former leader of the right-wing opposition in the Lok Sabha), formed out of the Janata Party of the late 1970s and with close links to the RSS and Sangh Parivar (a collection of right-wing Hindu groups). They campaigned on a high-caste, right-wing agenda, espousing the ideal of Hindutva, a Hindu homeland.

The BJP got its first taste of power in 1989 as part of the coalition government of V.P. Singh. This did not last for long. Advani started to campaign for the destruction of the Babri Masjid, which Hindus were claiming was built on the site of Rama's birthplace and of an earlier temple. He embarked on a country-wide *yatra* (pilgrimage) to raise support for the building of a new temple, culminating in a visit to the site at Ayodhya itself. Advani was arrested and the government fell. However, the campaign continued to gather support, and in 1992 hundreds of *kar sevaks* (Hindu volunteers) tore down the mosque. This led to some of the worst communal rioting India has ever seen, in which many Muslims and Hindus were killed, particularly in Mumbai. In 2002, Hindu extremist mobs in Gujarat killed and displaced thousands of Muslims in a frenzy of violence that erupted after a lethal fire started on a train of Hindu pilgrims. Numerous mosques and shrines were also destroyed, allegedly with the connivance of the BJP-led state government.

The BJP Chief Minister, Narendra Modi, was himself implicated in the carnage, after accusations that he expressly held back police so that rioters could kill and loot (accusations which were rebuffed in a subsequent government report). The darling of Gujarat's business community, Modi continued to enjoy great popularity in his home state in the subsequent years, where he held the position of Chief Minister from 2001 to 2014. Having won convincingly the state elections of 2012, he was catapulted to the leadership of the BJP, which defeated a fractured and unpopular Congress-led coalition in the national elections of 2013–14. The BJP is currently India's largest political party in terms of representation in Parliament and, with its 110 million members, arguably the largest political party in the world. In May 2014, Modi, the man much reviled by Indian liberals for his autocratic tendencies and con-

2008. The unholy alliance between reactionary, right-wing Hinduism as espoused by the BJP and economic liberalisation remained in opposition after the elections of 2009, which were a triumph for Congress, but since winning the 2013–14 national elections they have dominated the national government again.

Although at first neo-liberalism and a fantastical reworking of the religious past seem strange bedfellows, given the disruption neoliberal policies cause to people's lives, religion and an aggressive promotion of the national myth are useful tools for keeping the populace

Hindus at Dwarkadhish Temple, Mathura.

nections with far-right Hindu organisations, became India's prime minister. His cabinet has vowed to reform India's infrastructure and government, encourage economic development and improve health and sanitation standards.

During its period in power between 1999 and 2004, BJP-led national government gave 'saffronisation' momentum. Religious minorities came under attack, and schoolbooks were rewritten glorifying India's mythological 'Aryan' past, describing *kar sevaks* as heroes and vilifying Islamic contributions to society. Long after the fall of the BJP-led government, attacks against Dalits and Muslims have continued, and Christians, too, have been set upon by Hindu militants – as in Odisha (Orissa) in

onside while state and national governments push through unpopular measures.

In an Indian context this saw an individualisation of Hindu identity, while at the same time there was an attempt to homogenise a highly disparate and eclectic group of beliefs and practices. Modern Hinduism, at least as promoted by the Sangh Parivar, is increasingly coming to resemble evangelical Christianity. An individual's relationship with a deity and personal observance of ritual, rather than action for the social good, are seen as the key to salvation. Thus, limiting consumption and displays of wealth in the face of deprivation is of less spiritual importance than, say, taking part in the building of a new temple to Ram at Ayodhya.

This move away from Gandhian ideals has been accompanied by a more canonical approach to the religious texts. Writings such as the *Vedas*, *Bhagavad Gita* and *Ramayana* have acquired the status of historical document rather than spiritual tract; they are statements of absolute fact, rather than guides towards universal truths that are open to interpretation. Modern right-wing Hinduism is far more interested in having a rigid rule book of rights and wrongs than in the traditional subtleties of religious debate, which in the past made the Hindu world relatively inclusive and tolerant.

of the Nuclear Test Ban Treaty, became a nuclear rogue state watched nervously each time tensions rose on the Line of Control separating Indian and Pakistan-controlled Kashmir.

Gaining a nuclear arsenal was integral to India's desire to become a major player on the world stage. It has ambitions to have a permanent seat at the UN Security Council and wields considerable clout in climate-change talks. Geopolitically, India is now being courted by the US, which sees it as a strategic bulwark against the rising power of China. To this end, the US has proposed a nuclear coop-

Schoolchildren listen carefully at a school in Kerala.

As with any insistence on the observance of a series of rules, minority viewpoints have suffered. In India this has had the most noticeable effect on the country's 100 million-plus Muslims. The national myth promoted by the BJP is fiercely anti-Islamic. For all the recent peace talks between the two countries, the external bogeyman has been largely identified as Pakistan, something reinforced by the murderous terrorist attacks in Mumbai in 2008.

All this was brought into sharp relief in 1998, when India tested a series of nuclear devices at Pokhran in the Thar Desert, followed only 15 days later by an announcement from rival Pakistan that it too had successfully tested long range nuclear missiles. India, never a signatory

eration deal that would unilaterally bring India in from the cold. Highly controversial, it is seen by many nations as fatally undermining the Nuclear Test Ban Treaty and has even been problematic on the domestic front. In 2008 the UPA government faced (and won) a vote of no-confidence when the Left parties, in this case supported by the opposition BJP, withdrew their support, fearing undue US interference in India's internal affairs. The deal was finally approved by the US Congress in October 2008, but continues to be contentious; in July 2009 India identified two sites on which US nuclear reactors could be built, but an August 2010 nuclear liability law passed by the Indian government has further stymied progress. As of 2015 the agreement had not yet been fully implemented.

Gender issues

Womens' rights have crept up the political agenda in India, especially in the last few years. A huge outpouring of anger, both national and international, followed the news in December 2012 that a young female medical student had been gang raped on a moving bus in the city. Her subsequent death from injuries sustained in the attack, and mass demonstrations across the country at India's seeming inability to transform traditional attitudes to gender, prompted a fervent national debate and has raised the coverage of subsequent attacks, as well as begun to improve the seriousness with which rape is regarded by the country's law enforcers.

But there is, of course, a long way to go before entrenched attitudes are improved. The dowry system is still thriving, and payments can reach into many hundreds of thousands of rupees. Inheritance and property rights are another area in which women are heavily discriminated against, and, as the country remains in thrall to traditional social roles, women face discrimination in the workplace, not least in terms of the salary they can expect to earn.

Greater wealth for the middle class has not necessarily led to positive social changes for women. The problem of female infanticide is on the increase, with some areas of the country now showing figures of fewer than 850 girls to every 1,000 boys. Some of the worst districts are in wealthy regions such as the Punjab, Haryana and Gujarat. Ironically, rising standards of living have increased the availability of foetal ultrasound screening and abortion to families. With an ongoing social and economic prejudice against having daughters, the gap in the male-female population ratio has increased. Overall in India there are about 40 million fewer women than men, and the overall female-to-male birth ratio has fallen to around 914 girls to every 1,000 boys, with the trend getting worse, especially in the north.

As the lower castes begin to adopt the social mores of the rich and wealthy, aping their aspirational lifestyles, they are beginning to embrace the dowry system on a scale never seen before. So far from dying out (it is technically illegal), the system is becoming more widespread, and the demands on the bride's family are increasing to a ridiculous extent (asking for cars, foreign holidays and houses). This in turn puts even greater pressure on couples to produce a son, and as the practice of giving dowries spreads across the social spectrum, the fear is that there will be an even greater increase in the abortion of female foetuses and female infanticide.

On the other hand, it is true that in New Delhi, Mumbai and Bengaluru amongst other cities, young women are leading relatively free and independent lives, and wearing clothes

Walking home from school in Chettinad, Tamil Nadu.

The rate of female infanticide increases in proportion with wealth. Haryana, one of richest regions in the country, has only 857 girls per thousand boys – the worst child sex ratio in India.

that would not long ago have been considered 'immodest'. As with many things, middle-class women, with their access to education and health care, have seen their prospects and freedoms open up, while poorer women concern themselves with the struggle for survival. The vast majority of women all over India are still restricted to the domestic sphere.

South Indian vegetarian cuisine.

FOOD AND DRINK

With its increasingly discerning restaurant clientele pushing the quality of what is on offer ever higher, India is now, more than ever, a genuinely world-class culinary destination.

The cuisines of India are as diverse as the country's culture. From the tandoori cooking of the north to the spicy curries of the south, every region has its own distinct flavours. North India tends to rely on a variety of breads, predominantly *rotis*, chappatis, *parathas* and naan, as a staple, whereas a southern meal is incomplete without rice. The sauces of the North tend to be pungently spiced, and feature either butter or ghee, clarified butter, in almost every dish, whereas southern dishes are lighter and tend to include coconut. A further defining feature of the northern kitchen, and unheard of in the South, is the *tandoor* oven, used to produce a range of *tandoori* dishes. History has also had a strong influence on Indian cuisine. The Mughal rulers left an enduring legacy; Mughlai cuisine, twinned with the flavours of the Punjab, has long dominated the dishes of the North. The Portuguese occupation of Goa also left its mark, with *vindaloo* perhaps the most famous Portuguese-Indian collaboration.

Essential ingredients

Despite the regional variation, there are significant similarities, the most obvious being the use of spices, an integral part of Indian cuisine appreciated not only for flavour but also as appetite stimulators and digestives. Care is taken to ensure that the spices enhance rather than dominate the basic flavour. Traditionally, the ingredients in each meal were governed by the time of the year and classifications of heating or cooling foods, age, and even personality. Once there were also injunctions on the six *rasas* or flavours to be included in every meal: sweet, salty, bitter, astringent, sour and pungent. Each was believed to have its particular physical

Nuts for sale at the Zaveri Bazaar in Mumbai.

ANGLO-INDIAN CUISINE

Visitors coming to India having had Indian cuisine in restaurants at home may be surprised to discover just how different the real thing is. A simple explanation for this is that the majority of what pass for 'Indian' restaurants abroad are, in fact, Bangladeshi, meaning they serve a cuisine similar in style to that found in the Indian state of West Bengal but markedly different to that found elsewhere in the country. An added surprise is that many of the staples of 'Anglo-Indian' cuisine, *phal* and *balti* for example, simply don't exist in India, and even if they do, generally bear no resemblance to their namesakes elsewhere.

benefit and was prescribed in specific ratio to the others.

Other than spices, the important ingredients in Indian cuisine include milk and milk products, particularly ghee and *dahi* (curd or

To the orthodox Indian, a meal is 'pure' only if cooked in ghee (clarified butter), an emphasis that derives not just from its distinctive fullness and unique flavour but from its preservative qualities.

Samosa with lime.

yoghurt). Served to mitigate the chilli 'hotness' of some dishes, *dahi* is often mixed with vegetables or fruit and is lightly spiced to create the *raitas* of the north and the *pachadis* of the south. It's also churned and served in summer as lassi, a cooling drink.

Dals (split lentils) are common to most parts of the country. Regional preferences and availability have resulted in a bewildering variety, from the thick tamarind-flavoured *sambars* of the south and the sweetish dals of Gujarat to the delicious *makhani dal* of North India.

Vegetarian variety

The style of vegetable cooking is determined by the cereal or main dish with which they are served. Deep-fried vegetable crisps are perfect accessories to the *sambar* and rice of Tamil Nadu. The thick *avial* stew of Kerala cooked in coconut oil, or the *kaottu* in a coconut and gram sauce, are perfect for rice-based meals. *Sarson ka sag*, mustard greens, eaten with *maki ki roti* (maize bread), are a particular favourite in the Punjab, while the delicately flavoured *chorchori* of Bengal complements Bengal's rice and fish.

Ahimsa, or non-violence, is one of the central tenets of the Hindu faith, and by extension includes the practice of vegetarianism. The variety of vegetarian dishes readily available in India is perhaps unrivalled.

India presents a vast range of vegetarian cooking. The roasted and steamed food of the south is lighter than northern cooking. Rice is the basis of every meal. It is served with *sambar*, *rasam* (a thin peppery soup), vegetables, both dry and in a sauce, and *pachadi*. Coconut is used in cooked foods as well as chutneys. Made of fermented rice and *dal* batter, the *dosa*, *vada* and *idli* are South Indian snacks popular all over the country.

The semolina-based *upma*, cooked with curry leaves and garnished with nuts and copra, is another favourite. Other in-between bites found everywhere are the *samosa*, a three-cornered deep-fried pastry parcel with potatoes, and *pakoras* or *bhajiyas* – vegetables coated in a gram batter and deep-fried. In Gujarat, another region famous for its

SOUTHERN MEALS

Meals in the south revolve around rice, which comes in two forms: 'white' and 'red' (the latter being parboiled before it's dried so that the grain absorbs the goodness of the husk. Rice is eaten with *dal*-based soups, thin, sour rasams and the thicker *sambars*, often flavoured with tamarind. To these are added 'sambar powder', made of spices such as coriander and *methi* (fenugreek) seeds. Often they are finished by 'tempering'; chillies and whole spices are heated in oil until the important black mustard seeds 'pop', then poured on the top of the dish. Dry vegetable dishes are also served with rice, with curd (yoghurt) and fiery pickles.

vegetarian food, gram flour is used in bread-making and as a component of various dishes.

Kadi, made from *dahi* and gram with spices, is popular. *Gur* or *jaggery* (unrefined sugar) adds a hint of sweetness to piquant sauces, as does *am rasa*, the puréed pulp of mangoes eaten with *puris*.

Although Bengali food is never sweetened, it is customary to serve a sweet along with the other food as a foil to the hot chillies, or for a change in flavour. Possibly the 'purest' form of North Indian vegetarian food is the

This was the origin of the famous *tandoori* cooking including *tandoori* chicken and fish, *seekh*, *boti* and *barra kababs*. Among the *rotis* are the *naan*, the *tandoori roti*, and its richer equivalent, the *tandoori paratha*.

> In keeping with religious mandates, Gujarati (especially Jain) and Bengali vegetarian food is often cooked without the 'heating' or stimulating spices.

Fish curry is ubiquitous in South India.

Banarsi. Lightly spiced, many specialities are based on *panir* (soft cheese). A good source of protein, it is cooked in innumerable ways, with spinach (*palak panir*), in a gravy with peas (*matter panir*) or lotus seeds (*panir phulmakhana*).

Then there are the deep-fried or stuffed breads, made of combinations of refined and wholemeal flour; the golden puffs called *puris*, the *parathas*, *baturas* and so on. Most widely eaten is the simple chapatti, baked on a griddle.

Meat and fish delicacies

Muslim influence is most evident in the cooking of meats. The major contribution was the *tandoor*, the conical earthen oven from which emerged a delectable array of *kababs* and *rotis*.

The fastidious Mughals transformed local recipes, developing what has become known as Mughlai cuisine, with its luscious sauces of *dahi*, cream and crushed nuts. An amazing variety is on offer, including: the rich *kormas* and *nargisi koftas* (meatballs shaped around a hard-boiled egg) of Lucknow; the *pasandas* or mutton steaks cooked in an almond sauce; the biryani, a layered rice and meat concoction famous in Hyderabad; and a variety of *kababs* that literally melt in the mouth.

Laden with nuts, dried fruits and saffron, Kashmiri Muslim food is a gourmet's joy and has much in common with Persian food. *Haleem*, mutton pounded with wheat; *gaustaba*, incredibly light meatballs; and *rogan josh* are well-known Kashmiri specialities.

Vinegar lends a different taste to the meat dishes of Goa. Pork *sorpotel*, *vindaloo*, Goan sausages and chicken *shakuti* or *cafreal* are inimitable.

Fish, too, is prepared in many ways: the mustard-flavoured *macher jhol* and *malai* or cream prawns of Bengal, the chilli-hot curries of Andhra, the coconut and curry-leaf flavoured specialities of the south and the memorable fish and shellfish curries of Goa. *Hilsa*, a Bengali speciality, has spiky bones that support meltingly delicate flesh and requires careful chewing. Dried fish, misleadingly known as Bombay Duck, is cooked

Preparing pav bhaji, a favourite fast food of Mumbaikars.

with vegetables or *dals* and adds interest to the simpler fare of Maharashtra.

The Parsis also contributed interesting dishes, like *dhansak*, meat cooked with five different *dals* and an unusual blend of spices, and *patrani machi*, lightly spiced fish steamed in banana leaves.

Chutneys and pickles, sweet, sour, hot, or all three, stimulate the appetite and add relish to a meal. Many ingredients can be used: mint, coriander, mango, ginger, lime and vegetables with extravagant spices or just salt.

Sweets

Often too sweet for the non-Indian palate, the huge array of Indian confections and desserts are largely milk-based. Bengal is particularly well known for its confections. These include the *rasagulla*, *sandesh*, *rasamalai* and the steaming hot *gulab-jamuns*. Typical of the north are the *barfis* (milk cakes), some of pure milk, others of coconut or various types of nuts. Crisp golden *jelabis*, dripping with syrup, made even in the tiniest bazaars all over the country, are breakfast and teatime favourites.

Common northern desserts include *kheer*, the Indian equivalent of rice pudding, usually flavoured with cardamom, saffron, pistachios, almonds, cashews or dried fruit; *shahi tukra*, a variation on bread pudding; *phirni*, made of powdered rice and served in earthenware bowls; and *kulfi*, a rich nutty ice cream. Sweets from the south include Mysore *pak* and the creamy *payasam*, while the Gujaratis are partial to *srikhand*, made of drained, sweetened and spiced *dahi*. *Halvas* are created from ingredients as diverse as carrots, semolina, *dals*, eggs or even wholemeal flour.

Finally, there is the satisfying ritual of the after-dinner *masala pan*, which is praised for its digestive and medicinal, if addictive, properties. It is a combination of betel leaf, areca nut, catechu, cardamom, cloves and other fragrant ingredients.

Where to eat

Choosing where to eat can be a tricky business, with such a wide range of eateries, from street stalls to the swankiest restaurants, on offer. One solution is simply to follow the crowd; the most popular places tend to serve the tastiest and most hygienically prepared fare, although people's perceptions of 'tasty' may vary. The cheapest places – street stalls and the most basic restaurants – will typically have only a limited choice of dishes on offer: as often as not you get what you're given. Owners and staff are unlikely to speak English, or have menus, so be prepared either to point out what you want or to take it as it comes. *Thalis* in the North or *meals* in the South will generally include a variety of dishes, and are often replenished free of charge.

Next up would be the *dhaba*, or roadside restaurant. The most basic and traditional of these will double as truck stops, and often have only *charpois*, a wooden framed bed with a latticed cloth top, to sit on. They'll generally have a limited range of dishes, and while quality can vary, the food is often much better than the surroundings would suggest. More sophisticated examples of the *dhaba* now feature tables and chairs, menu cards in English, a wide range of dishes and overall can represent not only great value but a great eating experience as well.

Plush restaurants are becoming more and more common in the bigger cities, and often pride themselves on being 'multi-cuisine'. This typically means that Indian, Chinese and some Continental dishes will be on the menu, although all are likely to have at least an Indian twist to them. Five-star hotels tend to offer the finest dining experiences, with the whole range of international cuisines, from Thai to Mongolian to Italian and Lebanese, usually available in one or other of the best hotels in the biggest cities.

Water is about the only thing that most Indians would drink with a meal. Here again there are various categories; the cheapest restaurants are likely to serve only tap or well water, which should be strictly avoided. Next up is 'filter water', which is generally fine but quality will depend on the sophistication of the filter and regularity with which it has been maintained. The vast majority of bottled water in India is in fact 'filter water', but can generally be regarded as safe to drink, particularly if it comes from one of the nationwide brands. Top of the heap are the handful of genuine mineral waters on offer, distinguishable by their higher price and superior taste. The other drink which is taken with food is *lassi*, a yoghurt-based concoction famed for its cooling properties, useful in mitigating the effects of a hot, spicy meal. *Chai*, sweet, spicy, milky tea, is often served after a meal in the North, whereas coffee is the hot beverage of choice down South.

Cafés are becoming increasingly widespread, with several local, as well as one or two international, chains now operating in most major cities and towns. They have become very popular meeting places for both students and businesspeople, who often use them for activities as diverse as board meetings, interviews and matchmaking.

Soft drinks are available in all but the most remote locations and are generally safe; most of the popular local brands have now been either bought or eradicated by the major global companies.

India's relationship with alcohol is nothing if not complicated. Gujarat and Mizoram are the only officially dry states, with alcohol available to varying degrees everywhere else. Government-run 'English Wine & Beer Shops' are widespread, but vary significantly in what they offer. The 'English' has nothing to do with being from England, but instead denotes company-made alcohol, rather than local hooch. In smaller towns and villages, these shops will often serve hooch as well – locally made home brew that is responsible for hundreds of deaths every year and should be avoided at all costs,

Indian sweets.

despite the temptingly low cost. In all but the major cities these shops will offer a selection of Indian-made beers and liquors, often in quarter- or half-bottles intended for immediate consumption, making for something of a rowdy atmosphere come night-time. An increasingly wide range of well-priced international spirits is available in the big cities, although wine is still hard to come by despite some decent local produce. All restaurants technically require a liquor licence in order to serve alcohol. However, these are often expensive and/or difficult to obtain, meaning that many places will serve beer on the sly, often in mugs or teapots to disguise the contents in the event of a surprise police inspection.

FESTIVALS

India has a huge number of festivals throughout the year, from pan-Hindu celebrations to the appeasement of local deities and political parades.

Festivals are a part of daily life in India, perhaps an inevitability given the thousands of deities, saints, prophets and gurus who must be worshipped, propitiated and remembered. A large number of these festivals stem from Hinduism. Myriad practices and an enormous body of legend and history bring an extensive range of significance and association to most Hindu religious occasions.

There are numerous local and regional festivals but the most important are celebrated nationwide. The first of the significant pan-Hindu festivals to occur after the monsoon is Navaratri, or 'nine nights' (September to October). This is a major celebration of the goddess Devi or Shakti in her more fearsome aspects. At the end of Navaratri comes the day of **Dussehra**, the celebration of Durga's victory over Mahisasura, the buffalo-demon. Festivities often include fasting, and then the burning or submerging in water of effigies of the various Gods involved on Dussehra.

Divali, also known as 'festival of light' (usually October to November), is both a celebration of Rama's return from exile and of the goddess Lakshmi. Following the spring festival of **Vasant** (when the goddess Sarasvati is worshipped in January to February) the next major celebration, aside from **Pongal** (the southern harvest festival also known as Sankranti), is Sivaratri, the Shiva festival in February or March. This is followed in North India by **Holi**, the North Indian harvest festival. The festival year comes full circle with **Janmastami**, the birthday of Krishna, and **Ganesh Chaturthi** in August/September.

The Maha Kumbha Mela at Allahabad, on the confluence of the Yamuna and Ganges rivers, takes place every three years, and is the largest religious gathering in the world.

The North Indian springtime festival of Holi is a time of abandon and is celebrated by the throwing of coloured powders.

Brightly coloured powders can be found for sale during the Holi festival. The throwing of these powders symbolises the festival as a game that breaks down social conventions.

A statue of the Hindu god Lord Krishna.

NON-HINDU FESTIVALS

Islamic festivals occur throughout the year and range from major events to localised *urs* (the anniversary of a saint's death) held in *dargahs* (tombs) across the country. The most important of the pan-Islamic festivals are 'Eid-al-Fitr and 'Eid al-Adha, both dependent on the lunar calendar and so are moveable. The first celebrates the end of the fast of Ramadan and the second the end of the period of the Haj, or pilgrimage to Makkah (Mecca). The most important festival of Shia Muslims is Muharram, which mourns the matrydom of Hussain, the grandson of the Prophet.

The major festival of the Buddhist year is Buddha Jayanti, which takes place in April to May. It celebrates the birth of the Buddha and also his reaching of enlightenment. Jains commemorate a similar event at Dip Divali. This occurs 10 days after the Hindu festival of Divali and celebrates the liberation of the tirthankara Mahavira from the wheel of life.

Each Hindu temple has a festival in honour of the deity it enshrines, often accompanied by processions, music and important pujas (acts of worship).

Divali, the festival of lights, sees families set 'diyas', small oil lamps or candles, outside their doors to guide Rama back to Ayodhya, hopefully ensuring a prosperous year ahead.

Shivaratri, a festival held to honour the god Shiva's dance of creation that brought the world into being, and also his joining with his consort Parvati.

PERFORMING ARTS

From classical performances on the concert stage to brass bands playing at weddings, India's musical and dance traditions are many and varied.

India's performing arts permeate every aspect of society and culture, forming one of the richest complexes of music, dance and drama anywhere in the world. Perhaps most famous in the West for the classical music of northern India (also known as Hindustani music), there is also a separate, though related, classical tradition in the south (known as Karnatak music) and a myriad of separate local dance and theatre genres.

Hindustani and Karnatak music

The two classical music traditions of South Asia share certain common ideas and techniques, but in presentation, repertory and even instruments they are radically different. Broadly, the classical music culture of the north may be seen as a Muslim tradition, emerging from the Mughal courts. Indeed, many lineages of musicians (family and teaching pedigrees known as *gharanas*) trace their origins back to the famous performer Tansen who was employed at the court of Akbar (1556–1605).

In contrast, classical musicians in the south are overwhelmingly Hindu and trace their musical roots back to singer-saints of the 17th and 18th centuries. The three most famous of these (known as the 'musical trinity') are Tyagaraja (1767–1847), Syama Sastri (1772–1827) and Muttusvami Diksitar (1775–1835), whose compositions still form the backbone of the Karnatak repertoire.

Raga and tala

The works of these singer-saints also highlight a further difference between the two traditions. In general Hindustani music is improvised while Karnatak music is dependent on compositions (either written or passed

Musicians playing centa drums and ilatalam (cymbals) at a festival in Kerala.

down orally). There are, however, two concepts that they share – *raga* and *tala*, the first dealing with the organisation of pitch, the second with the organisation of rhythm and musical time.

Ragas are collections of notes (like a Western scale) that have a particular musical 'flavour' (the word *raga* comes from the Sanskrit for 'colour') and which must be performed in a certain way. The names of *ragas*, particularly in the north, often refer to the 'piece' being performed. So, you might hear musicians say they are going to play *Yaman*, *Bhairav* or *Desh* (all popular Hindustani *ragas*). In the south the piece will take its name from the text of the music being performed, although that too will be composed in a specific *raga*.

Tala is used to describe the repeating rhythmic cells (measured by the number of beats) that give the performance a rhythmic form. In the West we are used to hearing music with four-beat units (most popular music) or three beats (like a waltz), but in India these can be much more complex, especially in the south, with repeating *talas* of five, seven and eight beats being common. This complexity increases as musicians employ techniques of doubling or tripling the speed of the music within the *tala*.

Genres and instruments

Indian classical music is dominated by two different vocal genres, *khayal* in the north and *kriti* in the south. While there are numerous other musical forms, these are the two you are most likely to hear performed in concerts. *Khayal* is said to have been invented by Sultan Husain Sharqi in the 15th century, and it comprises two short, contrasting compositions (known as a *bandish* or *ciz*) that are used as a vehicle for improvisation. There is also a short, unaccompanied introduction that presents the notes of the *raga* about to be played.

In the instrumental adaption of *khayal* now familiar to many in the West, the performer (usually on either the sitar or *sarod*, both plucked lutes) gives a longer introduction, an *alap*, adopted from the more austere – and highly valued – vocal genre *dhrupad*. This presents a highly worked-out presentation of the *raga*, introducing each note in turn. The instrumental version of the *bandish* or *ciz* that follows is known as a *gat*, and this too gives the basic material for further improvisation.

Both the vocal and instrumental performances are accompanied by a number of other performers. The most prominent of these is the tabla player, who keeps the tempo and marks the *tala* on a pair of small kettledrums. Also on stage will be a *tambura*, a long lute a little like a four-string sitar that keeps a drone throughout the performance. At vocal performances you may also see either a *sarangi* (a short lute played with a bow) or a harmonium, that imitate the line of the soloist.

In the south the dominant form is the *kriti*. This is a devotional song form that grew out of the three-part *kirtana*. The composers of the

'musical trinity' developed the *kirtana* by adding a series of composed variations known as *sangati* to the form. *Kritis* are performed not only by singers but also on the *vina* (a large plucked lute) and sometimes the violin, now the most popular accompanying melodic instrument in South India.

Local traditions

As well as its impressive classical musical heritage, India is also home to numerous local performance genres, many of which are intimately tied in with the wider functioning

Vina player, Trivandrum, Kerala.

POPULAR MUSIC

Until recently, popular music in India was dominated by film songs from Bollywood and South Indian movies. While this still forms the bulk of the popular music heard in the country, there is a small but steadily growing indigenous pop, rock and dance music scene, prompted in part by the arrival of MTV on Indian televisions. Largely based in the major cities such as Delhi, Mumbai and Bengaluru, it has its greatest following among the newly wealthy young middle class. There are now several dozen indigenous rock bands, while on the dance scene *bhangra* is still popular, with many of the artists coming from NRI (non-Resident Indian) communities.

of South Asian society. Due to its inherently auspicious nature, music is used to mark calendrical festivals and rituals, such as the Ganapati *puja* or Holi, as well as being used in the worship of local deities. Weddings are one of the occasions that demand music, and there is a complex set of songs and processional music – usually performed by brass bands playing film songs – that forms part of the celebrations. These can make for quite a spectacle; visitors to the North during the auspicious winter months are likely to see a horse-mounted groom riding slowly down the road, followed by a quaintly uniformed, and singularly loud, brass band. Next in line will be the male wedding guests, all dancing to the beat blaring from speakers trundling along on home-made chariots towards the back of the procession, with a truck struggling along under the weight of a smoke-belching diesel generator bringing up the rear.

Classical dance

As with music, there are a huge number of dance forms in South Asia, some of them still undocumented. From these a select few have

Young dancers of Mohiniattam, a classical dance from Kerala.

DEVOTIONAL MUSIC

While all music in India is, at least theoretically, considered to be auspicious and so in some way devotional, there are certain types of performance that are used explicitly in praise of deities or in temples. Not restricted to Hindusim, there are songs from the Sikh holy book – the *Granth Sahib* – known as *kirtan*, and Muslim devotional songs known as *qawwali*, although the latter are more often heard in neighbouring Pakistan.

The most widespread devotional form, however, that you are likely to encounter is the Hindu *bhajan*. This is a collective song form usually performed in temples. Often the text is limited to a repetition of the name of the deity being praised and the performance is usually of call-and-response singing. The standard accompaniment is a *dholak* (a small barrel drum), small pairs of cymbals (usually called *tal*) and a harmonium. While performances are generally given by groups of non-professional devotees, there are professional *bhajan* groups who have made numerous recordings and even a sub-genre of pop *bhajans* with a strong rhythmic beat.

Other music-making you may encounter in South Indian temples is the processional music of the *periyar melam*, an ensemble consisting of long oboes called *nagasvarams* and *tavils* (very loud barrel drums). In Kerala temple festivals often include performances by large ensembles of drummers.

been identified as 'classical' dances – those with long and identifiable histories and with a body of laws (sastras) that govern their performance.

The style now known as *bharatanatyam* grew out of Tamil temple dance. The female dancers, called *devadasis*, would perform for the deity as part of temple rituals. Although the dancers were considered to be married to the deity, they were also taken as sexual partners by the temple priests or local king (the patron of the temple). This outraged Victorian sensibilities, and an 'anti-nautch campaign' (from the Sanskrit *naca* for dance) eventually led to the dancers being banned from temples in 1947.

At the same time a Brahman dancer and teacher, Rukmini Devi, sought to put elements of the dance on stage to promote an indigenous cultural identity in the run-up to Independence. It is this solo dance, accompanied by an ensemble of Karnatak music, that is now seen on the concert stage.

Another form of dance with a similar history is Odissi. This dance derives from the temple dancers at the Jagannath temple in Puri, Odisha (Orissa). In 1950, following the ban on temple dance, a group of scholars met to reinvent the tradition for performance on the stage, taking their ideas from temple sculpture and paintings.

The most popular classical dance in the north is *kathak*. Closely linked to the rise of Hindustani music at the North Indian courts – particularly the 'light' forms of *khayal*, *thumri* and *dadra* – it was traditionally danced by courtesans. The dance itself is characterised by fast pirouettes and rhythmic patterns created by the sound of the pellet bells worn around the dancers' ankles.

Dance-dramas and theatre

A slightly different form of performance is found in India's many dance-dramas. These use music and dance to tell a story, often one derived from the Hindu epics. One of the most spectacular performances you are likely to encounter is of *kathakali*. In this male Keralan dance form the characters – from the *Ramayana* or *Mahabharata* – wear dramatic costumes and make-up. The different colours used in the make-up give the audience a clue as to the role of the character; green is good, red is evil and white is for deities.

Andhra Pradesh also has a traditionally male-only dance-drama, *kuchipudi*, which is named after the village in the Krishna-Godvari delta where it originated. The stories portrayed by the dancer are taken from the life of Krishna and his consort Bhama.

As well as these classical dramas, there are many local theatre forms across India. In the north one of the more racy is the secular *nautanki*, unusual in that it only uses religious themes to denote concepts of good or evil and often draws on Muslim romance stories. In *nautanki* the actors use the drama to comment

A colourful Theyyam dancer in Bekal, Kerala.

The earliest textual source for South Asian performance traditions is the Natyasastra, thought to have been written by the sage Bharata around AD 150. In it he describes the practice of music, dance and theatre.

on current affairs, as they also do in the Tamil street theatre *terukkuttu*. More religiously-minded dramas performed at festivals are the *Ras* and *Ram lilas* of Braj and Varanasi that depict the lives of Krishna and Rama respectively, while both Kerala and Andhra Pradesh have shadow puppet theatres akin to those found in Indonesia.

CINEMA

In 1896, the Lumière Brothers' films were first shown in Mumbai; now India's film industry is even bigger than Hollywood, producing around 900 feature films a year.

Think of entertainment in India and you are bound to imagine the cinema. The biggest film industry in the world is characterised by big blockbusters that incorporate love stories, action, violence and song-and-dance routines. Gaudy sets and set pieces inhabit an imaginary world of glamour with an at times eye-wateringly tasteless array of costumes. That, at least, is the popular perception.

While there is some truth in this characterisation, the films are perhaps best seen as morality plays – good versus evil plays a prominent part – that draw on some of the conventions of traditional Indian theatre. Also, in recent years, more nuanced films have explored traditionally grey areas of morality (such as affairs and divorce in *Kabhi Alvida Naa Kehna*) or idealistic notions of unity and difference, in *Amar, Akbar, Anthony*, *Chak De India* and *3 Idiots*.

Huge amounts of money are made and invested in the cinema, and there have long been accusations of Bollywood's connections with the Mumbai underworld, perhaps adding an extra frisson of glamour for its vast number of adoring fans.

Bollywood, Kollywood, Tollywood

India's mainstream blockbusters are made by the three main regional films industries, Hindi cinema (Bollywood) made in Mumbai, Tamil films (Kollywood) from Chennai, and Telugu movies (Tollywood) made in Hyderabad. While Bollywood is generally held to be the biggest film industry in the world, at times Telugu output has beaten the Hindi industry and, overall, South Indian cinema is more productive than that in the north. South Indian cinema has even given Bollywood some of its biggest stars, including Sri Devi, Aishwarya Rai and A.R. Rahman, who

A scene from 'PK', the highest grossing Indian film in history.

FILM CITY

One of Asia's biggest studio complexes is just beyond the jaws of a fake shark that guards MGR Film City. This vast site on the outskirts of Chennai is funded by the state government. Here, 36 sets stand ready. Films are shot in Tamil and also dubbed into Malayalam, Telugu, Kannada and Hindi. Tourists are sometimes asked to be extras, especially on Raj-era films. Notable crossover successes into Bollywood include Sri Devi and Rekha. But the most powerful figure is Jayalalitha Jayaram, one-time starlet turned politician, who built the studio in memory of her lover M.G. Ramachandran, former chief minister and megastar.

have all made the transition to Hindi movies. The South Indian industry has also given birth to a number of highly influential politicians: M.G. Ramachandran, M. Karunanidhi and Jayalitha in Tamil Nadu, N.T. Rao in Andhra.

The first silent film made in India was *Raja Harishchandra* (1913) filmed in Mumbai, followed in the south by Tamil Nadu's *Kicaka Vadam* in 1917. While these were popular and the industry grew considerably during the 1920s, it was not until the advent of the 'talkies' in 1931 that India's close and passionate affair with the movies began in earnest. These early films were quite racy, featuring plenty of flesh and kissing, and it was not until Independence in 1947 that a form of 'moral censorship' came into play. The banning of the on-screen kiss and physical contact between a film's lovers led to inventive ways around the problem, and a whole host of wet-sari scenes, suggestive dances around trees and just-in-time fades.

Until the 1970s most films were romances, and the on-screen loves of stars such as Nargis and Sunil Dutt (who became real-life lovers after starring in *Mother India*, 1957), and Madhubala and Raj Kapoor were all-consuming topics of discussion among their many fans. This changed in the 1970s with the arrival of a new generation of actors, including Amitabh Bachchan. His appearance in the 1975 mega-hit *Sholay* ushered in an era of action movies, dubbed 'Curry Westerns' in homage to the Italian movies that inspired them.

While Sholay played on an appetite for violence, the 1990s saw the rebirth of the family drama and romance. Films such as *Hum Aapke Hain Hum*, *Raja Hindustani* and *Maine Pyar Kiya* managed the difficult task of promoting traditional family values while chaste but scantily clad actresses and muscle-bound heros flirted and revelled in material excess. In Bollywood the superstars of the period included Karisma Kapoor and Madhuri Dixit as well as Salman, Shah Rukh and Amir Khan. In the south, Rajnikant and Simran Bagga shot to fame. All of these actors continue to be popular, with Shah Rukh Khan the current King of Bollywood and Rajnikant having achieved near-godlike status in the South.

Film music

The popular music of India par excellence is film song (*filmi git*). It is heard almost everywhere, from shops and the backs of rickshaws to temples playing songs from devotional films (known as 'mythologicals'), as well as in the cinema itself. The first Indian 'talkie' was *Alam Ara*, made in Mumbai in 1931. Based in some respects on traditional Indian theatre, the plot was broken up by songs and dances that pushed the action forward and represented the passing of time. Not only were these early films extremely popular, but so were the songs associated with them, and thus the first pan-Indian form of popular music was born.

In the early films the actors and actresses sang themselves, but when recording technology allowed the songs to be dubbed in the late 1930s most film music became pre-recorded.

Anil Kapoor is well known internationally for his roles in '24' and 'Slumdog Millionaire'.

It was at this point that specialist 'playback singers' began their rise to superstardom. The biggest of these was, and continues to be, Lata Mangeshkar. Along with her sister Asha Bhosle and Geeta Dutt, her high-pitched voice has come to represent the ideal female vocal style. Of course the heroine had to have a hero, and the male singers Muhammad Rafi and Mukesh became as idolised as Lata and Asha.

The composers who write the songs, known as 'music directors', command huge payments and are almost as famous as the singers. While early music directors based their songs on traditional Muslim genres such as *ghazal* and *thumri*, soon composers such as the duo Shanker-Jaikishan,

S.D. Burman and the brothers Kalyanji Anandji were bringing ever more eclectic influences to bear on the music. These ranged from *bhajans* to jazz and Latin music to Western pop and rock.

Particularly influential were Western film scores like that for the Blaxploitation movie *Shaft* or the TV series *Mission Impossible*. Contemporary music directors, such as A.R. Rahman, are now global names, their music having spread through extensive NRI (non-resident Indian) communities or, in the case of Rahman, making it onto London's West End stage via his musical *Bollywood Dreams* and into Western

cinemas via his soundtrack for *Slumdog Millionaire*, for which he won an Oscar.

The New Wave

After Independence some film-makers were not drawn by the glamour and excess (or vulgarity, depending on your point of view) of Bollywood and turned instead to the French *Nouvelle Vague*. In India the initial inspiration came from the Bengali director Satyajit Ray (see page 295), who brought India into the international film scene with *Pather Panchali* (*The Song of the Road*, 1955). Later, aided by the government-funded

Bollywood star Shah Rukh Khan.

The actress Nagma.

THE TELEVISION REVOLUTION

For decades, until the early 1980s, television was controlled by government and concentrated on a heavy-handed mix of education and propaganda. It reached only 13 percent of the country. Then the focus shifted from social development to entertainment; the government liberalised the import of colour TVs and VCRs, and television proliferated, along with pirated videos.

The launch of Star TV in 1991 brought an entertainment channel, Star Plus, Prime Sports, MTV and the BBC World Service to Indian screens. In 1992, a Hindi channel was added to Star. Zee, with its talk shows, games, sitcoms and soaps, turned out to be a huge hit with the young and burgeoning middle classes. Stung by this

competition, Doordarshan, the Indian state-owned television network, launched an entertainment channel, Metro. Independent entrepreneurs also jumped into the fray by hiring transponders on various satellites and floating channels in Hindi and other Indian languages.

A substantial segment of this new programming was film-based, but social issues were tackled; one channel even took to telecasting a late-night 'adult' film on Saturdays. Now there are more than 500 channels across the country, and the major cities have access to over 100 cable and satellite channels, more than half of which are free. This has made India the world's third-largest TV market; 130 million households tune in daily.

Film Finance Corporation (FFC), other directors began to emulate his example. Mrinal Sen, also from Kolkata, was both critically and commercially successful with *Bhuvan Shome*, and soon directors were making films in other regional languages, especially Malayalam through the work of P. Bhaskaran and Ramu Kariyat (who made the critically acclaimed *Nilakkuyil* in 1957), M.T. Vasudevan Nair and Aravindan.

Despite a flowering of Hindi realist cinema during the 1980s (including films by Satyajit Ray), by the 1990s the New Wave had lost its way. Aside from one or two films by indigenous directors,

values, as well as innovations to the standard Bollywood format. Over the past few years, nearly all the highest grossing Indian films have been genre flicks: *3 Idiots* (2009), starring Amir Khan, and *Bajrangi Bhaijaan* (2015), starring Salman Khan, broke box office records, despite being feel-good comedy dramas. *Ghajini* (2008) was a dark psychological thriller, while *Don 2* (an action thriller; 2011), *Ra I* (a sci-fi superhero blockbuster; 2011) and *PK* (a satirical science-fiction comedy, which became the highest-grossing Indian film ever; 2014) were all radical departures from the Bollywood mainstream.

A Bollywood dance scene.

the headlines have been grabbed by expatriate film-makers, especially the controversial Deepa Mehta. Her films have tackled taboo subjects in India, such as lesbianism in *Fire* (1998) and the treatment of widows in *Water* (2005).

The future

While more 'art house' films from India have achieved audiences beyond the Subcontinent, such as Meera Nair's *Monsoon Wedding* (2001), Bollywood has gained a substantial following outside India, principally with expatriate South Asians resident in the US and UK. Because of the higher ticket prices, receipts from overseas markets often outstrip those in India itself, and have spurred a dramatic increase in production

Bollywood actors and actresses have found other ways to gain fame abroad. Shilpa Shetty's headline-grabbing encounter with the UK version of the reality TV show *Big Brother* in 2007 raised the profile of the industry (even if she subsequently found herself in trouble back home after being kissed in public by Richard Gere). The trade goes both ways, however, with the 'Big B' (as Amitabh Bachchan is known) revitalising his career by hosting *Kaun Banega Crorepati* (India's *Who Wants to be a Millionaire?*). In a final twist, Kaun Bangega Crorepati became the starting point for the massive international hit, *Slumdog Millionaire*, the 2008 Anglo-Indian rags-to-riches film which scooped eight Oscars.

ART AND ARCHITECTURE

A highlight of any visit to India is the wealth of artistic treasures, from exquisite temple architecture to ancient murals and sculptures and beautiful book illustrations.

For more than 2,000 years India has been witness to a succession of amazingly diverse artistic traditions. While Buddhist architecture and painting are now only found in the Himalayan valleys in the far north of India, temple construction and the fashioning of bronze and stone images for worship continue to be funded by wealthy Hindu and Jain patrons throughout the country. Indeed, Akshardham, reputedly the largest Hindu temple in India, was inaugurated in Delhi as recently as 2005.

Public mosques and tombs of saints are continuously refurbished and extended so as to serve the needs of India's substantial Muslim population. The descendants of India's royal families may have stopped building massive forts and sumptuous palaces, but many are successfully converting their ancestral residences into luxury hotels. Meanwhile, a new wealthy class of industrialists and IT specialists have begun to erect high-rise offices and ostentatious residences – the latest of which is 27 storeys high and includes three helipads, parking for 100 cars and employs 300 staff – and to collect the works of contemporary lauded Indian painters and sculptors.

In spite of this enthusiastic patronage, India is dotted with abandoned monasteries, temples, forts and tombs. Unesco has now inscribed 25 Indian properties on its prestigious World Heritage List, but India's historical legacy is still at risk from unprecedented urban development.

Buddhist shrines and monasteries

The earliest surviving architecture in India is Buddhist. From the 5th century BC onwards hemispherical earthen mounds known as stupas were raised to enshrine the relics of the

Ancient sculpture of a Hindu deity, State Government Museum, Chennai.

Buddha and his followers, and to symbolise the precepts of the new religion. Stupas built by the emperor Ashoka in the 3rd century BC at the various holy sites of Buddhism in North India, as well as in neighbouring Nepal and Sri Lanka, are faced with stone, and topped by umbrella-like stone finials that represented the ascending heavens.

The best-preserved stupa of this era is at Sanchi in Madhya Pradesh. Its hemispherical solid mound is surrounded by a pathway defined by a railing with monumental portals. Though built of limestone, the posts and lintels at Sanchi clearly imitate the details of timber construction. The portals are enlivened with relief carvings that illustrate episodes from the life of Buddha, though without any representation of the Master, since this was forbidden in early Buddhism.

Other reliefs at Sanchi depict popular tales, known as Jatakas, describing events from the Buddha's previous lives. Similar panels adorn the railings and portals of other stupas, such as those at Bharhut in Madhya Pradesh and Amaravati in Andhra Pradesh. These carvings are now on view in the Indian Museum, Kolkata, the Government Museum, Chennai, and the British Museum, London.

The Ajanta murals date back to the 2nd century BC.

Buddhist sites were also provided with monasteries, known as *viharas*, to accommodate the growing community of followers. Here, small residential chambers are arranged on four sides of a courtyard, often with a shrine in the middle of one side. Kitchens, wells and stores are generally located a short distance away. Constructed of brick, *viharas* survive today only in a dilapidated condition, as at Sarnath, on the outskirts of Varanasi in Uttar Pradesh. Among the carved sandstone images found here is a masterpiece portraying Buddha preaching the "First Sermon" in the deer park at Sarnath, dating from the 5th-century Gupta period, now displayed in the local archaeological museum. Here, too, is a magnificent polished sandstone lion capital that once topped a column erected by Ashoka.

Buddhist sculptures have also been found at numerous other sites in India, notably at Mathura in Uttar Pradesh. The finest is a Gupta-period Buddha dressed in a toga-like robe, with a full halo, now in the Government Museum, Mathura, Uttar Pradesh. Commemorative shrines, too, were erected at Buddhist holy sites, the most famous being that at Bodhgaya in Bihar, the site where Buddha attained enlightenment beneath the bodhi tree. The steeply pyramidal brick tower of the shrine dates back to the 7th century, but has been much altered in recent times.

A more complete idea of ancient Buddhist architecture and art may be had from the cave-temples of Maharashtra. Excavated into basalt cliffs, these monuments were intended as retreats for religious communities supported by local merchants. Shrines known as chaitya

BOOK ILLUSTRATION

In the Sultanate courts of the 13th–15th centuries book production was encouraged. The Mughals who followed were also a literary dynasty, with Babur, their 16th-century founder, having written his memoirs in the first guidebook to Hindustan, in which with the eye of a naturalist he described the different species of flora and fauna of the region of Hind. His son, Humayun, brought over the great painters Mir Sayyid Ali and Abd us-Samad from Persia. Almost 100 years later his grandson, Jahangir, wrote his memoirs and in a move to outdo Babur he employed the master painter of animals, Mansur, to illustrate his descriptions of the natural world.

The Emperor Akbar, who is reputed to have been illiterate, became a great patron of the arts, particularly painting. Illustrated histories of the Mughals were commissioned as official chronicles – the *Babur Nama*, *Timur Nama* and *Akbar Nama* – and artists recruited from all over India. One of the greatest works of the period, a vast illustrated version of the epic *Hamza Nama* on 1400 canvas folios, was produced by Akbar's atelier from 1562–1577. The style was bold and dynamic, fusing Islamic and Hindu elements, and heavily influenced the other Indian courts, where versions of the popular epics the *Ramayana* and *Mahabharata* were soon commissioned in the new style. Mughal painting introduced a quality of portraiture still unsurpassed today.

halls at Ajanta date back to the 2nd century BC, though examples from the 5th–7th centuries AD are also found at Ajanta and Ellora. Chaitya halls have nave-like interiors divided into triple aisles by lines of columns. The central aisles are roofed with barrel-vaulted ceilings that recall bamboo construction; these vaulted ceilings are expressed on the outside of the hall as horseshoe-shaped windows. The principal object of devotion inside chaitya halls is a monolithic stupa, embellished in later examples with sculpted images of the teaching Buddha. The halls have part-circular ends that define a pathway proceeding around the stupa.

Like brick-built *viharas*, rock-cut monasteries at Ajanta also have cells arranged around a square hall, with a shrine on one side accommodating a seated Buddha figure. The walls are covered with murals portraying Jataka stories, as well as scenes showing Buddha as a prince, ascetic and teacher, there being no prohibition on the representation of the Master by the 5th century. The Ajanta murals are the earliest Buddhist paintings to be found anywhere in Asia; but they are also vivid records of contemporary life in Indian palaces, cities, gardens and forests. Later examples of Buddhist paintings are found in the remote

> The depiction of the Buddha, the 'Enlightened One', in painting or sculpture, represented one of the highest aspirations of human art and thought.

sub-Himalayan valleys of Ladakh in Kashmir. The shrines of the monastic complex at Alchi, for instance, have their interiors cloaked in brightly coloured murals showing diverse Mahayana divinities. Dating from the 12th century and later, they reflect artistic and religious influences from neighbouring Tibet.

Hindu and Jain temples

Stone temples enshrining votive images of Hindu divinities as well as of Jain saints date back to the Gupta period. As in Buddhist architecture, the earliest examples are cut out of solid rock. The cave-temple on Elephanta Island in Mumbai harbour, excavated in the 6th century, consists of a spacious columned hall, or *mandapa*, with a central shrine housing a *lingam*, the

cosmic phallic emblem of Shiva. Scenes deeply sculpted into the surrounding walls represent Shiva as the dancer or the ascetic; seated in meditation or spearing demons; marrying his consort, the goddess Parvati; and playing dice with her on Kailash, their mountain home. At the end of the central aisle is a colossal bust of the god with three heads, those on the side representing Shiva's contrasting feminine and demonic aspects. Smaller Hindu cave temples of the same period are found at Mamallapuram in Tamil Nadu. These too are embellished with mythological wall-carvings, especially of

Carvings in the Elephanta caves, Mumbai. Both complexes are Unesco World Heritage Sites.

Vishnu asleep on the cosmic serpent, and the fierce goddess Durga.

Temples in North India

From the 7th century onwards, structural temples were constructed in two contrasting styles. The nagara temples of northern India have square sanctuaries topped by towers with curving profiles, known as *shikharas*. In later times these *shikhara* towers were multiplied and combined to create complex clustered forms. One of the best-preserved groups of fully evolved *nagara* temples is that at Khajuraho in Madhya Pradesh, dating from the 10th to the 11th centuries.

Dominated by clustered *shikhara* towers that soar dramatically above their sanctuaries, the Khajuraho temples are approached through a line of porches and *mandapas* with projecting balconies. The outer faces of their golden sandstone walls are covered with carvings of gods and their consorts, as well as magically protective prancing beasts, and human couples in provocative sexual postures. Temple interiors feature ornate columns with angled brackets sculpted as alluring maidens.

That the *nagara* style spread to eastern India is evident from temples in Bhubanesh-

Halebid temple detail.

war in Odisha (Orissa). Temple sanctuaries here are topped by vertical *shikhara* towers, which curve only at the very top to support heavy, disc-like ribbed finials. These towered sanctuaries are preceded by *mandapas* with pyramidal roofs. The climax of the Orissa style is represented by the 12th-century Jagannatha temple at Puri, celebrated for its chariot festival (hence the English word 'juggernaut'). The 13th-century temple at Konark, now reduced to a grandiose ruin, stands a few kilometres away. Its sculpted basement is covered with friezes of human figures, horses and elephants. Twenty-four gigantic wheels, carved in full relief, suggest that the temple was conceived as an allegorical chariot that

conveyed Surya, the Hindu sun god, across the heavens.

Nagara-style temples in Rajasthan are often dedicated to Jain saints, such as those in the 11th–13th-century complex at Mount Abu. Here, temple sanctuaries are preceded by columned *mandapas* roofed with domical ceilings, with angled bracket figures and pendant lotus flowers, all in exquisitely worked, white marble. The temple at Ranakpur, dedicated to Adinatha, the first of the 24 Jain saviours, dates from the 15th century. Its central sanctuary is topped by a clustered *shikhara* tower. This is reached through elaborate but identical *mandapas* on four sides.

Temples of the South

Temples in southern India and the Deccan are built in the contrasting *dravida* style, with multi-storeyed towers of granite or sandstone. Hindu shrines in this style dating from the 8th century are found at Kanchipuram in Tamil Nadu and at Pattadakal in Karnataka. Their outer walls are divided into niches framed by pilasters and filled with carvings of gods and goddesses. This same scheme is imitated in solid basalt in the colossal, monolithic Kailasanatha tem-

> Larger dravida temples with steeply pyramidal towers divided into multiple storeys are associated with the Chola rulers of Tamil Nadu in the 10th–11th centuries.

ple at Ellora in Maharashtra. The great Shiva temple at Tanjavur (Tanjore) has a tower that rises more than 65 metres (215ft) high. The walls beneath have double tiers of niches filled with magnificently carved images of Shiva. In later times temple towers tended to be built of brick and covered with brightly painted plaster sculptures. Such towers rise over the *gopuras*, or gateways, that lead into to the sacred compound. Among the largest *dravida*-styled monuments in Tamil Nadu are those at Srirangam and Madurai dating from the 16th–17th centuries. Here the religious monument is transformed into a vast walled complex, entered through *gopuras* on four sides. The interior is divided into courtyards, some with bathing pools, as well as extensive *mandapas*, columned corridors, and shrines dedicated to different gods and goddesses.

Dravida temples in southern India are also the settings for impressive works of Hindu art. Other than carvings on sanctuary walls, interior columns are often sculpted in almost three dimensions as lifelike leaping horses or fantastic beasts known as *yalis* ridden by armed warriors, as at Srirangam. Images of gods, goddesses and Hindu saints displayed in temple sanctuaries are cast in bronze with amazing elegance. The finest such bronzes are those dating from the Chola period,

> Prior to the introduction of paper in the 14th century, writings and illustrations were inscribed on palm leaves or parchment and 'bound' in wooden covers wrapped in cloth.

now displayed in the Government Museum, Chennai, and the Art Museum, Tanjavur.

Murals represent another aspect of *dravida* temple art. Ceiling paintings at Lepaksi in Andhra Pradesh, for example, illustrate Hindu legends, including the story of Shiva disguised as a forest hunter fighting the hero Arjuna. Here, too, are portraits of the governors who built the temple in the 16th century, accompanied by their elegantly dressed retinues.

A variant version of the *dravida* style is seen in the 12th-century Hoysala temples of Belur and Halebid. Built out of chlorite, these Hindu monuments are celebrated for their sharply carved figures of Hindu gods and goddesses, as well as minute friezes of animals and episodes from popular legends. Temple interiors at both sites are enhanced by polished, lathe-turned stone columns; angled brackets are fashioned as three-dimensional maidens posing beneath trees.

Mosques, tombs and palaces

With the establishment of Muslim power in Delhi at the end of the 12th century, the architecture and art of India came under the sway of well-established Islamic traditions imported from Iran and Central Asia. This is first seen in the mosques and tombs with pointed arches and lofty domes built for successive sultans in the 14th–15th centuries, a tendency that was to continue under the Mughals in the 16th and

17th centuries. Yet these Islamic buildings were essentially Indian since they were constructed out of local materials by local workmen. This is already evident from the Quwwat-ul-Islam mosque and adjacent minaret, known as the Qutb Minar, in Delhi, which are the first monuments to proclaim Muslim supremacy in India. Its prayer hall has a facade of pointed arches built of sandstone without any mortar, in the typical Indian dry masonry technique. Arabic inscriptions bordering the arches are enlivened by sculpted lotus embellishment similar to that found on temples. The same motifs decorate

Kailasanatha temple in Kanchipuram.

THE PEACOCK THRONE

Shah Jahan's legendary throne is said to have been made from 230kg (508lbs) of precious jewels, including rubies, emeralds, pearls and diamonds, among them the 105-carat Koh-i-noor, as well as 1,150kg (2,535lbs) of gold. When Nader Shah invaded India in 1738 he took the throne home with him to Persia as the world's most expensive souvenir. What happened next is something of a mystery: Nader Shah was assassinated, and nobody seems quite sure what became of the throne, with various theories attributing its fate to the Kurds, the British or the Iranians themselves. It was never seen again, although several imitations have been made.

the tapering flanged shaft of the nearby minaret that rises more than 72 metres (240ft) high.

Muslim religious architecture outside Delhi assumes a range of styles, reflecting the impact of regional building practices. Mosques and tombs in Ahmedabad in Gujarat, for example, have temple-like columns and corbelled domes, as well as perforated screens, known as *jalis*. The finest *jalis* in Ahmedabad are those in Sidi Sayyid's mosque of 1572; they are carved with astonishing skill to portray palm trees and creepers. Basalt is the medium of religious architecture in Bijapur in Karnataka. The Ibrahim Rauza, built in 1626, is roofed with an exaggeratedly bul-

The Mughal Era

Mughal architecture begins with the tomb of Emperor Humayun in Delhi, completed in 1571. This stands in the middle of a vast *charbagh*, or four-square walled garden with axial waterways, of obvious Persian inspiration. The tomb itself, raised on a lofty podium, has red sandstone arched portals facing in four directions; above rises a white marble dome with a slightly bulbous profile, revealing Central Asian influence. The next three Mughal emperors were also responsible for building grandiose garden tombs. The most famous of these is the Taj Mahal in Agra, Uttar Pradesh, built

Agra Fort.

bous dome framed by ornamental turrets and finials. The walls of the tomb chamber beneath are covered with superbly carved inscriptions and geometric patterns. The nearby Gol Gumbaz, the mausoleum of Sultan Muhammad Adil Shah, who died in 1656, has a colossal dome, some 44 metres (144ft) in diameter, making it one of the largest in the world. This is supported on an ingenious structural system of intersecting pointed arches. In the middle of Hyderabad in Telangana stands the Char Minar of 1591, named after its quartet of circular minarets, rising 56 metres (183ft) high. These frame the mosque elevated over the intersection of the two main streets of the city.

in 1632–53 by Shah Jahan for his beloved wife Mumtaz Mahal.

The Mughals also undertook ambitious military constructions. The Red Fort overlooking the Yamuna River in Agra is protected by massive ramparts and a deep moat, mainly the work of Akbar. The same emperor was also responsible for founding the nearby palace city of Fatehpur Sikri in 1571. Its audience halls, residential suites and pleasure pavilions of different designs are all built out of red sandstone, and have survived amazingly well. The great mosque nearby is entered through a lofty arched portal. In the middle of its courtyard stands the white marble tomb of Salim Chishti, the saint who predicted the birth of Akbar's son. Its veranda is lit by superb *jalis* with geometric designs.

In 1639 Shah Jahan founded his own new city, Shahjahanabad, in Delhi. Its Red Fort is entered through a great gateway facing the main street of the city. This leads via a covered bazaar to the audience hall that once housed the celebrated, gem-studded Peacock Throne. Beyond lie the private gardens and white marble residential pavilions, linked by waterways and scented fountains.

In spite of their grand planning and sumptuous ornamentation, Mughal palaces are now

> The Taj Mahal's perfect proportions and immaculate white marble cladding, enhanced by delicate pietra dura inlays of semi-precious stones, mark the high point of Mughal artistic achievement.

empty and forlorn. Nothing now remains of the woven carpets, embroidered textiles, silvered vessels and jade *huqqa* bowls that were produced in the imperial workshops. However, an idea of the Persian manner of these luxurious objects may be had from collections of Mughal art displayed in the National Museum, New Delhi, and Prince of Wales Museum (renamed the Chhatrapati Shivaji Maharaj Vastu Sangrahalaya), Mumbai. Here, too, are miniatures that portray the Mughal emperors and their nobles, as well as episodes from Persian epics and Hindu legends.

Realistic paintings of animals, birds and flowers prove that Indian artists took genuine delight in the world of nature. Evidence of this could be seen from the earliest miniatures, painted on palm leaves from the 11th century onwards, but really brought to prominence as an art form in their own right under Mughal rule.

Throughout the 17th and 18th centuries the Rajput princes of neighbouring Rajasthan were closely allied with the Mughals, with the result that their forts, palaces and arts were much affected by Mughal taste. Mughal-styled audience halls and residential apartments crowd the interiors of the citadels that mark the headquarters of the different Rajput families. The interior of the palace at Amber, capital of the Kachhwaha maharajas before their move to nearby Jaipur, even has a Mughal-styled

shish mahal, or mirrored hall. Here, countless tiny pieces of reflecting glass are set into the plastered ceiling to create a glittering interior. Palaces at Kota and Bundi are enlivened with murals that depict contemporary life, with Rajput rulers receiving visitors, riding in procession, hunting deer, enjoying performances of music and dance, and going on pilgrimage to Hindu shrines. Some Rajput palaces still preserve their royal art collections, as can be seen in the spectacular costumes, carpets, weapons and miniature paintings on display in the City Palace Museum, Jaipur.

Fatehpur Sikri, the work of the 16th-century emperor Akbar.

Here, too, mention must be made of the Sikh shrines of the Punjab, known as *gurudwaras*. Topped by Mughal-styled gilded domes, they commemorate the lives of successive Sikh teachers. The most famous Sikh monument is the Golden Temple in Amritsar, built by the fourth Sikh guru, Guru Ram Das, in the 16th century. A large tank was excavated, and the gold-covered temple built in its centre; the tank was then filled with water, the shimmering gold of the temple reflected on all sides to mesmerising effect.

Impact of Europe

The arrival of the Portuguese on the Arabian Sea coast in the early 16th century signalled the beginning of European influence. Italianate traditions were imported by the Portuguese for their cathedrals and monasteries in India, as is evident from the Baroque style of Sé Cathedral and Bom Jesus in Old Goa. The interiors of these churches are further enhanced with European-styled altarpieces created from gilded wood. Bom Jesus even incorporates the ornate marble tomb of Francis Xavier, the celebrated Jesuit saint. Ecclesiastical items produced in workshops in Goa under the Portuguese in the 17th and 18th centuries are displayed in the Museum of Christian Art in the Convent of St Monica, Old Goa. Churches in Puducherry show that Catholic architecture and art also flourished in India under the French.

It was, however, the British who had the most widespread impact on Indian architecture. The star-shaped forts that they constructed in the 17th century to protect their trading 'factories' at Chennai, Kolkata and Mumbai survive, though their ramparts and moats are now much dilapidated and overgrown. Churches within these forts display pedimented facades and pointed steeples

An evocative modern sculpture at the National Gallery of Modern Art in Delhi.

CONTEMPORARY INDIAN ART

In the years following Independence, Indian art was dominated by the Progressive Artists of Mumbai, including Ara, Souza, M.F. Husain, Raza, Ram Kumar and Kishen Khanna, most of whom are now at the top of the contemporary art ladder. Unlike the masters of the earlier Modern Movement, the Progressives styled their Indian themes in the modern European mould, and their followers have become increasingly influenced by the avant-garde movements of the West. This is one of the main reasons why so much contemporary work appears derivative. But it must be remembered that many artists are genuinely inspired by the modern urban environment with its Western influences. It is also important to note, when touring the galleries (the National Gallery of Modern Art in Delhi is a good place to start), that the hallmark of contemporary Indian art is diversity. Artists work in a wide range of media and with an immense variety of themes. It is possible to see everything from installations to narrative paintings, from landscapes to abstracts and works with Adivasi and local motifs.

A great place to gets to grips with what's hot on the contemporary scene is the December art biennale held in the southern city of Kochi (Cochin), whose faded Raj-era warehouses provide perfect backdrops for cutting-edge installations and video films, as well as painting and sculpture.

typical of Classical Revival architecture. A similar mode was also adopted for the civic monuments that represented English supremacy on Indian soil, notably Government House in Kolkata, begun in 1758, and the British Residency in Hyderabad of 1809. Neoclassical facades even graced the mansions of wealthy English merchants in Kolkata.

In the 19th century Gothic Revival became the preferred mode, not only for churches but also for urban projects. This is best seen in Mumbai, in the High Court (still called the Bombay High Court), Victoria Terminus railway station (now the Chhatrapati Shivaji Terminus, known as CST) and University Library, all built in the 1870s and 1880s. The turn of the 20th century was marked by the invention of the novel Indo-Saracenic style, in which European Gothic features mingled freely with domes and turrets derived from Mughal and Rajput architecture. This somewhat eccentric idiom was also sometimes chosen by Indian princes for their public buildings, as in the High Court and Osmania General Hospital in Hyderabad. Indo-Saracenic royal residences also sprung up, like the exotic palace of the Wodeyar rulers in Mysore, which even employs cast iron and stained glass imported from Glasgow.

For their own monuments the British preferred a more restrained version of Classicism, such as that practised by Sir Edwin Lutyens and Herbert Baker, principal architects of New Delhi. Completed in 1931, with broad boulevards, imposing civic monuments and garden bungalows, the new British capital was dominated by a central axis, at the end of which stood the Viceroy's House, now Rashtrapati Bhavan, residence of India's president. This domed building is an eclectic blend of Buddhist, Mughal and Rajput features, organised according to Classical proportions. In the course of the 20th century, European Modernism took widespread root in India, mostly at the hands of English and German architects employed by local princes. The masterpiece of Indian Modernism is Umaid Bhavan, now a heritage hotel, commissioned by the Jodhpur maharajas. Its lofty domed rotunda and splendidly appointed Art Deco apartments were completed in 1944.

Post Independence

Indian architecture after Independence displays a similar dependence on European models, especially once Le Corbusier and Louis Khan were invited to work in India in the 1950s. The layout and civic monuments of Chandigarh, new capital of Indian Punjab, reflect French urban ideals not necessarily suited to India. That the modernisation of Indian architecture is now an accomplished fact is obvious from the high-rise concrete and glass buildings that crowd most cities today. Some architects now seek an authen-

Basilica of Bom Jesus, Old Goa.

tic Indian aesthetic by reverting to traditional materials, such as sandstone and marble, and geometric patterns borrowed from earlier Indian Islamic buildings.

The same quest is taking place in the fine arts, with a new generation of Indian painters and sculptors drawing on indigenous themes. Some of these artists are concerned to reconcile the latest Western trends with a genuine Indian aesthetic. Although quality varies substantially, the discerning eye may pick out very accomplished and expressive works from the mediocre. Kolkata and Delhi are the best cities in which to find interesting art. Meanwhile, there is a vigorous revival of textile arts and village crafts.

HINDU DEITIES

Hinduism recognises a bewildering number of deities, from powerful Sanskritic gods, sometimes thought of as manifestations of one single divine entity, to local goddesses.

Hinduism has been called the 'religion of 330 million deities', a deliberate exaggeration merely intended to refer to the divine present in all beings. However, this claim does point to the vast number of gods and goddesses that this extremely heterogeneous religion embraces.

Some Hindus believe that the various incarnations of these deities (known as avatars) all descend from one central divine being known as Brahman, others that the Brahman manifests as three centrally powerful gods – Brahma, Vishnu and Shiva – known as the Trimurti, and others still that each deity is a distinct and separate entity to be worshipped in its own right. Of course, these are not necessarily mutually distinct positions and there are almost as many variations and gradations of belief as gods and goddesses.

The first deities that appear in the Hindu canon are those of the Vedas, powerful gods that personify elements of the temporal world. These include Agni, the god of fire, Indra, the god of thunder and war, Brahma and Surya, the sun god. These Vedic deities were supplanted by gods perhaps more familiar such as Vishnu (and his avatars, or incarnations, Rama and Krishna) and Shiva. The exploits of these gods are contained in a body of scriptures known as the Puranas.

Of great importance, although less canonical perhaps than Vishnu and Shiva, are the various aspects of the goddess (Devi or Shakti), from Sarasvati, the goddess of learning and music, to Durga, slayer of the buffalo demon Mahisasura. This manifestation of female power is considered vital for the balance of the universe and Devi is often seen paired with a male god as a consort, for instance Shiva and Parvati or Vishnu and Lakshmi.

Shiva is the oldest of all Hindu gods, dating back to the Harappan civilisation.

The son of Shiva and Parvati, Ganesh is the god of wisdom and auspicious beginnings, and he is invoked before setting out on a journey or a new venture.

The three gods that form the Trimurti, from left to right Brahma, Vishnu and Shiva, are considered the most powerful and important of the gods.

Two sadhus.

SADHUS

A feature of Indian religious life is the presence of numbers of sadhus (wandering hermits). They can be seen in cities and villages, in forests, on the banks of rivers and in the Himalaya. Usually dressed in saffron or ochre robes, their bodies smeared with ash and foreheads anointed with sandal-paste, the sadhus carry all their possessions with them: a bowl, a staff, a blanket. Some travel alone, others in small groups. Some have taken vows of silence, others preach or chant hymns. They are broadly divided into followers of Vishnu, Vaishnavas, and those of Shiva, Saivas. Those who worship Vishnu can be identified by three vertical lines painted on their foreheads (a *tilak*, usually in white and red), those for whom Siva is the object of devotion have a *tilak* of three horizontal lines.

This goddess, usually depicted with many arms and a garland of skulls, represents the most fierce and destructive aspect of Devi.

The monkey god, Hanuman, was Rama's helper during his battle against the demon Ravana. He is considered to be strong and loyal and is among the most popular Hindu deities.

Often the focus of devotional religion, bhakti, Vishnu is considered to have 11 avatars, or manifestations: Matsya, a fish; Kurma, a turtle; Varaha, a boar; Narasimha, a lion; Vamana, a dwarf; Parasurama, a man wielding an axe; Rama, the hero of the Ramayana; Balarama, an earlier incarnation of Krishna; Krishna, a well-loved god who appears in many stories; the Buddha; and Kalki, the horseman who will usher in the Kali Yuga, the age of destruction.

Paharganj, New Delhi.

The view from Jaisalmer Palace,
Rajasthan.

Riding an elephant on the beach, Havelock Island.

INTRODUCTION

The following chapters offer a detailed guide to the entire country, with principal sights clearly cross-referenced by number to the maps.

Mehrangarh Fort, Jodhpur, Rajasthan.

No one feels neutral about India. It slams you in the face with heat, spice and dirt, then seduces you with colour and sensual pleasure. Time distorts and assumes surreal yogic contortions: distances take longer to travel, minutes crawl during interminable waits, then vanish into a blur of hours, even days. The constant chaos can charm or repulse.

There are so many different facets of India: the 29 states, six Union Territories and the National Capital Territory of Delhi offer a bewildering number of travel options. Trekking to Adivasi villages in the Western Ghats is a physical challenge. Chugging across the Deccan Plateau in a three-tiered sleeper car while the other passengers snore is a mental one. The pride of an artisan working at a potter's wheel or loom is obvious; the appeal of rural villages trimmed with intricate murals is unforgettable.

A Bengal tiger.

Visit an old Portuguese fort or an ancient Jewish synagogue. Take refuge in a remote pleasure palace a full day's camel ride away from the rest of the world. Barter in a bazaar for old silver, new rugs, inlaid daggers, or go for the miniature paintings brushed with a squirrel's whisker, the antique opium boxes, or new jewellery made with crushed gemstones: it's all spread out before your eyes in a former caravanserai.

Other visitors come to India seeking something within themselves, some spiritual calm beyond the cacophony. Some enrol in meditation centres, others opt for social or environmental work, either can teach you something more about yourself.

India's travel experiences can be similarly uplifting, from boating down a river where elephants bathe, to the colour and spectacle of an esoteric religious festival. White-water rafting down the Ganges, practising yoga on a sunrise beach, tracking wildlife in game sanctuaries, climbing a Himalayan peak, sketching wildflowers in a hill station meadow, or examining erotic sculpture at Tantric temples: it would need immense stamina to undertake all the travel possibilities in India.

Some run away from India; others keep returning.

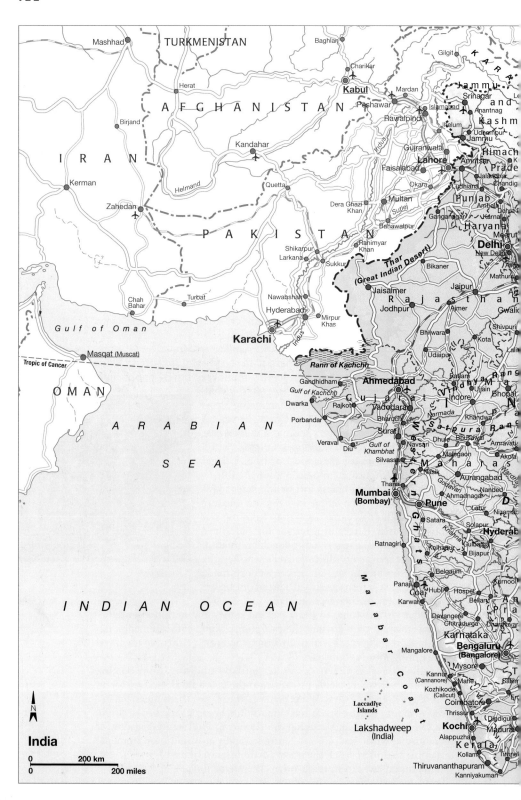

India

0   200 km

0   200 miles

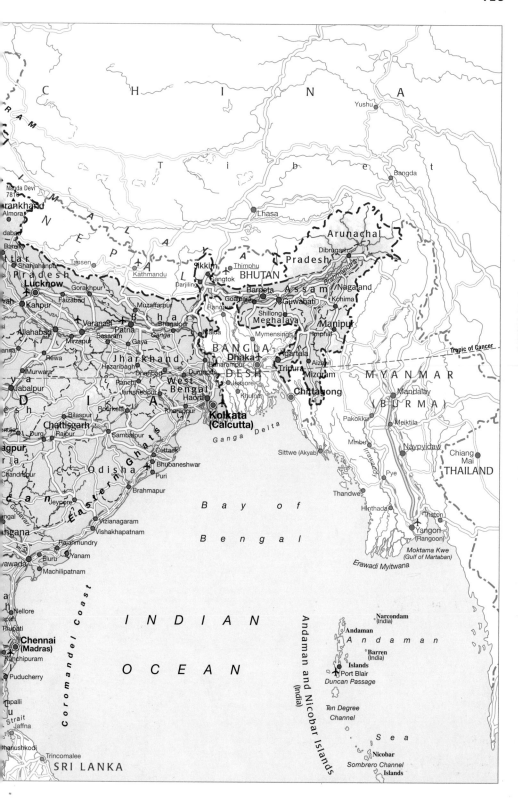

The mosque adjoining the Bara Imambara, Lucknow.

THE NORTH

Northern India covers a vast swathe of contrasting country, the dusty flatlands of the Punjab and the Gangetic plain giving way to the mighty Himalayas. The great Mughal cities of Delhi and Agra lie to the south.

Sarees for sale in a Delhi market.

Hot, dusty, crowded, loud and proud, this is the India of the popular imagination; but it can also be cold, calm, pristine and clean. Plains and mountains, chalk and cheese. The fertile flatlands are India's breadbasket, worked to good effect by the prosperous Punjabis. But move east and the good times fade; as the population increases, prosperity takes a nose dive, corruption cripples and industry blackens the horizon. Uttar Pradesh is the centre of much of India's politics, industry and divinity. Lucknow has witnessed the rise and fall of many of India's most influential political parties, as well as being the stage for the Uprising of 1857; its impressive array of architectural treasures bear witness to this turbulent past. Varanasi, on the Ganges and famed for its cremation ghats, is one of India's most intense experiences and not to be missed.

The mountains are another world entirely – of shining glaciers, flower-filled meadows and inaccessible ice peaks. Head north from the plains and it's all change, although the influence of the cities, and their increasingly well-travelled citizens, can still be felt, particularly in the 'hill stations'. Established by the British as places to

Cycle rickshaw on the streets of Delhi.

escape the summer heat of the plains, these days they tend to be popular with Indian tourists and honeymooners, leading to an intriguing blend of anachronistic charm and Indian kitsch. Keep heading north, though, and the green – and everyone – is gone. This is nowhere truer than in Ladakh, and particularly on the epic road that leads there from Manali, home to massive moonscapes and roads so high you can barely breathe.

A journey through this part of the country will do much to help unravel the complexities of its capital, Delhi, a compelling fusion of all things North Indian. From there it's a short hop to India's most iconic site, the Taj Mahal, a building so familiar and yet so achingly exquisite.

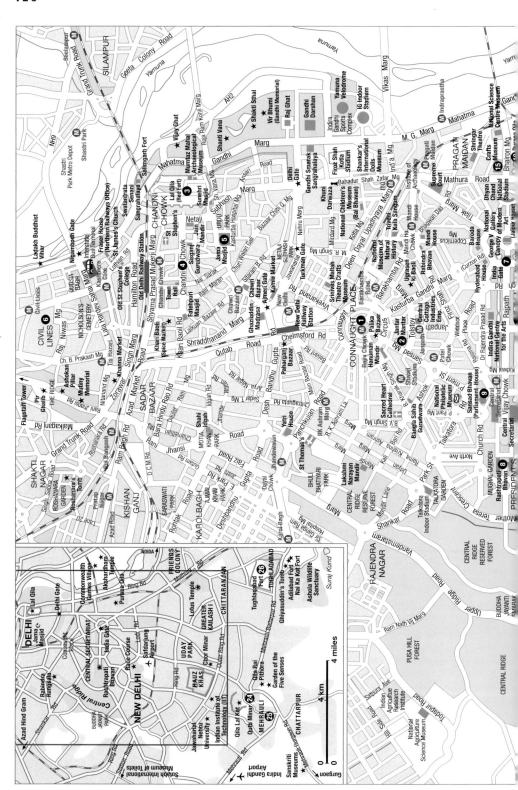

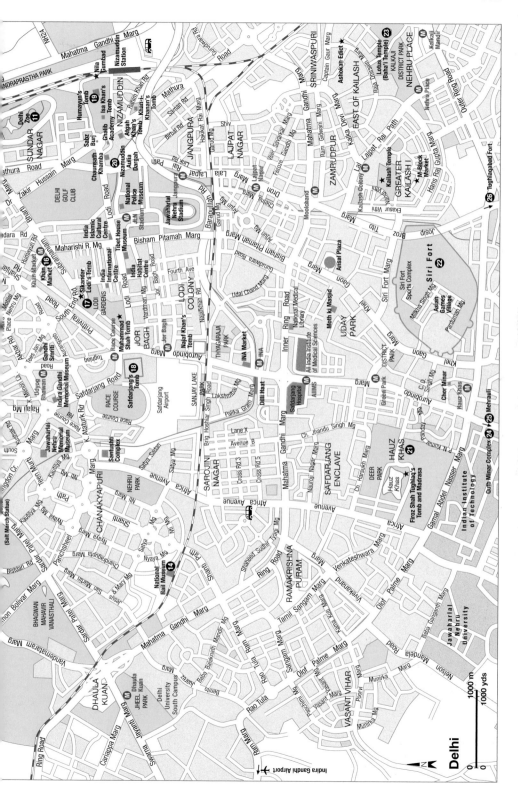

Delhi

Indira Gandhi Airport

DELHI

The capital of India presents an arresting combination of ancient and modern. And as a major cultural centre, Delhi offers a glimpse of the diversity of the country's many states.

I ndia's capital is one of the world's largest cities, both in terms of population and extent – and among its most vibrant and dynamic metropolises. The urban sprawl long ago erupted from the confines of the walled city built by Shah Jahan, these days known as Old Delhi, whose crowded lanes and markets are as densely populated, intense and bewildering to the outsider as any in Asia. A short distance to the south but a world away in terms of style and atmosphere, New Delhi was the elegant British riposte to the clutter of the old, designed with trademark Raj era bravado as a demonstration of colonial might. Ironically, independence was ushered in only a few years after New Delhi was completed and, from a population of fewer than 2 million at that time, has mushroomed into a vast megalopolis of over 22 million people.

Visitors to Delhi are likely to divide their time between the central and southern areas of the city, where most of the major sights can be seen and where most of the action is. It can be a tough place to fathom at times, but try not to focus exclusively on the sights and aim to do what you would do in a big city at home – enjoy the experience of seeing it all done so differently.

Devotions at the shrine of Sheikh Nizamuddin Aulia.

Expansion and reinvention

During the 1990s and early years of this century the city struggled to cope with the effects of rapid expansion – pollution, traffic congestion, shortages of water and power, continual construction – and an extreme climate. And while there is still a long way to go, more recently, as befits the capital of this rapidly developing country, Delhi has reinvented itself as the most forward-thinking and one of the best-run cities in India. Delhi's former Chief Minister Shiela Dixit

Main Attractions

Connaught Place
Lakshmi Narayan Temple
Lal Qila
Purana Qila
National Gallery of Modern Art
National Museum
Shrine of Sheikh Nizamuddin Aulia
Qutb Minar Complex
Garden of the Five Senses

must also take much of the credit – her administration clamped down on illegal building, attempted to clean up the city's streets and pushed through major infrastructure projects. The most prominent of these was the construction of a new metro system, which garnered country-wide praise for its swift progress and lack of corruption.

Pollution was tackled and curbed by a 2003 Supreme Court order that forced all public transport to convert from running on diesel to compressed natural gas (CNG), but drastic action has had to be taken to address the fact that Delhi's air quality is currently rated the worst of any major city in the world, thanks to the increased number of cars on the roads, construction site dust and wood-burning fires, amongst other things. In January 2016, a temporary alternate-day driving law – with private drivers only allowed to drive one day on, one day off – was announced, to attempt a cut in pollutants. The same measure was announced for a further fortnight in April 2016.

A further boost to the city came when it was awarded the 2010 Commonwealth Games. Although the games were used to justify much-needed improvements to the city's infrastructure, including a new international airport, some of this development was made at the expense of the poor. Large areas of slums were cleared and people dispossessed of what little they had in the name of beautifying the city. The Games themselves were not without controversy, with the athletes' village pronounced uninhabitable by the first groups of competitors to arrive, as well as minor building collapses and technical issues with the running of the events themselves. Less satisfactory still were the reports of wide-scale corruption in the build-up to the Games, the consequences of which are still being calculated. Reports into this corruption were commission, but to date, the findings have not been made public.

Delhi is one of the most expensive places to live in India, and has overtaken Mumbai as the most desirable,

TRANSPORT TO AND FROM DELHI

Buses: Long-distance buses arrive and depart from the Inter-State Bus Terminal (ISBT) at Kashmir Gate. Private bus companies offer more comfortable facilities than trains, but their services invariably travel through the night and have a notoriously bad safety record.

Flights: As befits the capital, Delhi is the major hub for all international and domestic flights, with daily arrivals from all over the world. Indira Gandhi International Airport was renovated for the Commonwealth Games in 2010. Domestic flights, on Indian and many other airlines, regularly depart to all areas of the country. The best source of up-to-date timetable information, and most convenient way to book flights on all airlines, is the website www.cleartrip.com.

Trains: As with air travel, Delhi is the major rail hub for India, with regular departures to almost everywhere in the country from the three main stations, New Delhi, Delhi and Nizamuddin. For foreign travellers, the tourist reservation facility on the first floor of New Delhi railway station offers an invaluable service, giving anyone in possession of an overseas passport access to special quotas. Without this booking facility, you'd be unlikely to be able to procure seats or berths on any trains departing from New Delhi – tickets sell out with days, or hours, of the reservation release time. Be warned, however, that touts hang around the entrance to the station attempting to divert tourists by claiming the office on the first floor is closed, or not the correct one, then taking them to private travel agents nearby where they'll be sold wait list or fake tickets. To book in the bona fide office you'll need your passport and receipts for any currency exchanges or withdrawals by ATM you've made in Delhi. Travelling by train will usually be a quicker and far more pleasant journey than by bus.

There are trains to Agra (many daily; 2–3hrs); Amritsar (many daily; 6–7hrs); Bengaluru (4 daily; 33–40hrs); Bhopal (many daily; 8–11hrs); Chennai (4–6 daily; 28–36hrs); Goa (4 daily; 25–30hrs); Jaipur (16–20 daily; 5–6hrs); Kolkata (6–10 daily; 18–26hrs); Lucknow (frequent service daily; 6–9hrs); Mumbai (many daily; 16–23hrs); Secunderabad (4–5 daily; 22–25hrs); Varanasi (7–8 daily; 12hrs).

attracting a greater influx of people than its great rival. While Mumbai remains the indisputable financial hub, Delhi is not only the political centre but increasingly the focus of much of India's cultural life. It is home to many of the country's leading fashion designers, as well as numerous writers, artists and musicians. It also has a booming retail sector, with glossy new malls springing up all the time and numerous chic boutiques in its colony markets. All these developments are epitomised by the vast new DLF Mall of India (www.dlfmallofindia.in), just over the state boundary in Gurgaon, the largest mall in the country.

The ancient cities of Delhi

Strategically located between the Aravalli hills and the Yamuna River, Delhi has been the site of more than a dozen cities. It is named after an earlier settlement, 'Dillika'. The first of the cities was Indraprastha, legendary capital of the Pandavas, epic heroes of the *Mahabharata*. Recent excavations at Purana Qila (Old Fort) date the settlement to between the 1st century BC and the 4th century AD.

The next documented city was Lal Kot, founded in the 8th century AD by Tomar Rajputs. It was captured and renamed Qila Rai Pithora by the Chauhan Rajputs in the 12th century. Later it was occupied by Qutb-ud-din, who founded the Delhi Sultanate and began construction of the Qutb Minar. The monuments and ruins from this era stand in and around the Qutb Minar complex in South Delhi. The ruins of Siri, a capital established by the Turkish Ala-ud-Din Khilji, can be seen around Hauz Khas colony. In 1320 Ghias-ud-Din Tughlaq moved to his fortress city of Tughlaqabad, east of Qutb Minar. His tomb, overrun by monkeys, stands across the road from the ruins.

Ferozabad, once the richest city in the world, was founded in 1351 by his successor, Feroz Shah Tughlaq, on the banks of the Yamuna River. The ruins of his palace and other monuments are situated in Feroz Shah Kotla, south of the memorials on the Ring Road.

Tomb of Bara Gumbad, Lodi Gardens.

They were followed by the Sayyids and the Lodis, whose tombs stand in Lodi Gardens, south of India Gate. Their defeat by the Central Asian invader Babur, in the 16th century, marked the end of the Delhi Sultanate and the dawn of the Mughal Empire. Din-Panah Fort (Purana Qila) was built above the Yamuna by Babur's son, the studious Humayun, who was forced to flee by Sher Shah, an Afghan invader. Sher Shah began constructing his new capital of Shergarh, but Humayun won back Delhi in 1555 only to die a few months later when he fell down his library stairs. Akbar, Humayun's son, moved his capital to Agra. His grandson, Shah Jahan, who built the Taj Mahal, returned to Delhi in 1638 to build the glorious Shahjahanabad. This walled capital, bound by 14 gates, included most of Old Delhi, Jama Masjid (Friday Mosque), the bazaars around Chandni Chowk and Lal Qila (Red Fort) from where he ruled his empire. Successive invasions from Persia reduced the power of the Mughals until the British took over Delhi in the 19th century.

In 1911, during the visit of King George V, Delhi was declared the capital of the British Empire in India. The present city of New Delhi, designed by Edwin Lutyens and Herbert Baker, was completed by 1931. Considered one of the great examples of colonial town planning, the architecture draws on European classical designs as well as Indian decoration, even though Lutyens famously declared his dislike of Indian buildings.

Around Connaught Place

The circular shopping arcade of **Connaught Place ❶** (properly Rajiv Chowk) forms the heart of modern Delhi. The colonnaded corridors were built for the British to be able to shop in style. Concentric roads create an Inner, Middle and Outer Circle lined with shops, restaurants, street stalls and cinemas. The underground **Palika Bazaar** on the Outer Circle has tiny shops overflowing with tourist tat and touts. The tourist theme continues to the north, with the backpackers' ghetto of **Paharganj Bazaar**, opposite New Delhi railway station. With

The Lakshmi Narayan Temple, aka Birla Mandir; an imposing example of Hindu architecture.

LUTYENS

Sir Edwin Lutyens (1869–1944), principal architect of New Delhi, was as versatile as he was prolific. Having initially honed his skills on a series of English country homes and gardens, and in doing so created a style almost entirely his own, he went on to design an array of public buildings and monuments around the world, including Westminster's cenotaph. But Delhi was his most ambitious project, an unprecedented opportunity to design a whole section of a city, and is perhaps his masterpiece. It is a unique blend of Classical British and Indian styles that continues to house much of the Indian government, as well as its president, and lends the city a character and elegance that would be unimaginable without Lutyens's grand vision and meticulous execution.

a huge concentration of cheap doss houses and eating places, it has been responsible for generations of cases of Delhi belly and the city authorities have recently moved in to close some of the worst fleapits and to try to improve the area.

To the southwest, Baba Kharak Singh Marg has a row of State Government emporia where regional handicrafts are sold at regulated prices. Opposite is **Hanuman Mandir** a temple dedicated to the monkey god Hanuman, helper of Rama and Lakshmana in the *Ramayana*, much revered by wrestlers. At the end of this road, to the left, rises the golden dome of **Bangla Sahib Gurudwara**, the city's principal Sikh temple and well worth a visit, particularly for those not planning to make the trip to the Golden Temple in Amritsar.

Going southwest along Sansad Marg (Parliament Street) is the red sandstone **Jantar Mantar ❷**, an open-air observatory built by Maharaja Jai Singh I of Jaipur (sunrise to sunset), a popular focal point for political protests. Constructed in 1724, it was the first of several observatories the ruler had built; others were later constructed in Jaipur, Ujjain, Varanasi and Mathura.

To the south, **Janpath** is the location of the huge **Central Cottage Industries Emporium** (CCIE), which offers a glimpse of the wide range of handicrafts available in India. Also here is the large, elegant Imperial Hotel, the only one to be included in Lutyens' designs for the new capital.

To the west of Connaught Place, on the aptly named Mandir (Temple) Marg is the **Lakshmi Narayan Temple**, otherwise known as the Birla Mandir. It was built in 1938 and financed by the industrialist B.D. Birla. M.K. Gandhi opened the temple but only on the condition that it should also be open to Dalits (then known as 'Untouchables'). The main celebrations take place here on Janmashtami (Krishna's birthday).

Old Delhi

The peaceful 18th-century **Qudsia Bagh** (gardens), near the Interstate Bus Terminal (ISBT) and Kashmir Gate, marks the northern boundary of the Mughal **Shahjahanabad** (often referred to as 'Old Delhi'), Delhi's seventh city.

The spectacular **Lal Qila ❸** (Red Fort; open Tue–Sun sunrise to sunset; charge) faces Chandni Chowk (meaning moonlit or silver crossroads), once the central avenue of a bazaar that is still an important commercial centre. A Persian couplet by Shah Jahan's court poet Amir Khusrau ('If there be paradise on the face of earth, it is this! Oh it is this! Oh it is this!') is inscribed on the walls of the Diwan-e-Khas (private audience hall), which once housed the legendary Peacock Throne and the Koh-i-noor diamond (later looted by Persian forces) (see page 107). Shah Jahan, the Mughal emperor whose paradise this was, built the immense red sandstone fort with its palaces and halls in 1648.

The entry point is Lahore Gate. Inside, passing through the Chatta

TIP

There are a number of useful websites for visitors to the city. A good all-round site is www.delhievents.com. Official government sites include: the Archaeological Survey of India (www.asi.nic.in), Delhi Government (www.delhi govt.nic.in) and Delhi Tourism, (www.delhi tourism.nic.in). For information on nightlife, see www.explocity.com.

TRANSPORT WITHIN DELHI

Delhi's ever-expanding metro network is generally the best way to get around town (see www.delhimetrorail.com for the latest information). Easy to use, single fares operate by means of a token that you hold by the reader at the start of your journey and feed into the machine at the automatic barrier when you exit the station. Fares are cheap, and services run from 6am to 11pm. A rail link to Indira Gandhi airport departs from New Delhi Station (express journey 20mins).

While autorickshaws can be the most convenient way to get around the city centre, it is often hard for visitors to negotiate a fair price for their journey. The Delhi government has put an extremely useful fare calculator online (www.delhitrafficpolice.nic.in/public-interface/auto-rickshaw-taxi-fare-calculator) which will give a good idea of what to pay.

Buses in Delhi are very crowded, if cheap. Stick to government-run buses, safer and more reliable than other operators'. The city authority recently inaugurated an entirely new fleet of modern vehicles.

Delhi's yellow-and-black **taxis** are difficult to flag down on the street and are best picked up at their transport company's kiosks, which can be found close to all the main markets or commercial areas. Two companies that are reliable, honest and can be booked by phone are: Mega Cabs, tel: 011-4141 4141, www.megacabs.com; Meru Cab, tel: 4422 4422, www.merucabs.com

Chowk covered market, one enters Shah Jahan's elaborate gardens. To the far right is the Mumtaz Mahal, possibly a former harem but now a museum with a collection of Mughal artefacts including miniatures, porcelain and costumes. Next to it are the Rang Mahal and Khas Mahal, the emperor's private apartments. The octagonal tower was used for royal public appearances (including that of Britain's George V and Queen Mary during their visit to India in 1931). Other buildings include the Diwan-e-Am (public audience hall), the royal baths, and the tiny white marble Moti Masjid (Pearl Mosque). Ugly concrete army barracks, a British addition to the fort, can also be seen dotted inside the massive walls. Now that the Yamuna has retreated, the fort, originally built on its banks, overlooks a large open ground, previously the site of Chor Bazaar (the thieves' market, now held near the Jama Masjid).

Chandni Chowk

Chandni Chowk ❹ is the main road leading from the Red Fort into the heart of Shahjahanabad, or Old Delhi. This now busy, crowded and noisy road was once an elegant boulevard with a canal running along its centre. Each street leading off the main road has its own speciality: silver and gold at Dariba Kalan, wedding paraphernalia and theatrical props at Kinari Bazaar, silk saris, copper and brassware and a fascinating wholesale spice market (with dried fruit and nuts from Kabul) at Naya Bazaar. On Chandni Chowk itself is the **Digambara Temple**, the oldest Jain temple in Delhi, and the **Bird Hospital**, where injured birds are nursed back to health.

The **Sispganj Gurudwara** (Sikh temple), **Sunehri Masjid** (Golden Mosque), and **Fatehpuri Masjid** (1650) are some of the sites crowded between stalls selling a jumble of wares, and the hawkers and touts. The Sisganj Gurudwara is one of the most important in the city, and is dedicated to the guru Tegh Bahadur – killed by Aurangzeb in the 17th century for refusing to renounce his faith. The famous sweetmeat shop of **Ghantewala**, established in 1790, is worth a visit. Specialities include *sohn halva* and *sohn papri* (caramelised sweets made with ghee, clarified butter).

Jama Masjid

South of Central Road, follow Dariba Kalan to the massive red sandstone and white marble **Jama Masjid** ❺ (Friday Mosque; open daily; charge; you must cover up to enter – robes are available for hire at the north gate), the focal point for Delhi's Muslims. Commissioned by Shah Jahan in 1644, the mosque can hold 20,000 people in its huge courtyard, in the centre of which is a tank used for ritual ablutions. The mosque and fort, opposite each other, were integral to the complex plan of the walled city. Outside of Friday prayers, it is sometimes possible to climb the southern minaret, although women are only admitted with a male companion.

Colonial architecture at the Jawarhalal Memorial Museum.

Raj Ghat

Eastward, behind the Red Fort, the Ring Road along the Yamuna river is connected by three bridges to the Trans-Yamuna residential areas. On the river bank from Red Fort south to ITO Bridge are the cremation grounds, now mostly used as memorial parks dedicated to national leaders such as Nehru, Lal Bahadur Shastri, and Indira and Rajiv Gandhi.

The biggest complex here is **Raj Ghat**, where M.K. Gandhi was cremated, and there are two museums dedicated to him. **Gandhi Darshan** (www.gandhismriti.nic.in; Tue–Sun 10am–5pm; free) has a good collection of paintings and photos, and charts the history of the *Satyagraha* (non-violence) movement. Close by is **Gandhi Smarak Sangrahalaya** (www.gandhimuseum.in; Thur–Tue 11am–5pm; free), which houses a display of Gandhi's personal belongings and has a library of recordings of his speeches.

North Delhi and The Ridge

British Delhi (which was strung out to the east of the Northern Ridge), with its cantonment bungalows and administrative buildings, begins to the north of Kashmere Gate. This area was known as the **Civil Lines ❻**, and a number of mementoes of British rule can be found here. One of the more beautiful is **St James's Church** (find the caretaker to ask for access). This was built in 1836 at the behest of James Skinner, a famous soldier of mixed race who, in the 19th century, formed an irregular cavalry brigade known as 'Skinner's Horse'. He initially fought on the side of the Marathas in their wars against other Indian rulers, but eventually joined the East India Company armies when the Marathas turned their attention to the British. With a large central dome and a cruciform plan, the church has a classical elegance not seen again in Delhi until the architecture of Lutyens and Baker.

Other remains of the era can be seen in the administrative buildings of the **University** campus and Delhi's most prestigious private school, **St Stephen's College**; many of India's upper crust have been educated either here or at 'Doon' School in Dehra Dun in the Himalayan foothills.

A more sombre reminder of the rule of the British can be found up on **The Ridge**. This wooded line of hills runs roughly northeast–southwest across the top of Delhi and acts in part as the city's 'lung' as well as being the refuge of much of Delhi's remaining wildlife. Here is the **Mutiny Memorial**, a neo-Gothic monument to the British and (loyal) Indian soldiers who died in the 1857 Uprising. Close by, to the north, is one of Delhi's **Ashokan Pillars**, placed here in 1867 after it had been reassembled from pieces returned from Kolkata.

At the highest point of The Ridge is the **Flagstaff Tower**, one of the earliest British buildings in Delhi. This spot was where the British civilians and wounded gathered during the 1857 Uprising while waiting for relief to arrive.

Shopping at Baba Kharak Singh Marg.

The British were not exactly modest when it came to celebrating their imperial ambitions in India. Delhi was used as the site of a number of *durbars* (processional celebrations), of which the most elaborate was that of George V in 1911 when he announced the relocation of the capital from what was then Calcutta to Delhi. The former *durbar* ground, just off K.B. Hedgewar Marg in the north of the city, is now known as Coronation Park and has been put to good use as a dumping ground for British monuments. The most impressive of these is a huge statue of George V that used to stand near India Gate.

West of the city centre, out in Mahavir Enclave, is one of Delhi's more unusual sites, the **Sulabh International Museum of Toilets** (www.sulabhtoiletmuseum.org; daily 10.30am–5pm, from 10am Apr–Oct; free). Set up by the social campaigner Dr Bindeshwar Pathak, the museum traces the evolution of sanitation from its earliest beginnings to the most modern flush systems (the mock-up of Louis XIV's 'throne' is quite something). The more serious side of the museum and the attached organisation is Dr Pathak's work in campaigning for better sanitation across India and for better treatment of India's sanitation workers, who come from the very lowest strata of the caste system and face considerable discrimination.

Rajpath and India Gate

Barakhamba (Twelve Pillar) Road leads southeast from Connaught Place to Mandi House Chowk, which is home to the **Rabindra Kala Sangam** (Triveni Theatre) and café, and various auditoria hosting regular performances of dance, music and theatre. The Rabindra Kala Sangam also contains the contemporary art gallery of the **Lalit Kala Akademi** (Mon–Sat 9am–6pm; free) and the **Sangeet Natak Akademi** museum, showcasing traditional musical instruments.

The next main thoroughfare leading off the Connaught Place hub is Kasturba Gandhi Marg, which runs to India Gate in the heart of Lutyens' New Delhi. The road is the location of the cultural centres of Germany and the UK, which have good libraries and reading rooms in addition to regular cultural events.

The area around **India Gate** ❼ formed the British administrative centre of Delhi with the local 'Champs Elysées' of **Rajpath** surrounded by lawns and shady trees, water channels and fountains. India Gate, a 42-metre (138ft) high archway, was built by Lutyens at the eastern end in 1931 to honour Indian soldiers who died during World War I and on the Northwest Frontier. There is an 'eternal flame' to commemorate those killed in the 1971 war with Pakistan. The area comes alive at sunset, when many locals gather with their families to enjoy the wide open spaces, fly kites, play cricket or eat an ice cream.

Rashtrapati Bhavan ❽, the presidential residence (former Viceregal

Kashmir Gate.

Lodge), can be seen at the western end of Rajpath with the circular **Sansad Bhavan** ❾ (Parliament House) nearby. The huge formal Mughal-style gardens of Rashtrapati Bhavan are among the finest in Delhi but are only open to the public from February to March (see www.presidentofindia.nic.in for more details). Flanking the approach to Rashtrapati Bhavan are the North and South Block Secretariats, housing the Ministries of Finance and Home Affairs, and Ministries of Foreign Affairs respectively (usually referred to in news reports simply as North or South Block).

To the west of Rajpath, behind Rashtrapati Bhavan, is Buddha Jayanti Smarak Park, part of the Central Ridge Reserved Forest. On the corner of Willingdon Crescent that runs alongside the park and Sardar Patel Marg stands the **Dandi Statue**. This impressive bronze shows Gandhi leading the demonstrators on his march to Dandi on the Gujarat coast to protest against the British imposing a salt tax.

Southwest of Rajpath is **Chanakyapuri**, the diplomatic enclave where the majority of foreign missions and embassies are located. Nearby is the **Santushti Complex** (opposite the Ashoka Hotel), with shops of Indian designers.

At the eastern end of Rajpath (by India Gate) are two magnificent residences, **Hyderabad House** and **Baroda House**, built for the two most powerful rulers of the so-called Princely States of British India. Along Rajpath is the headquarters of the **Indira Gandhi National Centre for the Arts** (www.ignca.nic.in), with an auditorium and a library. Beyond India Gate lies the National Stadium, used for hockey tournaments and a key venue for the 2010 Commonwealth Games.

Further east is **Pragati Maidan**, a huge exhibition complex. Facing its entrance stand the ramparts of the **Purana Qila** ❿ (entrance by the zoo; daily sunrise to sunset; charge also covers Archaeological Museum). The fort was built by Afghan ruler Sher Shah Suri (1540–5) and was taken over by Mughal emperor Humayun when he regained the throne in 1555–6. Its

The Nehru Museum.

A backstreet near Chandni Chowk.

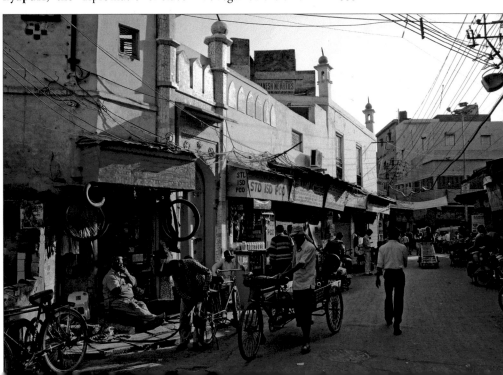

Qila-e-Kunha-Masjid is the best-preserved Lodi mosque in Delhi.

Just to the right inside the main gate
is the fort's **Archaeological Museum**
containing artefacts that date back
to the first human settlement here
in around 1000 BC. The well-pro-
portioned **Sher Mandal** pavilion, set
in beautifully maintained gardens,
was used as a library by the Mughal
emperor Humayun and was where he
fell to his death in 1555. Outside the
main entrance is an attractive park and
lake (once part of the moat) surrounding the fort.

Delhi Zoo ⑪ is nearby. With its
relatively large, open enclosures, it
is said to be one of the better examples in the country, but Indian zoos
are on the whole depressing places,
resembling concentration camps
rather than, at best, places to breed
endangered species (for further information visit www.petaindia.com and
www.zoocheck.com). The zoo shares
a border with the wealthy **Sundar
Nagar colony**, with some interesting shops specialising in jewellery
and antique artefacts.

*Faces of the new India
at the Pragati Maidan
conference centre.*

New Delhi museums

The area around Rajpath contains
a wealth of museums. The national
historical, archaeological and modern
art collections are all here, as are some
interesting sites relating to India's
political history.

South of Rashtrapati Bhavan is Teen
Murti Bhavan (www.nehrumemorial.nic.
in; Tue–Sun 9am–5.30pm; free), which
houses the **Jawaharlal Nehru Memorial Museum** in the prime minister's
former residence. Nehru's study, sitting
room and bedroom have been preserved,
and there is a very detailed exhibition of
the history of the Independence struggle. The modesty of the interiors reflects
well on one of India's greatest leaders.
The research library here is one of the
most important for studying modern
Indian political history.

The story of the Nehru/Gandhi
dynasty is continued at the **Indira
Gandhi Memorial Museum** (Tue–
Sun 9.30am–5pm; free) at 1 Safdarjang Road. This bungalow was
her residence and the place where
she was killed by her bodyguards.
Bloodstains are still visible at the
spot in the gardens. Inside you can
see her study and her wedding sari,
woven by Nehru. The path of her last
moments is marked by a glass walkway in the garden.

Close by, on Tees January Marg, is
the site of another political assassination, the **Gandhi Smriti** (also known
as Birla House: www.gandhismriti.nic.
in; Tue–Sun 10am–5.30pm; free),
museum and memorial, in the house
of the industrialist G.D. Birla. In the
garden, the place where Mahatma
Gandhi was shot in 1948 is marked by
a simple memorial. Again the route
taken by the assassinated leader is
marked out, this time by a series of
concrete 'footsteps'.

Southeast of India Gate is the
National Gallery of Modern Art ⑫
(www.ngmaindia.gov.in; Tue–Sun 10am–
5pm), in the former Delhi home of
Jaipur's royal family. Its impressive
permanent collection includes 1930s

paintings by Jamini Roy and Nandalal Bose and 18th-century Indian landscapes by Thomas and William Daniell. The ground floor is devoted to exhibitions of work by contemporary Indian artists and photographers.

The **National Museum** ⓭ (www.nationalmuseumindia.gov.in; Tue–Sun 10am–5pm), south of Rajpath on Janpath, is noted for its Indian sculpture and jewellery collections, Chola bronzes and a Buddhist gallery, including a carved Buddhist gateway from Sanchi. Among the most important artefacts here are those from the Harappan excavations at Mohenjadaro (including the famous small bronze statue of a dancing girl) and the holdings of Mughal manuscripts and miniatures. Especially good, on the second floor, is the Verrier Elwin collection of Adivasi art, from northeastern, central and southern Indian states.

The **National Rail Museum** ⓮ (www.nrm.indianrailways.gov.in; Tue–Sun 10am–5pm), lies just off Shanti Path in Chanakyapuri, and is well worth a visit. There are some interesting period coaches and a large array of steam engines, including the huge Garratt, built in 1930 in Manchester. As well as the informative indoor displays outlining the functioning of the modern Indian rail network, there is also an unusual working steam monorail that takes visitors around the site.

The **Crafts Museum** ⓯ (Tue–Sun 10am–5pm) on Bhairon Marg by Pragati Maidan has demonstrations by regional craftsmen, huts built in regional styles and a good crafts shop. The fascinating exhibition galleries have displays of Adivasi art, woodcarving and textiles. There are *bhuta* figures from Karnataka, brightly decorated Naga objects from the northeast and some wonderful bronzes from Odisha (Orissa). The textile galleries are superb – the collections run to over 22,000 objects – as well as some astounding embroidery, especially the Kashmiri examples. There are also weaving demonstrations.

Lodi Gardens

South of India Gate lie most of the sites of the former cities of Delhi. There are also many good shopping areas, such as **Khan Market** ⓰, which has a wide range of bookshops, cafés and restaurants, as well as upmarket stores selling everything for the house, including fresh flowers.

A short walk southwest along Subramaniam Road brings you to the beautiful **Lodi Gardens** ⓱ (sunrise–sunset), with fascinating tombs set in well-maintained lawns lined with rows of flower beds, immense trees, a bridge and walkways. At the Lodi Road end is the octagonal tomb of the Sayyid ruler **Muhammad Shah** (1434–44), and by the lake near Subramania Road is another octagonal tomb, of Sikandar Lodi (1489–1517). In the centre of the gardens is the large Shish Gumbad, another tomb from the Lodi period. The gardens are a favourite spot for families to picnic and for young couples to grab a few moments away from the watchful eyes of their parents.

Go immediately across Lodi Road to the entrance to **Lodi Colony**

SHOPPING IN DELHI

Delhi has everything from bookshops and crafts to high-end fashion from India's top designers. If you are after gifts and souvenirs the first place to head for is the enormous Central Cottage Industries Emporium (CCIE) on Janpath, an excellent, fixed price, one-stop shop for Indian crafts and fabrics (available by the metre). The second is Baba Kharak Singh Marg, where you will find many of the state government emporia. The most interesting market for general shopping is Khan Market. Here you will find branches of the clothing and interior design chains Fab India and Anokhi, the booksellers Bahri & Sons and more interior design from Good Earth and Oma.

Not far away in Lodi Colony Market (Jor Bagh) are the shops of some of India's finest fashion designers, including Manish Arora and Abraham & Thakore. Manish Arora, and many more Indian designers, can also be found at the swish Crescent at the Qutb mall in South Delhi. Other good places to explore for interesting boutiques include Defence Colony and the Santushti Complex.

For antiques, curios and pieces of traditional Indian art, you can't beat Haus Khas village, in Central Delhi, where numerous boutiques and hip galleries crowd the winding medieval alleyways. Perfect for reviving pitstops, rooftop cafés afford views of the surrounding ruins and tomb gardens.

Market in the colony of Jor Bagh. This has a number of upmarket boutiques and one of Delhi's best fish restaurants, Ploof.

East along Lodi Road is the **India Habitat Centre** (www.indiahabitat. org), a cultural and conference centre which hosts regular exhibitions and film festivals. Just a few hundred metres along from the centre, in the Institutional Area, is the **Tibet House Museum** (www.tibethouse.in; Mon–Fri 9.30am–5.30pm). It has some fine exhibits, including *thankas*, sculptures and a range of Tibetan musical instruments.

There are two other cultural institutes in the area: the tiled facade of the **India Islamic Cultural Centre** (Lodi Road; www.iiccentre.com), which holds conferences and temporary exhibitions, and the **India International Centre** (Max Mueller Marg; www.iicdelhi.nic.in), haunt of Delhi's intellectuals and academics. It is notoriously hard to get access to the IIC (you must be invited by a member), but if you can it has a superb library and a pleasant café.

Exhibits at the National Gallery of Modern Art.

Mughal tombs

Safdarjang's Tomb ⓲ (daily sunrise to sunset) and its adjoining rose garden are at the western end of Lodi Road just across Aurobindo Marg. This huge monument, dating from 1753, is the last significant piece of Mughal architecture to be built in Delhi. The gardens have been renovated and are now beautifully maintained.

At the eastern end of Lodi Road is **Humayun's Tomb** ⓳ (daily sunrise to sunset; charge). Set in beautiful gardens, the red sandstone monument is the finest Mughal building in Delhi (listed as a Unesco World Heritage Site in 1993) and was the prototype for the Taj Mahal. It was commissioned by Humayun's senior widow, Bega Begum, and completed in 1565. Also in the grounds are the remains of the octagonal tomb of Isa Khan. To the north, easily visible from the gardens, is the modern Damdama Sahib Gurudwara. Not far from the tomb complex is the **Nila Gumbad**, a blue-tiled late-Mughal tomb.

To the west of Humayun's Tomb is the shrine, or *dargah*, of the Sufi saint of the Chisti order, **Sheikh Nizamuddin Aulia** ⓴ (1236–1325), after whom the surrounding colonies are named. The *dargah* is a haven of peace in this busy Muslim area; the tomb of the saint is in a pavilion with beautiful marble screens (note that women are not allowed in the tomb itself). Also buried here are the Mughal emperor Muhammad Shah (1719–48) and the saint's disciple and poet Amir Khusrau. Qawwali singing sessions often happen after the evening *namaz*, making it a good time to visit, particularly on a Friday.

Heading south down Aurobindo Marg, past Safdarjung airport, brings you to the popular INA fruit and vegetable market consisting of warrens of covered shacks selling meat, fish, poultry and every imaginable household good. Across the road is the **Dilli Haat Food and Crafts Bazaar**, which provides a pavilion for regional craftspeople from all the Indian states and an opportunity to taste their varied

cuisine (10.30am–10pm) from the very hygienic stalls.

South Delhi

Just to the south of Dilli Haat is Delhi's Inner Ring Road. Crossing underneath the flyover, past the well-maintained gardens planted in memory of Rajiv Gandhi, brings you to South Delhi.

Lying to the west of Aurobindo Marg is one of the most attractive enclaves in South Delhi, **Hauz Khas Village ㉑**. Poised at the edge of a 14th-century water reservoir and madrasa, and the tomb of Firoz Shah Tughlaq, the narrow streets and calm air seem far away from the hectic traffic along the main road. Although the village has been transformed into a colony of expensive boutiques and art galleries (particularly good is the Village Art Gallery, which has a wide selection of modern and contemporary Indian art), it still retains much of its greenery and charm.

Monuments dot the area: the ruins of **Siri Fort ㉒**, now very overgrown and difficult to see, stand near the Asian Games Village complex to the east. Much of the area is open only to members of the sports facilities built for the 1982 games, but the residential village is worth a look for students of architecture. Designed by Raj Rewal, the well-conceived housing project takes its cue from the tightly packed cubist construction of traditional Indian urban architecture.

To the north of Siri Fort, at Hudco Place, Khel Gaon, is one of the first air-conditioned malls in Delhi, Ansal Plaza. Much loved by the middle classes who come here to eat and shop, it seems to have maintained its place alongside the super malls springing up further south.

Directly south of Nizamuddin in Nehru Place is the modern white marble, lotus-shaped **Baha'i Lotus Temple ㉓** (daily 9am–5.30pm, until 7pm in summer; free). Visitors must take off their footwear before entering the gardens around the temple itself. Standing on Kalkaji Hill, this iconic piece of Delhi architecture, designed by Fariburz Shah, was completed in 1986 as a pilgrimage site for the Baha'i faith. Nearby, the colony markets (M and N Blocks) of

WHERE

In addition to the Dilli Haat at the INA Market on Aurobindo Marg, there is another Dilli Haat in Pitampura, northern Delhi on Netaji Subash Place. There is a nominal entrance fee.

Indira Gandhi Memorial Museum.

TIP

The following venues host dance and music performances: India Habitat Centre (Lodi Road, tel: 011-2468 2001, www.indiahabitat.org); India International Centre (40 Max Müller Marg, tel: 011-2461 9431, www.iic delhi.nic.in); Kamani Auditorium (1 Copernicus Marg, tel: 011-4350 3351, www.kamani auditorium.org); Sangeet Natak Akademi (Rabindra Bhavan, Firoz Shah Road, tel: 011-2338 7246, www.sangeetnatak.gov.in).

The resplendent shrine of Sufi saint Sheikh Nizamuddin Aulia.

Greater Kailash offer some of the best shopping and finest restaurants in Delhi.

The Qutb Complex

At the southern end of Aurobindo Marg, past the Outer Ring Road and the Aurobindo Ashram, lies the district of Mehrauli. Here stands one of the most important sites in Delhi, the **Qutb Minar Complex** 24 (daily sunrise to sunset; charge), a Unesco World Heritage Site. The Qutb Minar itself is a remarkable 72-metre (278ft) -high tower, engraved with verses from the Qur'an. It was built in the 13th century by Qutb-ud-Din-Aibak, the first Muslim sultan of Delhi, to celebrate his victory over the Hindu kings. The first storey was finished by Qutb-ud-Din and the final two by his son-in-law Iltutmish (whose tomb lies nearby). The cupola that once sat on the very top was destroyed in an earthquake in the 19th century, and unfortunately visitors are no longer allowed up to the balcony that encircles the top of the first storey.

In the grounds, Aibak's **Quwwat-ul-Islam Mosque** is believed to be the oldest in India, built using parts of the demolished Hindu and Jain temples of Qila Rai Pithora. In the mosque courtyard is a 4th-century iron pillar, remarkable for having never shown any sign of corrosion.

Mehrauli

The ruins of **Lal Kot**, Delhi's first city, are spread across the surrounding district of **Mehrauli** 25. The village of the same name lies just to the south amid a labyrinth of old Indian bazaars. Among the most important monuments here is the octagonal tomb of Adham Khan, who was killed by the emperor Akbar. The building is known as the **Bhulbhulaiyan**. As well as the lovely *baoli* (step well), also worth searching out are the *dargah* of **Qutbuddin Bakhtiyar Kaki** (access for males only) and the nearby marble **Moti Masjid**.

In the south of Mehrauli are the colourful tombs of **Jamali Kamali**, and the **Hauz-i-Shamsi** reservoir commissioned by Iltutmish in 1230. On the northeastern corner of Hauz-i-Shamsi lies the **Jahaz Mahal**, a ruined Lodi pavilion.

Chattarpur

Beyond Mehrauli, towards the Haryana border and Gurgaon, are three more interesting sights. The first you come to is the **Garden of the Five Senses** (daily 9am–6pm, until 7pm Apr–Sept). Laid out by Delhi Tourism and opened in 2003, the extensive formal gardens are quite beautiful and full of running water and sculptures. The higher parts of the hill against which they are laid out have been left to the natural scrub of the area, and there are great views over the city.

Turn south again to see the spectacular modern temples and ashram complexes of **Chattarpur**. This is one of the largest temples in India, all carved white marble and huge statues, some of it in slightly dubious taste.

That is not a charge that can be laid against the nearby **Sanskriti Museums** (www.sanskritifoundation.org; Tue–Sat 10am–5pm; free). The beautifully laid-out displays in the three museums of Indian terracotta, everyday art and textiles make this one of the best museums in the city.

On the Mehrauli–Badarpur road, the 14th-century ruins of **Tughlaqabad Fort** ㉖ (daily sunrise to sunset; free) and **Adilabad**, Delhi's third city, dominate the landscape. Remains of ramparts, water-storage tanks and subterranean passages can be explored, but this area can be dangerous to visit alone. Beyond Tughlaqabad is the large tank at **Suraj Kund**. Excavations here have revealed some of the area's earliest settlements.

Gurgaon and NOIDA

To the far south through the expanding urban sprawl is Delhi's satellite city of **Gurgaon**, mostly comprising middle-class housing and shopping malls, including the vast new DLF Mall of India, the largest mall in the country, with parking space for 10,000. More huge malls are to be found in **NOIDA** (the New Okhala Development Area) across the river. Of most interest to visitors here is the enormous **Akshardham Temple** (www.akshardham.com). Built by the Swaminarayan Foundation and opened in 2005, this confection in sandstone and marble is impressive, if brash, and set in lovely gardens.

The spectacular tomb of Sikandar Lodi in the Lodi Gardens.

The Taj Mahal.

THE NORTHERN PLAINS

The flat, sunburnt plains of the Ganges and Yamuna rivers are India's breadbasket, home to almost 40 percent of the country's population and many of its greatest sights.

Between the soothing serenity of the Golden Temple to the west and the equally becalming Mahabodhi Temple to the east lies one of the most intense, tumultuous and unmissable parts of this extraordinary country. The further east you travel, the more like the wild west it becomes, from the almost military bearing and discipline of the Punjab's proud Sikhs to the apparent lawlessness of large swathes of Bihar. Between the two, Uttar Pradesh is considered by many to be the heartland of India – its soul enshrined in the incomparable Taj Mahal, its turbulent political life played out on the teeming streets of Lucknow, and religious sentiments laid bare on the burning ghats of Varanasi.

Through it all runs India's most sacred river, the Ganges, known locally as the Ganga. From its source in the high mountains of western Uttarakhand, it combines with an increasing number of tributaries as it heads eastwards, most famously at Allahabad where it merges with the Yamuna; by the time it discharges into the Bay of Bengal, the Ganges has drained an area of 1 million sq km (386,000 sq miles). The plains that the Ganges irrigates support one of the most densely populated areas in the world, all dependent on this great river for their very survival, a fact which only serves further

to elevate the Ganges's place in the Indian psyche.

Punjab and Haryana

The Punjab at one time extended northwest to the Indus River and was known to the Greeks as Pentopotamia, because of the five rivers that ran through it. The Persians named it *Panj* (five) *ab* (waters) – a name which has stuck. In 1947 its character, identity and soul were irrevocably torn apart by the atrocities of Partition. Pakistan was created in response to escalating

Main Attractions

Golden Temple, Amritsar
Agra Fort
Itimad-ud-Daula
Taj Mahal
Fatehpur Sikri
Vrindavan
Bara Imambara
Varanasi
Sarnath
Bodhgaya

One of the region's 320 million inhabitants.

Hindu-Muslim communal violence and unrest, but the abruptness of its birth left millions of non-Muslims on the Pakistan side of the border, and millions of Muslims on the Indian side. As each community attempted to realign itself via the only border crossing just west of Amritsar, the inevitable clashes developed into wholesale and horrific carnage. Of the 13 million people who attempted to traverse the frontier, over half a million lost their lives.

Although the larger part of the Punjab went to Pakistan, both Pakistan and India retained the name 'Punjab' for their respective states since Punjabi is spoken on both sides of the border.

It was this linguistic distinction that eventually led to the further division of the Indian Punjab in 1966 when the new states of Punjab (92 percent Punjabi-speaking), Haryana and Himachal Pradesh (predominantly Hindi-speaking) were born.

The wide-open plains of the Punjab have always been the main route into the country for invaders from the northwest, and have thus witnessed some of India's most momentous battles. Key to securing control of the Subcontinent, these northwestern flatlands were also a major prize in themselves: the region is one of the most fertile in the world, its productive soil

The Northern Plains

watered by the numerous rivers flowing down from the massive mountains to the north. Indian Punjab alone accounts for around 2 percent of the global wheat and cotton harvest.

Their impressive contribution to India's agricultural output notwithstanding, it is the gregarious, assiduous people of the Punjab who exert the largest influence on the country's character. The wide-ranging influence of Punjabi music, culture and cuisine on North India, and particularly Delhi, far belies the relative paucity of the Punjabi population – just 2 percent of the Indian total.

Haryana, also a major agricultural contributor, has more recently come to prominence as India's industrial powerhouse. Half of the millions of cars and motorbikes made in India are manufactured here, while Gurgaon, a Singapore-styled satellite city to the south of Delhi, has emerged as a major player in the IT sector.

Despite the linguistic division that separated the states in the 1960s, the people of the Punjab and Haryana have much in common.

Both Punjab and Haryana have more history than historical monuments, more facilities for tourists than places of tourist interest, and are generally seen as interesting places to stop off on the way elsewhere rather than destinations in themselves. Having said that, Amritsar's Golden Temple is without doubt one of India's star attractions, rated by many visitors as more impressive even than the Taj Mahal.

Historical sites

There are several Mughal monuments in Haryana, of which the most popular is **Pinjore Gardens** at the base of the Sivalik Hills, 20km (12 miles) north of Chandigarh on the road to Simla. Inside the Mughal battlements is a beautifully laid-out garden with fountains and cascades, designed in the 17th century by Nawab Fadai Khan, foster brother of Aurangzeb, one of the great Mughal emperors. The gardens also offer panoramic views of the Himalayas.

Close to Delhi is **Suraj Kund**, an 8th-century Hindu sun temple, and home to a huge handicrafts *mela* (fair) every February, while beyond lies

PUNJAB TRANSPORT

Amritsar has a fully fledged international airport, with flights to Asia, the Middle East, Europe and North America, as well as internal connections to Delhi, which are also available from Chandigarh airport. Both states are very well connected by train, meaning buses only need be used for the most far-flung places.

Amritsar: Shatabdi train service to Delhi and beyond (2 daily; 6hrs plus many slower trains) plus regular services to Pathankot (4 daily; 2hrs 30min).

Chandigarh: There is a Shatabdi (express) train service to Delhi (2 daily; 3hrs30min plus many slower trains) and Kalka (7–8 daily; 30–40min). For services to Amritsar and other destinations, you will need to go to Ambala and change. Buses are the best choice for points north: Shimla (4hrs), Manali (11hrs) and Dharamsala (8hrs).

Worshippers in the Dwarkadhish Temple, Mathura.

Badkhal Lake, with a resthouse overlooking its stretch of water.

Punjab and Haryana contain some of the earliest evidence of Indian societies. Archaeologists have found implements made of quartzite fashioned over 300,000 years ago. Agricultural tools made of copper and bronze prove the existence of rural communities around 2500 BC. Later excavations have unearthed whole cities built around that period.

It was through these two states that invaders from the northwest – Greeks, Turks, Mongols, Persians and Afghans – entered India, and where many battles were fought. Their sites are marked with commemorative stones and mausoleums of kings and commanders, with the most famous at **Panipat** (also the site of the shrine of the Muslim saint Abu Ali Kalandar) and Kurukshetra in Haryana. There are innumerable forts scattered all over the countryside, including those of **Bathinda**, **Faridkot** and **Anandpur Sahib** (see page 152). Both states have developed wildlife sanctuaries along lakes, swamps and rivers, equipped with attractive tourist bungalows, while Haryana Tourism has now started to offer 'farm holidays' in an attempt to remind Delhiites of the joys of the country.

Le Corbusier's city

Of the many things that Punjab and Haryana have in common, the most important is their shared capital, **Chandigarh ❶**. Prior to partition the Punjab was governed from Lahore, but once that city had been ceded to Pakistan, the Indian side of the newly bisected state was left without a capital city. The idea of building a brand-new, planned city, rather than expanding an existing one, appealed to Jawaharlal Nehru, India's first prime minister. He saw it as the perfect project to reflect the character and ambition of a brave, newly independent India. Since both states have laid claims to the city, it is administered by the Central Government as a Union Territory until a final decision regarding its future is made. However, in the same city reside governors of the two states; in the same office buildings but on different floors

Le Corbusier architecture at Chandigarh.

are their separate secretariats and their respective High Courts.

Beautifully located below the Sivalik Hills, Chandigarh presented a fascinating challenge for ambitious mid-20th-century architects. The concept was initiated by Albert Mayer, an American, and Matthew Nowicki, from Poland, but the project was then taken over by the famous Swiss-born French architect Le Corbusier, assisted by his cousin Jeanneret and an English husband-and-wife team, Maxwell Fry and Jane Drew. They settled on a grid design for the new city's streets, giving Chandigarh a different feel from anywhere else in India; with all those straight roads and roundabouts it is not unlike an eastern version of the British 'new town', Milton Keynes.

Le Corbusier himself designed most of its important public buildings, including the **Secretariat**, the **Legislative Assembly** and the **High Court**. For those who are interested in the city's design there is an **Architecture Museum** with displays of the original plans and models inside the Government Museum complex. Many of these buildings are on stilts, an architectural style copied by many private institutions and homes.

The city has for some years been generating headlines for the way its architectural heritage – from old chairs out of the Legislative Assembly building, to prints, pictures, tapestries, carvings and even door handles – are being removed and sold piecemeal by officials, who have no idea of their actual worth. Bought at auction by local junk dealers, many of the items – originally designed by Le Corbusier and his team and regarded as collectors' items in the West – find their way to international art houses where they are sold for huge sums; one manhole cover recently fetched an amazing £15,000 in a sale in London. While some are fixtures formerly condemned by bureaucrats as 'unfit for use' by the local administration, many are thought to have been illegally removed.

Chandigarh is a very green city, with a large variety of flowering trees. It has an extensive **Rose Garden** with over 1,000 varieties. The **Government Museum and Art Gallery** (www.

Nek Chand's Rock Garden.

TIP

Tourists are welcome to visit the Golden Temple, but must respect Sikh cultural traditions. Shoes and socks must be left at the entrance cloakroom (free), and visitors are expected to wash their feet by walking through the shallow bath at the entrance. It is also necessary to cover one's head with a scarf – these are provided at the entrance. There is an information office (usually open 7am–8pm) near the entrance.

The Golden Temple at Amritsar.

chdmuseum.nic.in; Tue–Sun 10am–4.30pm) was also designed by Le Corbusier and features a good collection of Gandharan sculpture and miniature painting. **Sukhna Lake**, a 15-minute walk east from the centre, is a pleasant place for a stroll, its wide boulevard a popular evening hangout.

Chandigarh's quirkiest and most charming attraction is without doubt Nek Chand's compellingly unique **Rock Garden** (Oct–Mar 9am–6pm, Apr–Sept 9am–7.30pm), just to the north of Sukhna Lake. The idiosyncratic Chand, after starting work in Chandigarh as a roads inspector in 1951, noticed on his travels large amounts of unclaimed, recyclable building material on the city's many construction sites. Ever enterprising, he decided to build a small garden in which these materials could be fashioned into attractive sculptures. He chose as his site a gorge within a demarcated green zone, the illegality of his endeavour obliging him to work at night for fear of discovery. And so it continued for 18 years until, in 1975, the authorities – presumably to their considerable surprise – discovered

Chand's garden. By this time it had grown to cover an area of 5 hectares (12 acres), and consisted of a series of painstakingly crafted courtyards, each containing hundreds of sculpted animals, musicians and dancers.

At this point the authorities should by rights have demolished the garden, but to their eternal credit decided instead to give Chand a workforce of 50, an annual salary and instructions to finish what he started. Today the garden covers 16 hectares (40 acres), attracts over 5,000 visitors daily and has received substantial recognition worldwide.

Temples of the Punjab

The Punjab's largest city is **Amritsar** ❷ with its **Golden Temple** (open 24 hours), the holiest of holy Sikh shrines, and, in the past, a flashpoint for religious and political conflict. These days it's a bustling but perfectly safe destination, the urban sprawl outside the old city walls much like elsewhere in India, which only accentuates the tranquillity of the temple within.

The site was stormed by government troops in 1984 in an operation

known as 'Blue Star', now seen by some observers as the most embarrassing in the history of the Indian Army. In response to escalating Sikh-Hindu violence, Sikh militants had established the Golden Temple as their military base, turning it in to a formidably fortified stronghold. By mid-1984 the militants had effectively taken the law in to their own hands and Indira Gandhi, prime minister at the time, decided that enough was enough and ordered military intervention.

The Indian Army envisaged a swift, one-sided assault, but had grossly underestimated the firepower of the Sikhs, who were equipped with machine guns and rockets. In the event it took the army three days of heavy fighting and the deployment of 20 tanks to take control of the temple; the official death toll stands at 493, but most eyewitness accounts put it in the thousands, the majority innocent pilgrims. Recriminations were wide-ranging, and the bloody episode led to the assassination of Indira Gandhi by her Sikh body-guards later the same year.

Amritsar was founded over 400 years ago by Guru Ram Das, the fourth of the 10 Sikh Gurus. His son and successor, Arjun, raised a temple in the middle of a pool, sanctified its waters and installed the Sikhs' holy scripture, the *Granth Sahib*, in its inner sanctum. The sacred pool – *amrit* (nectar) *sar* (pool) – gives the city its name. In 1803, the Sikh ruler Maharaja Ranjit Singh (1780–1839; see page 151) rebuilt the temple in marble and gold, since when it has been known as the Golden Temple. The Sikhs refer to it as the *Harimandir* (the temple of God) or *Darbar Sahib* (the court of the Lord).

Today the temple is a soothing, peaceful place to be, even if (or perhaps because) it is run with an almost military efficiency. It is worthwhile spending an hour or two in the temple complex (be sure to have your head covered and feet bare), listening to the hymn-singing and watching the thousands of pilgrims at worship.

There are a number of shrines of historical importance, notably the **Akal Takht** (throne of the timeless God) facing the temple where arms

The holy site at the confluence of the Yamuna and Ganges, Allahabad.

MAHARAJA RANJIT SINGH

Maharaja Ranjit Singh took over control of a small area of the Punjab from his father at the age of 11. After a series of successful campaigns, he persuaded the various Sikh factions to unite as one state under his leadership, taking the title of Maharaja in 1801. He soon waged the first of many battles, defeating an army in Gujarat before vanquishing the Afghans and taking control of Lahore. For the next 40 years he extended the boundary of his kingdom, eventually to bring Pashtun, Amritsar, Kashmir and all of present-day Punjab under his control. He was famed as a just leader whose court was composed of people of all religions and from every corner of the earth. His army was trained by French, German, British and American officers, and became the most efficient fighting force for miles around.

of the warrior gurus, their dresses and emblems can be seen, and the eight-storey **Baba-Atal Tower**. The temple kitchen, which provides food free of charge to all visitors, is well worth seeking out; in return for the free meal, diners are expected to help with either the preparation of the food or the washing-up afterwards. The 'chapatti factory' should not be missed. There's also a museum above the temple's main entrance, although it's decidedly not for the faint-hearted. It depicts Sikh conflicts over the years, with a number of interesting paintings leading up to more recent times, when photographs take over; some of the before-and-after shots of Sikh martyrs are especially gory.

Besides the Golden Temple, there is its Hindu counterpart, the 16th-century **Durgiana Temple**; and **Jallianwala Bagh** where on 13 April 1919, in one of the worst atrocities of British rule, General Dyer notoriously fired on a peaceful, unarmed crowd and killed at least 300 people, shocking the nation – and boosting the emerging independence movement. The garden has a

monument commemorating the event. Amritsar is also an important industrial and commercial centre and, away from the peace of the Golden Temple complex, is a busy and congested city.

Further afield

There are many other Sikh temples dotted around the Indian Punjab. In the foothills of the Himalaya by the Sutlej river in the northeastern corner of the state is **Anandpur Sahib** where, in 1699, the last of the Sikh gurus, Govind Singh, baptised the first five Sikhs into the militant fraternity he called the *Khalsa* ('the pure'). Here are several temples and a fortress, **Kesgarh**. In the plains west of Chandigarh, a large complex of temples, palaces and forts can be seen at **Sirhind**, while nearby **Patiala** was once the capital of one of the richest 'princely states', in British India: the Shish Mahal palace of the ruling family is worth a visit.

The industrial city of **Ludhiana**, some 125km (78 miles) west of Chandigarh, is known as the 'Manchester of India', but aside from being a good place to buy textiles there is little to see.

Indo-Pakistan border

Thirty kilometres (18 miles) to the west of Amritsar (and midway between Amritsar and Lahore) lies the Indo-Pakistan border, at a village called Wagah, although authorities in Amritsar are now keen for the crossing to be known as Attari, the name of the last stop on the Indian side, having decided that Wagah itself actually lies in Pakistan. There is a highly ritualised border closing ceremony here at sundown every day which is well worth seeing. The tallest soldiers from each country's respective armies perform a series of Monty Python-esque walks which culminate in the lowering of the national flags and the banging shut of the border gates, while the crowds on both sides shout patriotic slogans in an almost pantomime atmosphere, once described

Soldiers perform at the Indo-Pakistan border at Wagah/Attari.

by Michael Palin as 'chauvinism at its most camp'. The recent thaw in relations between the two countries, however, has seen a corresponding toning down of the ritual, at least on the Indian side, with the addition of a cursory handshake between the guards before the slamming shut of their respective gates.

Note that at the time of writing in early 2016, official advice warns against travel in the immediate vicinity of the border with Pakistan everywhere other than Wagah.

Kurukshetra

Haryana has very few famous sights of tourist interest; even so, it can rightfully claim to be the birthplace of the most sacred religious scripture of Hinduism. At **Kurukshetra ③**, situated on the main Delhi–Chandigarh railway line, a legendary battle was fought between two sets of cousins, the Kuruvas and the Pandavas. On the eve of the battle, Sri Krishna, an incarnation of Vishnu, persuaded Arjuna, the reluctant commander of the Pandava army, to wage war on his relatives.

This sermon, known as the *Bhagavad Gita*, discusses *dharma*, the moral principle of doing one's duty without consideration of reward, victory or defeat. Kurukshetra is full of temples and tanks where pilgrims come to bathe on auspicious days.

Also in Haryana, in Gurgaon district southwest of Delhi, is the **Sultanpur Bird Sanctuary**. Set up in 1971, the sanctuary is based around a *jhil*, or seasonal lake. A large number of species can be seen here in the winter months, including common hoopoe, white ibis and painted stork, as well as nilgai and blackbuck antelopes.

Uttar Pradesh

Uttar Pradesh (UP), with close to 200 million inhabitants, would be the world's fifth-most populous country if it were independent. As it is, the state is the heartland of the world's largest democracy, and politics here are lively. UP has a broad industrial base but is still predominantly agricultural, with wheat, maize, rice and sugar cane among the main crops. Its name means 'northern state' and it is made up of

Street food in Lucknow.

TURBANS

Varieties of the distinctive turban – known in India as a *pagri* or *dastar* – are worn by Hindus, Muslims and Sikhs, but it is the last group with which they are most associated. Uncut hair is one of the five 'articles of faith' which all baptised Sikhs are expected to wear, and turbans were thus adopted as a practical way of containing such untrimmed tresses. Typically, Sikhs use at least 4.5 metres (15ft) of cloth, sometimes stitched into a double width. You will see all shapes, sizes and colours. Often the hair is first wrapped into a bun and placed into a handkerchief. (On casual occasions, the outer turban may be left off.) Punjabi turbans tend to be neat and tidy, especially compared to the enormous desert turbans seen in Rajasthan, which are up to 7 metres (23ft) long. Turbans are a male preserve: women, also required to keep their hair uncut, usually drape a large scarf over their heads.

In traditional times, Sikhs wore a special protective turban known as dumalla into battle. It featured a chand tora, or crescent sword symbol held in place at the front with a chord of woven chainmail. Tied into various patterns, the chand tora helped protect the wearer against

slashing blades. You'll still see it worn by devout Sikh pilgrims at special ceremonial processions and festivals today, usually over in navy blue and saffron dumalla frequently reaching two or three feet in height.

Motorcycle helmets will not accommodate a turban. While helmets are compulsory for non-turban wearers, the law has been amended to allow Sikhs to ride motorbikes without them, although they must legally be at least 5 metres (16ft) in length – anything shorter having been deemed to offer inadequate protection. Protective goggles are strapped on, and fastidious city Sikhs use a dust cover, akin to a tea cosy, for two-wheeler rides around town (beard nets are also commonly seen).

It is considered a humiliating offence to knock someone's turban from his head. Abject apology is shown by removing one's own turban and placing it at another man's feet. In hot lands across the Muslim world, turbans protect men from the heat and blows to the head. Persian invaders brought a refined aesthetic to the Mughal courts, with turban gems and feather adornments to indicate status.

Detail from the Itimad-ud-Daula tomb in Agra.

The King's Gate, one of the entrances to the Jama Masjid at Fatehpur Sikri.

two regions. The larger part comprises the rich, alluvial, pancake-flat plain of the Ganges and its tributaries, while to the south, the Vindhya Hills rise to the edges of the Deccan Plateau. Although UP is famous worldwide for the Taj Mahal at Agra, it attracts devout Hindus to the many pilgrimage places along the River Ganges, which flows through the holy cities of Allahabad and Varanasi. Buddhists are drawn to the deer park at Sarnath where the Buddha preached his first sermon.

Fifteen percent of the population is Muslim, and in addition to its mosques and Sufi shrines, UP has some of the most prestigious Muslim theological colleges. For the visitor, the state's political, historical and religious importance can be witnessed in a heady mix of destinations, from the sensual intensity of Varanasi, to the architectural wonders of Lucknow and the breathtaking beauty of the Taj Mahal, so familiar and yet so striking.

Agra: city of the emperors

Synonymous with the Taj Mahal, **Agra ❹** is the prime destination on most tourist itineraries of India. Be warned that a visit can be a crowded, noisy and rather exhausting experience. It is often very smoggy, too, particularly in the winter months. If you can cope with the crowds and the endless hustle, though, Agra has more to offer than its famous mausoleum: the fort and royal tombs are suitably grand reminders of the Mughals' wealth and power, while the old part of town still feels like a medieval city, with narrow lanes and colourful shops selling local handicrafts.

The city achieved greatness under the Mughals, and particularly the emperors Akbar (1556–1605), Jahangir (1605–27) and Shah Jahan (1628–58). The Agra of today is, however, considerably less illustrious than its past glories might suggest. For obvious reasons it has never struggled to attract visitors, but as a result has felt little need to add to its attractiveness. This has also coloured the attitudes of the local residents who most frequently come into contact with tourists; rickshaw drivers, shopkeepers and hotel touts all seem to work on

UP TRANSPORT

Agra, Lucknow, Kanpur, Allahabad and Varanasi all have regular flights to Delhi. Timetables can be erratic during the winter months, when fog frequently disrupts services. Travelling between Delhi and Agra, you're always better off going by train – it's actually faster than flying. **Agra**: Regular train service to Delhi; quickest is Shatabdi express (1 daily; 2hrs plus many slower trains). Other destinations include Jaipur (9–11 daily; 3hrs 40 mins–5hrs 35 min), Varanasi (3–4 daily; 12–16hrs) and Kolkata (4–7 daily; 20–31hrs). **Lucknow**: Trains run to Delhi (29–34 daily; 7–10hrs), Agra (4–7 daily; 5–9hrs), Varanasi (28–35 daily; 5–13hrs) and Kolkata (6–9 daily; 19–30hrs). **Varanasi**: Trains run to Delhi (8–12 daily; 12–16hrs), Agra (2–4 daily; 10–16hrs), Lucknow (28–35 daily; 5–13hrs), Kolkata (6–9 daily; 12–26hrs).

the premise that however indifferently they treat their clientele, more will turn up tomorrow.

Perhaps wary of its reputation, many visitors choose to see Agra in a day and then sleep elsewhere – even a return day trip from Delhi is feasible, with the express train making the journey in just two hours. While the main attractions can be seen in this way, it's worth remembering that the translucent marble of the Taj Mahal is at its most impressive in the early light of dawn.

Agra Fort and the Taj Mahal

Agra Fort (daily sunrise–sunset), on the banks of the Yamuna River, is the city's other major sight, and offers great views of the Taj (unfortunately the entrance fee is no longer included with that of the Taj). The structure began to take shape from 1564. Akbar constructed the massive 2.4km (1.5-mile), 20-metre (65ft) -high surrounding walls of local sandstone. It was said of Agra Fort that 'from top to bottom the fire-red stones, linked by iron rings, are joined so closely that even a hair cannot find a way into their joints'.

Of the former '500 edifices of red stones in the fine styles of Bengal and Gujarat', only the Jahangiri Mahal still stands. This was the main part of the women's quarters, constructed in a local Indian style to suit the needs of the emperor's Hindu wives. Akbar's other buildings were demolished to make way for the imperial quarters of Shah Jahan, combining Hindu and Islamic styles of architecture. The Mussaman Burj (Octagonal Tower) is said to be the place where Shah Jahan was imprisoned by his son, spending his last years lying on his deathbed gazing out wistfully at the Taj Mahal. Today this view is still one of the fort's main attractions, giving a perspective of the Taj difficult to obtain elsewhere, the river in the foreground reflecting the impeccable symmetry of this most iconic of buildings.

The tomb of **Itimad-ud-Daula** (daily sunrise–sunset), across the river from the fort, is the most intimate of the three great monuments in Agra, but far less epic in scale than the other two. Itimad-ud-Daula was father-in-law and *wazir* (principal minister) to Emperor Jahangir. Nur Jahan, Jahangir's queen, undertook the construction of her father's tomb (1622–8) in white marble. Included in the design are some interesting details – the wine bottles, for example, are thought to have been a comment on the minister's penchant for alcohol, of which his daughter disapproved.

Also on the east side of the river, hidden behind the lovely nurseries along Aligarh Road, are the **Chini ka Rauza**, the tomb of Afzal Khan, a courtier to Jahangir and Shah Jahan, and, further on, the **Rambagh** gardens, believed to have been laid out by the Emperor Babur (both sites sunrise–sunset).

Within sight of Agra Fort is the **Taj Mahal** (www.tajmahal.gov.in; Sat–Thur sunrise–sunset). The world-famous tomb of Mumtaz Mahal, wife of Emperor Shah Jahan, this iconic

THE DIAMOND DALIT

Although she is no longer the Chief Minister of Uttar Pradesh, Mayawati Kumari has dominated politics in the state for the past twenty years, courting as much controversy as she has praise for her rags to riches rise to power. Born into a scheduled caste family, Mayawati was the first Dalit, or member of an 'Untouchable' caste, to become the head of any Indian state. She was also the youngest Chief Minister ever, when, at just 39, she first came to the position in 1995.

The turbulent nature of UP politics ensured Mayawati has enjoyed four spells in the top job to date. Her political career has been nothing if not colourful. One of her early slogans exhorted fellow Dalits to beat members of the upper castes with their shoe, and while her rhetoric has since mellowed, she's seldom been out of the headlines. Charges of corruption have continued to dog her, fuelled by her expansive property portfolio and diamond-laden public appearances, particularly on her own birthday. Modesty has never been her strong suit; she remains the only chief minister to have ordered a statue of themselves.

In a recent court case, Mayawati revealed that her personal fortunes ran to Rs111.26 crore ($20.3 million). Her lawyers claimed the wealth derived from donations from supporters, rather than backhanders from contractors in the Taj Heritage Corridor (see page 156), as has been alleged by the Indian CBI.

The Vishram Ghat on the Yamuna river at Mathura, Lord Krishna's birthplace.

building stands in a Mughal garden on a terrace beside a bend in the Yamuna. Mumtaz Mahal was married to the emperor for 19 years, during which she accompanied him on his military campaigns and shared his confidence on all matters of state. She bore 13 children, including the next emperor, Aurangzeb. In 1631 she died in childbirth. Shah Jahan was desolate and built the Taj Mahal in her honour. He was later deposed by Aurangzeb and imprisoned in Agra Fort. For more on the Taj Mahal, see page 170.

Akbar's capital

Early morning is the best time to visit **Fatehpur Sikri ❺** (daily sunrise–sunset), Akbar's imperial capital, 35km (20 miles) southwest of Agra. The remarkably well-preserved remains include the palace and the royal Jama Masjid (mosque) where the Sufi saint Shaikh Salim Chisti is buried. Akbar is said to have visited the saint on this site when he was anxious for an heir. He was told that he would have three sons, and when his words came true Akbar chose Sikri for his capital.

Fatehpur, 'town of victory', was built of sandstone quarried from the hill on which it stood. It was, however, only occupied for 14 years before Akbar shifted his capital to Lahore. The usual explanation is that this happened because the water ran out, but it may also have been for strategic reasons. The palace buildings draw on the style of Persian, Mughal and local Indian architecture, skilfully blended by Akbar to create a style all of its own.

The finest monuments include **Diwan-e-Khas**, where Akbar debated religious matters from a platform supported by an ornate octagonal pillar, and connected to each corner of the square building by suspended walkways, **Mariam's House**, home of Akbar's wife and intricately private in design, and the Jama Masjid. Already an imposing structure, the mosque was given further stature by the addition of the **Buland Darwaza**, a massive entrance gate built five years later to celebrate Akbar's victories in Gujarat.

While the buildings are all uninhabited today, the complex gives a uniquely well-preserved insight into how life in the royal Mughal courts was lived, and the extent of the luxury that the Mughal emperors enjoyed.

Sikandra

Akbar also designed his own resting place. The tomb, completed in 1613, is at **Sikandra** (daily sunrise–sunset), 12km (7 miles) northwest of Agra. The mausoleum is four storeys high; the first three are of red sandstone, the fourth of white marble containing the false tomb of the emperor. The real tomb, as in all such mausoleums, is in a crypt below. Outside, blackbuck wander the gardens.

Braj

The area around **Mathura ❻**, on the banks of the Yamuna river 30km (19 miles) north of Agra on the Delhi road, is known as Braj and is popularly believed to have been the birthplace and home of Lord Krishna. According

CONTROVERSIAL CORRIDOR

An example of Uttar Pradesh government-level apathy came in the form of the 'Taj Heritage Corridor', a commercially driven attempt to create a cordoned-off corridor running from the Taj Mahal to Agra Fort, lined with shopping centres, amusement parks and restaurants. The initial phase of the project required 2km (1.25-mile) of the Yamuna riverbed to be filled in, dramatically altering the river's flow and potentially undermining the Taj Mahal's foundations.

Both this work and the construction of a 1.5km (1-mile) -long boundary wall were allowed to go ahead before sense prevailed. Unesco threatened to reconsider their World Heritage status should the project continue, at which point the Minister for Culture stepped in. He had also discovered that the scheme, which cost Rs175 crore ($44 million), had not been approved by any relevant government agency. Attempts were made to prosecute Uttar Pradesh's Chief Minister for her role in the project (and the disappearance of funds earmarked for the development). The legal case against her fizzled out in 2011, after the Supreme Court quashed allegations that her assets of approximately Rs111.26 crore ($20.3 million) were disproportionate to her income, though unfinished construction works remain dotted along the Yamuna, awaiting demolition.

to legend, the young Krishna was brought up in a family of cowherds, where he performed miracles for the good of the villagers, and played tricks on them, and where all the *gopis* (milkmaids) fell helplessly in love with him. He was, Hindus believe, an incarnation of the god Vishnu. In one of the greatest Hindu texts, the *Bhagavad Gita*, Krishna explains the world and how best to live in it.

Mathura today is an industrial town notable for its oil refinery, but it has retained its religious pre-eminence. Highlights include the **Kesava Deo Mandir**, built on the spot where Krishna was born; the stepped tank, **Potara Kund**, where his clothes were washed; and the numerous riverside ghats, of which **Vishram Ghat** is best known. Pilgrims gather to bathe at the ghats on the Yamuna and to visit temples such as the **Dvarkadhish shrine** in the crowded marketplace.

Disciples of the Hare Krishna movement descend on Mathura from all over the world; it was also once a thriving centre of Buddhism and Jainism. Sculptures made by local artists between the 2nd century BC and the 6th century AD are on display at the **museum** (Tue–Sun 10.30am–4.30pm, closed second Sat of each month).

There are numerous sites associated with Vishnu around Mathura, although the most impressive is at **Vrindavan**, 10km (6 miles) to the north, home to many Hindu widows who earn a tiny sum each day singing hymns to the Lord. Among the fine temples are those to **Govind-dev** (1590); **Jugal Kishor**, **Radha-Vallabh** and **Madan-Mohan** (17th century); **Ranganathji** and **Shahji** (19th century); the **Vankebehari shrine**; and **Pagal Baba**.

Southern Uttar Pradesh

The area bordering Madhya Pradesh can be explored from **Jhansi** ❼, 188km (117 miles) south of Agra. Jhansi is dominated by its impressive hill **fort** (dawn–dusk), from where the Rani of Jhansi, one of the heroines of the Uprising against the British in 1857, directed her operations. There is a **museum** here (Tue–Sun, 10.30am–4.30pm; closed second Sat

FACT

Following the death of the local rajah of Jhansi in 1853, his widow, Rani assumed power. She was removed by the British, who reserved the right to assume control of any Indian state where there was no male heir. Rani returned during the Uprising of 1857, and the British force was routed. Having later fled to Gwalior, Lakshmibai was killed in battle. She is revered as a hero of independence.

Mughal-style colonnades at Agra Fort.

of each month) detailing the (mostly pre-British) history of the area.

From Jhansi it's a three-hour drive east to the village of **Khajuraho** (in Madhya Pradesh), renowned for its 1,000-year-old temples and erotic carvings (see page 276). The pilgrimage centre of **Chitrakut**, 235km (146 miles) east of Jhansi, looks like a mini-Varanasi, with ghats on the banks of the narrow Mandakani river.

Central and Eastern UP

The route from Delhi, 446km (277 miles) east to the state capital of Lucknow, passes through **Aligarh**, site of the Aligarh Muslim University founded by Sir Syed Ahmad Khan in 1875 to provide the Muslim community of India with a modern, scientific education.

Kanpur ❽, on the Ganges 70km (44 miles) southwest of Lucknow, is the state's leading industrial city, and as such holds little interest for visitors. In the Uprising of 1857 the British garrison at Kanpur (Cawnpore), home to some 400 British men, women and children, was besieged by Indian forces, and in the face of starvation

after 18 days agreed to an offer of safe passage. As they crossed the riverbank they were massacred. **All Souls' Memorial Church** (1875) contains the names of those who died.

Lucknow

Uttar Pradesh's state capital, **Lucknow ❾**, a two-hour journey from Kanpur, stands on the Gomati River, a tributary of the Ganges. It was once a city of gardens, but many have disappeared under the onslaught of offices, shopping centres and residential colonies. The city's skyline is now a heady mix of modern design and some of the most elegant examples of Indo-Saracenic architecture in the country, often used these days as municipal offices for some banal-sounding government departments, the kind of places that would be housed in grey concrete elsewhere.

If you enter the city via the airport at Amausi, you will pass **Dilkusha**, a former royal hunting lodge designed like a Ruritanian castle and a key site in the 1857 Uprising. Several British officers died here, including

Vishnu temple at Vrindavan.

General Havelock, who is buried in the **Alambagh**.

La Martinière College, one of the city's most extravagant estates, lies on its eastern outskirts. It was built as a home for the French businessman adventurer Claude Martin, who bequeathed his huge fortune to the running of educational institutions for Anglo-Indians. In front of Constantia, the college's main building, is the Lord Cornwallis, a cannon cast by Claude Martin and used in the Battle of Seringapatam against Tipu Sultan. Major Hodson, who killed the sons of the last Mughal emperor Bahadur Shah in Delhi, is buried in the park, as is Martin's Indian wife. Martin himself is buried in the basement of Constantia. Visitors are welcomed, but permission must be granted by the principal's office at the college's east end.

Further west is Claude Martin's former armoury, now the state governor's residence, and beyond it the Anglican church, post office and state legislature, built in 1932 when the capital of Oudh was shifted from Allahabad to Lucknow. Nearby is Lucknow's main shopping area, **Hazratganj**, the Gentleman's Market. On Hazratganj itself is the **Imambara Sibtainabad**, built by the last nawab, Wajid Ali Shah, as a mausoleum for his father.

On Shah Najaf Marg, heading north from Hazratganj, is the **Shah Najaf Imambara** and **Sikandarbargh**, a 24-hectare (60-acre) botanical garden named after the nawab's wife. West, along Rana Pratap Marg, is **Kurshid Manzil**, shaped like a moated English castle, now the La Martinière Girls School. Adjoining it is the **Taron Wali Kothi**, the nawab's observatory, now the State Bank of India.

En route towards the Residency further west, you pass Farhat Baksh, Claude Martin's principal residence, now the Central Drug Research Institute (no entry permitted). All of this area, as it leads to the Residency, was the scene of ferocious fighting during the Uprising.

A monument of more recent origin dominates the riverfront to the east of the city centre. Erected by the controversial former Chief Minister of Uttar Pradesh, Mayawati (see page 155), the extravagant Dr Ambedkar Memorial – a vast complex of sandstone ramparts, gardens, canals, walkways and statues sprawling over 21 hectares (53 acres) – was opened in 2009, at vast expense to the Indian taxpayer. Quite why one of the poorest regions in the country saw fit to spend a sum estimated at around $127.7 million when tens of millions of inhabitants remain malnourished and without access to clean drinking water, remains a subject of considerable debate.

The Residency

The **Residency Compound** (Tue–Sun 10am–5pm) is a complex that housed about 3,000 mostly European residents prior to the Siege of Lucknow in 1857. Only 1,000 survived the five-month conflict. There is a **museum** (same hours as the Residency) in the basement of the Residency itself, which gives a good idea of conditions at the time of

Vishram Ghats, Mathura.

Hussainabad Imambara was built during the 19th century by Nawabs of the Oudh Dynasty, shortly before the British took control of the city.

A busy street in Mathura.

the Uprising, and of the wretched struggle that the residents had to endure.

Bara Imambara

About 2km (1.25 miles) west beyond the Residency is the **Bara Imambara** (6am–5pm, closed during Muharrum). Built in the time of famine in 1784 as a food-for-work programme, it is an architectural marvel built without pillars, and contains a hall 50 metres (163ft) long with acoustics so good you can hear a paper tear at the other end. There is an entertaining maze on the upper floor. The entrance ticket also gives access to the **Hussainabad Imambara** next door, with its fabulous chandeliers and silver pulpit, the Picture Gallery housing portraits of the nawabs, the Hussainabad Clock Tower and the Jama Masjid. Also in this area, south of Victoria Park, is the **Chowk**, or the street of the silversmiths, that now sells items featuring the local style of embroidery (*chikan*) and other local handicrafts.

Dudhwa National Park

The only place in India apart from Assam where you can see rhinos in the wild, **Dudhwa National Park** ❿ was, inaugurated in 1977. Its location, that bit further from Delhi than Corbett National Park (see page 176), has meant that its infrastructure has developed at a steadier rate, but is now more than adequate, and offers an exceptional wildlife experience. The best time to visit is between February and April; the park closes between 15 June and 15 November. The best way to get around once there is by elephant, available for hire in Dudhwa itself.

The east of the Northern Plains

Faizabad ⓫ , 150km (93 miles) east of Lucknow, was for a time the capital of the province of Avadh. This busy town has fine monuments, including Bahu Begum's tomb and Gulab Bari, the mausoleum of one of the first rulers of Avadh, Shuja-ud-Daula.

Six kilometres (4 miles) east is the temple town of **Ayodhya**, standing on the banks of the Ghaghara River. This is believed by Hindus to be the capital and birthplace of Lord Rama, another incarnation of Vishnu and hero of the *Ramayana*. Popular devotion to Rama increased in the 16th century after Tulsi Das wrote his great version of the *Ramayana* in Avadhi – the language of the people. The nawabs of Avadh gave donations to various temples, and the oldest and most beautiful buildings of Ayodhya date from this period.

One of the most notable buildings is **Hanumangarhi**, the fort of Hanuman, the monkey god, greatest devotee of Rama, and Sita. Steep steps lead up to the main temple (dawn–dusk), where monkeys are ready to snatch offerings from pilgrims' hands. The peace of the town was broken in 1992 when Hindu extremists demolished a mosque that they believed stood on the birthplace of Rama, 'Ram Janambhoomi'. In July 2005 five Islamic militants attacked the makeshift Hindu temple that had been built on the site, and were gunned down by security forces. After a protracted delay, a

September 2010 court ruling decreed that the site be equally divided between the three feuding parties.

Gorakhpur ⑫, 130km (80 miles) east of Faizabad, is named after Guru Gorakhnath, a pre-medieval saint, whose temple and *matha* (monastery) stand here. During the Khichri Mela festival, culminating on 14 January each year, villagers offer rice and lentils, which are thrown onto a pile in front of an image of the saint. **Jaunpur**, on the road towards Varanasi, was one of India's foremost centres of cultural development in the 14th and 15th centuries, and today, while a shadow of its former self, is home to some partially ruined, but unique, Islamic architecture.

Buddhist sites

Khushinagar, 53km (33 miles) east of Gorakhpur, is identified as the spot where the Buddha left this world and attained *parinirvana* in the 5th or 6th century BC. Here the **Muktabandhana stupa** is said to have been built to preserve the relics of the Buddha by the Mallas who ruled at the time he died. A smaller shrine nearby contains a reclining statue of the Buddha.

Other pilgrimage sites within reach of Gorakhpur are **Piprahva**, 90km (56 miles) away, where the Buddha spent his early years, and **Lumbini**, 8km (5 miles) across the border with Nepal, where he is believed to have been born. To the west, near the Nepal border, is **Sravasti**, where the Buddha spent the rainy season for 25 years. The founder of the Jain religion, Lord Mahavira, a contemporary of Buddha, was also a frequent visitor to Sravasti. Two Ashokan pillars stand at the gate of the **Jetavana monastery**.

Allahabad

Despite its Muslim-sounding name (it was originally called Prayag, but was renamed by Akbar), **Allahabad** ⑬ is one of the most sacred places of Hinduism – in fact it is known as 'Tirth Raj', the king of pilgrimage

sites. The holiness is geographical: the town is located at the point where the Yamuna and the mythical Sarasvati rivers flow into the Ganges, some 188km (117 miles) southeast of Kanpur. At the sacred confluence a religious fair, the Magh Mela, is held each January and February, and once every 12 years the greatest religious festival of northern India, the Purna Kumbha Mela, takes place. To bathe at the confluence at the most sacred times is said to wash away the sins of many births; in 2001 an estimated 66 million people bathed here. Rowing boats will take you to the spot where the milky waters of the Ganges meet the blue waters of the Yamuna.

The city itself is crowded and somewhat dilapidated: **Anand Bhavan** (Tue–Sun 9.30am–5pm) the former home of the Nehru family and a nerve centre of the independence movement is the main sight.

At **Kausambi**, 45km (28 miles) away, are the ruins of one of the great metropolitan forts built during the first millennium BC. Courtyard houses were protected by massive

TIP

It is possible to travel from Gorakhpur in Uttar Pradesh to the border with Nepal at Sonauli (3hrs) from where there are buses to Kathmandu; minibuses run directly to Chitwan National Park from Gorakhpur. Nepali visas are purchased at the border.

Hazratganj, Lucknow's main shopping area.

FACT

The Kumbh Mela, held periodically at one of the four towns of northern India: Allahabad, Haridwar, Nashik and Ujjain, is by some margin the largest pilgrimage in the world. The 2013 event in Allahabad, a Maha ('Great') Kumbh Mela, which occurs once in 144 years, saw over 120 million visitors over a two-month period, including 30 million on a single day, making it the largest gathering in recorded history. In 2016, the Kumbh Mela will take place at Ujjain.

Street barber in Varanasi.

walls of burnt brick. Kausambi was occupied from the 8th century BC to the 6th century AD. Its main Buddhist stupa measured 25 metres (80ft) across.

Varanasi

The most sacred stretch of the Ganges is at **Varanasi** (Benares), one of the oldest living cities in the world and arguably the most intense, atmospheric place in the whole of India. For more than 2,500 years it has attracted seekers and pilgrims. Its heart lies between the streams of the Varuna and the Assi, which flow into the Ganges and give the city its name. Another name, 'Kashi', probably derives from the Sanskrit 'to shine or look brilliant'. That light is the god Shiva's, Varanasi is his home. Shiva literally means auspiciousness or happiness and, according to a local saying, every single pebble and stone in Kashi is Shiva. To his devotees, Shiva is the one great God. To die here in his city on the banks of the holy river is to achieve *moksha*, liberation from the cycle of life and death.

Death is not hidden in India. It is part of life, and one reason why you find cremation grounds in the very centre of Varanasi, and cremation ghats lining the river.

It is not uncommon to see muslin-wrapped bodies being carried through town and down to the river, placed on a funeral pyre and cremated in full public view. This unlimited access to the practical applications of the Hindu faith, the raw intimacy with death and the stifling intensity of the narrow lanes that lead down to the holy river often combine to leave visitors literally breathless, emotionally overcome but never unmoved, or unimpressed. Perhaps nowhere else in India can offer the visitor such an explicit crash course in the tenets of Hinduism; a visit to Varanasi goes a long way in helping to explain sights and sounds you might encounter elsewhere in India.

Dawn on the Ganges is a fabulous sight. The river flows south to north, with the city on the west bank, and fields and trees to the east. As the sun rises, the golden rays fall on the innumerable temples and 70 bathing ghats, on the priests under their tilted umbrellas, and devout Hindus taking a purifying dip. The one notable mosque on the skyline was built by the Mughal emperor Aurangzeb.

Rowing boats take visitors along the ghats from Assi in the north to Raj Ghat, a highly recommended experience. These trips have become so commonplace that the boats are entirely ignored by the local population, which ensures that the sights on offer remain fascinatingly authentic, and far from the micro-managed stage show that they could so easily have become.

Within the city, the **Vishvanath Temple**, built in the late 18th century, is the main Shiva sanctuary. It is closed to non-Hindus, but visitors can climb surrounding buildings to see the gilded dome. If Shiva is king of Varanasi, the goddess Annapurna is queen. Her temple is close to Vishvanath's. She is the perfect mother, a gentle goddess who provides food *(anna)* and life. Another of the city's busiest temples is in the south and dedicated

to Durga, one of its fierce goddess guardians. The temple is often called the **monkey temple** because of the hordes of red macaques which have made it their home.

Nearby is the most popular shrine to the monkey god Hanuman, the **Sankat Mochan**. One of Hanuman's main strengths is the ability to turn away difficulties, and on Tuesdays and Saturdays devotees gather to ask for his help. The chief priest lives in a house overlooking the Ganges on Tulsi Ghat where Gosvami Tulsi Das is said to have written his *Ramayana* epic.

Across the river is **Ramnagar**, home of the Raja of Benares, whose fort houses a private museum (10am–noon, 2–4.30pm). He is the patron of the Ramnagar Ram Lila, a traditional month-long enactment of the *Ramayana* (Oct and Nov).

About 6km (4 miles) to the north of Varanasi is **Sarnath**, the deer park where the Buddha preached his first sermon after attaining enlightenment, and returned to spend the rainy season several times during his life. It is one of the most important Buddhist

Anand Bhavan, the former family home of Jawaharlal Nehru, Allahabad.

The famous ghats at Varanasi.

pilgrimage sites. The most impressive of the ruins is the **Dhamekh Stupa**, which is said to mark the exact spot where the Buddha preached, and an Ashokan pillar from the 3rd century BC. The lion capital of the pillar, now the emblem of the Government of India, is one of several outstanding exhibits in the nearby **museum** (Sat–Thur 10am–5pm).

Bihar

The state of Bihar lies in the eastern Gangetic plain, occupying the area that was the seat of several of the most famous ancient Indian dynasties, as well as being the cradle of Jainism and Buddhism. The name Bihar is itself derived from *vihara* (Buddhist monastery). Although the state is situated on the fertile alluvial soils of the floodplain of the Ganges, this is one of the very poorest parts of India, all but untouched by the economic boom taking place in other parts of the country. Bihar is notorious for its rampant corruption, lawlessness, decrepit infrastructure and extreme divisions of caste, manifested

Millet threshing in the Patna area, Bihar.

in sporadic outbreaks of caste-based violence, adding to the state's lawless reputation. On one side are the brutal private armies of the landlords, and ranged against them, Naxalite insurgents with close links to the Maoist Communist Party of Nepal. Travellers visiting Patna and the major Buddhist sites should face few problems, but visitors travelling off the beaten track should be alert to the possibility of trouble.

The current Chief Minister of Bihar, Nitish Kumar, has made significant reforms in the time he has been in power. His efforts to improve the state's appeal to both public and private investors have met with the approval of the World Bank, who loaned the impoverished region US$225 million. This type of investment, particularly if private companies can be tempted to get involved, represents Bihar's best chance of rising out of its current predicament, and the recent signs are good, with the Bihari economy now one of the fastest growing in the country. Rajesh Singh, a Bihari with an MBA

from Mumbai University, decided to go back to Bihar to start a business, motivated as he admits by both 'good potential and good intentions'. He typifies exactly the kind of outlook and attitude that the state so badly needs, but several turbulent years later he's still battling against Bihar's traditional woes; asked if there was a harder place in the world to do business he replied, 'Maybe Somalia, they are shooting at you there!'

Patna

Patna ⑮, the capital of Bihar, is a city of more than 1 million people lying beside the Ganges, but feels more like a rural town run wild. Under the name of Pataliputra it was the capital of the Magadha Empire. Patna is divided in two by a large square, the Maidan. To the west lies **Bankipur**, a cantonment and administrative area with colonial buildings, including **Raj Bhavan**, the governor's residence; the **Maharaja's Palace**, now the Bihar State Transport Corporation; **Patna Women's College**, an early 20th-century neo-Mughal

complex; and 1920s bungalows for government officers.

The **Patna Museum** (Tue–Sun 10.30am–4.30pm) near the **High Court** houses a collection of Hindu and Buddhist statues and sculptures, 18 of which were stolen in 2006. Among the exhibits is a 15-metre (49ft) fossil tree said to be 200 million years old and the longest of its kind in the world. At the entrance of the hall, on the left, is the **Didarganji Yakshi**, a buff-coloured Mauryan sandstone statue of a woman, remarkable for her brilliant polish, her rounded breasts, her navel, and her aggressive belly and hips. It is considered to be one of the greatest examples of Indian art from any era. Between the Maidan and the Ganges stands the **Golghar**, a beehive-shaped structure, built in 1786 as a granary. It is 27 metres (88ft) high and can hold 150,000 tonnes of wheat. From the top there are fine views across the city. The new **Bihar Museum**, planned as a future replacement museum to house the Patna Museum's 20,000-plus item collection, was partly inaugurated in mid-2015 in

FACT

The Ganges river dolphin, also known as the susu or shushuk, still survives in the Ganges and its major tributaries in Uttar Pradesh and Bihar, as well as downstream in West Bengal. An endangered species, it is threatened by pollution and reduced water levels caused by irrigation schemes; adults measure over 2 metres (7ft) in length.

Dhamekh Stupa at Sarnath.

The faithful come to wash and pray on the ghats beside the Ganges at Varanasi.

Bailey Road, but the rest of the new museum is still under construction.

Old Patna lies to the east of the Maidan. In this district of bazaars, a few buildings stand out: the **Khuda Baksh Oriental Library**, which contains rare Islamic manuscripts, including some from the Moorish University of Córdoba in Spain; **Padri-ki-Haveli** (St Mary's Church), built in 1775; **Sher Shah Masjid** and **Patther-ki-Masjid**, mosques erected respectively around 1540 by Sher Shah, and in 1621 by Parvez Shah, son of Jahangir and Governor of India.

Haramandirji, a *gurdwara* in old Patna, is one of the holiest places in India for Sikhs. Guru Govind Singh, the 10th and last Sikh guru, was born and died here. The *gurdwara*, built in the 19th century around the room where the guru was born, is a white marble building housing a museum of the Sikh religion. On top is a terrace with marble kiosks from where one can watch the sun going down over the city while loudspeakers broadcast the recitation from the Holy Granth.

A market in Patna.

Near the *gurdwara*, and visited only by appointment with the owner, is **Qila House**, a private residence built on the ruins of Sher Shah's fortress, which houses a collection of jade, Chinese paintings, silver filigree work of the Mughal period, and a bed that once belonged to Napoleon.

At **Gulzaribagh**, further east near the Mahabir Ghat, is a former East India Company factory, now a government printing press. Visitors can see the opium godowns (warehouses), the former ballroom and the hall where Shah Alam II was crowned Emperor of Delhi (under the protection and patronage of the East India Company) on 12 March 1761. In the same area, to the south at **Kumhrar**, a park has been created around the remains of **Pataliputra**. Here are the foundations of Emperor Ashoka's palace, wooden beams from structures in the former city, ramparts, and the pond where Ashoka is said to have thrown the bodies of his 99 brothers – this was before his conversion to Buddhism.

The **Mahatma Gandhi Bridge** crosses the Ganges east of the city. On

the north bank, at **Sonepur** near the confluence of the Ganges and Gandak, an animal fair is held in October/November. Some 40km (25 miles) further north, **Vaishali** is the former capital of the Vajian Confederacy (6th century BC), probably the first republic in Asia. The Second Buddhist Council was held here in 383 BC. All that remains is an Ashoka pillar and ruins of Buddhist stupas.

About 30km (20 miles) from the Nepalese border is the town of **Motihari**, where Eric Arthur Blair, the future George Orwell, was born in 1903. Plans are afoot to make his old two-room house a heritage site. The road reaches the India–Nepal border at Raxaul, the main crossing point between the two countries.

Mughal monuments

Some of Bihar's finest monuments lie to the west of Patna. At **Maner**, 30km (18 miles) away, are two mausoleums. **Choti Dargah**, in a small Muslim cemetery, is the grave of Maneri, a 17th-century ascetic. **Bari Dargah**, on the high bank of an artificial pond, was built in 1620 by Ibrahim Khan, Governor of Bihar under Jahangir, as a mausoleum for Shah Daula, his religious preceptor. At **Sasaram** ⑯, on the Grand Trunk Road southwest of Patna, are monuments from the time of Suri (Afghan) rule, including 16th century Emperor **Sher Shah's Mausoleum**.

Further north on the Ganges, **Buxar** is the place where Rama is said to have fought the demon Taraka and received higher knowledge from the sage Vishvamitra. Rama is said to have left a footprint here at Ram Rekha Ghat. Nearby, in 1764, the British defeated the last independent nawab of Murshidabad, thereby adding Bengal and Bihar to their Indian possessions.

The cradle of Buddhism

Nalanda ⑰, 'the place that confers the lotus' (*nalam* means spiritual knowledge), lies 90km (56 miles) south of Patna. This is the site of **Sri Mahavihara Arya Bhikshu Sanghasya**, a monastic university that flourished from the 5th century until 1199, when it was ransacked by the Afghan invader Bakhtiar Khilji. Lord Mahavira, the last Jain Tirthankara, and Lord Buddha taught here. Nalanda developed as a centre of Buddhist learning.

Leaving Nalanda for Rajgir, the road passes the Nava Nalanda Mahavira Research Centre on Buddhism and Pali Literature and **Wat Thai Nalanda**, a small Thai temple.

Rajgir, or Rajgriha, the 'royal palace', 12km (7 miles) to the south, was the capital of the Magadha Empire in the 6th century BC. It is a holy place for both Jains and Buddhists. Lord Mahavira taught here for 14 rainy seasons. The Buddha, too, spent five rainy seasons at Rajgir. He had so impressed King Bimbisara on his first visit that, when he returned from Bodhgaya having attained enlightenment, accompanied by 1,000 disciples, the king built a monastery set in a bamboo park for this new order (*sangha*) of monks.

TIP

Most tourists travelling into Nepal take the bus from Patna to the border town of Raxaul/Birganj (5–6hrs), from where an overnight bus runs to Kathmandu, a further 11 hours away. Buses are slow and crowded.

BODHGAYA: HOLY CASH COW

Over 100,000 pilgrims and tourists visit Bodhgaya every year, making it easily Bihar's biggest attraction. The money these visitors spend should be bringing much-needed relief to this desperately impoverished area, however, it would appear that even the administration of this most holy site is not immune to the ills that beset the state as a whole.

Most serious amongst the accusations is that a branch of the ancient bodhi tree that sits on the temple grounds, said to be a direct descendant of the one under which the Buddha sat before attaining enlightenment in the 6th century BC, was severed in 2006 and sold in Thailand for a staggering 60 million rupees – US$1.5million.

Although the current administration has made significant improvements to the site, quite where the income generated under previous tenures ended up is still under investigation. Empty niches around the temple underscore the fact that numerous Buddha statues have disappeared, along with – allegedly – huge sums in donations, both from wealthy foreigners and Indian pilgrims. Priests are demanding that control of the temple's finances should revert to Buddhists and not be maintained by Hindus with no religious connection to the site.

The giant 20-metre (65ft) Buddha statue at Bodhgaya, which was installed in 1989, is a modern addition to the site.

Contemporary Rajgir, a small town, is located north of the ancient site that spreads over seven barren hills surrounding a valley. A 50km (30-mile) wall with watchtowers built of huge stone blocks used to run round the city. Its remains stand on the hills and at the north and south gates.

Passing by the remains of the **Ajatasatru Fort**, built in the 5th century BC, the road reaches a small square lined with shops. On the right is **Venuvana**, the bamboo park where the Buddha and his disciples lived. A small mound, now covered with Muslim graves, marks the site of the stupa and *vihara* built by Ajatasatru. In the park is **Karanda Tank**, where the Buddha is said to have bathed.

Also in the neighbourhood is a large temple built by the **Nipponzan Myohoji** – a Japanese movement whose aim is to spread peace by promoting Buddhism. The Centaur Hokke Club caters to the needs of Japanese pilgrims, offering traditional Japanese meals and accommodation. Burmese Buddhists have also

built a temple to the east of the fort, at the foot of Vipula Hill.

Further up the hill, past the **Pippla Cave** and the **Jarasandha-ki-Baithak** – a monastery built out of large blocks of stone – is the **Saptaparni cave**, site of the First Buddhist Council. To the south, a cylindrical stone structure, **Manyar Math**, is a former temple to Maninaga, a serpent demi-god referred to in the *Mahabharata*. Turning left, the road passes **Jivakamhavana**, the site of the mango grove presented to the Buddha, and reaches **Maddakuchchi**. From here one has to walk to **Gridhrakuta Hill**, considered the holiest place in Rajgir, where the Buddha delivered the majority of his sermons. From Maddakuchchi, an aerial chairlift leads to the top of **Ratna Giri** where Japanese Buddhists have built the **Vishva Shanti** (World Peace) **Stupa**, a huge white structure visible from miles around. Four golden statues, one on each side, recall the Buddha's birth, enlightenment, teachings and death.

Places of pilgrimage

Gaya, 90km (56 miles) southwest of Rajgir, is an important Hindu site. Lord Vishnu is said to have conferred upon Gaya the power to cleanse one's sins. Devotees flock here to perform ceremonies to clear their dead of the burden of sin they might have carried over to the next world. They take a holy dip in the Phalgu River and lay offerings of *pindas* (sweets) and ritual rice cakes on the ghats along its banks, before entering the **Visnupada Temple** (closed to non-Hindus), built by the Maharani of Indore in 1787 over the footprint of Lord Vishnu. Within the grounds of the temple stands a banyan tree that is said to be the one under which the Buddha spent six years meditating.

The Buddha attained enlightenment in **Bodhgaya** ⓲, on the Phalgu River 12km (7 miles) to the south. The story relates how he first meditated in nearby Dungesvari, eating one grain of rice a day for two years, then nothing for four years. Realising that mortification did not bring enlightenment, he moved to a cave where voices told him this was not the place. He then found a *ficus* – now known as the *bodhi* tree – and sat under it to meditate, vowing not to rise until he attained enlightenment.

Emperor Ashoka erected a shrine near the *bodhi* tree, replaced in the 2nd century by the present **Mahabodhi Temple**. In the 17th century, Hindus took over the temple as the Buddha is considered an avatar of Vishnu, and it is now managed by a joint Buddhist-Hindu committee.

Inside is a gilded statue of the Buddha, sitting cross-legged, with his right hand touching the ground in acceptance of enlightenment. Around the temple are votive stupas.

Along the western wall is the *bodhi* tree, or rather its latest successor. The original is believed to have been destroyed by Emperor Ashoka before his conversion to Buddhism. The replacement was cut down by

Ashoka's jealous wife. The next in the line was destroyed by Shasanka, a Hindu king of Bengal. The immediate predecessor of the present tree withered in the 19th century. Under the tree is the **Vajrasana**, the **Diamond Throne**, a stone slab marking where the Buddha was sitting when he attained enlightenment.

Along the north side of the Mahabodhi Temple, the **Chanka Ramana**, a platform built in the 1st century BC, marks the place where the Buddha walked in meditation. Carved stone lotuses indicate the spots where the lotuses sprang from his feet. South of the temple a statue of the Buddha protected by a cobra stands in the middle of a large lotus pond.

There are many non-Indian Buddhist monasteries in Bodhgaya, and most accept foreign students. More controversial are plans to build a huge bronze Buddha statue that will dominate the site (see www.maitreyaproject. org). The **archaeological museum** (Sat–Thur 10am–5pm) displays various sculptures, some defaced during the 12th-century Muslim invasion.

The Mahabodhi Temple at Bodhgaya marks the site where the Buddha attained enlightenment around 500 BC.

THE TAJ MAHAL

India's most famous sight is every bit as magnificent as it is hyped up to be. Visit in the early morning to avoid the crowds and the heat, or at night during the full moon.

In terms of design the Taj Mahal is the crowning glory of Mughal architecture. Its proportions are stunningly simple. Its height is equal to the width of the plinth on which it stands, while the height of its facade is equal to the height of the bulbous double dome above. It was built between 1631 and 1648 by Emperor Shah Jahan to house the tomb of his beloved wife Mumtaz Mahal, who died in childbirth. The design owes much to Humayun's tomb in Delhi and is believed to have been the work of Ustad Ahmad Lahori, a master architect. White marble, brought by elephant from Makrana 300km (188 miles) away in Rajasthan, adds to its ethereal beauty, as do the floral decorations, bands of black marble Arabic calligraphy, and carved marble screens. The queen's tomb is complemented by the four minarets, while to the west of the enclosure is a mosque and, to the east, its replica – known as the javab (reply). The latter cannot be used for prayer as its central arch does not face Mekkah (Mecca).

According to legend, Shah Jahan planned to build a similar tomb for himself on the other side of the river out of black marble, linked to the original by a black and white marble bridge, but it remained a dream. He is buried in the Taj Mahal beside his wife.

Visiting for the first time is magical, particularly if you avoid the worst of the crowds (tour groups start to arrive from 9am). The colour of the white marble varies with the light: if you have time, try to see it at different times of day. For an even more memorable experience, the site is open for two nights either side of the full moon.

The Taj Mahal is approached through formal gardens, far less impressive than they once were. For the traditionally desert-dwelling Muslims, watered gardens symbolise paradise.

The main entrance to the tomb features a corbelled arch – an Islamic innovation – with a so-called jali screen behind.

Shah Jahan (1592–1666) and his wife, Arjumand Banu Begum Mumtaz Mahal (d.1631). The Taj Mahal, Mumtaz Mahal's tomb, was built within sight of Shah Jahan's palace at Agra Fort.

Sunset view from across the Yamuna river.

BUILDING THE TAJ

Twenty thousand labourers were involved in the construction of the Taj Mahal, including sculptors, calligraphers and artists from as far afield as Syria, Iran and Baluchistan. One thousand elephants were involved in transporting building materials to the site, and precious stones were brought from China, Tibet, Sri Lanka and Afghanistan to be used in the inlay. An elaborate brick scaffold was built to mirror the shape of the tomb; when foremen voiced their concern at the length of time this would take to dismantle, Shah Jahan decreed that whoever took the bricks could keep them, and the scaffold disappeared overnight. The green lawns that dominate the garden are a British addition; having defaced the Taj during the Uprising, and reputedly even having planned to dismantle it and sell off the marble, Lord Curzon decided to right the wrongs of his predecessors and ordered a wholesale restoration project, completed in 1908.

No expense was spared in construction, with Italian craftsmen reputedly employed to work on the marble inlay.

Photographing India's most visited sight.

An example of the attention to detail displayed in the construction of the Taj is that the four minarets surrounding the main structure slant outwards, in order to prevent them collapsing onto the tomb in an earthquake.

THE HIMALAYAS

From the lush Kullu Valley to the arid heights of Ladakh, the Indian Himalayas are much loved by walkers, climbers and those in search of tranquillity.

Kashmiri men smoking a shisha pipe in Srinagar.

N o matter where you are in the Indian Himalayas, you're never far from a stunning view of a snow-capped peak, rushing waterfall or lush, cedar-lined valley. These can be seen in the company of thousands – Manali is still top of every Indian honeymooner's and snow-seeker's wish list – or entirely alone. The high-altitude deserts of Ladakh are guaranteed to make you feel supremely small, yet sustain a unique culture whose Tibetan-style monasteries and traditional farming practises have altered little since medieval times. Just as Islam dominates Kashmir, so Buddhism is the predominant religion across large swathes of both Ladakh and Himachal Pradesh, while the area is also home to some of Hinduism's holiest sites.

Visitors should note that they will need to obtain a Protected Area Permit to visit parts of Jammu, Kashmir, Himachal Pradesh and Uttarakhand.

Uttarakhand

The mountain districts to the north of Uttar Pradesh form the new state of Uttarakhand (known formerly as Uttaranchal), cleaved off from Uttar Pradesh in 2001. Hinduism regards mountains as the dwelling places of gods, and this stretch of the Himalayas is considered especially sacred as the source of the streams that join to form the Ganges and Yamuna rivers.

Less commercially developed than neighbouring Himachal Pradesh, Uttarkhand, and particularly its western Garwal region, offer some of the most unspoilt and beautiful destinations in the Himalayas. Although not particularly well served by either the air or rail networks, the state's roads are well maintained and make access to some of the highest peaks relatively straightforward.

The highest of those peaks is **Nanda Devi**, rising 7,816 metres (25,646ft)

Main Attractions

Nanda Devi National Park
Mussoorie
Haridwar
Corbett National Park
Simla
Kullu Valley
Dharamsala
Srinagar
Leh

above the eponymous National Park, a World Heritage Site owing to its exceptional natural beauty and populations of rare and threatened mammals (although one that is closed to all but a select quota of accredited mountaineers each season).

Dehra Dun ❶ at the foot of the hills is a fast-expanding town and capital of the new state. It is notable for its prestigious institutions, including the Wildlife Institute of India, the Forest Research Institute and the Indian Military Academy. On a ridge 30km (18 miles) beyond Dehra Dun – an hour by taxi – is the hill station of **Mussoorie**, a popular weekend break for Delhi-ites offering impressive views to both the south and north as well as an almost carnival atmosphere in the high season. It's also home to the Lal Bahadur Shastri National Academy of Administration, which trains entrants to the elite Indian Administrative Service, successor to the British colonial Indian Civil Service, and the Landour Language School, renowned as one of the best places in India to learn the Hindi language.

At **Haridwar ❷**, 50km (30 miles) southeast of Dehra Dun, the Ganges flows out of the mountains into the plains, making it one of the seven most sacred cities for Hindus. This is

one of the four places in India that hosts a Kumbha Mela religious festival once every 12 years (the others are Allahabad, Ujjain and Nasik). The evening *arati* (worship) of the River Ganges is held every day at **Har-ki-Pauri**, the main ghat, and the area along the riverbank to the south, dominated by the aptly named Bada (big) Bazaar, is well worth a wander for its many minor ghats and charming period *havelis*.

Rishikesh, a town of temples and ashrams surrounded by forest, is 25km (15 miles) upstream. The northern part of the town, **Muni-ki-Reti**, is very attractive, and the best views can be seen from either of the two footbridges suspended across the river, the Ram Jhula and the Laksman Jhula. Whereas Haridwar has a reserved, sanctimonious feel, Rishikesh seems somehow more on show, the sadhus and ashrams vying for the attention of the legions of foreign visitors who have been coming here since The Beatles' well-publicised stay with Maharishi Mahesh Yogi in 1968.

Sacred mountain sites

Haridwar, Rishikesh and Dehra Dun are the starting points for pilgrimages to the four most sacred places in the Indian Himalayas: Yamunotri, source of the Yamuna; Gangotri, source of the Ganges; and the Kedarnath and Badrinath temples, collectively known as the **Char Dham**.

Yamunotri can be reached from Dehra Dun or Rishikesh. The road stops 13km (8 miles) short of the temple at **Hanuman Chatti**. From here there is a trek along the riverbank. Pilgrims cook rice and potatoes in the water of a hot spring near the temple and offer it to the goddess Yamunotri.

The road to **Gangotri** ❸ runs steeply from Rishikesh to Narendra Nagar, Tehri (where a controversial dam has been built) and Uttarkashi before reaching Gangotri at 3,140 metres (10,300ft). From here it's a day's trek to **Gaumukh** ('cow's mouth'),

where the Ganges springs from the base of a glacier. A further day's hiking gets you to Tapovan, a grassy meadow used as the base camp for expeditions to Shivling, often referred to as the most beautiful mountain in the entire Himalayan range.

Further to the east, the road to **Badrinath**, home of Lord Vishnu, rises slowly from the steep valley of Deoprayag to the old Garhwal capital of **Srinagar**. From here the route climbs more steeply to **Joshimath**. The **Narsingh Bhagwan temple** here is the main centre of worship to Vishnu when his shrine at Badrinath is closed during winter. Joshimath is connected by India's longest cable-car ride (4km/2.5 miles), to **Auli**, one of the country's best-known ski resorts.

Beyond Joshimath, Govindghat is the starting point for treks to the majestic **Valley of Flowers National Park** ❹ (best seen June–Aug when it is carpeted with over 300 varieties of flowers thanks to the monsoon), and to the modern Sikh temple at **Hemkund**. The road continues up to Badrinath, with the **Kedarnath**

A terraced hillside in the Garwhal mountains.

TIP

The Indian ski scene offers a low-cost and very different experience from that in the West. There's a good range of equipment available in Auli (above Joshimath), and enough slopes, lifts and instructors to keep all but the most experienced skiers entertained. Kufri, 16km (10 miles) from Simla, is a centre for winter sports. The ice-skating rink is the only one in this part of the world. Skiing is also available at Narkanda, 64km (40 miles) from Simla, Solang, 10km (6 miles) from Manali, where a lift is under construction, and Gulmarg in Kashmir.

Tiger in Corbett National Park.

route branching off. The shrine at Kedarnath is dedicated to Shiva and contains one of the 12 *jyotirlingas*, or *lingas* of light. The temple stands at the head of the Mandakani river, in a stunning valley surrounded by snow-covered mountains.

Hill stations

In the Kumaon district to the east are the popular hill stations of Nainital, Ranikhet and Almora. **Nainital**, built around a lake surrounded by forested hills, was originally the summer capital of the government of United Provinces – as Uttar Pradesh and Uttaranchal were known under the British. It is by far the most developed of the three resorts, its proximity to Delhi guaranteeing floods of tourists in the peak season.

Naukuchiyatal, 25km (15 miles) from Nainital, is the most secluded and peaceful of the nearby lake resorts, while **Ranikhet**, home of the Kumaon Regiment of the Indian Army, is one of the least spoilt of the hill stations, very well maintained and devoid of the rampant over development found

elsewhere. **Almora** itself has nothing as such to recommend it, but is an ideal starting point for exploring the majestic oak forests of **Binsar**, or for visiting the 150 magnificent temples at **Jagesvar**.

Corbett National Park

Corbett National Park ❺ (Nov–June), 300km (186 miles) north of Delhi, is considered by many to be India's premier national park. Its pristine forests and meadows shelter a population of tigers (around 135), elephants and deer, and a variety of birds, including the maroon oriole, fairy bluebird, green magpie and red-breasted falconet. The Ramganga River provides a habitat for crocodiles and gharial, as well as the impressive mahseer fish. It was named after the hunter-turned-conservationist Jim Corbett, whose gung-ho adventures *The Man-Eaters of Kumaon* and *The Man-Eating Leopard of Rudraprayag*, are perennial best-sellers.

All individuals and vehicles require a permit to enter, which can be obtained from the reception centre in

Ramnagar. There is a choice of five different areas of the park to be visited, with Dhikala offering the widest range of accommodation as well as the greatest variety of wildlife.

Himachal Pradesh

The picturesque state of Himachal Pradesh straddles the Himalaya from the foothills to the high, remote valleys of Lahaul and Spiti, with a swathe of snowy peaks in between. Its capital, Simla, had the distinction of serving as the summer capital of India in the days of the British viceroys, a refuge for the sahibs from the heat of the plains.

In summer, the fragrance of fresh flowers pervades these enchanting hills and the coolness of the melting snow tempers the heat. The monsoon brings a spectacle of lush greenery and cascading waterfalls. Autumn is marked by pleasant sunny days, clear views and gorgeous sunsets. Winter brings snow.

The majority of Himachalis are Hindus, but Buddhism is also a major influence, particularly with the presence of the exiled Dalai Lama at Dharamsala and the large settlements of Tibetan refugees.

The state is predominantly rural and its towns are small. The traditional village house is of special interest: the lowest storey is occupied by the household cattle; the middle provides space for storing grain and other things, but also for sleeping in winter; the top floor (dafi) provides living space. These days, however, traditional lifestyles are becoming increasingly marginalised as tourists encroach in ever greater numbers. In this regard Himachal feels significantly more developed than neighbouring Uttarakhand.

Simla to Kinnaur

Simla ❻ (Shimla) lies on a ridge at a height of 2,100 metres (6,900ft). It was previously the official summer location for the government of British India, and much British influence survives in the upper town. It is linked to the plains by the Kalka–Simla narrow-gauge railway, with four departures a day in each direction: the train slowly winds its way up the picturesque mountainside in about six hours. The level ground of Simla's ridge is a favourite evening rendezvous, particularly Scandal Point, and the main street, the Mall (from which Indians were infamously banned), is the place for shopping.

In spite of its considerable growth since Independence, Simla, perhaps more than any other spot in India, is reminiscent of an attempt to recreate England in India. Its colonial domestic architecture and Christchurch (the second church to be built in North India) give it the air of a neglected Edwardian town. It was the setting of many of Rudyard Kipling's stories in his book *Plain Tales from the Hills*, and the bazaar below the ridge was famously described in his novel *Kim*.

Simla is a pleasant place to relax, although the centre of town gets very overcrowded during the peak

A grey langur with baby.

HIMACHAL PRADESH TRANSPORT

There is one airport operational in Himachal Pradesh – the Bhuntar Airport (the Kullu Manali Airport) with Air India providing service to Delhi, Kolkata, Dharamsala and Chandigarh. Train services are limited within the state, ensuring that most visitors either travel by bus or taxi.

Dharamsala: The closest mainline train station is at Pathankot, but this can be reached via the narrow-gauge Kangra Valley Railway. The closest station to Dharamsala is at Kangra Mandir, 20km (12 miles) away. Buses run from here to Pathankot (4hrs), Delhi (12hrs), Manali (10hrs) and Dehra Dun (13hrs).

Simla: The best and most scenic way to reach Simla is via the 'toy train'. From Delhi take a train to Kalka (6hrs), from where the narrow-guage locomotive winds its way up to Simla in a leisurely 5 hours. Onward journeys are by bus or taxi; buses leave regularly for Manali (10hrs), Dharamsala (10hrs) and Chandigarh (4hrs).

Manali: In the summer buses run to Simla (10hrs) and Dharamsala (10hrs), as well as over Rohtang Pass to Kaza (11hrs), Keylong (9hrs) and Leh (2 days including overnight stop in Sarchu). Share taxis/jeeps are also available for the journey to Leh.

Hill stations

The architecture and ambience of the Raj has been largely sidelined elsewhere, but high in the hills of India it still takes centre stage.

Perhaps nowhere in India gives as evocative an impression of life during the Raj as one of its many hill stations. Initially designed as summer retreats from the heat of the plains, these quaint throwbacks often include many of the components of the classic British summer holiday: donkey rides, pedalos, golf courses, rain, promenades, tea rooms, ice creams, gymkhana clubs and character-building walks through the woods. The clubs are especially antiquated, often requiring temporary membership to be arranged before entry, and enforcing strict dress codes of an evening, typically including a tie and jacket for men, who often have their own men-only bars on the premises.

There are hill stations dotted all over India, from the Nilgiri Hills to the Western Ghats, to Rajasthan and the Himalayas, but they all retain a remarkable similarity. Whatever the extent of modern additions,

Viceregal Lodge, Shimla.

a certain proportion of the buildings will always date back to the Raj, as will the interior decor and furniture. British-style churches are often a centrepiece. Menus are likely to include at least some British staples – bread and butter pudding, scones and apple pie are not unheard of.

Modern resorts

Hill stations have long been the favoured by Indian honeymooners, and are nowadays among the most popular short-break holiday destinations for the Metropolitan middle classes, which has spawned a rash of glitzy-looking hotels – round beds and mirrored ceilings are a regular feature, along with plate-glass exteriors and all mod cons.

Newlyweds aside, the number of Indian tourists hitting the hill stations in the summer is growing rapidly, meaning congestion has become a real problem in the typically narrow streets. Local businesses have developed to reflect this trend, with many of them now offering the latest electronic gadgets, trendiest fashions and designer shades – a glaring contrast with the old-fashioned provisions stores that often sit next door. Nationwide coffee-shop chains are also moving in, again often in close proximity to their traditional counterparts, as are international sportswear brands.

Adding to the mix are several other demographic groups: hill stations tend to have a fairly large military presence – they were originally used by the British as sanatoriums for their troops, and the tradition has lived on. Buddhist monks have established monasteries in many of the Himalayan hill stations and boarding schools are often located nearby, some attracting students from the world over.

The areas surrounding these towns are often the main attraction, typically thickly wooded and offering stunning views of the plains below and mountains above. Trekking and camping trips can be arranged in most places, and adventure sports such as paragliding, mountain biking and rock climbing are becoming increasingly widely available, a far cry from the traditional evening stroll down the promenade.

The other defining feature of India's British-era hill stations are the narrow-gauge trains which served as their principal link with the plains. These days, they've been superseded by roads but still survive as popular tourist attractions, and in the case of Darjeeling, Ooty and Shimla have been declared world heritage sites.

summer season, at which time it makes sense to stay in the outskirts, where there are excellent walks through the woods. The green slopes are covered with fir, rhododendron, pine and Himalayan oak.

One of the most popular walks is up to Jakhu Temple, 2km (1.25 miles) from Christchurch, dedicated to Hanuman, the monkey god, and appropriately enough surrounded by monkeys. Care should be taken with these extremely brazen animals – keep all food items firmly out of sight. The views from the top more than compensate for the obstacles en route, however.

Chail, 63km (39 miles) south of Simla, was once the summer capital of the Maharaja of Patiala and is now a lovely tourist resort. Its cricket pitch is reputed to be the highest in the world and certainly one of the most scenic. The town and its environs provide excellent facilities for fishing, tennis, squash, bird and wildlife enthusiasts.

Narkanda ❼, at a height of 2,700 metres (8,850ft), and 64km (40 miles) from Simla on the Hindustan–Tibet road, is famous for its apple orchards and scenery. It is one of the state's ski resorts, albeit one without any real skiing infrastructure, and is a convenient starting point for visiting the heart of Himachal Pradesh. Naldera, famous as a golf destination, and Mashobra, both a short detour from the main highway from Simla, make very peaceful places to relax, and both offer wonderful views of the higher peaks. Travelling east from Narkanda along the valley of the Sutlej River brings you to the border region of **Kinnaur**.

On the bank of the Sutlej, **Rampur ❽**, 140km (90 miles) from Simla, is one of the largest towns in the state and is a good place to pick up a permit to visit Kinnaur. It is noted for its three-day market fair, *Lavi*, which is held in November. While the days are spent in making bargains, the evenings are given over to song and dance.

Kinnaur is one of the most unspoilt and least visited regions of Himachal Pradesh. Its proximity to the Tibetan border makes it a restricted zone, but permits are now easy to obtain.

FACT

The 1st-century AD Greek traveller and philosopher, Apollonius Tyaneus, could have been describing much of modern-day Himachal Pradesh when he said: 'In India I found a race of mortals living on the Earth, but not adhering to it. Inhabiting cities, but not being fixed to them, possessing everything but possessed by nothing.'

The Kalka-Simla Railway was completed in 1903.

Rekong Peo is the main town, but a better place to head for is **Kalpa**, a little way along the main road, which has stunning views of the Kinner-Kailash Mountains and a wider choice of accommodation. Buses run from Rekong Peo and Kalpa to **Sangla** in the beautiful valley of the Baspa River.

There are some lovely treks in the region. The old Hindustan–Tibet road is recommended: starting in Sarahan, passing through Kalpa and continuing into Upper Kinnaur (for which a Protected Area Permit is needed) and the Rupa Valley. Another spectacular trek is the pilgrims' circuit of the Kinner-Kailash range.

The Valley of the Gods

The **Kullu Valley ❾** on the Beas river, at an altitude of 1,200 metres (3,900ft), is renowned for apple orchards, beautiful scenery, wooden temples and its music and dance. Its mountain surroundings offer scope for all manner of outdoor pursuits, including trekking, climbing, mountain biking, paragliding, skiing, rafting and angling.

The regional hub, **Kullu**, has fewer attractions to detain travellers than places further up the valley, although there are two Hindu shrines in the town that are worth seeing: the Raghunathji temple and the cave-temple of Vaisno Devi. Kullu really comes to life during the *Dussera* festival (usually in October), when tourists and locals flood into the town to see the spectacular procession of village deities. Carried on the shoulders of bearers in specially decorated palanquins, between 100 and 200 gold-faced devtas and devis (gods and goddesses) converge on Kullu's maidan, where they pay homage to the royal family's tutelary deity, Raghunathji. Accommodation should be booked well in advance at this time.

The most remarkable temple of the valley is **Bijli Mahadeva**, 8km (5 miles) southeast of Kullu and accessible only by a long flight of steep steps (with tremendous views from the top). It is built of large blocks of stone without the use of cement, and its 20-metre (65ft) flagstaff is reputed to attract lightning – considered an

Christ Church, Shimla.

expression of divine blessing. Every time the flagstaff is struck by lightning, the Shiva *lingum* (phallic symbol) inside the temple is shattered. It is put back together each time by the priest and stands until another flash repeats 'the miracle'.

Kullu's airport is at Bhuntar, 10km (6 miles) south of the town; flights to Delhi, Kolkata, Dharamsala and Chandigarh are available with Indian Airlines. Bhuntar also marks the turning-off point for the **Parvati Valley**, which runs to the northeast. Along the valley are the hot springs at **Manikaran**, a Sikh and Hindu pilgrimage town. Although this dramatically beautiful area is best explored on foot, dozens of foreigners have disappeared here over the past decade. Bodies washed downstream by the Beas River have confirmed that at least a dozen of these disappearances were the result of violent murders, but many more – perhaps as many as sixty – remain a mystery. Local police and journalists connect them with the local trade in charas, or marijuana resin. Another theory is that a large proportion of the disappeared are simply travellers who have settled in remote villages, and now live off hashish cultivation, having long outstayed their visas and passports. Either way, if you wish to trek here, take the precaution of hiring an experienced guide and travel in a group. Further towards Mandi, just south of the road tunnel, lies the turn-off to **Jalori Pass**, a protracted but picturesque route that leads to Narkanda and ultimately Simla. The road becomes particularly steep as it approaches the pass at 3,000 metres (10,000ft), and is best attempted in a four-wheel-drive. There is good accommodation available at **Shoja**, a great place to unwind far from the madding crowd.

The road from Kullu to Manali runs along the rushing torrents of the Beas. It is flanked by lofty mountains and spreading forests. Near Katrain is the small town of **Naggar**, where the Castle Hotel is said to be haunted. The town has been made famous by the late Russian painter Nicholas Roerich, whose **gallery** can be seen here (www.irmtkullu.com; Tue–Sun 10am–1pm, 1.30–5pm, until 6pm Apr–Oct). It is also increasingly popular as a less hectic alternative to Manali as a place to stay, with more and more hotels springing up in the area.

Manali

Manali ❿ is encircled by beautiful glades of deodars and flowering horse chestnuts. Traditionally an important trading centre, in recent years it has become a popular resort for Indian honeymooners and holidaymakers, as well as Western tourists, and can get overcrowded in the summer months.

The town is split into two parts: the New Town is where the bus-stand and most of the hotels are, while along The Mall (the main street) and over the Manaslu River is the more atmospheric old village, where it is possible to find accommodation in traditional houses. The Hindu **Dhungri Temple**,

The Himalayan foothills around the Kullu Valley are criss-crossed with hiking trails offering stupendous scenery.

Hindu pilgrim in the Himalayas.

dedicated to the goddess Hadimba, is believed to be more than 1,000 years old, while Manali's large Tibetan population has built two new *gompas* (monasteries).

Three kilometres (2 miles) up the valley are the hot springs of **Vashisht**. The temple complex here has separate outdoor baths for men and women. The Kullu Valley ends as the road passes the ski resort of **Solang** – the best place to learn to paraglide in northern India – and winds up through rocky ranges to the Rohtang Pass, gateway to the enchanting Lahaul and Spiti valleys and onwards to Ladakh.

Lahaul and Spiti

In the northeastern corner of Himachal Pradesh, across the 3,978-metre (13,050ft) **Rohtang Pass**, lie the two valleys of **Lahaul** and **Spiti** at a height of 3,000–4,800 metres (9,800–15,700ft). Both valleys are cut off from the rest of the world for much of the year, though this state of isolation is set to end as a new road tunnel beneath the pass nears completion.

While the road is only open from May through October, the 8.8km (5.5-mile) tunnel will provide a year round link to the two valleys beyond.

Rohtang, for the time being the only gateway to this spectacularly beautiful trans-Himalayan region, marks a stark climatic divide. In the summer monsoon, the climb from Manali is often misty or rainy, but on crossing the pass you tend to find a much brighter, sunnier day. Once on the far side, the culture of the valleys' inhabitants also contrasts with those of Kullu. Lahaulis are half-Buddhist, half-Hindu, while people from Spiti are of Tibetan origin and almost entirely Buddhist.

At the town of **Gramphu**, on the far side of the Rohtang Pass, the road from Manali splits: one route runs eastwards into the Lahaul Valley and then on to the Kunzum Pass and Spiti. The other, far better, surfaced route heads north to Ladakh via the district capital, **Keylong** (the only market between Manali and Leh).

Continue east to cross the **Kunzam Pass** at an altitude of 4,550 metres

Men woodworking in Himachal Pradesh's Kulu Valley.

(15,000ft) and then descend into the Spiti Valley. As well as cultural distinctions, there are pronounced climatic and topographical differences from one side of the pass to the other. While Lahaul is relatively fertile, with an almost Mediterranean look and feel, Spiti has a far more barren, almost lunar landscape. The Lahaul Valley is an important route to Ladakh, particularly for the army, but Spiti feels utterly remote, seeing far less traffic and giving the impression of having existed more or less in its current form for hundreds of years.

In Spiti, the town of **Kaza** is the place to plan treks and arrange Protected Area Permits, and is a good base from which to visit the spectacular *gompa* at **Kyi**, 12km (7 miles) away. Some of the world's greatest examples of Buddhist painting and sculpture can be seen 46km (28 miles) further up the valley in the Chos Khor Gompa at **Tabo**, founded in 996.

The Kangra District

Kangra is one of the most beautiful valleys in the Himalayas.

Dharamsala ⑪, the headquarters of the district at the foot of the Dhauladhar Range, consists of a lower and an upper town, its altitude varying from around 1,000 to 2,000 metres (around 3,300–6,600ft). Upper Dharamsala, better-known as **McLeod Ganj**, has since 1959 been the home of His Holiness the Dalai Lama and the Tibetan Government in Exile, and is the main tourist destination. While much of the accommodation is here, the smaller villages in the surrounding area are much quieter and can make excellent bases from which to explore the area; **Naddi** has particularly impressive views.

The large Tibetan population supports many organisations, including TIPA (Tibetan Institute of Performing Arts), which preserves and arranges performances of traditional Tibetan music and dance, particularly the drama *lhamo*. **Namgyal Monastery**, just below the bazaar in McLeod Ganj, makes a fascinating visit and an excellent first introduction to the Buddhist faith. Assuming he's in town, audiences with His Holiness

TIP

There is no end to the trekking possibilities in Himachal Pradesh, and the routes are generally far less crowded than in Nepal. Whichever route you opt for, however, it's always a good idea to hook up with a guide, best booked through an agency in Manali or Chamba. Quite apart from ensuring you don't lose your way, a guide will also help shop for the necessary provisions for the trek, arrange accommodation in villages and act as a translator.

There are an estimated 120,000 Tibetan refugees in India, and the region is naturally a focus for the Free Tibet campaign.

can be arranged through the security office by Hotel Tibet. Also well worth a visit is the **Norbulingka Institute**, 5km (3 miles) below the lower town. The institute was established with the aim of preserving the cultural heritage of Tibetan Buddhism, and has become a major seat of learning, offering classes in Tibetan language, crafts, Buddhism and meditation. There's also a small museum and a well-stocked library. In the lower town is the **Museum of Kangra Art** (Tue–Sun 10am–1.30pm, 2–5pm), housing a collection of miniature paintings and other local artefacts.

The ancient town of **Kangra** ⓬, 48km (30 miles) south, is well known for its temples, the most popular being the one dedicated to the goddess Vajresvari. Also worth visiting is the fort, once the palace of the local Katoch kings, with an outstanding view over the valley below.

Continuing south from Kangra, **Jawalamukhi** is one of the most popular pilgrimage sites in Himachal, notable for its 'eternal flame', where a fissure in the rock face emits a

constant stream of flammable gas. Off the road to Hoshiapur, **Pragpur** is India's first 'Heritage Village', painstakingly restored to depict life in the region hundreds of years ago, with the added benefit of a hugely atmospheric hotel. Some 34km (22 miles) southwest of Dharamsala are the 10th-century rock-cut temples of **Masrur**, similar in style to those at Ellora in Maharashtra (see page 258), though not as well preserved.

Chamba Valley

Further north, the romantic valley of **Chamba**, a former princely state, has few rivals for scenic beauty. Its valleys, meadows, rivers, lakes, springs and streams have a unique charm. The town of **Chamba** ⓭ is situated on the right bank of the Ravi river at an altitude of 900 metres (2,950ft). It is noted for its ancient Shiva and Vishnu temples, some of which date back to the 10th century. The **Bhuri Singh Museum** (www.bhurisingh museumchamba.in; Tue–Sun 10am– 5pm) is a treasure trove of exquisite paintings from the famous Kangra

A protector deity in a Tibetan Buddhist fresco, Dharamsala.

and Basohli schools and has a mass of material relating to the history of the region.

Among the innumerable fairs and festivals celebrated in Himachal Pradesh, the most important is the *Minjar* fair, held at Chamba around August to celebrate the coming of the rains and the flowering of maize. A procession of decorated horses and banners marks the beginning of the week-long fair.

Some 56km (35 miles) from Chamba town is **Dalhousie**, a quiet hill station located on five hills, which offer pleasant walking and superb mountain views. At the eastern end of the valley, **Brahmaur**, the ancient capital of Chamba, is famous for the Pahari architecture of its ancient temples and its lovely location, while **Nurpur** is known for its textiles.

In the Himalayan foothills

En route from the plains to the Kullu Valley, **Mandi** ⓮, on the left bank of the Beas river at an altitude of 750 metres (2,460ft), has several stone temples with beautiful carvings, but is otherwise of little appeal to the visitor. For the *Shivratri* Fair (February/March) devotees put the *rathas* (carriages) of their village family gods and goddesses on their shoulders and process to Mandi town. They present themselves at the **Raj Madhan Temple** and pay homage to Lord Shiva at **Bhutnath Temple**. On this day, a week-long fair of selling, music and dance begins.

Bilaspur lies 40km (25 miles) south of Mandi in the Siwalik Hills. Among the town's major attractions are **Vyas Gufa** (cave) and the **Lakshmi Narayan** and **Radheshyam temples**. The **Shri Naina Devi Temple**, which attracts thousands of pilgrims during its many fairs, is situated at the top of a triangular hillock just 57km (35 miles) from Bilaspur. This sacred place provides an unparalleled view of the holy **Anandpur Sahib**, the birthplace of a Sikh guru, on one side, and Govind Sagar (named after the guru) on the other.

Paonta Sahib, on the road between Dehra Dun and the small holiday resort of **Nahan**, is a pilgrimage

View of Chamba, and the surrounding scenery of the Ravi river valley.

Kashmir scenery.

centre for the Sikhs. Its impressive *gurdwara* (temple) on the bank of the Yamuna River is thronged by pilgrims during the *Hola* festival in March. **Renuka** is a picturesque lake town 45km (30 miles) northeast of Nahan. Kasauli, just above Chandigarh off the main Simla Highway, is the closest hill station to Delhi, but sees relatively few visitors, and offers attractive walks through the nearby pine forests.

Jammu and Kashmir

Although famed as one of the world's most beautiful mountain regions, Kashmir found itself isolated from India's tourist circuit in the mid-1990s, after six Western travellers were killed by a militant Islamist group. The tragedy brought to the world's attention a long-running insurgency that over the course of the following fifteen years would result in the deaths of thousands of Kashmiris and see the valley swamped by Indian military personnel. The slow rehabilitation of Kashmir as a destination took a major step forward when the

British Foreign Office finally revised its travel warning for the region in 2012, with visitor numbers increasing rapidly. Throughout all the troubles, neighbouring Ladakh, the eastern part of the state, had remained peaceful, and reaped the rewards in terms of tourism receipts, although it too remains a sensitive border area. Unfortunately, at the time of writing in early 2016, the British Foreign Office was once again warning against visiting the states of Jammu and Kashmir (including the tourist destinations of Phalgam, Gulmarg and Sonamarg, but excluding the cities of Jammu and Srinagar, and the region of Ladakh), due to an increased risk of kidnapping, shootings and grenade attacks.

Geography

The area is divided into three regions. Jammu occupies the plains, and is populated by Dogras and Punjabis, who are primarily Hindu and Sikh. Further north, Kashmir includes the Kashmir Valley and surrounding mountains that stretch from Banihal

Nain Singh, one of the first men to explore the Himalayas for the British.

REGIONAL TRANSPORT

During the summer months, both Air India and Jet operate daily flights to and from Srinagar and Leh. AI also fly to Jammu. However, in the winter, schedules may be disrupted for days on end by adverse weather conditions. Travellers on flights to Leh or Srinagar should also note that due to the increased security, no hand baggage is allowed in the cabins; you also have to check in at least three hours prior to departure. Jammu is the only railhead in the state. If you're flying direct to Leh, see page 428 for advice on altitude acclimatization.

Leh: In the summer months only, buses go to Manali (2 days, overnight in Sarchu) and Srinagar (2 days, overnight in Kargil). **Srinagar:** Buses go to Jammu, the closest train station (10hrs), Delhi (24hrs) and Leh (2 days, with overnight stop in Kargil).

north into Pakistan. The third region is Ladakh (see page 189).

The present border between India and Pakistan (known as the Line of Control) is the ceasefire line from the 1948–9 war. At Independence it was still undecided which country Kashmir was to enter. The Hindu ruler took his majority Muslim population into the Indian Union in 1948, under circumstances that are still heavily disputed. The referendum on the issue of accession, promised by Nehru, has never been allowed to take place. The British Foreign Office advise against all travel in the immediate vicinity of the border with Pakistan due to the danger of rocket attacks and bomb explosions.

Jammu

Jammu ⑮ is the only railhead in the state of Jammu and Kashmir. Situated amid the Siwalik Hills, its low elevation (300 metres/984ft) makes it hot and humid in summer. Traditionally it is a stopover on the way to the Kashmir Valley or for pilgrims visiting the Vaishnodevi cave temple, although as the scene of some of the most notorious and bloody terror attacks in the Kashmir insurgency, the town saw comparatively few foreign tourists until the recent lull in the dispute.

There are two temples of note in Jammu town; the **Ranbireshwar Temple**, dedicated to Shiva, and the **Raghunath Temple**, dedicated to Rama. Both temples were constructed in the 19th century under Dogra *rajas*. These kings were patrons of the arts, and there is a collection of miniatures from the Basholi, Jammu and Kangra schools on show in the **Dogra Art Gallery** (Tue–Sun summer 8.30am– 1.30pm, winter 10.30am–4.30pm).

Out of the town centre is **Bahu Fort**, which is perched on a hill across the Tawi River. Within the fort is a temple dedicated to Kali, the Hindu goddess of time and change. At the northern edge of town sits **Amar Mahal Palace** (Tue–Sun, 10am–noon and 3–7pm) now a museum with some fine Pahari miniatures, which provides an excellent view of the surrounding countryside and city.

Dal Lake in Srinagar, one of the most romantic spots in Asia. The picturesque houseboats and surroundings remain, but the lake itself is becoming increasingly polluted.

KASHMIRI PANDITS

The Kashmiri Pandits are something of an anomaly – Hindus in today's predominantly Muslim Kashmir. They are followers of a branch of Hinduism which was established long before Islam became the region's dominant religion. Following the start of Muslim rule, and the destruction of many Hindu temples at the start of the 1400s, large numbers of Pandits left the Kashmir Valley for other parts of India. Their numbers have continued to decline; from 15 percent in 1941, they now form just 1 percent of the Kashmiri population. Their influence, however, far outweighs their numbers, with many influential positions in Indian political life having been held by Kashmiri Pandits, including independent India's first and third prime ministers, Jawaharlal Nehru and Indira Gandhi.

WHERE

A resort that opened in 2009 has made the Srinagar–Leh drive even more enticing. Situated on the banks of the Sindh River, and with a backdrop of pine forest, Rah Villas Hotel is 12km (7.5 miles) before Sonamarg, and has 24 luxurious rooms in a nice building located in peaceful surroundings. For more details, visit the website at www.site.rah-villas-kashmir.com.

A skier in Gulmarg, Kashmir.

Kashmir

Srinagar , around 10 hours by bus from Jammu, is situated on the shores of Dal Lake in the heart of the beautiful Kashmir Valley. People still live on the houseboats on the lake, also the location of a daily floating vegetable market, and ringed by high mountains. A stay in one of the many houseboat hotels has traditionally been one of the main attractions of the city.

Several Mughal gardens are located on the boulevard that skirts Dal Lake: **Chasma Shahi**, built by Shah Jahan; **Nishat** and **Shalimar**, both with fountains, marble terraces and latticed marble pavilions; and the smaller garden of **Harwan**. Near Harwan are the ruins of a Buddhist college. There are several important mosques and *dargahs* in Srinagar. The huge **Jama Masjid** dates from the late 17th century. The **Shah Hamadan Mosque** is famous for the papier-mâché work on its walls and ceiling, and for its construction without nails or screws. Across the river is the stone **Pather Masjid** (1623). In Nagin the modern, lakeside **Hazrat-bal shrine** is said to preserve a hair of the Prophet Muhammad.

Elsewhere in the valley, **Pahalgam** (east of Srinagar) is from where pilgrims make a four-day trek to a Hindu shrine held sacred to the god Shiva, the **Amarnath Cave**. The high profile of the Indian military during the festival is a consequence of the terror attack of 2000, when Kashmiri separatists massacred thirty pilgrims and horsemen.

Off the road from Pahalgam to Anantnag to the south of Srinagar, at Mattan, are the ruins of the **Martand Temple** complex and a sacred spring. South of Anantnag are **Achabal**, site of elaborate Mughal gardens, and more gardens at **Verinag**, while towards Srinagar there are temple ruins at **Avantipur**.

Gulmarg and Sonamarg

An hour by road from Srinagar is the ski resort of **Gulmarg** , used as a backdrop for old Hindi films, a major attraction in the 1970s and now experiencing something of a renaissance following the completion of an 8km (5-mile) ski lift, the highest gondola in the northern hemisphere. Experienced skiers rave about the abundant snow and lack of other skiers – like skiing in the Alps but with none of the queues. There is, however, a serious avalanche risk; extreme care should be taken, particularly if attempting unpatrolled slopes. A good standard of ski equipment is available for hire, and there are plenty of English-speaking instructors on hand to guide beginners on the two nursery slopes, each of which has its own drag lift.

The alpine meadows at **Sonamarg** ⓲, once a popular stopping place for Ladakh-bound travellers, are also a viable alternative to Manali–Leh. If anything it's more picturesque and carries fewer health risks, as its highest passes are significantly lower than those encountered when coming via Manali.

Ladakh

The far-northern region of Ladakh was formerly a kingdom of western Tibet, but following invasions by the Dogras in the 19th century it was annexed by India. Geographically and culturally it has more in common with Tibet than with India and provides travellers with an insight into that fascinating region. The Ladakhi language is closely allied to Tibetan, and Buddhism is the predominant religion, although there are many Muslim Ladakhis. This identity, very different to the rest of the state, has led to calls for either separate statehood or for separate administration from Delhi as a Union Territory, in part to disassociate Ladakh from the troubles elsewhere in Jammu and Kashmir.

Ladakh was only opened to tourists in 1974; a measure of the region's limited exposure to the outside world up until that point came when the first commercial flight landed. Ever hospitable and considerate, the local population carried grass to the runway in order that the metal beast may have enough energy for its return flight. While things have of course moved on since then, the region retains a character and charm all of its own,

"Stakna", meaning "Tiger's Nose", is built on the summit of a high rock in the middle of the Indus Valley.

Alchi Monastery at Gompa.

and for many visitors is a magical, incomparable place.

The best time to visit Ladakh is June to September, when you can travel by road. Travellers either fly into Leh from Delhi or Srinagar, or cross the 5,328-metre (17,476ft) Tanglang Pass from Manali in Himachal Pradesh, although increasing numbers are now entering via Srinagar and Kargil.

The landscape changes from lush to stark as you emerge on to the Tibetan Plateau, the mineral-streaked mountains set against a brilliant blue sky. It is a tough 475km (295 miles) from Manali to Leh, the Ladakhi capital, but the two-day journey is certainly one of the most spectacular drives in the world. Flights to Delhi, Chandigarh and Srinagar operate all year at Leh, although winter flights can be suspended for days on end without warning owing to bad weather conditions, and summer flights are often heavily overbooked.

Whether you fly or travel to the region by road, expect to experience mild altitude sickness – either at the midpoint camp on the Manali–Leh Highway, or else on arrival at Leh.

Allow yourself a day or two to acclimatise by doing absolutely nothing. Drink plenty of water – 3 litres (6 pints) a day is not excessive – and not only when you are acclimatising, since the dry air and altitude mean you still have to take in a lot of fluid. Ladakh is a very sensitive environment and bottled water should be avoided at all costs. Take your own water bottle and fill it for a nominal fee with pressure-boiled water from one of the eco-projects such as Dzomsa, or else invest in a portable water filter, available from any good outdoor equipment shop.

The traditional staples of the Ladakhi diet are *tsampa* (roasted barley flour), yoghurt, salt tea and butter. Tibetan dishes are widely available, particularly *momos* (dumplings) and *thukpa* (noodle soup). The most useful word of Ladakhi for travellers is '*Jullay!*', which can mean 'hello', 'goodbye', 'please' or 'thank you'.

Leh

Arriving in **Leh** ⑲, particularly if coming by road, can be quite a

revelation. The arduousness of the journey is more than compensated for by the comforts on offer. The peak tourist season is the exact opposite of that in Goa, meaning that many of Goa's chefs and hotel staff move up to Leh in the summer. The resulting range of cuisine is especially impressive given the severity of the surrounding landscape; perhaps nowhere else on Earth can you enjoy a calzone pizza in the middle of a high-altitude desert.

Leh's bazaar was once a trading post on the route between India, China and Central Asia. When the Chinese border closed in the 1950s its importance soon declined, but it is still a pleasant place to wander, with numerous shops selling Kashmiri and Himalayan handicrafts.

The most ambitious walk in town is up to the imposing and partially ruined 16th-century **Leh Palace** (Apr–Sept daily 7am–4pm), home to the kings of Ladakh until the early 1940s, when the royal family moved out to Stok. If you are fit and energetic, you can visit the **Tsemo Gompa** (May–Sept daily 7–9am and 5–8pm), perched on Namgyal hill, above the palace. The narrow streets of **Old Leh** below the palace evoke the medieval town it once was; close by, on Main Street, is the new **Soma Gompa**. An interesting place to visit is the **Ecology Centre**, run by the Ladakh Ecological Development Group (LEDEG). The group aims to promote ecological awareness and sustainability through traditional methods. The centre has a library and craft shop. **Dzomsa**, at the end of Main Street, has an ecological laundry, recycling bins and pressure-boiled water, as well as local produce such as dried apricots and apples for sale.

The village of **Changspa** (a continuation of Leh to the west), with its small vegetable gardens and peaceful guesthouses, is a pleasant place for a stroll. At the end of Changspa Lane is the new **Shanti Stupa**. A steep line of steps leads up to this Japanese-built peace shrine, and the views from the top are wonderful; there is also a small café in which you can recover your breath.

TIP

It is quite difficult to change or obtain money in Leh, although there are now several ATMs (and a few places accept credit cards), so make sure you have plenty of cash. Internet connectivity is now fast, efficient and available all over town.

A row of stupas topped with gold crowns at Shey Buddhist monastery, Leh, Ladakh, India.

Ladakh's gompas

Within a day's journey of Leh are some spectacular *gompas*. It is easy to arrange a driver and guide from either a travel agency or the Taxi Operators' Union. Prayer halls in monasteries are decorated with silk hangings in auspicious colours and sacred paintings, called *thankas*, and the walls are lined with stacks of Buddhist texts swathed in silk. Shrines dedicated to the Buddha and Bodhisattvas were traditionally lit with smoky, pungent butter lamps (now largely replaced by oil lamps), and are heaped with offerings of incense, water, tea, food or money. Most monasteries charge entrance fees towards their upkeep and are administered by the Archaeological Survey of India.

Ladakh is also known for its 'oracles'. According to Tibetan Buddhist belief, an oracle is a person who goes into a trance to heal people or animals, or predict the future. Oracles are possessed by benevolent spirits, serving as their channels, for the good of all beings. Several monasteries and villages have a resident oracle;

Temple door decorated with tassels at Tikse monastery.

Mulbekh, on the Srinagar–Leh road, has one, as does Stok, the royal residence near Leh.

There are two basic routes around the monasteries, one up and one down the Indus Valley. The road leading south from Leh up the **Indus river** to Hemis Gompa passes a number of monasteries of importance, including the small but interesting **Sankar** monastery on the way out of town. Along this road is **Shey**, the 17th-century summer palace of Ladakhi kings, which houses the largest Buddha in Ladakh. The 600-year-old **Shey Gompa** is here, too. Hundreds of *chortens* – whitewashed reliquaries – can be seen scattered around the barren plains. **Tikse** is a large hilltop monastery noted for its monumental statue of the Maitreya Buddha.

Hemis ⓴ (45km/28 miles from Leh) lies across the Indus at the end of a winding road. Founded in the 1630s, it is the largest monastery in Ladakh, known for its festival in June which features a traditional dance-drama. The greatest treasure of the *gompa* is its enormous embroidered *thanka*, only shown every 12 years – the next display is in July 2016.

The road back to Leh on the southern side of the Indus travels past **Stagna**, noted for its images of Bodhisattvas, and **Matho**. Just before the bridge that crosses the Indus is a turn-off to the 18th-century **Stok Palace** (May–Sept daily 7am–7pm), the more recent home of the kings of Ladakh and of the present Gyalmo. The palace houses a well-labelled display of some of the royal family's most precious ritual and ceremonial objects.

Heading west from Leh, down the Indus, brings you to one of the most beautiful monasteries at **Alchi** ⓴.

Spitok and **Phyang** monasteries also lie along this route. Beyond Spituk, as the road emerges from a steep gorge, is the confluence of the Indus and Zanskar rivers. The view here is spectacular, and the different colours of the two waters can be

clearly seen. Beyond, up a newly paved road, is the monastery of **Likir**, a Gelugpa *gompa* with a small museum and beautiful prayer hall. A right turn after **Saspul**, noted for its apricots, and the bridge which takes you over the Indus and to Alchi, brings you via an impressive gorge to **Rizong** *gompa*, perched high up at the end of a valley and regarded as the most staunchly traditional of the region's monasteries.

Nubra Valley and beyond

Many areas previously out of bounds to travellers have now opened up. Chief among these is the **Nubra Valley ㉒**, which lies over the Khardung La (5,602 metres/18,370ft), one of the highest roads in the world. The valley itself is surprisingly green after the heights of the pass. Panamik, at the far end of the valley, has hot springs, while the most important local *gompa* is at Deskit. Somewhat improbably, there are also sand dunes close to Nubra itself, where descendants of the two-humped camels that once transported goods from China to India and back can sometimes be seen, although they are now quite rare.

The lakes of **Tso Moriri ㉓** and **Pangong Tso ㉔** lie to the southeast, each a three-day return trip from Leh – assuming a day's drive each way and two nights' stay at the water's edge. Tso Moriri is an important nesting site for the barheaded goose and brahminy duck. Some 130km (80 miles) long and wonderfully clear, Pangong Tso crosses over into Tibet proper. The small kingdom of **Zanskar** lies to the southwest, over a fearsome range of peaks. This remote area is cut off by snow for seven months of the year, and this limited access has helped to preserve its strong Buddhist identity. The capital, **Padum ㉕**, lies over the Pensi La (4,450 metres/14,600ft); the only other access to the city is to walk in along the Zanskar River.

Padum can presently only be reached by road from Kargil, but plans are under way to build a road north from Padum to the Leh–Srinagar highway. The completion of this road is expected to change the nature of Zanskar for ever, and so visitors are advised to get there sooner rather than later.

Trekking can be one of the most rewarding ways of exploring the region. Popular treks include the Markha Valley, which takes in the Nimaling Plain and the 5,200-metre (17,056ft) Kongmaru Pass; and the trek from Lamayuru to Alchi or Chiling, which has some stunning views. One of the best, but more arduous, routes is over to the beautiful Zanskar Valley, while Stok Kangri is the most easily accessed of the surrounding high peaks. Short treks may also be taken to the monasteries near Leh, and along the Indus. It is strongly recommended that you hire an experienced guide and ponies, that you have the necessary permits and are well equipped and provisioned. Ladakh has a delicate ecosystem, with little rain, and here supplies are scarce. Take as much food, water and fuel as possible, and bring all rubbish back out with you.

ALCHI MONASTERY

Perhaps the most exquisite of Ladakh's monasteries is that at Alchi, some 60km (40 miles) from Leh, west along the Indus. Unique in being built on the flat valley floor, Alchi was established in the 11th century by the Tibetan Kal-dan Shes-rab. Much of the monastery, now no longer in use but maintained by the monks of nearby Likir, is made of locally grown willow. However, it seems to have been constructed by artisans from Kashmir; their work is seen in the intricate woodcarving and painted ceilings. The paintings are some of the oldest and most extensive surviving examples of Kashmiri Buddhist art.

The earliest temple is that of Du-Khang, with its ornately carved doorway and walls decorated with mandalas. The walls of the three-storey Sum-tsek Temple are also covered with mandalas; the carving of the wooden structure is very fine. The square shrines of Lotsava Lha-Khang and Manjusri Lha-Khang are side by side; the walls of the latter are covered with representations of the 1,000 Buddhas. The figures in the temples are of Bodhisattvas, including Avalokitesvara and Manjusri.

Alchi is currently being restored, and there is a nominal charge to help with its upkeep; if you are with a local guide they will help you gain access to the locked shrines.

Ghadi Sagar Tank, Jaisalmer.

Dyeing fabrics in Rajasthan.

THE DESERT STATES

Easily accessed from either Delhi or Mumbai, the largely arid northwestern states of Rajasthan and Gujarat are India at its colourful best.

Amber Fort.

Rajasthan and Gujarat, with their predominantly desert climates, are unlike anywhere else in India. The tough geography has bred a culture of resilience, the monochrome landscape a famously fluorescent dress sense.

In Rajasthan in particular this has been twinned with a tradition of strong Maharaja rule, and while the Maharajas' power has waned over the last century, the legacy of their remarkable reign can be seen in the incredible forts and palaces that dominate the state. Many of these have now been turned into unique heritage hotels offering a fascinating taste of how royal life was lived. A-list destinations include the pink city of Jaipur, and the gorgeous lake and palaces of Udaipur, Jodhpur, Pushkar, the Shekhavati region and Mount Abu are all fascinating, and – as if that wasn't enough – Ranthambore is probably the best place in India to see tigers in the wild. Camel treks from the romantic citadel town of Jaisalmer offer another unmissable experience: the chance to step off the road and into the flat, arid scrubland of the Thar Desert, where a unique way of life survives despite the perennial shortage of water.

Water carriers in the Thar Desert.

The desert conditions of both states have led to traditions of music and dance, and arts and crafts, that are carried on to this day and are an added attraction of the region, both in terms of performances to be enjoyed and shopping to savour. Gujarat, although much less visited than its northern neighbour, is as a result much less touristy, and offers an altogether more authentic experience. While the cities are of no special appeal, it is the wide open spaces and vibrantly dressed residents of the Ranns of Kutch that are the real draw, with traditions and wildlife all of their own. This is also the only place in India, and one of the few remaining places in the world, where Asiatic lions can be seen in the wild.

Jain temple complex at Ranakpur.

RAJASTHAN

A desert state it might be, but India's 'Land of Kings' is bursting with colour and exuberance. Ornamental palaces, impregnable forts and painted towns all vie for attention.

From the salmon-pink facades of Jaipur to the indigo blues of Jodhpur, the ochre ramparts rising from Jaisalmer's sandflats to the red *havelis* of Bikaner, each city in Rajasthan has its own hallmark hue. Out in the countryside, the drabness of the landscape only serves to highlight the vibrancy of Rajasthani costumes: brightly dyed turbans, voluminous pleated skirts spangled with mirrorwork and intricately embroidered veils set against a backdrop of scrub and spindly *khejri* trees.

Always central to the region's identity, Rajasthan's flamboyance reaches its most arresting heights in the palaces and forts erected by the local Rajput maharajas. Bountiful trade and expedient military alliances with the Mughals paid for a building boom of lavish proportions in the medieval era, which lasted well into British rule. As a consequence, nowhere else in India can boast such exotic skylines. Royal abodes, combining the graceful lines of Islamic architecture with the desert kings' love of ornamentation, enclose beautifully preserved pleasure halls whose surfaces sparkle with mosaics of semiprecious stones and glass. From the courtyard gardens, exquisite cusped arched windows overlook cubic expanses of flat rooftops far below to the arid landscapes beyond.

Rajasthani woman.

Desert tourism

Drought has always haunted this dry northwestern corner of India, and continues to undermine the lives of Rajasthan's 60 million inhabitants, 70 percent of whom depend on small-scale agriculture for survival. Per capita income and levels of female literacy lag well behind the national averages, and access to health care, education and clean water remain the preserve of the region's affluent minority.

Yet in spite of such challenges, Rajasthan's distinctive culture

Main Attractions
Jaipur
Shekhavati
Pushkar
Ranthambore National Park
Udaipur
Ranakpur
Jodhpur
Jaisalmer

TIP

Arriving in Jaipur by train
or bus can be an
intimidating experience
for independent travellers,
due to the gangs of pushy
autorickshaw-wallahs that
pounce on visitors at the
stations. The best way to
avoid the hassle is to ask
your hotel or guesthouse
owner to send a driver to
meet you when you book
your room.

continues to flourish: this is where
the romantic vision of India comes
to life like nowhere else. Tourism has
boosted traditional arts and crafts,
and everywhere you travel in the
state you will come across wonderful
hand-woven textiles, wooden puppets
and silver jewellery, as well as capti-
vating performances of local dance
and music. The tourist influx of the
past few decades has also proved a
boon for the landowning Rajputs,
many of whose properties have been
converted into wonderful heritage
hotels, where you can experience life
inside a maharaja's palace at close
quarters, taking elephant rides to

tumbledown forts and exploring the
desert on camel back.

Geographically speaking, Rajasthan
is divided between a semi-arid zone
in the southeast, where the densely
populated plains are intersected by
perennial rivers and broken sandstone escarpments, and the flat,
parched Thar Desert to the west and
north. Between the two, the Aravalli
Hills ripple diagonally from northeast to southwest. Peaking at 1,722
metres (5,646ft) near the hill station
of Mount Abu, the range is draped
in forest and remote valleys, where
communities of subsistence farmers
and hunter-gatherer Bhils and other

minority Adivasi people still scrape a living from the land.

The first dwellers

It is now thought that the ancient cities of the Indus Valley had their precursors in northern Rajasthan. It seems that the area was inhabited by the Bhils and Minas people, who dispersed following the arrival of horse-riding nomads from the northwest some time around 1400 BC. These newcomers were here to stay, just like the Afghans, Turks, Persians and Mughals who followed, first in war then in peace, giving the Rajputs a martial ancestry.

From the reign of Harsha (7th century AD) to the time when the Delhi Sultanate was founded by the Muslims (AD 1206), Rajasthan fragmented into competing kingdoms. In the 16th century the Mughals made northern India their home. Winning over Rajasthan was the achievement of Akbar, who mixed military might with the soft touch of religious tolerance. His trump card was matrimonial alliances with the Hindu Rajputs, which turned them from dangerous enemies into faithful allies.

Many princesses from Jaipur and Jodhpur married into the Mughal royal line, but when the Mughals weakened, the Rajputs were quick to reassert their sovereignty. After the British captured Bengal in 1757, Rajasthan resisted, although by the beginning of the 19th century the British were in control. Rajputana was Rajasthan's old name under the British, 'land of the Rajputs', and the Maharaja of Mewar (Udaipur) was the acknowledged head of their 36 states. When India became independent, 23 princely states were consolidated to form the State of Rajasthan, 'home of rajas'.

The pink city

Jaipur ❶ (the city of *jai*, or victory), the capital of Rajasthan, was not always pink. The original city was light grey, edged with white borders and motifs. In honour of the visit in 1883 of the Prince of Wales, it was ordered to be painted the traditional colour of welcome, and it is this which has been retained in the picturesque Old City.

The city was laid out in 1728 in a simple grid pattern by a young Bengali, Vidyadhar Bhattacharya, architect to Maharaja Sawai Jai Singh II (of the royal lineage that had ruled from Amber, 11km/7 miles to the north, since the early 10th century). Seven blocks of buildings are divided by wide, tree-lined avenues; at the heart of the city is the palace, which covers a further two blocks. These rectangular divisions represent the nine divisions of the universe. The whole is surrounded by a crenellated wall with seven imposing gates (*pols*), still in use today. Each of the blocks houses *mohallas*, districts given over to the practice of various crafts or trades, from bangle-making to fabric dyeing to *minakari* (enamel work), for which Jaipur is famous.

Lying within easy reach of Delhi and Agra, the Rajasthani capital forms

Participating in Jaipur's Elephant Festival.

HERITAGE HOTELS

There's no better way to gain a sense of what life must have been like for residents of Rajasthan's historic properties than to spend a night or two in one. Small palaces and forts across the state have been converted by their owners to accommodate visitors. Some offer simple budget rooms in rambling, run-down wings, occupied by less affluent branches of old aristocratic families. Others have been restored to exceed their original splendour, augmented with swimming pools, ayurvedic health spas and other five-star trimmings. You may get to see traditional musicians, sleep in historic, mirror-encrusted bedrooms and lounge around on the terraces gazing across the desert. The decor is often spectacular, featuring antique furniture and traditionally decorated walls.

At the top of the range are the über-luxurious heritage hotels run by the maharajas of Udaipur, Jaipur and Jodhpur – the gargantuan Umaid Bhavan Palace on the southern outskirts of Jodhpur being the most astonishingly grand example. However, you can also stay in comparably sumptuous accommodation on remote country estates. Many offer nights in specially erected luxury camps, where guests can ride through the desert on camel or horse back, dine under the stars and sleep in traditional Rajasthani hunting tents.

a prominent port of call on northern India's popular 'Golden Triangle' of sights, attracting streams of visitors through the winter. Other than its flamboyant Rajput architecture, Jaipur holds one of the country's biggest bazaars, renowned above all for its handicrafts – particularly textiles and gemstones. Be aware, however, that a number of unscrupulous gem dealers are at work here – try to deal only with reputable companies that have been recommended to you by a trusted source.

Jaipur's palaces

The **City Palace** (palace and museum, daily 9.30am–5pm), occupying the most auspicious central portion of Jaipur's grid plan, formed the political hub of the maharaja's ambitious design, and remains the residence of Jaipur's royal family. Although its innermost enclosures date from the 18th century, other wings were added in subsequent eras, fusing Mughal and Rajput architectural motifs.

A series of ornamental gateways, large enough to admit processions of elephants, lead to the interlocking courtyards at the heart of the palace, many of whose pavilions, or *mahals*, are given over to the **Sawai Man Singh II Museum**. Armour, weapons, priceless carpets, state regalia, jewellery, miniature paintings, manuscripts and precious ritual paraphernalia make up the bulk of the collection, all lavishly decorated by craftsmen whom the Jaipur maharajas recruited from the courts of the Mughals as the empire lapsed into decline. Turbaned retainers with luxurious handlebar moustaches stand guard over the exhibits, the most famous of which is a pair of huge silver urns, 1.5 metres (5ft) tall and featured in *Guinness World Records* as the world's largest hand-made silver object. They were commissioned by Maharaja Man Singh II to transport Ganges water to London during a state visit in 1907, and allegedly held 8,181 litres (1,800 gallons).

Four exquisitely decorated doors lead to the innermost enclosure of the palace open to the public, the **Pitam Niwas Chowk** (Peacock Courtyard), from where you can admire the

RAJASTHAN TRANSPORT

Jaipur, Jodhpur and Udaipur are connected with regular flights to Delhi and Mumbai, and a few cities in Gujarat and South India. A new civil airport is also under construction near Jaisalmer which will provide a fast link to this remote desert area near the Pakistani border, rendering the overnight train from Jodhpur all but defunct when it is completed, likely in 2016. New Delhi is the nearest international airport.

With the main Delhi–Mumbai line slicing through the centre of the state, rail connections with India's metropolitan cities are fast and frequent. Train travel is generally safer and more comfortable than bus travel, although high demand for seats and sleeper berths means you have to book well in advance and for shorter trips between towns, buses are more convenient. Private firms operate comfortable "video coaches" on inter-city routes (book through travel agents), while the state transport company, RSTC, runs to all but the smallest villages.

Jaipur: Trains run to Agra (9–13 daily; 4–6hrs 30min); Ajmer (27–34 daily; 2–3hrs); Bikaner (6–8 daily; 8–10hrs); Delhi (16–19 daily; 4hrs 30min–6hr 30min); Mumbai (4–7 daily; 17–22hrs); Udaipur (3–4 daily; 12hrs). Buses go to Agra (hourly; 5hrs); Ajmer (hourly; 2hrs 30min); Bikaner (11 daily; 7hrs); Delhi (every 15min; 6hrs); Jodhpur (every 30min; 8hrs); Udaipur (hourly; 10hrs).

Jodhpur: Trains run to Bikaner (7–12 daily; 5–7hrs); Delhi (5–7 daily; 10hrs 30min–12hrs); Jaisalmer (4–8 daily; 6hrs). There are buses to Agra (1 daily; 10hrs); Ajmer (hourly; 5hrs); Bharatpur/Keoladeo (3 daily; 10hrs); Bikaner (hourly; 6hrs); Delhi (3 daily; 12hrs); Jaipur (every 30min; 8hrs); Jaisalmer (hourly; 5hrs 30min); Mount Abu (1 daily; 9hrs 30min); Udaipur (2 daily; 12hrs).

Udaipur: There are trains to Ajmer (4–6 daily; 5hrs); Chittaurgarh (6–8 daily; 2hrs); Delhi (2–3 daily; 12hrs); Jaipur (3–4 daily; 12hrs); Ahmedabad (1 daily; 10hrs 40min) and Mumbai (1 daily; 16hrs). Buses go to Agra (1 daily; 14hrs); Ajmer (hourly; 7hrs); Bundi (10 daily; 7hrs); Chittaurgarh (hourly; 3hrs 30min); Kota (10 daily; 6hr); Mount Abu (10 daily; 7hrs); Ranakpur (6 daily; 3hrs).

delicate exterior of the seven-storey **Chandra Mahal**, home to the present-day maharaja (Bhavani Singh) and his family.

The most photographed sight in Jaipur, however, is the **Hawa Mahal** (Palace of Winds; daily 9am–4.30pm), dating from 1799, which stands at the eastern perimeter of the palace, overlooking the bazaar. A five-floored confection of domed balconies, delicate cupolas and pierced stone *jali* screens, all painted Jaipur's trademark salmon pink, it is not in fact, a palace, but an extraordinary facade of 953 airy niches and windows, used by the royal women in *purdah* (secluded from the public) to watch the outside world of the streets below.

Immediately behind the Hawa Mahal, the Unesco World Heritage list-inscribed **Jantar Mantar** (daily 9am–4.30pm) stands in surreal counterpoint to the traditional Rajput splendour surrounding it. Made up of 16 colossal geometric structures which Maharaja Jai Singh – a keen astronomer – used to calculate celestial latitudes and planetary movements, it is one of five such complexes built at Hindu cities across India (the others are at Delhi, Mathura, Ujjain and Varanasi). Pride of place goes to the giant Bihat Samrat Yantra, an enormous sundial whose shadow moves 4 metres (13ft) each hour, enabling calculations of time down to intervals of five seconds. In times past, drummers stationed on the high gnomon arm (the part of the sundial that casts the shadow) used to sound the hours.

Around Jaipur

Immediately south of the old city, in the centre of the Ram Niwas gardens, stands the Albert Hall containing the **Central Museum** (www.alberthalljaipur. gov.in; daily 9am–5pm and 7–10pm). The ornate Indo-Saracenic building houses a rather disorderly collection of costumes, ivory, brasswork and jewellery, as well as some unintentionally amusing models of Rajasthani festivals, occupations and trades.

The stark desert hills encircling Jaipur are crowned by some impressive Rajput fortresses, whose ramparts reveal magnificent views over the city. *Jaipur Palace.*

FACT

Amber's painted elephants often suffer chronic dehydration and sunstroke, as well as foot problems and malnutrition, after hours of trudging to and from the palace. To alleviate their plight, the NGO Elephant Family provides water troughs, sunshades, a mobile veterinary clinic and training for their mahoots. Find out more at www.elephant-family.org.

Nahargarh Fort (daily 10am–5pm) is the best one to head for at sunset to enjoy a drink on the café terrace, with perfect views of the pink city fading to grey. Built in 1734 by Maharaja Jai Singh II to house his various concubines, it can be reached by road, or on foot (in just under an hour) via a footpath starting at the northwest corner of the palace.

Other popular escapes from the city include the **Royal Cenotaphs** (daily 9am–4.30pm) at **Gaitor**, just north of the palace complex, where elaborately carved white marble *chhatris* (cenotaphs) stand as memorials to Jaipur's former rulers, and the **Monkey Temple** at **Galta**. Hidden in a fold on the ridge overlooking the city's eastern limits, this Rama shrine plays host to troupes of splashing, squabbling macaques.

Amber and Samode

Amber (www.amberfort.org; daily 8am–6pm), 11km (7 miles) from Jaipur, was once the capital of the Minas – believed to be the original inhabitants of this area. Painted

Bikaner Fort.

elephants take visitors up the hill to admire the massive gateways, pillared pavilions and palaces that recall the glory and wealth of Amber's association with the Mughals: Raja Man Singh was the commander-in-chief of Akbar's army, while Mirza Raja Jai Singh was a powerful ally of Jahangir. Of special interest are the **Diwan i Am**, Jai Singh's audience hall, and the **Shish Mahal**, the Hall of Mirrors, where the walls are inlaid with exquisite mirrored motifs that dance to the flame of even a single candle.

A 20-minute uphill walk from Amber palace is **Jaigarh Fort** (daily 9am–4.30pm), opened to the public in the late 1980s after being sealed for decades following a rumour that an enormous quantity of gold was buried in vaults under deep reservoirs. This forced isolation ensured the complex's many palaces and temples remained better preserved than those further down the hill. Jaigarh was renowned for its arsenal, and one of the highlights of any visit to the fort, apart from the views back over Amber, is the **Jaya Vana**, the largest antique cannon in India, said to have been able to fire over a distance of 35km (22 miles), a feat requiring some 100kg (220lbs) of gunpowder.

Before leaving Amber, it's worth paying a visit to the splendid new **Anokhi Museum of Hand Printing** (www.anokhimuseum.com; Tue–Sat 10.30am–5pm, Sun 11am–4.30pm), housed in a grand old *haveli* at Kheri Gate, 10 minutes on foot from the fort. The collection charts the evolution of this quintessentially Rajasthani textile form, which uses carved woodblocks to pattern fabrics, with antique pieces displayed alongside examples of more recent, export-oriented garments.

Proceeds from the Anokhi Museum are used to support blockprinters working in the Jaipur area, the largest community of whom live in the village of **Sanganer**, 16km (10 miles) south of the city. This is the best place to see traditional dyers and printers in action, squeezed into rows of small shops lining the bazaar. Along the riverbanks, lengths of vibrant cotton are hung out to dry – a great photo opportunity. Since the 16th century, Sanganer has also been a major centre for paper-making: cotton scraps are used as raw material for manufacturing sheets of paper distinctively textured with flower petals, and bound into books.

Continuing north from Amber on the main Jaipur–Delhi road brings you to the turning for **Samode**, 42km (26 miles) from the capital, and the site of a spectacular palace hotel set among the Aravalli Hills. The building and its adjacent village served as the setting for the 1980s hit movie *The Far Pavilions*, based on the Raj-era romantic novel by M.M. Kaye. Its beautifully preserved Durbar Hall and Shish Mahal (Hall of Mirrors) are among the most delicate in Rajasthan. Non-residents are welcome to visit, but are required to pay a small charge.

Alwar and Sariska

National Highway No. 8 runs north from Jaipur to Delhi. About 60km (35 miles) from Jaipur a turning leads northeast to Alwar, picturesque and dotted with historical sites. En route, at **Bairath**, are ancient Buddhist rock edicts of Emperor Ashoka, a 3rd-century BC Buddhist *chaitya* (temple) and a painted garden pavilion built around AD 1600.

Founded in 1771, **Alwar** ❷ is one of the newest of the princely states of Rajasthan. Starting out as distant cousins of Jaipur, the Alwar Rajputs manoeuvred their way through the chaos of the 18th century, skilfully changing sides as necessary, until the British finally acknowledged and rewarded them for their help against the Marathas (even so, the affairs of Alwar remained troubled, with only a few scattered years of peace). Some handsome palaces survive, chief among them Raja Bakhtawar Singh's resplendent **City Palace** (1793), built from half the state exchequer – a high proportion even by feudal standards. An exuberant mix

Common langurs (Hanuman monkeys) at Amber Fort.

TIP

The Sariska Tiger Reserve is most easily approached from Alwar. Any of the buses heading to Jaipur pass the park gates. For safaris, Jeeps offer the best way of spotting wildlife; booking should be made through the Forest Reception Office opposite the Sariska Palace, near the main entrance.

of Mughal symmetry and Rajput extravagance, the building holds a small **museum** (Sat–Thur 10am–4.30pm), whose collection of miniature paintings, manuscripts, arms and furniture evoke the opulence of the Alwari court, which saw its heyday in the early 20th century, when the state was legendary for the pomp of its processions and tiger hunts.

Next to the palace stands a reservoir featuring delicate temples, kiosks and symmetrical flights of stairs. Considered a masterpiece of Indo-Islamic architecture, the highlight is the double-storeyed *chhatri* (cenotaph) commemorating the self-immolation *(sati)* of a favourite royal concubine, Moosi Maharani.

A second royal palace, 37km (23 miles) south of Alwar, once served as a hunting lodge, but is now a hotel on the outskirts of the **Sariska Tiger Reserve**. The sanctuary made international headlines in 2005 when it admitted that its tiger population (estimated at 28 in 2003) had been completely wiped out by poachers working in cahoots with park rangers.

However, a total of five tigers were reintroduced to the park in 2005–2009, with initial signs looking positive for their future survival. With or without the big cats, the reserve is still worth visiting for its abundant bird life and delightful scenery, dominated by the rippling, forested hills of the Aravalli range.

Deeg Palace

Another little-visited town on the fringes of Rajasthan that holds some unexpectedly fine architecture is **Deeg**, on the road between Alwar and Bharatpur, 34km (21 miles) southeast. The town became the second capital of a dynasty of Jat warrior-farmers who wrested control of the region from the Mughals through the 18th century. Hemmed in by a dry moat and 28-metre (92ft) walls, the fort they erected here saw some particularly fierce battles, but the **palace** – comprising a collection of finely proportioned pavilions overlooking an Indo-Islamic-style *charbagh* garden (Sat–Thur 9am–5pm) – is what most visitors come to see. Built in 1767, the

The cenotaph at Alwar's City Palace.

Gopal Bhawan is the largest of the buildings, and preserves much original furniture, including a swing said to have once belonged to the empress Nur Jahan, and which was brought to Deeg as booty after Maharaha Suraj Mal's daring raid on Mughal Delhi in 1762. It stands in front of the structure regarded as the finest of its kind anywhere in Rajasthan, the **Keshar Bhawan**, or 'Monsoon Palace', an ornately carved pavilion to which the royals used to repair in hot weather.

Shekhavati: decorated towns

The second northern road (National Highway No. 11) from Jaipur leads to the painted towns of **Shekhavati** ❸ and on to Bikaner. Once subordinate to the maharajas of Amber, the region asserted its independence in 1471 under Rao Shekhav – after whom it is named.

Being located on the caravan route connecting the Gujarat ports and Central India with Delhi, trade in opium, silk, cotton and spices flourished, attracting wealthy Marwari traders in the 18th and 19th centuries. Elaborate cenotaphs and reservoirs, temples and caravanserais stand as a testimony to the wealth produced by this commerce, but it was the tall houses (*havelis*) which the merchant families built to combat the heat and glare that best expressed the confidence and prosperity of the era. Dynasties competed with each other to erect the grandest, most elaborately decorated homes.

The walled courtyards where the women spent most of their lives, screened from the outside word in the seclusion of *purdah*, were enlivened with extravagant murals depicting mythological scenes of gods and goddesses in vibrant colours. The men, meanwhile, conducted their business on the white cotton mattresses of their sitting rooms, which were also richly embellished with scenes from the wider world, many showing modern contraptions – such as trains, hot air balloons and motor cars – which had not yet arrived in this corner of Rajasthan. Erotic motifs were also camouflaged in discreet niches.

Sambar deer.

FACT

The Rani Sati Temple in the town of Jhunjhunu, in northern Shekhavati, is the centre of an immensely popular cult revolving around a merchant's wife who committed ritual self-immolation on her husband's funeral pyre in 1595. Although banned since the time of the British, the custom of sati is still occasionally practised. An 18-year-old Rajput girl, Roop Kanwar, burnt herself to death near Jaipur in 1987, sparking national outrage.

Time has certainly taken its toll on this rich storehouse of traditional art, but enough survives to make a journey through the region worthwhile. Some of Shekhavati's most richly painted *havelis* line the sandy backstreets of **Nawalgarh**, 120km (74 miles) north of Jaipur, where a better-than-average crop of hotels provide congenial accommodation for trips deeper into the area. On the east side of town, the **Dr Ramnath A Podder Haveli Museum** (www.podarhavelimuseum. org; daily summer 8am–8pm, winter 8.30am–6.30pm) ranks among the few mansions to have been restored to their former glory. Nearby, the Moraka Haveli and Bhagton ki Choti Haveli hold the usual quirky mix of Hindu mythological scenes and images of British Victoriana.

Dundlod, 7km (4 miles) north, is the site of an old Rajput fort, converted into a small heritage hotel. But the most imposing of the region's former forts towers over the tightly packed lanes of **Mandawa**. Several large hotels scattered around the edges of town serve through traffic on the

tour-group trail, but these impinge little on the old-world feel of the bazaar and its disintegrating, charismatic *havelis*. **Fatehpur**, in the far west of the Shekhavati region on the road to Bikaner, sees far fewer visitors, in spite of the presence of the **Nadine Le Prince Haveli** (daily 9am–6pm), restored by the French artists whose name it bears. Some of the overpainting carried out has been criticised for being heavy-handed, but it conjures better than anywhere else the splendour in which the region's merchants must once have lived.

Bikaner: city of the desert

Bikaner ❹ 190km (118 miles) west of Fatehpur, was founded in 1488 – 29 years after Jodhpur. A younger but more intelligent son of Jodhpur's founder Rao Jodha, Rao Bika, was given an army and asked to seek his own fortune to avoid a war of succession. Thus Bikaner was founded in the heart of the wilderness called Jangaldesh. Perhaps the very bareness of the landscape spurred the human hand to create beauty.

A typical painted wall in the Shekhavati region.

Erected towards the end of the 16th century, unconquered **Junagarh Fort** (www.junagarh.org; daily 10am–4.30pm) harbours palaces, temples and pavilions of unrivalled refinement. None, however, are more sumptuous than the **Anup Mahal**, which is encrusted with red and gold filigree *(usta)*. Lavish frescoes, gilded stucco mouldings, floral patterns and enormous carpets (woven by former inmates of Bikaner jail) adorn the suitably grand **Durbar Hall**, where examples of Bikaner's renowned school of miniature painting are displayed.

By comparison, the home of the present-day royal, **Lalgarh Palace**, 3km (2 miles) to the north, is more restrained. Designed by Sir Swinton Jacob (architect of Jaipur's Albert Hall), it's less alluring than its predecessor, with some wings serving as a luxury heritage hotel. Dusty old photographs and royal memorabilia are showcased in the **Shri Sadul Museum** (Mon–Sat 10am–5pm).

Encircled by 6km (4 miles) of dark red sandstone ramparts, Bikaner's **Old City** is a warren of twisting, sandy streets, many of them lined by crumbling Jain temples and some of Rajasthan's most eccentric *havelis*. The latter date from the textile boom of the early 20th century and present an unlikely mix of styles, fusing Art Nouveau with Victorian Municipal brickwork. Call at the tourist office, in the RTDC Dholamaru Hotel on Pooran Singh Circle, for their leaflet outlining a 'heritage route' that strings together the old city's architectural highlights.

Around Bikaner

Outside Bikaner, the countryside is arid desert, dotted with mud villages still heavily dependent on camels for transport and agricultural work. Around 10km (6 miles) south of town, the **National Research Centre on Camel** (www.nrccamel.res.in; daily 2–6.30pm) makes an interesting visit, particularly at sunset when the herds return from the dunes. In addition to a breeding programme, investigations are being carried out here into the health-giving properties of camel milk, which appears to reduce the

TIP

Bikaner may be less well known as a camel-trekking destination than Jaisalmer, but several companies operate out of the town, taking visitors into infrequently visited desert areas where wildlife is abundant and traditional villages numerous. One commendable outfit is run by Vijay Singh Rathore (www.camelman.com).

Ajmer's busy markets.

TIP

During the annual Urs Mela festival, held in October to November, auspicious kheer pudding is cooked in the huge degs (metal vats) that stand inside the Dargah's main gates. Over-zealous devotees literally dive into the pans when it's ready, getting plastered from head to toe in the sweet rice porridge – an unmissable photo opportunity.

incidence of diseases such as tuberculosis and diabetes.

The village of **Deshnok**, 30km (19 miles) south of Bikaner, is an important Hindu pilgrimage site for local desert-dwelling people. Its presiding deity, Karni Mata, was a real historical figure, a miracle-working bard, or *charani*, who rose to become an influential cult leader in the 14th century, and who, after her death, was elevated to the position of the royal family's patron goddess. The shrine is famous above all for the fact that thousands of holy rats, or *kaba*, scamper across its marble floors after food that is brought for them by devout visitors. The rodents are believed to be reincarnations of Karni Mata's relatives; it is considered highly auspicious if one runs across your foot or, better still, nibbles your toe during a visit.

Ajmer and Pushkar

About 135km (80 miles) southwest of Jaipur lies **Ajmer** ❺, the most sacred of all Sufi pilgrimage places in India. Its Muslim history began

PUSHKAR'S CAMEL MELA

Over the fortnight leading up to the full moon of Kartika month (late Oct/early Nov), villagers from the desert regions of western India congregate around Pushkar Lake for the famous Kartik Purnima festival and camel-trading fair. Decked out in their finest traditional dress, they come to buy and sell livestock, strike marriage deals, meet with relatives and generally enjoy themselves after the annual harvest. The spectacle, set against a sea of 50,000 dusty camels and rolling dunes, ranks among the most compelling in India, though don't expect to be the only foreign visitor in attendance.

Next to the trading grounds, a funfair also takes place, complete with races, camel 'fancy fur' contests and other events. With all the camel-related entertainment, however, it's easy to forget that the festival is primarily a religious one, commemorating Brahma's marriage to Savitri and Gayatri. Hindus believe the waters of the lake can cleanse all sins and congregate in huge numbers around the sacred ghats, or steps, encircling the lake to bathe at dawn – an unforgettable sight.

Accommodation can be scarce over the festival period, the local tourism department and several upscale hotels erect temporary tent compounds on the sand flats around the town. The tents are fitted with fans, electric light, bathrooms and other mod cons. Book in advance through www.rajasthantourism.gov.in.

in 1193, when Sultan Muhammad of Ghori captured the town. The Persian saint, Khwaja Mu'inuddin Chisti, who had come with Ghori, settled and preached here. The **Dargah Sharif**, where the saint is buried, lies at the foot of Taragarh Hill. When Akbar took Ajmer in 1556 he made it his military headquarters and visited the tomb on foot to pray for a son. The request was granted and Ajmer's reputation soared. Large cauldrons (*degs*) were presented by Akbar to be filled with food for distribution among the pilgrims at the shrine; this continues today, but the original *degs* were replaced in the 19th century. Important monuments within the *dargah* include the delicate white marble mosque of Shah Jahan (*c.*1650).

The **Arhai din ka Jhonpra** mosque is just west of the *dargah*. This Sanskrit college was converted to a mosque in 1210 by Qutb-ud-Din-Aibak. It is one of the finest monuments of medieval India, with beautiful decorations and ornate calligraphic inscriptions.

Just off Station Road is Akbar's red sandstone palace, the **Daulat Khana**, where in 1610 the emperor Jahangir met the first envoy sent to India from the court of a British monarch. Sir Thomas Roe had been despatched to extract trading rights from the Great Mughal – he was only partially successful in this, but his efforts paved the way for what would, over the coming decades, snowball into the East India Company. Nearby is the **Nasiyan Jain Temple**, a depiction in gold of the Jain interpretation of the universe and well worth a visit.

Divided from Ajmer by the corrugated slopes of Nag Pahar (Snake Mountain), **Pushkar** ❻, 14km (9 miles) northwest, is considered high up in the hierarchy of Hindu places of pilgrimage.

Pushkar has one of the few temples in India dedicated to Brahma, the Creator. Here every year, on the full moon of Kartika month (Oct–Nov), hundreds of thousands of pilgrims gather to bathe in a sacred lake, believed to have been created when Lord Brahma dropped a lotus flower to earth. This is the occasion for one of the largest cattle and camel markets in Rajasthan, Kartik Purnima, where the abundance of colour, jewellery, turbans and moustaches is unmatched. Aside from the livestock market, traditional funfairs and races draw huge crowds. However, the exotic swirl of blue- and whitewashed temples, onion-domed pavilions and ghats enfolding the northern shores of the lake remain busy throughout the year, and have become a second home for the backpacker crowd in particular. Every morning and evening, drums and ringing bells accompany worshippers as they bathe in the sacred water, which Hindus maintain holds the power to cleanse the soul of all sin.

Flanking the town and lake are a pair of beautiful, low desert hills crowned by small temples. Dedicated to Lord Brahma's wives, Savitri and Gayatri, can both be reached via paved paths that make great walks, with tremendous views across the slopes of Nag Pahar to the south and the sand flats of the Thar spreading north and west.

Ranthambore

From Tonk, 95km (58 miles) south of Jaipur on the main road to Bundi and Kota, a road leads east to **Sawai Madhopur** where the royal Jaipur household used to come for tiger hunts accompanied by their VIP guests. Overlooking the wildlife sanctuary of Ranthambore, 13km (8 miles) from the town, is the fortress of Rao Hamir, which was conquered by Ala-ud-Din Khilji in the 14th century and then again by Akbar in 1569. Despite being in ruins, its palaces, temples and cenotaphs are well worth a visit.

Ranthambore ❼ is famous for its tigers, which can often be sighted prowling among the medieval ruins or in the shallows of the lake. The lure of such exotic wildlife has ensured that Ranthambore has become India's most visited national park – in spite of the fact its fragile tiger population is in perilous decline, with only an estimated 40 animals surviving. Tickets

Pushkar Lake.

FACT

It's easy to see why Rudyard Kipling, who stayed in Bundi as a guest of the local Rao in 1892, thought the extraordinary palace 'such a place as men build for themselves in uneasy dreams... the work of goblins'.

for safaris, which happen either early morning or late evening, are strictly limited, although you should be able to get hold of one through your hotel. Visiting the park is either in a jeep or in a larger 'canter' (a kind of open-top bus). In addition to the big cats (there are also leopards), the park supports blackbuck, hyena and several species of antelope. Ranthambore is also something of a hotspot for birding, with around 300 species on record. One of the park's defining sights is that of its resplendent wild peacocks perched on the crenellations of the old fort.

Jat states

The Jaipur–Agra road leads east to **Bharatpur** and **Dholpur** – unusually, both Jat states in the predominantly Rajput stronghold of Rajasthan.

Bharatpur Fort houses a museum with exhibits of mixed antiquity, but what makes Bharatpur famous is its 29-sq-km (11-sq-mile) **Keoladeo Ghana National Park** ❽ (daily dawn–dusk; charge), with the largest concentration and variety of bird

life in Asia. Prior to 1940, this was the favourite shooting ground of the British viceroys, with a record kill of 4,273 birds in a single day. Sunrise or sunset from October to February is the best time to see the birds.

A total of 375 species have been recorded here, of which around 150 are migrants from as far afield as Siberia and Europe. Among the numerous aquatic residents of the Keoladeo wetlands are giant Sarus cranes, which grow to the height of a human and sport striking scarlet hoods. Until 2002, the sanctuary also hosted a few nesting pairs of rare Siberian cranes, but sadly, none have been sighted since then. No one has been able to account for their disappearance, though it is known that the cranes are hunted during their epic high-altitude traverse of the Himalayas. Repeated droughts have also impacted on Keoladeo's bird life, drying up the wetlands entirely in 2007, when drastic measures to divert rainwater from surrounding fields into the lake were met with stiff resistance from farmers. A compromise has

Udaipur.

since been reached, meaning that the park now has at least some water during the winter months.

Southeast Rajasthan

Founded in 1342, the ancient kingdom of **Bundi** ❾ (from *bando nal*, 'narrow passage') in southeast Rajasthan lies well protected in the ranges of the rugged Aravalli Hills that drop into rocky ravines traversed by four narrow passes.

The secluded position of its capital screened it from the hybridisation that held sway elsewhere in the 19th century, even though the British virtually controlled its affairs from 1818. 'Bundi is deliciously behind the times,' wrote the maharaja of Baroda – a remark that, in many ways, still holds true today. No other town of comparable size in Rajasthan feels as untouched by modern trends.

Bundi's undisputed highlight is its **palace** (daily winter 8am–5pm, summer until 7pm), whose faded serpentine, ochre and red sandstone walls are reflected to magical effect in the **Naval Sagar** lake below. Incredible

ramps and stairs zigzag between the ramparts, overhanging balconies and forest of domes and cusped arches.

Unlike most of its counterparts elsewhere in the state, the palace shows little influence from Islamic architecture and is regarded as the purest example of Rajput style. Large areas of it are open to the public. Visits begin at the splendid Hathi Pol, flanked by statues of rearing elephants, and progress through a disorienting series of halls, *zenanas* (women's quarters), antechambers and enclosed courtyard gardens. Some of the finest murals surviving in all of India are to be found in the exquisite Badal Mahal, most of them depicting scenes from the life of Krishna in subtle turquoise, blues, greens and terracotta tones.

The **Chitra Shala** (same hours as the palace), just above the main palace, holds more refined frescoes painted in the 17th and 18th centuries. Immediately behind it a path leads steeply up the hillside to the ruins of the medieval **Taragarh Fort**, and massive television booster mast,

A bridal procession in Udaipur.

Udaipur textiles.

Rajasthani children on their way to school.

from where you get an unrivalled view over the rooftops.

Crammed with traditional shops and buildings, Bundi town itself is fascinating to explore on foot. Local guides will show you the way to hidden step wells – such as the **Raniji-ki-Baori**, embellished with carved panels showing the 10 avatars of Vishnu – and walled *havelis* on the lakeside.

The territory hereabouts was first claimed by Udaipur and later by Jaipur. Part of it was given in 1579 as patrimony for a favoured younger son, and this tract, set in the open plains, grew to be **Kota** ❿ – larger than its parent state and bustling with the youth of a commercial city. In contrast to secluded Bundi, Kota had to be on constant alert because its strategic location on the plains along the Chambal River drew the envy of Udaipur, Jaipur, the Marathas and also the British – to whom it was the first state to accede, due to the foresight of Zalim Singh, the regent. Spasmodic interludes of peace led to spurts of architecture and a mélange of pillared halls, kiosks,

commemorative gateways, carving and painting. Some of the finest frescoes and miniature paintings of India belong to the Bundi-Kota school. The **City Palace** at Kota abounds in ornamentation, and the first-rate **Maharao Madho Singh Museum** (Sat–Thur 10am–5pm) shows treasures from the ruler's private collection. The most exquisite room is the **Raj Mahal**, hung with paintings from the Mughal to British periods.

Udaipur

The royal house of Mewar, now better-known as **Udaipur** ⓫, is one of India's most rewarding cities to visit. It has two reasons for pride. The first is that its rulers, the Sisodia Rajputs, can trace their recorded history back 16 generations to Bapa Rawal (AD 728), whereas Jaipur and Jodhpur lag behind by 200 and 483 years respectively. The second is pride in being Hindu and not losing honour to Muslim invaders. Mewar resisted such alliances for at least 50 years longer than the other Rajput states. This sense of history and pride persisted during the

British period, earning them the highest gun salute in Rajasthan: 19 guns as against the 17 each of Jaipur, Jodhpur, Bundi, Bikaner, Kota and Karauli. Maharana Fateh Singh of Udaipur had the distinction of not attending the Delhi Durbar for King George V in 1911 (obligatory attendance being, essentially, a ritual of submission to a higher rank).

The Sisodias moved to Udaipur after their former seat, Chittor (Chittaurgarh), fell for the third time to the Mughals in 1567. More easily defensible, the new site soon acquired a profusion of magnificent palaces, lakes, temples and cenotaphs, grouped around the shimmering waters of Pichola Lake, which the family's chief annalist and historian, the East India Company Resident Colonel James Tod, famously applauded as 'the most diversified and... romantic spot on the continent of India'. In these drought-prone times, the waters of the lake come and go, but Udaipur's wondrous architecture retains its former splendour, floating with regal disregard above the guesthouses and hotels that have mushroomed on the slopes below it.

City palace of the Sisodias

First stop on an visitor's itinerary has to be the Sisodias' splendid **City Palace**, which surges vertically from the lakeside – an imposing wall of plain yellow plaster topped by a crowning layer of domes, golden finials, fluted pillars and whimsical arches, all facing east towards the rising sun (the Sisodias' royal symbol). Much of the complex is still occupied by the maharaja of Udaipur, but the most historic, and vibrantly decorated, portions have been allocated to the **City Palace Museum** (daily 9.30am–5.30pm).

An array of ostentatious mirror-work, mosaics, murals, porcelain tiles, glass inlay and semi-precious stones encrust every surface of the palace's interior. Wandering between the various halls you can trace the shift in emphasis from the glorious cusp-arched, onion-domed extravagance of Mughal times to the Bohemian-crystal, gilded stucco pomp of the Raj era. The most elaborate

The Lake Palace at Jaipur.

PEACOCKS

The national bird of India, Blue peacocks are particularly common in the state of Rajasthan. They have long held a cherished place in Indian culture, with the peacock feather a much-used motif in Indian temple art, and associated with many of the more popular gods, particularly Kartikeya, who rides on a peacock's back. Their sudden appearance in full fan mode can be both startling and alluring, and their haunting cry is believed to foretell rain. Although they tend not to fly long distances, the sight of a peacock in flight is compelling, the abundant tail feathers trailing behind making this one of the longest flying birds in the world. Such is the beauty of the omnivorous Blue peacock, it is even said to be able to charm snakes and steal their eggs.

decor appears in the famous Mor Chowk ('Peacock Courtyard'), in which 5,000 pieces of tinted glass were deployed to create the four peacocks adorning the walls.

Lake palaces

Other palaces were built on the lake itself, to which Udaipur's rulers used to escape the heat of high summer. The largest, **Jag Niwas**, dates from 1746 and today houses the unashamedly luxurious and romantic Lake Palace Hotel (note the hotel is no longer open to non-guests). To its south, the older **Jag Mandir** is where Prince Khurram, who was later to become Emperor Shah Jahan, took refuge in 1624; British refugees also sheltered here from the horrors of the 1857 Uprising.

In the Old Town, the tangle of narrow lanes winding from the stepped banks of the lake are lined by historic buildings in various stages of collapse. Among the few that have been restored is the **Bagore-ki-Haveli** (daily 11am–6pm), a 138-roomed mansion that

once belonged to the prime minister of Udaipur state. It now holds a small museum and concert hall where recitals of traditional Mewari music and dance are staged for tourists. Just up the hill, the **Jagdish Temple**, built in the mid-17th century, has a remarkable bronze statue of Garuda (a mythical bird) facing his revered Lord Vishnu. The fascinating shops and craftsmen's studios in the narrow streets of the bazaar justify lengthy exploration.

On the outskirts, **Shilpgram** (daily 11am–7pm) is a lively folk museum where reconstructed village houses from across western India showcase traditional arts and crafts of the region, while music and dance performances are held throughout the day on openair stages in front of them. A visit to Shilpgram can be easily slotted into a trip to the **Sajjangarh** hill palace, 5km (3 miles) west of the city. Built in 1883 by the royal family as a monsoon retreat, the now poorly maintained structure is of less interest in itself than the wonderful views that extend across the lake and hills surrounding Udaipur – especially serene at sunset time.

Forts and temples of Mewar

In the erstwhile princely state of Mewar there were three almost impregnable forts: **Chittaurgarh** (112km/70 miles east of Udaipur), **Kumbalgarh** (84km/52 miles north) and Mandalgarh (near Kota).

Set deep in the Aravalli Hills, **Kumbalgarh** ⑫ remains difficult to reach, even today, but more than repays the effort. The journey leads through delightfully unspoilt countryside – much of it farmed by minority Bhil tribespeople. The citadel itself, approached via seven fortified gates, occupies an eagle's-nest summit ringed by enormous ramparts that fall away dramatically to the hazy plains below. It takes two days, with a night under the stars halfway, to hike around them – an

Ranakpur.

adventurous trek that takes you past forgotten ancient shrines infested with jungle and monkeys, affording superb panoramas throughout.

The Jain temple complex of **Ranakpur ⓭**, 160km (100 miles) northwest from Udaipur, can be reached in a scenic hour's drive from Kumbalgarh, dropping through old-growth forest to the floor of a shaded, thickly wooded valley. Built in the mid-15th century of milk-white Makrana marble, the temples – important way-stages on the region's Jain pilgrimage circuit, but rarely visited by foreigners – are renowned above all for their intricately carved columns, no two of which are identical.

Chittaurgarh ⓮, also known as Chittor, became the first capital of Mewar in the early 13th century under the reign of Jaitra Singh (1213–53). The siege of Chittaurgarh in 1303 by the sultan of Delhi, Ala-ud-Din Khilji, is notorious. The sultan had heard of the beauty of Princess Padmini, wife of Maharana Rawal Ratan Singh, and determined to bring her back to his harem. Despite a courageous Rajput defence, the citadel was captured by the sultan's force. Rather than face dishonour, the women committed *johar*, mass suicide. Chanting verses from the *Gita*, they threw themselves on the funeral pyre.

Chittor was later recaptured by the Rajputs. Two centuries later, in 1535, it was attacked by the sultan of Gujarat, Bahadur Shah; a total of 13,000 Rajput women are said to have sacrificed themselves in the flames. But by far the bloodiest siege here was the one laid by the Mughal emperor Akbar 32 years later, in which the entire female population of the fort committed *johar* on a mass pyre, while their husbands and male relatives rode to an honourable death in battle outside the walls.

Spread over a huge, sheer-sided plateau, Chittaurgarh Fort holds monuments spanning nine centuries of Rajput history, from grandiose gateways to temples, palaces and stepped tanks. Its defining landmark,

however, is the 37-metre (121ft), nine-storey **Jaya Stambha**, or 'Victory Tower'. Ornately carved from top to bottom, it can be scaled via 157 internal steps for superb views over the town and fortress.

Mount Abu

Mount Abu ⓯, 100km (62 miles) west of Udaipur, is one of the most sacred places of Jain pilgrimage. According to the Jain tradition, Mahavira, the last of the 24 *Tirthankara* (saints), spent a year there. At an altitude of 1,220 metres (4,000ft), it is the only bona fide hill resort in Rajasthan. Many princes built summer bungalows and small palaces around Nakki Lake, and visitors flock there during the summer to take advantage of the cooler temperatures. The surrounding countryside attracts less attention, but its woods and boulder-studded hillsides are criss-crossed by woodcutters' trails offering some wonderful walks to viewpoints with panoramas extending westwards across the plains, far below, into Gujarat.

TIP

Guided walks into the forested valleys and hills surrounding Mount Abu town are organised daily from the Shri Ganesh Hotel. The routes cover some of the area's lesser-known, least accessible panorama and wildlife-viewing points, where bears, jungle cats and other rare species may be spotted.

Mount Abu.

FACT

The famous riding breaches named after the Marwari capital are said to have been invented by Regent Pratap Singh, who disliked the cloth wrappings worn around soldiers' shins and devised an all-in-one trouser alternative, based on traditional Rajput garb. The fashion spread to London after Singh's visit to Queen Victoria's Diamond Jubilee in 1887.

The main attractions in Mount Abu, and one of the great sights of Rajasthan, are the **Dilwara Jain temples** (daily noon–5pm; free). Of the five main shrines here, **Adinath** and **Neminath** display the finest carving in white marble. Adinath, the most celebrated, was built in 1031 and is dedicated to the first Tirthankar. The lotus ceiling in the main shrine is carved from a single block of stone. Neminath was erected in 1230 to celebrate the 22nd Tirthankar, and the **Hall of Donors** is particularly fine. Of the other three, the Chaumukha Temple is later and built of sandstone, the Risah Deo Temple is unfinished, while the Dagambar Temple is much less highly decorated. The 24 elite Chauhan clans of Rajasthan claim descent from the holy fire that springs from the central peak of the Abu, **Guru Shikhar** (1,772 metres/5,813ft), the highest point in Rajasthan and site of the much venerated Atri Rishi Temple. Mount Abu is particularly popular with Gujarati tourists, who come here to take advantage not only of the cooler climes but also the ready availability of alcohol – Gujarat is a dry state.

Jodhpur

The Rathores of Kanauj (in modern Uttar Pradesh) moved in AD 1211 to Marusthal – literally 'Land of Death' – the arid desert spreading westwards from heart of Rajasthan. Their territory, crossed by the major trade artery connecting northern India with the ports on the Gujarati coast, came to be called Marwar, and furnished them with untold riches.

In 1459, Rao Jodha ploughed much of the wealth gleaned from taxing this commerce in sandalwood, spices, copper and silk into the construction of a new stronghold at **Jodhpur** ⑯ after the Rathores old seat at nearby Mandore had proved too vulnerable. Thereafter, allegiances with the Mughals, whom the Rathores' helped in their conquest of Gujarat, saw the family's fortunes rise still further, but after the demise of Shah Jahan, Rao Jaswant Singh backed the wrong brother in the ensuing war of succession and was attacked by Aurangzeb,

The blue city of Jodhpur, as viewed from the Fort.

his subjects forcibly converted to Islam. Two centuries of fratricidal disputes and famines ensued before the city experienced a resurgence during the British colonial period.

The Raj era saw the construction of one of India's most decadent palaces, Umaid Bhavan, on Jodhpur's outskirts, but it is still the stupendous profile of the glittering **Meherangarh Fort** (www.mehrangarh. org; daily 9am–5pm) that entirely dominates the city. Floating 125 metres (410ft) above the rooftops of the old town, the citadel sprawls over a flat sandstone plateau, protected on all sides by sheer cliffs and a crust of crenellated ramparts. The approach to it winds through seven fortified gateways. Emerging from the last of these, **Loha Pol**, or 'Iron Gate', you'll see a series of *sati* stones showing the hand prints of royal widows burnt on the maharajas' pyres. The palaces within, sculpted from hard sandstone and marble, were designed to catch the breeze to keep them cool. An extensive museum displays howdahs, paintings, thrones, banners, doors, weapons, and a spectacular 17th-century tent made for Shah Jahan. The fort also boasts an excellent audio guide, available for hire at the ticket office.

The old city of Jodhpur below the fort is an intriguing place to explore. Its maze of narrow streets, where you'll find dozens of shops selling traditional *kathputli* puppets and mirror-inlaid textiles, is painted a striking shade of blue. Tourist guides will tell you the distinctive colour denotes the homes of Brahman families, but the truth is more prosaic: it derives from copper sulphate, traditionally added to limewash to deter termites and other insects.

Umaid Bhavan palace

Across town, the scrubby southern outskirts of Jodhpur are overshadowed by the monolithic bulk of **Umaid Bhavan** palace, built from red sandstone by famine victims in the 1920s and 1930s. It took 3,000 labourers more than a decade and a half to construct the 347-roomed behemoth, which centres on a gigantic domed hall. No expense was spared on the interiors. When the original fittings and furniture, ordered from Maples of London, were lost in a U-boat attack during World War II, Maharaja Umaid Singh ordered a new Art Deco look, embellished with oodles of Rajasthani gilt flourishes. It was among the most extravagant designs ever created, and stands as a fitting monument to the iniquities of Rajasthan's age-old feudal system.

One closed wing of the building remains occupied by the royal family, but the rest has been dedicated to a luxury heritage hotel; non-residents are, however, welcome to take tea and watch the peacocks patrol the vast lawns, and there's a small **museum** (daily 9am–5pm) displaying the usual array of royal treasures, regalia, hunting trophies and old photographs, alongside a video on the making of the palace.

Mehrangarh Fort.

FACT

Much of what we know about the history of Rajasthan is due to 23-year-old Lieutenant James Tod, who arrived in 1805 as the East India Company's representative. Over the next decade, he roamed across 'Rajpootana', compiling the royal genealogies, folklore, poetry and history he acquired along the way into the Annals and Antiquities of Rajasthan – the most authoritative account of the region ever written.

Gadi Sagar Tank.

North of Jodhpur

The Rathores' old capital of **Mandore**, 8km (5 miles) north of Jodhpur, boasts landscaped gardens surrounding temples and the *chatris* of the Marwar rulers. Sights include the **Hall of Heroes**, with larger-than-life figures painted in gaudy colours, and the temple of the black Bhairav and the white Bhairav (manifestations of Lord Shiva), where the idols are pasted over with layers of foil paper.

The **Osian Temple** complex (daily 6am–8pm; free), 65km (40 miles) north of Jodhpur, has 16 very fine Hindu and Jain temples, dating from the 8th–12th centuries. The first group, of 11, represents the earliest phase of temple-building in Rajasthan. The largest temple, **Mahavira**, has a sanctum dating from 783–93. As well as rich decoration, the halls are open, with balustrades rather than walls, to provide more light. This group also contains one of the few temples to Surya (the sun god). The second group is later and contains the fine 12th-century **Sachiya Mata Temple**.

Jaisalmer

Jaisalmer ⓱, land of the Bhatti princes, born of the moon, is by far the oldest Rajput capital, dating from AD 1156. The vision of its crumbling sandstone ramparts rising seamlessly from the desert sands, capped by carved temple towers and the domed kiosks of medieval palaces, is one of the most compelling in India, drawing tens of thousands of tourists each winter across the Thar from Jodhpur, a six-hour train ride to the west. The resulting commercialism has proven a mixed blessing for the town, but Jaisalmer remains – for all the signboards, touts and gimcrackery crammed into its narrow streets – undeniably beautiful. It's also the region's main springboard for camel safaris, offered by every hotel and guesthouse, and easily the most memorable way to engage with the unique landscape unfolding from the citadel walls.

Jaisalmer's fort, built in 1156 of soft yellow Jurassic sandstone, is like a city in miniature, enclosing a tightly packed warren of *havelis*, shops and hotels divided by narrow alleyways. A paved road winds to the square standing in

its centre, **Main Chowk**, which is overlooked by the five-storey facade of the **Palace of the Maharawal** (daily 9am–6pm). Royal heirlooms and medieval sculpture make up most of its interesting collection, but the architecture itself is the main attraction.

Tours wind up at the **Rani ki Mahal** (Queen's Palace), an ornately filigreed chamber that was rebuilt using funds donated by the NGO Jaisalmer in Jeopardy (www.jaisalmer-in-jeopardy.org). JIJ was set up to help forestall the fort's buildings from literally falling apart: the erosion of its foundations caused by a dramatic increase in water consumption over the past couple of decades has resulted in the collapse of several major landmarks, including parts of the palaces and two whole bastions.

Jaisalmer fort, together with five other hill forts in Rajasthan: Amber, Gagron, Kumbhalgarh, Ranthambore and Chittorgarh (www.hillfortsrajasthan. nic.in), were added to the Unesco World Heritage list in 2013.

Jaisalmer's havelis

In the town, wrapped around the base of the fort, stand many beautiful *havelis*, dating from the era when Jaisalmer formed an important outpost on the trans-Thar caravan route. Before the creation of the Indo-Pakistan border in 1947 brought overland trade with neighbouring Sind to an abrupt end, the bazaars here were stacked with exotic produce carried by camel across the sandy wastes to the west. The trade peaked in the 18th and 19th centuries, when vast sums were spent on building and decorating houses out of the malleable local stone. Jaisalmer's *silavats* (stone carvers) were famous all over western India, and their work continues to look as fresh as it did 100 or more years ago: projecting balconies, domes and window frames were all exquisitely sculpted into elaborate forms.

One of the finest examples is **Patwa Haveli** (also known as Patwon-ki-Haveli; daily 8am–7pm), constructed in the first half of the 19th century by a family of Jain traders. Further southwest on Gadi Sagar Road, **Salim Singh Haveli** (daily 8am–6pm) once belonged to a former prime minister and ranks among the town's top three period properties in the town, along with **Nathmali-ki-Haveli**, off Court Road, immediately north of the fort.

Flanked by ghats and little domed shrines, the **Gadi Sagar Tank**, on the south side of town, dates from 1367 and affords a lovely view of Jaisalmer's amber-coloured ramparts. The triple-arched gateway leading to it, the Tilon-ki-Pol, was commissioned in 1909 by a wealthy courtesan named Tilon, much to the displeasure of local worthies, who tried to get the structure pulled down on the grounds that it was built using ill-gotten gains. The maharaja eventually bowed to public pressure and ordered its removal, but Tilon outwitted everyone by having a shrine to Vishnu installed on the gate's upper parapet, thereby making any attempt to destroy it an act of desecration. The gateway stands to this day, forming the perfect frame for what must rank among the most perfect views anywhere in India.

TRIPS INTO THE THAR

There's no better way to explore the Thar Desert than on camel back, and in Jaisalmer, camel safaris are big business. Trips range from half-day tours of the outskirts to week-long expeditions, complete with luxury hunting tents, gourmet meals and performances by music and dance troupes. Two or three nights tends to be long enough for most people. Accompanied by a cook, English-speaking guide and camel man, you can plod around a constellation of mud-and-thatch villages, taking in some of the less accessible highlights in the desert around the town en route.

Topping most itineraries are the ruins of ancient Loduvra, capital of the Bhatti rulers before the foundation of Jaisalmer, and the Akal Fossil Park, where the fragments of huge Jurassic trees are scattered over a patch of remote desert. Some safari operators also start their tours at the photogenic village of Khuri, beautifully decorated with geometric white murals and mirror-encrusted mudwork. The honeypot of the safari scene, however, is Sam, 40km (25 miles) west of Jaisalmer, where a wedge of soft sand dunes attracts swarms of hawkers, guides, itinerant musicians and busloads of day trippers, which can make the whole experience of watching the fabled sunsets an anticlimax if you've spent days riding there.

INDIAN RAILWAYS

For a true taste of India, its people and landscape, nothing beats travelling by train on one of the most comprehensive networks in the world.

Indian Railways is a huge state-run conglomerate, the world's largest employer, with over a million staff. It moves 10 million passengers a day, yet still remains remarkably efficient – and uniquely poetic. There is no better way to get the pulse of the country than to view the changing scene from a carriage window.

The British laid most of the 62,000km (38,500 miles) of track in the 19th century, but it has been remarkably well maintained and modernised, while reservations are now computerised at most stations.

The stations themselves are hives of human activity, with passengers going one way, red-clad porters the other, and amongst them all a succession of hawkers selling everything from tea to snacks to peanuts to magazines, each belting out their sales pitch more exuberantly than the other. Things calm down a notch once you are inside the train, although silence is definitely rare: those same hawkers often find their way on board, families roam around, doors and windows open and close in a refreshingly un-automated manner.

The scenery can be breathtaking, particularly along the coasts, with the Mumbai–Goa stretch an all-time favourite. The hill railways of India are famous for their character and quaintness, often served by 'toy trains' – narrow carriages ride narrow rails at impossible inclines as forests and occasional panoramic views pass by on either side.

Riding on the roof of a train is less common than it was, but there are certainly exceptions, as these devotees returning from a Hindu festival in Mathura prove.

Waiting for the Darjeeling Himalayan Railway, nicknamed the 'Toy Train'.

A porter carries a passenger's luggage on the platform of a railway station.

The Royal Rajasthan on Wheels; the last word in luxury train travel.

RAIL TOURISM

There are a number of seasonal, super-luxury trains aimed at foreign tourists in India that are the last word in elegance on rails, faithful replicas of the private carriages of the former maharajas. Each runs on a unique route, taking in a selection of outstanding sites on the way, with the journey typically lasting up to a week. Whilst the rolling stock may be old-fashioned, the carriages have been refurbished to a high standard, with each typically featuring private cabins, wall-to-wall carpeting, a mini-bar and a kitchenette.

Best known of them all is the Palace on Wheels, which runs through Rajasthan and features two turbaned valets for each air-conditioned carriage, two dining cars and a luxuriously appointed bar. However, another service, Royal Rajasthan on Wheels (www.royalrajasthanonwheels.co.in), is even more luxurious, offering contemporary designs with all mod cons. Rajasthan is the most popular area for these trains, although there are a couple of services in the South as well, one plying the Mumbai Goa stretch mentioned above and the other taking a tour of the hills of Karnataka (see page 422).

hawker sells fruit on a train in Kolkata.

A train driver prepares his engine for a daily journey on the Darjeeling 'toy train'.

n Indian Railways network train passes through the hill ation of Araku Valley on the Kothavalasa-Kirandul railway ne on the East Coast Railway (Odisha and Andhra Pradesh).

A Lambada woman wearing traditional jewellery in Gujarat.

GUJARAT

A compelling mix of tradition and modernity, Gujarat lies off the main tourist trail, making it a rewarding destination for those keen to discover the 'real' India.

Through the blaring cacophony of bicycles, autorickshaws, cars and bullock carts, a motorcycle with large milk cans tied astride darts through the streets of Ahmedabad with its rider bedecked in a brilliant red turban, flashing golden earrings and a fierce moustache. He is a Rabari from the milk-vending community, who has adopted modern transportation while continuing to wear his traditional dress. He is the essence of Gujarat, where tradition and modernity combine in a vibrant, dynamic fashion.

Past and present

Archaeological finds at Lothal near Dhandhuka in Ahmedabad district and Rozadi in Saurashtra carry the history of this western corner of India back 3,500 years to the age of Harappa and Mohenjodaro. In legend, the epics and *Puranas* tell of how Krishna and his brother Balarama left Mathura and settled at Kusathali (Dwarka) on Gujarat's western coast.

The name 'Gujarat' derives from the Gurjaras, an immigrant people of obscure origin who entered India through the northern passes, made their way through the Punjab and settled in lands that came to be known as Gujarat from around the 10th century.

Gradually, a flair for maritime and mercantile pursuits developed a

spirit of enterprise and produced a prosperous Gujarati middle class that wielded considerable influence, with traders and artisans forming powerful guilds.

The state divides into three principal regions. In the northwest is semi-arid Kutch, while Saurashtra makes up the western Kathiawar Peninsula, between the gulfs of Kutch (Kachchh) and Khambhat (Cambay). The eastern parts of the state, including the capital Ahmedabad, make up the third region – mostly fertile

Main Attractions
Jama Masjid, Ahmedabad
Sun Temple, Modhera
Kutch
Somnath
Mount Girnar
Sasan Gir Lion Sanctuary
Diu Island
Palitana

Ornately carved temple, Ahmedabad.

Fishermen on the Rann of Kutch, a remote marshy area.

lands of wheat, cotton, peanut and banana plantations. The southern border area is hilly.

A less attractive side of Gujarat is manifest in the popularity of the Hindu chauvinist BJP, which runs the state government. This strain of militant Hinduism was seen at its worst during communal riots in 2002. After a terrorist attack on a train carrying *kar sevaks* (Hindu volunteers) to the disputed religious site at Ayodhya (see page 71), gangs of Hindus roamed the streets of Ahmedabad and other major centres, looting, killing and driving out Muslims. Eyewitnesses report the police standing by, or even helping, while the gangs did their worst, prompting speculation that members of the ruling BJP, then marshalled by Chief Minister Narendra Modi, were complicit in the violence (a charge of which he was officially cleared a decade later). By the time the troubles subsided, between 1,000 and 2,000 people had been massacred and 150,000 displaced, the majority of them Muslims. Modi was criticised

both in his home state and abroad for the government's failure to halt the carnage (the US revoked his visa), but this didn't stop him from winning a fourth successive term in 2012, nor being elected prime minister of India in 2014.

Ahmedabad

The reign of Sultan Ala-ud-Din Khilji of Delhi witnessed the creation of the first Muslim empire in India, and one of his earliest conquests was the wealthy kingdom of Gujarat in 1300. But it didn't last long: following Timur's attack on northern India, Gujarat broke off from the weakened Delhi Sultanate to form its own state. Before long, in 1411, Ahmad Shah I founded **Ahmedabad** ❶ as his capital, on the site of the ancient city of Karnavati.

Today, Ahmedabad's belligerent, swerving autorickshaws, modern Ashram Road with its hotels, shops and cinemas, and the heavily populated industrial sections of town, are all manifestations of its character as a great textile and commercial city

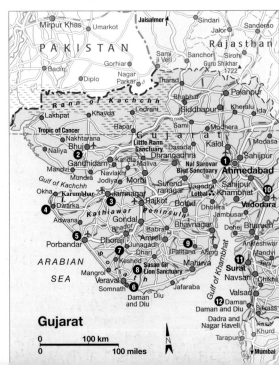

Gujarat

0   100 km
0   100 miles

GUJARAT TRANSPORT

Gujarat has several airports, the busiest being Ahmedabad. Bhuj is served by daily connections to Mumbai, as are Diu, Porbandar, Rajkot, Vadodara, Jamnagar and Bhavnagar.

Ahmedabad: Trains run to Mount Abu (17–24 daily; 3hrs 30mins–5hrs); Bengaluru (1–4 weekly; 36–38hrs); Chennai (1–2 daily; 33–34hrs); Delhi (6–9 daily; 16hrs 30min–19hrs); Dwarka (1–4 daily; 9–10hrs); Jaipur (7–11 daily; 9–13hrs); Jodhpur (5–12 daily; 9–10hrs); Porbandar (1–4 daily; 10hrs 30mins); Vadodara (47–55 daily; 1hr 30min–3hrs 30mins).

Vadodara: Trains run to Ahmedabad (46–58 daily; 1hr 30mins–3hrs 30mins); Delhi (12–15 daily; 11–14hrs); Jaipur (3–7 daily; 11–15hrs); Mumbai (51–54 daily; 5–9hrs 30mins); Porbandar (1–4 daily; 13hrs); Surat (every 30mins; 2hrs).

of western India. Omnipresent is the Sabarmati River, over which six bridges connect the new city with the old.

The city is famous for its Gandhi connections: India's future leader was born in Porbander, on Gujarat's south coast, but based himself in Ahmedabad during the run up to Independence in the 1940s – partly because of its textile industry (which he sought to revitalise as part of his Home Rule campaign against foreign imports) and partly because the city was a communal flashpoint whose rioting threatened to derail negotiations on the country's future.

Numerous examples of medieval architecture survive amid the hectic streets of the old quarter, sprawling from the river's east bank. In the city's 15th- and 16th-century heyday, the ruling sultans recruited local Hindu craftsmen to decorate the impressive mosques, forts and palaces they erected in the capital, and the result was a hybrid Indo-Muslim style of architecture quite distinct from that of their Mughal rivals. A particularly well-preserved example is the **Teen Darwaza**, a chunky, triple-arched gateway carved with a mixture of Islamic calligraphy and typically Hindu ornamentation. Around its base, a lively fruit and vegetable market spills across the surrounding streets on weekdays.

From the *darwaza*, walk east up Mahatma Gandhi Road – the Old City's principal thoroughfare – to the splendid **Jama Masjid** (1424), whose domed prayer hall is supported by 120 pillars, all ornately sculpted with patterns that wouldn't look out of place in a temple of the same period.

Opposite the mosque, the incense-filled **Tomb of Ahmed Shah I** (1442) is enclosed by arcaded verandahs, nowadays occupied by cloth merchants rather than the Sufi mystics and pilgrims who would once have gathered here. The tomb stands as an oasis of calm amid the chaos of appropriately named **Manek Chowk** nearby, where rows of traders dealing in silver jewellery lean against spotless white bolster-pillows, waiting

Gujarat is one of the best places in India to buy fabrics and handicrafts.

Gujarati textiles

Perhaps in reaction to the monochrome desert surroundings in which they are created, Gujarati textiles are spellbindingly vibrant, colourful and distinctive

Gujarat is synonymous with textiles both within India and the world over. A vast array of different types of cloth is still produced here, using traditional techniques unique to this region, and the results are dazzling.

Patterns and prints

Perhaps the best known of all Gujarati textiles is that made using the tie dye, or *bandhani*, technique. Small portions of muslin cloth, or *mulmul*, are bundled together using fine threads; when the cloth is subsequently dyed, the knotted portions of the cloth do not absorb the colour, leaving a pattern of clear sections of cloth. This process is then repeated several times to produce a multi-coloured, intricately patterned design. The main centres for this type of production are Jamnagar, Anjar and Bhuj.

High-end fashion in a Delhi boutique featuring Gujarati fabrics.

Block-printed cotton fabrics are equally popular. In this process a pattern is chiselled onto the surface of a small wooden block, and the block is then dipped in dye and pressed repeatedly against a cloth to produce a design. The results vary greatly from region to region, from the very fine detailing typical of the *Dhamadka* fabrics to the more freewheeling, geometric designs of the tribal *Deesa* prints. This type of textile is most commonly made along the Gondali River, whose waters are said to impart a particularly vibrant hue.

Mashru, a fabric produced from a blend of cotton and silk, was originally made all over India but is now found only in Gujarat. It was first made by Muslims as a way of getting round their prohibition on the wearing of pure silk, and is still popular all over the Muslim world. Patan is where most of this lustrous fabric is produced, with *ikkat* designs the most in demand.

Embroidery

The *patola* pure silk fabrics produced in Patan are prized for being completely reversible. They typically feature animal- or flower-based designs, as intricate on the front as on the back. Embroidery is another skill still widely practised in Gujarat, although its popularity has waned since its 17th-century heyday, when it was probably the foremost centre for commercial embroidery in the world. Marriage costumes, quilts, wall hangings and cradle cloths are all embroidered and often form an important part of the wedding dowry amongst the tribes of the Kutch, with all the women on the bride's side of the family working on the textiles to be hung or used in the bride's new home. Embroidery in the region forms part of a hidden language of caste and social status. You can tell where a woman comes from, which community she belongs to, what her husband does for a living, and even whether she has children or not from the style of mirror work adorning her clothes. Many of the age-old skills are being lost as families move away to the city and women have less time to devote to stitching and sewing.

Kutchi 'bling'

Of all the clothes made from these materials, it is the *abhas* worn by the tribal ladies of the Kutch region that have become the most celebrated, with the best examples being sold at auction houses in London and New York. These traditional costumes typically use bright colours, gold thread, sequins, mirrored glass and tie-dyed patterns to stunning effect: contemporary versions have now become popular amongst the fashion-conscious Indian elite.

for customers. On the upper floors of the buildings on this street are the carved wooden balconies, windows and doorways of old *havelis* (town houses); the most beautiful stand in **Doshivada-ni-Pol**.

Other famous Islamic monuments in the city worth seeking out include **Sidi Saiyad's Mosque** on Dr Tankaria Road, renowned above all for its twin windows of pierced stone, forming a lyrical design of a tree with palm leaves and curving tendrils. The 'shaking' minarets of **Sidi Bashir's Mosque** at Kalipur, just south of the railway station, are among only a few surviving examples of a kind of tower that used to be common throughout Ahmedabad, but which has all but disappeared. Founded on soft sandstone, the minarets sway when their inner walls are shaken – believed to be an anti-earthquake measure.

The **Calico Museum of Textiles** (www.calicomuseum.org; Thur–Tue, two-hour tour at 10.30am by arrangement only: calicomuseum@gmail.com, no baggage is allowed inside the galleries; free) in Shahibag is located in an old *haveli* which houses the Sarabhai Foundation, a public charitable trust. The exceptionally fine collections, which attract enthusiasts from all over the world, include rich brocades and fine embroideries from Kashmir, Gujarat and the southern states, all beautifully displayed. The museum is divided into two wings: the first, given over to its core (secular) gallery; the other portion exhibits religious or iconographic material. Photography is strictly forbidden in both.

Hridey Kunj (www.gandhiashram sabarmati.org; daily 8.30am–6.30pm; free), Mahatma Gandhi's ashram at Sabarmati, is a set of austere yet beautiful buildings nestling amid mango trees. It was from here that Gandhi experimented in non-violent methods of political struggle.

The simple museum, added later, is a fitting tribute. Designed by Charles Correa, a well-known Indian architect, it displays Gandhi's spectacles, sandals, photographs, a spinning wheel and some cloth spun by the great man.

Gujarat Vidyapith, a university established by Gandhi, has a vast collection of books, a museum, research centre and the Navjivan Press, which holds the copyright of Gandhi's works. It is located on the busy Ashram Road and visitors can shop for *khadi* (hand-spun) fabrics and other handmade village industry products at the nearby **Khadi Gramudyog Bhandar**.

Central Gujarat

The central region of Gujarat around Ahmedabad boasts numerous large, highly decorated step wells – *baoli* or *vav*. One of the finest specimens, the **Dad Hari-ni Vav**, stands in the northeast of the city. It was excavated in AD 1500 and decorated with typically Hindu motifs, despite having been paid for by a prominent

Ritual ablutions before worship, Jama Masjid.

member of the sultan's harem. Between 10am and noon, when the sun's rays penetrate its interior, is the best time to visit.

An even more spectacular example is the **Adalaj Vav**, located 19km (11 miles) north of the city, which Sanskrit inscriptions record was built by the wife of a local chief in 1498. Carved images of dancing girls, musicians, birds, animals and some erotic scenes adorn the walls, niches and pillars of the rectangular well. The most magnificent example of a step well, **Rani Ki Vav** (the Queen's Stewell), however, is located some 120km (75 miles) north of Ahmedabad, in Patan, on the banks of Saraswati River. It was built in the 11th century, most probably as a memorial to a Solanki dynasty king. In 2014 the site was added to the Unesco World Heritage list.

The **Sun Temple** at **Modhera**, a three-hour journey by road north of Ahmedabad, is one of the finest examples of Indian temple architecture. Built in 1026, during the reign of King Bhima of the Solanki dynasty, the shrine is dedicated to the sun god,

Surya. It stands on a plinth oriented towards to the east: during the spring and autumn equinoxes the main deity – which for the rest of the year is hidden in half-light – is illuminated by the rays of the rising sun. Elaborately carved figures of gods, goddesses, flowers, dancers, animals and mythical beasts adorn the red sandstone surfaces.

Lothal, 85km (52 miles) southwest of Ahmedabad, is of immense archaeological importance. Only discovered in 1954, and with excavation work still ongoing, a 4,500-year-old city has been unearthed, clearly discernible if only three bricks high. It has been linked to the contemporary remains at Mohenjodaro and Harappa in Pakistan. On the way it's well worth stopping off at **Nal Sarovar Bird Sanctuary**, particularly between November and February when a large number of migratory birds, including flamingos, make this their temporary home. It is best to get there before sunrise, hire a boat and be in a position to see the birds before they see you as the sun comes up.

Crowds gather for a Muslim festival at the Jama Masjid Mosque, Ahmedabad.

THE LAST SHIPYARD

An hour's drive south of Bhuj, Mandvi is a small seaside town that used to be one of the major ports in the region. Few vestiges of its bygone prosperity survive, but the riverbanks on the edge of town are the site of an extraordinary shipyard where ocean-going ships are still hand-made entirely out of wood, just as they have been for centuries. It takes teams of Muslim shipwrights an average of two years to construct each vessel, the largest of which fetch up to $500,000 from wealthy Gulf Arabs, who use them as pleasure craft. No written plans, and very few power tools, are used in the process. Visitors are welcome to look around any half-finished ships looming on the riverbanks; just turn up in working hours (any day except Friday) and seek permission from the foreman.

Kutch: isolation and refuge

Sandwiched between Indian Sau-rashtra and Pakistani Sind, Kutch (or Kachchh), in the far northwest of Gujarat, has always been a land apart. Until the recent construction of permanent road and rail links, the region used to be cut off for months on end by monsoon flood-waters flowing off the Aravalli range to its northeast. When these recede, they leave in their wake vast flats of cracked mud and salt, broken by opal-blue pools of brine and distant flocks of flamingo: in the north, the Great Rann, and in the south, its smaller sibling, the Little Rann. In the past, local Rabari camel herders knew the safe routes to the main-land, but nowadays the only foot-prints you're likely to find on the Ranns are those of arms smugglers, desperate salt miners and herds of wild asses.

This extreme physical isolation explains why Kutch has tradition-ally been a place of refuge for tribes, castes and clans fleeing persecu-tion elsewhere. Over the centuries, a mosaic of cultures evolved under the umbrella of the region's tolerant Hindu rulers, the Maharaos. In spite of depopulation, each has managed to preserve its distinct traditions, especially when it comes to costume, architecture, art and crafts, making this one of India's most colourful regions.

The survival of so many minor-ity cultures in Kutch is all the more extraordinary given the fact that on the morning of 26 January 2001 (India's Independence Day) the region was devastated by a massive earthquake in which an estimated 25,000 people were killed, and many more made homeless.

One of the worst-hit areas was the medieval walled town of **Bhuj** ❷, regional capital and site of the Maha-raos' medieval **palace**. Centrepiece of the complex is an opulent pleasure hall, the Aina Mahal, to which the king would repair to listen to poetry and compose music, soothed by dozens of delicate indoor fountains. Many of its ceilings collapsed in the earthquake, but the famous **Hall**

TIP

The best source of information on Kutch, and how to explore the craft villages lying to the north of Bhuj, is the caretaker of the Aina Mahal museum, Mr Pramod Jethi, who runs his informal tourist desk (Sat–Thur 9am–1pm, 3–6pm) from the palace's ticket counter.

Kite festival, Ahmedabad.

A Lambani gypsy forest dweller.

of Mirrors (www.ainamahalbhuj.com; Fri–Wed 9am–noon, 3–6pm) came through intact, as did most of its precious contents, which now form the basis of an engaging museum.

Kutch is renowned all over India for its handicrafts, especially embroidery and block printing. Each of the region's minority groups maintains its own styles and techniques, and the best way to experience them is to visit the villages where the work is carried out. The semi-desert area north of Bhuj harbours a major concentration of these, easily explored by renting a car, driver and guide for the day. As a primer, start your tour at the excellent **Kala Raksha Trust** (www.kala-raksha.org; Mon–Sat 10am–2pm, 3–6pm; free) in Sumrasar, 25km (15 miles) north of Bhuj, an NGO that is working to help preserve the region's crafts; there's a small museum and shop on site, and workshops where you can watch Rabari and Garasia Jat women at work.

With more time, it's possible to travel out to the fringes of Kutch for a taste of life on the **Ranns**. In the far southeast, the Little Rann is the site of the isolated **Wild Ass Sanctuary**, part of the Little Rann Sanctuary – a 4,850-sq-km (1,870-sq-mile) reserve set up to protect the rare Indian wild ass. Distinguished by their buff-brown coat and ridge of dark fur, these beautiful, shy animals survive on the mud and salt flats, retreating to grassy islets called *bets* when the monsoon floodwaters inundate the rest of the Ranns. The best way to see them is on a jeep safari, arranged through either of the two hotel resorts situated just outside the sanctuary (a 30km/18-mile drive from the nearest railhead at Viramgam).

Exploring Saurashtra

Saurashtra, or **Kathiawar** as it's also known, is the large, spatula-shaped peninsula forming the central heartland of Gujarat, flanked by the Gulf of Kutch to the east and Gulf of Khambhat (Cambay) to the west. Its district headquarters is **Jamnagar** ❸, a walled city with several gateways. The older parts are bursting at the seams, but many areas were planned as recently as 1914 and have a systematic layout of facades, squares, circles and broad streets.

The fort-like **Lakhota Palace** is located in a lake and approached over a stone bridge. It could accommodate 1,000 soldiers, and now houses a fine museum (Thur–Tue 10.30am–2pm, 2.30–5.30pm).

Dwarka ❹, 140km (86 miles) west of Jamnagar, was a flourishing port in ancient times, and a pilgrimage site – believed to have been established by Krishna 5,000 years ago. The **Temple of Dvarkadish** on the northern bank of Gomti Creek is typical of the architecture of old Hindu temples. It has a shrine, a large hall, a roof supported by 60 columns of granite and sandstone, and a conical spire 50 metres (160ft) high. The shrine is elaborately ornamented and has a sculpted figure of Ganesh over the entrance.

Gandhi's birthplace

For those who have a special interest in the life of Mahatma Gandhi, a visit to **Porbandar** ❺, his birthplace (90km/56 miles along the coast from Dwarka), is a pilgrimage worth planning. Gandhi was born in this quiet town in 1869, in his ancestral home. The house has been preserved as a museum (daily 7.30am–7.30pm; free). With its small rooms, trellised windows and carved balconies, it exudes an air of peace and tranquillity.

Driving along quiet coastal roads through Chorwad and Veraval you will reach **Somnath** ❻, 115km (70 miles) from Porbandar. Standing majestically on the shores of the Arabian Sea is one of the 12 most sacred Shiva shrines in India. Ransacked repeatedly by northern invaders and rebuilt successively in gold, silver, wood and finally in stone, it is said to have been built by Soma, the moon god, in penance and worship of the wrathful Lord Shiva, who had laid a curse on him. Nearby a temple marks the spot where Lord Krishna is said to have been accidentally killed by a hunter's arrow. Cymbals are played at dusk to mark the time for prayers.

Junagadh and Amba Mata

Junagadh ❼, in interior southern Saurashtra, ranks among the most ancient towns in India. Buddhist caves chiselled between 200 BC and AD 200 into the rocky hills surrounding it testify to the area's importance as an administrative and religious centre during Mauryan times, while the squat Maqbara tombs clustered in the centre of town recall the heyday of its 19th-century Muslim rulers.

Most visitors who pass through these days do so en route to **Mount Girnar**, an extinct volcano rising out of the plains 4km (2.5 miles) to the east. The massif, which reaches 945 metres (3,100ft), has five distinct peaks, joined by 8,000 or more stone steps that thread their way between a constellation of small Jain and Hindu shrines.

By far the most revered of the shrines is the temple dedicated to

Somnath.

FACT

Gujarat is India's most industrialised state, accounting for 20 percent of the country's GDP (including 50 percent of its petro-chemical production and 45 percent of its pharmaceuticals). The pollution resulting from rapid economic growth has made its cities among the filthiest on the planet. To fuel the boom, a series of super-dams have been built along the Narmada Valley, displacing millions and provoking outrage among civil-rights organisations.

The lions of Gir Forest are the sole remnant of a once extensive population of Asiatic lions.

Amba Mata, also known as 'Ambaji', the mother goddess, which attracts young couples from all over northwestern India petitioning for happy and fruitful marriage. The fifth peak, the one furthest from town, is associated with Kalika, the eternal aspect of Durga, and hosts a community of Aghora *sadhus* – hard-core Shiva-worshipping ascetics who demonstrate their renunciation of the temporal world by drinking out of human skulls, smearing themselves in ashes from funeral pyres and eating excrement.

Lions of the Gir Forest

Sasan Gir Lion Sanctuary ❽, 40km (25 miles) north of Somnath (www. girnationalpark.in; mid-Oct–mid-June, Thur–Tue 8–11am, 3pm–dusk; safaris daily at 6.30, 9am and 3pm, booking well ahead is advisable), is one of the last places in the world where Asiatic lions can be seen in their natural habitat. Efforts at conservation began in the **Gir Forest**. In 1900 the nawab of Junagadh, in whose territory most of the forest lay, had

invited the viceroy, Lord Curzon, for a lion *shikar* (hunt). When the viceroy accepted, a newspaper published a letter that questioned the propriety of an important person doing further damage to an endangered species. Lord Curzon not only cancelled his *shikar*, but also advised the nawab to protect the remaining lions, which he duly did. These days the Gir Forest is one of the most important game preserves in India, and a successful conservation project: early in the 20th century there were only 100 lions left here; now they number 523 (2015 census).

The Portuguese legacy

The Saurashtran coast always played an important role in the maritime trade between northern India and the Persian Gulf, and the first Portuguese navigators to explore the region were quick to see the strategic potential of a small island called **Diu**, on the peninsula's southernmost tip. In return for military assistance against the Mughals, Sultan Bahadur of Gujarat reluctantly

handed over control of the port in 1535, which the Portuguese managed to retain until Nehru expelled them by force in 1961.

Diu town, clustered on a promontory on the island's eastern tip, has retained plenty of Lusitanian character, with a crop of elegant Indo-Portuguese mansions and churches, and more liberal liquor laws than those prevailing on the mainland. A string of quiet beaches lying within easy reach of the town provide further incentive to stop by here for a few days, while birdwatchers are drawn by the migratory flamingos that stop on the mudflats lining the north of the island in early spring.

Bhavanagar district

Palitana ❾ in Bhavanagar district almost completes the full circle of Saurashtra. Just to the south is the **Shatrunjaya Hill**, the most important centre of Jain pilgrimage, with an incredible 863 Jain temples atop its twin peaks.

It is worth heading back in the direction of Ahmedabad via **Surendranagar** and **Wadhwan**. The ancestors of the stone-carvers of Wadhwan built Dwarka and Somnath. Skilled stone-carvers live and practise their craft near **Hawa Mahal**, a finely conceived but unfinished palace at the edge of the town. Traders in Surendranagar town have a vast collection of old embroideries and artefacts from all over Saurashtra.

Eastern Gujarat

The 'industrial corridor' of Gujarat lies due south of Ahmedabad. In its hinterland is the exclusively Adivasi belt, whose rural societies lead very different lives to those in the mercantile centres elsewhere in the state (see page 34).

The industrial city of **Vadodara ❿** (formerly Baroda), 115km (70 miles) southeast of Ahmedabad, was capital of one of the richest 'princely states' in pre-Independence India. The Old Town has a number of attractions associated with the ruling maharajas, including the once opulent **Lakshmi Vilas Palace**.

A Champaner mosque.

Vadodara serves as a springboard for trips to the deserted Muslim city of **Champaner**, 45km (28 miles) northeast. A wealth of intricately carved mosques, tombs and gateways bearing exquisite Islamic calligraphy survive from the late 14th century, when the town, then known as Muhammabad, served as the sultan of Gujarat's capital. Despite being classed as a Unesco World Heritage Site, it sees few visitors and has an almost forlorn feel.

Surat ⓫, on the east coast of the Gulf of Khambhat, was the first outpost established (in 1608) by the British East India Company and was on one of the old trade routes for silks, embroideries and spices. Today the city is the epicentre of one of India's fastest growing industrial areas, and a major diamond market accounting for 90 percent of India's diamond trade.

Despite its historic pedigree, however, the city holds few monuments of note. Pollution and appalling traffic rather than heritage architecture are likely to be your most lasting memories. That said, one colonial-era vestige warrants a detour. A fifteen-minute rickshaw ride from the centre off Kataragama Road, a weed-infested British cemetery holds the splendidly hybrid, domed mausoleums of the East India Company officials who died here between the seventeenth and nineteenth centuries, the grandest of them belonging to Sir George Oxenden (1620–69), the first governor of Bombay.

In the far south, the one location worth breaking a journey down the coast to visit is the former Portuguese outpost of **Daman ⓬**, where a 16th-century fort encloses a collection of grand Lusitanian churches and *palácios* overlooking the mouth of the Damanganga River. Only at Old Goa will you find Baroque facades so beautifully preserved. Daman's other claim to fame is its Union Territory Status (shared with Diu), which means its liquor licensing laws are more lenient than those of Gujarat – and why the town gets inundated most weekends by jeep loads of heavy-drinking Gujarati men.

A young woman and child, Diu Island.

Fishermen untangling their lines, Diu Island.

Tourist headgear for sale at Anjuna flea market.

WEST-CENTRAL INDIA

From the bright lights of Mumbai to golden
Goan beaches, the breathtaking ancient sites
and remote jungles of the interior, India's
west-central heartlands are full of interest.

Garlanded bus.

Washed by the Arabian Sea, the metropolis of
Mumbai, formerly Bombay, is the country's
most cosmopolitan city, and sets the pace for all
western India. The commerce and cinema of Mumbai
draw visitors from all walks of life, and increasingly
from all over the world; this is perhaps the only truly
international city on the Subcontinent. The hub of the
new India, Mumbai is the centre of business and industry that is defining the rise of the country's increasingly
global ambitions.

To the south, the lush Konkan coast extends
hundreds of miles to the formerly Portuguese
Goa, one of the first European toeholds in Asia.
A short flight from Mumbai, this is the water-
ing hole for the city's rich and has become a
hedonistic beach centre for clubbers, hippies,
backpackers, expats and artists – increasing numbers of them from Russian and the former Soviet
states. During the winter season it's a busy, bustling, vibey mix; the rest of the year is warmer
but more relaxed, and monsoon is a time of
thundering waves and spectacular skyscapes
above the forts and churches, with the winter
tourists long gone.

Sacred bull at Benaulim.

Inland from Mumbai, the forested hills of the
Western Ghats form a divide between the coastal
plains and the harsher environment of the Deccan plateau. The state
of Maharashtra is most famous for the magnificence of the cave art
at Ajanta and Ellora, but is also home to the interesting city of Pune,
hill stations in the cool heights of the Ghats, and several noteworthy
Hindu temples.

Further to the north and east, the sprawling state of Madhya
Pradesh in the heart of India is best known for the erotic art at
Khajuraho, impressive forts such as Gwalior and Mandu, and magnificent wildlife parks where tigers and leopards prowl by night. Cleaved
off from the eastern part of the state in 2000, Chattisgarh is a largely
rural backwater seldom visited by tourists; it has a large Adivasi population and some of India's largest surviving forests.

Shoemakers in Mumbai.

MUMBAI (BOMBAY)

Surrounded on three sides by the Arabian Sea, India's most populous city is also the country's glamorous commercial hub – a magnet for rich and poor alike.

The story of Mumbai is fascinating. From obscure, humble beginnings as a set of seven small islands separated by tidal creeks and marshes, the city has risen to become India's most important commercial and industrial centre. The seven islands have been merged into one and thus survive only as names of localities like Colaba, Mahim, Mazgaon, Parel, Worli, Girgaum and Dongri.

Modern Mumbai is booming. Home to the wealthy and the glamorous, it has long been India's Hollywood (its former name, Bombay, leading to the genre-defining 'Bollywood'), producing more films each year than any other city in the world. Nowadays, it is also the home of India's own fast-growing satellite and television industries, as well as a rapidly expanding call-centre and back-office support sector.

Mumbai has a vibrancy not found anywhere else in India, and which only exists in the world's biggest cities. Like all big cities – albeit in greater measure than most – Mumbai has its seamy side, its slums and its overcrowding, the foothills of poverty on which are built towering skyscrapers. And like all success stories, there have been chapters of intrigue, violence, happiness and calm, and the struggles of the pre-Independence years, when Mumbai became the political capital of nationalist India.

There is a sad history of violence in the recent past, although after each atrocity, the city has bounced back with impressive resilience. In the 1990s, communal riots between Hindus and Muslims were encouraged by the ultra-right-wing Shiv Sena, and its founder, Bal Thackeray. A series of anonymous bombing campaigns were widely interpreted as the Muslim backlash. In 1993, 10 huge blasts ripped apart key landmarks, among them the Air India building and Stock Exchange, while a car bomb killed 107

Main Attractions
Gateway of India
Cricket maidans
Victoria Terminus
Jyotiba Phule (aka 'Crawford') Market
Mangaldas Lane
Malabar Hill
Dr Bhau Daji Lad Museum
Elephanta Caves

Mumba Devi Temple, Kalbadevi.

outside the Gateway of India in 2003. A series of explosions on packed suburban commuter trains resulted in considerable loss of life in 2006, and in November 2008, parts of the city centre were targeted by terrorists in a three-day siege which left 173 dead.

Harbour city

Mumbai is ranged around a natural harbour at the northern end of India's tropical western shore, the Konkan Coast. With its port already developed by the British, the city grew rapidly following the opening of the Suez Canal in 1869. Today it handles more than 40 percent of India's maritime trade.

India's largest city now stretches 22km (14 miles) into the Arabian Sea. The maximum width of the composite island that constitutes metropolitan Mumbai is no more than 5km (3 miles). Into this narrow strip is squeezed the majority of the city's 18 million people, its major business and commercial establishments, its docks and warehouses, and much of its industry – including most of its

textile industry, which employs thousands of workers.

Tourists focus on the older, southern parts of Mumbai, in districts such as Colaba, Kala Ghoda and Fort. This is where you'll find the greatest concentration of Raj-era buildings and monuments, including the iconic Gateway of India, along with the city's most important galleries and museums. Most of the best accommodation and eating options are also in this area; the majority of visitors will find they'll stick to the southern tip of this city, with no need to head north until they're moving out of town. The Gateway also serves as an embarkation point for launches heading across Mumbai harbour to Elephanta Island, site of an ancient rock-cut cave complex where one of India's greatest archaeological treasures – a giant, triple-headed Shiva sculpture – peers out of the gloom.

The best time to visit Mumbai is during the relatively cool, dry winter period, between November and February. From March onwards, the humidity builds as temperatures rise inland on the Deccan plateau, sucking in moist air from the sea. After weeks of suffocating weather, the monsoon finally erupts in June, bringing curtains of heavy rain that obscure the view and flood the roads. The downpours peter out in October, but the humidity can last until well into November.

Mumbai's population

The Mumbai Municipal Corporation provides primary and secondary education in at least 10 languages, including English, and the city has developed its own patter, 'Bombay speak', which regular Hindi/Urdu speakers find rather comical. It is often caricatured in Indian films.

The Hindu population is largely Marathi, though most non-Marathi locals are also Hindus. The city's Gujarati population includes a large number of Jains.

TRANSPORT TO AND FROM MUMBAI

Mumbai's international airport – CST – is connected by direct flights to destinations worldwide. Its domestic neighbour serves as the region's principal gateway. Getting to the airports from downtown can take literally hours at peak times, so plan your trip accordingly. Or if you're only passing through between flights, consider booking a room in a hotel close to the airport.

Trains run to Ahmedabad (25–35 daily; 6hrs 30min–9hrs 30min); Aurangabad (4–5 daily; 7hrs); Bengaluru (5–9 daily; 23–26hrs 30mins); Chennai (3–4 daily; 23hrs 15mins–26hrs 30mins); Delhi (14–19 daily; 16–29hrs); Hyderabad (5–10 daily; 12–17hrs); Kolkata (4–7 daily; 30–38hrs); Pune (36–39 daily; 2hrs 40min–5hrs 15mins).

Private and inter-state buses run to destinations across central and southern India, often more frequently than trains. Although far less comfortable for long overnight journeys, it is usually easier to obtain tickets at short notice for bus travel than rail.

The government bus depot in Dadar handles express buses to destinations in Maharashtra, including Kolhapur (4–6 daily; 9–11hrs); Nasik (17 daily; 4hrs); Pune (half-hourly; 3hrs 30min–4hrs). For cities further afield, such as Goa, Ahmedabad and Bengaluru, you depart from Mumbai Central bus station.

When the Portuguese arrived, local Muslim nawabs ruled this corner of India, but they handed it over to the newcomers in 1534 in exchange for support against the Mughals. This was the beginning of Mumbai's large Christian (mainly Roman Catholic) population and its many churches, which led to two separate areas in the city becoming known as '**Portuguese Church**'. A few churches retain their Portuguese facades: **St Andrew's** in the suburb of Bandra is a fine example. There are also minor remains of Portuguese fortifications both on the main island and the much larger island of **Salsette** north of the city. At **Vasai** (Bassein), 50km (30 miles) from Mumbai, sprawl ruins of a Portuguese walled settlement.

In 1662 Charles II of England married Catherine of Braganza, a Portuguese princess. As part of the dowry, the British crown received the islands of Mumbai. They were leased to the British East India Company in 1668 at the princely rent of £10 per annum. This company of merchant-adventurers had for some time felt the need for an additional west-coast port, to supplement and ultimately to supplant Surat in Gujarat. Far-sighted governors, such as Gerald Augnier, began the construction of the city and harbour, inviting the settlement of Gujarati merchants and Parsi, Muslim and Hindu manufacturers and traders to help develop the city. This led to the settlement of all these communities in Mumbai.

Cotton boom town

The slow transformation of the swampy islands during the 17th and 18th centuries gave way in the 19th century to rapid change. In 1858, the Honourable East India Company returned them to the British crown. In the 1850s came the steam engine, and by the end of the century Mumbai was linked with central and northern India by the Great Indian Peninsular Railway and, some time later, with eastern India, too.

During this period, Mumbai became an important cotton town. In an early precursor of globalisation – albeit one that operated in reverse order to the typical 21st-century

FACT

Mumbai holds the record for the highest rainfall of any city in a single day. On 26 July, 2005, a drain-defying 942mm (37ins) deluged the Maharashtran capital, causing landslides and extensive flooding estimated to have killed 100 people. It also provoked a storm of criticism for the Shiv Sena municipality, who failed miserably to cope with the emergency and its aftermath.

Portuguese ruins at Vasai, north of Mumbai.

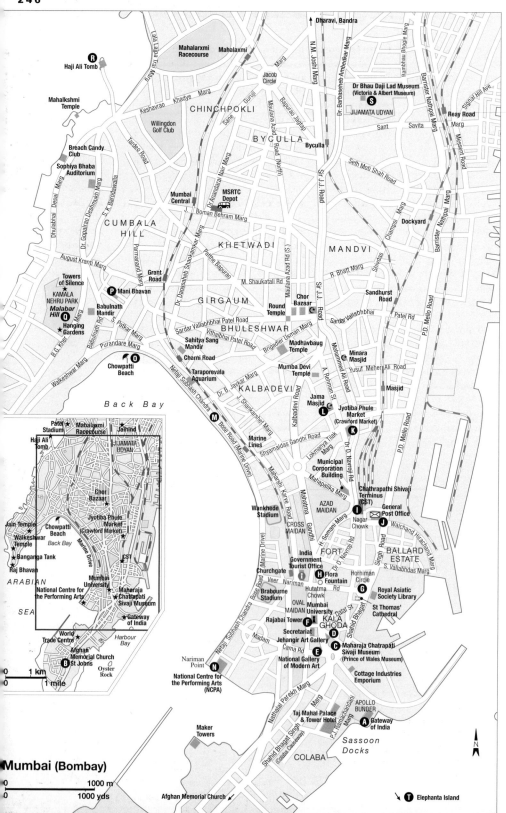

↑ Dharavi, Bandra

® Haji Ali Tomb

Mahalarxmi Racecourse

Mahalaxmi

Mahalkshmi Temple

CHINCHPOKLI

Dr Bhau Daji Lad Museum (Victoria & Albert Museum)

⑤

JIJAMATA UDYAN

Reay Road

Breach Candy Club

Sophiya Bhaba Auditorium

BYCULLA

Byculla

Willingdon Golf Club

Jacob Circle

Dockyard

Mumbai Central

MSRTC Depot

CUMBALA HILL

KHETWADI

MANDVI

Towers of Silence

KAMALA NEHRU PARK

Malabar Hill ⓠ

Hanging Gardens

Babulnath Mandir

ⓟ Mani Bhavan

Grant Road

GIRGAUM

Round Temple

Chor Bazaar

Sandhurst Road

BHULESHWAR

Minara Masjid

Sahitya Sang Mandir

Madhavbaug Temple

Charni Road

Masjid

ⓞ Chowpatti Beach

Taraporevala Aquarium

Mumba Devi Temple

KALBADEVI

Jama Masjid

ⓛ

Jyotiba Phule Market (Crawford Market)

Back Bay

Marine Lines

ⓚ

Patel Stadium

Mahalaxmi Racecourse

Jaihind

Haji Ali Tomb

UJAMATA UDYAN

Chor Bazaar

Municipal Corporation Building

Chathrapathi Shivaji Terminus (CST)

Jain Temple

Jyotiba Phule Market (Crawford Market)

Wankhede Stadium

AZAD MAIDAN

Nagar Chowk

General Post Office

ⓙ

Walkeshwar Temple

Chowpatti Beach

Back Bay

CROSS MAIDAN

ⓘ

Banganga Tank

CST

FORT

BALLARD ESTATE

Raj Bhavan

ARABIAN SEA

Mumbai University

National Centre for the Performing Arts

Maharaja Chatrapati Sivaji Museum

India Government Tourist Office

Churchgate ⓗ Flora Fountain

Brabourne Stadium

Hutatma Chowk

Royal Asiatic Society Library

ⓖ

St Thomas' Cathedral

World Trade Centre

Gateway of India

OVAL MAIDAN

Mumbai University

KALA GHODA

Afghan Memorial Church ⓑ St Johns

Harbour Bay

Oyster Rock

Rajabai Tower ⓕ

Secretariat

Jehangir Art Gallery ⓓ

Maharaja Chatrapati Sivaji Museum (Prince of Wales Museum)

Cama Rd ⓔ

National Gallery of Modern Art

ⓒ

Cottage Industries Emporium

Nariman Point ⓝ

National Centre for the Performing Arts (NCPA)

0   1 km

0   1 mile

APOLLO BUNDER

Taj Mahal Palace & Tower Hotel

ⓐ Gateway of India

Maker Towers

COLABA

Sassoon Docks

N

Mumbai (Bombay)

0   1000 m

0   1000 yds

Afghan Memorial Church

ⓣ Elephanta Island

model – raw cotton from Gujarat was shipped to Lancashire, spun and woven into cloth and brought back to Mumbai for sale all over India. Despite the competition, Mumbai's own cotton textile industry was established in the same period, thanks to the persistence of Mumbai's entrepreneurs. The outbreak of the American Civil War in 1861 and the opening of the Suez Canal gave further impetus to cotton exports, and the city's new-found wealth led to the construction of many impressive buildings.

Gateway of India

The district at the far southern tip of the peninsula, **Colaba**, takes its name from the Koli fisherman who originally inhabited the area when it was an island, prior to British rule. Koli shanty settlements still cower beneath the skyscrapers of **Nariman Point**. After reclamation work in the late 19th century connected it to the rest of the city, the main quayside (Apollo Bunder) served as the landing stage for the massive P&O steamers that brought the burra sahibs and memsahibs of the Raj to India.

Today, Colaba's defining landmark is the grandiloquent **Gateway of India** Ⓐ on the waterfront, a triumphant arch built to commemorate the visit of Britain's George V and Queen Mary for the Delhi Durbar in 1911. Its honey-coloured basalt, decorated with motifs inspired by the Indo-Muslim monuments of medieval Gujarat, catches the light of the rising and setting sun, changing from shades of gold to orange and pink. The King and Queen Empress never passed under the structure, and the monument is – somewhat ironically – better remembered nowadays as the place where the last detachment of British troops slow-marched to their waiting ships in 1947, marking the official end of imperial rule.

Day-trippers congregate en masse on the paved esplanade fronting of the Gateway, taking rides in silver-plated horse-drawn carriages (*gaddis*), having their pictures taken by itinerant photographers and running the gauntlet of balloon sellers and peanut vendors.

Surveying the scene imperiously from the background is the **Taj Mahal**

Using the older-style Mumbai taxis should work out around 40 percent cheaper than the newer air-conditioned models.

The fabric bazaar at Mangaldas Lane.

THE KOLIS

The earliest known inhabitants of Mumbai were a caste of fisherfolk called the Kolis, who are thought to have migrated here from the coast of Gujarat in prehistoric times. Their descendants still occupy patches of beach in the south of the city, hemmed in by skyscrapers. In spite of industrial pollution and real-estate pressure, the Kolis continue to maintain their traditional way of life. They're also something of a thorn in the side of the municipality and its landshark backers, organising marches to protest against over-fishing by trawlers and other factors threatening to squeeze them out. It was the Kolis who first worshipped the goddess Mumba Devi, whose name Maharashtran nationalists insist lies at the root of the word 'Bombay' – hence the Marathi 'Mumbai'.

The Parsis

Although not as influential as they once were, the Parsis are an example of India's cultural diversity, at once completely distinct and yet undeniably Indian

Parsis form a fascinating part of Mumbai's diverse ethnicity. Originally from Iran, these followers of the Zoroastrian faith left their homeland following the emergence of Islam in the 8th century. Mumbai has the greatest concentration of Parsis in India, and while their overall numbers may be small, their influence on the city is far greater than the numbers would suggest.

Migration

The earliest Zoroastrian migrants settled in Gujarat, and it was not until the 17th century, when the British East India Company began to establish Bombay as a trading post, that the Parsis moved south to take advantage of the new job opportunities on offer. They brought with them from Iran an indigenous caste system that they initially tried to maintain, but soon

The Brittania, a Parsi restaurant in the Fort area of Mumbai.

realised that their limited numbers made such a system impractical, and so abolished all castes apart from that of high priest. This in turn endeared them to the British, who had little patience for the vagaries of the Indian system, with one employee refusing to work with another purely for reasons of caste.

British schools were soon established and enthusiastically attended by the Parsi community, who in turn saw their literacy rates rise high above those of the Indian population (today they're at 98 percent, compared with a national average of 74 percent), and led to even closer ties with the British, who soon had Parsis installed in their most senior positions. From a community largely comprising weavers and small-time merchants, Parsis now rose to prominence as bankers and industrialists, and began to play an increasingly important role in the life of Mumbai as a whole.

Decline

By the end of the 19th century there were 48,000 Parsis living in Mumbai, accounting for 6 percent of the city's population, but since then their relative numbers have gone into decline; they now represent just 0.006 percent of the Indian population. One explanation for this is their longevity: 31 percent of Parsis are over 60 years old, against a national average of only 7 percent. Another statistical quirk is that for every 1,050 female Parsis there are only 1,000 males, against the national average of 933 females to every 1,000 males. Out-migration, particularly to the US and Canada, has also taken its toll.

The dwindling numbers are sharply reflected in the declining congregations at Zoroastrian fire temples, or agiaries, throughout the city. Fewer Parsis are also opting for the traditional way of disposing of deceased family members: by placing corpses on top of so-called Towers of Silence on Malabar Hill for vultures to devour their flesh.

Visitors to Mumbai are most likely to encounter Parsis at the long-established eateries around Colaba in south Mumbai. The most famous of these is Leopold Café, which achieved international notoriety after featuring in David Gregory Roberts' hit novel *Shantaram*, and, during the 2008 terrorist attacks, when gunmen opened fire on its crowded interior, killing 12 people.

For an insider's perspective on life in the Parsi community of post-Independence Mumbai, it's worth seeking out the novels of acclaimed expatriate writer Rohinton Mistry, which include *A Fine Balance* (1995) and the Man Booker Prize-winning *Family Matters* (2002).

Palace and Tower. After the Parsi industrialist J.N. Tata was refused entry to the 'European' hotel Watson's, he exacted revenge by constructing a far more opulent competitor nearby. It opened in 1903, and heads of state and celebrities have been passing through its doors ever since (Watson's, by contrast, closed decades ago). Legend has it that the architects who designed the building placed its entrance on the wrong side by mistake (the old main gate used to be on the landward-facing flank, behind a courtyard now occupied by the hotel pool). In fact the choice was intentional: it maximised the number of rooms with sea views.

The huge terracotta dome, Swiss gables and elaborate corner towers of the Taj have become almost as iconic of the city as the nearby Gateway of India. During the 2008 terror attack, TV reports and newspaper front pages the world over featured surreal images of the familiar grey-and-white edifice engulfed in flames and smoke. The building, however, has since seen a complete refit and continues to serve as Mumbai's premier five-star, hosting visiting dignitaries and cricket teams.

Colaba

Head down Colaba's main street, SBS. Marg (still better known by its pre-independence name, 'Colaba Causeway') for 10 minutes and you'll reach the gates of **Sassoon Docks**, where the city's trawler fleet lands its catch each morning. If you can cope with the overpowering stench, it's worth wandering around the quays to watch the fish being flung into crates of ice balancing on the heads of waiting porters, who carry them at top speed to the adjacent auction halls for sale. Hundreds of boats tie up here during the day, their flags, masts and rigs forming one of Mumbai's more arresting spectacles. This is also where you will see the city's signature dish, 'Bombay Duck', being dried in the salty breezes.

You'll need to jump on a bus, or catch a cab, to reach Colaba's other

notable Raj-era monument. Now dwarfed by the tower blocks of Nariman Point to the north, in its mid-19th-century heyday the **Afghan Memorial Church of St John the Evangelist** Ⓑ dominated the city's skyline. Consecrated in 1858 as a memorial to those who fell in the First Afghan War, it is a lovely piece of architecture, with Gothic arches and stained-glass windows. Plaques on the walls recall the names of officers who perished in the ill-conceived North-west Frontier campaign, along with the battle-scarred colours of the Bombay Army, annihilated in the infamous 1842 Retreat from Kabul.

Kala Ghoda

Immediately north of Colaba is the district known as **Kala Ghoda**, or 'Black Statue', referring to the equestrian figure of Edward VII that once presided over its main intersection. The statue has been removed, but the huge colonial buildings erected around it at the height of the cotton boom still stand as evocative reminders of the Raj at its peak. The most distinctive of them all is

Laundry at the dhobi ghats.

Mumbai's former name, Bombay, was almost certainly derived from the Portuguese 'Bom Bahia', meaning 'Good Bay'. In 1995 it was changed to reflect the area's pre-colonial roots. Mumbai is derived from 'Mumba Devi', a popular local Hindu goddess whose shrine was originally on the site of CST (VT) station. To make room, the deity was shifted uptown in the 1880s, where she still presides over a temple in the bazaar district (see page 253).

The national pastime played out on the Maidan.

the domed **Prince of Wales Museum**, now re-named the **Maharaja Chatrapati Sivaji Museum ⓒ** (www.csmvs. in; daily 10.15am–6pm), on Mahatma Gandhi Road (M.G. Road). A whimsical fusion of Gujarati, Bijapuri and British municipal architecture, the building is of as much interest as the fine collection of antiquities it houses. Treasures showcased in the Key Gallery, just inside the entrance on the ground floor, include inlaid Mughal daggers, Lucknowi *bidri* hookah pipes, and a handful of remarkable 5th-century terracotta bas-reliefs and busts, unearthed in the ancient Buddhist ruins of Mirapur Khas in 1909. On the first floor is the museum's famous collection of Indian paintings, among which are miniatures and illuminated manuscripts from Akbar's own library. Tibetan Buddhist artefacts, coins, Chola bronzes and some wonderfully ornate Gujarati woodcarvings occupy side rooms off the staircase leading to the top floor, where among an array of grizzly weapons hangs a suit of armour recently discovered to have belonged to Akbar.

The **Jehangir Art Gallery ⓓ**, next to the museum, stages regular exhibitions of contemporary art and crafts. On the opposite side of M.G. Road, completing the cultural triumvirate, is the **National Gallery of Modern Art ⓔ** (Tue–Sun 11am–6pm), where contemporary paintings and installations occupy an intriguing space converted from a former concert hall.

Bounding the west side of Kala Ghoda are the great **maidans** – open parks that once formed clear fields of fire for East India Company troops, and which now host cricket matches throughout the day. A phalanx of architectural behemoths dating from the late 19th century form a suitably imperious backdrop to the matches.

'A massive pile whose main features have been brought from Venice, but whose beauty vanished in the transhipment', was how G.W. Forrest described the former **Secretariat** in 1903, which today serves as the City Civil and Sessions Court. Next door, **Mumbai University** was designed by the Gothic Revival genius Gilbert Scott, of St Pancras fame. Its centrepiece, paid for by

the wealthy Parsi philanthropist, the aptly named **Cowasjee Readymoney**, is a high-roofed **Convocation Hall** whose church-like profile wouldn't have looked out of place beside the Thames. Jan Morris once categorised the library next door as 'Oxbridge Absolute'. In a similarly lofty Victorian style, the **Rajabai Clock Tower** , which overshadows both, once chimed the hours with 'Rule Britannia' and 'God Save the King'.

Fort

The name of Mumbai's financial hub, the **Fort** area is a throwback to the all-but-forgotten citadel the East India Company erected after it took possession of Mumbai's seven islands from the Portuguese in 1668. Once British military supremacy had been firmly established in the 19th century, the old ramparts and their three gateways were pulled down and the moat filled in to make way for a much grander downtown area that better expressed the achievements of the Raj. Now, only a few small fragments of the Georgian stronghold remain, but the Victorian streets that supplanted it are still impressive, accommodating the city's biggest banks, financial institutions and newspapers. It's a compelling district to wander around, especially after working hours, when legions of crisp-shirted employees congregate at the *pao bhaji* and tea stalls, girding themselves for the long slog home by train.

The main artery slicing from east to west through this part of town bisects **Horniman Circle** , an incongruously serene, shady oasis in the heart of the old city, ringed by wrought-iron railings and curved ranks of grand sandstone facades. Formerly known as 'Elphinstone Circle', after a former governor, the garden, which occupies the site of the old cotton auction and parade ground, is overlooked on its east side by the Doric columns and neoclassical pediments of the former **Town Hall**, home to the **Royal Asiatic Society Library** (Mon–Sat 10.30am–6.30pm). Along with copies of every book printed in India, the archives stored on its dusty shelves include more than 10,000 rare antique manuscripts,

FACT

The travel writer and critic Robert Byron was less than enthusiastic about British Bombay, which he described as an 'architectural Sodom'. Aldous Huxley was no more impressed: 'Architecturally', insisted the author of Brave New World, 'Bombay is one of the most appalling cities in either hemisphere'.

Tiffin wallah.

TIFFIN WALLAHS

In the rising heat of late morning, the streets around Churchgate Station are thronged with people pushing hand carts or bicycles laden with little aluminium tins. These porters, distinguished by their traditional Maharashtran 'Nehru caps' and baggy pyjamas, offer a delivery service unique to Mumbai, ferrying some 160,000 home-cooked lunches for local workers from the suburbs each day. They do it using a colour code painted on the lids of the tiffin tins – a system of staggering efficiency (only one box in 6 million goes astray, allegedly). Bill Clinton and Sir Richard Branson are among those who have come to see how they achieve such a success rate. Curious visitors can accompany the tiffin wallahs on their rounds, via a scheme run by the Nutan Mumbai Tiffin Box Suppliers Charity Trust.

among them a copy of Dante's *Divine Comedy* rumoured to be worth US$3 million – Mussolini once tried to buy it but was turned down. With its statues of old worthies, dark teak bookcases and paddle fans spinning listlessly overhead, the reading room feels lost in a delightful time warp.

On the opposite (west) side of the circle, **St Thomas' Cathedral** ranks among the oldest surviving buildings in the city. It opened on Christmas Day 1718, complete with cannon-proof roof, and is worth a visit for a browse of the memorial plaques to Company servants and soldiers, many of whom met with untimely, and often violent, deaths in the service of the nascent empire.

A five-minute walk west along V.N. Road brings you to **Hutatma Chowk** (Martyrs' Square), a busy intersection formerly known as **Flora Fountain** ⒽⒽ. The fountain in question, depicting a scantily clad Roman goddess of spring hewn from handsome Portland stone (nowadays covered with prosaic white paint), was erected in honour of the governor, Sir Henry Bartle Edward Frere, who built the new Mumbai in the 1860s. The rather less elegant memorial that has given the square its new name – Hutatma – commemorates those who lost their lives in the cause of setting up a separate Maharashtra state in the Indian Union.

Victoria Terminus

Continuing west from Hutatma Chowk, follow the route covered by a tidal wave of commuters each day as they pass between the Oval and Cross maidans to reach **Churchgate station**, a mass of blue-grey basalt and white Indo-Saracenic domes built in the 1890s, and now the headquarters of the Western Railway.

Churchgate and the other Victorian buildings lined up along the maidans may be imposing, but they're small fry compared with the mighty bulk of **Victoria Terminus**, to the northeast. Now renamed **Chathrapathi Shivaji Terminus** ❶ (CST for short), the headquarters of the **Central Railway** was by far the biggest station in the world when it was built in 1887 – a fitting monument to the Raj at the height of its powers. A British lion and recumbent Indian tiger flank the main gateway, as 'Progress', with arm raised prophetically above the massive central dome, looks down on the traffic swirling past. Inside, polychrome marble, polished Aberdeen granite and richly carved woodwork combine with friezes of carved stone animals and birds to stunning effect – not that the streams of commuters who pour past them have much time to admire the decor. CST remains India's busiest railway station.

A short walk southeast across hectic Nagar Chowk brings you to the **General Post Office** ❶, another splendid Raj-era vestige, considered as the pinnacle of Indo-Saracenic architecture, which sought to blend Indian elements with civic building. Wander into the cavernous central hall, with its circular stamp counter, for an inside view of the magnificent dome crowning the structure.

MUMBAI TRANSPORT

To travel downtown from the airport, it's easiest to take a prepaid taxi from the booth outside the main terminal. (Autorickshaws aren't allowed into central Mumbai.) Mumbai's fleet of ageing taxis has been radically overhauled. The new cars come in two categories: standard non-air conditioned, which are yellow-and-black; and blue air-conditioned 'Cool Cabs'. The latter charge 40 percent more. Drivers are happy to use their meters, but the actual fare is calculated using a 'conversion chart', which you're entitled to consult, though you usually end up haggling.

The cheapest way to get around town is by bus. The Brihanmumbai Electric Supply and Transport (BEST), operates a network that extends to every corner of the metropolis and its outlying suburbs. For journey planning, consult the website, www.bestundertaking.com, which has a user-friendly 'point to point' facility.

Casual visitors should probably avoid Mumbai's over-burdened suburban rail network. More than 6 million commuters travel on its decrepit trains each day – during peak periods, carriages carry three times their maximum capacities, resulting in what the rail company refers to as a 'Super Dense Crush Load'. A massive metro system is currently under construction. The first 12km (7.4-mile) section of line 1, including 12 stations, was inaugurated in 2014, but the full network is not expected to be rolled out until 2021.

Kalbadevi and Bhuleshwar

Kalbadevi, immediately north of CST and the maidans, is the city's main bazaar district: a jam-packed tangle of lanes lined with wood-galleried tenements and pistachio-hued mosques. Before venturing in, browse through the aisles of the British-era covered market on the corner of D.N. Marg and Lokmanya Tilak Marg. The arched entrances to **Jyotiba Phule Market ⓚ** (still widely known as Crawford Market are spanned by bas-reliefs of toiling, well-fed peasants designed by Rudyard Kipling's father, Lockwood. Inside are rows of brightly lit stalls where you can buy anything from wigs to parakeets – though be prepared to haggle hard. The market's future is under threat from developers.

Opposite the market, **Mangaldas Lane** is Mumbai's main fabric bazaar, leading to the heart of the Muslim district centred on the **Jama Masjid Mosque ⓛ**, with its green-washed domes and stucco-covered minarets. In the surrounding streets are many tiny shops selling perfume – a traditional Muslim trade. Keep heading north and you'll eventually arrive at the cream-and-turquoise-coloured tower of the **Mumba Devi Temple**, after whose deity the local municipality renamed the city.

Further north still, **Bhuleshwar** is one of the most charismatic corners of central Mumbai, its bazaars specialising in fresh flowers: lotus blooms, hibiscus and vibrant orange marigolds strung into garlands as offerings for one of the 85 Shiva temples in the neighbourhood. During the 18th and 19th centuries, communities from across western India settled here, and the cosmopolitan feel is clearly discernible in the architecture, which shows Gujarati, Rajasthani and Konkani influences. In a backstreet off the main market, near a couple of white marble temples, immigrant Jains founded the **Panjarapool animal sanctuary**, where 400 or more sleek brown *ghir* cows are cared for, along with countless stray pigeons, chickens and rabbits. Visitors can buy balls of fat and grain to feed to the fortunate foundlings.

Marine Drive

Surrounded on three sides by the sea, life in Mumbai draws much of its character from its beaches, seaside promenades and coastline. The long, gracefully curving **Marine Drive ⓜ** (Netaji Subhash Chandra Bose Road) links Malabar Hill to Fort and Colaba. It is flanked by a wide promenade, ideal for the early-morning jogger, evening walker and late-night stroller. During the monsoons the turbulent waves splash over the parapets.

Marine Drive ends at **Nariman Point**, and at the very tip of the promontory is the **National Centre for the Performing Arts ⓝ**, set up by the Tata Trust in 1966. One of India's premier cultural centres, it hosts exhibitions and puts on music, dance and drama performances. **Chowpatti ⓞ**, at the northern end of Marine Drive, is a stretch of sandy beach. In the evenings, it is crowded with people enjoying the cooling sea breeze and stalls

EAT

Wander around the 'Khau Gullies' ('eating lanes') of Fort or Churchgate at lunch time or just after offices close: **pao bhaji** – a spicy tomato and red-lentil mush served in a fluffy white roll – is the tired commuters' favourite. The other quintessential local snack is **bhel puri** – a scrumptious heap of rice, vermicelli, potato and crunchy pieces of puri mixed with chopped tomatoes, onions, coriander, and a twist of tamarind and lemon juice.

Bazaar at Mohammad Ali and Crawford roads.

EAT

The best place for a
quick pit stop while
visiting the Maharaja
Chatrapati Sivaji
Museum is the Kala
Ghoda Café in Ropewalk
Lane, at Kala Ghoda Fort
(www.kgcafe.in). It's a
café, a bakery and an art
gallery serving tasty
snacks, salads, desserts,
coffee and cold drinks
throughout the day
(8am–11.45pm).

*The coast by
Walukeshwar Temple,
Mumbai's
westernmost point.*

selling delicious Mumbai *bhelpuri* and
other snacks. Chowpatti is famous also
for its *kulfi* and ice creams. During the
Ganesh Chathurthi festival, processions from the city meet here with
images of Ganesh, which are then
thrown in the sea.

Tucked away in a suburban backstreet 10 minutes' walk north of the
Chowpatti seafront, the former house
of a wealthy diamond merchant is
where Gandhi used to stay on his
frequent visits to Mumbai. Gandhi
organised strikes among the city's
textile workers and addressed rallies
as part of his Satyagraha campaign
against British import policies. He also
launched the 'Quit India' movement
from here in 1942. **Mani Bhavan** ,
at 19 Laburnum Road (daily 9.30am–
6pm) has since become a museum to
the Mahatma, where exhibits include
one of Gandhi's famous spinning
wheels, his library and a collection of
letters, among them one written to
Hitler in the 1930s imploring him to
embrace peace.

To the north of Chowpatti Beach,
a long promontory bristling with

skyscrapers tapers into the Arabian
Sea. Fanned by the breezes of the bay,
Malabar Hill was from the time
of the city's birth favoured as a retreat
from the heat and frenzy of the Fort,
and to this day it holds some of the
most desirable, and expensive, real
estate in Mumbai.

The thick forest spilling down the
south-facing slopes of the hill were
chosen by Zoroastrian Parsi immigrants as the site of their mortuary
towers – the infamous 'Towers of
Silence', or *dhokmas*, where the bodies of the devout are traditionally
devoured by vultures so as not to
pollute the sacred elements of fire
or earth. Hindu cremation rituals,
meanwhile, are conducted, as they
have been for centuries, around the
Banganga Tank, an ancient reservoir
surrounded by shrines at the far tip of
Malabar Hill.

Banganga and its clutch of crumbling temples have become relative
backwater these days, but the same
cannot be said of the more modern
Mahalakshmi Temple on the northern side of Malabar Hill, dedicated

(appropriately enough for a city obsessed by the pursuit of wealth) to the goddess of prosperity. For non-Hindus, the chief incentive to come here is the dazzlingly colourful flower market leading to the main gates.

A short walk north of Mahalakshmi, on an islet joined to the mainland by the narrowest of tidal causeways, stands the mausoleum of **Haji Ali** Ⓡ, whose coffin local Sufi Muslims believe was washed up here after it was thrown into the sea in Sind, Pakistan. Beggars line the whole length of the slender walkway leading to the tomb, which attracts crowds on Thursday and Friday nights, when performances of devotional Qawwali music are staged in the courtyard.

Byculla, Dharavi and Bandra

In the heart of central Mumbai, **Byculla** district was once the powerhouse of the city's textile industry. Partly collapsed chimney stacks, derelict warehouses and the burnt-out shells of cloth mills recall the long-gone cotton boom.

Plans are always being put forward to transform this blot on the urban landscape, but so far only one renovation project of note has been carried out. In Byculla-East, the former **Victoria & Albert Museum**, now the **Dr Bhau Daji Lad Museum** Ⓢ (www.bdlmuseum. org; Thur–Tue 10am–6pm), was once applauded as 'one of the greatest boons the British have conferred on India' when it was constructed in 1872. A Palladian-style mansion set in a classical botanical garden, the building has been beautifully restored and merits a visit as much for its architecture as the collection of maps, prints, paintings and scale models relating the Mumbai's colonial history displayed inside. In a plot to its rear, a lone, carved-stone elephant was removed from Elephanta's cave temples by their Portuguese discoverers.

Two wildly contrasting aspects of the city face each other from opposite banks of filthy Mahim Creek, north of Byculla. On one side, **Dharavi** is a vast slum where over one million people live and work in dire conditions, without access to clean water and health care. Amazingly, some 15,000 small

School outing to the Victoria & Albert Garden, Byculla.

GANESH CHATHURTHI FESTIVAL

One of Mumbai's greatest spectacles is the Ganesh Chathurthi festival, a Hindu celebration held at the height of the monsoon in July and August. Under leaden skies, huge effigies of the god of good beginnings, Ganesh (also known as Ganapati) are paraded through the streets before being immersed in the sea. Crowds of hundreds of thousands gather to watch the event, dancing to the rhythms of the bands that accompany the brightly painted statues as they're carried towards the waves. The largest mass immersion of Ganesh idols takes place on Chowpatti Beach, at the northern end of Marine Drive. See the Maharashtra Tourism website (www.maharashtratourism.gov.in) for precise dates and other information.

The formerly light-hearted festival has, over the past decades, attracted some controversy. Right-wing Maharashtran nationalists nowadays use the event as a kind of rallying point, sponsoring processions which are marshalled by its cadres of aggressive, saffron-clad senaks – a symptom of the wider communalisation of Mumbai by the pro-Hindu Shiv Sena Party. Environmentalists also have reservations about the festival, claiming the plaster of Paris and paints used to create the idols seriously pollute the sand and sea water around Mumbai when they are immersed on its final day (in former times, *shadu maati*, a natural compound of clay was used to make the statues).

EAT

During the month of Ramadan, the streets next to the Minara Masjid, just off Mohammad Ali Road, are given over to a lively night market, where Muslims from across the city come to break their fasts. A mouth-watering array of grilled kebabs, pungent curries and piping hot rotis are on offer, as well as racks of traditional milk sweets. The market gets into its stride around 9pm and lasts through the night.

factories are crammed into the shanty town, turning over an estimated $1.4 billion annually. Most of these micro-businesses specialise in some kind of recycling: aluminium cans, soap scraps, leather cast-offs, oil drums and other unwanted materials are scavenged by Dharavi residents across the city and brought back here to be remade. The clock, however, may well be ticking on the slum. A $40-million redevelopment project is being pushed through by Mumbai municipality and private backers eager to get their hands on what is among India's most valuable real estate. As with all such projects in India, however, progress is slow. Since the original redevelopment was proposed in 2004, nothing has actually happened on the ground – a fact in part attributable to the raised profile of Dharavi since Danny Boyle's hit 2008 movie, *Slumdog Millionaire*, which was partly filmed in the area.

A vision of what Dharavi could well turn into if the developers have their way rises from the opposite shore of Mahim Creek, in the form of **Bandra** – north Mumbai's swankiest suburb.

This is where the city's affluent elite aspire to live, shop and party. The enclave, bounded on its seaward side by trendy Carter Road where the beau monde promenade on weekends, epitomises the self-assured, go-ahead side of modern India. Hip young things in imported shades and designer jeans hang out in the air-conditioned malls and bars, rubbing shoulders with the many foreign expats who've also made Mumbai their home in recent years.

In the far south of Bandra, the Catholic **Basilica of Mount Mary** attracts worshippers from the low-caste Hindu and Muslim communities on festival days: the church, founded by the Portuguese in the 17th century (but substantially rebuilt in the 20th century after a fire), holds a Madonna believed to possess miraculous powers. Wax models of body parts are piled with candles below the statue.

Elephanta (Gharapuri)

While the city of Mumbai has no ancient monuments, an hour's ride away by motor launch from the Gateway of India (Tue–Sun) is the island

The coast at Carter Road, Bandra.

of **Elephanta** ❶, site of a magnificent series of rock-cut cave temples (Oct–May Tue–Sun 9.30am–5pm (but boats leave Gateway only until 2pm, boats return to Gateway from noon until 5.30pm) with large, sculptured interiors, excavated in the 7th and 8th centuries.

'Elephanta' was the name given to the island by its Portuguese discoverers, after the stone elephant they found on the shoreline (this now resides in the Dr Bhau Daji Lad Museum). The same Portuguese mariners inflicted terrible damage on the devotional sculpture they encountered, using some of the deities for target practice. But these depredations have, miraculously, done little to diminish the splendour of the carvings, which continue to exert a powerful spell.

Reached via a flight of 100 stone steps, the pillared cave at the top of the island was dedicated to Shiva. Its centrepiece is the famous Trimurti (or 'Maheshmurti' figure as it's also known), a 6-metre (20ft) tall, triple-headed deity set in an alcove at the back of the cave. Although some debate surrounds the exact date the figure was carved, scholars are united in regarding it as the zenith of ancient Hindu art: no other statue in India emanates such a vivid sense of serenity.

Kanheri Caves

Some 40km (25 miles) north of central Mumbai, near Borivali station on the Western Railway suburban line, is the Sanjay Gandhi National Park. Encompassing tracts of teak forest that are rich in wildlife considering their proximity to the city, the reserve is a popular retreat from the urban sprawl below. It also protects the **Kanheri Caves** complex, one of Maharashtra's most important archaeological sites.

A total of 109 caves were excavated by Buddhist monks over a 700-year period between the 2nd and 9th centuries AD. They range from simple square cells to elaborately decorated monastery halls, connected by a network of steep, stepped pathways. The caves, and indeed the Sanjay Gandhi National Park as a whole, are best visited on weekdays; come here on Saturday or Sunday and you'll find the peace and quiet shattered by parties of noisy picnickers.

TIP

Tours of Dharavi, focusing on its economic successes rather than deprivation, are run by the outfit Slum Tours, based in Colaba. The tours include travel to and from the shanty town, and the services of a knowledgeable guide. For more, go to www.reality toursandtravel.com.

Kanheri Caves.

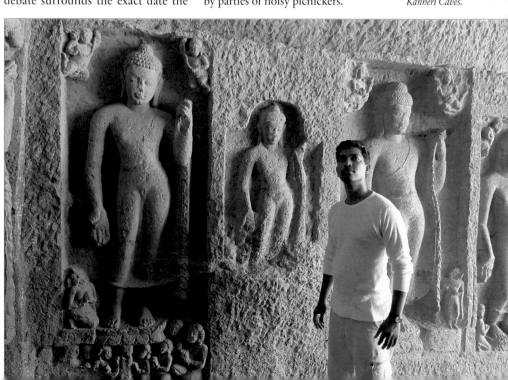

AJANTA AND ELLORA

The Buddhist, Hindu and Jain cave temples of these two magnificent sites are among the most important monuments in India.

'The finest gallery of pictures to survive from any ancient civilisation' is how historian John Keay described the Buddhist cave murals at Ajanta, 105km (65 miles) northeast of Aurangabad. Forgotten for nearly 1,000 years, the jungle site was only rediscovered by a party of British tiger-hunters in 1819. Today it is classified as one of Unesco's World Heritage monuments. The frescoes and sculptures date from around 200 BC to 650 AD, a period when Buddhism was acquiring some of the sensuousness of Hinduism. People used to the idea of Buddhist thought being essentially a negation of the senses will be startled by the voluptuousness of much of the imagery. Highlights include Cave 1 with its superb murals, and the painted ceiling of Cave 2, although for many people the dramatic setting coupled with the mystique of the caves is reason enough to visit.

Ellora, 25km (15 miles) northwest of Aurangabad, has 34 rock-cut temples representing the Buddhists (caves 1–12), Brahmanic Hindus (caves 13–29) and Jains (caves 30–34). The term 'cave temple' cannot convey the magnitude of the Ellora achievement. These caves were scooped out of the rocks 10 centuries ago, a feat comparable to carving an entire cathedral out of solid rock. The work usually began from the top of the temple and moved downwards to eliminate the need for scaffolding.

The centrepiece at Ellora is the Kailasa Temple. Its architects were not modest in their ambitions; Kailasa is, after all, the mythical mountain where the gods dwell. In its galleries are recreated various scenes from Shiva myths. One of them represents the eternal struggle between the forces of evil represented by Ravana, the demon king of Sri Lanka, and the forces of good represented by Shiva and Parvati.

Varaha, incarnation of Vishnu as a boar, at Ellora.

Kailasa Temple at Ellora, a representation of Shiva's mountain, was carved out of 85,000 cubic metres of rock.

Buddha flanked by apsaras (celestial nymphs) at Ellora.

...aintings represent the life of the Buddha at Ajanta.

...eclining Buddha in an Ajanta chaitya (chapel).

Ceilings at Ajanta are adorned by carved friezes.

THE AJANTA CURSE

Early efforts by 19th-century artists to document Ajanta's art treasures were bedevilled with disasters, leading to speculation that the site was gripped by a malevolent curse. English painter Robert Gill spent 27 years copying the murals, but lost his entire collection in the fire at London's Crystal Palace in 1866. Exactly the same thing happened to another folio of facsimiles when they were destroyed by fire at the Victoria & Albert Museum. A team of Japanese Buddhist artists also lost their copies, crafted on rice paper, after they were buried in an earthquake.

Subsequent attempts to preserve the world-famous wall paintings met with little more success. Restoration work commissioned by the Nizam of Hyderabad in the 1920s nearly destroyed the murals altogether, when the varnish applied began to crack and flake away, taking fragments of paint with it.

Attempts to record and preserve the artwork at Ajanta have proved extremely challenging. The Archaeological Survey of India now oversees all restoration work.

MAHARASHTRA, MADHYA PRADESH AND CHATTISGARH

These central provinces are rich in history, with breathtaking rock temples, forts and atmospheric ruins. The Western Ghats and swathes of the interior are home to some of India's largest forests.

T he contiguous states of Maharashtra, Madhya Pradesh and Chattisgarh encompass a vast area of central India. Between them, they hold enough ancient monuments, wildlife reserves, sacred pilgrimage towns and remote forests and mountain ranges to occupy even the most intrepid of travellers for several lifetimes. Yet, compared with other parts of the country, the interior of the Subcontinent sees comparatively few visitors.

Five major river systems flow through the region: the Naramada and Tapti in Madhya Pradesh, which rise in the far east of the peninsula and flow into the Gulf of Khambhat (Cambay); and the Godavari, Bhima and Krishna in Maharashtra, whose sources lie in the Western Ghats (here known as the Sahayadris) and run eastwards. By trapping the lion's share of monsoon rains blowing off the Arabian Sea to the west, the mountains form a precise divide between the lush, densely populated coastal lowlands of the Konkan, and the more arid uplands of the Deccan plateau, or '*desh*'.

A journey through India's core takes in the full spectrum of the country's history: from the earliest Buddhist caves and stupas of the Mauryan era, through the splendours

of medieval Hinduism at Khajuraho and Orcha, to the Afghan-influenced palaces and tombs of Mandu, and Maratha forts of the Maharashtran coastline. Along the way, forays into the central Indian *sal* forests for a glimpse of the wild tigers that roam there will bring you into contract with descendants of aboriginal tribespeople whose presence in the region – most prominent today in rural Chattisgarh – predates even the oldest stone monuments in the Subcontinent.

Main Attractions

Matheran
Lonavala Caves
Gwalior Fort
Khajuraho
Sanchi
Kanha National Park

Taking in the great panoramic views at Matheran.

Maharashtra

The Konkan coast

The narrow, well-watered coastal strip extending south from **Mumbai** ❶ ranks among the least explored corners of India. Known as the Konkan, few of the many tourists heading between Mumbai and Goa consider crossing it overland, but the 500km (310-mile) shoreline sandwiched between the Arabian Sea and the Western Ghats has some beautiful beaches and scenery, as well as a series of wonderful fortresses dating from the era when control of the region's maritime trade was a continual source of conflict. The Portuguese, Siddis, British and Marathas all established strongholds here at one time, some of them on offshore islands from which they traded in rice, precious stones, cotton and silk. In addition to these derelict citadels, the Konkan's settlements possess a distinctive atmosphere, as well as a uniquely fiery brand of coastal cooking.

Travel in the Konkan has always been a stop-start affair, thanks to the innumerable tidal rivers that flow across it, although the recent appearance of a high-speed rail link has made access far easier. That said,

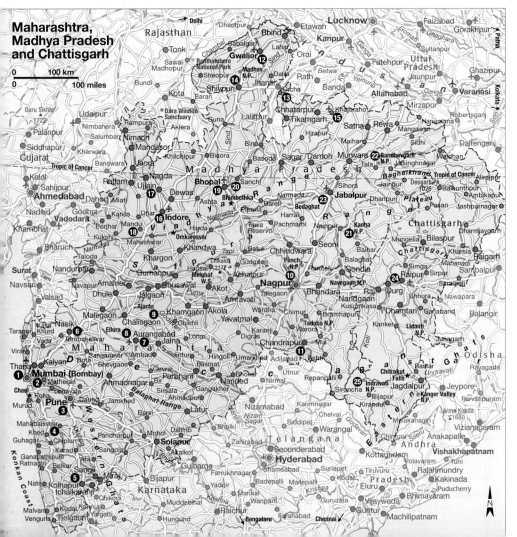

Maharashtra, Madhya Pradesh and Chattisgarh

as the Konkan Railway (www.konkanrailway.com) runs 10–25km (6–15 miles) inland for most of its course, you'll need to catch a combination of local ferries and buses to reach **Chaul**, on the banks of the Roha River, where overgrown basalt ramparts enclose all that's left of a once thriving Portuguese town. **Murud**, 33km (20 miles) further south (and 165km/102 miles from Mumbai), is the springboard for boat trips out to the spectacular island fort of **Janjira**, founded in 1511 by the Siddis, a dynasty descended from freed Abyssinian slaves who made their fortune providing armed naval escorts for Haj pilgrims travelling to and from Mecca. Rising sheer from the waves, the crumbling ramparts of Janjira afford sweeping views of the coast and surrounding countryside.

The next worthwhile stopover, **Ganpathipule**, lies over 200km (124 miles) south of Murud. A popular pilgrimage destination, it's most easily reached via the town of Ratnagiri on the Konkan Railway. Tens of thousands of Hindus pour through each year to pay their respects to a naturally formed image of the elephant-headed god Ganapati (Ganesh). Moreover, a magnificent white-sand beach extends in both directions of the seafront, backed by a string of pleasant hotels.

Coastal citadels

Accommodation and transport options thin out as you head further south, but it's worth venturing into this undeveloped area for the chance to visit **Sindhudurg Fort**, another spectacular island stronghold, located off the coast near the town of **Malvan**. It was built in 1664 by the Marathas and never conquered. The nearest train access is at Kudal station, 38km (24 miles) to the west.

The last, and most splendid, of the Konkan's chain of coastal citadels occupies a lonely promontory at **Vijaydurg**, where the old Bombay–Goa ferry used to dock. Facilities in the sleepy fishing village south of its main gateway are limited to a couple of local chai shops, but you'll have no difficulty in finding someone to show you the dirt tracks winding west across

TIP

Local *hodka* boats run throughout the day to Janjira Fort from Rajpuri jetty, reachable by autorickshaw from Murud town, 5km (3 miles) to the north. However, they will only depart once full – not a problem at weekends, when there are plenty of day trippers, but the cause of long waits on weekdays.

Karla Temple at the entrance to the caves.

THE MARATHAS

This whole region was once part of the Maratha Empire, which at its height stretched from Tamil Nadu to modern-day Pakistan and Bengal, a dynasty formed by the enigmatic Shivaji Maharaj. Pre-17th-century, the Marathas were known as fierce warriors but lacked cohesion. This all changed once Shivaji assumed leadership of the clan around 1650, and began to extend Maratha rule in all directions. For the next century or so, the Marathas took on all comers, until their defeat at the third battle of Panipat in 1761. The influence of this empire was substantial, representing as it did the re-assertion of Hindu rule in North India after a long period of Mughal dominance, and even today one of Maharasthra's most powerful political parties, the Shiv Sena, is named after Shivaji.

Tea, samosas and other snacks brought to train windows.

a treeless laterite plateau to a hidden series of exquisite shell-sand coves.

Matheran and Lonavala caves

A busy six-lane highway scythes inland from Mumbai, climbing through the verdant Western Ghats to Pune, and winding in tandem through the Sahayadri Hills with the rail line built by the British in the late 19th century. The cotton transported seawards along this route from the dark, volcanic-soiled fields of the Deccan fuelled the rapid rise of Bombay. In fact the niche in the range where the hills tumble to the coastal plains must have served as an important corridor for thousands of years, judging by the scale and magnificence of a crop of ancient rock-cut monuments overlooking it.

On a clear day, after rain has dampened the dust, you can see the outlying skyscrapers of Mumbai from **Matheran** ❷, a genteel British-era hill station situated 108km (67 miles) southeast of Mumbai. Yet a more stark contrast between two places it is hard to imagine. Spread over a flat-topped, sheer-sided mountain at an altitude

of 800 metres (2,600ft), Matheran is swathed in verdant forest and – thanks to the total absence of motorised traffic (it lies some distance off the main highway) – blissfully insulated from the ravages of the internal combustion engine. Aside from some delightful Raj bungalows, the main reason to visit the resort is the journey to it from the valley floor via a rattling old narrow-gauge railway. Once installed, there's little to do beyond enjoy the cool air, chew blocks of sticky, nut-encrusted local *tikki* toffee, and savour the panoramas from the various viewpoints that ring the ridge top.

Scattered around the town of **Lonavala**, back on the main highway further to the south, are three main clusters of Buddhist cave temples dating from the Satavahana period (2nd century BC–1st century AD) – collectively the finest crop of ancient monuments in the region after Ajanta and Ellora.

The closest cave to the town is **Bhaja**, 9km (6 miles) east, where a delicately carved facade in the basalt cliff opens to an apsidal-ended hall containing a bulbous votive stupa. **Karla**, 11km (7 miles) east, boasts a spectacular prayer hall writhing with wonderfully well-preserved sculpture depicting dancers, musicians, court scenes and elephants. Next to it, a shrine dedicated to the Hindu goddess-oracle Ekrivi is still a popular pilgrimage destination for members of the aboriginal Koli fishing community from Mumbai. By contrast, the cave temple at **Bedsa**, 12km (8 miles) east from the turning to Bhaja, is nearly always deserted, which allows you to savour the essential serenity that must have attracted Buddhist monks to this region in the first place.

Pune

Pune ❸, (170km/105 miles from Mumbai), was once the capital of the Maratha Empire. The British captured the city at the Battle of Koregaon in 1818 and developed it along the lines of an archetypal army garrison with

---

MAHARASHTRA TRANSPORT

Other than Mumbai, regional airports include Pune, Kolhapur, Aurangabad and Nagpur. All of the destinations covered in this chapter are accessible by express rail and bus services.

Aurangabad: There are trains to Delhi (1 daily; 22hrs 30mins); Mumbai (4–5 daily; 6hrs 45mins–8hrs).

Kolhapur: Trains run to Bengaluru (1 daily; 16hrs 45mins); Mumbai (2–3 daily; 11–12hrs 15mins); Pune (4 daily; 7–8hrs).

Nagpur: There are trains to Bhopal (17 daily; 5hrs 30min–7hrs 40mins); Chennai (3–6 daily; 15hrs 15mins–23hrs 30mins); Delhi (10–13 daily 14hrs–21hrs 45mins); Hyderabad (2–5 daily; 8hrs–14hrs 45mins); Indore (1 daily; 11hrs 45mins); Jabalpur (1–3 daily; 8–10hrs); Kolkata (7 daily; 17hrs 40min–24hrs 10mins); Mumbai (10 daily; 11–23hrs); Nasik (7 daily; 9–13hrs); Pune (3 daily; 15–17hrs).

Nasik: Trains run to Agra (3–4 daily; 17hrs 20mins–21hrs 15mins); Bhopal (7 daily; 9hrs–12hrs 20mins); Delhi (3 daily; 21hrs 20mins–25hrs 50mins); Jabalpur (10 daily; 11hrs 20mins–14hrs 55mins); Mumbai (35 daily; 3–5hrs); Nagpur (6 daily; 9–11hrs).

Pune: Trains go to Bengaluru (2–5 daily; 19hrs 15mins–22hrs 40mins); Chennai (3 daily; 20hrs–25hrs 45mins); Delhi (5 daily; 20–27hrs); Hyderabad (3–4 daily; 10–13hrs); Kolhapur (6 daily; 7hrs 50mins); Mumbai (every 30mins; 2hrs 35mins–5hrs); Nagpur (4 daily; 15–22hrs).

the usual uncluttered cantonment areas in distinct contrast to the busy, crowded old quarter. Industrialisation has inevitably changed Pune's character to a large extent. A metropolis of over 5 million inhabitants, it's now one of India's boom centres, with a rapidly expanding IT sector. Shiny new shopping malls, car showrooms, gold emporia and high-end, gated residential 'villages' on the outskirts are just some of outward signs of this recent prosperity; appalling traffic congestion and air pollution are others.

Well worth a visit is the **Raja Kelkar Museum** (www.rajakelkarmuseum.com; daily 10am–5.30pm), a wonderful showcase for the traditional Indian arts. It has 36 sections, which include carved palace and temple doors, 2,000-year-old excavated pottery, traditional Indian lamps and 17th-century miniature paintings. Of special interest are a collection of brass nutcrackers (some of them explicitly erotic) and padlocks (including a scorpion-shaped padlock whose 'pincers' lock together). The **Agha Khan Palace** (daily 9am–12.30pm and 1.30–5.30pm), with its Italianate arches and spacious, well-tended lawns, was an unlikely place for a prison, but at one time the British interned Mahatma Gandhi and his wife Kasturba here along with other leaders of the Congress Party. Kasturba died in the palace and a memorial has been erected in the grounds.

Mahadji Scindia, one of the Maratha ruling princes, constructed the small black-stone Shiva temple **Shinde Chatri** in the 18th century. His descendant, Madhavrao II, built an annexe in Mahadji's memory, although his architectural inspiration was not Indian, like Mahadji's, but southern European. The contrast in the two styles is a monument to the assimilative powers of Indian culture. Mahadji's *samadhi* (mausoleum) stands across a courtyard. There is a likeness of him in silver, topped by a flame-coloured turban. **Shanivarvada** (daily 8am–6.30pm), in the Old City,

was the palace of the Peshwa rulers who succeeded Shivaji's empire. It was built in 1736. All that remains from a massive fire in 1827 are its fortified walls, brass-studded gates, 18th-century lotus pools and the elaborate palace foundations.

The 8th-century rock-cut **Temple of Patalesvar** stands in the middle of Pune. Carved from a single boulder of awe-inspiring size, it is still used by worshippers. Other fine temples include the **Parvati Temple** on a hilltop on the city outskirts. A Muslim shrine, the **Qamarali Darvesh**, contains a celebrated 'levitating' stone.

Unrivalled views over the city and the table-topped mountains surrounding it are to be had from **Sinhagad Fort** (literally 'fortress of the lion') 24km (15 miles) to the southwest, where Shivaji notched up a landmark victory against the Sultan of Bijapur's army in 1670. Local legend has it that his right-hand man, General Tanaji Malsure, scaled its sheer precipice with a group of trusted lieutenants using ropes and giant monitor lizards especially trained for the purpose.

TIP

The easiest way to get around the three cave sites near Lonavala is to hire an autorickshaw or car for a half-day tour; count on around 4 hours for the whole trip. Soft drinks and bottled water are available at Karla. It's always a good idea to avoid weekends, when raucous crowds can spoil the atmosphere at the archaeological sites.

Deccan landscape near Karla.

Stupas carved out of the rock at the Bhaja Caves. The complex dates back to the 2nd century BC.

Votive stupa at the Bhaja caves.

Pune is also famous for being home to the Osho Ashram, now known as the **Osho International Meditation Resort,** which is centrally located a kilometre or so from the main train station, next to Koregaon Park. Established by the late and uniquely colourful Osho, this is still an immensely popular destination for spiritual travellers from the world over (see www. osho.com). On 13 February 2010 a bomb ripped apart a German bakery close to the Ashram, killing 17, including a number of international visitors.

Southern Maharashtra

In the heart of the hills south of Pune, **Mahabalesvar ❹** and **Panchgani** are cool hill stations that lend themselves to quiet walks with panoramic views. Horseriding is popular, and horses and ponies can be hired.

One of the most important pilgrimage centres in Maharashtra is **Kolhapur ❺**, 225km (140 miles) south of Pune, close to the border with Karnataka. In fact, it's often called **Dakshina Kasi** (the Varanasi of the south), due to its many temples and the ghats that

run down to the Panchganga River. The temple held in highest esteem is the **Mahalaksmi Temple** (Ambabai Temple), built in the 9th century. To the east of the city is **Kotiteerth**, a temple of Mahadev in the centre of a wide expanse of water.

Kolhapur was the capital of a former princely state and has some splendid palaces. These include the 18th-century **Raj Wada** (Old Palace; daily 10am–6pm; free) near the Mahalakshmir Temple, and a **New Palace** from the 19th century (Tue–Sun 9.30am–1pm, 2.30–6pm), 2km (1.25 miles) north of the city. Kolhapur is also known for its leather *chappals* (sandals). One of India's biggest annual pilgrimages, the **Pandhapur Yatra**, happens in June to July, and attracts over a million pilgrims. They walk from Pandhapur to Alandi, close to Pune, in 21 days, and numbers are rising every year; this is becoming one of *the* religious spectacles of India.

The Northeast

Nasik ❻, 150km (93 miles) northeast of Mumbai, is a holy city. It stands on the banks of the Godavari River, venerated by Hindus, and around 2,000 temples and numerous bathing ghats testify to its sanctity. It is also featured in an episode from the *Ramayana*: when Lakshana, Rama's younger brother, tiring of the efforts of the demon Surpanakha to persuade him to marry her, chopped off her nose, it fell where Nasik now stands. The *Kumbha Mela* (known in Nasik as the *Sinhastha Mela*), held once every 12 years, is the high point of a pilgrimage here, although the focus of the celebrations is at nearby Trimbakesvar. This is safest seen from a distance (at the 2003 *Kumbha Mela* several people were trampled to death).

According to legend, **Trimbakesvar**, 30km (18 miles) west of Nasik, was the site of a dispute which arose between the gods and the demons over the possession of a pot of nectar. In the mêlée, the nectar spilled, and some of

the drops fell on Trimbakesvar. The **Trimbakesvar Temple** has an important Shiva lingam and is an imposing monument with splendid carvings. An auspicious site in the neighbourhood is the nearby hill of **Brahmagiri**, source of the sacred Godavari River. As its name suggests, **Aurangabad** ❼, 370km (230 miles) from Mumbai, has a strong Muslim flavour. The city contains the mausoleum of Mughal emperor Aurangzeb's wife, the **Bibi ka Maqbara** (daily 8am–sunset; charge), a poor copy of the Taj Mahal. There is also an interesting medieval watermill, the **Panchakki**, by a Muslim shrine. Three kilometres (2 miles) from the Bibi ka Maqbara, there are 12 Buddhist caves excavated between the 3rd and 11th centuries AD. The most interesting are Nos 3, 6 and 7; carry a torch.

Daulatabad, 15km (9 miles) west of Aurangabad, has a massive hilltop fort, often described as 'totally impregnable' (daily 9am–6pm). The site dates from the 12th century, and the seven rings of fortifications are from the 15th–16th centuries. To deter invaders further there is a deep moat, once filled with crocodiles and crossed by a single bridge, after which is a dark labyrinth. The views from the top are spectacular. Close by are two sacred sites. At **Khuldabad** is the simple tomb of Aurangzeb (1707), surrounded by the graves of Muslim saints. The Hindu **Ghrusnesvar Temple** near Ellora was founded in the 8th century and houses one of the 12 *syambu jyotirlingas* ('self-born lingams of light'), and is an important pilgrimage centre.

Ellora and Ajanta

Among the most important monuments in India are the magnificent caves at Ajanta and Ellora, both featuring some of the world's most exquisite rock carvings.

Ellora ❽ (Wed–Mon sunrise–sunset) is easily accessed from Aurangabad, lying just 25km (15 miles) northwest of town. The caves here are richly adorned with Hindu, Buddhist and Jain carvings, with the highlight being the eighth-century Hindu Kailasa rock temple. They are best visited in the late afternoon, when their westerly aspect catches the light to mesmerising effect (see page 258).

The Buddhist caves at **Ajanta** ❾ (Tue–Sun 9am–5pm), 105km (65 miles) to the northeast of Aurangabad, not only contain sculptures, but remarkably preserved frescoes as well. Secluded deep in the Deccan backwoods, they were only discovered in the 19th century, which explains why the monuments escaped the depredations of invading armies. To protect the caves from the ravages of pollution, a fleet of environmentally friendly buses takes visitors up to the site.

As much as the caves themselves, Ajanta's position on a forested river gorge – with a spectacular waterfall during the monsoon – makes the place very special. Numbered from the entrance, caves 1, 2, 10, 16 and 17 are particularly fine, though all are worth a look. (See page 258.)

TIP

City buses run from Pune's Swargate stand to Sinhagad village throughout the day. Note that in recent years, heavy monsoon rains have caused damage to the road leading up to the citadel, which may be closed as a result. Check the status of the route at Pune's MTDC tourist information desk, on the concourse of the train station (Mon–Sat 9am–7pm, Sun 9am–3pm; tel: 020-2611 1720).

An alternative mode of transport in Pune.

The far northeast

Nagpur , in Maharashtra's far northeast, was the capital of the Bhonsle branch of the Maratha Empire. Each winter its imperial status is faintly recalled when today's rulers – that is, the provincial government – relocate here from Mumbai. At the geographical centre of India, the region is also famous for its oranges.

Ramtek, a hilltop temple 40km (25 miles) northeast of Nagpur, is so named because Rama, the popular incarnation of Lord Vishnu, stopped here with his wife Sita and brother Lakshmana when they were banished from Ayodhya. It is also associated with the India's greatest Sanskrit poet and playwright, Kalidasa, who wrote his 5th-century epic *Meghdoota* ('The Cloud Messenger'). A modern memorial to the bard has been erected on the hilltop.

To the southwest of Nagpur, **Wardha** is the alighting point for **Sevagram** and **Paunar**. The village of Sevagram is where Mahatma Gandhi lived in an ashram. This has been well preserved and is a place of modern pilgrimage. Paunar was made famous by one of Gandhi's disciples, Acharya Vinoba Bhave, who lived and died there. He is famous for his *bhudan* (land-gift) movement, which encouraged landowners to give away portions of their estates to landless labourers.

This part of India was until relatively recently covered with a vast swathe of jungle teeming with tigers and other wildlife, and although large areas have been cleared, some wild forests remain. East of Nagpur, **Navegaon National Park** protects one such area.

Chandrapur , 160km (100 miles) south of Nagpur, has a fort, several temples and makes a convenient base for a visit to **Tadoba**, Maharashtra's best-known sanctuary. In the park is a lake held to be sacred by local Adivasis; crocodiles thrive in large numbers. **Chikhalda**, 220km (135 miles) west of Nagpur, is the hill station of the region. The nearby **Melghat Wildlife Sanctuary** protects an area of thick jungle rich in wildlife.

Madhya Pradesh

In the heart of the Subcontinent, the large state of Madhya Pradesh – the

Bibi ka Maqbara, Aurangabad.

name means 'middle land' – is primarily comprised of upland plateaux and hills, interspersed with the deep valleys of rivers that flow east into the Bay of Bengal and west into the Arabian Sea. A large proportion of India's remaining forest is located here, with some of the finest deciduous hardwoods in the world – teak, sal, hardwickia, Indian ebony and rosewood. Bamboo is prolific in the hills, and there are magnificent fruit and flowering trees. The Mahadeo Hills of the Satpura Range are the home of the tiger, leopard and other forest animals. Madhya Pradesh is one of the hottest parts of India; in May and June temperatures regularly climb to 45°C (113°F) or more.

The state is also home to many Adivasi groups. Among the most populous are the Gonds, found across central and eastern parts. Western Madhya Pradesh is inhabited by the Bhils, a group of warriors who once held the powerful Mughal army at bay, while the east is dominated by the Oraons, now largely Christian.

Madhya Pradesh is known for its handicrafts, from the weaving of Chanderi and Maheshwar, to the carpet-making of Vidisha, Mandsaur and Sarguja. Other crafts include carpentry, pottery, textile printing and dyeing, metalworking, woodcarving and leather work.

Ancient monuments and sacred sites dominate most tourist itineraries. Approaching from the north, Gwalior's spectacular clifftop fort is the first sight worth pausing at en route to the exquisite medieval ruins of Orcha, from where a four-hour road trip takes you across rolling river plains to remote Khajuraho, site of some of India's most illustrious stone temples, famed for their erotic sculpture. Bhopal, the busy state capital, provides the best base for visits to the ancient Buddhist remains of Sanchi – like Khajuraho, a Unesco World Heritage monument – and to the prehistoric rock art of Bhimbetka. The other great archaeological site in the region is Mandu, where some remarkable, derelict Afghan-style palaces and tombs, dating from the early phase of Islamic expansion into peninsular India, sprawl over a high plateau above the Narmada River.

TIP

Tours of Ajanta and Ellora are easy to arrange from Aurangabad. Many itineraries take in both sites in a single day. A bus or taxi from Aurangabad to Ajanta takes around 2.5 hours, while Aurangabad to Ellora is just 45 minutes. Take a hat, mosquito repellent, comfortable shoes and a torch. Flash photography is not allowed inside the caves as it damages the pigment in the paintings.

Aurangabad caves.

TIP

A great place to soak up the religious atmosphere of the Narmada is the town of Maheshwar, 91km (56 miles) southwest of Indore, where an 18th-century riverside palace has been converted into a heritage hotel, the Ahilya Fort (www.ahilyafort.com). Maheshwar is also famous as a hand-loom centre, producing some of the country's finest hand-woven silk saris.

For wildlife enthusiasts, the state also offers a better than average chance of sighting tigers. In the far east along the border with neighbouring Chattisgarh, the national parks of Kanha and Bandhavgarh inspired the writings of Rudyard Kipling, and hold the largest populations of tigers in the country, as well as an abundance of other wildlife roaming one of the Subcontinent's last surviving areas of pristine *sal* forest.

Gwalior

In the far north of Madhya Pradesh (within easy reach of Agra), **Gwalior** ⑫ was established in the 8th century AD and named after Saint Gwalipa, a holy man who cured Prince Swaraj Sen of leprosy. The city is dominated by its hilltop **fort** (daily 8am–6pm), one of the most impressive in India. The Rajput palace of Raja Mansingh, the Gujuri Mahal, built 1486–1516, is the best-preserved section. Located at the northern end of the citadel, it retains much of its original Afghan-style turquoise, blue and green tiling, inlaid in intricate bands of geometric patterns and animal figures above domed kiosks and pierced-stone *jali* windows. The fort also has one of the finest museums of sculpture in the country (Sat–Thur 10am–5pm); its prize exhibit, now on display after years of being locked in the vaults for safekeeping, is a sensuously carved sandstone figurine of a smiling *salabhanjika* ('tree nymph') – often dubbed as 'India's Mona Lisa'.

At the southern end of the fort is the wonderful 8th-century **Teli-ka-Mandir** ('oil man's temple'), while close by is the modern **Sikh** *gurudwara* commemorating Guru Gobind Singh (1595–1644), who was imprisoned here. The steep road up to the Urwahi Gate passes a series of Jain sculptures dating from the 7th to 15th centuries, and the view from the battlements near the ornate pair of 11th-century **Sas Bahu temples** is simply breathtaking.

The current maharaja, Jyotiraditya Rao Scindia, inhabits part of the enormous **Jai Vilas Palace**, built in 1875 on a vast scale that drew on elements of Buckingham Palace, Versailles and various Baroque stately homes visited by its British architect, Colonel Michael Filose. No expense was spared when it came to fitting out the interiors, and you can see some of the more extravagant family heirlooms at the **palace museum** (Tue–Sun 10am–5pm), where exhibits range from the usual depressing array of dead tigers to some fine stone carving, Mughal miniatures, Persian rugs and Louis XVI furniture. The real pièce de résistance, however, is the cavernous durbar hall, where the Scindias received King Edward VII and his 1,000-strong entourage in 1875. It features a silver train set with which the maharaja used to serve brandy and cigars.

Gwalior has long been an important centre of Indian classical music. **Tansen**, the great musician of the court of Akbar, is buried in a 16th-century domed tomb, set in the pleasant grounds of his guru, Afghan prince

A sadhu (holy man) sits under the tree in front of Orcha's Ram Raj Temple.

Ghaus Muhammad's mausoleum, a kilometre or so east of the fort in the Old City. At the opposite (west) side of town, on Ustad Hafiz Ali Khan Road, is the **Sarod Ghar museum** (www.sarod.com; Tue–Sun 10am–1pm, 2–5pm; free), dedicated to the most ethereal of India's stringed instruments, the *sarod*. The mansion in which the museum is housed – itself a beautiful monument embellished with sandstone and marble courtyards – belonged to a family who produced a dynasty of virtuosos, among them Ajmad Ali Khan, one of India's great living musicians.

Datia, Orcha and Shivpuri

South of Gwalior are three of the loveliest places in Madhya Pradesh; Datia, Orcha and Shivpuri. Built in the early 17th century by the Bundela Rajput king, Bir Singh Deo, an ally of the Mughal emperor Akbar, **Datia**'s Narsing Dev Palace (dawn–dusk; free) towers over a small town on the main Delhi–Mumbai train line, 30km (18 miles) from the nearest big town, Jhansi. A maze of flying walkways, domed pavilions, hidden passages and terraces looking across the flat rooftops of the old quarter at its base, the palace is one of the most beautiful medieval monuments in India, though one that sees few visitors.

On the other side of Jhansi, **Orcha** ⑬ served as the Bundelas capital until Bir Singh Deo was killed by bandits in 1627, after which it went into sharp decline. Ransacked by various marauding armies over the years, it was finally deserted in the 18th century, since when little has changed. The undulating landscape is dotted with palace and fortress, temple and cenotaph. The architecture is a synthesis of traditional Hindu, hybrid Indo-Saracenic and ornate Mughal. One of the finest sights is the view of the stunning *chatris*, or cenotaphs, from across the blue river with green hills in the background.

About 100km (60 miles) from Gwalior is **Shivpuri** ⑭, the former summer capital of the Scindias of Gwalior. Located on the Vindhyan plateau, the contrast with the Gangetic Plain is immediate. Here

WHERE

Evocative sound and light shows are held nightly in Gwalior Fort, near the Gujuri Mahal (Man Singh Palace). From November to February, the English versions start at 8.30pm (or an hour later from March until October), and last for just under an hour. Guides for tours of the fort wait for clients at the main Urwahi Gate.

Gwalior's magnificent fort.

Adivasi winnowing rice.

are the two lakes of Sakhia Sagar and Madhav Sagar. Surrounding them is the **Madhav National Park**, home to deer, *chinkara* or Indian gazelle, sambar, blue bull, blackbuck, barking deer and four-horned antelope. Also seen are wild dog, and sloth bear. Bird life abounds and peacocks are to be seen in their hundreds.

Khajuraho

Deep in the Indian countryside to the southeast of Orcha lie the famous temples of **Khajuraho** 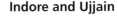. Over the course of the period from 950 to 1050 AD, the rulers of the Chandela dynasty built 85 temples, of which 22 survive, ornately carved with a staggering array of erotic sculptures. The sculptures depict the everyday life of the people and the court in the 10th and 11th centuries. This procession of life itself culminates in the inner sanctum sanctorum. The western enclosure houses the main temples (sunrise–sunset), and the **Archaeological Museum** (Sat–Thur 10am–5pm) is nearby. For more on Khajuraho, see page 276.

Indore and Ujjain

The rapidly growing industrial city of **Indore** ⑯ is located on the Malwa plateau in western Madhya Pradesh, an area known for its cotton fields. On its periphery is **Devas**, where the novelist E.M. Forster lived while working as private secretary to the local maharaja, an experience that provided the material for his travelogue, *The Hill of Devi*.

The land of Malwa is sacred, and two of the 12 *jyotirlingam*, or naturally occurring lingam, are located at the **Mahakalesvar Temple** at **Ujjain** ⑰, 60km (35 miles) from Indore, and **Mandhata** at **Omkaresvar**. For Hindus, these two places enjoy a sanctity equal to Varanasi. Every 12 years Ujjain has the great fair of *Kumbha Mela*, or *Simhastha* as it is called locally. The *mela* moves every three years between Ujjain, Allahabad and Haridwar on the Ganges, and Nasik on the Godavari River.

The sacred river at Ujjain is the **Sipra**. The gods and the *asuras* (demons) fought for 12 days for possession of the *kumbh*, or pot, of *amrit*, nectar of immortality, that came from the churning of the milk-ocean. As they fought, four drops fell on the places where the *Kumbha Melas* are now held. Every 12 years, millions of Hindus congregate to worship at these spots. Ujjain is also a centre for textile dyeing using vegetable dyes and hand-carved teak blocks. The *chipas*, or dyers and printers, are found at **Bherugarh**.

Mandu

Mandu ⑱, the capital of the Sultanate of Malwa, lies in hilly country 90km (55 miles) southwest of Indore. The approach is impressive; there is a chasm, a deep wooded ravine crossed by a narrow bridge, and on the skyline before you is the largest-standing fortified city in the world – its walls have a circumference of more than 75km (45 miles). The **Bhangi Gate**, a fearsome defensive bastion, leads to lakes and groves, gardens and palaces. The **Jahaz Mahal**, or ship palace, floats on its lake, and the **Hindola Mahal**, or swing palace, appears to sway gently in the breeze.

The **Jama Masjid** has acoustics so perfect that a whisper from the pulpit is heard clearly in the furthest corner of the huge courtyard. There is also the **Nikanth Temple**, a standing monument to the tolerance of Emperor Akbar.

Close by is the **Reva Kund**, said to be filled by the waters of the Narmada River, some 25km (16 miles) to the south and 600 metres (2,000ft) lower down. Legend has it that Sultan Baz Bahadur met his future queen, Rupmati, on the banks of the Narmada when out hunting. He married her on a promise that he would bring the Narmada to Mandu, and Reva Kund is the fulfilment of that promise. On its banks he built a palace for himself and, further up, at the very edge of the escarpment, a pavilion for Rupmati, from the terrace of which she could see the Narmada as a silver thread on the horizon. There is a sheer drop of 600 metres (2,000ft) from the pavilion terrace to the plains of Nimar below.

Bhopal and Sanchi

The state capital, **Bhopal** ⑲, was tragically put on the world map in 1984 by the gas leak from a pesticide plant owned by the US multinational Union Carbide, which killed at least 2,000 and affected hundreds of thousands of others. With compensation still not paid to the victims, the city remains under the disaster's shadow, yet, with its moderate climate, splendid situation on the shores of three lakes, and magnificent Muslim monuments and museums, holds plenty of interest to visitors. The architect Charles Correa designed **Bharat Bhavan**, a fabulous multi-arts centre; it contains a **Museum of Man** (Tue–Sun 10am–6pm) that displays striking exhibits. Also noteworthy are the **Archaeological Museum** and **Birla Museum**, with good displays of sculpture. Bhopal is one of the greatest centres of art

and culture in the country, and is well endowed with art galleries, museums and theatres. The city was founded in the 10th century by Raja Bhoj. The **Bhojpur Temple**, even in its ruined state, speaks of the greatness of this king, as do the remains of the magnificent **Tal** Lake, which once covered 600 sq km (230 sq miles) and whose destruction in the 15th century by Sultan Hosang Shah of Malwa altered the climate of the region. Thirty km (18 miles) south is **Bhimbethka**, where more than 500 caves with Neolithic rock paintings have been discovered. Five periods have been identified, from the prehistoric Upper Palaeolithic to the early historical and medieval.

At **Sanchi** ⑳, 46km (28 miles) northeast of Bhopal, a great stupa covers relics of Gautama Buddha. Noted for exquisite carvings in honey-coloured stone, Sanchi is classed as a Unesco World Heritage site. Aside from the hemispherical mounds still in place, the site's chief treasures are the finely carved railings adorning the entrance arches to the main monument, the

FACT

In 1610, Sir Thomas Roe, British emissary to the court of Emperor Jehangir, believed he and his companions were the only Englishmen in the Subcontinent. Imagine their amazement when, amid the ruins of Mandu, they met a traveller called Thomas Coryate, who had walked all the way there from Somerset. Unlike Roe, Coryate never made it home again: he died the following year of dysentery in Surat.

SLOWLY DOWN THE NARMADA

From its source high on the Amarkantak plateau, the Narmada River flows for 1,282km (810 miles) across the state of Madhya Pradesh, via a giant rift valley through the Vindhya and Satpura ranges. It's held to be sacred by Hindus: a mere glimpse of its waters can cleanse the soul of sin. The holiest of the pilgrimage sites along its banks is **Omkaresvar**, a tiny islet, where one of the country's 12 most venerated Shiva lingams is enshrined.

The ultimate act of veneration that can be accorded the river, however, is its parikrama, or circumambulation. The great walk begins at the river mouth, near the Gujarati town of Bharuch on the Arabian Sea, and from there heads east to the source in the Maikal Mountains at Amarkantak, where it reverses direction to return to the sea – a trip that typically takes two years to complete on foot.

Recent decades have seen religious activity on the Narmada disrupted by a massive – and highly controversial – dam building project. Opponents of the **Sardar Sarovar** scheme point to the fact that, far from benefitting poor farmers in the region, the multi-billion-dollar development has displaced millions of impoverished villagers, many of them the local Adivasi (aboriginal) people.

The Great Stupa at Sanchi.

Great Stupa, built by the Mauryan emperor Ashoka in the third century BC. Northeast of Sanchi are **Vidisha** and **Udaygir** (8km/5 miles) and **Gyaraspur** (50km/30 miles), the cradle of Mauryan civilisation.

Kanha National Park

The setting for Rudyard Kipling's *The Jungle Book*, **Kanha National Park** and its sister sanctuary, **Bandhavgarh** , in the far east of Madhya Pradesh, are perhaps the state's top attractions. These magnificent parks feature grassy meadows, home to chital deer, barasingha (swamp deer) and blackbuck, and thick jungles teeming with leopards, bears, monkeys and a significant population of tigers. The best times to visit are from December to March, and comfortable accommodation is available in both parks.

Pachmarhi and Bedaghat

Pachmarhi, a former British hill station in the Satpura range 210km (130 miles) southeast of Bhopal, offers some wonderful forest walks, some to remote prehistoric rock-art sites with sweeping views across the distant plains.

Bedaghat is 22km (14 miles) from Jabalpur, in eastern Madhya Pradesh. Here the Narmada River flows through a 5km (2-mile) gorge, between towering white marble cliffs, particularly spectacular on full-moon nights. Below the gorge are the **Dhuandhar Falls**, literally 'smoky falls' – a location beloved of Bollywood moviemakers. Jabalpur is the most convenient place to stay whilst visiting the gorge.

Chattisgargh

One of the least known and least urbanised parts of India, the sizeable state of Chattisgarh came into being in 2000, when it was cleaved off from the eastern parts of Madhya Pradesh.

Some 44 percent of the land is covered by trees, accounting for around 12 percent of the remaining forest in India. Beneath the surface lie some of the richest mineral deposits in the world, and these deposits are starting to be exploited. Mining, huge power plants, steel mills, aluminium factories and copper-smelters are already here, with little benefit to Adivasi populations.

Around the state

Raipur , capital of Chattisgarh, is located in the middle of the state and is the transport hub for the entire region. Largely industrial and expanding rapidly, the city is said to have been founded by the Kalchuri king Ram Chandra near the end of the 14th century, although there seems to have been a settlement on the site since the 9th century. Sights in Raipur include a ruined fortress and a 17th-century temple.

Some 80km (50 miles) east of Raipur is the important site of **Sirpur**. It is mentioned as early as the 5th century AD, and excavations in the area have revealed many ancient temples, as well as two Buddhist monasteries. Two of the most important buildings still standing are the brick-built

Jahaz Mahal.

Lakshmana, and the finely decorated Gandesesvara temples.

In the **Kanger Valley** around 140km (90 miles) south of Raipur en route to Jagdalpur, the hilly landscape is covered in some of India's most extensive forests. Close to the pleasant city of **Jagdalpur**, the **Tirathgarh Falls** decorate the hills with a 250-metre (820ft) lace of froth, before disappearing into **Kotamsar**, whose limestone rocks produce caves full of stalactites and stalagmites. This part of Chattisgarh is the home of the Bison Horn Marias, whose dances and drumming can be seen at festivals. West of Jagdalpur are the impressive **Chitrakut Falls** on the Indravati River.

In the same area west of Jagdalpur is the **Indravati National Park and Tiger Reserve** ㉕ (Dec–June) in the Dantewara region. This is one of the state's main attractions but, owing to the activities of Naxalite revolutionaries, entry is intermittently restricted; contact the Chattisgarh tourist office for more details (tel: 0771-4224 600; www.chhattisgarhtourism.net).

Chattisgarh's Adivasi people

About one-third of the Chattisgarh's population are Adivasi. The most numerous are the Gonds, who once ruled much of central India. They inhabited the Satpura and Kymore ranges and their major branches, the Maria and the Muria Gonds, live in the Bastar region. Another numerous group are the Christian Oraons.

The Adivasis of Chattisgarh have retained their identities and customs, largely because previous state governments have treated them with sensitivity. As a result, quality crafts may be found all over the state, from household and agricultural items made from bamboo to attractive jewellery made from a variety of metals, beads, cowries and feathers. Woodcarving is another widely practised skill. Similarly, wall and floor paintings display a high degree of skill, particularly traditional *pithora* paintings made to mark life-cycle ceremonies such as marriage and childbirth. These usually include the depiction of a horse, which in the past was considered an auspicious animal to sacrifice.

FACT

During the Hindu festival of Maha Shivratri (Feb–Mar), tens of thousands of pilgrims flock to Pachmarhi for the ascent of a sacred mountain, Chauragarh, 10km (6 miles) from town. The crush can make the climb perilous, but come outside the festival and the ancient 24km (15-mile) track to the summit makes a superb hike. The peak is crowned by a thicket of Shiva's tridents, and gives magnificent views over the Vindhya range.

Chitrakut Falls.

KHAJURAHO

The temple complex of Khajuraho in northern Madhya Pradesh comprises one of the greatest collections of medieval Indian temple art.

The astounding temples at Khajuraho were built under the reign of the Chandellas, who controlled a large area of the northern Deccan between AD 950 and 1310. Important not only for their exquisite sense of architectural form and proportion, their facades are fabulously decorated with a myriad of deities, nymphs and, most famously, erotic carvings depicting a mind-boggling variety of sexual acts. Although the Chandellas were a Hindu dynasty, there are both Hindu and Jain temples at the site; the latter are almost all concentrated in a compound at the eastern end of the site and tend to be more modest in size and less highly decorated than the major Hindu shrines.

Many of the surviving 22 temples (there were originally around 85 scattered across the surrounding countryside) are in a remarkable state of preservation. This is due mainly to their relative isolation. When the early Muslim invaders of the Delhi Sultanates arrived in the 10th century they destroyed or defaced many Hindu shrines. Khajuraho was at the time far removed from the centres of conflict, and so was ignored, and the temples were gradually forgotten by the outside world. By the time they were 'rediscovered' by British scholars in the late 19th century, they had been surrounded by thick jungle for centuries.

This isolation also posed problems for tourists until a new railway line opened in late 2008 between the site and Mahoba (63km/39 miles away), making access much easier. In addition to local services, trains run straight through from Delhi five times a week, taking around eight hours to reach Nizamuddin overnight.

A good time to visit Khajuraho is in March during the annual 10-day dance festival, when India's leading classical dancers perform on the podium of the largest temple, Kandariya Mahadeva.

Dating from c.1025, the Lakshmana Temple was the first built in the Khajuraho style, where all elements of the temple are architecturally unified.

The temples are designed to lead one's eyes from ground level ever upwards to the ultimate heaven, Kailasa.

Covered with exquisite carvings, the lofty, square bulk of the Duladeo Temple, dedicated to Shiva. It is believed to date from around 1130.

The towers of the shrines seem almost fantastical as they rise from the archaeological park.

The Lakshmana temple is dedicated to Rama's brother and companion in his fight against the demon Ravana.

Erotic carvings at the Kandariya Mahadeva Temple.

EROTIC SCULPTURES

The Kandariya Mahadeva Temple is considered to be the greatest achievement of the Khararaho temple builders' art. It, more than any other, demonstrates a perfection of form and silhouette that seems scarcely credible on first sight. However, it is also famed for its exceptional decoration and particularly its erotic sculpture.

When the British first encountered the temples they were shocked (and, no doubt, secretly titillated) by such flagrant displays of what, to their eyes, was pornography. This was, of course, to misunderstand the intention behind the sculpture. To the medieval Hindu mind the unity of the male and female principles bound the universe together; sexual union was not only considered a manifestation of this perfect union but also a homage to the creation of the universe itself. Related to this metaphysical ideal was Tantra, a form of physical devotion, akin to yoga, that sought this unity through sex. Above all, however, these are very humane carvings, celebrating an essential part of human existence and can be, at times, a little tongue-in-cheek: look out for the nymph who part hides her face in either amusement or embarrassment, and for the man having sex with a horse.

Another example of the temple's erotic carvings.

Dining at sunset, Baga.

GOA

Home to India's most popular and renowned beach resorts, the former linchpin of Portugal's vast Asian trade empire has evolved a uniquely hybrid culture that still lures Europeans to its shores.

Until the arrival off its shores in 1510 of Alfonso Albuquerque's fleet of Portuguese *caravelas*, Goa was merely one among many small ports dotted along India's southwest coast that owed its existence to the trade in horses with Arabia. For many centuries, the warring Hindu and Muslim empires inland had imported stallions bred in the Persian Gulf, exchanging them for Indian spices and diamonds. Albuquerque recognised that a huge fortune could be made by any country possessing a navy strong enough to control this trade. He promptly identified Goa as the perfect base for his country's expanding maritime empire, annexing it from Yusuf Adil Shah, the Sultan of Bijapur, in a ferocious battle at the mouth of the Mandovi River.

Over the ensuing century and a half, the tiny colony blossomed into Asia's most prosperous – the nexus of a trade network stretching from Macau to Brazil, with a population greater even than that of Rome or Lisbon. Glittering Baroque churches and high-roofed *palácios* rose above the palm canopy, and the bazaars of the old Rua Direita groaned under the weight of gold, silks and precious stones. But the boom was short-lived. Outmanoeuvred by rival European powers, the Portuguese eventually lost their grip on their sea-borne trade; the harbour silted up and thousands of Goans perished from disease.

Portugal, however, held on to their colony for 451 years (a much longer lifespan than that of the British Raj), only relinquishing control after Nehru sent in the Indian army in 1961. A tidal wave of changes were unleashed by the 'Liberation' (which some Goans still refer to as 'the Invasion'), but the state has nonetheless preserved its Indo-European identity.

Main Attractions
Panaji
Calangute
Anjuna Beach
Vagator Beach
Benaulim
Palolem
Old Goa

A Portuguese colonial mansion, Siolim.

Goa's European influences

Although brutally imposed by the Portuguese, Christianity now coexists harmoniously with indigenous Hinduism, and the two have intermingled over the years, giving rise to unique forms of architecture, cuisine, dress and language. Wherever you travel in Goa you will come across whitewashed, gabled church facades, and as many flatteringly tailored, Catholic-style dresses as saris, while – most noticeably – every town and village sports an abundance of bars and liquor shops.

European-influenced attitudes to alcohol are only one reason why Goa has become a favourite holiday destination for sun-starved Europeans. Its exquisite beaches – washed by the warm surf of the Arabian Sea, and backed by ranks of swaying coconut trees – provide enough incentive in themselves. On the other hand, development has spiralled out of control in places, with whole villages smothered by luxury resorts. Yet while it's fair to say that none of Goa's beaches have come through the tourism revolution

entirely unscathed, a few relatively quiet stretches of coast survive where you can see what the place must have been like three or four decades ago, when it was visited only by homesick Goan expats and a handful of intrepid hippy travellers.

Regulations concerning the purchase of property in Goa were always considerably more liberal than elsewhere in India, leading to Europeans of all nationalities and professions making Goa their home.

Over time, however, these regulations were consistently abused, with the Russians in particular buying up huge swathes of shorefront property, leading eventually to a clamping down on foreign investment. The contrast between the high and low seasons couldn't be more marked. From October to February the state is inundated with tourists of all descriptions; trendy young Mumbaikars looking to party hard, backpackers, Russian package tourists and jet-setting celebs. Outside these months it is a different place: hotter and wetter but calmer and less frenetic, with only the permanent residents still around.

Away from the beaches, the remains of the former Portuguese capital at Old Goa, in addition to pockets of decaying colonial architecture elsewhere, offer the most memorable day trips inland, with a glimpse of the 'real' Goa that was, and far fewer visitors throughout the year than on the coast.

Churches and carnivals

As you travel through Goa's villages, the imprint of four and a half centuries of Catholicism is evident. The Portuguese came not only to conquer, but also to preach. Presiding over every village, commanding the hilltops, hugging the shores of rivers, are sparkling white churches, crosses and small shrines, built mostly in the 16th and 17th centuries in the Gothic and Baroque styles.

GOA TRANSPORT

Flights: Goa's airport, Dabolim, is a 45-minute drive south of Panaji. A fleet of new taxis are on hand to shuttle travellers to and from the large terminal building that replaced the one erected in the 1990s to serve charter tourists.

In addition to international flights from Europe (mainly Russia) and the Gulf, it is served by frequent daily flights from Mumbai (14–15 daily); Delhi (7–8 daily); Bengaluru (6–8 daily); Chennai (1 daily).

There are also daily flights to Hyderabad, Jaipur, Kochi, Kolkata, Pune and Thiruvananthapuram.

Trains: Goa is on the Konkan Railway, connecting it with Mumbai and Maharashtra to the north, and coastal Karnataka and Kerala to the south. There's also a broad-gauge line running east into the Deccan – handy for visits to the ruins of Hampi.

Trains run from Madgaon (Margao) station in south Goa to Delhi (3–5 daily; 30–38hrs); Ernakulam/Kochi (4–10 daily; 15hrs); Gokarna (1–2 daily; 1hr 50mins); Hospet (for Hampi; 4 weekly; 7–8hrs); Mangalore (8–14 daily; 5–6hrs); Mumbai (12–22 daily; 11hrs 15hrs 30mins); Pune (1–2 daily; 12hrs); Thiruvananthapuram (1–2 daily; 16–20hrs); and Udupi (8–13 daily; 4hrs).

On the feast day of the patron saint – and every village has one – the whole village is in attendance. The image of the saint, brightly decorated, is carried in procession by priests and laity to the chanting of prayers and litanies, recited or sung, accompanied by a violin or even a brass band.

Goa's Carnival takes place in February, and towns and villages celebrate for three days. Processions of floats and dancers attract huge crowds of revellers from out of state, and the Kingfisher beer and Indian whiskey flow freely.

Panaji

Panaji (Panjim) ❶, the capital of Goa, situated on the southern bank of the Mandovi River, is centred on a church and the square in front of it. **Largo da Igreja** (Church Square) is an impressive ensemble, dominated by the dazzling Baroque facade of the **Church of the Immaculate Conception**, its proportions emphasised by the white-balustraded stairway in front. Built in 1541, its twin towers were the first signs of 'home' for

the sailors who made the long voyage from Lisbon.

Panaji has several squares, the houses lining them rising directly above the wide streets. Most of these villas, painted in pale yellow, green or deep rose, with their embellishments picked out in white or some contrasting colour, feature shell windows opening onto wrought-iron balconies. Particularly quaint is the old residential area of **Fontainahas**, where narrow cobbled alleys weave past closely knit houses with tiled roofs, overhanging balconies and carved pillars, much as one would expect to find in any provincial town in Portugal. Winding streets echo to the splutter of motorcycles and the chatter of locals. Given an expensive facelift in 2004, when Panaji was nominated as the permanent venue for India's international film festival, the broad riverside boulevard running along the Mandovi is fronted by some of the grandest public buildings, including the old **Secretariat**, converted by the Portuguese in 1615 from the Adil Shah's former palace.

Painted trees mark the site of a full-moon beach party, an increasingly rare occurrence in Goa.

House at Fontainahas, Panaji.

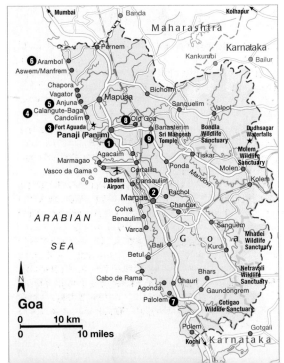

TIP

Goa is unique in India for having motorcycle taxis. Riding bikes distinguished by yellow mudguards, 'pilots' – as they're better-known – charge less than autorickshaws for short trips across town, and cut more quickly through the rush-hour traffic jams. You'll find them waiting outside the bus stop in Panaji and at ranks around town.

Anjuna.

Further west, the **Menezes-Braganza Institute** (www.imbgoa.com; Mon–Fri 9.30am–1pm, 2–5.45pm; free) is the most imposing of many civic structures erected during the governorship of Dom Manuel E'Castro (1826–35), Panaji's 'Founding Father'. Spectacular panels of traditional Portuguese *azulejos* (painted ceramic tiles) enliven the main entranceway, depicting scenes from the nationalistic epic of Luís Camões, *Os Luisadas*, including one where admiral Vasco Da Gama encounters the Zamorin of Calicut on his first voyage to India in 1498.

Margao and Mapusa

Headquarters of Goa's most fertile district (Salcete), **Margao ❷** is the second-largest town in Goa. Some 27km (17 miles) south of Panaji, an indication of its former prominence is the number and size of Portuguese-era *palácios* surviving in the well-to-do north of town. The grandest, boasting deep-pillared verandas, high pitched roofs and huge oyster-shell windows, line the streets radiating from the **Largo da Igreja**, a red-dirt square

where the massive **Church of the Holy Spirit** (Mon–Sat 9am–5.30pm; free) stands as one of the finest surviving late-Baroque churches in India.

Keep heading west from the rear of the church along Lourenço Road for around 200 metres/yds and you will arrive at the granddaddy of all Margao's colonial mansions, **Sat Banzam Gor**. Built in 1790 by a private secretary of the Portuguese viceroy, the house boasts an elegant Rococo facade, colour-washed in oxide-red and white, and five textbook Goan roof gables. The Da Silva family, descendants of the original owners, still live in the house, but do not encourage casual visits.

Goa's beach culture

Strung along Goa's 100km (60-mile) coastline are some superb beaches – stunning stretches of golden sand and surf edging the aquamarine expanse of the Arabian Sea. **Fort Aguada ❸**, 10km (6 miles) west of Panaji, is near the luxury resorts at **Sinquerim** beach and the popular package resort of **Candolim**.

GOAN PALÁCIOS

Nothing encapsulates the elegant hybrid nature of Goan culture quite as well as the architecture of its colonial-era mansions, or *palácios*. While many fine specimens line the older streets of Panaji, Margao and Mapusa, the most photogenic nestle amid the paddy fields and palm groves further inland. They date from the middle phase of Portuguese rule, a time when high-ranking, Goan-born officials and merchants were making profits from trade in opium and gemstones, as well as commercial interests in Portugal's African colonies. Many amassed vast fortunes, which they spent converting their ancestral homes according to the fashionable European styles of the day.

Around traditional Hindu courtyards would be piled sumptuous Classical facades with fancy Rococo mouldings. Flights of formal steps would lead to gabled entranceways, where long stone seats were set along deep verandas. Inside, Belgian crystal chandeliers, Macau porcelain and ornately carved furniture embellished sumptuous salons and ballrooms.

Of the few surviving ancestral Goan homes open to the public, by far the most impressive is the Braganza-Perreira/Menezes-Braganza house, in **Chandor**, 13km (8 miles) east of Margao in south Goa and the wonderful Palacio do Deao in Quepem (www.palaciododeao.com), half an hour further southeast. Both are open to the public.

North along the coast 6km (4 miles) from Fort Aguada is **Calangute** ❹ beach, favoured by bus-loads of day trippers from other Indian states. This long stretch of beach, lined with restaurant shacks, ends at the mouth of a small river in **Baga**, around which sprawls the liveliest of the state's resorts, attracting a mainly young, hard-drinking crowd. Across the river are a few good cafés and restaurants.

A walk along a cliff-side path that skirts the ocean leads to **Anjuna beach** ❺, also approachable by road, 4km (2.5 miles) north of Calangute. Traditionally popular with hippies, this beautiful beachfront is fringed with coconut palms, and the gentle sea makes it ideal for bathing, except in the afternoons when local tourist groups descend to view the 'naked foreigners', or during the famous Wednesday flea market.

Around the corner from Anjuna are the superb white-sand beaches of **Vagator**, centre of Goa's vestigial trance-dance scene. For excellent views of the coastline, climb up to the ruined Portuguese fort at the fishing village of **Chapora**.

Further north still, the broad Chapora River marks the border with Goa's northernmost district, reached via an impressive concrete bridge. The first village in this area, Morjim, has been colonized by long-staying, big-spending Russians and consequently has an unwelcoming atmosphere, but a more relaxed vibe holds sway at nearby Aswem and Mandrem, where a row of chic beach restaurants, lounge bars and boutiques have become the first choice of international A-listers and celebs (Brad and Angelina, Paris Hilton and Kate Moss have all dodged the paparazzi here in recent years).

Finally, in the far north, **Arambol** ❻ is where all the alternative types migrated to when Anjuna became too hectic. Fronted by a wonderful white sand beach, the village is the place to come to dabble in yoga and other holistic therapies, and offers accommodation and top local seafood at a fraction of the price of spots further south down the coast.

Mapusa market.

For the week preceding the Feast of St Francis on 3 December, Catholics from across the state, and beyond, travel to Old Goa to worship at the mausoleum of St Francis Xavier. Many families sleep under the stars to bag the best pews for Mass, held at dawn in the Basilica. Every 10 years, the event takes on a more intense complexion when the incorruptible corpse of the saint is displayed for veneration: the last 'Exposition' was held in 2014.

Traditional boat at Palolem beach.

Colva beach, 25km (15 miles) south of Panaji, with a 25km (15-mile) stretch of silver-grey sand running to Cabo de Rama, is a remarkable sight. Dozens of super-luxurious hotel resorts have mushroomed here, and the formerly pristine beach is no longer tranquil. **Benaulim**, 2km (1.25 miles) south, has a better beachfront, while a further 40km (25 miles) south in **Canacona** district the rocky coast harbours beautiful beaches such as **Agonda**, currently the quietest resort in the state, and **Palolem** ➐, now the destination of choice for most backpackers who winter in Goa.

The full-moon party scene for which Goa was once famous has, thanks to a clampdown by the local government and police, all but fizzled out over the past decade. Instead, you can party at one of several nightclubs dotting the north coast. Tito's, in Baga, is the most famous, but Cuba Cubana, on a hilltop at nearby Arpora, is more popular with foreigners. Further north in Vagator, the Nine Bar and Hilltop's DJs spin textbook Goa trance, the brand of techno that grew out of the 1990s

beach raves – for a mainly Indian and Russian crowd.

Old Goa

No trip to this corner of India is complete without a visit to the 16th- and 17th-century delights of **Old Goa** ➑, 'Rome of the Orient', with its magnificent churches, sumptuous buildings, stately mansions and broad streets.

The **Sé Cathedral** Ⓐ (Cathedral of St Catherine) remains one of the greatest monuments of the Portuguese colonial period. Completed in 1619, it is the largest Christian church in South Asia, and a grand example of Renaissance architecture. The cathedral's 80-metre (260ft) aisle culminates in a richly carved gilt altarpiece – one of the finest in India. There is a font in the church, possibly a vessel of Hindu origin, said to have been used by Goa's patron saint, St Francis Xavier. Within the compound of the cathedral, but facing the opposite direction, is the **Church of St Francis of Assisi** Ⓑ, with a stucco ceiling and a profusion of carvings.

The majestic **Basilica of Bom Jesus** Ⓒ is famous as the site of St

Francis Xavier's mausoleum. It's a beautiful building, blending neoclassical restraint with Baroque exuberance and a flamboyant late-Renaissance facade. The Jesuits were the first Christians to undertake large-scale missionary activity in Portugal's new Asian possessions – the *Estado da India* – and Francis Xavier, a Basque priest, was their most successful emissary. Housed in a small chapel in the basilica's south transept, his supposedly incorruptible remains are Old Goa's most revered relic

The **Church of St Cajetan D**, near the ferry wharf, complete with two belfries and a cupola, was modelled on the Basilica of St Peter in Rome by its Italian architect. Also near the riverbank stands the **Chapel of St Catherine E**, built on the site of the bitterest fighting during Albuquerque's conquest of Goa in 1510.

A few minutes' walk up the road from the basilica is **Monte Santo** (Holy Hill) where one, allegedly haunted, tower of the **Church of the Augustinian Monastery F** is all that remains of a once-splendid vaulted structure. Adjacent to the ruins stands the **Convent of St Monica**, once one of the largest nunneries in the Portuguese Empire.

Past the convent's buttresses, on a grassy mound at the edge of a steep slope, is the shell of the **Church of Our Lady of the Rosary G**, one of the earliest to be built in Goa. It contains the intricately carved alabaster tomb of Dona Caterina, wife of the 10th viceroy and the first Portuguese woman to hazard the arduous voyage to India.

The Goan interior

The interior of Goa is quite different from the coastal areas, and sees very few tourists. Those who were determined to preserve their ancient faith in the face of Portuguese proselytisation removed their deities from the coastal shrines and fled to the mountainous interior.

The **Sri Mangesh Temple 9** (dedicated to Lord Shiva) and the **Shanta-Durga** (to goddess Parvati) and **Nagesh** temples, 22km (13 miles) east of Panaji near Ponda, are among the most frequented in Goa. Ornate, Baroque interiors and several-storey *dipmals* – elaborate lamp towers – are unique features of these fine Goan Hindu shrines.

Morjim beach.

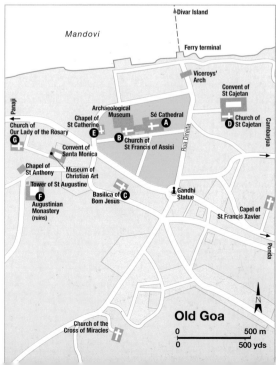

Old Goa

সুন্দর পথ ঘাট,
সেতু সুন্দর,
ক্রিয়বাসীর কাছে
বাড়ায় কদর।

EAST AND NORTHEAST INDIA

Bordering the Bay of Bengal, India's eastern corner is a distinctive and colourful part of the country, anchored by the city of Kolkata. Almost cut off from the rest of India, the remote northeast features on few visitors' itineraries.

Temple decoration, Sikkim.

East and northeast India might be the least visited regions in the country, but that is merely a result of their geographical isolation, rather than any lack of appeal. The teeming flood plains of the Ganges River in Jharkhand and the great Brahmaputra in Assam contrast with the sparsely populated, forested hills of the northeastern borderlands, the Himalayan north and the wild Odishan hinterland. In coastal Odisha (Orissa), startlingly ornate temples attract throngs of worshippers, notably at the Konark Sun Temple with its great carved chariot and annual dance festival. The original juggernauts (giant, hand-hauled chariots that carry the gods through the streets) come from the main temple in Puri and continue to rumble through the city once a year. Adivasi tribal groups in Odisha, though usually isolated from outsiders, add spice to weekly markets near the Adivasi crossroads of Koraput.

On the Ganges delta south of Kolkata, and bordering Bangladesh, is one of India's great wilderness areas: the extensive Sunderbans swamps, protected by national park status, and a major draw for adventurous wildlife-lovers. Fishermen wear masks on the back of their heads to fool swimming tigers, who reputedly will only pounce on a prey's back.

View at Darjeeling.

Kolkata (formerly Calcutta), despite its undeserved, and now outdated, reputation for misery, has gracious mansions, a horseracing track and cricket pitches dating from the British Raj. Pavement hawkers, rickshaw pullers, and political activists help to give the city of Kali a chaotic frenzy. Conversations are easy to strike up with opinionated and widely read Bengalis. To the north, where the plains give way suddenly to the foothills of the Himalaya, is Darjeeling. The largest hill station in the east, it is reached by an 88km (55-mile) journey on a 'toy' train that provides dramatic Himalayan views and steaming cups of home-grown tea. Sikkim adds orchids to this compelling list of attractions.

The northeastern states are almost cut off from the rest of the country by Bangladesh, and are remote in other ways. Away from the Brahmaputra lowlands this is a remote region of forested hills and Christian tribes.

KOLKATA (CALCUTTA)

From its beginnings as a small east-coast trading settlement, Kolkata (formerly Calcutta) became a city of palaces in the heyday of the Raj. Today it is recognised as a vibrant cultural centre.

U ntil 1999, when it took on the local Bengali name of Kolkata, the capital of West Bengal was known to the world as Calcutta. Its history dates back to 1686, when Job Charnock, chief of the East India Company's factory in nearby Hugli was looking for new factory sites and selected a group of three villages – Kalikata, Govindapur and Sutanuti – where Armenian and Portuguese traders had already settled. A factory was established in Kalikata on 24 August 1690, and Calcutta was born. A fort was built, named after King William I.

The community's lifestyle was marked by the profile of the European population, most of whom were young bachelors. Punch houses, brawls and duels were common. The young 'writers', as Company employees were called, usually lived with local mistresses, their 'sleeping dictionaries'.

In 1773, Calcutta became the headquarters and nascent capital of the British administration in India. By that time, the European population had swollen from a few hundred to 100,000 through the arrival of new writers, traders, soldiers and what the administration called 'cargoes of females'. The city was flourishing, a home away from England with an Esplanade and a Strand.

Decline set in after 1911, when Delhi usurped Calcutta as the British

Indian capital. Following Independence, and the flow of refugees across the newly created borders, the city suddenly had more people than it could house. The 1971 Bangladesh War brought a further, rapid influx which brought the city's infrastructure to the verge of collapse. Since then, the overcrowding situation has gradually improved.

Kolkata today

Kolkata is the third-largest city in India, with a population of around

Main Attractions

Fort William
The Maidan
Victoria Memorial
St Paul's Cathedral
Indian Museum
Kali Temple
Botanical Gardens
Salt Lake

Market by Haora Bridge.

Kolkata (Calcutta)

0   1000 m

0   1000 yds

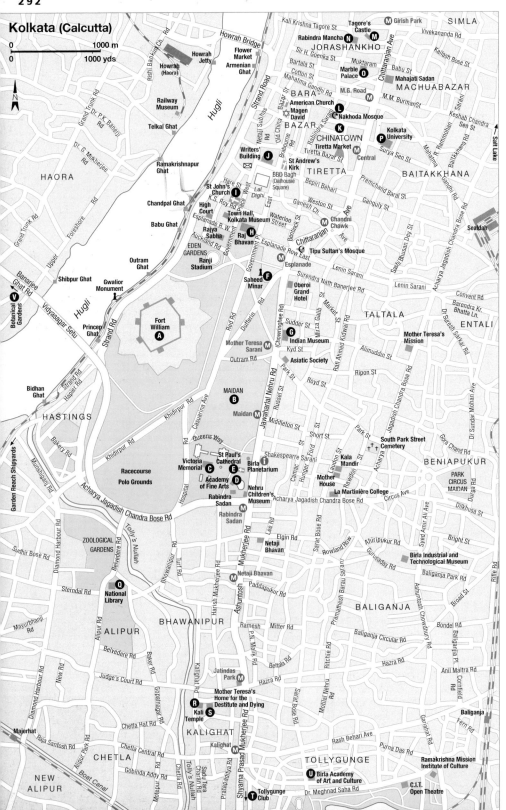

SIMLA

JORASHANKHO

MACHUABAZAR

BARA

BAZAR

CHINATOWN

TIRETTA

BAITAKKHANA

HAORA

TALTALA

ENTALI

HASTINGS

MAIDAN

BENIAPUKUR

PARK CIRCUS MAIDAN

Botanical Gardens

Garden Reach Shipyards

ZOOLOGICAL GARDENS

BALIGANJA

ALIPUR

BHAWANIPUR

Baliganja

KALIGHAT

CHETLA

TOLLYGUNGE

NEW ALIPUR

between 4.5 and 14.2 million (depending on where you draw its boundaries). Long something of a byword in the West for third-world poverty, descriptions of its misery, however, are somewhat exaggerated these days. With its Soviet-designed metro and an efficient one-way system for traffic, Kolkata has the feeling of a well-run city. There are also a large number of well-maintained parks, especially the huge Maidan in the heart of the city.

Kolkata is a lively place: there is always something happening, be it a religious celebration, concert, cricket match, theatre or movie festival, or political demonstration; and although decaying, the architectural heritage is still there. Most of the city's main attractions are on the east side of the Hugli River, between the two bridges. The budget accommodation is centred around Sudder Street, while the more upmarket hotels are slightly further south on Park Street, but both are within walking distance of the town centre.

The city's reputation as a city of intellectuals and culture is unrivalled in South Asia. It was the home not only of India's first, and so far, only Nobel laureate for literature, Rabindranath Tagore in 1913, but also its first Oscar winner, Satyajit Ray in 1991, 'in recognition of his rare mastery of the art of motion pictures, and of his profound humanitarian outlook...' During the 20th century, the city also produced some of India's most important painters and sculptors, including Jamini Roy and Nandalal Bose. It retains a strong tradition of left-wing politics and, until 2011, was ruled by one of the world's longest-standing Communist administrations, the Left Front, which led the city's municipal and state administrations for 34 years. Marxist rule has always been a very pragmatic form of Communism, however, with the Bengali Party adopting some of the most free-market- and multinational-friendly policies in India. Although not a Communist political party, the current government, headed by the Trinamool Congress, is also left-leaning.

The Saheed Minar. In the 19th century, the monument was used by Young Bengal nationalists to hoist the French flag as a sign of rebellion against the British Raj.

The Edward VII statue in front of the Victoria Memorial.

TRANSPORT TO KOLKATA

Buses: Long-distance buses depart from the Esplanade Bus Terminal near the Shahid Minar at the northern end of the Maidan. Most places can be reached by train, though, and the journey by rail will be safer and far more comfortable.

Flights: Netaji Subhash Chandra Bose international airport, still widely known by its old name, Dum Dum, is the main gateway into eastern India. The domestic terminal is by the international one and serves almost all other parts of India.

Trains: Regular long-distance trains run from the city's Haora (Howrah), Kolkata and Sealdah stations to most other destinations in India. Kolkata to: Delhi (6–8 daily; 16hrs 20mins–26hrs); Chennai (2–5 daily; 26hrs–28hrs); Mumbai (4–7 daily; 26hrs–35hrs); New Jalpaiguri, for Darjeeling (11–15 daily; 8–12hrs); Guwahati (4–6 daily; 17–22hrs).

The Maidan

Kolkata was built around **Fort William** . On its western side is the **Strand** and the **Hugli River**, a branch of the Ganges. On the eastern side is the **Maidan** Ⓑ, a huge open park established in 1758 by Robert Clive, who cleared tracts of forest around the new Fort (now the eastern headquarters of the Indian army) in order to open up lines of fire for the guns.

The main construction on the Maidan is the **Victoria Memorial** Ⓒ (Tue–Sun 10am–5pm, gardens 5.30am–7pm daily), an awe-inspiring domed building made from white marble quarried in Rajasthan. It has been beautifully maintained and sits in some of the most attractive gardens in the city. Inaugurated in 1921 by the then Prince of Wales, it houses an excellent collection of Victorian memorabilia as well as a huge number of items on Bengal and elsewhere in India, including paintings (the *Elephant Procession at Jaipur* is among the best), miniatures and manuscripts. The most interesting display, however, is the new **Calcutta Gallery**, describing the history of Kolkata from a small village to its inception as a trading port, and up to the Independence struggle. There are lots of fascinating documents and models, including a mockup of an entire 19th-century street. In the park in which the memorial stands are statues of Queen Victoria and Lord Curzon. Here people picnic, couples hold hands beneath the trees and tourists squint through the strong light at the magnificent building.

Behind the memorial, on AJC Bose Road, is the **Presidency General Hospital** where, in 1898, Sir Ronald Ross identified the carrier of malaria, the female anopheles mosquito. South of the Maidan is the **Racecourse**, opened in 1819, and in its central oval are the **Kolkata Polo Club** grounds where the game has been played since 1861.

To the southeast is Cathedral Road starting at **Rabindra Sadan**, a concert hall named after Rabindranath Tagore. The nearby **Academy of Fine Arts** Ⓓ (daily 10am–5pm; free) has a collection of textiles, miniatures, Mughal swords, Tagore memorabilia and some examples of modern Bengali art.

Birla Planetarium.

SPORTING POWERHOUSE

Kolkata produces a disproportionate number of India's greatest sports stars. It is home to that great crucible of Indian cricket, Eden Gardens, and excels at the national sport, with one of India's most successful Test cricket captain, Sourav Ganguly, among the city's favourite sons. But unlike other cities in the country, it doesn't end with bat and ball – Kolkata is India's most football-mad metropolis, home to many of the country's top clubs as well as the oldest football league in Asia. And the list goes on: Leander Paes, with 12 tennis Grand Slam doubles titles to his name, is Calcuttan; the oldest golf club in the world outside Britain is here, as is the world's oldest polo club. Even rugby union, that most un-Indian of sports, gets a look in, with the oldest international tournament, the Calcutta Cup, named after the city.

The adjacent **St Paul's Cathedral** **E** (daily 9am–noon, 3–6pm, Sunday services 7.30 and 8.30am, 6.30pm) was consecrated in 1847. It is a tall Gothic building with rows of fans hanging from a wooden ceiling, stalls and pews of heavy wood, and a stained-glass window by Edward Burne-Jones, *The Destruction of Sodom*. On the walls are commemorative slabs to the British killed during the 1857 Uprising and those who lost their lives in various wars. Near the cathedral are two attractions that children might find interesting. The **Birla Planetarium** (daily, shows in English 11.30am, 4 and 6pm) is one of the largest in the world. The **Nehru Children's Museum** (www. nehrumuseum.org; Wed–Sun 11am– 7pm) is also worth a look. The latter displays a collection of toys and two dioramas of the *Ramayana* and *Mahabharata* shown in 61 scenes.

At the northern end of the Maidan, just behind the noisy bus terminal, is the 48-metre (158ft) high **Saheed Minar** **G** (Ochterlony Monument). It was erected to celebrate Sir David Ochterlony's victories in the Nepal Wars, but has been renamed Saheed Minar to honour martyred freedom fighters.

Nowadays the Maidan is a 24-hour show. At sunrise joggers appear, as do the West Bengal Mounted Police on their horses; army units perform their morning drills; goats and sheep browse on the course of the **Calcutta Golf Club**. Later, the trams start bringing people to work. Football or cricket then takes over, and people gather under trees near the **Gandhi Statue** and the **War Memorial**. At night, crowds congregate around **Sri Aurobindo's Statue** opposite the Victoria Memorial.

Eden Gardens, north of the Maidan, is the famous site of test-match cricket, and as the venue for the World Cup of 2011. It is festooned with banners proclaiming the Kolkata Knight Riders, the Indian Premier League team part-owned by Bollywood heartthrob Shahrukh Khan. The park was laid out on the site of Respondentia Walk, a fashionable promenade, and the pagoda here was brought to Kolkata from Prome in Burma by Lord

The festival of Durga puja in September or October is a big event in the city calendar.

SATYAJIT RAY

One of Kolkata's most famous sons is the film director Satyajit Ray (1921–92). So far the only Indian director to win an Oscar, which he received in 1991 for Lifetime Achievement, Ray was a visionary, almost single-handedly responsible for developing an Indian 'new wave' of art-house cinema.

Born in Calcutta in 1921 to a family of prominent artists, Ray started his working life as a graphic designer for an advertising agency, then moved on to produce book jackets for a local publisher. His move into cinema came in the late 1940s after he served as a location scout for the French director, Jean Renoir, who was filming his movie *The River in Bengal*. Renoir encouraged Ray to film, on a shoestring budget, his first feature, *Pather Panchali* (1955). The story of a young boy, Apu, growing up in a Bengali village was a great success, both in India and abroad, and Ray and his cameraman Subrata Mitra went on to complete what became known as the *Apu Trilogy* with *Aparajito* and *Apu Sansar*.

Although this is considered his greatest work, Ray subsequently made many other films, including Charulata (1964), the *Calcutta Trilogy* (1970–5) and his first Hindi/Urdu film *Shatranj ke Khilai* (The Chess Players, 1977). For detailed information on the great director's life and individual films, see www.satyajitray.org.

Kolkata has a greater number of churches than any other large Indian city.

Visiting the Indian Museum.

Curzon. Not far away, in the middle of a roundabout, is a statue to Bengal's most famous freedom fighter, Subhas Chandra Bose. His life is celebrated in Netaji Bhavan on Elgin Road (see page 300).

Chowringhee

To the east of the Maidan, **Chowringhee** (now Jawaharlal Nehru Road, although many people still use the old name) was once a jungle path leading to the Kali Temple. Together with the **Esplanade** at the Maidan's northern edge, it is home to late 19th-century buildings such as the **Oberoi Grand** and the Indian Museum. Chowringhee's glory is no more: many of the facades are decaying and the elegant old buildings are being displaced by modern high-rise developments. Hawkers, shoe-shine boys, beggars and touts crowd the pavement.

The huge **Indian Museum** Ⓖ (www.indianmuseumkolkata.org; Tue–Sun, Mar–Nov 10am–5pm, Dec–Feb 10am–4.30pm), certainly the largest in the country if not all of Asia, lies at the northern end of Jawaharlal Nehru

Road. It was founded in 1814 but was not opened to the public until 1878. Also known as the *jadu ghar*, 'house of magic', the sprawling complex is dreadfully run-down (be warned that the toilets are unusable), but it is still worth the effort to visit.

The 36 galleries contain a large variety of exhibits, and you will need to put aside a whole morning or afternoon to see the best of them. Prize archaeological items include a 3rd-century BC Mauryan lion capital, artefacts from Mohenjadaro and Harappa, and pieces from the 2nd-century BC stupa at Bharut in Madhya Pradesh. The museum also contains extensive geological and natural history galleries (although these are a legacy of rather unenlightened research methods). In addition there are collections of textiles, Kalighat paintings, miniatures and sculpture, including many Gandharan works and some impressive Pala bronzes. The new painting galleries are particularly good, with collections of Bengali art.

Raj Bhavan Ⓗ on Esplanade Row East was built in 1803 by Governor-General Wellesley, who believed that India should be governed 'from a palace, not from a counting-house'. Towards the river are the **Rajya Sabha** (Assembly House), the old **Town Hall** and the **High Court** built in 1872 on the model of the Gothic belfry of Ypres in Flanders. The Town Hall has been restored and now houses the **Kolkata Museum** (Mon–Fri 11am–6pm), which outlines the history of the city through models, paintings and interactive displays.

To the north of Raj Bhavan is **St John's Church** Ⓘ, built in 1784. Inside is a celebrated *Last Supper* by Zoffany. Job Charnock, the founder of the city, was buried in the cemetery here. In the garden stands the monument to the victims of the infamous 'Black Hole', when 146 British prisoners were crammed into a small room after Fort William was stormed in 1756, and 113 suffocated and died.

BBD Bagh

Beyond St John's is **Dalhousie Square**, renamed **BBD Bagh** in memory of three brothers, Binoy, Badal and Dinesh, who were hanged for having conspired to kill Lord Dalhousie, the Lieutenant-Governor of Bengal.

Facing the tank that once used to be Kolkata's only source of drinking water stands the **Writers' Building ❶**, seat of the West Bengal government. It was built in the late 19th century. The first buildings that stood here – constructed as far back as 1690 – housed 'writers' (clerks) of the East India Company, hence the name. Security is tight, and photography strictly forbidden. Opposite stands **St Andrew's Kirk**, opened in 1818 and built on the site of the old Court House. A cool retreat from the baking square outside, it is reputed to have the best church organ in India.

The offices of Kolkata's most prestigious companies – tall Victorian buildings, with Art Nouveau staircases, brass signs, marble floors and wood panelling – form a gracious parade along the old Clive Row, now **Netaji Subhas Road**. These streets are now choked with hawkers, cars and taxis. Even the **Stock Exchange** has spilled over onto the street opposite Jardine Henderson's. The Stock Exchange building on the corner of Lyon's Range, erected in 1917, houses a number of official bodies and associations. In India Exchange Lane, near the **Jute Balers Association**, speculators on the jute market operate from booths equipped with telephones projecting from the buildings along the street. Buyers shout their orders to sellers who stand in the street.

Chinatown

Starting at the northeastern corner of the Maidan, in **Bentinck Street** there is a succession of Chinese shoemakers, Muslim tailors and sweet and tea shops. **Tiretta Market** nearby, named after its former owner, a friend of Casanova who had to flee Venice, sells dried fish, vegetables and meat.

Chinatown ❸ is in Tangra, where the Chinese settled at the end of the 18th century. This area was a Cantonese town, but since 1962, when Indian and Chinese troops clashed at the frontier, it has been greatly reduced. There are still some 5,000 Chinese citizens – though the community has been greatly depleted by emigration – and most of the Chinese buildings have disappeared along with the Chinese-language newspapers that used to be printed here. Tangra still has a different feel to other areas of the city, and there are a number of Chinese restaurants, mostly producing a *Chinjabi* fusion of Indian and Chinese dishes.

In **Old China Bazaar**, west of Brabourne Road, Parsis have an *agiary* (fire temple), the Ismailis have a mosque, and the Gujarati Jains a **temple** (daily 6am–noon, 3–7pm), one of the most charming in Kolkata. There are also two synagogues, one of which, **Magen David**, was built in 1884. Kolkata's Jews came from Iraq in the 19th century and formed a

EAT

The dishes found in the small local restaurants of Chinatown bear little resemblance to authentic Chinese regional creations. A very Indian mix of spices is added to noodles and fried rice, resulting in what has become an exceptionally popular fusion of Indian and Chinese cooking. For authentic Chinese food, try Beijing or Mainland China.

KOLKATA TRANSPORT

Travelling north–south between Dum Dum and Tollygunge through central Kolkata is easy on the metro. India's first mass rapid transport system, the Russian-designed network was inaugurated in 1984 and now has six constantly expanding lines in addition to its central axis

This main line extends further south to Garia, while a new line is due to connect Salt Lake and Haora (Howrah); several other lines are also being built. Kolkatans are justly proud of their metro which, although showing signs of age, still manages to be cheap and punctual. Trains run from 6.45am until 10.45pm Monday–Saturday and from 9.50am until 10.45pm on Sundays. For more info, visit www.kolmetro.com.

Suburban rail services, by contrast, are of little use to most visitors.

Kolkata is currently the only city in India with a tram network and this can be a good way to get around the city centre. Most routes run between around 6am and 9pm.

Elsewhere in the city there is an extensive, if crowded, bus service, but it is generally best to pick up a taxi or autorickshaw. As elsewhere in India, these are supposed to use their meters, but it can be very hard to persuade them to do so. Negotiate hard and you will soon get a feel for what is a reasonable fare.

To cross over from Kolkata proper to Howrah, numerous ferries operate from various ghats along the river. The journey is short and cheap.

FACT

Kumartuli's god effigy workshops are busiest between August and November, over the period covering the city's popular Durga and Kali festivals.

prosperous community, but emigration to Israel, the US and the UK since the end of World War II has left less than 100 Jewish families in the city.

Off Old China Bazaar Lane stands the **Armenian Church of Our Lady of Nazareth**. It was built in 1724 and is said to have the oldest working clock in Kolkata. Arriving as traders from the Persian city of Isfahan in the 17th century, the Armenians were already here and in Chinsura, upriver on the Hugli, when Job Charnock founded the city. A grave in the church cemetery is dated 1630. In and around Kolkata, the Armenians, of which there are now only a few hundred, have several churches, a school, a club and also one of India's best rugby teams.

Along Chitpur Road, now Rabindra Sarani, stands the **Nakhoda Mosque** ⓛ, built in red sandstone with four floors. The model was Akbar's tomb at Sikandra near Agra. It has room for a congregation of 10,000. The area around the mosque is full of Muslim shops and some good restaurants.

North Kolkata

The adjacent areas of Jorashankho and Pathuriagata, in north Kolkata, are two of the oldest in the city, with streets lined by grand, colonnaded mansions and other buildings dating from the hey day of the Raj. Among them on Darpanarain Tagore Lane is **Tagore's Castle** ⓜ, built in 1867 and originally a theatre, whose extravagant towers, turrets and crenellations were inspired by those of the fairytale Bavarian castle of Neuschwanstein. Overbuilt structures and tenements have, unfortunately, altered its silhouette.

At the end of Dwarkanath Tagore Lane is **Rabindra Mancha** ⓝ (Tue–Sun 10.30am–4.30pm; charge), an 18th-century house where the poet Rabindranath Tagore was born in 1861, and where he died in 1941. Tagore House also puts on Bengali music and dance performances. Adjoining the house is a library and **Rabindra Bharati University**, the Tagore Academy. The university's museum (40-minute tours in English Nov–Jan 7pm, Feb–June 8pm) is devoted to the poet's life and to

Courtyard at the Indian Museum. The Italianate building dates from 1878.

the Young Bengal movement, as well as a collection of almost 2,000 of Tagore's paintings.

In **Kumartuli**, further north, lives a community of artisans making clay images of the goddesses Durga, Lakshmi and Sarasvati for festivals. In **Rajabazar** on Badni Das Temple Road are four Jain temples of the Digamber sect, built at the end of the 19th century. Known collectively as the **Parasnath Mandir**, the best-known is that dedicated to Sital Nath. Its architecture is a mixture of Mughal, Baroque, neoclassical and local styles, and its interior is decorated with mosaics, coloured glass, mirrors, coloured stones, crystal and marble.

On Muktaram Babu Street at Chorebagan ('the thieves' garden') is the **Marble Palace ⓞ** (Tue, Wed, Fri and Sun 10am–4pm; free; visits must be arranged in advance from the Tourism Information Centre, 3/2 BBD Bagh, tel: 033-2248 8271, or from a regional tourist office). This charming, eccentric building was commissioned in 1835 by Raja Mullick and built in Italian marble. The raja's descendants still live here, but most of it can be visited. In its dark halls are assembled paintings, clocks, statues, crystal and china. Among them there is said to be a Napoleon by Houdin, one Arnold, one Gainsborough, three Rubens and a statue by Michelangelo. In the yard is the family temple, and a collection of parrots, doves and mynahs.

Kolkata University ⓟ on College Square was founded in 1857 and moved to this location in 1873. It has, in the past, been the scene of many demonstrations, and many of its walls are periodically covered with political graffiti. In the **University Senate** building is the **Ashutosh Museum** (Mon–Fri 10.30am–5pm, Sat 10.30am–1.30pm; free), presenting a collection of Pala sculptures, terracotta pieces, bronzes and examples of Bengali traditional art.

The **Indian Coffee House**, on Bankim Chatterjee Street, is the traditional meeting place for the city's intellectual and student circles.

On R.N. Mukharji Road, to the west of BBD Bagh, is the **Old Mission**. This was built in 1770 by a

EAT

While you're in the University District, be sure to drop by the famous Indian Coffee House at 15 Bankim Chatterjee St, a favourite meeting place for generations of freedom fighter, revolutionaries and poets.

Grandiose imperial architecture at the Writers' Building.

One of the numerous shrines at the Kali Temple.

Swedish missionary and is the oldest church in Kolkata.

Behind Chowringhee is the old European quarter. It is an area of mansions slowly being replaced by modern buildings. **Park Street**, the main thoroughfare, was laid during the first quarter of the last century. The **Freemasons' Hall** on this street was built in the 19th century and houses the oldest Lodge outside Britain.

The **Asiatic Society** (www.asiaticsocietycal.com; free), also at the beginning of Park Street, was founded in 1784 by Sir William Jones. It houses a permanent exhibition of oriental manuscripts, prints and paintings that can be visited on request.

Park Street used to be called European Burial Road and once ended at the **South Park Street Cemetery**, the oldest in Kolkata. Here are buried Major General Charles 'Hindoo' Stuart, an Irishman who adopted the Hindu religion; Robert Kyd, founder of the Botanical Gardens; William Makepeace, Thackeray's father; Rose Aylmer, 'who died of eating too many pineapples'; the poet Henry Derozio,

Street life on the Strand.

founder of the Young Bengal movement; and Sir William Jones, the father of the Asiatic Society.

Another landmark is **La Martinière College** on Acharya Jagadish Chandra Bose Road, founded by a Frenchman, Claude Martin. A former bodyguard to the French Governor of Pondicherry, Martin later joined the service of the East India Company and ended his career as a Major General. He died in 1800, bequeathing his fortune to set up schools in Lyon (France), Kolkata and Lucknow, and donated a sum of Rs50,000 to the Church of the Sacred Heart in Chandernagore. Nearby, in Bhawanipur, is **Netaji Bhavan** (Tue–Sun 11am–4pm) on Elgin Road, the house from which Subhas Chandra Bose, the nationalist leader, escaped during World War II to establish the Indian National Army in Japanese-occupied Southeast Asia. It is now a museum with a collection of photographs and letters written during his campaign to rid India of the British.

On Gurusady Road is the **Birla Industrial and Technological**

Museum (www.bitm.gov.in; daily 10am–5.30pm). The well-displayed galleries are arranged by theme (Life Sciences, Transport and Electricity, for example) and have interactive models.

South Kolkata

The south of the city is essentially residential, with several wealthy neighbourhoods. Warren Hastings's first residence, at Alipur, now an institute of education, is said to be haunted by its former owner.

The **National Library** ⓠ, on Belvedere Road, was once the Winter Viceregal Lodge (www.national library.gov.in; Mon–Fri 9am–8pm, Sat–Sun 9.30am–6pm; free but application for membership necessary). The collections are extensive and are divided into sections corresponding to the major Indian languages. The **Zoological Gardens**, close to the National Library, were established in 1876. Like all Indian zoos, a visit here can be a very depressing experience.

Kalighat is a pleasantly traditional middle-class neighbourhood on **Tolly's Nullah**. In 1775 Colonel Tolly drained the silted canal to bring Ganges water to the **Kali Temple** ⓡ. The present *mandir* was built in 1809 by Sobarna Chowdhury on the site of a 16th-century Kali temple, although some kind of shrine has probably been here since early times. The Kali Temple is said to stand on the spot where Sati's little toe landed after her dead body had been dismembered by Vishnu and scattered across the earth; this was to stop Shiva's destructive dance of mourning.

The temple is still owned by the founder's descendants, the *paladas*, who have a monopoly over rituals. Pilgrims make offerings to Kali (an *avatar* of Sati) of milk mixed with Ganges water and *bhang* (cannabis). Human sacrifices are known to have taken place, but today only goats are sacrificed. Kali's image, inside the central shrine, is made of black marble, and the goddess is seen with four arms, garlanded with a chain of human heads, and with a hand, tongue and eyebrows made of gold; her eyes and tongue are painted blood-red.

The temple is closed to non-Hindus, and at times the streets around the shrine can feel slightly unsafe to visitors. The fervour of the devotees is fascinating, but with the animal sacrifices that take place daily, those of a sensitive disposition might want to observe the goings-on from a distance. The market outside the temple is very lively, and there is a huge amount of religious paraphernalia on display.

Next door, the late Mother Teresa's (1910–97) **Home for the Destitute and Dying** ⓢ, or Nirmal Hriday, is the first of several missions run by her Sisters of Charity in the city. The nuns, in their white saris, can be seen all across town. Mother Teresa was beatified in 2003 by Pope John Paul II and the date for her canonisation as a saint has been set for September 2016 – but she remains a controversial figure both in India and abroad.

TIP

People interested in volunteering at the Home for the Destitute and Dying (the Home of the Pure Heart, Nirmal Hriday) should contact the Mother's House in advance at: Missionaries of Charity, 54 A.J.C. Bose Road, tel: 033-2249 7115.

Shoe shining and repairs outside the main bus station.

Shaving on the street.

Tollygunge

There are more temples further south on Chetla and Tollygunge roads. Nearby is the **Tollygunge Club** ❶. An indigo plantation was laid out here in 1781 by the Johnson family. Later the exiled family of Tipu Sultan lived in the Johnson mansion, which was subsequently converted into the club. It became the Tollygunge Club in 1895 and offers its facilities (golf, tennis, squash and a swimming pool) to visitors on a daily basis. Come in the evening to see Kolkata's 'great and good' having a drink and eating the somewhat institutional food; it offers a real insight into how the city's middle class operates and interacts. It is also possible to stay here (contact the club secretary in advance at: 120, Deshapran Sasmal Road, tel: 033-2417 6022, www.tollygungeclub.org).

Stalls in the market outside the Kali Temple.

Those of the middle class not enjoying themselves in the verdant surrounds of the Tolly are likely to be found not far away at Kolkata's largest shopping complex, **South City Mall**. Rather incongruous given the run-down surroundings, this is a large, glass-fronted, air-conditioned mall, complete with food court and international chains.

Northeast of Tollygunge, around **Rabindra Sarovar Lake**, are rowing clubs and the **Birla Academy of Art and Culture** ❶ (www.birlaart.com; Tue–Sun 3–8pm; free) on Southern Avenue, a museum that is never crowded, with a whole floor of miniatures from all the major schools, a modern art gallery and a collection of old statues.

The **Ramakrishna Mission Institute of Culture** on Gol Park, near the lake, is a branch of the Ramakrishna Mission of Belur Math. It has a school of languages, a library, a museum of Indian art and a Universal Prayer Room.

Along the Ganges

From the ghat near the Garden Reach shipyard, a ferry periodically crosses to the **Botanical Gardens** ❶ (Tue–Sun 7am–5pm). Set up in 1787, these once boasted the largest banyan tree in the world. The trunk was struck by lightning in 1919 and was subsequently removed. About 1,500 offshoots remain, forming a circle with a diameter of more than 10 metres (33ft). It is also the location of the Central National Herbarium of India.

The **Metiaburuz Shi'ite Mosque**, where the last nawab, Wajid Ali Shah, was exiled, on Garden Reach Road was built and lavishly decorated by the royal family of Avadh in the 19th century.

The riverside ghats off Strand Road, like any on the Ganges, are most active at dawn and sunset. During festivals thousands of devotees converge on **Babu**, **Outram** and **Princep ghats** to immerse clay images of Durga, Kali, Lakshmi or Sarasvati into the river. Other communities hold festivals too. On Chat, Biharis dip fruit in the river and Sindhis, on Chetti Chand, immerse statues of the god Jhulelal. On Strand Road, in January, a transit camp is arranged for the thousands of pilgrims on their way to the holy island of Sagardwip. Every morning the ghats swarm with people washing and praying.

On the riverfront promenade is the **Gwalior Monument**, called the 'Pepper Pot' because of its shape, and erected to commemorate a British victory in the Maratha Wars. At Princep Ghat dinghies are available for hire on an hourly basis.

The 1941 **Haora Bridge** over the Hugli has eight traffic lanes, which is not enough for the daily flow of trams, buses, trucks, rickshaws, pedestrians, buffaloes, sheep, goats, taxis and bullock carts. On hot days its length can increase by 1 metre (3ft). It has been supplemented by a new **Vidyasagar Setu** suspension bridge at Hastings, 3km (2 miles) south.

Salt Lake

On the northeastern edge of Kolkata, on the way to the airport, is the new town of Bidhannagar, more popularly known as **Salt Lake**. Initially laid out in the 1950s, it has developed into one of the most attractive parts of the city, at the heart of which is a large park. Mostly comprising blocks of middle-class residences, it is also the location of the very swish Hyatt Regency, and one of the city's largest shopping malls, City Centre. **Nicco Park** (www.niccoparks.com; daily 10am–8pm) is an amusement park on the south side of Salt Lake. The somewhat optimistically named **Wet-o-Wild Beach Tropicana** (daily 10am–8pm), the city's best public swimming complex, is entered through Nicco Park.

Not far away, where the Eastern Bypass crosses J.B.S. Halden Avenue, is another good destination for families, **Science City** (www.sciencecitykolkata.org.in; daily 9am–8pm). The striking complex of rounded buildings accommodates a large interactive museum of science and technology, including a state-of-the-art planetarium and a particularly good display on tectonics and earthquakes.

A rather different complex is found in a large park just across from the Salt Lake Stadium. **Swabhumi** (daily 10am–6pm) has a food court serving dishes from all parts of India, a crafts village, heritage shopping complex and an auditorium which puts on performances of traditional music and dance.

The great banyan tree at the Botanical Gardens.

Darjeeling houses.

Map on page 309

WEST BENGAL, ODISHA AND JHARKHAND

From the swamps of the Sunderbans to the peaks of the Himalayas, this diverse region has attracted traders and colonisers, poets and philosophers, all of whom have left their mark.

The three states that make up the eastern part of the Indian Peninsula, West Bengal, Orissa – now renamed Odisha – and Jharkhand, see relatively few visitors compared to other parts of the country, but are nonetheless full of interest. Among the attractions are ancient temples, wide beaches, the world's largest mangrove forest, centres of culture and tea gardens clinging to the lower slopes of the Himalayas.

Bengal is known for its strong intellectual tradition as well as important historical sites, many of which shed light on the early years of European trade and conquest in India. Odisha has some of the holiest places in Hinduism in the temples of Puri and Bhubaneshwar, as well as some important Buddhist sites. The extravagant size and coastal location of the Hindu temples give them an atmosphere all of their own: they seemingly blend in to the surrounding landscape, and more than warrant the journey to see them. Jharkhand, carved out of the forested tracts of the Chota Nagpur plateau, is the home of a number of Adivasi (tribal) groups, as well as being the location of heavy industry, with India's largest steelworks.

West Bengal

West Bengal stretches from the Himalayas to the Bay of Bengal. Early mention of Bengal can be found in the Mahabharata and in Ptolemy's *Geography*. Bengal was then a seafaring nation, sending traders to Sri Lanka, Sumatra and Java and being visited by Greeks, Chinese and Persians.

From the end of the 19th century onwards Bengal was one of the most prosperous territories of the British Empire. Temples were built, the Bengali language was enriched by poets and writers such as Bankim Chandra Chatterjee and Rabindranath

Main Attractions

Sunderbans
Darjeeling
Darjeeling Himalayan
   Railway
Druk Thupten Sangag
   Choling Monastery, Dali
Bhubaneshwar
Jagannath Temple, Puri
Sun Temple, Konark

Sikkimese man and child.

Tea picking. Whereas some coarser grades of tea are cut with shears, Darjeeling teas are all hand-picked.

Early colonisers

Along the Grand Trunk Road, on the right bank of the Hugli just north of **Kolkata ❶**, are sleepy little towns with palaces, old churches, riverfront promenades and colonial houses and cemeteries – remains of the old Danish, Dutch and French settlements. The Grand Trunk Road is reached by the Bally Bridge crossing the Hugli at **Dakshinesvar**, 20km (12 miles) north of Kolkata, where, on the left bank, stands the 9th-century **Kali Bhavatarini Temple** complex containing a central temple to Kali, one to Radha-Krishna and 12 small temples to Shiva. The philosopher Ramakrishna once lived here, and his room is now a museum.

Downstream across the river is **Belur Math**, headquarters of the Ramakrishna Mission, founded by Ramakrishna's disciple Vivekananda. The main building, the **Sri Ramakrishna Temple**, 75 metres (246ft) long and

Tagore, and religious philosophers such as Ramakrishna and Vivekananda emerged.

35 metres (115ft) high, reflects Ramakrishna's call for harmony between religions. The gate is Buddhist, the structure above the entrance South Indian, the windows and balconies Mughal and Rajput, and the floor plan is that of a Christian cross.

The first foreign settlement north of Kolkata was at **Serampore**, 25km (15 miles) from Kolkata. The Danish East India Company carried on trade here from the late 17th century until 1845, when the Danes sold all their possessions in India to Britain. In 1799 William Carey, an Englishman, and two fellow Baptist missionaries established a press here and were pioneers of printing in several Asian languages.

In 1819 Carey founded the **Serampore College**, which was incorporated in 1827 as a university by Danish Royal Charter. Still active, the college is now a Baptist theological institute. It stands on the banks of the Hugli, among other 18th- and 19th-century mansions. Slightly inland is **St Olaf's Church**, built in 1747.

A gate bearing the motto of the French Republic, *Liberté,*

Egalité, Fraternité, marks the entrance to **Chandernagore**, a French *Etablissement* almost continuously from 1673 to 1952. A French atmosphere still persists along the shaded Quai Dupleix, now Strand Road, with its public benches exactly like those in Parisian parks.

The Dutch settled at **Chinsura**, 1km south of Hugli, in 1625 and ceded it to Britain in 1826 against Bencoolen in Sumatra. A Dutch barracks, church and cemetery still remain from that period. Chinsura's Armenian community constructed **St John's Church** in 1695 and, once a year, on St John's day, in January, the Armenians of Kolkata gather here to hold religious services. To the north, on the riverside, is the **Imambara**, a Shi'ite place of worship with a clock tower donated by Queen Victoria.

The Portuguese founded nearby Bandel de Ugolim, now **Hugli**, in 1580, and controlled most of the trade passing through Bengal, until the arrival of other European nations. The **Church of Our Lady of Bandel** is all that remains of the Portuguese past. Consecrated in 1599, it was rebuilt after being destroyed by Shah Jahan in 1632, but without the usual exuberance of Portuguese churches. It has remained a pilgrimage centre. Even today, each Christmas Eve, a Mass is celebrated.

Bengal's holy cities

There are two temples at **Bansberia** ❷, 6km (4 miles) north of Hugli. The small **Vasudeva Temple**, constructed in the 17th century, has sculptured terracotta tiles representing ships, Portuguese soldiers and scenes from the *Ramayana*. **Hangsesvari Temple**, with its 13 towers, was founded in the early 19th century. Rajah Deb started building it following a dream, but died before completion. His widow was about to commit *sati* (self-immolation), but was rescued at the last moment by the religious reformer Ram Mohan Roy, founder of the Brahmo Samaj movement. She lived on and completed the temple.

Tribeni, 50km (30 miles) north of Bansberia, is a holy place at the confluence of two rivers where twice a year, at Dussera and during the festival of Varuna, the god of water, pilgrims visit the little **Benimadhava Temple** complex and take a bath in the Ganges. On the southern side is the **Darya Zafar Khan**, Bengal's oldest Muslim building, erected in the 13th century using material from dismantled Buddhist and Hindu temples.

Nawadwip ❸, 125km (78 miles) north of Kolkata, also known as **Nadia**, is built on nine formerly distinct islands on the Ganges, called Bhagirathi here. It was the capital of Bengal in the 11th and 12th centuries and is among the holiest of places in West Bengal. Chaitanya Mahaprabhu, said to be an incarnation of Vishnu, taught the Vaishnava philosophy here in the 16th century. Every year in March, over 500,000 pilgrims come to Nadia for the *padikrama*, a pilgrimage on foot that takes them along a 50km (30-mile) loop around places and

REGIONAL TRANSPORT

Flights: The major hub for the region is Kolkata's Netaji Subhas Chandra Bose airport, but most large cities, such as Bhubaneshwar and Ranchi, have domestic airports served by low-cost airlines as well as the major carriers, Indian Airline and Jet Airways. The exception is Darjeeling, where the nearest airport is the military runway at Bagdogra near Siliguri (from where you have to take a taxi). However, most places are just as easily reached by rail – the exceptions being areas subject to the ongoing Nazalite-Maoist insurgency, where all travel is inadvisable.

Trains: West Bengal, Odisha and Jharkhand are well served by rail services. Bhubaneshwar is on the main line north–south along the east coast, Puri is on a branch line off the main line at Khurda Road, while Ranchi takes a little more time and effort but is still straightforward to reach from Kolkata or, better still, Patna. West Bengal has numerous local passenger services, while the narrow-gauge railway from New Jalpaiguri up to Darjeeling is one of the great India travel experiences.

Bhubaneshwar: Kolkata (Haora) (13–17 daily; 7–8hrs 30mins); Puri (15–21 daily; 1hr 40mins–2hrs)

Ranchi: Kolkata (Haora) (2–3 daily; 7hrs 30mins–9hrs); Patna (4–6 daily; 9–12hrs)

New Jalpaiguri–Darjeeling: (1 daily, dept. 8.30am, arr. 4pm. From Darjeeling the train departs at 10.15am, arr. 5.45pm)

temples associated with Chaitanya. Nearby is Sri Mayapur, the headquarters of the International Society for Krishna Consciousness (ISKON).

Murshidabad and Malda

Some 50km (30 miles) north of the battlefield of Plassey, **Murshidabad** ❹ was the capital of Bengal in 1705, when the *diwan* (Mughal viceroy) of Bengal, Bihar and Odisha, Murshid Kuli Khan, transferred his capital here from Dacca. Most of the monuments are ruined, but Siraj-ud-Daula's grave at Khusbagh (across the river), Murshid Kuli Khan's tomb inside the Katra Mosque and the Jafarganj cemetery can still be seen. There are also palaces; the Jafarganj Deorhi, where Siraj-ud-Daula was assassinated; and **Hazarduari**, the nawab's palace, built in 1837 in Gothic style, now a museum containing old arms, china and special plates called *ghauri* used by the nawab that, it was believed, would crack if the food were poisoned (Sat–Thur 10am–5pm). Murshidabad is still well known for its fine silk and ivory carving.

Nearby, at **Baranagar**, are a number of 18th-century terracotta temples. Further north, about 340km (210 miles) from Kolkata, is the town of **Malda** ❺, formerly called English Bazaar, a foreign settlement dating from 1680, where the Dutch, the French and then the East India Company carried on trade.

Gaur, nearby, was the capital of the Pala and Sen dynasties. The now deserted city was destroyed by the Afghan rulers of Bengal, and you can see the Barasona Baroduari Mosque completed in 1526; the Feroze Minar, a minaret built in 1486; the ruined Chika Mosque with Hindu idols on the doors and lintels; and the now dilapidated Lattan mosque. Portions of Hindu monuments from Malda were used to build the new capital of **Pandua**, where the most important building is the Adina mosque.

South to the Sunderbans

The **Sunderbans** ('beautiful forest' in Bengali) ❻ formed by the Ganges-Brahmaputra delta, start south of Kolkata and extend across the northern

Sunrise in the Sundarbans.

shore of the Bay of Bengal. A Unesco World Heritage Site, two-thirds of which is in Bangladesh, this is an area of marshy mangrove jungle, the largest estuarine forest in the world. It is also the land of the Royal Bengal Tiger, which swims and has been known to attack fishermen.

There are few roads, and water transport is often the only way of communication. A permit is required to enter the area. Check with the West Bengal Tourist Promotion Board for the latest information, particularly regarding the **Sudhanyakali** and **Sajankali** wildlife sanctuaries. The chances of seeing a tiger are slim, but there are estuarine crocodiles, the largest in the world, usually seen sleeping on mudflats along the river, as well as fishing cats, water monitors and turtles.

At **Bratacharingam**, 15km (9 miles) south of Kolkata, on the road to Diamond Harbour, is **Gurusaday Museum** (Tue–Sun 10am–5pm), a collection of Bengali traditional art: terracotta temple plaques, clay figurines, wood sculptures, Kalighat paintings, scroll painting and *kanthas*, which are used cotton saris, stitched together and embroidered.

On the Hugli, at the end of Budge-Budge Road, branching off Diamond Harbour Road, is **Achipur**, named after Ah-Chi, the first Chinese to migrate to Bengal in modern times (end of the 18th century). His red-painted grave facing the river is probably the only Chinese tomb along the Ganges. There is also a Taoist temple with inscriptions dating back to the 18th century. On every Lunar New Year, the Chinese community of Kolkata comes here on a pilgrimage, transforming this Bengali village into a Chinese community for one day.

Diamond Harbour ❼, 50km (30 miles) down the Hugli from Kolkata, a natural harbour, is a former stronghold of Portuguese pirates. Remains of their fort can be seen along the riverfront.

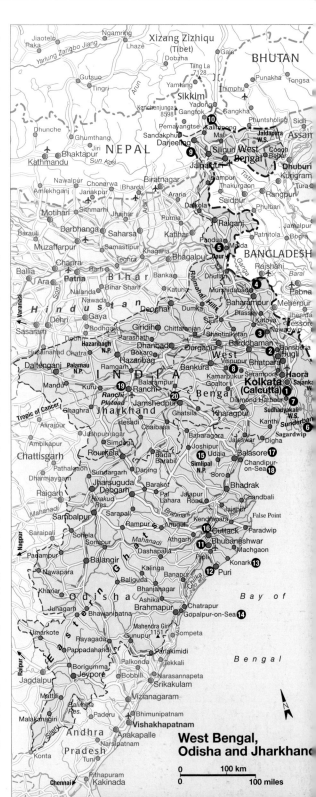

West Bengal, Odisha and Jharkhand

0   100 km
0   100 miles

The last island before the ocean is **Sagardwip**, where the Ganges meets the sea. Every year, in mid-January, a religious festival, Gangasagar Mela, is celebrated here. Over half a million pilgrims take a holy dip and then converge at the **Kapil Muni Temple**. On the west coast of the Bay of Bengal 240km (150 miles) southeast of Kolkata, on the Odisha border, is **Digha**, which has a good beach, and is very popular with Indian tourists.

West of Kolkata

The **Tarakeshwar Temple**, 57km (35 miles) west of Kolkata, is built around a black stone lingam of Tarakesvar Babu, an avatar (incarnation) of Shiva. It is of little architectural interest but is one of West Bengal's most active pilgrimage centres. At Sivaratri in February and Kastamela in August, barefooted pilgrims carry Ganges water from Kolkata to the temple in earthen pots decorated with flowers and pour it over the lingam.

Kamarpukur, 60km (37 miles) further west, a group of three hamlets surrounded by paddy fields, is religious

philosopher Ramakrishna Paramhansdeb's birthplace. There is a temple with a marble statue of Ramakrishna.

Visnupur ❽, 200km (125 miles) west of Kolkata, was the capital of the Malla kings. In the 17th and 18th centuries Visnupur became an important cultural centre, developing its own distinctive style of brick-built temple architecture, as well as being a centre for *dhrupad* singing.

The most impressive building in Visnupur is **Rashmancha**, a Vishnu shrine that takes the form of a flat pyramid-like structure resting on the arches of three circumambulatory galleries.

Nearby, opposite the Tourist Lodge, stands **Dalmadal**, a huge cannon almost 4 metres (13ft) long, whose boom saved the city from the Maratha armies in 1742. There are temples all over the city, most of them dedicated to Radha and Krishna. The most remarkable among them are: the **Kalachand Sri Mandir**; the **Shyam Rai Mandir**, perhaps the finest terracotta temple in Bengal, decorated with scenes from the *Ramayana* and the *Mahabharata*; **Jor Bangla**, covered with tiles depicting naval battles and hunting scenes; the **Madan Mohan**, dating from 1694; and **Madan Gopal**, almost resembling a church more than a temple, with its five towers.

North of Visnupur, 136km (85 miles) from Kolkata, is **Shantiniketan**. In 1861 Rabindranath Tagore's father founded an ashram here. The poet spent most of his Nobel Prize money to make it an educational institution. Here the poet revived the traditional Indian way of teaching in the open air, under a tree, in close contact with nature. Shantiniketan soon became one of the hubs of intellectual life; one of the university's most famous alumni is the late Indira Gandhi.

An annual festival is celebrated nearby at **Kendubilwa,** the birthplace of Jaidev, another great Bengali poet and keen propagator of Vaishnava philosophy. In mid-January, Bengali bards,

The Toy Train at Darjeeling station.

known as *bauls*, gather for a four-day non-stop recital of the poet's work.

The pilgrimage centre, **Tarapith**, 80km (50 miles) from Shantiniketan, is a small village dominated by a temple to Tara, an avatar of Kali, whose third eye is said to have landed here.

North Bengal

North Bengal includes the hills and mountains of the Himalayas around Darjeeling as well as the district known as the Dooars that lies on the edge of the plains in the Terai. Having more in common with the Tibetan-influenced peoples to the north, it is culturally very different to the rest of Bengal. There has been unrest for a number of years, with the Gorkha Janmukti Morcha demanding separate statehood for the area under the name of Gorkhaland (you will see graffiti demanding this along with the yellow and green flags of the Gorkha indepedence movement everywhere). So far nothing has come of their agitations, but strikes and protests can shut down the district for weeks at a time.

Darjeeling Himalayan Railway

Every year at the beginning of the monsoon, the viceroys of India, and after 1911 the lieutenant governors of Bengal, would move to **Darjeeling** ❾ (also spelt Darjiling), situated at an altitude of 2,134 metres (7,000ft), facing the Himalayas. In the 1840s tea-planting was introduced in the area and Darjeeling 'orthodox' tea is now famous for its delicate flavour. Darjeeling is a three-hour drive up a winding road from Bagdogra airport near Siliguri (where there is also a railway station). It can also be reached from New Jalpaiguri railway station by the **Darjeeling Himalayan Railway**, a Unesco World Heritage Site.

Completed in 1881, the line climbs 1,500 metres (5,000ft) over 88km (54 miles) through mountains and tea gardens, reaching its highest point at the station of Ghoom (2,225

metres/7,300ft), before rounding the spectacular Batasia Loop with its amazing views and dropping down to its final station at Darjeeling.

The steep ride takes around seven hours – at one point the train goes so slowly that one can buy from hawkers alongside – and the train is now pulled by oil-fired locomotives, converted from the original coal-burning rolling stock. During the monsoon the service may be disrupted as the track can be in danger of being washed away. Another sporadic disruption comes from strikes demanding separate statehood for the region; these can stop services for days or even weeks.

Darjeeling

Darjeeling is an abrupt change from the plains, its population being largely Nepali, Lepcha, Tibetan and Bhutia. At the town centre is the **Mall**, Darjeeling's commercial street, lined with souvenir shops. The Mall leads to **Chaurastha**, a square where there are cafés, hotels and a good bookshop with many interesting books on India and Tibet. A Nyingmapa Buddhist

---

THE GREAT HEDGE OF INDIA

The taxing of salt was controversial throughout the period of British rule in India. Having taken control of all salt production in the then 'presidency' of Bengal in 1788, the British East India Company decided to impose a tenfold increase in the salt tax. Naturally this was an unpopular move, and led to the widespread smuggling of salt into the region, mainly from the princely states which were not under direct British rule. The British response to this was to build a series of customs offices on the major transport routes into the state. When this proved ineffective, it was decided that the only solution was a continuous, impenetrable barrier. Initially running between Delhi and Agra, the line, which for the most part consisted of thick, live hedge, eventually covered over 4,000km (2,500 miles) and was patrolled by a staff of 14,000. It extended from the Punjab in the east to Odisha (Orissa) in the west, and eventually came to be known as the Inland Customs Line. The sums of money involved were colossal; by 1877 the salt tax was earning the British government £6.3 million per year, but meant that the average worker was having to spend at least a month's salary a year just to keep his family in salt. The line was abolished in 1879 but the tax lived on, instead imposed at the point of manufacture, and survived Gandhi's famous protest march of 1930 before eventually being rescinded post-Independence.

Wall painting of a lama at Druk Thupten Sangag Choling Monastery.

Sherpa tea stall in the hills above Darjeeling.

monastery, Dorjeling, 'the place of the thunderbolt', once stood on **Observatory Hill** but was destroyed by the Nepalis in the 19th century. A Shiva temple now occupies the site, although the central shrine is shared by both Hindu and Buddhist priests and the surrounding trees are festooned with prayer flags.

On Birch Hill to the north stands the Shrubbery, the residence of the governor of West Bengal, and further down along Birch Hill Road is the **Himalayan Mountaineering Institute**, once headed by the late Tenzing Norgay, the Sherpa guide who conquered Everest with Sir Edmund Hillary on 29 May 1953. A museum displays the equipment used (www.hmi-darjeeling.com; daily 9am–1pm, 2–5pm, entry through zoo; closed Tue during the winter).

The **Zoological Park** specialises in high-altitude wildlife – yaks, Himalayan black bears, pandas, but it also has four Siberian tigers. They are housed in open enclosures, but even so the conditions are very cramped and the animals look rather miserable (daily 9am–6pm; charge includes entry to the Mountaineering Institute).

Dominating the Mall is the **Planters' Club**, which visitors can join and where they can stay on a daily basis. The **Lloyd Botanical Gardens** (Mon–Sat 6am–5pm; free) were laid out in 1878 on land donated by the owners of Lloyd's Bank, and boast an impressive collection of Himalayan and Alpine flora. Nearby is the Tibetan Refugee Self-Help Centre with its temple, school, hospital, and a shop selling carpets, textiles and jewellery.

A little way out of town towards Ghoom is the **Druk Thupten Sangag Choling Monastery** at Dali. Although the building is only a little over 20 years old (it was founded by the lama Thuksay Rimpoche, who died in 1983), it is beautifully constructed, with a wonderfully decorated facade and an impressive prayer hall (ask one of the monks to show you inside if it is not too close to the evening prayer time at 5pm; donations to the monastery are appreciated).

South of Darjeeling

Mount Kanchenjunga can be seen from Observatory Hill, but a much better view of the peak is that from **Tiger Hill**, 10km (6 miles) south of Darjeeling. Taxis take visitors there to watch the sunrise. On most winter days the range can be clearly seen, with Kanchenjunga (8,598 metres/28,208ft) in the middle, flanked by **Kabru** (7,338 metres/24,074ft) and **Pandim** (6,691 metres/21,952ft). To the right are the Three Sisters, **Everest** (8,850 metres/29,035ft), **Makalu** (8,482 metres/27,828ft) and **Lhotse** (8,500 metres/27,887ft), and to the east, Tibetan peaks.

With a plunging view of the plains, **Kurseong** (1,458 metres/4,783ft), 35km (22 miles), marks the point where the Toy Train starts running parallel to the road. Southwest of Ghoom lies **Mirik**, a hill station set in attractive forests. It has an

artificial lake in a small valley where boats can be hired.

Ghoom (perhaps more aptly called 'gloom', as it sits in the mist for much of the year) has an important Buddhist temple and one of the highest railway stations in Asia. The **Yiga Cholang Gelugpa Buddhist Temple** was built in 1875 and hosts a 5-metre (16ft) statue of Lord Buddha. To reach the temple, follow the signs leading up the narrow street off the main road, just down from the station on the Darjeeling side. There is another small Tibetan monastery on the left-hand side of the main road a little further on that is often confused with the older temple.

A five-hour drive (57km/35 miles to the west) from Darjeeling via Ghoom is the trekking centre **Sandakphu**, which is situated 130km (80 miles) from Everest as the crow flies. As well as being the most convenient place from which to start a trek, Sandakphu is worth a visit just to see its particularly fine view of the main Himalayan range.

Make sure you take your passport if you wish to go any further as there is a checkpoint at the entrance to the village. Much of what lies beyond runs along the Nepal border, and there are military checkpoints at regular intervals.

If you are in need refreshment – as you probably will be if you have come from Darjeeling – then the Hotel Khangchendzonga opposite the jeep-hire booth is a good place to eat noodles and *momos*.

Sandakphu is also the place to rent a jeep to take you up to **Phalut** (3,596 metres/11,700ft) for spectacular views of Kanchendzonga. Many of the vehicles here date back to the 1940s, left behind by General Slim's army at the end of World War II. The 'road' up to Phalut (22km/14 miles from Sandakphu) is very rough, indeed spine-breaking, but the views en route are wonderful, as are the moss-laden rhododendron forests you pass through. At the top is a small trekkers' guesthouse and a tea stall; take warm clothes, as the wind can be bitter.

Gorkha women carry heavy loads on the hill of Darjeeling Mall.

Prayer flags adorn the trees outside a Buddhist temple in the Darjeeling hills.

Kalimpong

Kalimpong ⑩, east of Darjeeling, is reached after a two-hour journey. Winding its way among forests and tea gardens, the road crosses the one-lane bridge over the Teesta River, near its confluence with the Rangeet at Pashoke, finally reaching Kalimpong, 51km (32 miles) from Darjeeling. The Lepchas say the two rivers are lovers who fled the mountains to hide their love. One came down in a straight line, led by a partridge, the other zigzagged, led by a cobra, and they were united at Pashoke. Kalimpong was once the starting point for the land route to Tibet. Twice a week, on Wednesday and Saturday, a *hat* (market) is still held here selling spices, fruit and traditional Tibetan medicines, textiles, wool and musk.

There are two Gelugpa Buddhist monasteries in Kalimpong. **Tharpa Choling** at Tirpai houses a library of Tibetan manuscripts and *thanka*, while **Zangdog Palrifo Brang Monastery**, on Durpin Dara Hill, is smaller and of more recent construction.

FACT

In 2007 and 2008 parts of rural Odisha, particularly the predominantly Adivasi Kandhamal District, saw terrible communal violence. While there has long been enmity between the two communities, the killing of the Hindu leader Swami Lakshmananananda in 2008 by Maoist insurgents unleashed attacks against the state's Christians, and the situation has remained tense, with sporadic outbreaks of violence in the years that have followed.

Darjeeling barber.

East of Kalimpong, along the Bhutan border, are the **Dooars**, a tea garden and jungle area little-known to tourists, which can be reached by rail from New Jalpaiguri and by plane via Cooch Behar or Bagdogra. At **Jaldapara** there is a wildlife sanctuary, home to one-horned rhinos, elephants, deer, gaur and wild boar. The Tourist Lodge at nearby **Madarihat** is a villa on stilts built entirely in timber. Nearby is Phuntsholing, across the border in Bhutan.

Odisha (Orissa)

Most visitors to Odisha seek out the state's ancient temples, Adivasi villages or the wide beaches, although this part of eastern India is also known for its destructive cyclones, which move in off the Bay of Bengal; in 1999 a huge storm hit, killing thousands of people and destroying many buildings.

Ancient seafarers from Odisha set up colonies in Burma and Java. Buddhism became the religion of the kingdom of Kalinga, as Odisha was called, soon after the faith was established – spreading down from Bodh Gaya just to the north. Buddhist universities flourished at Nrusinghanath and Ratnagiri, near Cuttack.

Modern Odisha remains an intensely religious state where devotion is focused on Lord Jagannath, an incarnation of Vishnu. A visit to one of the state's major temples is like nowhere else in India; the sense of unflinching devoutness is unsurpassed, giving an immediate idea of the continuing importance of religion in daily Odishan life, and the impression that this is a practice that will continue for centuries to come. Not surprisingly, many elements of Odishan culture stemmed from its temples, where the most remarkable erotic statuary can be found and where Odissi, a style of religious dance, originated. Odissi was traditionally performed by resident temple dancers (*maharis*) devoting their lives to the temple god. When temple dance was outlawed the style began to disappear, but Odissi has been revived as a performing art.

Bhubaneshwar

Bhubaneshwar ⑪, capital of Odisha since 1956, is a city of temples. There were once more than 1,000 of them, and many are still active. Unlike in nearby Puri, most of the temples in the city, with a notable exception, will admit non-Hindus into the temple compound. A large number are located around **Bindu Sarovar**, a tank that is believed to receive water from all the holy rivers of India. The **Lingaraj Temple** to the south, built in 1014 to the glory of Shiva, is certainly the most impressive. A massive wall surrounds a 45-metre (150ft) high *deul* (temple), as well as minor temples to Parvati, Gopalini and Bhubanesvari. All are decorated with a profusion of sculptures of deities, nymphs and amorous couples. Entry is prohibited to non-Hindus.

Vaital Deul is a typical 8th-century temple with an oblong roof (*khakhara deul*). It is decorated with stone figures of Durga, such as the eight-armed Mahishasuramardini, on the northern wall, piercing the left shoulder of Mahisasura, the buffalo-headed demon, with her trident. Within the sanctum, another avatar (incarnation) of Durga, eight-armed Chamunda, often hidden by a drape, sits on a corpse, with an owl and a jackal on each side. She wears a garland of skulls.

Sisiresvara Temple, next to Vaital, is adorned with sculptures of lions, elephants, the gods Ganesh and Kartikeya, and the Avilokitesvara Buddha seated cross-legged and accompanied by a deer and a *nag* (cobra), illustrating the strength of the Buddhist influence in Odisha. The **Uttaresvara Temple** situated on the north bank of the lake has undergone extensive restoration.

Parasuramesvar is one of the oldest of a group of temples located east of the lake. Built in the 7th century, it is still well preserved and is decorated with a four-armed Ganesh, a two-armed Kartikeya mounted on a

FACT

Odishan temples in the Nagara style, seen at their best in Bhubaneshwar, have a distinctive architectural style. The *mandapa* (hall) that leads to the inner sanctum is decorated with horizontal lines called *pida*. This striated appearance also carries over to the temple tower (*rekha deul*) where the convex soaring lines of the building are decorated with sculpture and the characteristic horizontal divisions known as paga.

Druk Thupten Monastery.

peacock and killing a snake, as well as amorous couples and rampant lions.

Muktesvara is the gem of Odishan architecture. The entrance to the temple compound is through a sculptured *torana* (gateway); the *jagamohana* (porch) has diamond-shaped latticed windows and a richly decorated interior. Temple, gateway and walls are covered with figures of female warriors, erotic scenes, elephants, women, monkeys in various comic scenes, women worshipping lingams and *naginis* (half-snakes, half-women). On each side of the *deul* is a grimacing lion face, flanked by smiling *ganas* (dwarfs). Just to the northwest is the more recent and less ornate **Siddhesvara Temple**.

Bhubaneshwar's **Rajarani Temple** (daily dawn to dusk; charge) is another fascinating place. Like the temples at Khajuraho (see page 276), it is particularly noted for its sculptures of women in sensuous poses, as well as the sculptures of the eight 'guardians' placed at cardinal points around the main structure.

Bhubaneshwar has two museums worth visiting. The **Odisha State Museum** (www.odishamuseum.nic. in; Tue–Sun 10am–1pm, 2–5pm) displays Hindu, Buddhist and Jain sculptures, and early Odishan palm manuscripts. The **Handicrafts Museum** has a collection of traditional art, including Cuttack silver filigree. The **Tribal Museum** (www. scstrti.in; Tue–Sun 10am–5pm; free) is in a cluttered government office, but has a decent bookshop of manuscripts and maps.

Around Bhubaneshwar

West of Bhubaneshwar, on the immediate outskirts, are two hills, **Udayagiri** and **Khandagiri**. Both were once inhabited by Jain ascetics who lived in cells excavated in the rock. Khandagiri has fewer caves than Udayagiri, but a small Jain temple still stands on top of this hill.

At **Dhauli**, a hill 8km (5 miles) south of Bhubaneshwar, there is an example of Emperor Ashoka's edicts. Sculpted elephants mark the site where in 262 BC, the Mauryan

Siddhesvara Temple, Bhubaneshwar.

emperor defeated Kalinga troops, slaying 100,000 people and taking 150,000 captive. This scene of bloodshed is said to have turned Ashoka away from violence and led him to embrace Buddhism. To commemorate Ashoka's acceptance of Buddhism, substituting the ideal of *dharmavijaya*, spiritual victory, for *digvijaya*, military conquest, Japanese Buddhists have built a white **Peace Pagoda** on top of the hill.

At the former Buddhist university site of **Ratnagiri**, northeast of Bhubaneshwar, there are the remains of three monasteries, a number of ruined temples and several stupas.

South to Puri

Some 10km (6 miles) to the south of Bhubaneshwar is **Pipli**, a small village specialising in appliqué work in vivid colours unique to this area. Further on, **Puri ⑫**, 60km (37 miles) southeast of Bhubaneshwar, is the holiest place in Odisha for Hindus, and one of the biggest pilgrimage centres anywhere in India. The city was at one time a flourishing port identified with ancient Dantpur.

Puri is known for its cult of Jagannath, originating, some say, in the times when the people of Odisha worshipped trees, hence the practice of carving his image in wood. According to the more popular legend, however, the Lord appeared in King Indrodyumna's dream and commanded him to build a temple for him. The king complied, having the images carved out of a single log of wood found floating in the sea, as the Lord had enjoined in the dream. His temple lies in the midst of a huge complex of buildings housing more than 5,000 priests and temple staff. The climax of Jagannath worship is the spectacular Rath Yatra festival (also known as the Car festival) celebrated every summer at the **Jagannath Temple**, said to commemorate Krishna's journey from Gokhul to Mathura.

Although the beach at Puri is one of the best in India, the seas can be very rough, with strong and erratic currents. Caution is advised. *Nolia*, lifeguards, easily recognisable by their white, cone-shaped straw hats, are not always alert. Be sure to watch

Muktesvara Temple, Bhubaneshwar.

JAGANNATH TEMPLE, PURI

Known as the 'White Pagoda' by the mariners who used it in colonial times as a navigational aid while sailing between Madras and Calcutta, the Jagannath Temple was originally built in the 12th century. The main building is 65 metres (213ft) high, surmounted by the mystic wheel *(chakra)* and the flag of Vishnu. It is surrounded by a wall 6 metres (20ft) high. Non-Hindus are not permitted to enter the temple, although you're allowed to peek over the wall from the library opposite, whose roof terrace affords a bird's-eye view into the complex. About two weeks before the annual festival of Rath Yatra, held in June and July, the images of Jagannath and his brother, Balabhadra, and his sister, Subhadra, are given a ritual bath. On the first day of the festival, the deities are placed on *rathas*, chariots 12 metres (40ft) high, with wheels 2 metres (7ft) in diameter. Jagannath's chariot is decorated in yellow stripes; Subhadra has a red chariot; Balabhadra's is bright blue. All three are preceded by four wooden horses, but are actually drawn by hundreds of devotees from the temple to Gundicha Mandir (Garden House), 8km (5 miles) away, where they stay for seven days. The rituals completed, the deities ride back to their temple. Every 12 years, the images are replaced by new ones. The old images are then buried in a secret ceremony.

Ornate sculptures adorn the Sun Temple at Konark.

A fishing village along the coast from Puri.

the fishermen come ashore through the surf.

Konark

Going north, 33km (20 miles) from Puri, is **Konark** (Konarak) , a former centre of Odishan Buddhism, an active port (now silted up) and, in ancient times, a centre for sun worship. A temple to the Sun God was built here in the 9th century. The present **Sun Temple** was erected in the 13th century and took 16 years to complete; 1,200 artisans were employed on the task. In its original form the temple consisted of a 70-metre (230ft) high *deul* with a 40-metre (130ft) *jagamohana*, representing the Chariot of the Sun; drawn by seven impetuous horses, the chariot rode on a dozen pairs of eight-spoke wheels.

Worship of the sun is thought to pre-date Hinduism, and still maintains a special reverence among Hindus, the sun being considered the only incarnation of God that can be seen on a daily basis. The sun god is known as Surya, the lord of excellence

and wisdom; yoga practitioners will be familiar with the *surya namaskar*, a series of stretches designed to greet the rising of the sun.

The *deul* collapsed in the middle of the 19th century and one horse is missing. The temple no longer stands on the shore since the sea has receded 3km (2 miles). Despite its dilapidated state the Sun Temple stands out as a fine example of Odishan architecture. Two lions guard the pyramidal entrance of the Sun Temple, and on each side of the temple stands a colossal war elephant and a warhorse trampling fallen warriors. Gentler scenes – erotic sculptures of couples in sensuous contortions, depictions of nymphs and court scenes, musicians, floral motifs and elephants – are also carved on the ruins.

South along the Odishan coast

Along the coast south of Bhubaneshwar is **Chilka Lake**, a 1,100-sq-km (425-sq-mile) shallow inland sea, separated from the Bay of Bengal by a sandy ridge, and spreading over 75km (47 miles) from north to south. From Barkul, the Odisha Tourist Development Corporation operates a two-hour cruise to Kalijai Temple offshore, and to Nalabar Island. The lake supports an abundance of fish and shellfish, and from mid-December to mid-January migratory birds spend the winter here. Further south, 95km (59 miles) from Bhubaneshwar, **Gopalpur-on-Sea** was, during the time of the British Raj, one of the finest beach resorts in eastern India.

Adivasis live in the district of **Koraput**, the Southern Hills area, and come mostly from the Austro-Asiatic Munda group. In the Northern Hills bordering West Bengal and Bihar, **Simlipal National Park** is one of India's most attractive forests; its 2,750 sq km (1,062 sq miles) are populated with tigers and wild elephants.

Northern Odisha

About 15km (10 miles) north from Bhubaneshwar is **Nandanakanan**, a park set in the Chandka Forest, where animals are kept in natural surroundings. The main attractions are four white tigers, one-horned rhinos, white-browed gibbons and African lions. There is also a **Botanical Garden**, with a rosarium, Zen temple and a cactus house.

Cuttack ⑯, the former capital of Odisha, is situated on a narrow river island 19km (12 miles) north of Bhubaneshwar. There are a few historical remains, including the blue granite **Barabati** Maratha fort, stormed by the British in 1803; **Qadmam-i-Rasul**, a walled compound with corner towers, containing three 18th-century mosques and a domed building housing footprints of the Prophet Muhammad engraved on a circular stone. The shrine is visited by both Muslim and Hindu worshippers.

Further north, **Balasore** ⑰ is one of the earliest British settlements in India, granted to the East India Company in 1633. The Kutopokhari Temple at Remuna is a seat of Vaisnava culture and has an 18-arm granite statue of Durga. Bhudhara Chandi at Sajanagarh, built in the 16th century, contains a three-faced image of Shakti. Panchalingeswar on Devagiri Hill is a temple with five stone lingams. To the east is the small resort of **Chandipur-on-Sea** ⑱, with a beach where the sea recedes by 5km (3 miles) at low tide. This is a good place from which to visit Simlipal National Park.

Jharkhand

To the east of Odisha and the south of Bihar is (along with Chattisgarh) the most recently created state of Jharkhand, cleaved off from Bihar in November 2000 and largely comprising the mineral-rich Chota Nagpur plateau. A large part of the population is Adivasi (over a quarter of the population are classified as 'tribals'), speaking Mon-Khmer languages. The main peoples are the Santhal, Bedia, Birhor, No, Khond, Munda and Oraon. Some still lead a hunter-gatherer existence, although the majority have become sedentary and cultivate maize and millet, and raise cattle and fowl. About 60 percent are Christian. Many Adivasi groups face severe discrimination, and in desperation have left their traditional villages to find work in the state's new industrial cities. Enduring poverty in the region accounts for the long-running Naxalite-Maoist insurgency which has rendered the remote districts along Jharkhand's border with Odisha off-limits to outsiders for the past decade. In 2006, Prime Minister Manmohan Singh described the conflict as 'the single biggest internal security challenge ever faced by our country'. An estimated 12,000 people have been killed in violent encounters since the start of hostilities in 1990, yet little international attention has been attracted by what many regard as a de facto civil war.

> **TIP**
>
> Parts of Odisha and Jharkhand, together with Bihar, are notorious for bandits, who have been known to target foreigners' hire cars. Avoid travelling on the road after dark and be on your guard. These regions have also been affected by violence against certain minorities as well as the political Naxalite struggle against landlords.

Konark's Sun Temple.

WHERE

The Hazaribagh National Park is about 90km (55 miles) from Ranchi on the Chota Nagpur plateau. Its 186 sq km (71 sq miles) are mostly covered by thick forest and the park is crossed by a number of rivers that have cut gorges down into the plateau. Part of Project Tiger, it has, alas, few tigers, but is a good place to try to spot sambar, nilgai and sloth bears – or would be if the area weren't awash with bandits and Naxalite guerrillas.

A woman performs morning rituals to celebrate Samba Dashami, a festival unique to Odisha.

Ranchi

Ranchi ⑲, the former summer capital of Bihar, suffered something of a loss of identity when its trees were cut to make room for a new industrial town. A few colonial buildings remain: the **Eastern Railway Hotel**, the **Lutheran Church** and **St Paul's Anglican Church**, and some eccentric villas on Kanke Road, near Ranchi Hill. Beyond the bazaar area, on top of Ranchi Hill, overlooking Ranchi Lake, stands a **Shiva Temple** of limited interest compared to the 17th-century fortified Jagannath Temple at Jagannathpur near the airport. It is open to non-Hindus. The city is also home to the **Tribal Research Institute and Museum** (Mon–Fri 8am–6pm, Sat 8am–1pm), which has a large ethnographic collection open to the public.

Jharkhand has a great deal of forest cover (though this is being steadily depleted through logging), and there are many beautiful sites within easy reach of Ranchi. Three spectacular waterfalls lie within 40km (25 miles) of the capital, the **Hundru**, **Dassam**

and **Johna falls**, and a little further are the **Panch Ghagh falls** (55km/35 miles from Ranchi; so called because it has five cascades in a row) and the **Hirni falls** (70km/44 miles away).

Rajrappa, situated at the confluence of the Damodar and Bhairavi rivers, is a lively pilgrimage site sacred to the goddess Chinamastika. Not too far away, **Palamau National Park**, 140km (87 miles) west of Ranchi, is both a Project Tiger site and a good place to spot elephants, particularly in the pre-monsoon months of March and April.

India's industrial heartland

Jharkhand's mineral wealth is the richest in India and accounts for most of the state's income. In addition to substantial deposits of coal and iron ore, there are also reserves of bauxite, copper and mica.

Jamshedpur ⑳, 170km (106 miles) southeast of Ranchi, is the property of Tata Steel . The city has grown up around the first and most productive steel plant in India, built back in 1912 by the Parsi industrialist Sir Jamshedji Tata, after whom the city is named.

East of Ranchi is 'the Indian Ruhr', an industrial zone spreading along the Damodar River into West Bengal. In the northeast of Jharkhand is the city of **Dhanbad**; this sits on the largest coal reserves in India and is dominated by collieries, technical institutions and research centres. Just to the west is **Bokaro**, the site of India's largest steel complex. To the northwest of Dhanbad, the **Parasnath Hill** is a religious centre noted for its 24 Jain temples of both the Svetambara and Digambara sects, the most interesting ones being the **Samosavan**, **Bhomia Baba** and **Parasvanath**. Of the 24 Jain Tirthankaras, 20 attained nirvana here. Prospective visitors to this area should seek advice before travelling as many of the rural districts between the industrial centres are effectively held by Naxalite-Maoist rebels and too dangerous to cross.

A coalmine at Jharkhand.

Looking over Darjeeling and Kanchenjunga.

THE NORTHEAST

Situated in a sensitive border area with limited road access, the northeast is India's predominant Adivasi region. As restrictions ease, visitors have a greater chance to explore this fascinating region.

I ndia's northeastern states, with the exception of Sikkim, are largely cut off from the rest of the country by Bangladesh, and as such form one of its most beautiful, spectacular and least visited areas. The landscape ranges from the steamy valley of the mighty Brahmaputra River with its World Heritage Site national parks, to the high mountains of Sikkim and the forested hills of the Adivasi states that border Burma (Myanmar) and Bangladesh.

Over the last few decades it has been difficult to gain access to the 'seven sisters' of Assam, Tripura, Meghalaya, Arunachal Pradesh, Nagaland, Manipur and Mizoram, but more recently the situation has improved. Although there are still the rumblings of insurgencies in Assam, Nagaland and, especially, Manipur (at the time of writing in early 2016, the British Foreign Office was still advising against all travel to Manipur due to a risk from insurgent groups, mainly in rural areas), much of the region is free from trouble and more than repays the effort required to reach what is India's most remote region. Visitors require permits and forward planning is essential.

Sikkim

Sikkim is India's highest state, with several peaks over 6,000 metres

(19,700ft). Kanchenjunga, at 8,598 metres (28,208ft) the third-highest mountain in the world, is believed to be the abode of a god of the same name, a fiery character with a red face who wears a crown made of five skulls and rides a snow lion.

Until the 18th century, the inhabitants of Sikkim were mainly Lepchas, cultivators of Mongol origin who came from Tibet in the 8th century. The first kings of Sikkim were the Namgyals, descended from the Minyaks of Tibet. Khye-Bumsa,

Main Attractions

Gangtok
Rumtek Monastery
Kaziranga National Park
Shillong
Tawang
Kwairamband Bazaar, Imphal

Applying make-up for the Goshta Astami drama in Manipur.

TIP

Pelling is a small town in western Sikkim, just beyond Pemayangtse. It is becoming increasingly popular with visitors from the plains below, and has a large number of basic hotels. As well as Pemayangtse, there are a couple of other attractions nearby: the Sanga Choelling Monastery, thought to be the oldest in Sikkim, and the peaceful Khecheopalri Lake, which is said to be in the shape of the Buddha's foot.

The fluttering of the flags in the breeze is considered by Buddhists to be an act of devotion.

a Namgyal prince, helped in the building of the Sakya Monastery in Tibet in 1268. He befriended the Lepchas and swore a blood brotherhood with their chief, Thekongtek. When Thekongtek died, the Lepchas turned for leadership to Guru Tashi, Khye-Bumsa's fourth son, who was consecrated king *(chogyal)* in 1642. In 1700 the Bhutanese invaded Sikkim and the young *chogyal*, Chador, was forced into exile. He built monasteries at Pemayangtse and Tashiding and invented the Lepcha alphabet. He was assassinated in 1717 on the orders of his pro-Bhutanese half-sister, Pei Womgmo.

In the early 19th century the East India Company entered the Himalayas with a view to opening up trade with Tibet. In 1814, in the Anglo-Nepal Wars, Sikkim sided with the Company and received parts of the Nepali Terai (an area of grasslands, marshes and forests at the foot of the Himalayas) as a reward. As a friendly gesture, King Tsugphud Namgyal gave the East India Company the hill of Darjeeling for development

as a resort. Relations soured and, following a quarrel over the illegal collection of taxes by the British in Sikkim, the British annexed the Terai and established a protectorate over the kingdom. Since the 18th century, Nepalis have flowed into Sikkim, and now constitute 75 percent of the population.

When British rule in India ended, the government of independent India entered into a similar arrangement with the *chogyal*. Sikkim was not wholly merged with the Indian Union. In 1975, however, the Sikkim Parliament voted for the incorporation of the kingdom into India. The monarchy was abolished and Sikkim became a state.

Gangtok

The capital, **Gangtok** ❶, 'the hill made flat', lies at an altitude of 1,640 metres (5,400ft), facing Kanchenjunga. It is reached by road from Darjeeling, Bagdogra airport (110km/70 miles) or New Siliguri railway station (125km/77 miles). The most important building in the town is

---

ENTRY PERMITS

Entry to some areas of India's northeast can be problematic. Although the government is keen to open the region up to tourism, and restrictions are being eased all the time, it is wise to apply for any permits at least four weeks before you travel.

At present foreign travellers do not need permits to enter Assam, Tripura or Meghalaya, although they may be required to register on arrival and departure. Permits are required to visit the entire state of Nagaland, parts of Mizoram and parts of Manipur. Although visitors need a permit to enter Sikkim, this is largely a formality, and it can be issued along with your visa or at the Sikkim border at Rangpo. For Arunachal Pradesh the regulations are less straightforward: you will need to apply for a Protected Area Permit and travel in a group of at least two people; the permit lasts for 30 days from the time of entry.

All permits are much easier to obtain through an agency. Alternatively you can apply in person to the Foreigners' Regional Registration Office, A.J.C. Bose Road, Kolkata. They might refer you to the Ministry of Home Affairs, Foreigners' Division, Lok Nayak Bhavan, Khan Market, Delhi. There are also registration offices in Siliguri and Darjeeling. Wherever you apply you will need passport photographs and a photocopy of your passport.

the **Chogyal's Palace**, usually closed to visitors except for the Tsuklakhang Royal Chapel, where ceremonies are held. The palace itself opens once a year, during the last week of December, for the Pong Labsal festival, during which lamas wearing masks perform a dance to Kanchenjunga around a banner-pole.

The **Research Institute of Tibetology**, built in 1958 by the last *chogyal* to preserve Tibetan culture, houses a library of more than 30,000 books on Buddhism, astrology, medicine and philosophy, as well as a collection of *thankas* (Tibetan religious paintings on cloth). The **Deer Park** was set up in homage to a Bodhisattva who was reincarnated as a musk deer. The **Orchid Sanctuary** is where 250 different types of orchids bloom. Nearby is a **Tibetan Refugee Craft Centre** and the well-known **Hotel Tashi Delek**.

Monastery treks

The **Rumtek Monastery**, 24km (14 miles) west of Gangtok, is one of the most famous in Sikkim. It belongs to the Karmapa school, a reformist branch of Tantric Buddhism founded in the 15th century. The monastery, built in the 1960s, is a replica of one in Tibet destroyed at the time of the Chinese takeover.

About 100km (62 miles) further west, **Pemayangtse** has a **Red Hat Ningmapa Monastery**, built in 1705. Its walls and ceilings bear frescoes of gods and demons. A one-day trek north leads to **Tashiding Ningmapa Monastery**, dating from 1706. A longer trek can be organised from Pemayangtse. As the path approaches **Kanchenjunga ❷**, the altitude rises to 4,270 metres (14,000ft) and terraced rice paddies and barley fields give way to apple orchards, then fir trees and mountain lakes. **Yakshun**, reached after six hours, is a small town where the first *chogyal* was crowned in 1642. The next stages are **Bakkhin** (five hours) and **Dzongri**

(six hours), with a close-up view of Kanchenjunga.

Assam

Assam, meaning undulating, best describes this state of rolling plains dissected by the Brahmaputra and its many tributaries. One of the world's widest rivers, at places the Brahmaputra spills across several kilometres, making it impossible to see the opposite bank. The river often floods during the July monsoon, and in successive years recently Assam has experienced terrible deluges, due largely to excessive deforestation, in which more than a million people have been displaced.

Early Assamese history

The name Assam is probably derived from the Ahoms – the dynasty that ruled Kamrupa, as Assam was known, from the 13th to the early 19th century. Legend has it that the first king of Assam was Narakasur, son of the Hindu god Vishnu and Dharitiri (Mother Earth). Narakasur was killed by Vishnu for his unreligious

The northeast is home to some 700 species of orchid.

behaviour and was succeeded by his son Bhagadatta.

From the earliest times Assam has been a melting pot of peoples. In 1228, the Ahoms, a Buddhist people from northern Thailand, raided Assam and defeated the ruler of Kamrupa. They established their own kingdom with their capital in Charideo (now Sibsagar). The Ahoms converted to Hinduism, but there are isolated villages in Upper Assam where Buddhist customs are still practised and the inhabitants speak Shan Thai. The Ahoms established a powerful kingdom that flourished along the south bank of the Brahmaputra. On several occasions the Mughals tried to subdue the 'rats of Assam', but each time the Ahoms proved more than a match for the invaders.

British rule

The Ahom dynasty's grip on power started weakening from the 17th century. In 1792 Burma invaded Assam and the king, Gaurinath Singh, was forced to ask the East India Company for assistance. The Anglo-Burmese War of 1824–6 was followed by the Treaty of Yandaboo, whereby Burma ceded a large part of northeast India, including Assam, to the British. The colonists

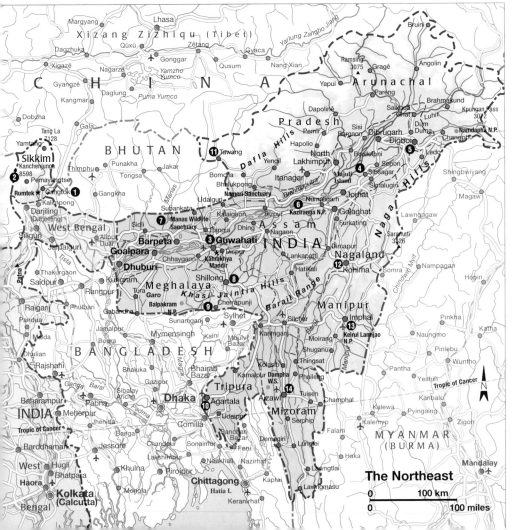

The Northeast

0   100 km

0   100 miles

gradually established their hold over the region, and during World War II Assam played a strategic role as an important supply route to both China and Burma.

A testament to Assam's British legacy can be seen in the region's 300 tea estates. Braving the inhospitable terrain and climate, the British, with the help of labourers from central India, transformed large areas of malaria-infested tropical jungle into well-manicured carpets of tea for which the state is renowned.

Modern Assam

Since Independence in 1947 Assam has been fragmented into several smaller states. Today it only occupies the plains of the Brahmaputra Valley, south of Arunachal Pradesh and the kingdom of Bhutan. The fragmentation has deepened the crisis facing Assam. Its major problem is a growing imbalance between ethnic Assamese and immigrants – Bengali Hindus displaced by Partition in 1947 and Muslim immigrants fleeing poverty in Bangladesh.

The fear of being swamped by outsiders triggered a popular student-led revolt in the 1980s, which snowballed into violent secessionist movements. The ULFA and Bodo militants now have a powerful presence in the state and are waging wars against Indian Army soldiers. As a result, Assam was shut to foreign tourists until the 1990s. The state is now open, but visitors should be aware of the political situation and take reasonable care when travelling around.

Guwahati

Pragjyotishpur, the ancient capital of the Kamrup kings, is now **Guwahati** ❸, a city with a population of around 600,000 people. Despite its dramatic location on the south bank of the Brahmaputra, Guwahati is not a pretty city. However, there are spectacular views of the river from the hill 3km (2 miles) southeast of the centre where

Raj Bhavan, the governor's residence, and **Belle Vue Hotel** are situated.

Close to the railway station, opposite the Dighali Pukhuri tank, is the **State Museum** (Tue–Sat 10am–4pm, summer until 5pm, closed alternate Sat), housing rare stone sculptures from the Kamrup period. Guwahati features some unusual temples: on a small promontory along the river is the 10th-century **Sukhlesvar Janardhan Temple**, which was rebuilt in the 17th century. It has a statue of Lord Buddha in a rare coexistence with Hindu deities. Nearby, in the middle of the river on **Umananda** (Peacock Island), is a small Shiva temple, which can be reached by boat from one of the ghats along the bank. During the winter months there's a daily sound and light show on Assamese history on the adjoining island.

Navagraha Mandir, the Temple of Nine Planets, is located on Chitrachala Hill. The temple was an astrological centre, hence the city's earlier name of Pragjyotishpur, the 'Eastern City of Astrology'.

Numerous varieties of local tea: over half of India's tea comes from Assam.

Indian tea

Although tea has only been grown on a commercial basis in India since the early 19th century, it is a vital part of Indian life.

Chinese tradition points to India as the original home of tea. A Brahman, Dharma, went as a missionary to China. He was so tired that he fell asleep on reaching his destination. When he awoke, he was so angry at his own weakness that he tore out his eyebrows. The hair took root and became tea plants. He ate the leaves and fell into meditation.

The early tea trade

Tea had been identified in Assam by English travellers as early as in the last years of the 18th century. When the East Indian Company's monopoly of importing tea into Britain from China was abolished in 1823, the Honourable Company decided to look into the possibility of growing tea in India.

Expeditions were sent to Assam, and in 1826, following the Burmese Wars, the Company's troops brought back a tea bush as evidence of the existence

Picking tea on an estate near Darjeeling.

of tea in the area. On Christmas Eve 1844, the Governor General, Lord Bentinck, officially announced the discovery of tea in India and called for the development of the industry. Production started in Assam in 1836, in Bengal in 1839, and in the Nilgiris in the south in 1863. Plantations were introduced around Darjeeling in the early 1840s. The bushes were not indigenous; they had been smuggled out of China.

Workers for the plantations, which the Assamese were not keen to work on, were imported from Central India. Many of them were Adivasis and hired as indentured labourers, effectively slaves. The conditions were terrible, and a huge number of workers died from hunger and disease. Even today the overwhelmingly female tea workers are poorly treated.

The first Indian teas were of low quality, and Chinese experts were brought to Assam to supervise the processing of tea leaves. India became a major grower and, by 1900, was supplying Britain with 150 million pounds of tea against 15 million brought from China.

Modern tea production

Today, India is the second world's largest producer of the fragrant leaf, after China, with an output of 1.2 million tonnes (total world production: 5 million tonnes). India's area under tea (564,000 hectares/1.4 million acres) is the second largest in the world. More than half of Indian tea is grown in Assam, one-quarter in West Bengal and one-fifth in the southern Nilgiris.

There are two sorts of Indian tea. CTC tea, the most common, takes its name from the Cut-Twist-Curl process in which the leaf is broken. It gives a strong liquid of dark colour. Most CTC production is for the home market. "Orthodox" teas have a lighter colour (they are said to be "bright") and yield a weaker liquid: one kilo makes 350 cups against 500 for CTC tea. Most of the Orthodox tea is exported, the best varieties being Darjeeling and Assam Golden Flower Orange Pekoe.

Some 60 percent of the Indian production is sold through auctions, including all export teas. There are auction centres at Guwahati, in Assam; Kochi, Coimbatore and Coonoor, in the south; and at Siliguri and Kolkata, in West Bengal. The Kolkata centre has two auction rooms (one for the home market, the other for exports), and the largest tea-tasting room in the world.

From having been consumed only by the hill peoples 150 years ago, tea has become the national drink of India. However, on average, each cup of tea consumed by an Indian is matched by approximately six consumed by an English person.

Guwahati's most important temple is **Kamakhya Mandir**, 10km (6 miles) southwest of the city centre along the banks of the Brahmaputra on Nilachal Hill. Legend goes that to stop Lord Shiva's fearful dance of destruction, provoked by the sight of the dead body of his consort, goddess Shakti, the lesser gods dismembered and scattered her body far and wide. Shakti's *yoni* (reproductive organ) landed on Nilachal Hill. Kamakhya is one of India's main centres of the Tantric cult, and human sacrifices were once common here.

Along Guwahati's boundary wall and water tank one can still see the ruins of the original temple destroyed in 1553 by Kalapahar, a powerful Brahman who converted to Islam after being ostracised by his community for marrying a Muslim princess. The present structure, with its high beehive spire and long turtle-back hall, is typical of early Assamese religious architecture.

The pilgrimage to the hillside mosque of **Pao Mekkam** 25km (15 miles) to the southwest of Guwahati, is said to be the equivalent to one-quarter, or a *pao*, of a Haj to Mecca. The state's Buddhist heritage can be seen at the site of Hajo's Hayagribha Maghadeva Mahadap temple, west of Guwahati. It is believed by some devotees that this was the place where the Buddha attained enlightenment.

Around Assam

Some 175km (108 miles) to the northeast of Guwahati lies **Tezpur**, widely regarded as the cultural capital of Assam. Historical ruins here date back as far as the 4th century, and the local orchid sanctuary has an amazing collection of rare species.

Travelling east, about 370km (230 miles) from Guwahati along the south bank of the Brahmaputra is the old Ahom capital of **Charideo**, now called **Sibsagar** ❹. Few monuments have survived Assam's monsoons and the tropical undergrowth that threatens to overrun every abandoned structure. Among those still standing are the water tank along with adjoining Devi, Shiva and Vishnu temples, an oval-shaped pavilion from where the kings

Majuli Island in the Brahmaputra River.

watched elephant fights and the *char-ideo* (necropolis) of the Ahom kings.

Around 100km (62 miles) northeast of Sibsagar, surrounded by dense forests, are the oil towns of **Duliajan** and **Digboi** ❺. The British struck oil here in 1867 and built India's first refinery at Digboi.

Assam also has what may be the largest river island in the world, **Majuli**. The centre of Assamese Vaisnaivism, the island is dotted with *satras*, monasteries whose white-turbaned monks are renowned for their chimeric dance-plays and music. The island is also a haven for many species of birds.

National parks

Kaziranga National Park ❻, 230km (145 miles) northeast of Guwahati, is the principal sanctuary for the Indian one-horned rhinoceros. Nearing extinction at the turn of the 20th century, it's now being rehabilitated, with numbers now up to 2,400 and rising. Despite stringent protective measures, a number are still poached every year, and their horns

An Indian one-horned rhinoceros cools off in a water hole at Kaziranga National Park.

are smuggled to traditional medicine markets in East Asia.

The majority of visitors are restricted to visiting only the central of the three ranges that make up the park, and while much of it is covered in tall grass, making sightings difficult, there are enough clearings to make a visit worthwhile. In addition to the rhinos, elephants, deer, bison and a variety of bird life can also be seen. The closest railway station is at **Furkating**, 75km (46 miles) away, or alternatively plenty of buses come here from Guwahati, 220km (136 miles) away.

To the northwest, 176km (109 miles) from Guwahati, is the **Manas National Park** ❼, a thick tropical jungle set along the Bhutan border. The park is a sanctuary for several endangered species, including tigers, leopards and elephants as well as rhinos. The river flowing through the park is an angler's paradise for *mahaseer*, a local variety of carp. Angling camps are also organised on the Jia Bharali River in the **Nameri Sanctuary**, 200km (124 miles) from Guwahati,

NORTHEAST TRANSPORT

Buses: In many areas you will have to rely on the local bus service, or hire a jeep and driver. Buses are usually quite reliable, but for most northeastern states you must travel as an organised group: transport is usually organised as part of the package.

Flights: The gateway for travel into the northeast is Kolkata. There are airports in Guwahati, Argartala, Dibrugarh, Imphal and Shillong. The airport for Sikkim is Bagdogra, from where you must take a taxi up to Gangtok (there is a pre-paid counter in the airport).

Trains: Rail services are limited to the Brahmaputra Valley and run, via Guwahati, on broad-gauge tracks as far as Dibrugarh. A narrow-gauge line runs north of the broad-gauge line from Guwahati to Murkongselek.

also a good place to see wild elephants, rare turtles and even tigers.

Meghalaya

Meghalaya, 'the abode of clouds', south of Assam, was previously part of Assam. It became a separate state of the Indian Union in 1972. It is a hilly region, and very foggy in winter, causing the traffic police to dress in fluorescent clothing. It is inhabited by three Adivasi groups: the Garos in the west, the Khasis in the centre, and the Jaintias in the east. They originally constituted independent little township kingdoms, the Seiyams, which the British annexed one by one to British India in the 19th century.

The Garos are Tibetan. They once practised human sacrifice as part of their local religion. In 1848, under a treaty with the British, they agreed to stop displaying skulls in their houses. Archery stakes, a peculiar local form of gambling using arrows, is still a common amusement.

The Khasis are Mon-Khmers related to the Shans of Burma. Their religion, Seng Khasi, holds that God is everywhere and should not be represented or adored in a specific form. There are no temples, just prayer halls for specific celebrations. The Khasis adorn themselves in jewellery made of gold and amber. To commemorate their dead, they erect *mawbynnas*, monoliths arranged in groups of three or more that can be seen in most villages. The Pnars, generally known as Jaintias, are closely related to the Khasis. The three peoples have matrilineal and matrilocal family systems. Missionaries in the 19th century converted most of them to Christianity but old traditions persist, especially their dances. A major dance festival, the *Shat Suk Myasiem*, the Festival of the Joyful Heart, is held in Shillong in April. In November, the Garo 100-drum festival in Tura celebrates the end of the harvesting season.

Shillong ❽, the capital of Assam until 1972 and of Meghalaya since then, lies 100km (60 miles) south of Guwahati, a three-hour drive through hills covered with pineapple and betel plantations, and pine forests. It passes along **Bara Pani** (Umian Lake).

TIP

Shillong Peak, not far from Shillong on the way to Cherrapunji, is 1,961 metres (6,430ft) high, the highest point in the district. Outside of the monsoon (May–September) and when not shrouded in mist and fog it gives magnificent views over the city and surrounding area.

Religious art in a Vishnu Monastery.

Incense at a Buddhist temple in Arunachal Pradesh.

Shillong has been called the 'Scotland of the East' because of its climate and its location at an altitude of 1,500 metres (4,900ft). Here the British and rich Bengalis built cottages, a golf course and polo grounds. It is a small city with a market, **Bara Bazaar**, selling Nepali silver and Khasi gold jewellery, spices and textiles. Shillong spreads across hills covered with English-style country houses, the largest being **Raj Bhavan**, the summer residence of the governor of Assam and Meghalaya, and the **Pinewood Hotel**. Nearby are the **Ward Lake** and **Botanical Garden**. The highest point in the state is **Shillong Peak** (1,965 metres/6,440ft), which offers a fine view of the neighbouring hills.

Cherrapunji ❾, 56km (35 miles) to the south, was infamous as the world's wettest place, until the record was broken by nearby **Mawsynram, 15km (9 miles) northwest**, which on average receives just under 12 metres (470ins) of rain annually. The most interesting spot is **Mawphluang**, 24km (15 miles) further south, a barren and windy

Shillong's Bara Bazaar.

plateau covered with monoliths. The road takes you along the side of a spectacular gorge. This whole region is riddled with caves, many with spectacular formations and river passages.

Access to **Garo hill country** from Shillong is difficult, via Guwahati and then southwest to **Tura**. The villages in this region have retained their traditional architecture and some traditional buildings, like the bachelors' dormitory at Rongreng (Williamnagar). The highest point in the Garo Hills is Nokrek Peak (1,412 metres/4,630ft); the rich flora in this area is now protected as part of a biosphere reserve. The hill region is also home to a variety of fauna, including India's only ape, the Hullock gibbon, as well as elephants and tigers.

Tripura

Well-forested Tripura was the former princely state of Tipperah. The population, mostly of Tibeto-Burmese origin, took up Vaishnava Hinduism early, and was ruled by rajas until Indian Independence. Other major groups in Tripura are the Kukis – related to the

Shans of Burma – Chakmas, Moghs, Lusharis and Riangs. Tripura had been at war with her neighbours when the British, taking advantage of a feud between Maharajah Krishna Manikya and the nawabs of Bengal, intervened and established a protectorate. Following Independence, Tripura joined the Indian Union in 1949 and became a state in 1972.

Agartala ❿, the capital, is a burgeoning city town of 522,000 people, surrounded by hills on three sides. One of the main sights is the large **Ujjayanta Palace**, built 1899–1901 by Maharaja Radha Kishore Manikya. Much of the building is very fine and is set in pleasant Mughal-style gardens; it is now the home of the State Legislature. The **Pushbanta Palace** was erected in 1917 by Maharaja Birendra, a philanthropist who helped Rabindranath Tagore to finance the Shantiniketan University in Bengal. The palace is now the residence of the governor of Tripura. The **Tripura Government Museum** (www.tripura.nic.in/museum; Mon–Sat 10am–1pm, 2–5pm) has an interesting array of archaeological finds as well as a good display of Tripura crafts.

In Udaipur (55km/34 miles from Agartala), the ancient capital of Tripura, is the temple to **Tripura Sundari**. Said to be built on the spot where the right foot of Sati fell, it is also known as Kurma ('turtle') Pith as its shape resembles a turtle's back. By the temple is a pool containing enormous turtles which you can feed.

Arunachal Pradesh

North of Assam lies Arunachal Pradesh, kept isolated for years by its strategic location on the frontier between India and China. The area has 1.4 million inhabitants divided into 82 different peoples, the largest groups being the Apatanis, Khamptis, Padmas and Miris. Most are Buddhists. It can get very cold in Arunachal, even in the summer, so it is advisable to take plenty of warm clothing.

Itanagar, the state capital, has a couple of interesting sights, including Itar Fort, a brick-built citadel said to have been constructed by the Ahoms, and the Jawaharlal Nehru Museum, which

Khasi archers, Meghalaya.

has good coverage of the state's customs and peoples.

At **Tawang ⑪**, over the Sela Pass (4,215 metres/13,820ft), is India's largest Buddhist monastery. Founded in 1642, this Gelugpa *gompa* (monastery) is where the 6th Dalai Lama was born. The monastery is very similar to those in Tibet, with colourfully painted windows and murals, and there is also a huge gilded statue of the Buddha. The monastery celebrates its major festival in December/ January. However, perhaps the main attraction is its spectacular location, at an altitude of 3,050 metres (10,000ft); the views and surrounding scenery are breathtaking.

To the east, near the border with China and Burma, the Brahmaputra forms a lake, **Brahmakund**, before entering the plains of Assam. Bathing here is believed to wash away one's sins, and Hindus come by the thousands on Makar Sankranti Day in mid-January. The old road to Mandalay begins at **Ledo**.

In the south of the state is the **Namdapha National Park**, which has retained much of its pristine state due to its inaccessibility. It covers a wide variety of environments, ranging from around 200 metres (650ft) to 4,500 metres (14,750ft) above sea level. The remote sanctuary is home to the very rare Hoolock gibbon, and four cat species – tigers, leopards, clouded leopards and snow leopards – as well as a population of red pandas.

Nagaland

Remote Nagaland is inhabited by a variety of Tibeto-Burmese peoples, speaking more than 20 different dialects, the largest groups being the Aos, Angamis and Konyaks. These Nagas were once headhunters, however, the practice was abandoned two generations ago.

The Cacharis, one of the Naga peoples, once established a Hindu kingdom at **Dimapur** from where they used to raid Assam and Burma. The Ahoms of Assam established their authority over the Cacharis at the end of the 17th century. However, as soon as Burma invaded Assam in 1816, the Naga raids on the plains were resumed. In 1832, the British, while establishing a road link between Assam and Manipur, met the Nagas for the first time. For a few years they made attempts to control them, Naga raids being followed by punitive expeditions. In 1879 the British outpost at **Kohima ⑫** came under Naga siege for a month. A state of permanent peace was finally reached in 1889.

During World War II the Japanese and the Indian National Army launched an attack on Kohima, taking half of the city in 1943. The objective was to reach Dimapur, a vital railhead for supplies to British Army units in forward areas. Kohima proved to be the furthest point west reached by the Japanese. The War Cemetery at Kohima contains Commonwealth graves, and a memorial with the inscription: 'When you go

Red pandas are an endangered species found in the Himalayan foothills of north-eastern India at altitudes between 2,000 and 4,000 metres (6,500–13,000ft).

home tell them of us and say, "For your tomorrow we gave our today.'"

In the war against the Japanese, the Nagas were of great help to the Allied forces, carrying supplies to the front, evacuating the wounded and spying behind enemy lines. Following Indian Independence, some Nagas grouped in a Naga National Council and demanded autonomy. But soon successionist elements were asking for independence, with the aim of uniting the estimated four million Nagas living on both sides of the Indo-Burma frontier. In November 1975, at Shillong, the government of India and Naga leaders reached an agreement whereby the Nagas accepted the Indian Constitution, but there are still occasional outbreaks of violence, and visitors may encounter army checkpoints.

Naga villages are usually perched on hills and are surrounded by a stone wall. One, **Barra Basti**, is a suburb of Kohima. To the east of Kohima, at the railhead of Dimapur, are the remains of the former capital of the Cachar Hills razed by the Ahoms in 1536.

The best way to see the region is on foot between November and May. You have to apply for a Protected Areas Permit, and stick to officially designated circuits, visiting sanctioned sights. Chief among the attractions is the annual Hornbill festival, held in a village near Kohima in the first week of December. Sponsored by the government as an attempt to foster social integration between the state's indigenous inhabitants, it attracts Naga tribes people from across the region, dressed in traditional finery. Expect displays of dance, song, wrestling and archery competitions, as well as a chilli-eating contest, beauty pageant, rock concert and car rally.

Manipur

This is another former Princely State on the Burmese border. Meitheis, a Tibeto-Burmese people related to the Shans, form 60 percent of the population. They live in the valleys and have developed *Jagoi*, a Manipuri dance style which is performed at festivals and is accompanied by the

Yongchak (bitter gourd) is a highly prized local vegetable. Together with chillis and fermented fish, it forms a major part of yongchak eronba, Manipur's best-known dish.

Thukpa, Tibetan noodle soup. Tibetan cultural influences are in evidence in parts of Arunachal Pradesh.

Striking a bargain at Imphal's Kwairamband Bazaar – a large market run entirely by women.

pung (a double-headed barrel drum). The 29 other peoples, most of them Tibeto-Burmese and now mostly Christian, form one-third of the population and live in the hills. The largest of these groups are the Lotha, the Konyak and the Nagas.

Manipuris are reputedly fierce fighters. They excel in martial arts, including: *thangta*, practised by both men and women, and accompanied by drumming; the spear dance *(takhousarol)*; the sword fight *(thanghaicol)*; and wrestling *(mukna)*. The Manipuris have a history of conflict with their neighbours in Arakan and other border regions of Burma, which they invaded in 1738. In 1819, the raja of Manipur, who previously had paid tribute to the Burmese crown, did not attend the coronation of Burma's new king, Bagyidaw. The Burmese sent out a punitive expedition. The Anglo-Burmese War was caused partly by this incursion.

Burma was defeated, and by the Treaty of Yandaboo, on 24 February 1826, recognised British sovereignty over Manipur. After years of relative peace, a revolt took place in 1891 during which the British chief commissioner of Assam was killed. The rising was crushed and its leader, Tikenderjit Singh, the maharaja's brother, hanged. There was trouble again in 1930, when a self-styled prophet, Jadonang, announced the imminent departure of the British. He was executed and the priestess of his cult, Rani Gaidiniliou, who was only 17, was sentenced to life imprisonment. She was released when India gained its independence.

In 1944, the Indian National Army and the Japanese put Imphal under siege from March to June. They were repulsed, and in March 1945, General Slim's 14th Army marched to Mandalay from the Manipur hills. The war cemeteries that commemorate those who died are outside of Imphal on the Dimapur road and are kept in a very good condition. In 1949 Manipur became a Union Territory and a fully fledged state of the Indian Union in 1972, although secessionists still continue to fight for independence.

Imphal ⓭, the capital, can be reached by road from Kohima after a 130km (80-mile) drive. The most impressive sight is the huge **Kwairamband Bazaar**, a women's market selling food and crafts. The **Manipur State Museum** (Tue–Sun 10am–4.30pm) has a good display of Adivasi artefacts. Also worth seeing are the two well-maintained war cemeteries, the Raja's Palace and Royal Polo Grounds. Nearby, at **Langthabal**, is the Raja's Summer Palace. **Moirang**, 45km (28 miles) from Imphal, has the **Thankgjing Temple**, dedicated to a forest god, and is also known as the headquarters of the Indian National Army.

Mizoram

The former Lushai Hills District, Mizoram is bordered by Bangladesh on one side and Burma on the other. The region has deep river gorges, the sides of which are densely forested with bamboo. Related to the Shan, Mizos are a group of peoples (Lushais, Hmars, Pawis) that came relatively recently to India. They started raiding tea plantations in 1871. The British retaliated and established control over the area in 1872, but could not establish peace until 1892. The British then introduced the Inner Line system. Only missionaries were allowed through. As a result, 95 percent of the population is Christian, and literacy has reached 86 percent in some areas. At Indian Independence Mizoram became a Union Territory, and was granted full statehood in 1987.

The capital, **Aizawl** ⓮, is built along a ridge. In town is Bara Bazaar, the central shopping area where local people in traditional costume sell their produce, including river crabs in small wicker baskets. The small **Mizoram State Museum** (Mon 1–4pm, Tue–Fri 10am–4pm, Sat 10am–2pm) has an interesting collection of local artefacts. Other places of interest include the **Dampha Wildlife Sanctuary** on the Bangladesh border, and the busy town of **Champhai**, from where you can visit the traditional Mizo village of **Ruantlang**.

The Mizoram Mountains.

Fisherman at dawn, Lighthouse Beach, Kovalam.

View across the Western Ghats near Munnar.

THE SOUTH

India's steamy tropical south is the most relaxed part of the country. Wonderful food, cool green hill stations, a smattering of sandy beaches and an exuberant culture are all reasons to visit.

Schoolgirl with jasmine flowers in her hair.

All five states of South India, as well as the Lakshadweep and Andaman Islands, lie deep within the tropics, a possible reason for the more languid pace of life; on the whole, this is a laid-back region in comparison with the hustle of the north.

South Indian women twine fragrant jasmine blossoms into their hair, while many of the men still wear the traditional *lunghi*. Patterns made from flower petals or crushed and coloured rice, known as *kolam*, enhance the entrances of temples and households. Rice is the staple grain here, and people devour heaps of the stuff from clean banana leaves. Phrasebook Hindi won't get you very far in this region, where most languages are Dravidian. Linguists would need Telugu in Hyderabad and Telangana, Kannada in Bangalore, Tamil in Chennai (Madras), and Malayalam in Kochi, but English is widely understood.

The vast Deccan plains, the rainforests of the Ghats, and two long coastlines distinguish the south. Temples are truly colourful: each deity is brushed with a vibrant hue, and the steep temple tops look as chaotic and crowded as a bazaar. Kerala is noted for its elephants and exuberant festivals. Hyderabad, the gateway to South India, has been

The Shore Temple at Mamallapuram.

famous since Marco Polo's time for the skills of its Islamic craftsmen and the grandeur of Golconda Fort. This glory is almost surpassed by Hampi, a deserted stone city in the midst of rural Karnataka. The pubs of Bengaluru (Bangalore) resemble those anywhere in the world, reflecting the city's status as India's most forward-looking city. Chennai values, and strives to preserve, its heritage of music, dance and commerce. While it has retained its charm, the South is now throwing off its slightly dreamy traditional image and is the driving force behind India's thriving new technology and software industries.

Across the waters of the Bay of Bengal lie the scattered islands of Andaman and Nicobar, home to indigenous peoples, tropical jungles full of exotic birds and clear blue seas teeming with aquatic wildlife. Off the west coast is the beautiful, remote island chain of Lakshadweep, complete with perfect white-sand beaches.

The view from the Charminar, Hyderabad.

KARNATAKA, ANDHRA PRADESH AND TELANGANA

Karnataka is one of the most appealing states in India, with beautiful scenery, evocative ruins and some fascinating cities. Less visited by tourists, Andhra Pradesh and India's newest state of Telangana have some impressive sights including temples, palaces and ruined forts.

The states of Karnataka, Andhra Pradesh and Telangana lie on the threshold of India's deep south, straddling the Subcontinent from the lush Malabar and Coromandel coasts via the largely inhospitable Deccan plateau. This huge area encompasses a little of everything that India has to offer, from the pulsating, high-tech megacities of Bengaluru and Hyderabad to the dry, arid expanses of the Deccan plateau and the lush greenery of the Nilgiri Hills. Parts of these states are devastatingly poor and underdeveloped, while the finest residences of the states' capitals rival those anywhere in the world. This has always been a region of enormous strategic importance, and has been home to some of the country's greatest dynasties, including the Nizams of Hyderabad and Wodeyars of Mysore. The resulting historical legacy can be seen in the stunning array of palaces, forts, monuments and museums that dot these three states; although Andhra Pradesh and Telangana in particular see relatively few visitors, this region is one of India's most colourful, and is not to be missed.

Karnataka

Created in 1956 from the former state of Mysore, Karnataka is one of India's most varied states, with a series of distinct regional landscapes.

A narrow fertile coastal strip to the west – the so-called Konkan coast – is flanked by the hills of the Western Ghats, their well-watered slopes sustaining dense tropical forests famed for their teak, rosewood and bamboo. With much of the moisture from the rain-bearing monsoon expended on the ghats, the Deccan plateau to the east is a much drier region. In the southwest lie the hills and valleys of the Kodagu (Coorg) district. Amid the profusion of dense tropical rainforests in the Southern

Main Attractions

Bengaluru (Bangalore)
Mysore
Somnathpur
Belur
Halebid
Sravanabelagola
Hampi
Gokarna
Charminar, Hyderabad
Golconda Fort

Mysore resident.

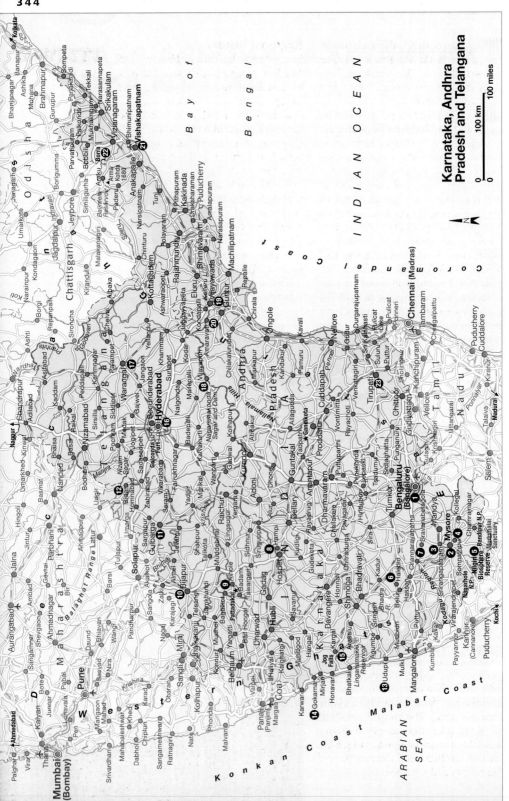

Karnataka, Andhra Pradesh and Telangana

Ghats roams the Indian elephant, the gaur and the long-tailed langur, the last frequently breaking into the silence of the sun-freckled forest with gossipy chatter.

Karnataka has a population of around 61 million, and its people are as varied as its land. The northerners are predominantly Lingayats, followers of the 12th-century scholar-saint Basavanna. A Hindu reformer, his message was spread through rhythmic prose called *vachanas*. In the south around Mysore, the rich farming community of Vokkaligas dominates. Their rivalry continues in Karnataka's politics today. The state has one of India's most noticeable wealth gaps between well-off urbanites (notably in Bengaluru) and impoverished village dwellers.

Coastal Karnataka is inhabited by fisherfolk whose forebears traded with ancient Mesopotamia, Persia and Greece. Portuguese influence can be seen in Mangalore, where the Christian community and its churches were established in the 16th century. Chikmanglur, along the border with Kerala, is a major coffee-growing district. Adivasi communities live mostly in the north and the west. The Coorgs of the Kodagu region on the border with Kerala have a distinctive culture of their own.

The principal language, Kannada, has a rich tradition of poetry and prose. The earliest classic, *Kavira-jamarga* (9th century), and Kannada inscriptions from the 5th century, indicate its antiquity.

Karnataka's traditional theatre, *bayalata* (see page 352) has many forms, the best-known of which is *yakshagana*. These dance-dramas take their themes from Hindu epics, and the performers appear in elaborate costumes. The traditional crafts of Karnataka include silk weaving, sandalwood- and ivory-carving, Bidri work from Bidar and the popular red clay tiles of Mangalore.

Regional history

Successive Buddhist, Hindu and Muslim rulers dominated this part of southern India, leaving a trail of architectural wonders such as Bijapur, Hampi, Aihole and Badami. Chandragupta Maurya, India's first emperor, was believed to have converted to Jainism in the 4th century BC at Sravanabelagola.

The Hindu Chalukyas (6th–8th century AD) were followed by the Rashtra-kutas and other princely houses before the Hoysalas of the Vijayanagar Empire established the capital of their vast empire at Hampi in the central eastern region of the state.

The demise of the Vijayanagar Empire in the 16th century was followed by a period of Muslim rule. Hyder Ali and his son Tipu Sultan, rulers of the Kingdom of Mysore in the south, were defeated by the British in a battle at Srirangapatnam in 1799, and the British restored the former Wodiyar Rajas of Mysore as governors. The present state government meets at the Vidhana Soudha in the capital, Bengaluru.

The Bull Temple at Bengaluru is in south Indian Dravidian style.

Bengaluru (Bangalore)

The booming city of **Bengaluru ①** (formerly Bangalore) derives its name from *Benda Kaluru*, 'place of boiled beans'. It was originally founded in 1531 by a local chieftain, Kempe Gowda, who built a mud fortress here that was later extended by Hyder Ali and Tipu Sultan. During the British Raj the pleasant climate – Bengaluru's altitude of 920 metres (3,020ft) means temperatures are relatively low – made it a popular garrison town with attractive parks and gardens. In recent times the city has become a research centre for science and technology and the vibrant hub of India's dynamic hi-tech industries. The addition of the computer software industry attracted people from all parts of India and, with a population approaching 6 million, Bengaluru is rapidly becoming overcrowded and congested; it is now India's third-largest city.

A major transport centre, Bengaluru presents the modern face of India and has some of the country's best accommodation, some excellent restaurants and lively bars. These abound in the

Downtown Bengaluru.

area around M.G. Road, Brigade Road and St Mark's Road. The shopping is good, too: try **Commercial Street** for clothes and jewellery, and for contrast visit the colourful city **vegetable and fruit market** on Avenue Road, and the Old Town with its narrow lanes and bazaars. Bengaluru is also famous for its cinema halls. **The Plaza** on M.G. Road and the **Galaxy** on Residency Road show first-run English films. As a university town, it has several music festivals, usually featuring local bands.

The few local sights include public buildings such as the 46-metre (150ft) **Vidhana Soudha** (Secretariat and State Legislature) at the northwest corner of **Cubbon Park ④**, which is floodlit during weekends and holidays. The peaceful 1,200-hectare (3,000-acre) park was laid out by the British viceroy in 1864. Other notable buildings including the red Gothic **High Court** and **State Central Public Library** stand at its edge.

Another park, the **Lalbagh Botanical Gardens ⑧** (daily sunrise–sunset) in the south of the city, was laid out in the 18th century by Tipu

Sultan and Hyder Ali, and contains India's largest collection of rare tropical and subtropical plants, with trees from Iran, Afghanistan and Europe, and a glasshouse similar to the former Crystal Palace in London. Lalbagh is the venue for flower shows in January and August. The low hill at its centre affords tremendous views over the city. **Tipu Sultan's Palace** Ⓒ on Avenue Road southwest of the market is now a museum (daily 9am–5pm).

The ultra-modern **ISKCON Sri Radha Krishna Mandir** (www.iskcon bangalore.org; daily 4.15–5am, 7.15am–1pm, 4–8.20pm), a Hare Krishna temple, is located on Chord Road, 8km (5 miles) north of the centre. Long queues form to enter the colossal structure, said to be the largest temple complex in the world. Its main hall – surmounted by a pyramid of tinted glass, four huge, Dravidian-style *gopura* towers and an enormous golden dome and finial – centres on a suitably massive gilded chandelier, protruding from the ceiling in the form of an inverted lotus flower.

Also in Bengaluru is the headquarters of the **Art of Living Foundation**, the spiritual and humanitarian organisation founded by New Age guru and Hindu evangelist Sri Sri Ravi Shankar (not to be confused with the classical sitar player). The focal point of the state-of-the-art Ved Vignan Mahavidyapeeth, or VVM campus, is a massive, five-storey meditation hall, built entirely of marble in the shape of a lotus, with 1,008 stone petals encrusting its exterior. Inside, adoring audiences, drawn mostly from the city's English-speaking elite, gather on the polished marble floor to listen to the teachings of their long-haired, bearded *guruji*, who sits on a stage in flowing silk robes – a British journalist, Edward Luce, once remarked that the scene 'looked as if Jesus were shooting a shampoo advertisement.'

The Karnataka State Tourism Development Corporation (KSTDC) at Badami House, N.R. Square, offers city tours and excursions to **Bannarghatta National Park**, 21km (13 miles) to the south, which runs a wildlife safari and has a crocodile and

Venkataramanasvami Temple next to Tipu Sultan's palace.

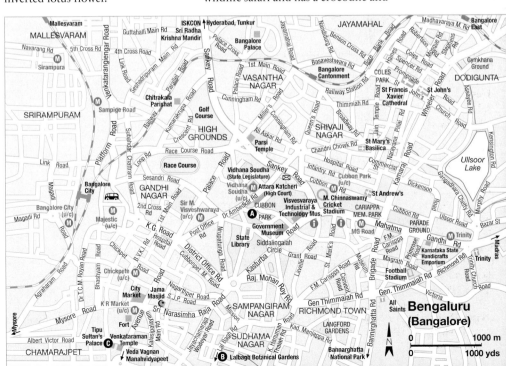

snake farm (Wed–Mon), and to the **Sai Baba Ashram** 20km (12 miles) to the east at Whitefield.

Princely Mysore

The town of **Mysore** ❷ lies 140km (86 miles) southwest of Bengaluru. Once the capital of a former Princely State, it is now a busy city but retains an undeniable character and charm. The moderate climate adds to the appeal, as does the pride that the city seems to take in both its past and its present – Mysore is often referred to as the cleanest city in India. In October the festival of Dasara (Dusshera) is celebrated with royal splendour, and has become synonymous with the city, as the maharaja leads a richly decorated procession that includes elephants and horses, flowers and incense, through the city streets.

The former Wodiyar maharaja's huge, fairytale-castle **palace** (daily 10.30am–5.30pm; charge) was built at great cost by a British architect in 1912 in the Indo-Saracenic style. A part of it is still the residence of the current maharaja. The interior is an amazing medley of striped pillars, stained glass, carved doors (including one made of solid silver) and mosaic floors. An extravagant mural depicting the great Mysore Dasara procession of 1930 lines the walls of the octagonal Kalyana Mandapa, the royal wedding hall. It took a team of four artists 15 years to paint, and presides over a vast hall filled with crystal chandeliers and gaudy Belgian stained glass. An adjacent room features a magnificent ceiling carved from teak. The palace's pièce de résistance, however, is its open-sided, colonnaded Durbar Hall, where the maharaja once hosted audiences while seated on a throne made from 280kg (615lb) of solid Karnatakan gold. Mughal-style inlaid marble adorns the ceiling arches, and fine views over the city and surrounding hills extend from an outer balcony, raised on heavy circular pillars. Every Sunday night, and all through Dusshera, the contours of the palace's exterior are illuminated by 97,000 light bulbs, to mesmerising effect.

The **Sri Jayachamarajendra Art Gallery** (daily 8.30am–5pm), housed in the Jaganmohan Palace to the west of Mysore Palace, features paintings dating from the 19th century, including works of Raja Ravi Varma and traditional Mysore gold-leaf paintings. **St Philomenas' Church**, built in Gothic style during the 1930s, has beautiful stained-glass windows. It is one of the largest churches in India.

For the best panoramic views over the city scale the 1,000 steps leading to the top of **Chamundi Hill**, 3km (2 miles) southeast of the centre, where a 12th-century temple dedicated to Durga (the Mysore royal family's patron goddess) houses a deity made of solid gold. En route, you pass a succession of minor shrines and, at around the halfway point, a stately 5-metre (16ft) -tall Nandi bull, Shiva's vehicle, sculpted from a single block of black granite – an object of popular veneration.

The central area around Sayaji Rao Road is full of places to eat and shops

On the streets of Mysore.

selling the sandalwood and incense for which Mysore is famous. It's a pleasant walk from here to **Devaraja Market**, which sells flowers, fruit, spices and conical piles of vibrantly coloured *kumkum* powders. The city is also renowned as a silk-weaving centre, and visitors are welcome to visit the government-run **Karnataka Silk Industries Factory**, 4km (2.5 miles) from the centre (Mon–Sat 10am–noon, 2–4pm) to watch the weavers and giant looms in action. Finely brocaded, gold-edged saris are sold in the factory showroom, and at many emporia clustered around K.R. Circle and along Mandavadi Road.

Srirangapatnam

The remains of Tipu Sultan's capital, **Srirangapatnam ❸**, occupy an islet in the Kaveri River, 14km (9 miles) from Mysore. The site was originally named after the Sri Ranganaswamy Temple, built in the 8th century and, miraculously, untouched by the devastating battles fought around it in later years.

The summer palace of the royal family, **Daria Daulat**, stands 1km (0.6 mile) east of the temple. Built as a guesthouse, the low colonnaded structure boasts elaborately decorated interiors, with tiger-striped pillars and lavish murals, including one showing Tipu's historic victory over the British at Polliore in 1780. The great leader and his father were both entombed 3km (2 miles) east in the Bijapuri-style **Gumbaz Mausoleum** (Sat–Thur 10am–5pm), a square granite structure topped by a whitewashed brick-and-plaster dome. Carved rosewood doors, exquisitely inlaid with ivory, lead into the tomb's hushed inner sanctum, which is lined with Tipu's trademark tiger stripes.

The Hoysalas, who ruled over central Karnataka between the 11th and 13th centuries, erected a series of distinctive, richly decorated temples across their domain, blending northern and southern styles of Hindu architecture. The **Keshava Vishnu Temple** (daily 7.30am–5.30pm), outside the rural village of **Somnathpur ❹**, a couple of hours' bus ride east of Mysore, is widely regarded as the finest of the crop. Like its counterparts elsewhere in the state, it's built on a star-shaped plan and mounted on a high plinth, though here the bewilderingly ornate sculpture is what most impresses. Resplendent images of deities, hewn from lustrous steatite (soapstone), adorn the upper walkway surrounding the shrine, which is encrusted from top to bottom with delicate stonework.

Nilgiri Biosphere Reserve

The remote **hill country** in the far southwest of Karnataka, straddling the state border with Kerala, encompasses an area of extraordinarily rich biodiversity. Although under threat from hydroelectricity projects, overgrazing, road-building and illegal logging, the dense evergreen and mixed deciduous forests of the Western Ghats hold around one-third of all India's flowering species, as well as an array of large fauna, including jungle civets, Indian

Descending the stairs to the open loggia at the front of Tipu Sultan's Palace.

THE TIGER OF MYSORE

Tipu Sultan (1750–99), the redoubtable Muslim ruler of Mysore state, became infamous in the annals of British India for his audacious military campaigns, which – along with those of his father, Hyder Ali – proved a perennial menace to East India Company ambitions in the far south. Tipu learnt early in his career that the way to defeat European armies was to dish out a taste of their own medicine, and consciously emulated his adversaries' military tactics. With support from the French, he deployed well-drilled, well-equipped infantry, cavalry and artillery (including much-feared ranks of 'rocket men'), notching up a series of crushing victories over the course of four 'Mysore Wars'.

Tipu ranked among the very few Indian leaders ever able to dictate terms in a treaty to defeated British generals. His nemesis, however, arrived just short of his 50th birthday in 1799, when an army of 30,000 East India Company regulars and sepoys, led by Lord Wellesley and his brother Arthur (later the Duke of Wellington of Waterloo fame) descended on his capital at Srirangapatnam, 14km (9 miles) from Mysore. Badly let down by his French allies at the last minute, 'the Tiger of Mysore' died defending a breach in the fort's walls – a scene immortalised in Wilkie Collins's novel *The Moonstone*. The British then plundered his palace; numerous artefacts are on display at the Victoria and Albert Museum in London.

The giant, 80-metre (260ft) figure at Sravanabelagola.

Mysore's Royal Palace.

bison (gaur), elephants and vestigial population of tigers.

The vast **Nilgiri Biosphere Reserve** , encompassing the Subcontinent's largest area of protected forest, was created from an amalgam of five separate national parks abutting the watershed of the range. Two of these – **Nagarhole** and **Bandipur** – lie within Karnataka, within easy reach of Mysore. At Bandipur, the more frequented of the pair, you can trek or take jeep safaris around the lower slopes of Gopalswamy Betta peak (1,455 metres/4,770ft), though sightings of large animals are only likely towards the end of the dry season, from late February through to May. Nagarhole, to the north, was decimated by fire in 1990s after disputes between the Forest Department and local tribal people over grazing rights erupted in a spate of arson attacks from which the wildlife population has yet fully to recover.

North of this area lies the Kodagu, or **Coorg**, region, dubbed the "Scotland of India". It is an extraordinarily beautiful place, famed for its abundant tea and coffee estates which have traditionally brought much prosperity to the region, and have turned the hills into waves of vibrant green. Many of the estates have now opened guesthouses which offer a supremely relaxing experience in stunning surroundings. The **Chikmagalur** region to the north of Coorg is equally beautiful and, in addition to the greenery, boasts the picturesque and historical town of **Sringeri**.

Sravanabelagola

Hassan (118km/73 miles northwest of Mysore) provides a base for exploring the region's top Hoysala temple towns, **Belur** and **Halebid** ❻, whose medieval shrines are embellished with some of India's most intricate Hindu sculpture. Belur's main draw is the painstakingly decorated **Channekeshava Temple**, the only remaining Hoysala temple still in use. Make sure you look up and take the time to appreciate the exquisitely fine ornamentation higher up the building. Arguably the most outstanding example of Hoysala temple architecture is **Hoysaleswara Temple** in Halebid; its uniquely extravagant exterior is a major work of art in itself. The third place worth heading to for Hoysala temple exuberance is **Somnathpur**, just 33km (20 miles) east of Mysore. The **Keshava Temple** here is the only example of a complete temple, and is again a marvel of decorative design.

The sacred Jain site of **Sravanabelagola** ❼, by contrast, holds monuments whose power to impress lies more in their jaw-dropping scale than decoration. Revered as the place where the Mauryan emperor Chandragupta starved himself to death in 300BC, the pilgrimage town, located around 50km (31 miles) east of Hassan, is dominated by a gigantic, 80-metre (260ft) colossus depicting the naked male figure of Gomateshwara. Said to be the largest free-standing sculpture in the world, it dates from the 10th century and provides the focus for the extraordinary **Mahamastakabhisheka festival**, held

every 12 years (the next one is scheduled for 2017). At the end of the celebrations, a week of increasingly intense rituals culminates with the pouring of a vast quantity of holy water, sandalwood paste, spices, milk, flowers, ground jewels and gold dust over the statue's head from a specially erected scaffold or even, as in 2005, from a helicopter.

Hampi

In northern Karnataka, on the banks of the Tungabadhra River close to **Hospet**, lies the deserted city of **Hampi ❽**, capital of the great Vijayanagar Empire from the 14th century and one of India's archaeological highlights (Vittala Temple, 8.30am–5.30pm; Royal Enclosure 8am–6pm). Hampi was destroyed in 1565 after the Battle of Talikota, in which the Vijayanagar army was defeated by the Bijapur confederacy. Its many temples and palaces are a World Heritage Site. It made its fabulous wealth from the spice and cotton trade, and at one time had a population of half a million people. The spectacular landscape is dotted with ruins and huge boulders, and is best explored by bicycle.

Among its many sights, the **Vittala Temple** is noted for its sculptural details; the **Royal Enclosure** houses the remains of the **Lotus Mahal**. For more on Hampi, see page 362.

Badami and Aihole

The boulder-studded tableland to the northwest is scattered with remnants of the Chalukyas, a powerful and expansionist dynasty which ruled the region, indeed most of southern India, between the 6th and 8th centuries. At **Badami**, a five-hour bus ride north of Hospet, the cliff faces of a gorge slicing between two low sandstone hills are pock-marked with cave temples (daily sunrise–sunset). More evocative ruined temples, decorated with accomplished carvings, are piled around the shores of Agastya Lake, an artificial tank at the foot of the gorge east of town, which is thought to date from the 5th century.

Archaeological remains spanning 600 years, including no less than 125 ancient shrines, lie around the village of **Aihole ❾**, an hour and a half's bus ride north of Badami. Founded on an age-old cultural fault line between the Brahmanical north and Dravidian south of peninsular India, the temples exhibit traits from both traditions. They also cover a long period and therefore plot the evolution of Hindu temple architecture, from the simpler designs such as the **Lad Khen Temple** to the more sophisticated style of the village's main draw, the **Durga Temple.**

The same is true of nearby **Pattadakal**, 25km (16 miles) from Badami, which served as a coronation site for its Chalukayn rulers from the 6th century onwards. Its finest vestiges are a group of temples inspired by the Pallava shrines of Kanchipuram, in Tamil Nadu, and were probably the grandest and most ornate in all of India at the time of their construction.

Karnataka's far north

The northernmost region of Karnataka, beyond the Krishna and

TIP

Badami is connected to Bijapur (132km/82 miles north) and Hubli-Gadag (128km/80 miles south) by a metre-gauge line, covered by five or six trains daily. You can also get there by direct bus from Hospet (near Hampi) – a bumpy six-hour ride across Karantaka's central cotton belt.

Intricate sculpture at Halebid.

SHOP

In the bazaar occupying the back streets of Bidar's old quarter, south of the fort, are workshops of metal-workers specialising in a now rare form of art called *bidri*. A Damascene technique originally devised by Persian silversmiths, it first arrived in the region with the Bahmanis in the 15th century. Deccani *bidri*, nowadays used to embellish everything from vases to betel nut boxes, is distinguished by swirling floral motifs in silver on dark backgrounds. Bidar's most famous workshops line Siddiq Talim Road.

Tungabhadra rivers, comprises a high, arid plateau – the Deccan or 'Desh' – whose dark volcanic soils today provide the Subcontinent with most of its cotton. From the late 14th century, renegade Muslim dynasties fled into this hostile border zone to carve out kingdoms beyond the reach of their tyrannical overlords, the Delhi Sultans, and later, the Mughals, who never managed fully to subjugate the area but would, by the death of Aurangzeb in 1707, all but exhaust their imperial coffers attempting to do so.

Over time, control of the Konkan's maritime trade, coupled with successful campaigns against the wealthy Vijayanagar Empire (whose capital was only a short march to the south at Hampi), furnished vast fortunes which the Deccani Sultanates lavished on splendid fortifications, palaces, mosques and tombs in their stronghold cities.

The most impressive and best-preserved of these is **Bijapur** ❿, capital of the Adil Shahis, often dubbed in tourist literature as 'the Agra of the South' or 'Palmyra of the Deccan' for the scale and ornate style of its monuments.

Bijapur's heyday extended over the reign of Adil Shah II (1627–57), a time when the dynasty's treasuries filled with booty from the plunder of Vijayanagar. His tomb, the mighty **Gol Gumbaz**, is the most conspicuous building in the city, if not in all of southern India, and stands as an eloquent reminder of the dynasty's formidable power – which extended at its height across most of the south. At almost 40 metres (132ft) in diameter, the great dome surmounting the mausoleum is the second-biggest in the world after St Peter's in Rome.

Bijapur's other famous tomb is an architectural gem conceived on a much smaller scale. Set in a walled compound on the opposite side of the city, the **Ibrahim Rauza** (daily dawn–dusk) is believed to have been commissioned by the wife of the Sultan Ibrahim Adil Shah (1580–1626), and certainly possesses a more delicate, feminine aura, with slender minarets, fountains and finely domed cupolas embellishing a pair of twin tombs that face each other from opposite sides of a raised plinth.

The first dynasty to establish supremacy on the Deccan, after migrating into the region from Afghanistan, were the Bahmanis. At their former capital, **Gulbarga** ⓫, 160km (100 miles) northeast of Bijapur, remnants of a fort developed by Allauddin Bahmani cover several hectares and include the **Jami Mosque**, an expansive structure in the style of the mosque at Córdoba in Spain. The interior arches are so designed and the pillars so placed that the pulpit can be seen unobstructed from any part of the hall. Gulbarga's most visited monument, however, is the **tomb of Saiyid Muhammad Husaini Gisu Daras** on the northeast edge of town. 'Bandah Nawaz', as the the Sufi saint is today affectionately known, was the spiritual mentor of the Bahmanis, and his tomb has, ever since his death in 1422 at the ripe old age of well over 100, been the most

KARNATAKAN ENTERTAINMENT

One of the most memorable experiences that Karnataka has to offer is an evening spent outdoors, sitting on a straw mat watching a *bayalata* (field play). These traditional dramas, which depict the exploits of heroes and heroines from Hindu epics such as the Ramayana and Mahabharata), may run from early evening until sunrise. The performances are an amalgam of music, dance and drama, featuring spectacular costumes and make up. An easygoing atmosphere prevails throughout: local people will be delighted to see a foreigner attend and any of them who speak English will ensure you understand the intricacies of plot and character.

When the fields are flush with water, there is another sight popular in Karnataka and not to be missed: the annual *kambala* (buffalo race). Held in a paddy field, the race is contested by pairs of specially trained racing buffaloes, egged on by men riding behind them. To start the race the driver jumps up, his hand cocked, his whip held high, and the huge animals lunge forward, bellowing, their hooves churning the muddy waters and sending their wet spray into the hot air, their eyes wide, wild and white. The races are a good excuse for some serious gambling, and a highly charged atmosphere is guaranteed.

important object of Muslim veneration in the Deccan.

Few travellers make it as far northeast as **Bidar** ⑫, another important Muslim capital, which emerged in the 1420s following the death of Bandah Nawaz and the ensuing break-up of the Bahmani dynasty. But the town, 284km (176 miles) northeast of Bijapur and 136km (84 miles) from Hyderabad, holds some of the most beautiful Islamic relics in all of southern India. On its northern edge, 10km (6 miles) of ramparts and fortifications enclose a campus of crumbling palaces and mosques, some of which boast fine mother-of-pearl inlaid stonework, sumptuous woodcarving and magnificent views over the surrounding countryside. The old quarter to its south is dominated by the tile-encrusted minaret of a 15th-century madrasa, its facade enlivened with bands of Islamic calligraphy and patches of green, blue and yellow ceramics.

The Konkan coast

The narrow coastal strip dividing the Western Ghats from the Arabian Sea, known as the Konkan or *Dakshini Kannada*, is in many ways a region apart from the rest of Karnataka, boasting its own language (Konkani), seafood-rich cuisine and a long history of contact with foreign traders and invaders. Thanks to the high-spec NH-17 Highway and Konkan Railway, travel along the coast is these days a far more straightforward affair than it used to be, when progress was hampered by frequent river crossings on slow, flat-bottomed ferries.

Beyond the largely uninteresting port city of **Mangalore**, close to the Keralan border, the first essential stop on any journey along the Konkan should be **Udupi** ⑬, a pilgrimage town par excellence. Its heart, surrounded by a square and broad bazaar, is the Krishna Temple founded by the Hindu saint Madhva in the 13th century. The site is famed above all for the spectacular festivals held within it in January and February, when gigantic wooden chariots capped with bulbous domes made of brightly coloured pennants are dragged by devotees around the sacred precinct.

The view from Sravanabelagola, a sacred site for Jains.

A similar ritual is staged several times each year at **Gokarna** ⓮, another ancient Hindu temple town to the north of the coastal belt, not far from Goa. Unlike Udupi (a *vaishnava* site), most of Gokarna's shrines are dedicated to Shiva or to his associated deities. Top of most pilgrims' hit list, after they have taken a purificatory dip in the step-lined **Kooti Theerta tank** on the east side of town, is the **Mahabaleshwar Temple** on the western side of the town's main street. Within its smoke-blackened core resides one of India's most revered Shivalinga, said to have been dropped here by the arch-demon Ravana during his epic struggle with Rama.

Gokarna is also a place of refuge for long-staying hippie travellers from Western countries, thanks to the presence over the headland from town of a string of delightful sandy coves, reachable on foot or by fishing boat. In recent years, a handful of luxury hotels have started to mushroom on the bare laterite hillsides overlooking **Om Beach**, the most picturesque of the string (its name derives from the shape of its twin bays, thought to replicate the auspicious Hindu Om symbol). Otherwise, the pace of change in this staunchly traditional corner of India is slow, allowing visitors to savour what much of the country must have been like before Independence.

South of Gokarna, accessed by taking the road heading inland from the village of Honavar, are the **Jog Falls** ⓯. The Sharavati River plunges over four cataracts here as it descends from the heights of the Western Ghats to the coast.

Telangana

Telangana, situated on the Deccan Plateau and drained by the Krishna and Godavari rivers, was a region in the Princely State of Hyderabad, which accessed to the Union of India in 1948. When India's states were reorganised along linguistic lines in 1956, Telangana was incorporated into the new state of Andhra Pradesh, comprised of Telugu-speaking peoples. In the years that followed, there were many movements to create a separate state out of the poorer northern districts of Andhra Pradesh, where people felt that their interests were often ignored by the state's politicians who hailed from the coastal and southern regions. Finally, the new state of Telangana was formed out of 10 districts of Andhra Pradesh and came into being in June 2014. The new state's population is predominantly Hindu and Telugu-speaking, while its capital city is Hyderabad, which is also serving as the capital of Andhra Pradesh, although only until 2024 at the latest.

Hyderabad-Secunderabad

Hyderabad ⓰ is the capital of both Telangana and Andhra Pradesh and India's fifth-largest city. It has a population of around 6.8 million, although the figure is closer to 7.7 million when the entire urban area is included. An acute scarcity of water and overcrowding at Golconda, 11km (7 miles) to the west, led Muhammad Quli of the

TELANGANA TRANSPORT

Flights: Hyderabad's impressive Rajiv Gandhi International Airport, 22km (13 miles) south of the city, is regarded as the most modern and efficient in India. It has direct flights to/from the UK, a few other European hubs and all large Indian cities. AeroExpress shuttle buses run to and from the centre every 30mins.

Rail: The major rail hub in the state is Secunderabad (for Hyderabad). Trains also run from Hyderabad but it's a long haul. **Hyderabad:** Trains run to Mumbai (6–10 daily; 14–17hrs 30mins). From **Secunderabad** trains run to Bengaluru (1–3 daily; 12–13hrs); Chennai (2 daily, 12–14hrs); Tirupati (4–6 daily; 12–15hrs 30mins). **Warangal:** Trains connect with Chennai (9–12 daily; 9–13hrs); Mumbai (1 daily; 20hrs); Tirupati (3–7 daily; 10–13hrs); Vijayawada (30–41 daily; 3–6hrs).

Qutb Shahi dynasty to build the new capital of Hyderabad on the banks of the Musi River in 1591. In 1687 the Mughal emperor Aurangzeb over-threw the dynasty and appointed his former general as viceroy. This dynasty of Asaf Jahi, which declared its inde-pendence after Aurangzeb's death, ruled as the Nizams of Hyderabad until 1949. The seventh and last ruling Nizam, Osman Ali Khan (1911–50), was famous for his eccentricities and enormous wealth, said to have been derived from diamonds and other gems mined by his ancestors around Golconda – which, in the 17th cen-tury, was the diamond centre of the world. At Independence in 1947 he expressed a wish to join Pakistan, a position he managed to maintain until 1949, when riots in the city gave the Indian army the excuse they needed to invade.

Traditionally a cosmopolitan cen-tre of learning and the arts with a reputation for friendliness and hos-pitality that still exists today, the old town of Hyderabad and its twin city, the modern Secunderabad, are separated by Hussain Sagar Lake. Besides being a major centre of com-merce and industry, transport and communication, Hyderabad is also a processing centre for pearls from the Middle East, Japan and China. It is considered the centre for Islam in South India and yet on the lake is the world's largest statue of Buddha.

In recent years Hyderabad has become, along with Bengaluru, the centre of India's software and hi-tech service industries. The districts of Ban-jara and Jubilee Hills are now full of expensive villas and flashy shopping malls where the newly wealthy mid-dle class congregate. Hitec City, a lit-tle further out, is where many of the multinational companies, including Microsoft and Oracle, have their head-quarters in large, modern glass-fronted buildings. This is in striking contrast to the narrow backstreets around the Charminar and the relentless poverty of the surrounding countryside.

The Old City

The main Mahatma Gandhi Road cuts straight through Hyderabad City,

Hyderabad's Charminar is surrounded by busy streets.

Vishakapatnam Beach, Andhra Pradesh.

Pearls and traditional bangles for sale in a Hyderabad bazaar. The city is famous for its glass bangles.

past the central shopping area around Abids Circle, and across the Tank Bund (a popular local promenade overlooking the lake) to continue onwards into Secunderabad. The old walled city area is anchored by Hyderabad's most famous landmark, the **Charminar** Ⓐ (literally 'four towers'; daily 9am– 5.30pm). Floodlit in the evenings, this magnificent square archway supported by four 56-metre (184ft) towers was built in 1591 to commemorate the end of a local plague. It is covered with a yellow stucco mixed from powdered marble, gram flour and egg yolk. There is a tiny mosque on the second floor where royal children studied the Qur'an.

Nearby stands one of the largest mosques in India, the black granite Mecca Masjid, said to have bricks made of red clay from Mecca over the central archway. Old bazaars with narrow cobbled lanes lined with rows of tiny shops selling spices, grain, perfume oils and Hyderabadi specialities such as seedless Anabshahi grapes, surround the Charminar. The pearl market has varieties of seed pearl, rice pearl and round pearl, sold loose by

Locals in Hyderabad.

weight, or strung into jewellery. Lad Bazaar, a narrow street, is the traditional centre for bridal accessories and bangles (Hyderabad is particularly noted for its glass bangles). To its east is a quadrangular complex of palaces built by the nizams.

The **Salar Jung Museum** Ⓑ (www. salarjungmuseum.in; Sat–Thur 10am– 5pm), on the southern bank of the Musi River, is the largest single-person collection of art and artefacts in the world. Salar Jung was a minister at the court of the Nizams, and his collection of over 43,000 objects and 50,000 rare books and manuscripts includes a good selection of European artworks and some wonderful decorated manuscripts from all over the Islamic world. The large Mughal jade collection in the museum is outstanding.

The neoclassical Falaknuma Palace, about 4km (3 miles) south of the Charminar, served as the royal guesthouse for the Nizams. Built in 1884, it is an imposing structure (set on a hill to maximise its impact) with an opulent interior that has now been fully

restored by the Taj group and opened as a luxury hotel.

Elsewhere in the city

Other places of interest include the Bagh-e-Aam (Public Gardens), which are the location of the ornate Legislative Assembly building, dating from the early 20th century. The **State Archaeological Museum** **C** (Tue– Sun 10.30am–5pm) is also located here. The collections of Chalukyan, Buddhist and Kakatiya sculpture are particularly fine.

A good spot for sunset views is Kala Pahad (Black Mountain), where the Birla Venkatesvara Temple is perched on the hilltop. On the adjacent hill, Naubat Pahad, is the Planetarium (daily 10.30am–8pm), with regular shows in English at 11am, 4 and 6pm. Hyderabad's Nehru Zoological Park, in the southwest of the city, is said to be one of the better zoos in India, but the condition of the animals is still depressing.

Leaving the city in the direction of Golconda Fort brings you to the burial ground of the Qutb Shahi

rulers. Despite being built over a long period of time, their **tombs** **D** (Sat– Thur 9am–4.30pm) are remarkable for the unity of their design. They all have a central dome, more or less onion-shaped, rising from a lotus-petal calyx, a small dome, minarets and stucco decoration. Most graves are of black basalt with calligraphic inscriptions. At the centre of the enclosure is the hamam, the baths built by Sultan Quli. The simple interior space is impressive, with a beautiful inlaid platform.

In the furthest outskirts of the city is Ramoji Film City, centre of the Telugu film industry and the largest production complex in the world. It is possible to visit on guided tours (www.ramojifilmcity.com; 9am–5.30pm) which give a fascinating insight into the gaudy, glamorous world of Indian cinema. Elsewhere are the new Botanical Gardens, covering 48 hectares (120 acres) and opening in stages, and the Shilparamam Crafts Village out in Madhapur. The latter has stalls and workshops of craft workers from all over India.

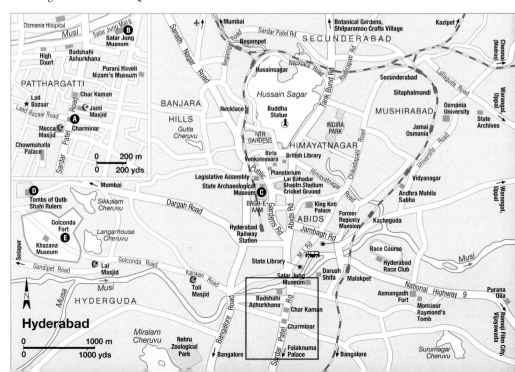

Around Hyderabad

The major sight outside Hyderabad is magnificent **Golconda Fort ⓔ**. Pochampalli, a village east of the city, is noted for its silk saris and ikat weaves.

Further afield is **Warangal ⓱**, 145km (90 miles) to the northeast. This 12th- to 13th-century capital of the Hindu Kakatiyas was renowned for its now abandoned brick-and-mud fort, a massive structure protected by two rings of walls and a moat. There are a few Chalukyan Shiva temples in the hills around Warangal and, some 30km (19 miles) east of Warangal, the Ramappa Temple in Palampet is said to be the best-preserved example of Kakatiya temple architecture in India.

Andhra Pradesh

Geologically one of the oldest parts of South Asia, Andhra Pradesh has stunning landscapes of hilly, rock-strewn plateaux, fertile river valleys, and a long coastline to its east. Yet it can be difficult to explore. The harsh climate – hot and dry for most of the year, interrupted by the flooding of rivers during the monsoon months – can make life very difficult. Cyclones frequently hit the coastal areas during May, October and November, paralysing transportation; the pre-monsoon period from April to June is baking hot, with temperatures regularly topping 45°C (113°F).

The state of Andhra Pradesh, the first formed on a linguistic basis, was created in 1956 after a period of considerable political agitation. The predominantly Hindu Telugu-speaking parts of the Presidency of Madras were combined with the former territories of the Princely State of Hyderabad, hitherto ruled by a Muslim nawab. In 2014, a new state of Telangana was formed out of 10 districts of Andhra Pradesh, which included the city of Hyderabad, although it remains the de jure capital of Andhra Pradesh until a new capital city is selected, no later than 2024.Buddhism, Hinduism and Islam have all flourished in Andhra. Ashokan accounts from the 3rd century BC refer to a people called the 'Andhras'. Later, the Satyavanas ruled from Amaravati and were Buddhist patrons.

Andhran culture

Telugu, the principal language of the state, has a rich literature that can be heard in its *padyams*; rolling, sonorous prose narrations of rural life, customs and festivities. Andhra has strong traditions of music and dance, too. *Kuchipudi*, a dance drama originating in the fertile delta of the Krishna and Godavari rivers, is thought to have developed out of the local *yaksagana* theatre. Of the skilled craft workers of Andhra some of the finest specialise in wood-carving; those from Kondapalli near Vijayawada fashion colourful toys and figures that portray village life. *Bidri* workers from Bidar create delicate designs, inlaid in silver or gold on matt-black gunmetal hookahs, vases, boxes and jewellery. The weavers use distinctive weaves and dye techniques, and are famous for their rich brocades,

GOLCONDA FORT

The huge and once-impregnable Golconda Fort (Sat–Thur 9.30am–5pm), situated on a steep granite hill 11km (7 miles) west of Hyderabad, was built by the Qutb Shahi dynasty, which ruled during the 16th and 17th centuries. It was their capital until 1590, when the king moved to his new city of Hyderabad, and was used by the last of the Qutb Kings in the 17th century as a bastion against Mughal attack. The fort was encircled by immense walls with 87 semicircular bastions and eight gates with elephant-proof spikes. Famous for its ingenious acoustics, a remarkable hot-and-cold-water supply system, natural air conditioning and Turkish baths, the remains of its once-splendid palaces and gardens give an idea of its former grandeur, when diamonds and rubies embellished the walls of the Queen's Palace – a hint at where the Qutb Shahi dynasty's extraordinary wealth originated. In their day, the mines of Golconda were the only known source of diamonds in the world, and merchants from as far afield as Persia, Africa and Europe travelled here to purchase them. World famous gems that originated in the kingdom, and which were once stored in the Golconda sultans' treasuries include the Koh-i-Noor ('Mountain of Light') and exquisite blue Hope Diamond (aka 'Le Bleu de France'). The views over the city from the topmost point are truly spectacular. Golconda is easily reached by local bus or autorickshaw from central Hyderabad.

ikats, silks and *himru* fabric – a mixture of silk and cotton.

Nagarjunakonda Dam

Around 170km (106 miles) southeast of Hyderabad you will find the **Nagarjunakonda Sagar and Dam** ⑱. Built in 1960, this reservoir submerged an entire valley, which had been home to a series of ancient civilisations. Important Buddhist monuments have been reconstructed at a museum within the ruins of a fort on an island, which was once the top of a 200-metre (650ft) hill. Boats leave three times daily from Vijayapuri between 9.30am and 1.30pm, the last boat returning at 4.30pm, and the trip takes about 45 minutes. The entrance charge covers the boat journey and access to the site and **museum** (Sat–Thur 9am–4pm).

In the area to the east of Nagarjuna is the important pilgrimage site of **Srisailam** (the 'holy hill'). Within the walls of a moated fort on the south bank of the Tungabhadra River, just before it joins the Krishna, are eight temples and a **museum** (Sat–Thur 10.30am–5pm). The latter has a good collection of Alampuri sculpture.

Vijayawada and Amaravati

On the banks of the Krishna river, the ancient city of **Vijayawada** ⑲, 240km (150 miles) east of Hyderabad, was once visited by the Chinese traveller Hieun Tsang. It shows traces of its past in the two ancient Jain temples and the cave temples nearby, and also the hilltop **Kanakadurga Temple**, devoted to the patron deity of the city. It is now a busy commercial centre, and most travellers only pass through in transit along the east coast.

Vijaywada is useful to the visitor as a base from which to visit **Amaravati** ⑳, 30km (19 miles) to the west, the site of early Buddhist settlements. Here the remains of a 2,000-year-old Great Stupa are embellished with carvings depicting the life of the Buddha. A small **museum** (Sat–Thur

9am–5pm) displays statues of the Buddha, although most of the sculptures are kept in either the Government Museum in Chennai or the British Museum, London.

A journey across the beautiful Krishna-Godavari delta to the coastal town of **Machilipatnam**, 70km (43 miles) to the east, makes an interesting excursion. Here you can still see the *kalamkari* process of printing cloth using a *kalam* (pen) and woodblocks. Also within striking distance of Vijaywada is **Kondapalli**, famous for its production of wooden toys, painted with vegetable dyes to stunning effect; there's also an impressive 14th-century fort.

The northeastern coast

The naval base and shipbuilding centre of **Vishakapatnam** ㉑ (known as 'Vizag') on Andhra Pradesh's northeast coast is the fourth-largest port in India. Its twin city, **Waltair**, was built as a resort town by the British and still retains shady avenues, charming bungalows and marvellous views. Set on a beautiful curving bay, Vizag is

Golconda Fort.

Red-hot chilli harvest in the Andhran countryside.

Paddy fields in the Araku Valley.

delineated by two hills to the north and south. **Kailasa Hill** (to the north) is topped by well-maintained gardens, at the centre of which is a monumental pair of statues of Shiva and Parvati. There is also a small tourist train that runs around the park. While you can take the winding road up (toll fee), it might be more fun to take the cable car to the top (although following an inquiry into an accident in February 2016, the service is presently suspended).

The view from **Dolphin's Nose** (so called because of its shape), the southern hill, is even more spectacular – especially from the **lighthouse** at the end of the road (daily 3.30–5.30pm), although there are plans to convert this to a private hotel.

Unfortunately, apart from the beach at **Rushikonda** (11km/7 miles north of Vizag) swimming is extremely dangerous along this stretch of coast. At the quiet former Dutch settlement of **Bhimunipatnam** (24km/15 miles from Vizag) there are some striking colonial graves by the seashore. Between Vizag and Bhimunipatnam are a number of Buddhist sites, while the **Godavari River** provides some worthwhile sites, most noticeably the scenery close to the gorge and the temple architecture at **Draksharaman.**

There is a 13th-century Orissan-style Hindu temple and hot springs at **Simhachalam** up in the forested Eastern Ghats nearby, and **Mukhalingam**, close to the border with Odisha (Orissa), has some superb examples of Orissan-style temple architecture. A 70km (43-mile) journey inland (best done by train) brings you to the Adivasi area of the **Araku Valley** on the border with Odisha. There are coffee estates around the towns of Ananthagiri and Chintapalli that lie at the entrance to the valley. Also here are the impressive **Borra caves** ㉒ (daily 10am–1pm, 2–5.30pm). Discovered in 1807 by the British geologist William King, they are one of the natural wonders of Andhra. The Gosthani river that flows from the caves takes its name ('cow's udder') from the colour of the milky calcium carbonate in the water.

ANDHRA PRADESH TRANSPORT

Flights: Visakhapatnam Airport is the only international airport in Andhra Pradesh, 12km (7.5 miles) north of the city. It has flights to many Indian cities including Chennai, Delhi, Mumbai, Hyderabad, Kolkata, Tirupati and Vijayawada, and a few international connections to Dubai, Kuala Lumpur and Singapore.

Rail: The major rail hub in the state is Vijayawada. Most important sites are reachable by rail, apart from Amaravati and Nagarjunakonda (which are accessible thanks to bus tours run from Vijayawada).

The line that runs over the Eastern Ghats into the Araku Valley (twice daily from Vizag) is one of the most scenic journeys in South India – the tourist office in Vizag offers daily guided tours.

Tirupati is most easily reached by rail from Chennai (3 daily; 3–4hrs).

Vijayawada: Trains connect with Chennai (19–27 daily; 7–9hrs), Secunderabad (26–36 daily; 5–7hrs); Visakhapatnam (34–41 daily; 5–7hrs).

Visakhapatnam: Trains run to Chennai (9–11 daily; 12–16hrs); Mumbai (2–4 daily; 26–29hrs); Secunderabad (11–16 daily; 12–15hrs); Tirupati (3–7 daily; 12–17hrs); Vijayawada (34–41 daily; 5–7hrs).

The Adivasi heritage of the region is celebrated in Araku with the **Museum of Habitat** (daily 10am–1pm, 2–5pm). The collections here have a large array of fascinating Adivasi household objects, jewellery and musical instruments, many displayed in re-creations of traditional housing.

Southern Andhra

Tirupati ㉓ is famous for the **Lord Venkatesvara Temple**, which stands on nearby Tirumala Hill. Receiving between 30 and 40 million pilgrims annually, this is officially world's busiest pilgrimage sites, as well as one of the wealthiest. The efficient temple administration (www.tirumala.org) deals with between 60,000 and 100,000 visitors daily, and operates an 18-hour-a-day *darsan* (view of the deity) regulated by a token system: pilgrims receive a token from one of several offices, which tells them which time to enter the queue, after which it takes about two hours to enter the temple. Many pilgrims shave their heads as a pledge, or to thank the deity. The hair is used to make wigs, which are sold locally and exported. The steep road up the hill has 57 hairpin bends and lovely views.

At **Chandragiri** (Sat–Thur 10am–8.45pm, sound and light show in English at 7.30pm), 11km (7 miles) from Tirupati, are the Raja Mahal and Rani Mahal, late Vijayanagara structures of the 17th century. These palaces lie within a moat and formidable battlements. 25km (15 miles) in the other direction from Tirupati are the stunning temples of **Sri Kalahasti**, a place that really comes alive during the Mahashivaratri festival but which is worth a visit any time.

Thirteen kilometres (8 miles) east of Hindupur is the temple town of **Lepaksi**. On a little hill is the **Virabhadra Temple**, built in 1530, famous for its frescoes of deities. A monumental **Nandi**, the biggest in India, proudly raises its head 1km (0.6 mile) away.

The barren landscape can be surveyed from a number of impressive forts, including **Penukonda** about 35km (22 miles) north of Hindupur. Here there is a massive encircling wall and a pavilion on the hilltop. Nearby is the elegant Gagan Mahal (a royal pavilion), still in good repair. The fort at **Gandikota**, to the east of Anantapur, is poised above a gorge carved out by the Pennar River.

Northeast of Penukonda is the small village of **Puttaparthi**, location of the ashram of the controversial spiritual teacher, mystic and self-proclaimed philanthropist Sai Baba (see www.srisathyasai.org.in) Large crowds visit the site to attend rituals and bhajan (sacred hymn) sessions, despite the fact the guru passed away in 2012.

About 25km (15 miles) on from Gandikota are the temples at **Tadpatri**, easily reached by rail from Chennai. The **Ramalingesvara Temple** was built in the 15th century and the **Venkataramana** in the early 16th century. They are a mix of Chalukyan and Chola architecture, with exuberant Vijayanaga decoration.

Making an omelette at Vijaypuri.

HAMPI

The ruined capital of the Vijayanagar rulers is one of the greatest sights in South India, the location being as much part of the magic of the place as its historical remains.

The Vijayanagar Empire (1336–1565) was one of the largest in India, spreading across much of the South, and its rulers accrued a great deal of wealth. This helped build one of the medieval world's most opulent cities, Hampi, described by the Muslim envoy Abdul Razaq in 1443 as 'such that the pupil of the eye has never seen a place like it and the ear of the intelligence has never been informed that there existed anything to equal it in the world.' As well as being a centre for trade and crafts, its rulers were also great patrons of the arts, contributing much to the development of South Indian music, sculpture and architecture.

The Vijayanagar kings were Hindu, although they allowed the practice of other religions, and they themselves followed a variety of deities (including Virupaksa and Vittala, whose temples remain as important monuments). This cosmopolitan city was, however, to be wiped out in 1565 following the declaration of war by the Muslim sultanates to the north. The court fled and the city was sacked, never to be reoccupied. The remains were listed as a Unesco World Heritage Site in 1986 and they still have the ability to conjure up at least an idea of the splendour that must once have held sway here.

Hampi's monuments are now spread across a magical landscape strewn with granite boulders, and fall into three main areas: the sacred centre around the Virupaksa Temple, where recently shops and other businesses were bulldozed as part of a government attempt to 'sanitize' the site; the Royal Enclosure and the Vittala Temple. The site was naturally well defended, protected by rocky hills on three sides and to the north bounded by the River Tungabhadra, which also provided water for the city.

The Virupaksa Temple, with its towering gopuram (temple gateway).

This huge monumental sculpture of Vishnu in his incarnation as a lion is carved from a single boulder.

The elephant stables of the Royal Enclosure.

The Lotus Mahal, a skilful blend of Hindu and Islamic architecture.

THE ROYAL ENCLOSURE

This area in the south of the site was the location of the palaces of the Vijayanagar rulers, and also where the administrative functions of the state were carried out. Perhaps the most notable monument here is the Ramachandra Temple, the place of worship of the ruler and located between the royal court and the residence. As well as some beautifully carved pillars, in three bands around the outside wall of the temple are reliefs that tell the story of the Ramayana. There are a number of step wells and tanks on the site, but the most lovely is the Queen's Bath, a square basin overlooked by cantilevered balconies. The women of the court had their own quarters and the most famous structure of these is the Lotus Mahal, pictured above. The final notable monument in the Royal Enclosure is the elephant stables, a row of 10 chambers with high vaulted entrances in different architectural styles.

The Vittala Temple complex is considered to contain some of the finest sculpture from the Vijayanagar period.

Devotees who come to Hampi take a ritual bath in the Tungabhadra river.

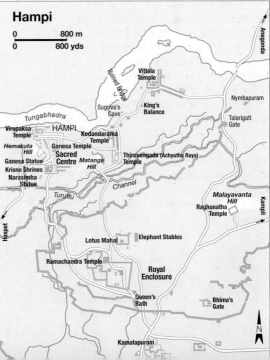

Hampi

0   800 m
0   800 yds

Anegonda

Vittala Temple

Ruined Bridge

Sugriva's Cave

King's Balance

Nymbapuram

Tungabhadra

Talarigatt Gate

HAMPI

Virupaksa Temple

Kodandarama Temple

Hemakuta Hill

Ganesa Temple

Sacred Centre

Ganesa Statue

Matanga Hill

Thiruvengada (Achyutha Raya) Temple

Krisna Shrines

Narasimha Statue

Turuthu

Channel

Malayavanta Hill

Raghunatha Temple

Kampli

Lotus Mahal

Elephant Stables

Hospet

Ramachandra Temple

Royal Enclosure

Queen's Bath

Bhima's Gate

Kamalapuram

N

CHENNAI (MADRAS)

Chennai (formerly Madras), capital of Tamil Nadu, hugs India's sandy southeast shore. The least pressured of the country's four big urban hubs, it is a stronghold of Tamil culture.

The major metropolis of the South, Chennai – known as Madras until 1996 – is India's fourth-largest city, home to around 4.7 million inhabitants and sprawling for miles along the coast of northern Tamil Nadu. The area has been inhabited since as early as the 1st century, but really came to prominence as a major port from the 1500s onwards. The Portuguese and the Dutch both had bases here, but it wasn't until the arrival of the British East India Company in 1639 that the city began to take shape.

The city today is a curious mixture. While it retains the legacy of the British Raj, and is, in some ways, a conservative bastion in social and religious matters, it is also the Bollywood of South India and, simultaneously, a stronghold of traditional Tamil culture. There are churchyards, staid residential areas and prim gardens side by side with giant-size cut-outs of cinema heroes and heroines, painted in bright colours and dotted with flashing sequins.

As if this contrast were not enough, Chennai has reinvented itself over the last few years. Now one of the south's booming software and call-centre hubs (rivalling Bengaluru and Hyderabad), the centre is sprouting glossy new high-rise buildings and shopping malls, patronised by the city's middle class. Not quite so fortunate, however, are Chennai's poor and lower castes, still greatly in evidence on the city streets.

Most of the city's sights are easily reached from the city centre, which is also where most of the accommodation options are to be found. The colonial Fort area is just to the north of the city centre, while the wider, more open spaces tend to be found to the south, with a number of attractions, particularly for children, dotted along the scenic East Coast Road to Mammallapuram.

Main Attractions
Fort St George
The Marina
M.G.R. Memorial
Anna Salai
Chennai Music Academy
St Andrew's Kirk
Kapalesvara Shiva Temple

A Mylapore jeweller.

As in most Indian cities, Chennai's buses are frequently overcrowded and difficult for foreigners to use.

Climatically, this corner of India goes from hot to hotter and hottest, with relief brought by the northwest monsoon in June and July, and the southeast monsoon in November and December, when sea breezes bring a cool freshness to the land and the beaches are beautiful in the early hours and late evenings. The sea here, on the east coast – romantically named the Coromandel Coast – is not as inviting for the swimmer as India's western Malabar coast (the wicked undertow making it very dangerous), but the city beaches hum with groups of picnickers and strolling families. At night, lights from fishing boats can be seen glowing over the dark waters.

Chennai is also the gateway to Tamil Nadu, and makes an excellent introduction to Tamil culture, food, customs and people. Vegetarian food is available in restaurants serving delicious hot 'meals' with boiled rice, lentil curries and tiny portions of vegetables, while the famous fried *dosa* and steamed *idli* have come to be identified with Tamil Nadu.

Portrait of Queen Victoria at the Fort St George Museum.

Fort St George

The British East India Company established one of its earliest seats of power in India in the former Madras, and the construction of **Fort St George** Ⓐ was begun around 1640 – making it the oldest colonial structure in the country. The fort was often attacked by Indian and French forces, yet it continued to expand. Today its buildings house the Tamil Nadu Government **Secretariat** and the **Legislative Assembly**. A feature of the East India Company architecture is the use of Madras *chunam*, a glittering whitewash of limestone mixed with crushed seashells. The *chunam*-coated walls of the buildings are dazzling.

Within the fort, a number of other early buildings still stand, of which **St Mary's Church** (daily 9am–5pm; free) is the most interesting. It is the earliest English building surviving intact in India and the oldest Anglican church in Asia, consecrated in 1680. The interior of the church is whitewashed, but there are also elaborate carved wooden panels. The church was the venue for the marriage of Robert Clive, victor of

TRANSPORT TO CHENNAI

Chennai is one of India's major international airports, as well as a important hub for internal flights on a variety of domestic airlines.

There are two main railway stations, Chennai Central and Chennai Egmore, so check on your ticket where your train departs from. **Trains** run from Chennai to: Bengaluru (9–13 daily; 5–7hrs); Delhi (4–5 daily; 27–36hrs); Hyderabad (3–4 daily; 12–14hrs); Madurai (11–18 daily; 8–12hrs); Thanjavur (7–10 daily; 6–9hrs); Tirupati (3 daily; 3–4hrs).

Long-distance **buses**, including those to Mamallapuram, depart from Mofussil Bus Terminus in southern Chennai – one of the largest in Asia, it is well-run and clearly signposted. In reality visitors will probably only use it to reach Mamallapuram (2.5 hrs, over 20 departures daily).

the Battle of Plassey in 1759 – which marked the beginning of formal British rule in India.

The **Fort St George Museum** (Sat–Thur 9am–5pm), housed in what was built as the Public Exchange, gives a good overview of the early British colonial lifestyle. A marble statue of Cornwallis by Thomas Banks greets visitors, with various storehouses and the city's first bank occupying the ground floor. The first floor, now a gallery of colonial portrait art, was once the coffee shop where merchants and officials met for gossip and trade. Other items on display include uniforms, coins, weapons and books. Perhaps the most intriguing artefact is Anstruther's Cage, a small wooden box used by the Chinese to imprison a British army officer captured in 1840 during the First Opium War, who was subsequently kept in the cramped space for six months.

Other fort buildings of note include the **Old Government House** and the **Banqueting Hall** (Rajaji Hall), built for the governor's official entertainment during the Clive period. The architectural style drew inspiration from the classical Greeks and Romans – with Doric, Corinthian and Tuscan pillars, entablatures and friezes much in evidence.

The **Marina**, extending almost 13km (8 miles), is a wide, sandy – and in places rather dirty – beach and one of Chennai's most popular meeting places. A 2010 renovation and litter drive went a long way to tidying up the beachfront. It's worth coming down here at sunset to witness the crowds and the entertainment – **Elliot's Beach** in Besant Nagar is a slightly more low-key alternative. Facing the sea are the 19th-century **Presidency College** and the **Senate House** of the **University ⓑ**. The university building and its grounds are noted examples of the Indo-Islamic style popular in Indian public architecture in the late 19th century.

Opposite the university is the **Anna Samadhi**, a large marble-clad lotus commemorating C.N. Annadurai, who led the Dravidian movement to political power and changed the social and political structure of Tamil Nadu. Beside it is a memorial to **M.G. Ramachandran**, a much-loved film star and chief minister.

Anna Salai and environs

Anna Salai ⓒ (previously Mount Road) is Chennai's main shopping street. Higginbotham's, one of India's best-known bookshops, is here. There are other bookshops worth checking out nearby: Landmark Books in Spencer Plaza is said to be one of Asia's largest bookstores, while Giggles in the Connemara is recommended for its knowledgeable owner and eclectic stock.

Chennai is famous for its silk emporia where silk saris, scarves, and material for suiting and dresses are available by the yard. The Government-run Co-optex shops have an extensive range of fabrics, and Poompuhar, the Government Handicrafts Emporium, has good bronzes. Both these are on Anna Salai, along with a number of other

Traffic in the Anna Salai district.

state emporia. At the junction of Anna Salai and Binny Road is Spencer Plaza, an air-conditioned complex with a large number of different shops. On Binny Road itself is the Art Deco Taj Connemara hotel.

To the north of the busiest part of Anna Salai are many of the newer landmarks of the city, most of them 100–150 years old. On Pantheon Road, where the **Pantheon** was home to public entertainments in Arthur Wellesley's (later the Duke of Wellington) day, is the magnificent, though dreadfully run-down, **State Government Museum** (www.chennaimuseum.org; Sat–Thur 9.30am–5pm). Established

in 1846, it has one of the finest collections in the country including a rare collection of sculptures from Amaravati in Andhra Pradesh, belonging to the Buddhist period, 2nd century AD. The white limestone sculptured medallions and panels tell the story of the life of the Buddha. The Bronze Gallery has a superb collection of Chola bronzes (9th–13th century AD). Some are barely 4cm (1.5 ins) tall, while others measure over half a metre (1.5ft). All are iconographically sophisticated. The dancing Shivas, Durgas and Ganapatis and the famous Rama, Lakshmana and Sita group are the pride of the museum.

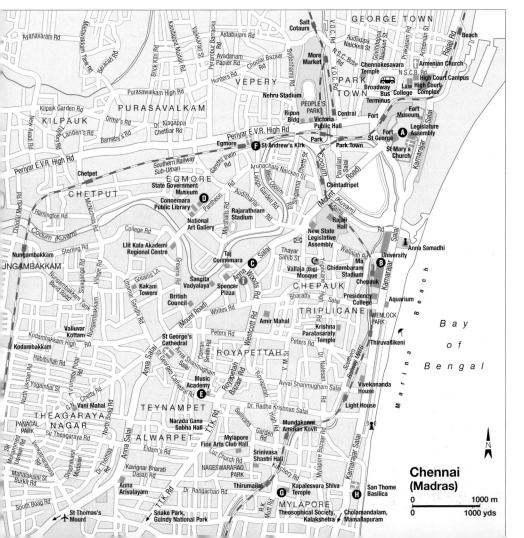

Chennai
(Madras)

Next door to the State Government Museum is the **National Art Gallery** (Sat–Thur 9.30am–5pm; admission included with State Government Museum), with a permanent exhibition of Indian painting. In the newer wings is a gallery of contemporary art where temporary shows are held. The nearby **Connemara Public Library** is one of the country's four national libraries to which every book published in India must be sent.

In performing arts, of all the city's concert halls, the **Music Academy** ⓔ is the most renowned. It puts on music and dance programmes by eminent artists for discerning audiences, which inspires the performers, whether of Karnatak music or *Bharata-natyam*, to memorable heights. Check out other venues, such as the **Krishna Gana Sabha** (www.krishnaganasabha.org), particularly during the Chennai Festival in December and January, when you can see performances by South India's finest dancers and Karnatak musicians.

Beyond, at no. 601, is **The Park** hotel – set in what was once the city's Gemini Film Studios, where a number of classic Tamil movies have been shot. Now a luxurious design hotel, its bar, club and rooftop pool are a magnet for Chennai's young middle class looking to spend their call-centre salaries.

Egmore and George Town

Beyond the Government Museum is **Egmore**, once the Indian town that complemented the colonial town of Fort St George. Now a commercial centre, it has a number of interesting colonial buildings. Egmore Railway Station, the Chennai Medical College, the Ripon Building and Victoria Public Hall are all worth seeking out. Perhaps the most magnificent Indo-Saracenic complex in the city, however, is the **High Court** and **Law College** campus to the northeast of Egmore, bordering on George Town. Its large, ornately-domed towers are surmounted on *chatris* (pavilions), while the windows are given a characteristic arch striking

a nice balance between imperial pomp and local architectural forms.

Not far from Egmore Station is **St Andrew's Kirk** ⓕ. It bears a passing resemblance to St Martin-in-the-Fields in London and was built by James Gibbs in 1818–21. The towering steeples and the strength of the pillars of the facade make it a city landmark.

North of both Egmore and Fort St George is the district of **George Town**. Now quite run-down, its tightly packed grid of streets is nonetheless worth exploring. Within this trading district are some of the oldest temples and mosques of British Chennai and the churches of the first Protestant missionaries. The twin **Chennakesavara** and **Chennammallikesvara** temples, and the beautifully maintained **Armenian Church**, are among the most interesting places of worship in the city.

Mylapore

One of the most interesting parts of Chennai lies just south of the city centre. This is **Mylapore**, with a tank, market area and old Brahman houses. At the evening bazaar, crowds of people,

The M.G.R. memorial commemorates Maruthur Gopala Ramachandran, film star, prominent Tamil nationalist and political leader who died in 1987.

THE "SEASON"

The most popular classical music and dance festival in India is the Chennai 'season', an annual event that began 65 years ago, when the Chennai Music Academy was founded and began organising conferences at which various aspects of Karnatak music and *Bharata-natyam* were the chief topics of discussion. The conferences were accompanied by day-long programmes comprising instrumental and vocal concerts and dance recitals. It is still held at the Academy today, running for three weeks from mid-December to early January. Artists consider it an honour to be invited to perform at its concerts, and devotees of South Indian music and dance come from all over the country to attend.

Several other art-promoting societies *(sabhas)* have sprung up in Chennai, and all now organise 'seasons' during the same period. They include the Tamil Isai Sangam, Brahma Gana Sabha, Narada Gana Sabha, Krishna Gana Sabha and the Mylapore Fine Arts Club. Listings of what's on are published every day in *The Hindu*.

Finally, if you're in the region any time in January, try to catch the annual Chennai Sangamam arts festival, which sees performances of south Indian folk music and dance, martial arts and street plays taking places at various open-air venues across the city; admission to all events is free.

freshly bathed, make their way to the **Kapalesvara Shiva Temple G**. The vibrantly colourful sculptures inside and all over its towering *gopuram* (temple tower) are among the most spectacular sights in Chennai. The temple is dedicated to Shiva in the form of a peacock *(mayil)* from which the town receives its name *(mayil-puram*, 'peacock town', which became Mylapore). The central shrine (closed to non-Hindus) has a Shiva lingam, behind which is the large temple tank. Timings can be sporadic – afternoon is the best bet. Almost as old is the **Krishna Paratasaraty Temple** on Triplicane High Road further to the north.

Mylapore is well known for its jewellers, who specialise in making gold-plated 'dance jewellery sets'. Silver ornaments are dipped into a gold solution, and bright-pink tissue paper is then placed into pre-moulded grooves before being capped with a pale pink stone. The result mimics the ruby-studded gold traditional patterns required for classical dance. The classic headpiece comprises a *rakodi*, worn just above the flowers in the hair,

Gopuram detail at Kapalesvara Shiva Temple.

flanked by a stylised sun and moon. Ear ornaments come in three parts: a chain, a dangler, and a support for the lobe. Around the neck is a choker, plus a half-moon-shaped pendant *(padakkam)* suspended from a longer chain. A *vanki* bracelet grips the upper arm and is heavier than the standard gold bangles jingling at the wrist. A broad ornamental belt, called an *odyanan*, completes the costume. Sometimes a *sarpam* hair ornament snakes around the long plait for a final golden touch.

San Thome and Adyar

On the coast to the east of Mylapore lies the district of San Thome, named after the St Thomas the Apostle. **San Thome Basilica H** is on the Main Beach Road: it is believed that Thomas was martyred on what is called **St Thomas's Mount** and that his remains were enshrined in this church. The modern crypt marks where he is thought to have been buried and is an important pilgrimage spot for Indian Christians.

The **Theosophical Society** (www.ts-adyar.org; Mon–Sat 8.30–10am, 2–4pm) has its headquarters on the banks of

the Adyar River south of Mylapore. It houses a vast library of books on religion; in the gardens that lead up to the river and the sea is a sprawling banyan tree, said to be one of the largest in India.

Local attractions

The places described below are easily reached by bus from Chennai's new, and very well-organised, **Mofussil Bus Terminal**, which lies in the west of the city at Koyambedu.

South of the city in Thiruvanmiyur is **Kalakshetra** (www.kalashetra.net), an academy of music and dance set up by Rukmini Devi, the doyenne of Indian dance. Her efforts to re-establish temple dance after it had been banned led to the creation of *Bharatya-natyam*, now India's most prominent classical dance form. The academy organises dance programmes.

On the East Coast Road (ECR) south of Chennai is **Cholamandalam**, the artists' village, where exhibitions, poetry readings and other programmes take place. At Muttukkadu, 28km (17 miles) from Chennai, is **Dakshina Chitra** (www.dakshinachitra.net; Wed–Mon 10am–6pm). This is an exemplary museum featuring a number of rescued examples of South Indian village architecture. It aims to preserve and promote traditional crafts.

Outdoors, the attractions in the area immediately south of Chennai include the **Guindy Deer Park** and the **Snake Park** (Wed–Mon 9am–5.30pm; no bags allowed inside). The former has species of black buck, chital (spotted deer) and numerous monkeys. The Snake Park is the only major reptilium in India, founded by the American conservationist Romulus Whitaker. Beside the Deer Park is the large campus of Chennai's branch of IIT (the Indian Institute of Technology). These are the most prestigious science universities in the country, and competition for admission to the courses is extremely fierce. Continuing south down the coast you'll come to **Madras Crocodile Bank Trust and Centre for Herpetology** (www.madras crocodilebank.org; Tue–Sun 8.30am– 5.30pm), an incredibly large collection of different varieties of crocodiles, well worth a visit.

TIP

Try to catch a *Bharata-natyam* performance while you're in Chennai, a contemporary interpretation of one of South Asia's oldest dance traditions. The dancers once came from a highly trained community of temple dancers, known as *devadasis* or 'servants of god', but are now mostly from urban middle-class backgrounds.

Indo-Saracenic architecture near Egmore Railway Station.

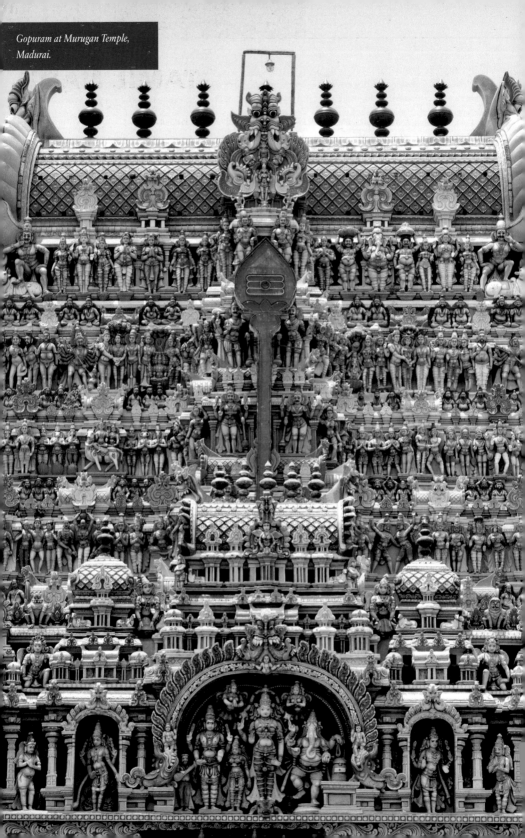

Gopuram at Murugan Temple, Madurai.

TAMIL NADU

South India's outstanding temple architecture is just one of the highlights of **Tamil Nadu**, which stretches from the sand dunes of the east coast to the cool **Nilgiri Hills** in the west.

Tamil Nadu has a reputation for being conservative, devoutly religious and fiercely proud of its ancient culture, and while this may still largely hold true, a gradual transformation is taking place as the state increasingly deals with the outside world. There is a definite 'otherness' to Tamil Nadu, its language and culture unlike anywhere else in India. **Chennai ❶** (see page 365) is the usual starting point for a tour of this most southerly of Indian states.

Tamil politics

A feature of Tamil temples is the presiding orthodox Brahmins, who still dress in white dhotis and display forehead markings, half-shaven scalps and long hair at the back twisted into single plaits. A sacred thread always stands out against their bare chests. Although a minority community, Tamil Brahmins continue to exert much influence in national and international affairs.

   In reaction to centuries of Brahmin rule, a pan-Dravidian movement gathered pace after Independence, claiming that Brahmanical rule and influence were a symbol of northern domination. In 1967, a party championing the lower castes, the DMK, won power under C.N. Annadurai. The DMK was a breakaway party from the DK of P.E.V. Ramaswamy

which initially campaigned for a separate country of 'South India'. The film star M.G. Ramachandran (known by his initials as M.G.R.) took over as Chief Minister a decade later, controlling the splinter-party AIADMK and attracting a huge level of support. On his death he was succeeded by his former co-star and 'companion', Jayalalitha Jayaram. Voted out in 1996 over allegations of corruption, undaunted, and still attracting fierce loyalty from her supporters, she entered parliament and

A typical convenience store in Tamil Nadu.

led her party into coalition with the BJP in 1998. This relationship soon soured, and when she withdrew her support the central government fell. She regained power in Tamil Nadu but her party, the AIADMK, was trounced by its bitter rival, the DMK under M. Karunanidhi, in the 2004 general election. In a further blow, he also took control of the state during the elections to the legislative assembly in 2006. Despite his advancing years, Karunanidhi continues to contest the chief minister's post with his arch adversary Jayalalitha, who has been in power five times since 1991. Jayalalitha was voted into office once again as chief minister of Tamil Nadu in 2015.

Language was an important element in the pan-Dravidian movement and today still remains a vital part of Tamil politics. The adoption of Hindi as the 'national language' (seen as another manifestation of northern arrogance) was greeted with horror in the south, and its official imposition can still spark off riots.

Tamil Nadu has a long coastline, stretching down to Kanniyakumari at the very southern tip of India. The tsunami that hit Southeast Asia at the end of 2004 badly affected the Tamil Nadu coast, but most of the obvious damage

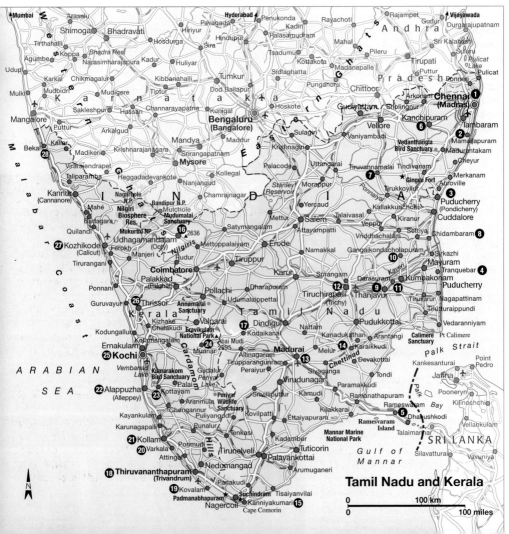

Tamil Nadu and Kerala

has now been cleared up. Generally the major tourist sights – including the Shore Temple at Mamallapuram and the city of Puducherry – escaped largely unscathed.

Mamallapuram

The first major destination south of Chennai is **Mamallapuram** ❷ (daily, ticket sales 6am–5.30pm, sites until 6pm; one ticket covers all sites), a tiny village by the sea and an extraordinary showcase for Tamil art. One of the great highlights is **Arjuna's Penance** or the **Descent of the Ganges**, the world's largest bas-relief, 27 by 9 metres (764 by 288ft) and one of the major masterpieces of Indian art. It is a beautiful composition of hundreds of deities, humans and animals, set around a natural cleft in the rock. Dominating the scene is a 5-metre (16ft) -long elephant leading a procession of elephants to the scene of the penance by the cleft, where Arjuna stands on one leg to propitiate Shiva to help him win back the kingdom of the Pandavas.

The best-known landmark of Mamallapuram, however, is the **Shore Temple** (daily 6am–6pm). Standing by the sea, now protected by a wall that hides its facade but saves it from the elements that are fast eroding it, this twin granite spire has perfect proportions and a wealth of sculpture. It is also unique in that it includes shrines for both Shiva and Vishnu. The temple's architecture, much of which dates to the 7th century AD, has been declared a World Heritage Site.

The 2004 tsunami that hit the coast here particularly hard did not damage the Shore Temple but did carry off an enormous amount of sand. In the process it has uncovered the foundations of another huge monument, lying a few hundred metres to the south of the Shore Temple, apparently also dating from the Pallava era. The huge waves also uncovered a long wall running north of the Shore Temple, and in the moments before it formed, exposed traces of even more intriguing ruins on the seabed approximately 400 metres/yards off shore which, when explored later,

Cycle rickshaws are becoming increasingly rare all over India.

TAMIL NADU TRANSPORT

Flights: Aside from the international airport in Chennai (see page 366), Tamil Nadu is well served by internal flights, with airports at Coimbatore, Salem, Puducherry, Madurai and Tiruchirapalli.

Trains: Railways wind throughout the state from the principal hubstations at Madurai, Erode, Tiruchirapalli and Nagercoil. Tamil Nadu's Blue Mountain Railway, built by the British in the 19th century to form a year round, narrow-gauge link between the Tamil plains and hill station of Ootacamund, is now listed by Unesco as a World Heritage Site, along with the one running up to Darjeeling in northeastern India.

Madurai: Chennai (14–22 daily; 9–12 hours); Mumbai (1–3 daily; 33hrs); Mysore (1 daily; 14hrs 20mins); Tiruchirapalli (13–23 daily; 3hrs).

Kanniyakumari: Chennai (1–2 daily; 13hrs 30mins).

Nagercoil: Chennai (4–7 daily; 13–15hrs); Madurai (8–14 daily; 4–5hrs).

Puducherry: Chennai (2 weekly; 3hrs 30mins–4hrs).

Buses: The Tamil Nadu network is one of the best in the country. Some places in the state, especially in the hills, are only accessible by road. Useful services include those between Udhagamandalam and Coonoor (11 daily; 1hr) and Kodaikanal and Mettupalayam (2 daily; 7.5hrs). Another important route is that between Chennai and Mamallapuram (4 daily; 3hrs).

The monkeys at Mamallapuram are very bold, and have been known to steal food and drink from visitors' hands.

Arjuna's Penance, the world's largest bas relief, at Mamallapuram.

turned out to date from AD 500–800, the height of the Pallava period. This has led to renewed speculation about the old belief that the Shore Temple was originally one of seven 'pagodas'– an assertion seemingly confirmed by reports by early European travellers to this coast.

The other wonders of Mamallapuram are the *mandapams* – caves scooped from the hillsides and ornamented with pillars and great sculptured panels that are an integral part of the excavation – and the *rathas*, monolithic rock-cut shrines that have inspired generations of South Indian temple-builders. In the **Krishna Mandapam**, the serenity of a pastoral scene is ensured by Krishna protecting the earth from a storm's fury with his massive umbrella, the Govardhana mountain. In the **Varaha Mandapam**, Vishnu in his incarnation as Varaha the boar bursts from the ocean clutching the rescued Earth Goddess. Lastly, in the **Mahisasuramardini Mandapam**, the goddess Durga, astride a lion, battles the powerful buffalo-headed demon Mahisasura.

To the south of the Shore Temple, along a road lined with stalls selling stone carvings for which Mamallapuram is famous, are the **Five Rathas** (daily 6am–6pm), named after the Pandava brothers, the heroes of the *Mahabharata*, and their wife Draupadi. These carved structures are thought to have been used as small shrines. They are in the shape of wooden *rathas* (temple chariots), and each is incomplete, yet remains an architectural gem. Also in this arena are a magnificent free-standing elephant and an exquisite Nandi, the sacred bull. There are four other *rathas* elsewhere in Mamallapuram.

Other notable sights include the **Trimurti Cave** and the **Adivaraha Temple**, where worship still continues, and scores of individual pieces of sculpture, of *yalis*, monkeys and other mythical and living creatures. There is also a smaller, open-air museum of scattered sculptural treasures from around the site. In tribute to the skills of the ancient sculptors, a college of sculpture is

run in the township, not only granting degrees but turning out some excellent work.

Tamil Nadu's European enclaves

Tamil Nadu's long coastline is washed by diverse influences. **Puducherry ❸** (previously Pondicherry), the former French colony, is listed as a Union Territory for administrative purposes (although it is now lobbying for full statehood). In addition to Le Club – one of the best French restaurants in South India – Puducherry has French-speaking rickshaw drivers, Vietnamese restaurants, the tastiest bottled water in India and Goubert Salai, the cleanest seaside promenade in the country. In parts of the town you'd be mistaken for thinking you were in France – a visit here is a definite contrast to anywhere else in the state, and also has some excellent shopping opportunities.

Just north of Puducherry lies the New Age community of Auroville, founded in 1968. The city is made up of attractive, experimental housing, and at its centre is the huge Maitri Mandir meditation centre. Travellers can stay in Auroville to learn more about the place and to participate in voluntary development projects.

Outside Puducherry is **Arikamedu**, an historic site where the famous British archaeologist, Mortimer Wheeler conducted excavations in the 1940s, revealing a Graeco-Roman trading centre of the early Christian era. The discovery proved what Roman texts had already suggested: that a flourishing trade in dyed muslins and spices (particularly pepper) existed between Rome and this stretch of the Coromandel coast in ancient times.

Some European settlements on the Tamil Nadu coast are more obscure. The adventurous traveller can experience what is left of the former Danish settlement of **Tranquebar ❹** (100km/62 miles south of

Puducherry) by walking through the old gate, with its coat of arms, down to the sea. A memorial to the first Protestant missionaries to visit India remembers Bartholomew Ziegenbalg and Heinrich Plutschau, while overlooking the deserted beach, the remnants of Dansborg Fort and a Lutheran church, the oldest in India, recall this almost forgotten episode in European colonization of India's southeast coast. The former Governor's bungalow has been converted into a delightful heritage hotel, the Neemrana Group's Bungalow on the Beach.

Tamil temples by the sea

The **Ramalingesvara Temple** on **Rameswaram Island ❺**, 150km (93 miles) southeast from Madurai, severed from the mainland by a cyclone in the 15th century, is one of the holiest spots in India. This is believed to be the place where Rama stopped to worship Shiva after his conquest of Lanka. It is believed that the two lingams in the sanctum of the magnificently

The Krishna Mandapam at Mamallapuram.

Cave temple (mandapam) at Mamallapuram.

sculpted **Ramanatasvami Temple** were installed on this spot by Rama himself. The temple, it is said, took 350 years to complete; its crowning glory is a magnificent 1,220-metre (4,000ft) -long pillared corridor that surrounds the main quadrangle.

Walk away from blaring, devotional songs playing on loudspeakers and catch a bus as far as it will go to the extreme tip of the island for a holy bath at **Dhanushkodi**. Walk back to the bus stop, 3km (2 miles) across a perfect circle of sand dunes. A pilgrimage to Varanasi is said to be complete only after bathing at Dhanushkodi. The town was once a thriving port linking India to Sri Lanka, only 20km (12 miles) away across the Gulf of Mannar, until it was devastated by a cyclone in 1964. At the time of writing in early 2016 plans were afoot to reintroduce the ferry service between Dhanushkodi and Sri Lanka following the cessation of hostilities in the long-running civil war in Sri Lanka, though no precise date for the resumption of the service has yet been decided.

Tamil temple towns

Those with an interest in temple architecture could travel on to Kanchipuram, Tiruvannamalai, Chidambaram, Thanjavur and Tiruvarur, Tiruchirapalli (Trichy) and Srirangam or Madurai. Although each temple town has a distinct character, they share common elements. Processions of the god or goddess are accompanied by the loud temple ensemble of *nagasvaram* (a long oboe with a piercing tone) and *tavil* (barrel drum, played with a stick in the left hand and fingers clad in plaster 'thimbles' on the right). The music from the procession is considered very auspicious. The overpowering fragrance of incense and jasmine and marigold garlands, the sight of hundreds of slippers piled up outside temple *gopurams* and the thousands of pilgrims pressing forward for a better view of an idol being paraded on a palanquin are common to all temples during festivals. Visitors should note that many Tamil temples forbid non-Hindus to enter the inner

The tank at the Kamakshi Temple, Kanchipuram.

sanctum, although they are usually free to wander around the rest of the complex.

Kanchipuram

Known as the 'golden town of a thousand temples', **Kanchipuram ⑥** has about 125 officially recognised shrines, all of them centuries old. Dating back to the early Jain kingdoms, Kanchipuram was successively capital of the Pallavas, the Cholas and the Rajas of Vijayanagara. The height of Kanchi's glory was as the capital of the Pallavas Empire from the 6th to the 8th century, when Mamallapuram and Mylapore were its great ports. All that is left of that era are its magnificent temples.

The **Kailasanatha** Temple has an added courtyard, and a high *vimana* crowning the inner sanctum. Prototype carvings of Shiva, accompanied by his consort and mythical beasts known as *yalis*, set the standard for carvers. The largest of the town's temples is **Ekambaresvara**, dedicated to Shiva and with a famous '1,000-pillar' *mandapam* (columned

hall). The town's silk weavers are renowned for their skill and their use of colour and intricate patterns.

Vellore, with its impressive 16th-century fort, lies a further 60km (40 miles) west of Kanchipuram, while **Tiruvannamalai ⑦**, 100km (63 miles) to the southwest of Chennai, is one of the holiest sites in South India, and certainly one of the largest temple complexes, sprawling over 10 hectares (25 acres). The earliest part of the temple, the inner sanctum, dates back to the 11th century, while the huge *gopuram* was built during the Vijayanagar period (14th–16th century).

East of Tiruvannamalai is the 700-year-old **Gingee Fort**, with its battlements stretching over three hills. A Vijayanagara fort that the Marathas, the Mughals and the French added to over the years, Gingee has within its walls several richly carved temples, a palace, a harem and a mosque. It had an interesting system of plumbing and water storage, the remnants of which can still be seen. Towering over all of them is Rajagiri, a steep hill 150 metres (500ft) high.

Street dogs are numerous all over India.

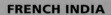

FRENCH INDIA

Puducherry lies on the coast of Tamil Nadu, 150km (93 miles) south of Chennai. It came under French rule in the mid-18th century and was finally returned to India in 1954. The town was originally divided by a canal. On one side was the **Ville Blanche** for the French inhabitants and on the other the **Ville Noire** for the Indian population. **Government Park** formed the heart of the city, around which the **Raj Nivas** (residence of the lieutenant governor) and other official buildings are now located. Near the railway station is the Gothic-style **Sacred Heart Church**.

The streets of the old French area are cobbled in the traditional way, and the waterfront area is designed to resemble Nice. A great way to savour the faded Gallic ambiance is to stay at one of the handful of lovely heritage hotels that have opened up in the French enclave.

Ten kilometres (6 miles) from the town are the **Sri Aurobindo Ashram** and the international community of **Auroville**, which was designed by the French architect Roger Auger. The ashram was set up by the Bengali philosopher Sri Aurobindo, who played an active role in the Indian independence movement. His teachings were preserved by his French-born spiritual companion, Mirra Alfassa, who became known as "The Mother".

Chidambaram

Beyond Gingee you begin to enter the heartland of Tamil Nadu, and especially the Chola, the fertile Kaveri delta. The temple at **Chidambaram** ❽, the Chola capital from the 10th to the 14th century, is dedicated to Shiva in his form as Nataraja (Lord of the Dance). The temple management is the sole preserve of a group of Brahmins known as Diksitars, recognisable by a single tuft of hair over their foreheads.

Much of the temple as seen today was built by the Chola emperors. Massive *gopurams* soar over great entrances. There are several shrines in the temple complex, including one for the god Vishnu. The inner sanctum enshrines the god in his dance pose. Adjacent to it is the sanctum of the goddess, whose name here is Shivakamasundari, 'the beautiful woman who evoked the love of Shiva.' An unusual shrine is one without an image in it; this is known as the secret of Chidambaram – the implication being that god is to be found everywhere. The roof of the temple is gold-plated.

Eye-poppingly bright garlands of flowers are given as offerings to deities in Hindu temples.

As befits a temple dedicated to the god of dance, poses now adopted by the classical *Bharata-natyam* style are sculpted around the shrines and on the gateways.

Tamil Nadu's World Heritage sites

In **Thanjavur** (**Tanjore**) ❾ (260km/160 miles southwest of Chennai), the former Chola capital set in the Kaveri delta paddy fields, the **Brihadesvara** Temple dominates the landscape. This, along with two further Chola temples at Gangaikondacholapuram and Darasuram, was added to the Unesco World Heritage List in 1987, cited for their importance not only as architectural gems but also their continued significance as places of worship.

The Brihadesvara Temple was constructed in the 10th century by Rajaraja I and features a *vimana* (sanctuary of the god) more than 60 metres (200ft) high (the tallest in India) and entrance towers (*gopurams*). Subsequent Chola temples add subsidiary shrines and extended *mandapams* or pavilions to the architectural plan. Unlike other temples in the south, the *gopurams* of this temple (aptly called the 'Big Temple') are dwarfed by the *vimana* over the sanctum. The exquisitely sculpted *gopurams* lead to a vast courtyard in which the main temple stands, guarded by two enormous *dvarapalakas* (sentries) carved out of single stones. Separated by a corridor and facing the sanctum is a Nandi (Shiva's bull).

Inside the sanctum stands a *lingam*, symbol of the god Shiva, which is reputed to be the largest in the country. The corridors around the sanctum in which devotees circumambulate, going from left to right, have many sculptures; some wonderful Chola frescoes have also been discovered here.

Close by, to the northeast, is the **palace** (daily 9am–6pm). Remnants of the fort that surrounded the palace can still be seen, and a 58-metre

(190ft) -high lookout remains in good shape. Members of the former royal family of Thanjavur continue to occupy some apartments in the inner recesses, but the palace is now used mainly as an art gallery and to house the Saraswathi Mahal Library. The Sangita Mahal is a music hall with great acoustics.

The **art gallery** (daily 9am–1pm, 3–6pm) was set up in 1951. Initially established by the district collector who rescued many pieces from surrounding villages, the gallery houses some of the most beautiful sculptures of the Chola period, mainly from the 9th to the 14th century, and a magnificent collection of Chola bronzes, including some unique representations of Shiva Nataraja. The sculptures include freestanding pieces (many of them from Darasuram) as well as groupings. One of the most beautiful of the ensembles shows Shiva as a handsome mendicant, making the chaste wives of several *rishis* fall in love with him.

Within the art gallery is the **Rajaraja Museum** (daily 9am–6pm) which

houses Chola artefacts, many excavated from the site of the palace of Rajendra Chola at Gangaikondacholapuram. These exhibits include coins, terracotta objects, carved conch shells and metal vessels and measures.

One of the greatest collections in India is in the **Saraswathi Mahal Library** (10am–5.30pm library Thur–Tue, library museum daily), housed in another part of the palace. The Maratha rulers of Thanjavur in the 17th and 18th centuries were enlightened monarchs who patronised art and culture. The greatest of them, King Serfoji, started the library. An engaging and infinitely curious intellectual, he collected not only manuscripts and illuminations but also books in many European languages. There are over 40,000 items in the collection, and they include rare books on the arts and sciences, many of them written on palm leaves.

More Tamil temple towns

Close to Thanjavur is the town of **Tiruvarur**, birthplace of the South Indian 'trinity' of composers,

Traditional kitchen knives for sale in Karaikkudi.

Ekambaresvara Temple, Kanchipuram.

THE DANCE OF SHIVA

As one of the holiest sites in South India, it is fitting that Chidambaram should have an origins story to match. It is said that the god Shiva performed his cosmic dance – or tandava – here after humbling several conceited *rishis* (sages) who believed they had acquired extraordinary powers through their rigorous austerities. Other sages, as well as the gods and goddesses, begged to see the dance, and Shiva agreed to perform for them in the forest of Thillai (another name for Chidambaram). The situation acquired an additional piquancy when the guardian of the forest, Kalika Devi (in reality Sakti, the consort of Shiva), challenged him to a dance contest. By performing movements which she as a modest woman could not, Shiva defeated her. He concluded his performance with the dance of bliss. In response to the *rishis*' request, Shiva dances the cosmic dance for all time to come in Chidambaram, as depicted in the beautiful bronze image in the temple. Some of the finest of all the Chola idols show Shiva in this distinctive pose, with his four harms gracefully raised, standing on one leg crushing the demon Apasmara, which signifies victory over ignorance. The surrounding flames represent the Universe, the snake writhing around his waist the divine force residing in all life, and calm expression on his face indicates detachment from the world.

EAT

To dismiss the notion that only mild vegetarian *thalis* are available in South India, try fiery Chettinad cuisine, which uses lamb, quail, crab and many spices and lichens for flavouring. The Chettinad area of southeastern Tamil Nadu is also famous for its merchant traders' palatial houses with woodwork in carved Burma teak.

Tyagaraja, Muttusvami Diksitar and Syama Sastri. **Gangaikonda-cholapuram** ❿ is about 64km (40 miles) northeast of Thanjavur. This elaborate name means 'the City of the King Who Conquered the Ganges', and commemorates the triumph of Rajaraja's son Rajendra. He invaded the north and conquered many territories, reaching the Ganges in the process. On his return he built a city, and a **Brihadesvara Temple** which is almost the equal of the eponymous temple in Thanjavur. Some even assert that the sculptures in this temple are superior. This small village is all that remains of a grand 11th-century city, but the temple is a remarkable monument. Modelled on the Thanjavur Temple, it too has a large enclosure, at the centre of which is a shrine containing a huge Shiva lingam. Close by is a small museum with finds from local excavations (daily).

Darasuram ⓫ , close to Kumbakonum, has a magnificent Shiva Temple, the **Airavatesvara Temple** built by the Chola king Raja Raja II in the

12th century. Because of neglect over the centuries, much of the temple has crumbled, but what remains reveals a gem of Chola architecture and sculpture. The main shrine with a 26-metre (85ft) -tall *vimana* (superstructure) and the shrine of the goddess are in a fair state of preservation. The entrance hall is shaped like a chariot, and the steps leading up to it give a musical ring when struck. The exuberance of the sculptures makes one wonder what the temple must have been like in its heyday. Sculptures and remnants of paintings create a whole world of dancers and acrobats, and depict a variety of scenes from everyday life. It was known as 'the temple of perpetual entertainment'.

Tiruchirappalli (Trichy)

Tiruchirapalli ⓬ is dominated by a 90-metre (300ft) -high rock fort containing 7th-century rock-cut temples. At the top of 437 steps is the Tayumanasvami Temple, crowned with a golden *vimana*. From the fort there are remarkable panoramic views (daily 6am–8pm).

Coconuts and bananas, sold as offerings outside the Minakshi Sundaresvara Temple, Madurai.

The **Sriranganathasvami Temple** in nearby **Srirangam** is one of the holiest temples for devotees of Vishnu, and its annual winter festival (December to January) attracts thousands of people. It is a rather confusing complex since it was built over the centuries. Surrounded by crumbling granite walls, with 21 ornamental towers, most parts of the temple are open to non-Hindus. The main charm of Srirangam is that it is a living temple – much like Madurai's Minaksi Temple.

Madurai

Madurai ⑬, a bustling town to the south of Tirucharapalli, is Tamil Nadu's main transport hub after Chennai, and as such tends to end up featuring in most visitors' itineraries at some point. This is no bad thing – it is the site of another great Vijayanagar temple, the **Minakshi Sundaresvara Temple,** perhaps Tamil Nadu's most popular, with thousands of visitors from all over the world coming to it every day. Dedicated to the goddess, and consort of Shiva, this is said to be the biggest temple in the country. Its four towering *gopurams* with their brightly painted sculptures are spectacular. The 1,000-pillar *mandapam* here has some beautifully carved columns and displays of art. Other special sights include a monolithic statue of Ganapati, and the temple tank, where the god Indra is believed to have bathed.

The splendour of the Nayak rule in Madurai is evident in the remains of the **palace of Tirumalai Nayak** (daily 9am–1pm, 2–5pm), the most famous king of the Nayak dynasty. The palace originally occupied an area of approximately 210 by 300 metres (700 by 1,000ft), and consisted of many fine apartments and galleries, as well as gardens, tanks and fountains. Much of it is gone now, except for the great audience hall, a three-sided pavilion; the courtyard, supported by pillars 18 metres (60ft) high and 4 metres (12ft) in circumference; and

an unsupported dome over 18 metres (60ft) high.

Also worth a visit is the **Gandhi Memorial Museum** (www.gandhimmm.org; Sat–Thur 10am–1pm, 2.45–5.30pm), located in the historic Tamukkam Palace. It contains a comprehensive account of the struggle for independence in India, and of course a more specific collection on the life of Mahatma Gandhi. On the road out to the airport is a **Murugan Temple** that backs onto a large granite hill. The brightly painted facade and *gopuram* are especially fine. Young trainee Brahmins can be seen racing from their school behind the temple in time for *pujas*. Further around the monolith is a small **rock-cut temple** dating back to the Pallavas. This is an especially calm and peaceful spot with monkeys playing in the trees that grow below the towering rock.

Chettinad

On the coastal plain between Tiruchirapalli and Madurai is the **Chettinad** region, homeland of the Chettiar merchant community. Their ancestral

TIP

For more on the life of Swami Vivekananda, pay a visit to Kanniyakumari's Wandering Monk Museum, on Main Road, where 41 panels give a detailed account of his travels and philosophies.

Inside Minakshi Sundaresvara Temple.

villages, now partly deserted, have some of the finest family mansions in South India. In the 19th century the Chettiars were known as the bankers of South India, and their immense wealth was poured into gold, jewellery and, most impressively, their houses. Covering entire blocks, their interiors contain pillars of teak, satin wood and granite, intricately carved teak doors, and Italian marble floors. The walls are gleaming white, covered with a paste made from lime, egg white and *myrobalam* fruit.

Some of the finest mansions can be found in **Karaikkudi** , the largest village in the region, and nearby **Kanadukathan**. After Independence, the wealth of the community diminished and the money was no longer available to maintain these luxurious dwellings, and now many of them are uninhabited. The Chettiars have, however, left a culinary legacy of peppery meat-based dishes, flavoured with unusual spices and dried fruits. While it is impossible to gain access to most of the houses, even those that have been well maintained, one or

two enterprising families have begun to open up their mansions as attractive hotels, giving visitors a peek into what was an extraordinary world.

Kanniyakumari

At the southernmost tip of India, **Kanniyakumari** ⑮ occupies a unique position in the mythology, as well as the geography, of the Subcontinent. Close to 2 million Hindu pilgrims travel here each year to worship at the temple dedicated to the Virgin Goddess, Kanya Devi, whose weathered stone walls overlook the place where the waters of the Bay of Bengal, Indian Ocean and Arabian Sea merge. It's considered particularly auspicious to bathe at the ghats extending into the waves below the shrine during the full-moon phase of April, when you can watch the sun set and moon rise on the same horizon.

Standing offshore, their bases lashed by surf, is a pair of rocky islets, one of which sports a giant, 29-metre (92ft) image of the Tamil poet-saint Thiruvalluvar. The

Devotees at Minakshi Sundaresvara Temple.

colossus, inaugurated in 2000, took 150 workmen more than a decade to build, at a cost of more than US$1 million. On the other island rests a memorial to the 19th-century spiritual leader and Hindu reformer, Swami Vivekananda, one of the figures responsible for introducing yoga and Vedic philosophy to the West. The spot marked the culmination of the two-year journey which the sage made across the length and breadth of India in 1890: on reaching Kanniyakumari, he plunged into the sea and swam out to the rock, meditating for three days on the country's past, present and future. Just over a century later, 400 people were stranded on the islet after the Boxing Day tsunami laid waste to much of the coast hereabouts.

Kanniyakumari's religious associations aside, the town can – thanks to its crowds, ugly concrete architecture and overzealous hawkers – come as a bit of a disappointment if you've travelled here expecting a mystical atmosphere. However, there's plenty of old-world ambience on offer

at **Suchindram**, 12km (7.5 miles) northwest, whose spectacular Sithanumalayan Temple was founded 1,000 years ago in Chola times; its most famous monuments are a collection of exquisitely carved musical pillars, which emit notes when struck. Ancient Tamil epigraphs may also been seen on a boulder in the main *mandapa* assembly hall. Unlike most shrines in the region, the inner sanctum – unique in India for holding a deity that represents all three gods of the Hindu Trinity – is also open to non-Hindus.

Interesting stopping-off points on the way down to Kanniyakumari include **Tirunelveli**, 70km (44 miles) to the north. Reputed to be one of the oldest cities on the Subcontinent, Tirunelveli is home to Tamil Nadu's largest Shiva temple. Fifty kilometres (31 miles) east of Tirunelveli lies the largely industrial port town of **Tuticorin,** which is home to India's foremost pigeon-racing club.

West of Kanniyakumari lies **Nagercoil**, with its temples and churches, and beyond Nagercoil the palace at

19th-century Chettiar mansions at Kanadukathan.

Yoga, spas and retreats

Whether you are looking to find yourself or your figure, or just want to get away from it all – India offers all manner of yoga programmes, health spas, ashrams and retreats.

Yoga originated in India, and while it is now practised worldwide, the Subcontinent is still seen as the centre of the discipline. Thought to have developed from the Buddhist/Hindu tradition of meditation, yoga strives to enhance both physical and mental well-being, with the intake and exhalation of air also playing a vital role. In the strictest interpretations of both the Hindu and Jain faiths, the ultimate goal of yoga is the achievement of *moksha*, meaning liberation from suffering, the only way to break the cycle of life and death.

The benefits of yoga are myriad, from improved strength, flexibility and tone to reduced symptoms in osteoarthritis and rheumatoid arthritis patients. Balance and core strength are enhanced through the holding of the various *asanas*, or poses, and the weight-bearing nature of some of the exercises has been shown to benefit women approaching

Yoga on the beach.

menopause, delaying the onset of osteoporosis, or thinning of the bones. The psychological benefits are equally wide-ranging; yoga is often prescribed to those dealing with depression, anxiety or stress, and many practitioners report a generally heightened sense of well-being, improved powers of concentration and deeper sleep.

Schools of yoga

There is now a vast array of different schools of yoga, each emphasising a slightly different aspect of its practice. At the most energetic end of the scale is 'power yoga', of which the most common form is *Ashtanga*, in which participants are encouraged to keep moving throughout the class, using a selection of *vinayasas* sequences of movements that link the principal poses together without pause. This makes for a strenuous, fitness-orientated workout. At the milder end comes *Hatha* yoga, which concentrates on far gentler poses, with a significant proportion of the class dedicated to exercises in breathing and meditation.

There are a huge number of opportunities to practise yoga in India, from informal drop-in classes in local parks, sample classes at gyms and hotel spas to ashrams and retreats and even university-level courses. While some type of yoga will be accessible almost wherever you go in India, anyone looking for a specific type of course should plan in advance, as the best-known institutes tend to be oversubscribed.

Ashrams and spas

However, ashrams and retreats are not exclusively yoga-based, with many different experiences on offer – from super-luxurious spa-type places where pampering is the main aim, to a more general focus on well-being which may include some yoga but will also offer activities such as ayurvedic spa treatments, meditation, exercise and diet control. These are dotted all over the country, often run in conjunction with an established hotel or spa centre.

At the other end of the scale are bare-bones ashrams, which can be austere, with basic accommodation, a strictly no-frills vegetarian diet and a high level of reverence expected for the residing guru; some even forbid talking. But for an authentic, grassroots experience, they are hard to beat.

In North India, Rishikesh is the place to go, its location on the banks of India's most spiritual river, the Ganges, providing the perfect setting. Head south and you will be spoilt for choice, with well-established centres of learning in Pune, Mumbai, Mysore, Trivandrum and Chennai.

Padmanabhapuram (Tue–Sun 9am–1pm, 2–5pm). The splendid fort and palace set out around four courtyards were once the seat of the maharajas of Travancore, before the capital moved to Thiruvananthapuram, in modern-day Kerala, in 1790.

Inside, slatted screens and window panes of mica cast a magical light into the carved rooms cooled with natural air conditioning created by the use of inner courtyards. An imposing royal bed, formed from a single granite slab, is placed on a gleaming black floor made from egg whites and burnt coconut shell. Murals adorn many of the walls (though the best of them, in the raja's former meditation room, are closed to the public), and in several of the larger rooms collections of antique furniture and miniature paintings are displayed. The **palace museum** (Tue–Sun 9am–5pm) has a fine collection of murals, stone sculptures and beautiful woodcarvings.

The Southern Ghats

Forming a mighty barrier between the Tamil plains and the Malabar coast, the Southern Ghats are the last major manifestation of a 1,400km (870-mile) chain of mountains running along the flank of peninsular India. The range reaches its highest in the far south around the conjunction of the Karnataka, Tamil Nadu and Kerala borders, where it's known as the Nilgiris, or 'Blue Mountains'.

Peaks nudging 2,700 metres (8,850ft) soar above a vast tract of evergreen forest and inaccessible valleys, falling to a belt of tea gardens. Because they block the eastward march of the monsoon clouds billowing off the Arabian Sea between June and October, the Nilgiris soak up a huge amount of rain – around 2.5 metres (8ft) in less than six months. This ensures an exceptional biodiversity: one-third of all the Subcontinent's flowering plants are present in the forests here, along with elephant, bison (guar), panther, viable populations of tiger and dozens of other rare mammals, birds, reptiles and insects.

It was to hunt and collect these magnificent animals that the first British explorers ventured into the

TIP

There are four trains that make the journey down the Nilgiri Blue Mountain Railway to Conoor. Passengers wishing to travel on to Chennai should take the one that continues to Mettupalayam, a main-line station served by regular connections to the Tamil Nadu capital.

Decoration on Sri Ranganathaswamy Temple in Tiruchirapalli.

TODAS

The Todas are an isolated tribal people living on the Nilgiri plateau on the Kerala–Tamil Nadu border. Despite their relatively low number, which has been around 800 for the last century or so, their extreme isolation has made them the subject of much anthropological research. The central focus of their religion, and therefore much of their life, is the buffalo; they have traditionally made their living as dairy farmers. Their sociological framework was originally based on a model of fraternal polyandry, wherein the same woman would be married to all the brothers in a family, although the practice is now thought to have largely died out. Although they had started to abandon their traditional bamboo huts, called *munds*, in favour of concrete houses, recent years have seen a resurgence in *mund* building.

Fresh coconut water makes a refreshing drink in the heat of South India.

area in the early 19th century. Until then it had remained the exclusive territory of Adivasi (aboriginal) tribes such as the Todas, who inhabited the upper valleys, rarely descending to the plains. When John Sullivan, Collector of Coimbatore, and his detachment of Indian sepoys hacked their way to the head of the Hulikal Ravine in 1819, they discovered a huge, saucer-shaped depression ringed by high ridges and fed by rivers crashing through virgin forest. Sullivan was quick to see the potential of this lost Eden and, after purchasing land of the local Toda for Rs1 per acre, moved there with his family in 1822 to establish a tea estate.

Snooty Ooty and the Blue Mountain Railway

Within a couple of decades, Ootacamund had mushroomed into a prosperous settlement, to which increasing numbers of Brits started to flee to escape the heat and humidity of the plains. By the 1880s it had acquired all the trappings of a Home Counties

Granite rock formation near Madurai.

Victorian town, complete with Anglican church, botanical gardens, a racecourse and, most infamously, a Members' Club whose verandas and lawns became synonymous with the Raj at its snobbiest.

'Snooty Ooty', now known as **Udhagamandalam** ⓰ (its original Toda name), survived Independence and, thanks to its cool climate, continues to thrive as a hill resort, though little of the British era's stiff-upper-lipped gentility has endured in the centre of town. Plenty of evocative Raj-era bungalows, however, nestle on the outskirts, while the surrounding hills offer limitless scope for walkers, with treks leading into the high Nilgiris, where isolated Toda outposts lie scattered in the forest. The more traditional of these, comprising wagon-shaped huts of bamboo and thatch, attract a trickle of curious visitors, but the Todas remain for the most part suspicious of outsiders, most of their land having been taken from them by successive governments, and their numbers decimated by disease, poverty and alcoholism.

Perhaps the best way to spend your time in downtown Ooty is simply to wander around, taking in the semi-ordered, tourist-tinged chaos of it all. There are, however, several worthwhile sights; the **Botanical Gardens** (daily 7am–7pm) are exceptional, with a wide range of plants, and fossils, from both the local vicinity and elsewhere. The museum at the **Tribal Research Centre** (Mon–Fri 10am–5pm; free) gives a good insight into the lives and cultures of the local tribes, and the quirky **Thread Garden**, (www. threadgarden.com; daily 8.30am–7.30pm) featuring a collection of extremely realistic-looking plants made entirely from coloured thread, has to be seen to be believed.

A busy highway winds up to Ooty from the industrial city of Coimbatore on the plains, but the authentic way to travel there is on the **Blue Mountain Railway**. Built between 1890 and 1908, the narrow-gauge line today functions as one of the Subcontinent's last steam railways, retaining its original locomotives and rolling stock intact. The secret of its survival is the old 'Swiss Rack' system of cogs and bars by means of which it ascends 1:12 gradients, unmanageable for more modern machines. Passing through 16 tunnels in the course of its 46km (28-mile) journey from the railhead at Mettuppalaiyam, the rattling ride ascends for four and a half hours across misty tea gardens and *shola* forest.

Its principal stop en route is Conoor, a dishevelled plantation town whose scruffy bazaar of tin-and-stone houses clusters in a valley at the top of the Hulikal Ravine. There's nothing much to see or do here, beyond shop for top-grade Orange Pekoe tea and pungent essential oils in the market, but Conoor's high fringes hold several attractive heritage hotels and homestays in British-era buildings. One of the great pleasures of the Nilgiris is to sit in flower-filled gardens, sipping fine Orange Pekoe and gazing across the valley to the tea estates, while the engines of the Blue Mountain

Verdant landscape around Udhagamandalam (Ooty).

Railway chuff, wheeze and screech their way to and from Ooty.

Kodaikanal

Further south, the Palani Hills form a spur of the Southern Ghats projecting into the Vagai plain, some 120km (75 miles) northwest of Madurai. At an altitude of 2,000 metres (6,560ft), the massif's principal hill station is **Kodaikanal** ⑰ ('Princess of Hill Stations'), a less brash, greener version of Ooty, surrounded by beautiful forest. It was founded by American missionaries in the 1840s around an artificial, star-shaped lake, now known as **Kodai Lake**, and remains a popular destination particularly among Tamil honeymooners, who enjoy pedalo rides and strolls along the escarpment enfolding the southeastern edge of town. **Coaker's Walk** is the main path, and the views across the plains from the lip of the cliffs here are breathtaking, stretching most of the way to Madurai. The attractive **Bryant Gardens** (daily sunrise–sunset; free) are close to the start of Coaker's Walk, and also the place to start the 7km (4-mile) trek to **Pillar Rocks**, another stunning viewpoint.

Kodai is also renowned for its prestigious International School, whose students hang out in the cafés around the bazaar. One of India's premier educational establishments, offering International Baccalaureat diplomas to pupils drawn from more than 30 countries, KIS boasts a trademark hiking and outdoor programme that makes great use of the many trails winding through the wilder corners of the Palani Hills. In recent years these have started to attract the attention of trekkers: numerous guides nowadays work out of local beauty spots, offering routes ranging from half-day rambles around the town to more adventurous forays involving overnight says in Forest Rest Houses.

A lesser known but perhaps more relaxing hill station is **Yercaud**, just north of Salem which is 150km (93 miles) north of Kodaikanal. There's not an awful lot to do here, which is the whole point of coming – there are some good hotels and the surrounding hills are stunning.

High in the hills above Ooty.

Tamil Nadu's wildlife sanctuaries

As might be expected from a state bounded by mountains and the Coromandel coast, there are still a few pockets of natural jungle, coastal wetland and coral islands where wild animals and birds can thrive. On the coast, **Vedanthangla** and **Point Calimere**, 315km (196 miles) south of Chennai, play host to a large number of migratory birds during the winter monsoon. **Mudumalai**, in the Nilgiri foothills, 67km (42 miles) northwest of Ooty, is home to the gaur (Indian bison), wild elephants and a handful of tigers. The **Annamalai Sanctuary**, 70km (43 miles) northwest of Kodaikanal, harbours lion-tailed macaques. Access to these sanctuaries is easily granted upon arrival, though it is wise to book accommodation, elephant rides and jeeps in advance.

Lesser-known sanctuaries (which require special government permits) offer the naturalist an extraordinary chance to view rare species. **Mannar National Marine Park**, for example, is clustered around 21 low-lying, uninhabited coral islands in the Gulf of Mannar. The sanctuary is the home of the endangered sea cow, the dugong. Myriad other aquatic life forms are also supported by the park's coral reef, as well as more than 100 varieties of seaweed and grass, which change the depths of green in the seabed. Permission to land on the islands can be granted only by the Chief Conservator of Forests in Chennai, if you convince him that you have a genuine professional reason for visiting. Fears have recently been raised about the long-term survival of the islands, which seem to be slipping into the sea, possibly due to illegal sand extraction.

The **Mukurti National Park**, home of the Nilgiri tahr (an endangered species of mountain goat) and a few tigers, located high in the Nilgiris, also has restricted access. Permission may be obtained from the Nilgiri Wildlife Association in Ooty, but can take a few days. Clefts of tropical rainforest (*shola*) combine with grassland in a beautiful landscape. The altitude (1,800 metres/6,000ft) gives the park a temperate climate while supporting a variety of tropical wildlife.

Wild elephants at Mudumalai.

KERALA

Between the ancient creation myth of Kerala and the modern political fact is a land of lush, physical beauty that contains a rich storehouse of legend, history, culture and tradition.

W hen the victorious warrior-goddess Bhadrakali selected a place on Earth where she would reside she chose Kerala in the southwestern corner of India, and today the *thattakkam*, Kerala's local equivalent of a parish, is always under the divine jurisdiction of a goddess. Although legend declares that the land of Kerala was formed when Parsurama, an incarnation of Lord Vishnu, threw his mighty battle-axe into the Arabian Sea, the fertile land that emerged was not established as an Indian state until 1956, with the integration of three Malayalam-speaking areas, Malabar and the two former Princely States of Cochin and Travancore.

Kerala's attractions are focused mainly in the south, within easy distance of the capital, Thiruvananthapuram, where the beautiful white-sand beaches around the resort of Kovalam attract streams of sun worshippers throughout the winter months. Further north, the densely populated backwaters area forms a distinctive tropical environment, its tangled canals, rivulets and lakes screened from the main transport routes of the coastal strip by a wall of intense greenery. A fleet of converted rice boats cruise these idyllic waterways, allowing you to explore the region in great comfort

Vizhinjam.

and style from towns such as Kollam and Alappuzha.

The backwaters peter out as they approach Kerala's biggest city, Kochi (formerly Cochin), a sprawling metropolis divided between modern Ernakulam on the mainland, and the historic district of Fort Cochin across the water. Lined by some of India's oldest colonial buildings, the fort's narrow streets are packed with visitors from all over the world, just as they were 400 years ago, when they formed the hub of India's maritime spice trade.

Main Attractions

Padmanabhapuram
Kovalam
Varkala
Kuttanad (backwaters)
Periyar Wildlife Sanctuary
Eravikulam National Park
Munnar
Kochi-Ernakulam

Spices, tea and coffee

Spices such as cardamom and turmeric – along with tea and coffee – remain the economic mainstay of the interior, where thick forests and river valleys give way to grassy summits approaching 3,000 metres (9,800ft). Coffee plantations spread across the foothills of the Western Ghats, tea grows at higher altitudes and, in southern Kerala, there are acres of rubber trees.

On the coastal plains the landscape is dominated by tall, elegant coconut palms. No part of this tree is wasted, and the state has a flourishing coir (fibre) industry. The Malabar coast grows the world's best pepper, and half of Europe engaged in power struggles to command supplies of this small, pungent berry. Cardamom and cashew nuts are other important cash crops, and no compound is without a few banana trees. The fertile land also supports two or three annual harvests of rice.

Modern values

Nilgiri thar at Eravi-kulam National Park.

Kerala made its impact on modern India when, in the state's first elections in 1957, it formed the world's first democratically elected communist government – controversially dismissed by the Congress government in Delhi after intense lobbying by Indira Gandhi. The CPI (M), which soon regained power with a huge popular mandate, was led by the great E.M.S. Namboodiripad, who pushed through sweeping land reform, educational and health care programmes. As a result, Kerala has the most equitable land distribution in India, near-total literacy and low rates of poverty, which is remarkable considering it is the Indian state with the least natural resources.

This high level of literacy (which is also due to the enlightened educational policies of the hereditary rulers of Travancore), coupled with relatively few employment opportunities in Kerala itself, has led to Keralites finding work all over India and in the Gulf States. Gulf workers are an important source of income for the state, sending much of their money home to their families – as seen in the proliferation of 'Gulf houses', some of them extraordinary fantasies built of concrete in defiance of the climate and environment; towns such as Chavakad have become 'little Dubais'.

Women in Kerala have traditionally had a higher profile than elsewhere in India. The Nambudiri Brahmans and Nairs practised matrilineal inheritance, and women were in charge of running family property. Although this system has now largely broken down, high literacy levels have empowered Keralan women, and they tend to have more freedom than their counterparts in other states.

Multi-faith Kerala

Kerala not only has Hindus, Muslims, Christians and Jews, but many different castes and communities – all with their own customs and

traditions and styles of dress, food, jewellery and marriage. Perhaps these contrasting elements explain the genuine religious tolerance found in Kerala, a state remarkably free from the communal violence that haunts other parts of India.

Here a Marxist politician might prostrate before a Hindu shrine, a Muslim contribute to a temple festival or a Christian make a Hindu pilgrimage, and buses display the religious icons of three faiths. Saint George is particularly popular across all communities, as he is thought to offer protection against snake bites.

Performance arts

Kerala has extraordinarily rich theatre. There is the Sanskrit drama of *Kutiyattam*, the lyrical dance of *Mohiniattam*, the religious fervour of *Krishnattam* and, above all, the spectacular magnificence of *Kathakali*. All these dramas evolved out of the religious beliefs of their participants and, despite their highly dramatic presentation, are less a theatrical performance than an act of worship.

The spectacular *theyyams* of Malabar demonstrate this concept when the fantastically costumed god-actors dance before shrines, possessed with the spirit and power of their Dravidian deities.

Costume and make-up play an important part in these ritual dramas. It is worth arriving early at a *Kathakali* dance drama to watch the pre-show transformation of the actors as they apply bright make-up, and don masks and ornate skirted costumes weighing up to 35kg (77lbs).

Only during the monsoon months of June to August is it difficult to find some ritual, ceremony or festival taking place. Although non-Hindus are not usually permitted to enter Keralan temples, temple festivals are accessible and visible to all. In central Kerala the use of elephants brings a regal quality; there can be few sights to beat 50 or more caparisoned tuskers assembled before the Vadakkunathan Temple in Thrissur on the day of the Thrissur Pooram. Temple festivals are invariably

> **TIP**
>
> Recitals of Kathakali, specially tailored for the short attention spans of foreign audiences, are staged each evening at several locations around Fort Cochin. Two of the most popular are those laid on by the Cochin Cultural Centre (www.cochinculturalcentre. com) and Kathakali Centre (www.kathakalicentre.com).

KERALA TRANSPORT

Flights: Kerala has three civil airports (at Thiruvananthapuram, Kochi and Kozhikode). Although most flights passing through them are services to and from hubs in the Gulf States, domestic carriers maintain links with cities elsewhere in India. Book as far in advance as possible, especially if you intend to fly to Goa. Direct flights to the former Portuguese enclave do not run daily and are in particularly high demand, meaning travellers frequently have to make the long dog leg northeast to Hyderabad, or even all the way north to Mumbai, to catch a connecting flight.

Trains: Along Kerala's main railway line, which runs the length of the state via the coastal strip, trains are fast and frequent. Many continue north to the Konkan Railway and Mumbai. In addition, a couple of branch lines peel east across the Ghats into neighbouring Tamil Nadu, and a line also links Alappuzha and the backwaters. South of Kerala, the main line skirts the tip of the peninsula at Kanniyakumari before bending north into the Tamil plains and Chennai. Tickets should be be booked in either Thiruvananthapuram or Kochi, where dedicated tourist reservation facilities exist, allowing foreign travellers to access special ticket quotas.

Buses: Long-distance bus services tend to be much slower than the train, but seats are easier to come by at short notice than on popular rail services. As elsewhere in the country, buses are recommended for shorter journeys.

Trains

Kochi/Ernakulam to: Alappuzha (13–17 daily; 45mins–1hr 50mins); Bengaluru (3–7 daily; 10–14hrs); Chennai (9–12 daily; 11hrs 45mins–16hrs); Kanyakumari (2–3 daily; 7hrs 25mins–10hrs); Kozhikode (12–19 daily; 4hrs–5hrs 30mins); Mumbai (6–10 daily; 27–39hrs); Thiruvananthapuram (every 30mins; 3hrs 30mins–5hrs 30mins).

Kozhikode to: Kochi/Ernakulam(13–18 daily; 4hrs–5hrs 30mins); Mumbai (6–9 daily; 17–22hrs).

Thiruvananthapuram to: Alappuzha (10 daily; 2hrs 40min–3hrs 15mins); Bengaluru (2 daily; 16–18hrs); Chennai (4–5 daily; 16hrs 30mins–18hrs 45mins); Kanyakumari (3 daily; 2hrs 45mins–4hrs); Kochi/Ernakulam (every 30mins; 3hrs 30mins–5hrs 30mins); Kozhikode (11 daily; 7hrs–10hrs 30mins); Madurai (3 daily; 6hrs 40mins–9hrs); Mumbai (3–5 daily; 25–30hrs); Varkala (15–20 daily; 45–1hr 25mins).

TIP

Buses run to
Padmanambhapuram
Palace from
Thiruvananthapuram's
Thampanoor bus stop,
via Kovalam junction. All
services heading to
Nagercoil or Kanniyaku-
mari pass the site. Aim
to arrive as early in the
morning as possible,
before the heat builds.
Taxis also run the route,
for pre-fixed routes
displayed on boards at
taxi ranks.

accompanied by traditional music. Look out for the *panchavadyam* (literally 'five instruments') drum and trumpet ensembles that accompany processions, the loud but virtuosic *cenda melam* drum-orchestras and the drumming genre *tyampaka*.

Southern Kerala

Attractions are plentiful in the capital, **Thiruvananthapuram** ⑱ (Trivandrum), former seat of the maharajas of Travancore, and set around seven low, wooded hills. The temple of **Sri Padmanabhasvami** that the maharajas built to honour Lord Vishnu physically dominates the bustling Old City. Reflected images of its majestic gateway towers, designed not according to traditional Keralan principles but in typical Tamil-Chola style, shimmer in the waters of the adjacent bathing tank, where devout worshippers bathe before entering. Unfortunately, the complex is closed to non-Hindus – a rule enforced by bare-chested *ambalavasis* guards – which means few foreign visitors get to peek inside at the temple's main

deity, a massive image of a reclining Vishnu which worshippers peer at through openings in the floor of a special stone platform. Sri Padmanabhaswami made international headlines in 2011 when the state's high court ruled that its custodians should conduct an inventory of the valuables sealed inside the temple's treasury. A vast hoard of antique gold and precious stones was duly discovered, valued at a staggering $40–200 billion, making this the world's richest place of worship. A decision has yet to be made on what to do with the treasure – many in Kerala would like to see it displayed in a special museum – but its most likely resting place will be the secret vault under the deity where it was discovered.

The Travancore family's rather more dowdy royal heirlooms are displayed in their former residence, the **Puttan Malika Palace** (Tue–Sun 8.30am–12.30pm, 3.30–5.30pm), next to the temple. With its elegant gables, elaborately carved pillars and enclosed courtyards, the complex is a wonderful example of regal Keralan architecture. A fine collection of musical instruments and dance costumes bears witness to the fact the Travancores were passionate patrons of the region's arts, particularly music. A festival held annually in the grounds here celebrates the memory of one member of the dynasty, Raja Swathi Thirunal (1813–46), renowned as one of Kerala's greatest composers. Singers and instrumentalists from all over the country perform in the grounds, with Puttan Malika's illuminated walls as an atmospheric backdrop.

Fort, the old quarter around the temple and palace, remains a bastion of traditional arts. At the **Margi School** (www.margitheatre.org), in the west of the district, you can watch students learning Kathakali dance drama. Regular performances are also held here of the more archaic *kutiyattam*. Many of the rigorous physical

AYAPPAN

Between December and January each winter, the roads and holy places of Kerala are thronged by bus parties of bare-chested, barefooted men and boys, wrapped in distinctive black *lunghis*. Punching the air and shouting sacred chants as they walk around (in a manner not unlike football fans), these noisy groups are devotees of Lord Ayappan, a Hindu deity whose principal shrine is a remote forest temple at Sabarimala in the Western Ghat mountains, 200km (124 miles) inland. Also known as Shasta, the temple is only open for these two months each year and cannot be reached by motor vehicle. It has been estimated that around 1.5 million people make the journey to it on foot, walking 61km (38 miles) from the nearest village. This massive event, held to be the world's second-largest pilgrimage after the Muslim Haj, culminates on the night of Makara Sankranti, when a 'celestial pillar of light', or *makara jyoti*, mysteriously appears on a hilltop on the opposite side of the valley.

Men of any age may participate in the march, but females between the ages of nine and 50 aren't allowed. Before embarking on the trip, Ayappan devotees must make a 41-day penance, wearing the trademark black *lunghi* and necklace of *tulsi* seeds, and abstaining from sex, eating meat and cursing.

exercises you'll see the students being put through here originated in Kerala's own form of martial art, *kalarippayattu*. The CVN Kalari Sangam, southeast of the temple, ranks among the state's most highly reputed teaching institutes; visitors are welcome to attend early morning training sessions (daily from 7am; free) in the gym's traditional red-earth-floored sparring pit.

North of the city centre, in a park popular with picnickers and strollers, stands Thiruvananthapuram's **Napier Museum of Arts and Crafts** (Tue–Sun 10am–5pm), housed in an extraordinary Indo-Saracenic building designed by Robert Fellowes Chisholm for Lord Napier (a former governor) in 1880. Inside, its lavishly patterned walls, cases of jewellery, ivorywork, Chola bronzes and Keralan woodcarvings are somewhat upstaged by the showy Raj-era architecture. Also worth a visit, in the northern corner of the park, beyond the city zoo and botanical gardens, the **Shri Chitra Art Gallery** (Tue–Sun 10am–5pm) features paintings by Raja Ravi Varma

– a minor Keralan royal who became hugely popular in the late 19th century for his realist depictions of curvy, sari-clad women and mythological scenes – alongside some luminous Himalayan landscapes by Russian mystic Nicholas Roerich.

Before the Travancores shifted the capital to Thiruvananthapuram at the end of the 19th century, their principal palace lay 63km (39 miles) further south, across the modern Kerala-Tamil Nadu state border. Reachable in a half-day trip by bus or taxi, **Padmanabhapuram** is regarded as the finest surviving example of Keralan architecture (see page 387). Sixty-three kilometres (40 miles) to the northeast of Trivandrum city lies **Ponmudi**, the closest hill station to the Keralan capital. The drive to get there is stunningly scenic, winding its way past tea estates and waterfalls, and the town itself, although small, makes an excellent trekking base.

Kerala's best beaches

Among Kerala's excellent beaches, the best-known is **Kovalam** ⑲, located

Local village festivals in Kerala often involve the use of ornate and bizarre costumes and headdresses.

The Krishna Temple at Guruvayur.

Fishing nets at Cochin.

16km (10 miles) south of Thiruvananthapuram, where facilities at all levels are available. Except for the tourist trade near the beach itself, life in the surrounding countryside and the fishing settlements in the area goes on very much as in the rest of rural Kerala. Ayurvedic massage is relaxing after a swim in rough waters, and masseurs are ready on shore to oblige. Massage using herbal oils is said to be most effective at the moment the monsoon breaks in early June.

A ramshackle agglomeration of hastily erected hotels, the resort extends across the paddy fields and palm groves inland from a trio of separate coves, each with their own distinct character. Most foreign tourists, including an ever-increasing number of charter holidaymakers from Russia, congregate on Lighthouse beach, whose arc of golden sand is overlooked by the red-and-white-striped tower of the eponymous Kovalam lighthouse. At night, the revolving lamp casts its beam across a strip of brightly lit café-restaurants and the crashing surf to a horizon dotted with the lamps of tiny inshore fishing boats.

Get up early enough in the morning and walk around the low, rocky promontory dividing Lighthouse beach from its neighbour, Hawa beach, and you'll be treated to one of the quintessential spectacles of the Keralan coast: teams of local fishermen, dressed in cotton turbans and Madras-chequed *mundus (lunghis)*, hauling huge nets ashore with ropes.

Hawa beach comes to an abrupt end at a sheer-sided headland, crowned by the five-star Leela hotel, but the sands – empty save for a few fishing boats – continue on the opposite side, spreading north for as far as the eye can see.

Heading in the other direction, south from Kovalam, tourism development is more marked once you're past the port of **Vizhinjam**, a former regional capital divided between low-caste Hindu and Christian fishing communities. The shoreline beyond Vizhinjam breaks into a succession of small coves, backed by a large, gated hotel complexes specialising in

Ayurvedic therapies. Eventually, the cliffs yield to the shimmering expanse of Chowara beach, which stretches south for 17km (10.5 miles) to the mouth of the Neyyar River, where a large island in the backwaters shelters another cluster of luxury hotels.

Varkala ⓴, 54km (32 miles) north of Thiruvananthapuram, is an attractive village with a less commercialised, fine sandy beach at the base of dramatic red cliffs. Though tourists come for the beach, it is also one of Kerala's major Hindu pilgrim centres: guided by local priests, families immerse the ashes of recently deceased relatives in the waves, while ranks of foreign sun worshippers slurp tropical fruit cocktails, play volleyball and practise yoga poses nearby. High above them, a row of bamboo and palm-leaf cafés noses over the cliff edge, offering ideal spots to gaze at the sunsets over the Arabian Sea.

To escape Varkala's tourist scene you can amble 4km (2.5 miles) north along the laterite-paved coast path leading to neighbouring Odayam, where a handful of small guesthouses huddle in the coconut groves behind

a small, black-sand cove. Fishing is still an important part of the economy in these parts. The mostly Muslim fishing villages are conservative, and it is important not to cause offence by bearing too much flesh. Even in Varkala, topless sunbathing is definitely taboo.

Kuttanad: the backwaters

About 20km (12 miles) north of Varkala is **Kollam** ⓴ (Quilon), a cashew-nut port that once served as the hub of the Malabar Coast's spice trade, attracting Arab, Greek, Roman and Chinese ships. These days, however, most of the boats passing through here are en route to the **Kuttanad** backwater region to the north, for which Kollam serves as a gateway. Many visitors also stop over on their way to the famous ashram of Amma, 'the hugging saint', and Amritpuri, 33km (20 miles) north.

Among the few surviving relics of the town's former prominence is the British Residency, on the shores of Ashtamudi Lake, just north of the centre. A stately 250-year-old mansion, it was built in an idiosyncratic, Keralan-British fusion style typical of the

Map on page 374

TIP

Lifeguards patrol Lighthouse beach to ensure swimmers do not fall foul of the treacherous currents that rip through the bay at certain phases of the tide. Fatalities occur every season. Always stay within the limits of the safety flags and obey the whistles of the lifeguards.

Theyyam dance.

TIP

Kottayam is famous as the source of Kerala's most widely read daily, the *Malayalam Monorama*, published here since 1890 and boasting a state-wide readership of around 1.5 million. Non-Malayalam speakers can browse its English edition online at www.manoramaonline.com.

mid-18th century, when attitudes to local traditions were still more respectful rather than dismissive. Inside the building, which nowadays houses an atmospheric Government guesthouse, a vast teak table, giant Chinese pickle jars and walls hung with military lithographs gather dust.

The most popular cruise in the backwaters is the eight-hour trip between Kollam and **Alappuzha** ㉒ (Alleppey). Two companies run the route: the State Water Transport Department (SWTD) and the District Tourism Promotion Council (DTPC), both of which have offices at Kollam's main boat jetty (on the west side of town) where you can purchase tickets. The boats depart at 10.30am sharp, and stop for lunch at **Karunagapalli**, where shipbuilders construct *kettuvallam* rice barges out of jackwood planks sewn together with coir rope. Halfway through the journey, 10km (6 miles) east of Chengannur, is **Aranmula**, famed for both its **Parthasarathi Temple** and its unique metal mirrors. Equally unique is the boat 'race' held here every year on the last

day of Onam (Aug–Sept) as part of the Vallamkali festival. It commemorates the crossing of the river by Krishna, who is thought to be present in all the boats taking part, meaning they are all obliged to cross the finish line at the same time in deference to the god.

Alappuzha itself is a bustling, typically Keralan market town, set on a grid plan formed by intersecting canals. In colonial times, these formed an important link between the interior and the sea. Coir, cashews, spices, rubber, tea and coffee were transported via the backwaters to the *godown* warehouses lining the town's waterways and shipped to Europe from a long pier, whose rusting remnants still preside over Alappuzha's desultory beach. These days, hotels and cruises form the mainstay of the area's economy, with over 400 tourist barges plying the backwaters.

Vembanad and Kottayam

The northeastern fringes of Alappuzha are dominated by a vast inland lake, whose waters stretch for almost 100km (62 miles) to the edge of Kochi.

Kovalam is Kerala's main beach resort.

Encompassing more than 1,500 sq km (580 sq miles), Vembanad Lake is one of India's largest bodies of water and is also a busy transport artery, connecting the coastal strip and backwaters with the foothills. During the winter, literally hundreds of rice barges may be seen drifting across its glass-like surface, and local ferries chug between the towns and villages lining its shores.

Vembanad's eastern flank was chosen by the British missionary Henry Baker as the site of an experimental rubber and fruit farm in the 1820s. After Independence, this estate was ceded to the government and turned into the **Kumarakom Bird Sanctuary** (dawn–dusk), an important nesting site for winter migrants, while Baker's residence was converted into the first of the many luxury hotels that now encrust the shoreline. Arundhati Roy's Booker Prize-winning novel *The God of Small Things* was set in this area; and both Baker and his former home feature in the book.

One of the reasons for Kumarakom's success as a tourist destination is its proximity to **Kottayam ㉓**, 10km (6 miles) further inland. Rubber plantations in the surrounding countryside form the bedrock of the town's legendary prosperity, which has fuelled exceptionally high rates of literacy – high-earning expats now account for as much income hereabouts as rubber. The majority of local estates, and the booming Kottayam publishing industry, are dominated by Syrian Christians, for whom this is an important centre. A pair of ancient churches, 5km (3 miles) northwest at Valliapalli and Cheriapalli, testify to their long presence in the area.

Thirty kilometres (18 miles) east of Kottayam is **Palai**, commonly known as the Vatican of India. It holds a world record for being the Christian parish with the largest number of priests in the world: 151 and counting! There are naturally a large number of churches in the area, including Alphonsa Church, a popular pilgrimage destination which houses the mortal remains of St Alphonsa of India, the first person of Indian

FACT

Arundhati Roy, author of the Booker Prize-winning novel *The God of Small Things*, was born and raised in Kerala. Many of the characters and places that appear in the book were derived from real-life people and locations in the backwaters near Kottayam, including the infamous 'History House', the residence of a former rubber planter and now a luxury hotel.

Vizhinjam.

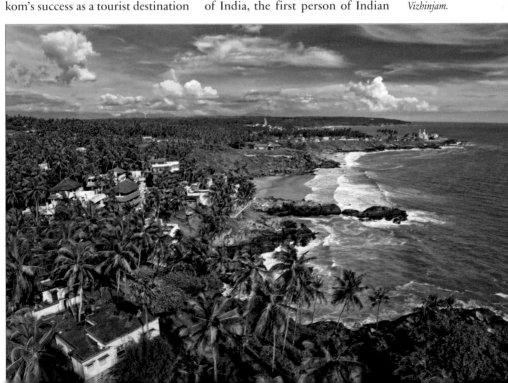

FACT

India is the world's third-largest producer of pepper, and most of the 70,000 tonnes it ships annually are either grown or sold in Kerala. Mantancherry, Kochi, used to be the site of the Inter-national Pepper Exchange, whose functions were recently superseded by the online India Pepper and spice Trade Assocation (IPSTA).

origin to be canonised as a saint by the Catholic Church.

The Ghats

Inland from Kottayam, the flat country of the backwaters is soon interrupted by tracts of low, wooded hills and rubber plantations, which gradually steepen as they approach the shirt-tails of the Western Ghats – the highest mountain range in South India. Because it blocks the eastward advance of the monsoon weather systems, this chain of peaks, culminating at an altitude of 2,695 metres (8,840ft), soak up astonishing levels of rainfall between June and November; most regions receive 3–4 metres (10–13ft) over these six months, and some get as much as 9 metres (30ft). The result is one of the planet's richest eco-systems: 4,000 species of plants thrive on the Ghats' western flanks, where stands of giant teak trees give way to montane rainforest and deciduous woodland, before finally yielding to open grassland. In high valleys, the British took advantage of the moist weather and cooler temperatures to

plant vast coffee and tea estates, and these – together with cardamom and spice plantations – still dominate the landscape of many districts.

For visitors, however, the main incentive to travel into the Keralan mountains is the chance to spot wildlife in one of several reserves established in the region. By far the best-known of these is **Periyar Wildlife Sanctuary**, near the market town of Kumily, close to the Tamil Nadu border, where the former hunting reserve of a maharaja is now protected as an official sanctuary. The park, among the most visited in India, centres on a convoluted reservoir where, from the comfort of a boat deck or bamboo raft, you can sight grazing herds of wild elephant, and even, on rare occasions, one of the handful of tigers that survive in the surrounding forests. In an attempt to protect its fragile populations of fauna from poachers, the Periyar Tiger Reserve has implemented a radical scheme whereby local forest-dwelling minority people are employed as guides, wardens and hotel staff in the park

Toddy tapper at Alappuzha.

– the idea being that if local villagers gain direct financial benefit from the sanctuary, they are less likely to indulge in illegal hunting. So far, the initiative seem to have been extremely successful, with animal numbers on the increase and local poverty on the wane. For details of the reserve's tips, go to www.periyartigerreserve.org.

Another sanctuary worth making a detour to visit is **Eravikulam National Park** (www.eravikulam.org; Apr–Jan daily 8am–4.30pm), a four-hour drive north of Periyar, not far from the tea station of Munnar. High up near the watershed of the Ghats, the reserve is the last bastion of the Nilgiri tahr, a rare species of mountain goat that survives on the grasslands of the range's uppermost ridges and peaks. The tahr was almost wiped out by hunters during the colonial era, but revived after American biologist Clifford Rice attracted herds to his camp using salt licks; dozens of semi-tame tahr hang around outside the park gates at Vaguvarai.

As the site of the Western Ghats' most beautiful tea gardens, **Munnar**

㉔ fully deserves a couple of days out of anyone's itinerary. The stiff-upper-lipped gentility of the Raj still very much holds sway at the famous High Range Club, on the south side of town, where you can sip gin and tonics in a bar lined with hunting trophies and the dusty pith-helmets of long-deceased British tea-planters.

Kochi-Ernakulam

One of the most atmospheric old cities in the south, **Kochi-Ernakulam** **㉕** (Cochin) is well worth a day or more's exploration. It can be reached from Alappuzha by water, but boat traffic on the way to this major port and naval base is heavy, and many prefer to travel by road or rail. Ferries connect the islands of **Willingdon**, **Bolgatty**, **Gundu** and **Vypeen** to the southern peninsula of Fort Cochin and Matancherry and to the commercial centre, **Ernakulam**, on the mainland. Semitic traders from Yemen and Babylon used to import dates and olive oil in exchange for peacocks and spices, and Kochi is still an important spice port – its *godowns* (warehouses),

Colourfully decorated trucks are a common sight on India's highways.

Fertile land in the Western Ghats.

Heavy load.

Hill people.

smelling of pungent spices, are a hive of activity.

Most of the interest is concentrated in the Fort area. **Matancherry Palace** (Sat–Thur 10am–5pm; charge), on the eastern side of the peninsula, was built in 1557 by the Portuguese in exchange for trading rights, and then repaired by the Dutch (renaming it the Dutch Palace) in 1663, although its architectural style is Keralan. Its frescoes, dating from the 17th century, depict Indian epics in extraordinary vegetable colours. The Royal Bedroom is particularly splendid, featuring a series of 45 murals relating the tale of the *Ramayana*. In the heart of the Fort area is the oldest European church in India, **St Francis's**, dating all the way back to 1506. Vasco de Gama died here, and was originally buried in the cemetery before his remains were removed to Portugal 14 years later.

Jew Town, a settlement that dates back a millennium, still thrives with antiques and spice shops. Lying to the south of Matancherry Palace, the small Pardesi synagogue here is used by the diminishing Jewish community; most families have left for Israel. The synagogue is floored with blue-and-white tiles from Canton, no two of which are the same.

There is little trace of the Arabs, Phoenicians, Romans and Greeks who traded at the port. Old colonial churches and warehouses recall the Portuguese, Dutch and British settlers with faded elegance, while the Chinese fishing nets that line Fort Kochi's northern shore hark back to the era when the harbour was jammed with massive junks from Canton. The nets are operated by a cantilevered system of counterweights and they have become a visitor attraction in their own right.

The **Chottanikkara Temple** 30km (18 miles) west of Kochi attracts a growing number of pilgrims who seek release from evil spirits, and the long iron nails driven into the huge tree near the sanctum of the goddess testify to their successful exorcism.

Northern Kerala

Leaving Kochi by crossing to Vypeen island and heading north, you pass a pair of Portuguese forts before rejoining the mainland. Just beyond Azhikod is **Kodungallur**. Steeped in history, this settlement is thought to have been the ancient port of Muziris, visited by the Romans. The followers of the Prophet Mohammed also came early to Kerala, and although the **mosque** at Kodungallur is a brash, modern concrete structure, its interior is still the cool and serene original of India's oldest mosque.

Travelling further north up the coast from Kochi takes you past the turn-off to the **Palakkad Gap** (Palghat), the lowest point in the Western Ghats, at **Thrissur** ㉖. This is the site of one of Kerala's most important temples, **Vadakkunnatham**, which legend says was founded by Parasurama. Each year in May, the broad avenues outside it host the annual Pooram festival, the largest and most exuberant temple festival in the state, featuring dozens of lavishly

caparisoned elephants and ear-splitting drum orchestras. Thrissur's small **Archaeological Museum** on Town Hall Road (Tue–Sun 10am–5pm) has interesting examples of temple art. The Krishna Temple at **Guruvayur**, 30km (18 miles) from Thrissur, is the most sacred place in Kerala. The temple painters from this town are particularly skilled. Like most Keralan temples, access is for Hindus only.

Kozhikode ㉗ (Calicut), capital of northern Kerala, was known to the Phoenicians and ancient Greeks, who both traded spices here. These days, the town's economy rests not on exports, but on the remittance cheques of its many emigrants resident in the Gulf States. The **Pazhassi Raja Museum** (Tue–Sun 9am–1pm, 2–4.30pm) and **Krishna Menon Art Gallery and Museum** both have interesting displays. Krishna Menon was a prominent Keralan politician after Independence.

Close by, at **Kappad**, 16km (10 miles) from Kozhikode, is the place where Vasco da Gama first landed in India in 1498. Further north, past the French enclave of **Mahé**, is the attractive coastal town of **Kannur** (Cannanore). The town is home to the Mopplah community, originally of Arab descent; the picturesque streets of **Mopplah Town**, just south of **Fort St Angelo**, are well worth exploring, as is nearby **Payyambalam beach**. The town's other claim to fame is its weavers, of whom many work at the **Kanhirode Weavers' Cooperative Society** (www.weaveco.com), which welcomes visitors. Further north again is the atmospheric **Bekal Fort** ㉘, overlooking a beautiful beach. Although often referred to as Tipu Sultan's Fort, it was originally built by the Kadamba Kings before coming under Tipu Sultan's control, and then finally passed into the hands of the East India Company.

Roughly 60km (37 miles) inland from Kannur is the **Waynad** district, an area of rainforest interspersed with tea and coffee plantations, many of which now operate as guesthouses and offer a supremely tranquil experience. The journey there from the coast, and continuing on to Mysore, is one of India's most scenic.

EAT

The food stalls lined up next to Fort Cochin's Chinese fishing nets are a great source of delicious local seafood. You can pick the fish you want straight from the nets, and watch it grilled or pan-fried in front of you. The quayside is busiest just after sunset.

Munnar street life.

CRUISING KERALA'S GREEN BACKWATERS

In these southern lagoons women catch mudfish with their bare toes and Chinese fishing nets leave phosphorescent streaks across night waters.

'It was warm, the water. Greygreen. Like rippled silk./ With fish in it./With the sky and trees in it./And at night, the broken yellow moon in it.' In these lines from her novel *The God of Small Things*, Keralite author Arundhati Roy evokes a sense of place and the reflective pace of life beyond the mainstream.

The backwaters of Kerala are a tangle of brackish channels fed by rivers just inland from the Arabian Sea. They extend from Kochi south to Alappuzha, where peppercorns are still traded silently, using hand signals shared by the buyer and seller.

Progress here can be slow as the shallow waterways are often choked with water lilies and duckweed. A recent menace has been the proliferation of the water hyacinth, which has bred so successfully it now makes passage through some of the canals impossible and starves the life underneath of light. Sadly, this is only one indicator of the ecological threat this lovely landscape faces. Many of the lakes are now polluted and have been reduced through land-reclamation.

Life on the waterfront

The backwaters are neither an untamed wilderness like Florida's Everglades, nor are they a waterfront cityscape like Venice. They are a bustling tropical townscape, interlaced by slender canals. Housewives trim the hibiscus, schoolgirls with ribboned plaits walk up the nearest gangplank, and livestock travels downstream. Local industries such as rope-making can be viewed unobtrusively from on deck.

With trademark woven mats protecting their cargo, backwater boats cater to everyone from commuting locals to pleasure cruising, multi-day trippers.

Nearly one third of Keralans are Christian, and stunningly preserved churches dot the dark green landscape. Their architecture is a reminder of the Portuguese presence along the Malabar coast.

Travelling the backwaters of Kerala on a converted rice barge allows visitors an authentic view of life at water level.

Nature's energy drink, coconuts and their water are a mainstay of Keralan cuisine and one of the best ways to beat the heat.

COCONUT PALMS

The rural and urban landscape of the Malabar coast is dominated by the coconut palm. The trees that sway over these backwaters are put to use in a dozen ways – virtually nothing is wasted.

Each tree produces around 80 nuts a year. Copra is the dried coconut flesh from which workers extract cooking oil and soap. Coir is the fibrous outer husk, which is stripped and kept for months in unsightly heaps, soaking in the shallows. It is then dried stiff and beaten. The short fibres are twisted into rope or woven into mats for the table or floor. Family coir workshops abound in the backwaters.

Coconut palm fronds are prized for thatching roofs against the rain, or are fashioned into sun hats or baskets. The liquid is drunk fresh or fermented into a potent liquor. Coconut milk, prepared with the white flesh, is often used for cooking, and the grated flesh is a staple for sweets. Tree trunks are sawn into boards for boatbuilding or house construction. If they are not burnt as fuel, the hard shells are polished and made into salad bowls or carved hair ornaments.

Found nowhere else in India, these cantilevered fishing nets were introduced to the region by Chinese seamen in the 16th century.

Boat racing is a serious business in Kerala. The biggest snakeboats require 100 oarsmen to row to a chanted beat.

Children on coracles on the backwaters.

OFFSHORE ISLANDS

India's offshore archipelagos, the Lakshadweep
group in the Arabian Sea and the Andaman and
Nicobar Islands in the Bay of Bengal, are fringed
with coral reefs and mangrove swamps, and are
home to unique groups of indigenous peoples.

The myriad small islands which make up the Lakshadweep and Andaman archipelagos are remote, entrancingly beautiful and way off the beaten tourist trail. Anyone seeking the quintessential white-sand, palm-fringed, turquoise-watered tropical beach experience – without the tourist crowds – will not be disappointed. Some parts of all the Andaman and Nicobar Islands are off limits to tourists to protect indigenous tribes, but the rest of the islands are available to tourists if they obtain a Restricted Area Permit.

Lakshadweep

Scattered some 200–400km (124–248 miles) west of the Keralan coast are the Lakshadweep Islands. Some speculate that the name derives from the estimates of early sailors, who imagined at least 100,000 (one *lakh*) of these coral islands and atolls. In fact, there are only 22 (depending on how they are counted), of which just 11 are inhabited by some 65,000 people. The group is a continuation of the Maldives, and the small islands are similarly characterised by beautiful white-sand beaches fringed with palm trees and translucent lagoons; the islanders of Minicoy, further to the south than the main group, have a great deal in common culturally with the Maldives.

From the 13th century, the islands were ruled by the rajas of the Keralan kingdom of Kannur, and a large proportion of the population are descendants of the settlers who came here from that part of Kerala. To the Portuguese and other European mariners, these were the Laccadive Islands. They were under British control from 1877 until Independence.

The climate is tropical throughout the year, with daytime maximum temperatures ranging from 32° to

Main Attractions
Kavaratti
Kalpeni
Agatti
Bangaram
Kadmat
Port Blair

*An Indian bull elephant cooling off,
Havelock Island.*

TIP

A permit is required by all foreign travellers to the Andaman and Nicobar Islands. These are issued on arrival and are valid for 30 days (extendable to 45 days), allowing travel and overnight stays to a strictly designated list of destinations in the archipelago. Permits and passports are checked on disembarkation at all islands.

35°C (90° to 95°F). The southwest monsoon arrives in May and it rains, on and off, until the end of September. During this period, the islands are harder to reach, and transit between islands may have to be by helicopter as the sea can become extremely rough.

Being largely of Keralan descent, the islanders were originally Hindu, as the prevalent systems of caste and of matrilineal inheritance bear out. However, most converted to Sunni Islam, which had been established on the islands from as early as the 7th century. Today the vast majority of islanders are Muslims. The people speak a dialect of Malayalam, the only exception being Minicoy island, where Mahl (the language of the Maldives) is spoken. Coconut farming and fishing are the main occupations, along with some dairy and poultry farming.

These are some of the few unspoilt coral islands left in the Indian Ocean, and they have an exceptionally sensitive environment. Tourism by non-Indian nationals is officially restricted to the islands of Bangaram and Kadmat. It may, at times, also be possible to stay at the tourist resort close to the airport on Agatti. Transfer from Agatti to Bangaram and Kadmat is by boat.

Around the islands

The capital of the island chain is **Kavaratti ❶**, headquarters of the administration of Lakshadweep and home to around 11,000 people. The Ujra Mosque here has an ornately carved ceiling, said to be made of driftwood. **Kalpeni**, to the southeast, has a spectacular lagoon containing three uninhabited islands, Tilakkam, Pitti and Cheriyam; Kalpeni has been developed for internal tourism and has watersports facilities and tourist huts. Evidence can still be seen of a huge storm that devastated the island in 1847. The southernmost island is **Minicoy**. The predominant industry here is tuna fishing and canning. There is also a 50-metre (165ft) lighthouse built by the British in the 19th century.

The three islands likely to be of most interest to foreign tourists are Agatti and its minuscule neighbour

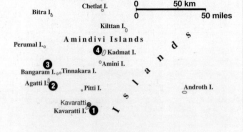

Lakshadweep

Bitra I.
Chetlat I.
Kilttan I.
Amindivi Islands
Perumal I.
❹ Kadmat I.
Amini I.
❸
Bangaram I. Tinnakara I.
Agatti I. ❷
Pitti I.
Androth I.
Kavaratti
Kavaratti I. ❶

Suneli I.
Cannanore Is
Cheriyam I.
Kalpeni I.

Nine Degree Channel

Minicoy I.
Eight Degree Channel

0   50 km
0   50 miles

GET TO LAKSHADWEEP

As access to the Lakshadweep islands is controlled and limited by the Indian government, foreign tourists must book through one of two tour operators. The only airport is at Agatti, from where onward travel is by helicopter or boat.

For Bangaram Island Resort, contact CGH Earth (previously the Casino Group), tel: 00 91-0484 301 1711, www.cghearth.com; for Kadmat, contact Lacadives, tel: 00 91-022 666 27 381, www.lacadives.com. Both operators offer PADI-registered diving packages for experts as well as those for beginners.

Indian Airlines operate six flights weekly between Agatti and Kochi. The other option is to take a ship from Kochi (see www.lakshadweep.nic.in for details of tours and latest schedules), stopping off at several islands en route. Journey time is between 14 and 20 hours.

Bangaram, northwest of Kavaratti, and Kadmat further to the northeast.

Agatti ❷, on the edge of a stunning lagoon, is the location of the only airport in the island chain. A 20-seater Indian Airlines plane connects with Kochi. Visitors who are heading to Bangaram either take a helicopter or embark on a two-hour boat ride. **Bangaram ❸** is uninhabited apart from its resort complex, and is also situated on a beautiful clear lagoon. **Kadmat ❹**, usually reached by helicopter, has small-scale tourist development and a breathtaking beach with superb diving.

The marine life on the reefs and within the lagoons is impressive. As well as a huge variety of corals, there are over 1,000 species of fish, including butterflyfish, clownfish, wrasses, parrotfish, goatfish and lionfish. Among the more spectacular sights are the turtles, harmless sharks and manta rays, and visitors may also encounter dolphins in the lagoons.

Glass-bottomed boats, snorkels or scuba gear are available for close-up encounters, and the resorts offer scuba and snorkel training. If you are planning on diving you will need a certificate of health from your doctor.

The Andaman and Nicobar Islands

The Andaman and Nicobar islands lie 1,220km (760 miles) southeast of Kolkata across the Bay of Bengal, or 'Kala Pani' (Black Water), as this cyclone-prone sea was traditionally known. Their existence was reported in the 9th century AD by Arab merchants sailing towards the Straits of Sumatra, but with dense forests, mangrove swamps and shark-infested seas, the 572 islands were considered fit only for political prisoners and Malay pirates. Their development as a tourist destination, attracting scuba-divers, birdwatchers and honeymooners, has happened only in the past three decades. Most of the islands, however, are Adivasi (tribal) reserves and only a limited number are open to visitors – and the Nicobar group remains off-limits. The best time to visit is from December to April.

The aboriginal inhabitants of the Andamans, comprising several

The vast majority of islanders are Muslim.

GET TO THE ANDAMANS

Flights: Port Blairis connected to Chennai and Kolkata by direct daily flights on Indian Airlines and Jet Flying time is 2hrs.

By sea: It takes between three and five days to travel from Kolkata (departures once per fortnight) and Vishakapatnam (monthly); conditions on board the poorly maintained government vessels are often extremely uncomfortable, the food poor and sanitation less than ideal. Within the islands, government ferries run from Port Blair to Havelock Island (2–3 daily; 2hrs–2hrs 45min); Little Andaman (5 weekly; 8–12hrs); Long Island (4 weekly; 7hrs); Neil Island (1–2 daily; 3hrs); Rangat Bay (1 daily; 8hrs). There is also a private catamaran service between Port Blair and Havelock which leaves at 8.30am and returns at 4pm; see www.makruzz.com for details.

Nicobar pigeons are easily identified by their beautifully coloured, iridescent plumage. They are resident in parts of Indonesia and, as the name suggests, the Nicobar islands.

Traffic moves along a street in Port Blair.

independent tribes known collectively as the Andamese, are among the most isolated peoples on earth. The exact date of their arrival on the islands is not known, but is thought to have been at least 60,000 years ago, and in all likelihood formed part of the large-scale migration of humans from Africa to Asia, which began some 100,000 years ago. From that time until the arrival of the British in 1789, they lived in complete isolation, with no contact with the outside world or even each other – they lived so separately that they don't understand each other's languages.

The largest group on Little Andaman are the Onges. They are hunter-gatherers, who collect honey and spear fish, and ritually paint their bodies with clay. The Sentinelese are an elusive group of 200 people, who have been known to fight off intruders with poisoned arrows. They adorn themselves with body paint, beads and bone. The Jarawa, with a population of 240, have a large reserve on South Andaman.

The first Westerners to set foot on the islands were the Danes, who established a settlement in the Nicobars, but left in 1768 due to poor health conditions. The British Indian government annexed both groups of islands in 1872 and built a prison at Port Blair for prisoners serving life terms. The jail was used mainly for political prisoners engaged in the Independence struggle, and it was in Port Blair, while under Japanese occupation during World War II, that the Indian flag was first raised.

The arrival of the British saw many of the indigenous people perish through disease, alcoholism and, according to some sources, deliberate attempts to wipe them out. There were approximately 5,000 Andamese when the British arrived, but this number had fallen to just 600 by 1901. Throughout the 20th century, the tribes were known for their fierce attempts to maintain independence; a European anthropological party that attempted to land on one of the islands in the 1970s was repelled by a flurry of arrows. They left gifts of modern appliances, including metal buckets and spades, only to find that

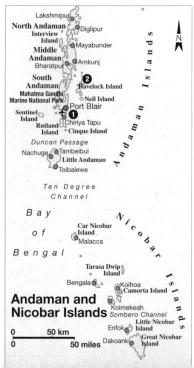

Andaman and Nicobar Islands

0   50 km
0   50 miles

upon their return some time later they were subjected to the same aerial bombardment; only this time the arrows had metal tips.

The Jarawa tribe, who live closest to Port Blair, began to initiate contact with the settled population in 1997, and have slowly increased their interaction with the capital – some Jarawan children are now attending schools outside their reserve. The building of the Great Andaman Trunk Road in the 1970s, which runs straight through the Jarawa reserve, has had a huge impact on the lives of this tribe, including several outbreaks of common diseases such as measles. In reaction to this, a law was passed to try to protect the Jarawa from such contact, and from the widespread encroachment on their land. All visits to Jarawa territory are forbidden by government law, a law unfortunately flouted by government travel agencies, which take Indian tourists to visit the Jarawa on a daily basis.

On 26 December 2004 the islands were hit by the enormous tsunami that also devastated parts of Southeast Asia. The damage was overwhelming, particularly in the Nicobars and on Little Andaman. More than 3,000 are officially listed as having been killed, and thousands more displaced, but the main areas visited by tourists, including Port Blair and Havelock, although affected by the earthquake, were protected from the tsunami itself.

Port Blair and South Andaman

Port Blair ❶, on the island of South Andaman, is the capital and only sizeable town (population 108,000) in the archipelago. It was named after Lt Reginald Blair, who conducted a survey of the area in 1789. The British, however, only gained control over the Andamans after 1857, and used this outpost of empire as a penal colony right through to 1947.

The **Cellular Jail**, where 400 freedom fighters were held during the struggle for Independence, is now a museum (Tue–Sun 9am–noon, 2–5pm). There is also an **Anthropological Museum** (Tue–Sun 10am–12.30pm, 2–4pm), which has mini-reproductions of villages of local peoples. Across the harbour is **Viper Island**, where executions

TIP

If you are staying on the east coast of Havelock Island, away from the main market, finding a rickshaw to take you anywhere can be tricky – consider hiring a scooter; rates are reasonable, there is very little traffic and the roads are generally well surfaced.

Fishermen inspect their catch on the Andaman Islands.

TIP

It's worth remembering that although the Andamans are 1,000km (620 miles) east of the Indian mainland, they are still within the same time zone as the rest of the country. This means that sunrise and sunset are disconcertingly early – at around 5.30am and 5.30pm respectively, which makes for an early start to the day if you want to enjoy the fleeting cool hours of morning, and correspondingly long evenings.

Mangrove trees grow on a beach on North Passage Island, Andaman Islands.

used to take place, and **Ross Island**, guarded by World War II Japanese bunkers, and now a peaceful spot grazed by numerous chital deer.

Around one hour south from Port Blair (there are four daily buses), **Chiriya Tapu** has a beautiful beach and some good snorkelling. For truly spectacular snorkelling and scuba-diving, the village of Wandoor is the gateway to the **Mahatma Gandhi Marine National Park**: it is likely you will have to sign up for a tour in Port Blair. If you want to experience the pristine tropical forest, **Mount Harriet** has some superb walking trails: take the ferry from Port Blair to Hope Town, from where the starting point is a short bus ride. Alternatively, it is easy to hire a scooter, but extreme caution is advised on the unpredictable roads.

Elsewhere in the Andamans

Havelock Island ❷, around 2.5 hours by boat to the northeast of Port Blair, has an abundance of fabulous beaches, and is the main focus of tourism in the archipelago. Unsurprisingly given its location much closer to Thailand

than India, Havelock is reminiscent of many of the Thai islands, not just in its physical beauty but also in the way that tourism seems poised to take off – think Koh Samui in the mid-1990s. There is still a very relaxed feel to the place, with the majority of the island still uncultivated jungle – the drive from the west to east coasts is spectacular. The choice and range of accommodation is expanding every year, and the diving is superb, with costs amongst the lowest anywhere in the world, encompassing anything from one-off dives to officially recognised courses, right up to instructor level.

The stunning sea life is not solely the preserve of the certified diver – snorkelling excursions are plentiful, and there's even a glass-bottomed boat at **Elephant Beach**, one of the most popular snorkelling sites. Access is either via a 3km (2-mile) trek through the jungle or by boat – there are generally wooden longtail motorboats, known as *dunghis*, on most of the more popular beaches, with the owners open to offers for excursions around the island. Be warned, however, that

these are noisy contraptions, and have very little stability at low speeds!

Although most of the accommodation is strung out along the east coast, between beaches No. 2 and No. 5, the shoreline here is not as enticing as on the west coast – the beaches are narrow, and the water shallow and rocky underfoot.

Make the trip to the west coast, though, and the stunning **Radhanagar beach** (or Beach No. 7) awaits you. Wide and long, with squeaky clean sand and pristine, aquamarine waters, this is a beach that bares comparison with the best in the world. The only downside to this paradise is the sandflies, but a liberal application of baby oil seems to stop the little critters grabbing hold and biting. If you are there at sunset, you might even see an elephant belonging to the nearby Barefoot Resort strolling on the beach returning from the jungle where it spends its day feeding.

Another great place to spot elephants is the **Elephant Training Camp**, on the east coast just south of Kalapathar village. Follow the sandy trail through the forest to reach the enclosure – again these elephants tend to be feeding in the forest by day, so early morning or late evening are the best times to visit. There are an increasing number of options for excursions from Havelock, some of which include overnight camping on other islands. Check out www.barefoot-andaman.com for more details.

Just to the south, **Neil Island** is quieter, but just as beautiful, with an increasing number of backpacker-type hotels, as well as snorkelling and diving sites every bit as good as on Havelock.

The large islands of **Middle Andaman** and **North Andaman** are further off the beaten track, covered in thick forests. Some tribal areas are off-limits. The island of **Little Andaman**, devastated by the 2004 tsunami, has rebuilt its small-scale settlements and has started to make a few tentative steps into the world of tourism, with package tours from Port Blair including elephant safaris to remote waterfall sites in the interior organized by the snappily titled Andaman and Nicobar Islands Forest Plantation Development Corporation Limited (ANIFPDCL).

Havelock Island.

Fish off the coast of Havelock Island.

Temples and palaces line the banks
of the Ganges at Varanasi.

Transport

Getting There 418
  By Air 418
  Overland 418
Getting Around 418
  Air Travel within India 418
  Boats 419
  Buses 419
  Cars and Taxis 420
  Driving in India 420
  Railways 420
  Rickshaws and Tongas 423

A – Z

Accommodation 424
Admission Charges 424
Begging 425
Budgeting for Your Trip 425
Children 425
Climate 425
Crime and Safety 425
Customs 426
Disabled Travellers 426
Electricity 426
Embassies and Consulates ... 426
Etiquette 427
Gay and Lesbian Travellers 427
Health and Medical Care 428
Insurance 430
Internet 430
Maps 430
Media 430
Money Matters 430
Nightlife 431
Opening Hours 431
Outdoor Activities 431
Photography 431
Postal/Courier Services 431
Public Holidays 432
Restricted/Protected
  Areas 432
Shopping 432
Telephones 432

Time Zone 433
Tipping 433
Toilets 433
Tourist Information 433
Visas and Passports 434
Water 434
What to Bring 434
Women Travellers 434

Language

Traveller's Hindi 435
  Basics 435
  Pronouns 435
  Verbs 435
  Prepositions, adverbs
    and adjectives 435
  Questions 436
  Days of the week 436
  Months 436
  Relatives 436
  Health 436
  Travel 436
  Food 436
Traveller's Tamil 437
  Basics 437
  Verbs 437
  Prepositions, adverbs
    and adjectives 437
  Days of the week 437
  Questions and 'and' 437
  Pronouns and relatives 437
  Health 437
  Food (Sappadu) 437
Glossary of Commonly
  Used Terms 438

Further Reading

History 439
Society, Culture and Religion . 439
Fiction 440
Travel 440
Food, Language and Images .. 441
Wildlife 441

TRANSPORT

GETTING THERE AND GETTING AROUND

GETTING THERE

By Air

The vast majority of visitors arrive in India by air. Mumbai and Delhi airports are the major entry points, although a few international flights from Europe use Kolkata (Calcutta), Chennai (Madras) and Bengaluru (Bangalore). There are direct, non-stop flights between India and the UK (where many transatlantic passengers can change) on Air India (www.airindia.com), British Airways (www.ba.com), Virgin Atlantic (www.virgin-atlantic.com) and Jet Airways (www.jetairways.com), and one-stop flights on a number of other carriers, including Emirates, Qatar, Gulf, Etihad and KLM. There are also charter flights in season from UK airports to Goa. These flights are laid on for package tourists, but spare tickets are sometimes sold off to independent travellers, often at bargain prices.

India also has extensive air connections with other countries in Asia and the Gulf, with international flights from Sri Lanka, Nepal, Pakistan, the UAE and many other places. There are also direct non-stop flights from New York to Delhi and Mumbai on Air India (and also to Delhi on United Airlines), and from Sydney to Mumbai on Qantas.

The major airports all have left-luggage facilities, porters and licensed taxis, as well as duty-free shops in both the arrival and departure halls and banks (open 24hrs).

International airport contacts

Indira Gandhi International (IGI) Airport, Delhi
www.newdelhiairport.in

Tel: 0124-337 6000
Chhatrapati Shivaji International Airport, Mumbai
www.csia.in
Tel: 022-6685 1010
Netaji Subhas Chandra Bose International Airport, Kolkata
www.kolkatainternationalairport.com/
Tel: 033-2511 8036
Chennai International Airport, Chennai
Tel: 044-2556 0551
Kempegowda International Airport, Bengaluru
www.bengaluruairport.com
Tel: 1800-425 4425

Overland

India shares land borders with Pakistan, Nepal, Bangladesh, Bhutan, China and Burma. There are currently five border posts where visitors can cross between India and Nepal, four with Bangladesh, one with Pakistan, and one with Bhutan. The borders with China have long been closed to travellers. The same is true of Myanmar (Burma), although this may well change over the coming years if the promised opening of the Ledo Road across the mountains from Assam goes ahead.

For the adventurous, it is theoretically possible to take the train from the UK to India (there's a comprehensive overview of the route at www.seat61.com/India-overland.htm, which is also an excellent resource for all train information about India). The route is via Istanbul, Tehran to the end of the rail line at Bam, from where you would need to get a bus to Zahedan, from where a very basic twice-monthly train travels to the Pakistani border at Quetta, from where you can travel

on to Lahore or Karachi. There is currently only one train service between India and Pakistan. It runs twice a week (usually Monday and Thursday) from Delhi via Amritsar to Lahore, crossing the border at Wagah/Atari.

GETTING AROUND

Air Travel within India

There's been an incredible explosion in domestic air routes within India in recent years, with new operators entering the fray on a regular basis (and going bust just as regularly). Almost every city of any size is now served by frequent flights, and there is fierce competition on more popular routes. Fares vary widely. Those on the more upmarket carriers, like Jet Airways, can be relatively expensive, although fares

Cut Your Carbon

Air travel produces a huge amount of carbon dioxide and is one of the main contributors to global warming. Where possible, take the train while in the country, as this produces less CO2. It is possible to offset your 'carbon load' by, for example, having trees planted as a 'carbon sink'. A number of organisations can do this for you, and many have online 'carbon calculators' which tell you how much you need to donate. In the UK, travellers can try www.climatecare.org or www.carbon neutral.com; in the US, log on to www.climatefriendly.com or www.sustainabletravelinternational.org.

TRANSPORT

Buses are frequently crowded.

on the low-cost carriers can often be an absolute bargain.

The domestic airline market is in an almost constant state of turbulence at present, as airlines swallow one another up, re-brand, or simply go bust. In addition, the two government-owned airlines, the flagship international carrier, Air India and the domestic operator, Indian Airlines, merged in February 2011, which has led to a certain amount of confusion in terms of services and schedules. Just how volatile the Indian airline industry has become was underlined in October 2012 after Kingfisher, backed by the liquor tycoon Vijay Malia, was forced to ground all its flights, leaving passengers stranded and crew unpaid across the country.

Tickets for all the following airlines can be booked online.

Domestic airlines in India

Air India
www.airindia.com
Tel: 011-2462 4074
The national carrier operates a small number of domestic services between Mumbai and Delhi, Kolkata, Bengaluru, Chennai and Thiruvananthapuram.
Air India Express
www.airindiaexpress.in
Mumbai head office tel: 022-2279 6330 (for other offices see website). Low-cost subsidiary of Air India, with a good range of domestic services.
Go Air
www.goair.in

Tel: 020-2566 2111 or 09223-222 111
Low-cost airline based in Mumbai, with flights to Goa, Kochi, Delhi, Srinagar and Ahmadabad.
IndiGo
https://book.goindigo.in
Tel: 911-2466 3838 or 099-1038 3838
Low fares and an impressive number of destinations nationwide.
Jet Airways
www.jetairways.com
Tel: 3989 3333 prefixed with nearest city code (eg in Delhi, call 011-3989 3333).
India's leading private airline, with a huge network and high standards – although tends to be more expensive than other domestic carriers.
Spicejet
www.spicejet.com
Tel: 965-400 3333 (mobile users tel: 0987-180 3333)
Low-cost carrier, based in Delhi, serving around 20 destinations across the country.

Boats

Apart from river ferries there are very few boat services in India. The Andaman Islands are connected to Kolkata, Chennai and Vishakapatnam by boat, as well as to each other. Kerala has a regular passenger boat system, and a number of services operate from Alappuzha and Kollam (formerly Alleppey and Quilon), including the backwater trip between the two. In addition, luxury cruises on the Brahmaputra

and Ganges Rivers are operated by the Indo-British outfit, the Assam Bengal Navigation Company (www. assambengalnavigation.com; tel (UK): 44-1572-821121).

Buses

Virtually every part of the country is connected to India's extensive and well-developed bus system, which complements the railway system and also goes to places where trains can't reach (especially up in the mountains). Services range from clapped-out old rust buckets on more rural routes to deluxe, state-of-the-art air-conditioned express coaches on the major highways.

Although it's difficult to generalise, buses can often be a bit faster and more convenient than trains – services are often more frequent, and frequently don't have to bother buying tickets or making reservations in advance. On the downside, they're generally less comfortable, particularly for long

Reservation Forms

To reserve a ticket you must first fill out a Reservation Requisition Form, which will be available from one of the windows in the booking office. The form is in the local language on one side and English on the reverse. In addition to the obvious information such as where you wish to leave from and go to and when, to fill in the form you also need to know:

The train number and name. You can get this from a timetable, or, if the train departs from the station you are booking from, it is usually displayed on a board in the booking office.

The class you wish to travel and whether you require a berth (for overnight journeys, or any journey between 9pm and 6am), or only a seat.

Whether you require a lower, middle or upper berth. An upper berth is a good idea as it can be used throughout the day, whereas the other two may only be used for sleeping 9pm–6am.

Foreign travellers should also fill in their passport numbers in the column that asks for your Concession Travel Authority Number, which is needed if the ticket is issued under the foreign tourist quota.

A – Z

LANGUAGE

journeys, and not quite as safe either.

Buses are either operated by private companies or by the local state government. Again, it's tricky to generalise, but private buses tend to be a bit more comfortable, with padded seats and tinted windows, and the drivers more reckless.

On many buses you can just buy a ticket on board, although on others you'll have to purchase a ticket before getting on. Bus terminals in larger cities can sometimes be a bit confusing, with numerous different counters for different destinations. It's also possible to reserve a seat on many buses.

Baggage is usually carried in the boot or squeezed under your seat, although it sometimes ends up on the roof, in which case it's worth keeping an eye on it during stops en route (or better still, attach it to the roof rack with a small lock and chain).

Local city buses are generally less useful. All the major cities have their own services, but it's usually hard work to figure out which buses go where, and they can often be unbearably crowded too, particularly during the rush hours. It's generally much easier just to catch a rickshaw or taxi.

Cars and Taxis

For longer tours, you might consider hiring a **car with driver**. These

Urban Metros

The **Delhi Metro** (www.delhimetrorail.com) opened in 2002 and has revolutionised transport in the city. Services run from 6am to 11pm. There are currently six lines and the network is set to expand enormously by 2020.

India's first metro system, far smaller than Delhi's, was inaugurated in **Kolkata** way back in 1984. The second line is currently under construction. An underground system is also being built in **Mumbai**, a massive construction project, whose first 12-km line featuring 12 stations was inaugurated in 2014, is not expected to be fully rolled out until 2021. Bangalore has also acquired two lines and Chennai one line, and work is scheduled to start on brace of others in Hyderabad, Jaipur, Kochi, Ahmedabad, Lucknow and Pune, to name but a few cities.

Delhi's rapidly expanding Metro is a great way to get around the city.

generally cost about US$35–50 a day and can be arranged through tourist offices, hotels or travel agents. Costs vary depending on the size and condition of the vehicle and whether or not it's air-conditioned. Alternatively, you can usually hire a car with driver for a day – again, easily arranged through local tourist offices and hotels.

The local yellow-top black **city taxis** are metered, although with constant hikes in fuel prices, charges may be higher than indicated on the meter. If so, this will be prominently stated in the taxi and the driver will – in theory – have a card showing the excess over the meter reading that can be legitimately charged.

When arriving in India, most international airports (including Delhi, Mumbai, Chennai and Bengaluru) offer a system of **prepaid taxis**, running to fixed prices, which will save you the bother of having to haggle a fare yourself or dealing with unscrupulous drivers. Elsewhere, enquire at the information desk for the going rate for a journey to your destination before getting into the taxi; and make sure the meter is 'down' before you embark. In some cities, for example Mumbai, taxis have fare charts which, when applied to the amount on the meter, give the correct fare.

Driving in India

Driving in India is not for the faint-hearted. Roads can be congested and dangerous, and there are many

unwritten rules which you'll need to be aware of. City roads can often be (or appear to be) totally anarchic, and although things are a lot more peaceful in the countryside, route-finding can often be a problem. In general, it's far better, and quite often even cheaper, to hire a car and driver. If you do decide to drive, you should have an international driving licence (although this might not be insisted on if you have your driving licence from home).

Information regarding road conditions can be obtained from national and state automobile associations. Useful **contacts** include: the Automobile Association of Upper India (AAUI), C-8 Qutab Institutional Area, Behind Qutab Hotel, New Delhi 110 016, tel: 011-2696 5397, www.aaui.org; the Western India Automobile Association Lalji Narainji Memorial Building, 76 Veer Nariman Road, Churchgate, Mumbai 400 020, tel: 022-2204 1085, www.wiaaindia.com; the Automobile Association of Eastern India, 13 Promothesh Barua Sarani, Kolkata 700 019, tel: 033-2486 5131, www.uraaei.org; and the Automobile Association of Southern India, 187 Anna Salai, Chennai 600 006, tel: 044-2852 1162, www.aasindia.in.

Railways

Rail travel is by far the most enjoyable way to get around the country – although standards of cleanliness in some classes, and punctuality, may not be what you're used to back home. There are three basic types of train. The best are the 'Super-fast' services: air-conditioned trains on major inter-city routes. These include the excellent 'Shatabdi' daytime-only expresses, and 'Rajdhani' services, which link Delhi with cities nationwide. The second category are the 'Express' or 'mail' inter-city services, which are also generally fast and – if you book a seat in one of the more expensive carriages – comfortable. It's generally best to avoid the third category of train, the painfully slow 'passenger' services, which tend to take forever to get anywhere. There are also a number of special tourist trains. For an excellent overview of Indian railway services, check out the authoritative website www.seat61.com/India.htm.

Fares are generally low, especially if you travel in a non-A/C class, although the price of a long-haul first-class ticket can often be as much as (or even more than) the comparable air fare.

Comprehensive **timetable** and fare information is available at www.indianrail.gov.in, or the more user-friendly www.cleartrip.com.

Retiring rooms (for short-term occupation only) are available at over 1,100 stations on a first-come first-served basis, but these are usually heavily booked. All first-class waiting rooms have couches for passengers using their own bedding. At New Delhi and Howrah stations, a Rail Yatri Niwas offers accommodation for transit passengers which can be booked in advance.

Cloakrooms are available at most stations where travellers may leave their luggage, but bags must be locked and may be subject to an x-ray scan for security purposes. Be sure not to lose your reclaim ticket and check opening times of the cloakroom for collection.

Very useful prepaid **taxi** and/or **auto-rickshaw** services are available at some of the largest stations.

Remember to check which station your train departs from and allow at least half an hour to find your seat/berth. Lists of passengers with the compartment and seat/berth numbers allotted to them are displayed on platforms and on each carriage an hour before departure. The station superintendent and the conductor attached to the train are usually available for assistance.

On Shatabdi and Rajdhani trains the fare includes **food**, drinks and snacks. In other classes (except second class unreserved) veg and non-veg meals (often surprisingly good) can be ordered from the carriage attendant. Failing that, whenever the train stops the carriages are invaded by itinerant hawkers selling all sorts of food, while roving hawkers also dish up endless supplies of tea and coffee – the endless calls of *chai-chai-chai* or *kafi-kafi-kafi* providing an emblematic soundtrack to all Indian railway journeys.

Classes of travel

Indian Railways has no fewer than eight different **classes**, of varying degrees of comfort (although most trains will only have three or four different types of class). Sleeper compartments consist of two- or three-tier bunks: during the day, the bottom bunk is used for seating; reserving a top-bunk means you can lie down even in the middle of the day if you want to.

In descending order of price, the various classes are:

Air-conditioned first class AC (AC1) Very comfortable compartments with lockable cabins of two or four berths each, arranged in two tiers.

AC 2-tier (AC2) Two-tier bunks in open-plan carriages (not compartments) arranged in groups of six berths with curtains that pull across to provide privacy.

AC 3-tier (AC3) Like AC 2-tier carriages, but with three-tier bunks. The middle berths fold down when not used for sleeping.

AC executive chair class (EC) Found only on the most important Shatabdi services. Spacious seating (four seats across) in A/C carriages.

AC chair class (CC) The standard class on Shatabdi services. Like executive chair class, but with slightly more cramped seating (six seats across, rather than four) and plainer carriages.

First class (FC, non A/C) This type of compartment is being phased out, and is increasingly rare. They consist of non A/C lockable compartments containing two or four berths.

Sleeper class (SC) The most common class, with open-plan carriages divided into partitions of six berths with ceiling fans.

Second class unreserved Open-plan carriages of hard seats (no bunks). Can get horribly crowded.

Obviously, in the hot summer months A/C can be a worthwhile option. The major drawback with A/C carriages is that they usually have tinted and/or scratched/dirty windows, which means you don't

Indian Railways Online

The excellent Indian Railways website at www.indianrail.gov.in is a comprehensive, if unwieldy, source of information. You can check timetables for all trains here, as well as fares and current availability, and find out what classes are available on which trains.

It's also now theoretically possible to buy tickets online at www.irctc.co.in, though in practise you'll need book weeks in advance: Indian Railways require customers wishing to pay using credit or debit cards registered abroad have to send a photocopy (or scan) of their passport to India for verification first. A code will then be sent to you which you'll need to key in when you book online – a cumbersome process outlined in fine-grain detail at www.seat61.com/India.htm – from outside India. The private travel booking site Clear Trip (www.cleartrip.com) is much better set up than Indian Railways, with a clearer, faster interface, but again, foreign tourists are subject to Indian Railways arcane booking rules and required to verify their identity by sending passport copies in advance. All in all, you're invariably better off advance booking by means of an Indrail Pass which buys you access to special quotas on popular trains and thus nearly always ensures reservations on your desired day of travel – especially worthwhile for onward journeys by rail shortly after arrival in India.

If you really fall in love with the railways and want to learn more, try the excellent Indian Railways Fan Club site at www.irfca.org.

get a great view of the countryside outside. Sleeper class and second class unreserved, by contrast, just have metal grilles over open windows, which means you'll get a better view, and also benefit from pleasant breezes when the train is in motion.

Carriages have a mix of Western and Indian-style toilets – the latter are usually cleaner and less unpleasant, assuming you can keep your balance while squatting in a moving train.

Basic bedding (two sheets, a pillow and a blanket) is provided in first class AC, AC 2-tier and 3-tier, and is also available from the attendant for Rs20 in first class. No bedding is provided

Travelling by train is a unique Indian experience.

in sleeper class, so you might want to take your own.

Reservations

Reservations are required for all classes other than second class unreserved, and reserving well in advance is strongly recommended. Reservations may be made up to 60 days in advance. Many stations now have very efficient computerised booking counters from where you can book any ticket for any route. In the larger cities, the major stations have tourist sections with English-speaking staff to reduce the queues for foreigners and non-resident Indians buying tickets. Tourist offices at railway reservation centres are helpful in planning itineraries and obtaining reservations (International Tourist Bureau, New Delhi railway station, tel: 011-2334 6804; 24/7). There are tourist offices at New Delhi, Mumbai Churchgate, Kolkata Fairlie Place, Chennai Central, and some other popular tourist destinations.

The bottom line, however, is that reserving a railway ticket can be a pain, given the fact that you've got to visit the station in person and then probably queue, often for a long time. One good option is to get a local travel agent or your guesthouse/hotel to send someone to the station to buy a ticket for you. They'll charge you for this, of course, but the sums involved are usually fairly modest (typically around Rs250), and are well worth it

for what they'll save you in terms of time and hassle.

If there are no available places on the train you want, then you have a couple of options. Certain trains have a tourist quota that may be available. Other options are to take a wait-listed ticket or the more assured reservation against cancellation (RAC). There's also an 'emergency' quota, available only on the day of travel. The booking clerk should be able to advise you on how likely you are to get a reservation.

Your best option, however, is to try for a ticket under the Taktal scheme. This operates on trains (marked with a 'T' in timetables) on major inter-city routes, with 10 percent of the seats only being released for sale five days before departure. The catch is the price. You'll pay a surcharge for a Taktal reservation, but more importantly you'll also have to pay for the cost of a ticket for the whole of the train's journey from originating to terminating stations, regardless of how much of this route you intend to use.

Cancellations (for which you will need to fill in the same form as for a reservation) can be made with varying degrees of penalty, depending on the class and how close the cancellation is made to the time of departure.

Luxury trains

Since the advent of the Palace on Wheels (www.palaceonwheels.net) in the early 1990s, luxury trains have proved an enduringly popular

option with high-end visitors to India. Half a dozen of these super-swish locomotives now operate around the country. All adopt a similar formula, taking opulent carriages formerly used by local maharajas – or ersatz versions of them – and following routes around the tourist highlights of a given region. They're all government run by state tourism development corporations, but can be booked abroad through private agents – in fact, it's often cheaper to do just that as agents benefit from discounts which they usually (but not always) hand a part of back to customers. One thoroughly dependable London-based operator who offers the most competitive rates is SD Enterprises (103 Wembley Park Drive, Wembley, Middlesex HA9 8HG; tel: 0208-903 3411, www.indiarail.co.uk). In India itself, a recommended specialist is Indian Luxury Trains (tel: +0091-981-833 6340; www.indian luxurytrains.com).

The Deccan Odyssey (www.deccan-odyssey-india.com)
This plush train starts in Mumbai, and heads south down the Konkan coast, pausing at Ratnagiri and the Maratha fort at Sindhudurg en route to Goa, before swinging north again

Indrail Passes

The Indrail Pass gives unlimited travel on the entire rail network for periods of between 12 hours and 90 days and can be good value if you plan on travelling nearly every day – or if you wish to gain access to seats or berths at busy times through the special tourist rail pass quota. They are available to foreign nationals and Indians resident abroad and are paid for in foreign currency. Indrail passes considerably reduce time getting reservations; you pay no fees and no sleeper berth surcharge for night journeys for any class of accommodation.

In the UK the pass can be obtained through the very efficient S.D. Enterprises Ltd, 103 Wembley Park Drive, Wembley, Middlesex HA9 8HG; tel: 020-8903 3411, www.indiarail.co.uk. They can also book single-journey tickets in advance for you. In India, the Indrail pass can be bought at Railway Central Reservations Offices in Chennai, Kolkata, Mumbai Central, Mumbai CST and New Delhi.

A Delhi autorickshaw.

through Kolhapur to Aurangabad, for Ellora and Ajanta Caves. Tariffs hover around US$425/night, making this among the least expensive options.

The Golden Chariot (www.golden chariottrain.com). Taking in the highlights on the southern Indian state of Karnataka, the Golden Chariot follows a varied route through some fabulous scenery, and stops at some memorable locations. Rather than start at Bengaluru, we recommend you skip the first, rather dull couple of stages and pick the train up in Mysore, from where it calls at the Hoysala temple sites around Hassan, the ruined city of Hampi, the ancient Hindu capitals of Badami and Aihole, then arrives at Goa. The same train also follows a longer route stringing together the highlights of Karnataka with those of Kerala and Tamil Nadu, the 'Splendor of the South' tour. Tariffs for both start at around US$440/night.

Maharajas' Express (www.maharajas-express-india.com)
An über-luxurious alternative to the Palace on Wheels is the Maharaja's Express, which offers weekly departures on a range of five inter-city routes across India. Tours last between four and eight days and cost from around US$600/night

The Palace on Wheels (www.palaceonwheels.net). India's original and most famous luxury train, the Palace on Wheels, leaves Delhi every Wednesday afternoon from September to April and stops at Jaipur, Bharatpur, Chittaurgarh, Udaipur, Sawai Madhopur, Jaisalmer, Jodhpur, Bharatpur and Agra,

returning to Delhi on the eighth day. Tariffs range from around US $4,275–5,750 depending on the season, or $US520/night.

Royal Rajasthan On Wheels (www.royalrajasthanonwheels.co.in) This lavishly appointed train is run by the same outfit as the Palace on Wheels, and follows a similar route around the highlights of Rajasthan, only with a detour east to Varanasi via the temples at Khajuraho. Prices from $2,000–4,500 depending on length of the tour.

India also has a number of charming 'toy trains' which run from the plains up to certain hill stations. These include the narrow-gauge tracks up to Udhagamandalam (Ooty) in the Nilgiris, the line from New Jalpaiguri to Darjeeling, and the track between Neral and Matheran near Mumbai, as well as the broad-gauge service (known as the Himalayan Queen) between Kalka and Simla.

Rickshaws and Tongas

The most convenient, and typically Indian, way of getting around is by rickshaw. These come in two types: a cycle rickshaw (an oversized tricycle-type contraption with a seat for two people on the back), and motorised three-wheelers, known as autorickshaws or simply '**autos**'.

Autos are, like taxis, supposed to use a meter, although you'll only very rarely find one that's working, or a driver who's prepared to use it. In practice this means haggling every time you use an auto. *Always* agree a **fare** with the rickshaw driver before

you set off to avoid arguments later. It's often tricky to know what a good fare is – and you'll inevitably pay a bit more than the locals (and possibly a lot more if you're not keen on bargaining). It's a good idea to check the latest going rates at your hotel or guesthouse to get an idea of what it should cost to get wherever you're going. And if the first auto driver won't agree to the fare you want, just walk away. There will probably be 10 more just around the corner.

As well as one-off journeys, you might also want to hire a rickshaw (either auto or cycle) for the day in order to make a tour of the local sights. Again, check the going rate at your hotel and make it clear that you only want to visit the sights, and don't want to be dragged off to endless local shops where he will earn commission en route.

Auto-rickshaw rides can be fun but noisy – and sometimes decidedly hair-raising, as the driver ducks kamikaze-fashion through the traffic, dodging buses and lorries. **Cycle-rickshaws**, by contrast, are significantly slower than autos, but can be a lot more peaceful – if you're not in any particular hurry. Again, make sure you agree a fare before you set off. Many visitors are unhappy at the thought of being pedalled along by cycle-rickshaw wallahs, many of whom are clearly under-nourished and pitifully thin, although of course the fact is that they need your custom – and you can always give them a good tip at the end.

Note that rickshaws are not allowed into central Mumbai; the only transport options are the well-developed bus service or the reasonably priced taxis.

There are also an increasingly tiny number of hand-pulled rickshaws in central Kolkata – that is, rickshaws pulled by men on foot. The idea of being pulled along by another human being might seem distasteful to many visitors, but these rickshaws perform a useful function during the monsoon when the streets flood and the other rickshaws will not work – and also provide a living for the impoverished pavement-dwellers who pull them.

Finally, in quite a few towns it's still possible to travel by tonga. These traditional horse-drawn carts can be pretty to look at, although many of the horses are in a pitiable condition and are clearly mistreated by their (often equally impoverished) owners. Agree the fare before you set off, and expect to pay roughly what you would in a cycle-rickshaw.

A – Z

A HANDY SUMMARY
OF PRACTICAL INFORMATION

A

Accommodation

Accommodation in India ranges from ultra-cheap flophouses to opulent palaces of former maharajas. At the bottom of the scale are plenty of small-scale budget guesthouses and cheap tourist hotels. Those catering to foreign tourists are usually reasonably clean and cheap, though the mattresses tend to be thin and lumpy and plumbing limited to a squat loo and bucket bath. Away from tourist hotspots there are plenty of mid-range hotels aimed at local business travellers – again usually with good standards of comfort and cleanliness, though often lacking character. Air-conditioning will be optional. In addition to standard rooms, they'll also offer a 'deluxe' category, with greater space and comfier beds, and possibly frills such as a minibar-fridge and large, flat-screen TV. The air-con units will also be more modern and quiet. Many of the state tourist corporations run similarly bland but comfortable mid-range establishments, often described as tourist bungalows. Rates will be relatively low, but standards of maintenance and service in these places not comparable with hotels in the private sector.

While other mid-range options had been something of a rarity, there are now an increasing number of places catering to the older, or more discerning traveller who has perhaps done the backpacking thing but doesn't want to go the five-star route, or to the well-travelled Indian middle classes. Be aware, though, that mid-range pricing does not always mean

the standard will be better than the budget place next door – watch out, in particular, for the trick of naming a new hotel after a popular older one.

Going upmarket, India has some of the world's most memorable places to stay, many of them occupying the former palaces, forts and havelis of the country's erstwhile maharajas and other ruling elites, as well as many fine old Raj-era piles such as the Taj in Mumbai. These places include world-famous heritage hotels like the Taj Lake Palace in Udaipur. Expect to spend several hundred dollars a night or more in such establishments. The two leading chains, Taj and Oberoi, boast dozens of superb properties countrywide. Heritage doesn't always equate with expense, however, and there are innumerable less ostentatious boutique options, particularly in Rajasthan and Kerala, ranging from old havelis through to rustic hilltop forts to former hunting lodges and tea planters' bungalows in the hills many of which offer oodles of atmosphere.

When it comes to national parks and tiger reserves, choice has expanded considerably over the past decade. In addition to lower-mid-range government motels, you now also have a broad range of high-end safari lodges, with accommodation offered in luxury tents, boutique-style mud-and-thatch huts and honeymoon lovenests with their own plunge pools and deep verandahs. Prices tend to be top whack, running to hundreds of dollars per night, but will include the services of a qualified guide, as well as a Jeep and driver for safaris.

In beach resorts have also become much more sophisticated in past years. At the top of the scale are uber-luxurious complexes centred on huge, curvi-form pools, where the rooms recreational facilities and sports provision are international quality, and restaurants gourmet standard. Essentially five-stars-on-sea, such places do, however, possess much less character than boutique hotels of a comparable standard, where the décor will be more stylish and individual. Here, the vibe will be less formal and designer interiors like something out of a magazine.

Well-to-do families with beautiful old country mansions dominate the so-called heritage homestay market. Like boutique hotels, these tend to be far less anonymous that five stars. You're welcomed as part of the family by your hosts, who'll chat with you at meal times and show you around their estate or local village – all of which can make for a very memorable and rewarding time, particularly if you have children in tow.

Wherever you stay, when checking in, ask to see two or three rooms before handing over your money. Check that lights, fan work, hot water and A/C work, and that the price is clear. Check for taxes and hidden extras. And it is always worth trying to haggle a discount.

Admission Charges

Admission charges at India's museums and tourist attractions vary widely: from a couple of rupees at minor sites up to Rs750 for the Taj Mahal. Many of the country's major sites are run by the Archaeological Survey of India (ASI), with typical entrance fees between Rs100 and Rs750. Entrance to national parks is generally around Rs600–800, plus transport costs.

B

Begging

Visitors to India will encounter people asking for alms, especially in the cities, around holy shrines and on railway journeys. Many of them are physically disabled and have few other options for survival. Small amounts of money will be gratefully received. Try to give discreetly or you might attract unwanted attention. If you are unsure about whether to give or not, simply follow what other people are doing.

Budgeting for Your Trip

India can be either very cheap or incredibly expensive. Living on a shoestring, you could conceivably scrape by on as little as US$20 per day, although most backpackers probably spend around twice this amount or more. For around US$60–80 per day you can stay in comfortable mid-range hotels, eat well and perhaps hire your own car and driver. If you want to really push the boat out, however, you'll be looking at $150–200 per day (and possibly much more than this) – there are plenty of top hotels now charging US$500 per night, or more. Obviously, travelling as a couple is a lot cheaper than going solo, and the big cities are a lot more expensive than the countryside – Mumbai, in particular, is notoriously pricey.

C

Children

Indians love children and are very tolerant of them, making India a very easy place to travel with kids. Children will find the sights and sounds just as rewarding as adults. The problem is that little ones tend to be more easily affected by the heat, unsafe drinking water and unfamiliar food seasoned with chillies and spices. In case of diarrhoea, rehydration salts are vital. To avoid the risk of rabies, children should be vaccinated and kept away from stray animals, especially dogs and monkeys. It is difficult to find nappies and places to change them, so consider bringing a supply of disposables – though bear in mind if you do the absence in most of India of regular waste disposal. Washables may be messier, but at least you won't be leaving your mess behind you. A changing mat is essential. For touring, walking and hiking, a child-carrier backpack is well worth its weight, though you might consider a stroller if you plan to do much travelling in airports and train stations.

Climate

India's climate ranges from the permanent snows of the Himalayas and the tropical conditions along the coasts, to the continental climate of inland areas. There are also many regional and seasonal variations. In general, the best time to visit is after the southwest monsoon.

October to March is the cool season and the best time of year in Peninsular India. The weather is beautifully predictable in winter, with blue skies and bright sunshine in most areas. Parts of the south and east see a brief spell of rain from the northeast monsoon, while snow and sleet make the extreme north very cold and often inaccessible.

Summer, from April to June, is very hot and dry for most of the country, and humid along the coasts. The hills are particularly lovely at this time of the year.

The southwest monsoon begins to set in along the western coast towards the end of May, bringing respite from the heat and varying amounts of rain as it moves across the rest of the country through June and July and withdraws by late September. Northeastern India has heavy rain during this season, making it one of the wettest regions in the world.

Crime and Safety

Generally speaking, India is a safe place to travel, but a tourist is a natural target for thieves and pick-pockets, so take the usual precautions and keep money, credit cards, valuables and passport in a money belt or pouch well secured with a cord around your neck. A protective hand over this in a crowded place could save you a lot of heartache and hassle.

Do not leave belongings unattended, especially on a beach. Invest in good strong locks (available in India) for your bags. Chaining luggage to the berth on a train, or to your seat on a bus, is a precaution that travelling Indians often take.

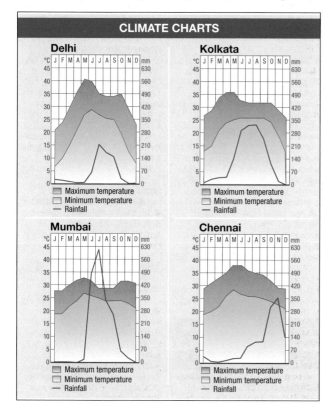

CLIMATE CHARTS

Delhi
°C J F M A M J J A S O N D mm

Kolkata
°C J F M A M J J A S O N D mm

- ▢ Maximum temperature
- ▢ Minimum temperature
- — Rainfall

Mumbai
°C J F M A M J J A S O N D mm

Chennai
°C J F M A M J J A S O N D mm

- ▢ Maximum temperature
- ▢ Minimum temperature
- — Rainfall

TRANSPORT

A – Z

LANGUAGE

Watch your luggage, especially during loading and unloading.

Credit-card frauds do exist, so make sure that shops and restaurants process your card in front of you.

Another sensible precaution is to keep a photocopy of your passport and visa, traveller's cheque numbers and receipts, ticket details, insurance policy number and telephone claims number, and some emergency money in a bag or case separate from your other cash and documents. If you are robbed, report the incident immediately to a police station (be patient: this can take hours).

Parts of inland Odisha (Orissa), Jharkhand and southern Bihar are known for their extreme poverty, persecution of Christian minorities and bandits and are notably less safe than other areas in India. Travel to the states of Jammu and Kashmir, as well as Manipur and the immediate vicinity of the Pakistani border, was being advised against by the British Foreign Office at the time of writing in early 2016. Before you travel, it's always best to check your government's current advice on foreign travel: https://www.gov.uk/foreign-travel-advice; http://www.state.gov/travel/.

Customs

At present, currency declaration forms for amounts of cash in excess of US$5,000 must be completed at customs on arrival. Prohibited articles include certain drugs, live plants, gold and silver bullion, and coins not in current use. All checked luggage arriving at Delhi airport is X-rayed before reaching the baggage collection area in the arrival hall. Duty-free imports include 100 cigarettes (or 25 cigars), 2 litres (4.2 pints) of alcohol, and a reasonable amount of personal effects, including binoculars, laptop, sound recording instruments, etc. Professional equipment and high-value articles must be declared or listed on arrival with a written undertaking to re-export them. Both the list and the articles must be produced on departure. As this formality can be a lengthy process, allow extra time, both on arrival and at departure. For unaccompanied baggage or baggage misplaced by the

Emergency Numbers

As of March 2016, there is an India-wide number covering all three emergency services (police, fire and ambulance) on **112**.

Sign in Kolkata.

airline, make sure you get a landing certificate from customs on arrival.

Export of antiques (over 100 years old), all animal products, and jewellery valued at over Rs2,000 (in the case of gold) and Rs10,000 (in the case of articles not made of gold) is banned. When in doubt about the age of semi-antiques, contact the office of the Archaeological Survey of India in Delhi, Mumbai, Kolkata or Chennai (www.asi.nic.in).

D

Disabled Travellers

Although disability is common in India, there are very few provisions for wheelchairs and special toilets. The roads are full of potholes, and kerbs are often high and without ramps. It may be hard to negotiate street obstacles, beggars, or steep staircases. On the other hand, Indians will always be willing to help you in and out of buses or cars, or up stairs. Taxis and rickshaws are cheap, and the driver, with a little tip, will probably help. You could employ a guide to help with obstacles. Another option is to go with a paid companion. In the UK, **Tourism For All** (7A Pixel Mill, 44 Appleby Road, Kendal Cumbria LA9 6ES; tel: 0845-124 9971; www.tourismforall.org.uk) can put you in touch with someone.

Some package holiday operators cater for travellers with disabilities, but ensure that your needs have been understood before making a booking.

E

Electricity

The voltage system in India is 220V AC, 50 cycles. DC supplies also exist, so check first. Sockets are normally of the two round-pin variety, but do vary. Take a universal adaptor for British, Irish and Australasian plugs. US and Canadian appliances will need a transformer. Be aware that both power cuts and surges are not uncommon – more expensive hotels will have generator back-up, others will not.

Embassies and Consulates

Australia
www.india.embassy.gov.au
Delhi: Australian High Commission
1/50 G Shantipath, Chanakyapuri, Delhi
Tel: 011-4139 9900
Mumbai: Consulate General
Level 10, A Wing, Crescenzo Building, Opp MCA Cricket Club, G Block, Plot C 38-39 Bandra Kurla Complex, Mumbai 400 051
Tel: 022-6757 4900

Canada
http://india.gc.ca
Delhi: Canadian High Commission
7–8 Shantipath, Chanakyapuri, New Delhi 110 021
Tel: 011-4178 2000
Mumbai: Consulate General
Indiabulls Finance Centre, 21st Floor, Tower 2, Senapati Bapat Marg, Elphinstone Road (West), Mumbai 400 013
Tel: 022-6749 4444

Ireland
www.irelandinindia.com
Delhi: Embassy
C 17 Malcha Marg, Chanakyapuri, New Delhi 100 021
Tel: 011-4940 3200

New Zealand
www.nzembassy.com/india
Delhi: High Commission
Sir Edmund Hillary Marg, Chanakyapuri, Delhi 110 021
Tel: 011-4688 3170

Mumbai: Consulate General
Level 2, 3 North Avenue, Maker Maxity, Bandra Kurla Complex, Mumbai 400 051
Tel: 022-6131 6666
Chennai: Consulate
Maithri, 132 Cathedral Road, Chennai 600 086
Tel: 044-2811 2472

UK

http://ukinindia.fco.gov.uk/en
Delhi: British High Commission
Shantipath, Chanakyapuri, New Delhi 110 021
Tel: 011-2419 2100
Mumbai: British Deputy High Commission
Naman Chambers, C/32 G Block Bandra Kurla Complex, Bandra (East), Mumbai 400 051
Tel: 022-6650 2222
Kolkata: 1A Ho Chi Minh Sarani, Kolkata 700 071
Tel: 033-2288 5172
Chennai: 20 Anderson Road, Chennai 600 006
Tel: 044-4219 2151
Goa: British Nationals Assistance Office Goa
303-304 Casa del Sol, Opposite Marriott Hotel Miramar, Panaji 403 001
Tel: 0832-663 6777

US

Delhi: Embassy
Shantipath, Chanakyapuri, New Delhi 110 021
Tel: 011-2419 8000
http://newdelhi.usembassy.gov
Mumbai: C-49, G-Block, Bandra Kurla Complex, Bandra East, Mumbai 400 051
Tel: 022-2672 4000
http://mumbai.usconsulate.gov
Kolkata: Consulate General
5/1 Ho Chi Minh Sarani, Kolkata 700 071
Tel: 033-3984 2400
http://kolkata.usconsulate.gov
Chennai: Consulate General
Gemini Circle, Chennai 600 006
Tel: 044-2857 4000
http://chennai.usconsulate.gov

Etiquette

Removing one's shoes before entering someone's house, or a temple, mosque or gurdwara (Sikh temple) is essential. Wearing socks or stockings is usually permissible.

The traditional *namaskaram* greeting with joined hands has been largely (if not completely) replaced by the Western handshake, particularly in cities, although women often prefer not to shake hands with men – don't offer to shake hands with a woman unless she first holds out a hand to you. Kissing and embracing in public is frowned upon; in rural areas, even men and women holding hands can provoke curious stares. (Although the sight of Indian men holding hands with other Indian men is common.)

Leather goods of any kind should not be taken into temples, as these are regarded as impure and can often cause offence. Menstruating women are also usually forbidden from entering Jain temples (although of course no one's going to check).

Photography is prohibited inside the inner sanctum of many places of worship. Do obtain permission before using a camera. Visitors are usually welcome to look around at their leisure and can sometimes stay during religious rituals. For visits to places of worship, modest clothing is essential. In Sikh temples, your head should be covered. In mosques, women should cover their head and arms and wear long skirts. A small contribution to the donation box (*hundi*) is customary.

When eating with your fingers, remember to use only the right hand.

Avoid pointing the soles of your feet towards anyone as this is considered a sign of disrespect. Don't point with your index finger: use either your extended hand or your chin.

G

Gay and Lesbian Travellers

Homosexuality is still a taboo subject for many Indians. Sexual relations between men are technically illegal and punishable with long prison sentences, although in practice this is highly unlikely – harassment and arrests are more of a risk, especially as cruising in public could come under public disorder laws. The subject of legalising homosexuality in India continues to be under review – watch this space. There is no similar law against lesbians. While general attitudes are discriminatory, things are changing slowly, and at least the issue of gay and lesbian rights is starting to be discussed, due in no small part to Deepa Mehta's 1998 film *Fire*, which depicted an affair between two married women, and the 2004 film *Girlfriend*. However,

Festivals

There are many festivals in India but few public holidays. Here is a selection of the annual highlights in India's festival calendar. In addition, every town, village and temple celebrates its own during the year. See page 92.
Jan–Feb
Pongal. This is the most celebrated harvest festival in South India; typically lasting four days, it involves the painting of elaborate *kollams* (floor paintings) and the preparation of *pongal*, a rice, sugar and nuts confection which gives the festival its name.
Holi. Full-moon festival welcoming the arrival of spring. Indians typically celebrate by throwing vast quantities of dyed water and paint over one another. Not for the faint-hearted.
August
Raksha Bandhan. A festival dedicated to the brother-sister relationship, celebrated most prominently in North India, during which brothers and sisters tie coloured strings on each other's wrists.
Sept–Oct
Dussehra. Ten-day festival celebrating the victory of good over

evil, particularly Rama's triumph over Ravana and Durga's over Mahishasura.
Oct–Nov
Diwali. India's biggest national celebration, the 'Festival of Lights', commemorates the homecoming of Rama and Sita with the lighting of innumerable oil lamps and the setting-off of vast quantities of fireworks.
Nov–Dec
Pushkhar Camel Fair. One of India's most celebrated events, with thousands of camels converging in the Rajasthani Desert while a mass Hindu bathing ritual takes place in nearby Pushkar Lake.
Moveable
Kumbh Mela. India's greatest religious celebration, held periodically at one of the four towns of northern India: Allahabad, Haridwar, Nashik and Ujjain, leading up to the Maha Kumbh Mela, held every 144 years. The last one, in Jan/Feb 2013 at Allahabad, the world's biggest festival, attracted 120 million pilgrims.
Eid-ul-Fitr. India's largest Muslim festival, celebrating the end of the holy month of Ramadan.

TRANSPORT

A – Z

LANGUAGE

gay and lesbian travellers should be discreet and avoid any public displays of affection (as should heterosexual couples). On the plus side, hotels will think nothing of two men or women sharing a room.

Good websites with useful information and links include (for gay men) www.indiandost.com, http://gaydelhi.tripod.com, www.bombaydost.co.in, www.humsafar.org and www.gaybombay.org, and (for lesbians) www.sangini.org.in.

H

Health and Medical Care

Altitude sickness

This can occur above 2,500 metres (8,200ft). Watch for symptoms of breathlessness, palpitations, headache, insomnia and loss of appetite. With total rest, travellers usually acclimatise within 48 hours. It is important that fluid intake is maintained; at least 4 to 6 litres per day is recommended.

Inhaling a few breaths from an oxygen canister can provide immediate relief in a mild attack. A severe attack, brought on by climbing too high or quickly, is marked by dizziness, nausea, vomiting, convulsions, severe thirst, blurred vision, drowsiness, weakness or hearing difficulties.

The only cure is to descend to a lower altitude at once. Lung damage from lack of oxygen can be permanent if untreated. Allow several days to acclimatise before attempting to re-ascend in easy stages. In acute cases, seek medical advice.

A previous trip with no symptoms does not mean that a traveller is immune to altitude sickness. It can strike anyone, and being fit does not prevent the problem.

Two other, extremely serious and potentially fatal, conditions can occur at high altitude, primarily to mountaineers: pulmonary oedema and cerebral oedema. The first is the filling of the lungs with fluid (symptoms include coughing up frothy fluid, irrational behaviour and fatigue); the only cure and treatment is to descend immediately. The second is a swelling of the brain (symptoms here include headache, hallucinations and disorientation, eventually resulting in coma); immediate descent is essential to prevent death. To reduce the swelling it is also possible to give 4mg dexamethasone three times per day, although this is a powerful drug and should only be given with medical supervision or in an emergency.

Diarrhoeas

Traveller's diarrhoea is usually caused by low-level food poisoning and can be avoided with a little care. When you arrive, rest on your first day and only eat simple food; well-cooked vegetarian dishes, a South Indian *thali* and peeled fruits are perhaps best. An upset stomach is often caused by eating too many rich Indian meat dishes (usually cooked with vast amounts of oil and spices) and failing to rest and let your body acclimatise.

Drink plenty of fluids (although it's best to avoid unboiled or unfiltered tap water). When in doubt, stick to soda, mineral water or aerated drinks of standard brands. Avoid ice as this is often made with unboiled water. All food should be cooked and eaten hot. Don't eat salads and always peel fruit.

With all cases of diarrhoea, including dysentery and giardia described below, it is not a good idea to use immobilising drugs such as loperamide (Imodium) and atropine (Lomotil), unless you absolutely need to bung yourself up for, say, the duration of a bus journey, as they prevent the body ridding itself of infection. The most important thing to do in cases of diarrhoea and/or vomiting is to rehydrate, preferably using oral rehydration salts.

Dysentery and giardia are more serious forms of stomach infection and should be suspected if the diarrhoea lasts for more than two days.

Dysentery is characterised by diarrhoea accompanied by the presence of mucus and blood in faeces. Other symptoms include severe stomach cramps and vomiting. Bacillic dysentery comes on quickly and is usually accompanied by fever. It may clear up by itself but its usual treatment is with 500mg of ciprofloxacin or tetracycline twice daily for five days. Do not take the powerful antibiotic chloramphenicol as it can have dangerous side effects. Amoebic dysentery has a slower onset and will not clear up on its own. If you suspect you have amoebic dysentery you should seek medical help as it can damage the gut. If this is not available then self-treat with 400mg of metronidazole (Flagyl) three times daily with food for seven days. Avoid alcohol when taking metronidazole.

Hospitals

In an emergency you can call an ambulance by dialling 102 (although depending on how ill you are, you might find it better just to jump in a taxi/rickshaw and make your own way to the nearest hospital). For other forms of assistance following an emergency, contact East West Rescue, 38 Golf Links, New Delhi, tel: 011-2469 8865, www.eastwestrescue.com. They operate over the whole country and have an extremely good reputation. As a rule of thumb, the new generation of modern, privately run hospitals, such as those founded by the Apollo chain, are better equipped and offer conditions and care closer to what you may be used to back home. Should you require any serious medical treatment in and Indian hospital, proof of medical insurance cover will be handy.

Chennai
Apollo Hospital, 21–22 Greams Road Tel: 044-2829 0200; www.apollohospitals.com

Delhi
All India Institute of Medical Sciences, Ansari Nagar Tel: 011-2658 8500; www.aiims.edu Safdarjang General Hospital, Sri Aurobindo Marg Tel: 011-2616 5060 Hyderabad/Secunderabad

At a Kali festival in Kolkata.

CARE Hospitals, Nampally
Tel: 040-3041 7777; www.care
hospitals.com
Kolkata
Birla Heart Research Centre, 1-1
National Library Avenue
Tel: 033-3040 3040; www.birlaheart.
org
Medical College Hospital, 88 College
Street
Tel: 033-2212 3741; www.medical
collegekolkata.org
Mumbai
Prince Aly Khan Hospital, Nesbit Road
Tel: 022-2377 7900; www.agakhan
hospitals.org

Insect bites and stings

Bed bugs can be a problem in cheap
hotels; look out for the marks of
squashed insects on the walls and
floor around the bed. Leeches can
also be a problem in wet jungle
areas; remove with a lighted match or
cigarette, or salt.

Giardia is a similar infection
caused by a parasite. Like amoebic
dysentery, it comes on slowly and its
symptoms include loose and foul-
smelling diarrhoea, feeling bloated
and nauseous, and stomach cramps.
Giardia will not clear up on its own
and will recur; its treatment is the
same as for amoebic dysentery.

Malaria

This mosquito-borne disease is very
serious and potentially fatal. There
are two common strains in India,
P. falciparum and *P. vivax*, both
carried by the Anopheles mosquito.
Symptoms are similar to acute
flu (including some or all of fever,
shivering, diarrhoea and muscle
pains), and an outbreak may come
on as much as a year after visiting a
malarial area. If malaria is suspected
then medical attention should be
sought as soon as possible.

Malaria risk varies in different
parts of the country (see the useful
malaria map at www.fitfortravel.nhs.
uk). Malaria prophylaxis is not always
considered necessary (and will never
be needed at high altitudes above
2,500 metres/8,200ft); discuss your
needs with your doctor or health clinic
before travel.

The usual anti-malarial protection
for India consists of a combination
of daily proguanil (Paludrine) and
weekly chloroquine (Avoclar, Nivaquin)
tablets. These can now be bought
across the counter in the UK, and
your pharmacist can advise you on
the correct dosages (usually 200mg
of proguanil daily and 300mg of
chloroquin weekly). This is at present

the only safe prophylaxis during
pregnancy. However, the combination
is at best 70 percent effective and
doesn't always work in areas of high
risk. Another drawback with this
regime is that you have to start taking
these tablets a week before you
arrive, and continue for a month after
you've returned home.

An alternative and much stronger
anti-malarial drug is mefloquine
(Lariam), taken weekly. However, this
should not be taken by people with a
history of epilepsy or mental illness,
and there has been much anecdotal
evidence of long-lasting and serious
side effects (although medical
evidence suggests that these are no
more likely than with the proguanil/
chloroquin combination). In the UK
mefloquine is only available as a
private prescription.

Other anti-malarial drugs include
doxycycline and the recently developed
atavoquone-proguanil combination
marketed as Malarone. This is
recommended for areas of chloroquine
resistance (such as Assam) and
is taken once a day. Malarone is
expensive, but has the great benefit
that you only have to start taking it the
day you arrive in a malarial area, and
continue for a week after. Other drug
regimes are not effective against both
strains of the disease.

The best, and only certain,
protection against malaria is not to
get bitten. Sleep under a mosquito
net impregnated with permethrin,
cover up in the evenings and use an
effective insect repellent such as DEET
(diethyltoluamide). Burning mosquito
coils, which are easily obtainable in
India, is also a good idea.

Skin problems

Prickly heat is a common complaint
caused by excessive perspiration. Try
to keep the skin dry by using talcum
powder and wearing loose-fitting
cotton clothes. Fungal infections
are also common, especially during
the monsoon, and can be treated by
exposure to the sun and/or by the
application of Canesten cream.

Sun exposure

The power of the sun is obvious on
the plains and in tropical India, but
also be careful in the mountains,
where thinner air makes the sun very
powerful, even if it feels cooler. Cover
up and use a high-factor sunscreen
and lip balm, even if it is cloudy.
Overexposure can also lead to the two
conditions below:
Heat exhaustion is common, and
indicated by shallow breathing, a

rapid pulse or pallor, and is often
accompanied by leg cramps,
headache or nausea. The body
temperature remains normal. Lying
down in a cool place and sipping
water mixed with rehydration salts
or plain table salt will prevent loss of
consciousness.
Heatstroke is more serious, and
more likely to occur when it is both
hot and humid. Babies and elderly
people are especially susceptible. The
body temperature soars suddenly and
the skin feels dry. The victim may feel
confused, then pass out.

Take them quickly to a cool room,
remove their clothes and cover them
with a wet sheet or towels soaked in
cold water. Call for medical help and
fan them constantly until their body
temperature drops to 38°C (100°F).

Vaccinations

No inoculations are legally required to
enter India, but it is strongly advised
that you get vaccinations against
typhoid (Typhim Vi gives protection
for 3 years), hepatitis A (Havrix gives
immunity for 1 year, or up to 10 years
if a 6-month booster is given), polio
(a booster is needed every 5 years)
and tetanus (booster injection every
10 years). You may need to show
proof of a yellow fever inoculation if
arriving from an infected area. Other
diseases, against which vaccinations
might be considered, particularly for
longer trips, include meningitis, rabies
and Japanese B encephalitis. There is
no vaccination against Dengue fever,
occasionally contracted in India. The
only protection is to avoid being bitten
(see also Malaria).

Bring along a personal medical
kit to take care of minor ailments.
This should include anti-diarrhoea
medication, a broad-spectrum
antibiotic, aspirin, clean needles, and
something for throat infections and
allergies would be a good idea. Take
your regular medications, tampons,
contraceptives and condoms, as
these may be difficult to find in shops.

Also include plasters, antiseptic
cream and water-purification tablets.
All cuts, however minor, should be
cleaned and sterilised immediately
to prevent infection. Locally available
oral rehydration powders (such as
Vijay Electrolyte) containing salts
and dextrose are an ideal additive
to water, especially when travelling
in the summer months or when
suffering from diarrhoea. If oral
rehydration salts are not available
then one teaspoon each of salt and
sugar in 500ml of water is a useful
substitute.

TRANSPORT

A – Z

LANGUAGE

I

Insurance

It is always advisable to obtain good travel insurance to cover the worst possible scenario, and make sure that your policy covers what you need (for instance, that it covers activities like trekking or whitewater rafting, if you're planning on doing these, or that it covers valuables such as expensive cameras or camcorders). Take a copy of your policy and keep a copy of the emergency medical numbers separately as a safeguard.

Internet

Internet access is widely available, either in guesthouses and hotels or in dedicated cybercafés – although away from the big cities connections can be slow and unreliable, with antiquated dial-up connections and frustrating service interruptions. Charges are usually around Rs50–60 per hour – or cheaper in larger cities.

M

Maps

Obtaining good maps of India can be difficult; the government forbids the sale of detailed maps in border areas, which includes the entire coastline, for security reasons; those which can be bought may not be exported.

Some good maps to bring along with you are: Bartholomew's 1:4,000,000 map of South Asia; Lascelles map of the same scale and Nelles Verlag maps. Other highly recommended maps are the Eicher series of detailed city maps, including those of Delhi, Chennai and Bengaluru, and their India Road Atlas.

Tourist offices can supply visitors with larger-scale city maps. The most detailed are held by the Survey of India, Janpath Barracks A, New Delhi 110 001.

Many of these maps are available from www.indiamapstore.com.

Google's map coverage of India is improving all the time, and provides the most accurate topographical reference tool, even if street labelling can be erratic. StreetView is still a distant dream. Attempts were made by Google India in 2012 to photograph go-ahead Bengaluru, but the initiative was stopped by the security-conscious government.

Media

An essential part of India's vibrant political and intellectual life, the press and broadcast media cover a wide political spectrum and have a long and honourable tradition of holding those in power to account. Star, Asia's biggest media company, provides news and entertainment channels.

Newspapers and magazines

The large number of English-language dailies and hundreds of newspapers in Indian languages provide a wide and critical coverage of national and international events.

Among the better-known national English-language dailies are the Times of India (www.timesofindia. indiatimes.com), the Indian Express (www.indianexpress.com), The Hindu (www.thehindu.com) and The Hindustan Times (www.hindustantimes. com). All dailies have Sunday editions. The main newspapers in Delhi are the Asian Age (www.asianage.com; good for political gossip) and The Pioneer (www.dailypioneer.com), for which both Churchill and Kipling used to write.

The top news magazines include India Today (www.indiatoday.intoday. in), Outlook (www.outlookindia.com) and the exemplary Frontline (www. frontlineonnet.com). There are also excellent general-interest magazines such as Sanctuary Asia (www. sanctuaryasia.com; specialising in South Asian natural history), and travel magazines like Outlook Traveller (www.outlooktraveller.com) and India Today Travel Plus, which give current information on local cultural events. Other useful news websites include www.samachar.com, with links to leading Indian newspapers, and the pioneering and irreverent www. tehelka.com, which has played a leading role in exposing government corruption scandals.

There are several glossy magazines in English, including Society (www.magnamags.com), many film magazines and city magazines such as Delhi Diary (www. delhidiary.in) and Time Out (www. timeout.com) with its 10 city online editions, including Delhi, Hyderabad, Chennai, Jaipur and Mumbai, plus women's magazines such as Femina (www.femina.in) and Verve (www. vervemagazine.in) and Indian editions of Cosmopolitan and Elle.

Television and radio stations

Doordarshan is the government TV company and broadcasts programmes in English, Hindi and regional languages. Satellite television is available almost everywhere – hotel TVs usually provide 40-plus channels. The main provider is Star TV (the Asian version of Sky), which incorporates the BBC World Service and MTV, as well as providing its own sports and movies channels. NDTV is a local 24hr news channel that provides good coverage of Indian news and politics. Other stations include Channel V (a local youth-oriented music channel) and the pop and youth culture-oriented Zee TV (in Hindi and other Indian languages).

All India Radio (AIR) broadcasts on the short wave, medium wave and, in Delhi, Mumbai and Chennai, on FM (VHF). The frequencies vary – you can check programmes online at http://all indiaradio.org.

Money Matters

The Indian currency is the rupee (subdivided into 100 paise). Coins come in denominations of 10, 20, 25 and 50 paise (although these are increasingly rare) and 1, 2 and 5 rupees. Notes come in 5, 10, 20, 50, 100, 500 and 1,000 rupees. Officially, it's illegal to import or export Indian rupees, although you're unlikely to be checked. Indian banknotes often become incredibly ragged with use. Don't accept torn banknotes, which can prove almost impossible to get rid of (even beggars look upon them with scorn, and giving ruined notes to alms-seekers can be construed as insulting). In addition, getting small change in India can be a real challenge. Break large-denomination notes wherever possible, and hoard small change.

The easiest way to access your money in India is via credit or debit card. Almost all towns now have at least one ATM which accepts foreign cards. Visa is the most widely accepted, followed by MasterCard and then American Express; Diners Club is less widely recognised. Credit cards are also increasingly accepted by hotels, restaurants, large shops, tourist emporia and airlines. A number of banks will issue rupees against Visa, MasterCard and (to a lesser extent) Amex. It's worth checking that your card will be valid in India, however. Credit-card fraud means that many banks now automatically block the use of their cards in foreign ATMs unless you call them and ask that they unblock your card for the duration of your visit.

Many tourists still opt to carry a small stock of traveller's cheques with them to guard against the loss of their credit card, or problems finding an ATM which will accept it. Stick to major brands such as American Express, Visa and Thomas Cook, preferably denominated in US dollars or pounds sterling.

N

Nightlife

Outside of the sometimes dubious pleasures of Goa, and the burgeoning prosperity of Mumbai, India is not famed for its nightlife. However, things are slowly changing in other large cities, too, as the young middle classes adopt more Western lifestyles. Many places are in the large, luxury hotels, all of which have strict admission policies. Bars are still largely a male preserve and lone women may find them intimidating. For up-to-date listings check out www. explocity.com.

O

Opening Hours

Government offices are officially open 9.30am–6pm Monday to Friday, but most business is done between 10am and 5pm with a long lunch break. Post offices open from 10am–4.30pm Monday to Friday, and until 12 noon on Saturday. However, in most of the larger cities, the Central Post Office is open until 6.30pm on weekdays, 4.30pm on Saturday. On Sunday some open until noon. Major telegraph offices are open 24hrs.

Banking hours are Monday to Friday 10am–2pm and Saturday 10am–noon for most foreign and nationalised Indian banks. Some operate evening branches, while others remain open on Sunday and close on another day of the week; some open 9am–1pm. In larger cities many banks now have 24hr ATMs, often guarded, which are very convenient and safe. All banks are closed on national holidays, on 30 June and 31 December for balancing the books.

Shops open from roughly 10am–7pm, some closing for lunch. Although Sunday is an official holiday, different localities in major cities have staggered days off so that there are always some shopping areas open.

Most businesses close on public holidays.

Outdoor Activities

Trekking

There's superb trekking throughout the Indian Himalayas and compared to neighbouring Nepal, routes are still pleasantly peaceful and un-touristed. The main starting points for treks are Leh, Darjeeling, Manali, Gangtok and Garhwal, and around Kinnaur in Himachal Pradesh, with a wide variety of routes. Possibilities include treks through the Singalili range near Darjeeling (taking in Kanchenjunga, the world's third-highest peak); between remote Buddhist monasteries and villages in the uplands around Leh; along the pilgrimage routes around Garhwal; or through Sikkim's high-altitude rhododendron forests.

There are also numerous trekking possibilities in the Western Ghats in southern India, particularly in the extensive highland forests of the Nilgiri Biosphere Reserve, which straddles the borders of Tamil Nadu, Kerala and Karnataka and offers many, still largely unexplored, hiking possibilities, including walks in or around the Bandipur, Nagarhole and Mudumalai wildlife sanctuaries. There are further trekking possibilities in Rajasthan, particularly up in the Aravalli Hills around Mount Abu.

Watersports

Diving

The best diving in India is far away from the mainland in India's two tropical archipelagos. There are superb coral reefs at the **Andaman Islands** (trips can be arranged from Port Blair) and at the tiny **Lakshadweep Islands**. Unfortunately, the cost of getting to either of these places (and the expense of staying at Lakshadweep) is something of a deterrent. On the mainland, **Goa** is the principal diving spot, with several operators now offering trips, although the limited underwater visibility is a drawback (operators have to ferry divers four hours south down the coast by boat to dive off Anjevid Island, where there's less silt in the water)

Whitewater rafting

A number of rivers in northern India offer challenging and spectacular whitewater rafting as they tumble down through the Himalayas. Some of the best places to go rafting are Kullu, Manali, Leh, Risikesh and Gangtok. The Indus River near Leh

offers a particularly scenic (although fairly staid) ride, and you can also go **kayaking** here. Rafting is best from around June to August, when water levels are at their highest.

P

Photography

Digital photography is well supported in India, and virtually every town now has at least one photo lab where you can download and burn images to disc, purchase memory cards and get help with technical troubleshooting.

Colour print film, developing and digital printing facilities are available in all cities. Colour slide film has fast become a rarity and labs capable of processing can only be found in major cities.

Protect your camera and film from excessive exposure to heat, dust and humidity, and note that there are strict restrictions on photography of military installations, bridges and dams, airports, border areas and Adivasi/restricted areas. In general, most Indians are delighted to have their picture taken, although it's still polite to ask permission (and, if using a digital camera, to show them the results afterwards). Note, too, that some people in more remote areas, women in particular, may be less enthusiastic about being snapped. Exercise caution and polite restraint.

Postal/Courier Services

The internal mail service is efficient in most areas. It is advisable to affix stamps to letters or postcards yourself and hand them over to the post office counter for immediate franking rather than to post them in a letter box, or to use one of the private courier services, which are generally efficient and amazing value.

Sending a registered parcel overseas is a complicated and time-consuming process. Most towns have only one main post office, but there is often confusion between Delhi and New Delhi. New Delhi's main post office is near Connaught Circus, while Delhi's main post office is between the Red Fort and Kashmir Gate in Old Delhi.

Courier services

An (expensive) alternative to regular post is to use a courier service. Both FedEx and DHL have offices in all major towns. An alternative to courier services is the government Speedpost service, which delivers parcels

TRANSPORT

A – Z

LANGUAGE

fractionally faster than airmail but at far cheaper rates than couriers.

Public Holidays

26 January: Republic Day.
15 August: Independence Day.
2 October: Mahatma Gandhi's Birthday.
25 December: Christmas Day.

R

Restricted/Protected Areas

Andaman and Nicobar Islands, and Lakshadweep

Some parts of all these island archipelagos are out of bounds to foreign tourists in order to protect indigenous inhabitants (Andamans and Nicobar) but other parts of the islands are available to foreign tourists, provided that they obtain a Restricted Area Permit at Port Blair, while a Protected Area Permit is required to visit some of Lakshadweep Islands.

Sikkim

Tourists need a Restricted Area Permit to visit parts of Sikkim (available at the border at Rangpo, or in advance from an Indian embassy). You'll need an additional Protected Area Permit (available from the Sikkim Tourism offices in Gangtok) to visit the entire state of Sikkim.

The northeast

Assam, Meghalaya and Tripura are currently free of restrictions. Permits are required to visit parts of Arunachal Pradesh, the entire state of Nagaland, parts of Mizoram and parts of Manipur. All visitors to these areas are officially required to travel in groups of at least four, although this rule is sometimes waived on payment of an additional fee. The best way of obtaining a permit is to book a tour through a local operator (see below). Alternatively, contact the Foreigners' Division of the Ministry of Home Affairs, Lok Nayak Bhavan, Khan Market, New Delhi, or the Foreigners' Regional Registration Office, A.J.C. Bose Road, Kolkata (apply four weeks in advance). You may also be able to obtain a permit through Indian embassies abroad, though apply at least two months in advance.

The north and northwest

Parts of the northern states of Jammu and Kashmir, Himachal Pradesh

and Uttarakhand and also parts of the northwestern state of Rajasthan require a Protected Area Permit to visit. The situation changes frequently so it's better to check before you travel to India with India's Ministry of Home Affairs at http://boi.gov.in/content/restricted-protected-area.

Local tour operators include Gurudongma Tours & Treks (www.astonishingindiatours.com), Jungle Travels India (www.jungletravelsindia.com), Purvi Discover (www.purviweb.com) and, for the south, Aadi Kerala (www.aadikerala.com).

S

Shopping

India can be a very rewarding place to shop – perhaps no other country on Earth produces such a dazzling array of handicrafts in such a huge variety of forms. **Textiles** are ubiquitous, from the traditional *khadi* (homespun cotton) garments championed by Gandhi through to brilliantly coloured mirrorwork Rajasthani fabrics and sumptuous Mysore and Varanasi silks. Clothes come in all shapes and sizes, from beautiful traditional saris (those from Kanchipuram in Tamil Nadu are particularly famous) and *shalwar kameez* through to contemporary designs using traditional fabrics, such as those sold by the excellent Anokhi, Soma and Fabindia chains.

Kashmir is the traditional centre of India's carpet industry (made in both wool and silk), producing world-class rugs – sometimes at world-class prices. Colourful **dhurries** (the Indian version of the *kilim*) are made in many parts of the country and are likely to make less of a dent in the wallet.

Gold, silver and jewellery can be found everywhere. Jaipur is famous for its gems (although not all are genuine – shop with caution), and is also good for silver, as are many other places in Rajasthan. Metalware is popular, too: brass and copper trays, plates, statues and enamel inlay-work, or the beautiful *bidri* designs made in Karnataka.

Carved sandalwood figures and elaborately worked wooden panels are a speciality of the south, while superb marble inlay-work *(pietra dura)* can be found in Agra. Pottery, lacquerware and cane goods are common, while leatherware is also often excellent, either made into bags or fashioned into traditional shoes, or *jutis*. Miniature paintings make particularly beautiful souvenirs,

ranging from Persian-style Rajasthani miniatures on paper or silk through to Tibetan *thangkas* (religious paintings).

There are thousands of shops selling all manner of handicrafts all over the country. Most states run their own chains of handicrafts shops, and these so-called **government emporia** are usually a good place to see what's on offer and get an idea of roughly how much things should cost – prices are fixed here, although generally a bit more expensive than elsewhere. Away from the government emporia, **bargaining** is the order of the day. Note that antiques and semi-antiques are governed by strict laws limiting their export; also beware of fakes. The export of skins, furs and ivory is strictly forbidden. Major **credit cards** such as Visa and MasterCard are widely accepted in shops, but don't let your card out of sight as credit-card fraud is common (multiple copies of card receipts are often made and then charged later on).

T

Telephones

India's telephone system is improving year on year, and international calls can now be dialled direct to all parts of the world. Calling from hotels can be extremely expensive, with surcharges up to 300 percent, so check rates first. Mobile telephones are everywhere in India, and your own phone may well work while you are there (though you should check in advance with your network provider). If not, you can buy local pre-paid SIM cards from most of the local mobile phone companies, who have shops on every high street. The set-up process involves filing forms with passport photos, but can be completed in around half an hour.

Privately run telephone services with international direct-dialling facilities are widespread. Advertising themselves with the acronyms STD/ISD (standard trunk dialling/international subscriber dialling), they are quick and easy to use. Some stay open 24hrs. Both national and international calls are dialled direct. To call abroad, dial the international

Dialling Codes

To call India from abroad, dial the international access code, followed by 91 for India, the local code less the initial zero, then the number.

Shopping in downtown Bengaluru.

tel: 011-325 0880
email: goito@global.co.za
UK
26-28 Hammersmith Grove, London,
W6 7BA
tel: 020-7437 3677
email: info@indiatourismlondon.org
US
3550 Wilshire Boulevard, Suite #204,
Los Angeles, CA 90010
tel: 213-380 8855
email: la.indiatourism@gmail.com;
1270 Avenue of the Americas, Suite
#303, New York, NY 10020
tel: 212- 586 4901
email: m.vashist@nic.in.

access code (00), the code for the country you want (44 for the UK, 1 for the US or Canada), the area code (without any initial zeros) and the number. Some booths have an electronic screen that keeps time and calculates cost during the call. Prices are similar to those at official telecommunications centres.

Indian telephone numbers are all 10 digits long (including the area code minus the initial zero). Mobile phone numbers also consist of 10 digits, starting with a '9'.

Home country direct services are available from any telephone to the UK, US, Canada, Australia, New Zealand and most other countries. These allow you to make a reverse-charges or telephone credit-card call to that country via the operator there. If you cannot find a telephone with home country direct buttons, you can use any phone toll-free by dialling 000, your country code and 17 (except Canada, which is 000-167). US international access codes are: MCI 000 126 and 000 127; Sprint 000 137; and AT&T 000 117.

Time Zone

India is 5.5 hours ahead of Greenwich Mean Time; 10.5 hours ahead of Eastern Seaboard Time.

Tipping

There's no harm in expressing your appreciation with a small tip, although be aware that many upmarket hotels and restaurants automatically add a 10 percent service charge to their bills, so there's no need to tip further (unless you particularly want to). If service isn't included, a tip of around 10 percent is generally a good rule of thumb.

Porters at railway stations expect around Rs20 a bag. Rickshaw and taxi drivers won't expect to be tipped, although of course they'll appreciate

it if you do – or just letting them keep the change, assuming it's not too much, does equally well. If you have been a house guest, check with your host whether you may tip his domestic helpers (for instance, the driver or cook) before doing so.

Toilets

Traditional Indian 'squat' toilets are becoming increasingly rare, with Western-style sit-down toilets now the norm. It's still a good idea to carry your own supply of toilet paper, however. Public toilets (in Hindi, *sulabh*), are few and far between, and are almost always stomach-churningly horrible. If you get caught short it's best to head for the nearest reputable hotel.

Tourist Information

The Ministry of Tourism has a good website (www.incredibleindia.org), with a lot of useful information on obtaining visas, places to visit and tour operators. One excellent general site is www.indiamike.com, a popular travel forum run by US India-phile Mike Szewczyk, with lively chat rooms and a useful number of members' travel articles.

Indian government tourist offices abroad

Australia
Shop 35, Level 1, Stockland Piccadilly, 133 Castlereagh Street, Sydney, New South Wales 2000
Tel: 61-2-92672466,
E-mail info@indiatourism.com.au.
Canada
60 Bloor Street (West), #1003, Toronto, Ontario M4W 3B8
tel: 416-962-3787
email: info@indiatourismcanada.ca.
South Africa
PO Box 412 542, Craighall 2024, Hyde Lane, Lancaster Gate, Johannesburg 2000

State tourism websites

Andaman and Nicobar Islands
www.andamans.gov.in
Andhra Pradesh www.aptdc.gov.in
Arunachal Pradesh www.arunachal
tourism.com
Assam www.assamtourism.gov.in
Delhi www.delhitourism.gov.in
Goa www.goatourism.gov.in
Gujarat www.gujarattourism.com
Haryana www.haryanatourism.gov.in
Himachal Pradesh www.hptdc.nic.in
Karnataka www.karnatakatourism.org
Kerala www.keralatourism.org
Lakshadweep www.lakshadweep
tourism.com
Madhya Pradesh www.mptourism.
com
Maharashtra www.maharashtra
tourism.gov.in
Odisha (Orissa) www.orissatourism.
gov.in
Rajasthan www.rajasthantourism.
gov.in
Sikkim www.sikkimtourism.travel
Tamil Nadu www.tamilnadutourism.
org
Telangana www.telanganatourism.
gov.in
Uttaranchal www.uttarakhandtourism.
gov.in
Uttar Pradesh www.uptourism.gov.in
West Bengal www.wbtourism.gov.in

Local tourist offices

Below is a list of government tourist offices in the major cities:
Agra 191 The Mall Tel: 0562-222 6378
Aurangabad Tourist Reception Centre, (1st Floor) MTDC Holiday Resort, Near Goldie Cinema, Station Road Tel: 0240-233 1217
Bengaluru KFC Building, 48 Church Street Tel: 080-2558 5417
Bhubaneshwar Paryatan Bhawan, Lewis Road Tel: 0674-243 2203
Chennai 154 Anna Salai Tel: 044-2846 1459
Delhi 88 Janpath Tel: 011-2332 0342

TRANSPORT

A – Z

LANGUAGE

Hyderabad/Secunderabad Ground Floor, Balayogi Paryatak bhavan No 6-3-870, Green Lands, Begumpet Tel: 040-2340 9199
Jaipur State Hotel, Khasa Kothi Tel: 0141-237 2200
Kochi/Ernakulam Willingdon Island, Kochi Tel: 0484-266 9125
Kolkata 4 Shakespeare Sarani Tel: 033-2282 1475
Mumbai 123 Maharishi Karve Marg, opposite Churchgate Tel: 022-2203 3144
Domestic Airport Tel: 022-2615 6920
International Airport Tel: 022-2832 5331
Varanasi 15B The Mall
Tel: 0542-250 1784

V

Visas and Passports

All visitors (apart from citizens of Nepal, Bhutan and Maldives) require a visa to enter India and need to obtain it in advance. Tourist visas are issued for six months from the date of issue (not entry). Note that anyone leaving India on a tourist visa will not be allowed to re-enter within two months, although exceptions are made in certain cases – these need to be arranged in advance. India has recently simplified the visa application process and the e-Tourist Visa Facility (eTV) is now available to nationals of 113 countries. To get a visa you'll need to apply online (https://indianvisaonline.gov.in/visa), pay for your visa with a credit or debit card and after your application is processed (usually three to four days), you will receive your eTV by e-mail. Print it and carry with you when you arrive at one of 16 airports in India, including Delhi, Mumbai, Kolkata, Hyderabad and Goa.

Tourist visas cannot be extended; you must leave the country and

The phone system has improved.

re-enter on a new one two months later. It may be difficult to apply for a new visa from neighbouring countries. Five-year visas are also issued to businessmen and students. In addition to visas, special permits are required for certain areas, while other areas are out of bounds to foreigners altogether.

If you stay for more than 180 days, you must get a tax-clearance certificate before leaving the country. These can be obtained from the foreigner's section of the income tax department in every city. Tax-clearance certificates are free, but take bank receipts to demonstrate that you have changed money legally.

W

Water

Tap water, especially in larger cities, is generally chlorinated and (in theory, at least) safe to drink, although it's best to stick to bottled or filtered water, since the unfamiliar micro-organisms in tap water can precipitate mild stomach upsets.

What to Bring

Clothing

Travelling in southern India, or the North during summer, it is best to wear cotton. Avoid synthetics. In the North during winter, sweaters and jackets are required. Cotton shirts, blouses and skirts are inexpensive and easily available throughout the country. Remember to bring swimwear.

In winter a sweater – preferably two, one light and one heavy – as well as a jacket or an anorak are necessary, especially in the North, where daily temperature differentials

Weights and Measures

The metric system is used everywhere. Precious metals, especially gold, are often sold by the traditional tola, which is equivalent to 11.5 grams. Gems are weighed in carats (0.2 grams).

Two characteristically Indian expressions which you'll probably come across are *lakh* (100,000) and *crore* (100 *lakh* or 10 million).

can be quite wide. Lighter clothing would be adequate in the South and along the coast. Comfortable footwear, trainers for winter and sandals for summer, is essential. 'Trekking' sandals are excellent for wearing in India as they are tough and provide good protection to your feet. Teva and Reef are good brands to look out for.

For your own convenience, women should not wear sleeveless blouses, miniskirts and short, revealing dresses. Cover up – it's a good idea in the Indian sun anyway – locally available *shalwar kamiz* (also known as *churidar*), a long tunic top worn over loose trousers, are ideal.

Other Essentials

If travelling away from the major cities or big hotels, take a sheet sleeping bag, pillowcases and medical kit among other items. Sun block (vital in the mountains) are not readily available, so they should be brought with you, along with cosmetics and tampons. A hat or scarf to cover your head is a sensible item. A mosquito net and a basin/bath plug are also useful in smaller hotels, which often do not have them.

Women Travellers

'Eve-teasing' is the Indian euphemism for sexual harassment. Take the normal precautions, especially on crowded local public transport (crowds are a haven for gropers). Do not wear clothes that expose legs, arms and cleavage; *shalwar kamiz* are ideal, and a shawl is handy to use as a cover-all when required. Despite a justified uptick in media coverage of more serious sexual assaults, these are still rare on tourists, but if something should happen, call for help from passers-by. On the up-side, there are 'ladies-only' queues at train and bus stations, and 'ladies-only' waiting rooms at stations and compartments on trains.

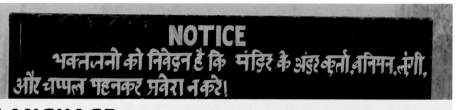

LANGUAGE

UNDERSTANDING THE LANGUAGE

With 18 official languages, hundreds of others and countless dialects, India can present a linguistic minefield. Luckily for the traveller, English is often understood, and it is usually possible to get by in all but remote, rural locations. However, attempts to speak the local language are always appreciated. The language most widely spoken in the North is Hindi, while in the South, Tamil is spoken in Tamil Nadu, Malayali in Kerala, Kanad in Karnataka and Marathi in Maharashtra.

Attempts to speak the local language are, however, always appreciated. The language most widely spoken in the North is Hindi, while in the South, Tamil has the highest profile.

Indian languages are phonetically regular, based on syllables rather than an alphabet. Important differences are made between long and short vowels, and reteroflex, palatal and labial consonants – listen hard to get a feel for the vocabulary below. There are various systems of transliteration, and you may see many of the words below spelt different ways in English. Where a consonant is followed by 'h' this is an aspirated sound, 'c' is usually pronounced 'ch' (followed by 'h', 'chh'), and 'zh' in Tamil stands for a sound somewhere between a reteroflex 'l' and 'r'.

TRAVELLER'S HINDI

Basics

Hello/goodbye *Namaste*
Yes *Ji ha*
No *Ji nehi*

Perhaps *Shayad*
Thank you *Dhanyavad/shukriya*
How are you? *Ap kaise hai?/Ap thik hai?*
I am well *Me thik hu/thik hai*
What is your name? *Apka nam kya hai?*
My name is (John/Jane) *Mera nam (John/Jane) hai*
Where do you come from? *Ap kahan se aye?*
From (England) *(England) se*
How much (money)? *Kitna paise hai?*
That is expensive *Bahut mahenga hai*
Cheap *Sasta*
I like (tea) *Mujhe (chai) pasand hai*
Is it possible? *Kya ye sambhav hai?*
I don't understand *Mujhe samajh nehi*
I don't know *Mujhe malum nehi*
Money *Paisa*
Newspaper *Akhbar*
Sheet *Chadar*
Blanket *Kambal*
Bed *Palang*
Room *Kamra*
Clothes *Kapre*
Cloth *Kapra*
Market *Bajar*

Pronouns

I am *Mai hun*
You are *Ap hain*
He/she/it is *Voh hai*
They are *Ve hain*

Verbs

To drink *Pina*
To eat *Khanna*
To do/make *Karna*
To buy *Kharidna*
To sleep *Sona*
To see *Dekhna*
To hear/listen to *Sunna*

To wash (clothes) *Dhona*
To wash (yourself) *Nahana*
To get *Milna or pana*

Prepositions, adverbs and adjectives

Now *Ab*
Right now *Abhi*
Quickly *Jaldi*
Slowly *Dirhe se*
A bit *Bahut*
A little *Tora*
Here *Yaha/idhar*
There *Vaha/udhar*
Open *Khola*
Closed *Bund*
Finished *Khatam hai*
Big/older *Bara*
Small/younger *Chota*
Beautiful *Sundar*
Old *Purana*
New *Naya*

Knowing a smattering of the local language will enrich your experience.

Questions

What is? *Kya hai?*
Where is? *Kahan hai?*
Why? *Kyun?*
Who is? *Kaun hai?*
When is? *Kab hai?*
How? *Kaisa?*
Most straightforward sentences can easily be turned into a question by putting *'kya'* on the front and raising the pitch of the voice at the end of the sentence, eg *'Dhobi hai'*, 'There is a washerman', *'Kya dhobi hai?'*, 'Is there a washerman?'

Days of the week

Monday *Somvar*
Tuesday *Mangalvar*
Wednesday *Budhvar*
Thursday *Guruvar*
Friday *Shukravar*
Saturday *Shanivar*
Sunday *Itvar*
Today *Aj*
Yesterday/tomorrow *kal*
Week *Hafta*

Months

January *Janvari*
February *Farvari*
March *March*
April *Aprail*
May *Mai*
June *Jun*
July *Julai*
August *Agast*
September *Sitambar*
October *Aktubar*

Newspapers in a variety of languages.

November *Navambar*
December *Disambar*
Month *Mahina*
Year *Sal*

Relatives

Mother *Mata-ji*
Father *Pita-ji*
Sister *Behen*
Brother *Bhai*
Husband *Pati*
Wife *Patni*
Maternal grandmother *Nani*
Maternal grandfather *Nana*
Paternal grandmother *Dadi*
Paternal grandfather *Dada*
Elder sister (term of respect) *Didi*
Daughter *Beti*
Son *Beta*
Girl *Larki*
Boy *Larka*
Are you married? *Kya ap shadishuda hai?*
Are you alone (male/female)? *Kya ap akela/akeli?*
How many children have you got? *Apke kitne bache hai?*
How many brothers and sisters have you got? *Apke kitne bhai behen hai?*

Health

Doctor *Daktar*
Hospital *Aspatal*
Dentist *Dentist*
Pain *Dard*
I am ill *Main bimar hun*
I have been vomiting *Mujhe ulti ho rahi thi*

I have a temperature *Mujhe bukhar hai*
I have a headache *Mere sir men dard hai*
I have a stomach ache *Mere pat men dard hai*
I have diarrhoea *Mujhe dast ar raha hai*
The English word 'motions' is a common expression for diarrhoea.

Travel

Where is (Delhi)? *(Dilli) kahan hai?*
Bus station *Bus adda*
Railway station *Tren stashan/ railgari*
Airport *Hawai adda*
Car *Gari*
How far is it? *Kitni dur hai?*
In front of/opposite (the Taj Mahal) *(Taj Mahal) ke samne*
Near *Ke nazdik/ke pas*
Far *Dur*
Ticket *Tikat*
Stop *Rukh jaiye*
Let's go *Chele jao*
I have to go *Mujhe jana hai*
Come *Ayie*
Go *Jayie*

Food

I want (a thali) *Mujhe (thali) chahiye*
Without chilli *Mirch ke bina*
Little chilli *Kam mirch*
Hot *Garam*
Cold *Thanda*
Ripe/cooked *Pukka*
Unripe/raw *Kachcha*

Basics

Mirch Chilli
Namak Salt
Ghee Clarified butter
Dahi Yoghurt
Raita Yoghurt with cucumber
Chaval Rice
Panir Cheese
Pani Water
Dudh Milk
Lassi Yoghurt drink
Nimbu pani Lime water
Tandur Oven
Pilao Rice cooked with *ghee* and spices
Biriyani Rice cooked with vegetables or meat
Mithai Sweets

Breads (Roti)

Puri Deep-fried and puffed-up wheat bread
Chapatti Unleavened flat bread
Nan Leavened flat bread
Tandoori roti Similar to *nan*
Paratha Chapatti cooked with *ghee*

Vegetables (Sabzi)

Palak Spinach
Aloo Potato
Gobi Cauliflower
Bindi Okra
Pyaz Onion
Matter Peas
Tamata Tomato
Baingain/brinjal Aubergine
Dal Dried pulses

Meat

Gosht Lamb
Murg Chicken
Machli Fish

Fruit

Kela Banana
Santra Orange
Aum Mango

TRAVELLER'S TAMIL

Basics

Hello Vanakkam
Goodbye Poyvituvarukiren
(Reply Poyvituvarungal)
Yes Amam
No Illai
Perhaps Oruvelai
Thank you Nandri
How are you? Celakkiyama?
What is your name? Ungal peyar yenna?
My name is (John/Jane) Yen peyar (John/Jane)
Where is the (hotel)? (Hotel) yenge?
What is this/that? Idu/Adu yenna?
What is the price? Yenna vilai?
That is very expensive Anda vilai mikavum adikum
I want (coffee) (Kapi) Vendum
I like (dosa) (Dosai) Pudikkum
Is it possible? Mudiyuma?
I don't understand Puriyadu
Enough Podum
Toilet Tailet
Bed Kattil
Room Arai
Train Rayil
Sari Pudavai
Dhoti Vesti
Towel Tundu
Sandals Ceruppu
Money Punam
Temple Kovil

Verbs

To come (imperative) Varungal
To go (imperative) Pongal
To stop (imperative) Nillungal
To sleep Tungu
To eat Sappidu
To drink Kudi
To buy Vangu

Hindi Numbers

1 ek	**30** tis
2 do	**40** chalis
3 tin	**50** pachas
4 char	**60** sath
5 panch	**70** setur
6 che	**80** assi
7 sat	**90** nabbe
8 arth	**100** sau
9 nau	**1,000** hazar
10 das	**100,000** lakh
20 bis	**10,000,000** kror

To pay (money) Punam kodu
To see Par
To wash (clothes) Tuvai
To wash (yourself) Kazhavu

Prepositions, adverbs and adjectives

Quickly Sikkirum
Slowly Meduvaka
A lot Mikavum
A little Koncam
Here Inge
There Ange
This Idu
That Adu
Now Ippodu
Same Ade
Good Nalla
Bad Ketta
Hot Karam
Cold Kulirana
Dirty Acattam
Clean Cattam
Beautiful Azhakana
Sweet Inippu
Big Periya
Small Cinna
Old Pazhaiya
New Pudiya

Days of the week

Monday Tingal
Tuesday Cevvay
Wednesday Putam
Thursday Viyazhan
Friday Velli
Saturday Ceni
Sunday Nayiri
Today Inraikku
Week Varam
Month Matam
Year Varutam

Questions and 'and'

How? Yeppadi?
What? Yenna?
Who? Yar?
Why? Yen?
Where? Yenge?
When? Yeppodu?

How much? Yettanai/Yevvalavu?
Questions in Tamil are usually formed by adding a long 'a' to the last word of a sentence (usually the verb), eg 'Ningal venduma?' 'What do you want?'. 'And' is formed by adding 'um' to the end of the nouns (with an extra 'y' if the noun ends in a vowel), eg 'Kapiyum, dosaiyum', 'Coffee and dosa'.

Pronouns and relatives

I Nan
You Ningal
He/she/it Avan/Aval/Avar
We (including addressee)/ (excluding addressee) Nam/Nangal
They Avakal
Man Manidan
Woman/girl/daughter Pen
Boy/son Paiyan
Children Pillaikal
Baby Pappu
Mother Amma
Father Appa
Husband Kanavan
Wife Manaivi

Health

I am sick (vomiting) Utampu cariyillai irukkiradu
I have a pain Vali irukkiradu
I have diarrhoea 'Motions' irrukkiradu
Doctor Taktar
Help! Utavi cey!

Food (Sappadu)

Tunnir Water
Sadum Rice
Puzham Fruit
Kaykuri Vegetables
Pal Milk
Mor Buttermilk
Minakay (iilamal) (without) chilli
Tengay Coconut
Mampazham Mango
Valaippazham Banana
Kapi Coffee
Ti Tea

TRANSPORT

A – Z

LANGUAGE

Iddli Steamed rice cakes
Dosai Pancake made from fermented dough
Vadai Deep fried snack made of *dal*
Rasam Thin, spicy soup, usually with a tamarind base
Sampar Thick soup made from *dal*
Poriyal Dry vegetable curry
Kolikarri Chicken curry
Attukkari Lamb curry
Mils 'Meals', similar to a North Indian *thali*, traditionally served on a banana leaf
Payasam Sweet milk-based dish served at festivals

GLOSSARY OF COMMON TERMS

Acha OK, good, I understand, really?
Ahimsa Non-violence
Air cooler Fan that blows air through wet straw or similar
Angrez Foreigner
Ashram Spiritual retreat or community
Auto (rickshaw) Three-wheeled, scooter-engine conveyance, tuk tuk
Avatar Traditionally an incarnation of a god, but now used more broadly
Bagh Garden
Bandar Monkey
Bandh General strike
Banian T-shirt or vest
Baori Step well, meaning a well accessed by an elaborate series of stairways
Bhang Dried marijuana, sometimes added to lassi
Bhangra Punjabi dance music
Bharat India
Bidi Small, leaf-rolled cigarette
Bindi Red dot worn on forehead
Brahmin Highest Hindu caste of priests
Burqha All-concealing dress worn by Muslim women
Basti Slum
Cantonment Military area of town
Caste Hindu equivalent of class system, based on occupation
Chalo Let's go
Charbagh Traditional Persian-style garden, divided into four quarters
Charpoi Traditional bed, made of rope woven across wooden frame
Choli Sari blouse
Chowk Junction
Chokidar Guard/caretaker
Coolie Porter
Crore 10 million
Dacoit Bandit
Dalit Lowest Hindu caste, previously known as 'untouchables'
Dhaba Basic restaurant, often at side of the road
Dharamsala Basic accommodation for pilgrims
Dhobi Clothes washer

Dhobi Ghat Area where clothes are washed, often next to a lake or river
Dhoti Long skirt worn by men, pulled up between legs and tucked in
Dhurrie Cotton, flat woven carpet
Diwan-i-Am Public audience hall
Diwan-i-khas Private audience hall
Dowry money or goods traditionally given to groom's family by bride's parents during wedding
Durgah Shrine of Muslim saint
Eve teasing Sexually harassing women
Fakir Muslim ascetic
Ganesh Elephant-headed god of good fortune
Ganj Market
Gaon Village
Garh Fort
Gari Vehicle, normally car but also bike, train, etc
Geyser Water heater
Ghat Either steps leading down to a lake or river or a range of hills
Ghazal Urdu devotional/love song
Godown Warehouse
Gompa Tibetan monastery
Gulli Alley
Gurudwara Sikh temple
Hanuman Monkey god
Hati Elephant
Haveli Elaborate old walled mansion
Hijra Eunuch
Hindola Swing
Imam Muslim leader
Imambara Shiite tomb
Jali Ornately carved screen
Jhuggi Slum
Kabaddi Traditional sport, a bit like tag
Kameez Long shirt worn by women
Khadi Homespun cloth
Khalsa Sikh brotherhood
Khol Black eyeliner, often used on baby boys to ward off evil spirits
Kurta Long shirt worn by men
Lakh 100,000
Lok People
Lungi Skirt/sarong worn by men, particularly in South India
Mahabharata Epic Hindu poem of mythology
Mahal Room or palace
Mahout Elephant trainer
Maidan Open square in city
Mali Gardener
Mandala Circular painting particularly popular in Buddhism
Mandi Market
Mandir Temple
Marg Street or road
Masjid Mosque
Mehndi Henna, often used to paint intricate designs on ladies' hands and feet, particularly for weddings
Mela Festival
Memsahib Madam
Nadi River
Namaskar/Namaste Traditional greeting

Tamil Numbers

1 *onru*
2 *irandu*
3 *munru*
4 *nanku*
5 *aindu*
6 *aru*
7 *yezhu*
8 *yettu*
9 *onpadu*
10 *pattu*
11 *patinonru*
12 *pannirandu*
20 *irupadu*
30 *muppadu*
40 *rarpadu*
50 *aimpadu*
60 *arupadu*
70 *alupadu*
80 *yenpadu*
90 *tonnuru*
100 *nuru*
100,000 *latcam*
10,000,000 *kodi*

Namaz Muslim prayers
Namkeen Crunchy savoury snacks (often dubbed 'Bombay Mix' in the West).
Nilgai Blue bull, a type of antelope
NRI Non-Resident Indian
Nullah Small stream
Paise Penny, but more commonly used to mean money in general
Panchayat Village council
Pandit Priest or expert
Peon Office drudge
Prasad Sacred food which has been offered to and blessed by a deity in a Hindu temple
Puja Ritual in which offering is made as act of devotion
Qawwali Sufi singing
Qila Fort
Ramadan/Ramzan Annual Muslim month of daytime fasting
Sadhu Hindu ascetic
Sahib Sir
Salwar Kameez Shirt and trouser combo worn by women
Sambhar deer
Sati Traditional act of a wife setting fire to herself at her husband's funeral
Scheduled Castes Official term for members of Dalit castes
Singh Literally 'lion', common surname amongst Sikhs and Rajputs
Stupa Buddhist monument
Sufi Muslim mystic
Tabla Twin drums
Tal Lake
Wallah 'Man', used as suffix to denote occupation, eg chai wallah, dhobi wallah, etc
Yatra Pilgrimage

FURTHER READING

HISTORY

The Discovery of India, by
Jawaharlal Nehru. Revealing history
by India's first prime minister, which
tells as much about the author as
its subject.
Freedom at Midnight, by Larry Collins
and Dominique Lapierre. Gripping
popular history of the birth of the
Indian nation.
A History of India, Volume I, by
Romila Thapar. New edition of this
highly acclaimed history. Volume 1
traces the history of South Asia from
ancient times through to the Delhi
Sultanate. Volume II, by Perceval
Spear, continues from the Mughals
to the assassination of M.K. Gandhi.
India: a History, by John Keay. A one-
volume history by a well-respected
writer. Also by Keay is the brilliant
India Discovered, telling the story of
how British scholars and adventurers
helped India rediscover its ancient
past.
The Last Mughal, by William
Dalrymple. Ground-breaking
revisionist history of the 1857
Uprising in Delhi and its bloody
aftermath, drawing on hitherto
forgotten records in Urdu.
***Liberty or Death: India's Journey
to Independence and Division***, by
Patrick French. Readable and well-
researched account of the freedom
struggle and Partition.
***The Nehrus and the Gandhis:
an Indian Dynasty***, by Tariq Ali. A
gripping account of India's famous
political family. Now out of print,
but second-hand copies can still be
found.
***Tea: Addiction, Exploitation
and Empire***, by Roy Moxham. A
fascinating history of the skulduggery
and economics behind one of India's
most valuable crops.
They Fight like Devils, by D.A.
Kinsley. Stories from Lucknow during
the Great Uprising in 1857.
***Traders and Nabobs: the British
in Cawnpore 1765–1857***, by Zoe
Yalland. Fascinating account of the
early days of the Raj until the Uprising,
focussing on the city of Kanpur.

Travels of Ibn Batuta, by Ibn Batuta
and Tim Mackintosh-Smith. The story
of a 14th-century adventurer.
White Mughals, by William
Dalrymple. This page-turning account
of the controversial marriage between
a high-ranking British official and
a teenage Hyderabdi princess in
18th-century frames a sympathetic
account of the early British Raj.
Wicked Women of the Raj, by Coralie
Younger. Stories about the women
who married Indian Rajas.
The Wonder That Was India, by A.L.
Basham. Learned historical classic in
idiosyncratic, rapturous prose.

SOCIETY, CULTURE AND RELIGION

The Argumentative Indian, by
Amartya Sen. Reflections on culture,
history and identity by India's Nobel
Prize-winner.
A Book of India, by B.N. Pandey.
A real *masala* mix of philosophies,
travellers' notes, poetry and literary
trivia, revealing a quixotic India.
Changing Village, Changing Life,
by Prafulla Mohanti. Wry account of
village life in Orissa (Odisha).
Everybody Loves a Good Drought,
by P. Sainath. Stories from India's
poorest district, by an award-winning
investigative reporter who looks at the
human face of poverty.
Gods, Demons and Others, by R.K.
Narayan. Retellings of some of India's
most popular religious myths by one
of the country's greatest writers.
Also worth looking out for are his
retellings of ***The Ramayana***, based on
the Tamil Kamban version, and ***The
Mahabharata***.
India: A Literary Companion, by
Bruce Palling. Another compilation
of impressions taken from literature,
letters and unpublished diaries,
skilfully presented.
***Indira: the Life of Indira Nehru
Gandhi***, by Katherine Frank.
An in-depth biography of one of
post-Independence India's most
charismatic leaders.
In Spite of the Gods, by Edward Luce.
Definitive but accessible account of

the economic rise, against all the
odds, of modern India.
An Introduction to Hinduism,
by Gavin Flood. Perhaps the
best general introduction to the
complexities of this diverse religion.
I Phoolan Devi, by Phoolan Devi
with Marie-Thérèse Cuny and Paul
Rambi. The autobiography of an
illiterate low-caste woman who
fought convention, led a gang of
bandits and surrendered to the
Indian government after years on
the run. When freed from prison,
she went on to win a parliamentary
seat. A controversial insight into
caste politics.
India, by Patrick French. Wide-ranging
portrait of modern-day India, and how
it came to be the country it is.
Maximum City, by Suketu Meta.
A compelling anatomy of Mumbai
depicted through a series of life
stories of hitmen, dancing girls, cops,
movie stars, poets, beggars and
politicians.
***May You Be the Mother of a
Hundred Sons***, by Elisabeth
Bumiller. Women's issues tackled
head-on: everything from dowries to
infanticide, with dozens of poignant
interviews. Though its statistics may
be somewhat out of date, the issues
still hold as true as ever.
A Million Mutinies Now, by V.S.
Naipul. The misanthropic scholar
returns to seek his roots and finds a
cast of characters not easily pigeon-
holed. A more positive follow-up to his
earlier, jaundiced, ***India: A Wounded
Civilisation***.
Plain Tales from the Raj, ed. Charles
Allen. First-hand accounts from
ex-colonialists.
***South Asia: the Indian Subcontinent
(The Garland Encyclopedia of
World Music)***, ed. Alison Arnold.
The ultimate reference work on the
performance traditions of South Asia,
written by leading academics.
***Temptations of the West, or How to
be Modern in India, Pakistan and
Beyond***, by Pankaj Mishra. Insightful
travelogue by the author of *Butter
Chicken in Ludhiana*.
**Unbound: 2,000 Years of Indian
Women's Writing**, ed. Annie Zaidi.

Anthology of texts produced by Indian women over the last 2,000 years.

FICTION

Calcutta Chromosome, by Amitav Ghosh. A scientific thriller set in India, New York and Egypt.
Clear Light of Day, by Anita Desai. The difficulties of post-Partition India seen through the eyes of a Hindu family living in Old Delhi.
Delhi, A Novel, by Kushwant Singh. A bawdy saga that takes us through 600 years of temptresses and traitors to unravel the Indian capital's mystique. Narrated in turns by a eunuch, an irreverent wag, potentates and poets. Superb. (It took this popular author 20 years to write.)
The English Teacher, by R.K. Narayan. Narayan depicts infuriating and endearing characters which inhabit Malgudi, a composite South Indian village. Also, in various editions, **Malgudi Days**, a series of short stories.
A Fine Balance, by Rohinton Mistry. Beautifully written, sad story of two tailors who move from their village to the city.
The Gift of a Cow, by Premchand. The great Hindi novelist's tragic classic about the hardships endured by a North Indian peasant.
The God of Small Things, by Arundhati Roy. The Kerala backwaters are evoked in a hauntingly personal novel set in a small village pickle factory in the 1960s. **Hungry Tide**, by Amitav Ghosh. An atmospheric novel set in the Sunderbans swamps.
In Custody, by Anita Desai. The last days of an Urdu poet, made into a beautiful Merchant-Ivory film.
Kanthapura, by Raja Rao. A lyrical novel about a village in Karnataka which implements Gandhi's methods of non-violent resistance to British rule.
Kim, by Rudyard Kipling. The wonderful adventures of a boy who wanders across North India in search of the Great Game.
Midnight's Children, by Salman Rushdie. Rushdie burst onto the literary scene with this dazzling novel of post-Independence India.
The Moor's Last Sigh, on Mumbai, is another tour de force set in India's south.
A New World, by Amit Chaudhuri. Naturalistic contemporary tale of divorced Indian man, resident in America, who takes his young son

back to his parents in Kolkata for the holidays.
A Passage to India, by E.M. Forster. The classic novel of the misunderstandings that arose out of the East–West encounter. After a mysterious incident in a cave Dr Aziz is accused of assaulting a naive young Englishwoman, Adela Quested. The trial exposes the racism inherent in British colonialism.
Pather Panchali, by Bibhutibhushan Banerji. Outstanding Indian novel which outdoes the film by Satyajit Ray, depicting richness of spirit amid poverty in Bengal.
The Raj Quartet, by Paul Scott. Four novels – **The Jewel in the Crown, The Day of the Scorpion, The Towers of Silence** and **A Division of Spoils** – set during the last days of the British Raj and charting its decline and fall.
A River Sutra, by Gita Mehta. Gently wrought stories which linger in the imagination.
The Romantics, by Pankaj Mishra. East meets West in Banaras.
Samskara, by U.R. Anantha Murthy. A tale of a South Indian Brahman village in Karnataka, where one Brahman is forced to question his values. Beautifully translated by A.K. Ramanujan.

Send Us Your Thoughts

We do our best to ensure the information in our books is as accurate and up-to-date as possible. The books are updated on a regular basis using local contacts, who painstakingly add, amend and correct as required. However, some details (such as telephone numbers and opening times) are liable to change, and we are ultimately reliant on our readers to put us in the picture.

We welcome your feedback, especially your experience of using the book "on the road". Maybe we recommended a hotel that you liked (or another that you didn't), or you came across a great bar or new attraction we missed.

We will acknowledge all contributions, and we'll offer an Insight Guide to the best letters received.

Please write to us at:
Insight Guides
PO Box 7910
London SE1 1WE
Or email us at:
hello@insightguides.com

The Scent of Pepper, by Kavery Nambisan. This beautifully written family saga is set in South India.
Shantaram, by Gregory David Roberts. Epic tale of Mumbai slums and underworld, as well as rural Indian life – a real page-turner.
A Suitable Boy, by Vikram Seth. A huge and multifaceted novel set during the run-up to Independent India's first elections, which centres around a mother's search for a suitable husband for her daughter. Highly recommended.
Train to Pakistan, by Kushwant Singh. This is a gripping story of the excesses of Partition, penned when scars of the divided Subcontinent were still fresh.
2 States, by Chetan Bhagat. Humorous take on the difficulties of inter-community marriages in modern-day India, by India's most successful English-language novelist ever.
Untouchable, by Mulk Raj Anand. Grinding tale of poverty and discrimination.
The White Tiger, by Aravind Adiga. Insightful account of the workings of modern India, as told in a series of letters to the Chinese premier. Winner of the 2008 Man Booker Prize.
Women Writing in India: 600 BC to the Present, ed. Susie Tharu and K. Lalitha. Wonderful and eclectic anthology bringing to light the neglected history of Indian women. Volume 1 includes writings from 600 BC to the early 20th century; volume 2 concentrates on the 20th century alone.
Yaarana: Gay Writing from India, ed. Hoshang Merchant, and, **Facing the Mirror: Lesbian Writing from India**, ed. Ashwini Sukthankar. Anthologies of short stories, extracts from novels and poetry from gay and lesbian Indian writers.

TRAVEL

Butter Chicken in Ludhiana: Travels in Small Town India, by Pankaj Mishra. An urban Indian novelist casts a jaundiced eye over modern Indian life.
City of Djinns, by William Dalrymple. The respected travel writer's account of a year spent in Delhi, full of historical references.
Desert Places, by Robyn Davidson. A woman's story of living and travelling with the desert nomads of Rajasthan.
Exploring Indian Railways, by Bill Aitken. Highly informed and occasionally idiosyncratic tour of the

Indian railway system written by a clear enthusiast.

A Goddess in the Stones, by Norman Lewis. The founder of Survival International travels among the Adivasis of Bihar and Odisha (Orissa). ***The Great Hedge of India***, by Roy Moxham. One man's bizarre quest to find the hedge that marked the old British customs line. Very entertaining and packed full of historical detail. Recommended.

Leaves from the Jungle: Life in a Gond Village, by Verrier Elwin. Very entertaining account of this early anthropologist's stay with a Central Indian Adivasi group.

The Smile of Murugan, by Michael Wood. Account of a journey through Tamil Nadu, which reveals the ancient roots of the region's religious traditions.

Sorcerer's Apprentice, by Tahir Shah. Travelogue of the author's attempts to learn the secrets of illusion and fraud of India's street magicians.

FOOD, LANGUAGE AND IMAGES

Dakshin: Vegetarian Cuisine from South India, by Chandra Padmanabhan. An excellent guide to wonderful foods of South India.

Hanklyn-Janklin, or a Stranger's Rumble Tumble Guide to some Words, Customs and Quiddities Indian and Indo-British, by Nigel B. Hankin. Lives up to its title and is a delightful reference work.

Hobson-Jobson. The 1886 glossary on which Hankin modelled his modern etymology. The pair complement each other.

India: Decoration, Interiors, Style, by Henry Wilson. Exquisite photography of a number of North Indian palaces and houses (in Delhi and Rajasthan), demonstrating the inventiveness and sense of design to be found in this part of India.

Lucknow City of Illusion, by Rosie Llewellyn-Jones. Historical survey of the city with photos from the Alkazi collections.

The Raj at Table, by David Burton. This culinary history of the Raj is one of the most entertaining books on British India ever written, approaching the subject via an exploration of the ways in which the formidable British memsahib made her mark on Indian culture – and vice versa.

WILDLIFE

A Book of Indian Birds, by Salim Ali. The classic guide to Indian birds, suitable for novices and experienced birdwatchers.

The Last Tiger, by Valmik Thapar. A history of conservation of the tiger and Thapar's current views on how to save it from extinction.

Pocket Guide to the Birds of the Indian Subcontinent, by Richard Grimmett, Carol Inskipp and Tim Inskipp. Illustrated guide for keen ornithologists.

CREDITS

Insight Guide Credits

Distribution
UK, Ireland and Europe
Apa Publications (UK) Ltd;
sales@insightguides.com
United States and Canada
Ingram Publisher Services;
ips@ingramcontent.com
Australia and New Zealand
Woodslane; info@woodslane.com.au
Southeast Asia
Apa Publications (SN) Pte;
singaporeoffice@insightguides.com
Hong Kong, Taiwan and China
Apa Publications (HK) Ltd;
hongkongoffice@insightguides.com
Worldwide
Apa Publications (UK) Ltd;
sales@insightguides.com
Special Sales, Content Licensing and CoPublishing
Insight Guides can be purchased in bulk quantities at discounted prices. We can create special editions, personalised jackets and corporate imprints tailored to your needs.
sales@insightguides.com
www.insightguides.biz

Printed in China by CTPS

Editor: Sarah Clark
Author: David Abram, Magdalena Helsztyńska-Stadnik
Head of Production: Rebeka Davies
Update Production: AM Services
Picture Editor: Tom Smyth
Cartography: original cartography Berndtson & Berndtson, updated by Carte

Contributors

This eleventh edition of *Insight Guide India* was commissioned by **Sarah Clark** and updated by prolific travel writer **Magdalena Helsztyńska-Stadnik**. She builds on the previous work of frequent Insight contributor **David Abram**. A freelance author and photographer specialising in India, David first visited the country in the early 1980s and has since written more than a dozen guides to the country, and contributed numerous items for radio and magazines. Other original contributors include **Matt Barrett**, **Maria Lord**, **Gavin Thomas**, **Roy Moxham**, **George Michell** and **Jan McGirk**.

The principal photographers for this book were **Britta Jaschinski**, who covered much of the country, **David Abram**, who focused on the area around Goa, and **Julian Love**, who photographed Delhi and the northern plains.

The index was compiled by **Penny Phenix**.

About Insight Guides

Insight Guides have more than 45 years' experience of publishing high-quality, visual travel guides. We produce 400 full-colour titles, in both print and digital form, covering more than 200 destinations across the globe, in a variety of formats to meet your different needs.

Insight Guides are written by local authors, whose expertise is evident in the extensive historical and cultural background features.

Each destination is carefully researched by regional experts to ensure our guides provide the very latest information. All the reviews in **Insight Guides** are independent; we strive to maintain an impartial view. Our reviews are carefully selected to guide you to the best places to eat, go out and shop, so you can be confident that when we say a place is special, we really mean it.

Legend

City maps

	Freeway/Highway/Motorway
	Divided Highway
	Main Roads
	Minor Roads
	Pedestrian Roads
	Steps
	Footpath
	Railway
	Funicular Railway
	Cable Car
	Tunnel
	City Wall
	Important Building
	Built Up Area
	Other Land
	Transport Hub
	Park
	Pedestrian Area
	Bus Station
	Tourist Information
	Main Post Office
	Cathedral/Church
	Mosque
	Synagogue
	Statue/Monument
	Beach
	Airport

Regional maps

	Freeway/Highway/Motorway (with junction)
	Freeway/Highway/Motorway (under construction)
	Divided Highway
	Main Road
	Secondary Road
	Minor Road
	Track
	Footpath
	International Boundary
	State/Province Boundary
	National Park/Reserve
	Marine Park
	Ferry Route
	Marshland/Swamp
	Glacier / Salt Lake
	Airport/Airfield
	Ancient Site
	Border Control
	Cable Car
	Castle/Castle Ruins
	Cave
	Chateau/Stately Home
	Church/Church Ruins
	Crater
	Lighthouse
	Mountain Peak
	Place of Interest
	Viewpoint

INDEX

Main references are in bold type

A

accommodation 424
heritage hotels 201
luxury tents 188, 201
Achabal (J & K) 188
Achipur (WB) 309
admission charges 424
Advani, L.K. 82
Agartala (Tri) 333
Pushbanta Palace 333
Tripura Government Museum 333
Ujjayanta Palace 333
Agatti (Lak) 411
Agonda (Goa) 284
Agra (UP) 154
Agra Fort **155**, 156
Chini ka Rauza 155
Itimad-ud-Daula tomb 155
Rambagh gardens 155
Red Fort 108
Taj Mahal 55, 108, 109, 155, 156
agriculture 21, 147, 153
coconuts 394, 410
coffee 23, 345, 350, 394, 402
rice 21, 23, 394
rubber 402
spices 394, 402
tea 23, 61, 311, 327, 328, 350, 389, 394, 402
wheat 21
Ahmedabad (Guj) 108, 225, 226
Calico Museum of Textiles 229
Doshivada-ni-Pol 229
Gujarat Vidyapith 229
Hridey Kunj 229
Jama Masjid 227
Khadi Gramudyog Bhandar 229
Manek Chowk 227
Sidi Bashir's Mosque 229
Sidi Saiyad's Mosque 229
Teen Darwaza 227
Tomb of Ahmed Shah I 227
Aihole (Kar) 351
Durga Temple 351
Lad Khen Temple 351
air travel 418
to/from Bihar 164
to/from Chennai (TN) 366
to/from Delhi 130
to/from Goa 280
to/from Gujarat 226
to/from Jammu and Kashmir 186
to/from Karnataka 346
to/from Kerala 395
to/from Kolkata (WB) 293
to/from Madhya Pradesh 268
to/from Maharashtra 264
to/from Mumbai (Mah) 244
to/from Punjab & Haryana 147
to/from Rajasthan 202
to/from Tamil Nadu 375
to/from Telangana 354
to/from The Northeast 330
to/from Uttarakhand 175

to/from Uttar Pradesh 154
to/from West Bengal, Odisha and Jharkhand 307
Aizawl (Miz) 337
Mizoram State Museum 337
Ajanta (Mah) 105, 241, 267
tours 269
Ajmer (Raj) 210
Arhai din ka Jhonpra mosque 210
Dargah Sharif 210
Daulat Khana 210
Nasiyan Jain Temple 210
Akal Fossil Park (Raj) 221
Akbar, Emperor 38, 53, 54, 104, 132, 154, 155, 156, 201
Alappuzha (Ker) 400
Albuquerque, Alfonso 279
Alchi (J & K) 192, 193
Alexander the Great 49
Alfassa, Mirra 379
Aligarh (UP) 158
Allahabad (UP) 161
Anand Bhavan 161
All-India Muslim League 63
Almora (Utt) 176
Alwar (Raj) 205
City Palace 205
Amaravati (AP) 359
Amarnath Cave (J & K) 188
Amba Mata temple (Guj) 234
Ambani, Mukesh 81
Ambedkar, B.K. 73
Amber (Raj) 109, 204
Anokhi Museum of Hand Printing 204
Diwan i Am 204
Jaigarh Fort 204
Jaya Vana 204
Shish Mahal 204
Amritsar (Pun) 147, **150**
Durgiana Temple 152
Golden Temple 70, 109, 147, 150
Jallianwala Bagh 152
amusement parks
Nicco Park (Kolkata) 303
Wet-o-Wild Beach Tropicana (Kolkata) 303
Anandpur Sahib (HP) 185
Anandpur Sahib (Pun) 148, 152
Kesgarh 152
Andaman & Nicobar Islands 23, 409, 411, 341, 432
transport 411
visitor permits 410
Andhra Pradesh 358
climate 358
Anjuna (Goa)
beach 283
Annadurai, C.N. 367, 373
Annamalai Sanctuary (TN) 391
Annapurna 163
antiques, exporting 426
Apollonius Tyaneus 179
Araku Valley (AP) 360
Arambol (Goa) 283

Aranmula (Ker) 400
Aravalli Hills (Raj) 200
archaeology 148, 230, 257
architecture 103
Architecture Museum (Chandigarh) 149
British colonial 132, 177
Goan 282
havelis 207, 209, 214, 216, 221, 229
Indo-Muslim 227
Indo-Saracenic 111, 158, 252
Islamic 161, 199
modern 111
religious buildings 103
temples 315
urban cubist 141
Arikamedu (TN) 377
art and crafts 345
ancient cave art 258
bas relief art (Mamallapuram) 375
Calico Museum of Textiles (Ahmedabad) 229
Crafts Museum (Delhi) 139
deity images 299
Didarganji Yakshi (Patna) 165
embroidery 228, 232
fine art 103, 110, 111, 293
Kala Raksha Trust (Guj) 232
Kanhirode Weavers' Cooperative Society (Kannur) 405
metal-work 352, 358
Napier Museum of Arts and Crafts (Thiruvananthapuram) 397
of Madhya Pradesh 269
of Rajasthan 200
of the Adivasi people 275
Shilparamam Crafts Village (Hyderabad) 357
shipbuilding 230
shopping for 432
stone carving 235
textiles 111, 204, 228, 232, 270, 283, 358, 359
Tibetan Refugee Craft Centre (Gangtok) 325
wood crafts 358, 359
art galleries. *See* museums and galleries
arts, performance 94. *See also* theatres and performance venues
arts season (Chennai) 369
Bharata-natyam dance 371
classical music and dance 94, 270
devotional music 96
film music 99
Natyasastra 97
Odissi dance 314
popular music and dance 94
raga and tala 94
Tibetan music and dance 183
traditional dance-dramas 97, 345, 352, 358, 395, 396

traditional music and dance 181, 197, 396
Arunachal Pradesh 333, 432
climate 333
Ashoka, Emperor 50, 166, 169, 232, 316
Assam 289, 325
Aswem (Goa) 283
Augnier, Gerald 245
Auli (Utt) 175, 176
Aurangabad (Mah) 267
Bibi ka Maqbara 267
Panchakki 267
Aurangzeb, Emperor 38, 55, 57
Auroville (TN) 377, 379
autorickshaws 423
Delhi 133
Jaipur (Raj) 200
Avantipur (J & K) 188
Ayodhya (UP) 71, 82, 160
Hanumangarhi 160
Ayurveda 398

B

Babur, Emperor 54, 104, 132
Backwaters (Ker) 393
Badami (Kar) 351
Badkhal Lake (Har) 148
Badrinath (Utt) 175
Baga (Goa) 283
Bairath (Raj) 205
Baker, Herbert 111, 132
Bakkhin (Sik) 325
Balasore (Odi) 319
Bandhavgarh National Park (MP) 274
Bandipur National Park (Kar) 350
Bangalore. See Bengaluru
Bangaram (Lak) 411
Bangladesh 289
creation of 71
Bannarghatta National Park (Kar) 347
Bansberia (WB) 307
Hangsesvari Temple 307
Vasudeva Temple 307
Baranagar (WB) 308
Bara Pani (Umian Lake) (Meg) 331
Barra Basti (Nag) 335
Bathinda (Pun) 148
Bay of Bengal 23, 289, 310
bazaars. See markets and bazaars
beaches 10, 22
Andaman & Nicobar Islands 414
Goa 280, 282
Gujarat 235
Karnataka 354
Kerala 22, 393, 397, 405
Konkan coast 241
Lakshadweep Islands 409, 411
Maharashtra 262, 263
Mumbai 253, 255
Odisha 317, 318, 319
Tamil Nadu 366, 367
Beatles, The 175
Bedaghat (MP) 274
Bedsa cave temple (Mah) 264
begging 255, 425
Bekal Fort (Ker) 405

Belur (Kar) 107, 350
Channekeshava Temple 350
Belur Math (WB) 306
Sri Ramakrishna Temple 306
Benaulim (Goa) 284
Bengaluru (Kar) 341, 346
Art of Living Foundation 347
cinemas 346
Commercial Street 346
Cubbon Park 346
High Court 346
ISKCON Sri Radha Krishna Mandir 347
Lalbagh Botanical Gardens 346
State Central Public Library 346
Tipu Sultan's Palace 347
vegetable and fruit market 346
Vidhana Soudha 346
Bhagavad Gita 36, 157
Bhaja cave temple (Mah) 264
Bharatpur (Raj) 212
Bharatpur Fort 212
Bhavanagar (Guj) 235
Bhave, Acharya Vinoba 268
Bhima River (Mah) 261
Bhimbethka (MP) 273
Bhimunipatnam (AP) 360
Bhindranwale, Jarnail Singh 70
Bhopal (MP) 273
Archaeological Museum 273
Bharat Bhavan 273
Bhojpur Temple 273
Birla Museum 273
Museum of Man 273
Tal Lake 273
Bhrugarh (MP) 272
Bhubaneshwar (Odi) 106, 305, 315
Bindu Sarovar 315
Handicrafts Museum 316
Lingaraj Temple 315
Muktesvara Temple 316
Odisha State Museum 316
Parasuramesvar Temple 315
Rajarani Temple 316
Siddhesvara Temple 316
Sisiresvara Temple 315
Tribal Research Museum 316
Uttaresvara Temple 315
Vaital Deul 315
Bhuj (Guj) 231
palace 231
Bhutan, border with 314
Bidar (Kar) 353
Bihar 164
Bijapur (Kar) 352
Gol Gumbaz 108, 352
Ibrahim Rauza tomb 108, 352
Bijli Mahadeva temple (HP) 180
Bikaner (Raj) 208
Anup Mahal 209
Durbar Hall 209
Junagarh Fort 209
Lalgarh Palace 209
Old City 209
Shri Sadul Museum 209
Bilaspur (HP) 185
Lakshmi Narayan Temple 185
Radheshyam Temple 185
Vyas Gufa cave 185
Binsar (Utt) 176

birdlife 28, 153, 212, 230, 391.
See also national parks and wildlife sanctuaries
cranes 212
flamingos 235
owls 26
peacocks 28, 212, 215
waterfowl 28, 193
Bison Horn Marias 275
'Black Hole of Calcutta' 296
Blue Mountain Railway (TN) 389
boating 303
boat trips and cruises 419
Ganges 163
glass-bottom boat trips (Lak) 411
Kerala backwaters 393, 400
Bodhgaya (Bih) 104, 167, 168
archaeological museum 169
Chanka Ramana 169
Mahabodhi Temple 169
Vajrasana (Diamond Throne) 169
Bokaro (Jha) 320
Bolgatty Island (Ker) 403
Bollywood 243
Borra caves (AP) 360
Bose, Nandalal 293
Bose, Subhas Chandra 65, 296, 300
Brahmagiri (Mah) 267
Brahmakund (ArP) 334
Brahmaputra 289
Brahmaputra River 21, 323, 325
Brahmaur (HP) 185
Brahmins 32, 49, 373
Braj (UP) 156
Bratacharingam (WB) 309
Gurusaday Museum 309
Buddha 40, 104, 154, 161, 163, 167, 168, 329
Bulsara, Farok. See Mercury, Freddie
Bundi (Raj) 213
Chitra Shala 213
Naval Sagar 213
palace 213
Raniji-ki-Baori step well 214
Taragarh Fort 213
business hours. See opening hours
bus travel 419
Bihar 164
Delhi 130, 133
in Tamil Nadu 375
long-distance buses 293, 366, 395
to/from Jammu, Kashmir and Ladakh 186
to/from Nepal 167
Buxar (Bih) 167
Byron, Robert 251

C

Calangute (Goa) 283
Calcutta. See Kolkata
Camel Fair. See Kartik Purnima, under festivals and events
camel treks 197, 209, 220, 221
Cameron, James 19
Canacona (Goa) 284
Candolim (Goa) 282

Carey, William 306
cathedrals. See churches
caves
  Ajanta (Mah) 258, 267
  Amarnath (J & K) 188
  Bhimbethka (MP) 273
  Borra (AP) 360
  Elephanta (Mumbai) 244, 257
  Ellora (Mah) 258, 267
  Kanheri (Mah) 257
  Kotamsar (Cha) 275
  mandapams (Mamallapuram)
    376
  Trimurti (Mamallapuram) 376
  Vyas Gufa (Bilaspur) 185
Chail (HP) 179
Chamba (HP) 184
  Bhuri Singh Museum 184
Chamba Valley (HP) 184
Champaner (Guj) 236
Champhai (Miz) 337
Chandernagore (WB) 307
Chandigarh (Pun & Har) 148
  Architecture Museum 149
  Government Museum and Art
    Gallery 149
  High Court 149
  Legislative Assembly 149
  Rock Garden 150
  Rose Garden 149
  Secretariat 149
  Sukhna Lake 150
Chandipur-on-Sea (Odi) 319
Chand, Nek 150
Chandor (Goa) 282
Chandragiri (AP) 361
Chandrapur (Mah) 268
Changspa (J & K) 191
  Shanti Stupa 191
Chapora (Goa) 283
Char Dham (Utt) 175
Charideo. See Sibsagar
Charnock, Job 296
Chatterjee, Bankim Chandra 305
Chattisgarh 241, 261, 274
Chaul (Mah) 263
Chauragarh mountain (MP) 275
Chennai (TN) 341, 373
  Anna Salai 367
  Anna Samadhi 367
  Armenian Church 369
  Banqueting Hall 367
  Chennakesavara Temple 369
  Chennammallikesvara Temple
    369
  Connemara Public Library 368
  Egmore 369
  Elliot's Beach 367
  Fort St George 366
  Fort St George Museum 366
  George Town 369
  Government Museum 107
  High Court and Law College 369
  Kalakshetra 371
  Kapalesvara Shiva Temple 369
  Krishna Gana Sabha 369
  Krishna Paratasaraty Temple 370
  Legislative Assembly 366
  Marina 367
  MGR Film City 98

Mofussil Bus Terminal 371
Music Academy 369
Mylapore 369
National Art Gallery 368
Old Government House 367
Pantheon 367
Park hotel 369
Presidency College 367
San Thome Basilica 370
Secretariat 366
Senate House 367
shopping 367
St Andrew's Kirk 369
State Government Museum 368
St Mary's Church 366
St Thomas's Mount 370
Theosophical Society 370
transport 366, 370
University 367
Cherranpunji (Meg) 332
Chettinad (TN) 383
Chidambaram (TN) 380, 381
Chikhalda (Mah) 268
Chikmagalur (Kar) 350
children 425
Chilka Lake (Odi) 318
Chinsura (WB)
  Imambara 307
  St John's Church 307
Chinura (WB) 307
Chiriya Tapu (A & N) 414
Chitrakut Falls (Cha) 275
Chitrakut (UP) 158
Chittaurgarh (Raj) 217
Cholamandalam (TN) 371
Chota Nagpur plateau 22
Chottanikkara Temple (Ker) 404
churches 280
  Afghan Memorial (Mumbai) 249
  All Souls' Memorial Church
    (Kanpur) 158
  Armenian (Chennai) 369
  Armenian Church of Our Lady of
    Nazareth (Kolkata) 298
  Augustinian Monastery (Old Goa)
    285
  Basilica of Bom Jesus (Old Goa)
    110, 284
  Basilica of Mount Mary (Mumbai)
    256
  Chapel of St Catherine (Old Goa)
    285
  Holy Spirit (Margao) 282
  Immaculate Conception (Panaji)
    281
  Lutheran (Ranchi) 320
  Our Lady of Bandel (Hugli) 307
  Our Lady of the Rosary (Old Goa)
    285
  Padri-ki-Haveli (Patna) 166
  Sacred Heart (Puducherry) 379
  Saint Paul's Anglican (Ranchi)
    320
  San Thome Basilica (Chennai)
    370
  Sé (Cathedral of St Catherine) (Old
    Goa) 110, 284
  St Andrew's Kirk (Chennai) 369
  St Andrew's Kirk (Kolkata) 297
  St Andrew's (Mumbai) 245

St Cajetan (Old Goa) 285
St Francis (Kochi) 404
St Francis of Assisi (Old Goa) 284
St James's (Delhi) 135
St John's (Chinsura) 307
St John's (Kolkata) 296
St Mary's (Chennai) 366
St Olaf's (Serampore) 306
St Paul's Cathedral (Kolkata) 295
St Philomena's (Mysore) 348
St Thomas Cathedral (Mumbai)
  252
Churchill, Winston 62
cinema. See film and television
  industry
climate 22, 23, 425
Clive, Robert 294, 366
clothing 434
  jodhpurs 218
  traditional dress 199
  turbans 153
Coimbatore plateau 23
Colva (Goa) 284
Coorg (Kar) 350
Corbett, Jim 26, 176
Corbett National Park (Utt) 176
Coromandel Coast (TN) 22, 366
Coryate, Thomas 273
cotton 60, 245
couriers. See postal and courier
  services
cricket 179, 250, 294, 295
crime and safety 11, 73, 164, 181,
  425
  bandits 319, 320
  civil unrest 311, 314, 327, 335
  ethnic violence 329
  Naxalite-Maoist insurgency 275,
    319, 320
  terrorism 71, 186, 187, 226, 243
Curzon, Lord George 171, 234
customs regulations 426
Cuttack (Odi) 319
  Barabati fort 319
  Qadmam-i-Rasul 319

D

da Gama, Vasco 57, 405
Dakshina Kasi. See Kolhapur
Dakshinesvar (WB) 306
  Kali Bhavatarini Temple 306
Dalai Lama 177, 183
Dalhousie (HP) 185
Dal Lake (J & K) 188
Daman (Guj) 236
Dampha Wildlife Sanctuary (Miz)
  337
Darasuram (TN) 382
  Airavatesvara Temple 382
Darjeeling Himalayan Railway
  (WB) 311
Darjeeling (WB) 289, 311
  Chaurastha 311
  Himalayan Mountaineering
    Institute 312
  Lloyd Botanical Gardens 312
  Mall 311
  Observatory Hill 312
  Planters' Club 312

Zoological Park 312
Dassam waterfall (Jha) 320
Datia (MP) 271
  Narsing Dev Palace 271
Daulatabad (Mah) 267
Deccan plateau 22, 343, 352
Deeg (Raj) 206
  Gopal Bhawan 207
  Keshar Bhawan 207
  palace 206
Dehra Dun (Utt) 174
Delhi 109, **129**
  Adilabad ruins 143
  Akshardham Temple 103, 143
  Archaeological Museum 138
  Ashokan Pillars 135
  Baha'i Lotus Temple 141
  Bangla Sahib Gurudwara 133
  Baroda House 137
  Bhulbhulaiyan 142
  Bird Hospital 134
  Central Cottage Industries
    Emporium 133, 139
  Chanakyapuri 137
  Chandni Chowk 132, 134
  Chattarpur 143
  Civil Lines 135
  Connaught Place 132
  Crafts Museum 139
  Dandi Statue 137
  Delhi Zoo 138
  Digambara Temple 134
  Dilli Haat Food and Crafts Bazaar
    140
  DLF Mall of India 131, 143
  Fatehpuri Masjid 134
  Feroz Shah Kotla 131
  Flagstaff Tower 135
  Gandhi Darshan 135
  Gandhi Smarak Sangrahalaya
    135
  Gandhi Smriti 138
  Garden of the Five Senses 143
  Ghantewala 134
  Gurgaon 143
  Hanuman Mandir 133
  Hauz-i-Shamsi tomb 142
  Hauz Khas 131
  Hauz Khas Village 141
  history 131
  Humayun's Tomb 108, 140
  Hyderabad House 137
  India Gate 136
  India Habitat Centre 140, 142
  India International Centre 140, 142
  India Islamic Cultural Centre 140
  Indira Gandhi Memorial Museum
    138
  Indira Gandhi National Centre for
    the Arts 137
  Iron Pillar 51
  Jahaz Mahal 142
  Jamali Kamali tomb 142
  Jama Masjid 132, 134
  Janpath 133
  Jantar Mantar 133
  Jawaharlal Nehru Memorial
    Museum 138
  Kamani Auditorium 142
  Khan Market 139

Lakshmi Narayan Temple 133
Lalit Kala Akademi 136
Lal Kot ruins 142
Lal Qila 132, **133**
Lodi Colony Market 139, 140
Lodi Gardens 132, 139
Mehrauli 142
Moti Masjid 142
Muhammad Shah tomb 139
Mutiny Memorial 135
National Gallery of Modern Art
  110, 138
National Museum 109, 139
National Rail Museum 139
New Delhi 129, 132
Nila Gumbad 140
NOIDA 143
Old Delhi 129, 133
Paharganj Bazaar 132
Palika Bazaar 132
population 129
Pragati Maidan 137
Purana Qila 131, **137**
Qudsia Bagh 133
Qutb Minar Complex 52, 107,
  131, 142
Qutbuddin Bakhtiyar Kaki 142
Quwwat-ul-Islam Mosque 142
Rabindra Kala Sangam 136
Raj Ghat 135
Rajpath 136
Rashtrapati Bhavan 111, 136
Red Fort 109
Safdarjang's Tomb 140
Sangeet Natak Akademi 136, 142
Sansad Bhavan 137
Sanskriti Museums 143
Santushti Complex 137
Shahjahanabad. See Old Delhi
Sheikh Nizamuddin Aulia shrine
  140
shopping 139, 143
Siri Fort 141
Sispganj Gurudwara 134
South Delhi 141
St James's Church 135
St Stephen's College 135
Sulabh International Museum of
  Toilets 136
Sundar Nagar colony 138
Sunehri Masjid 134
Suraj Kund 143
taxis 133
The Ridge 135
Tibet House Museum 140
transport 130, 133, 143, 420
Tughlaqabad Fort 143
University 135
websites 133
Desai, Morarji 69
Deshnok (Raj) 210
Devas (MP) 272
Devi, Rukmini 371
Dhanbad (Jha) 320
Dhanushkodi (TN) 378
Dharamsala (HP) 183
  McLeod Ganj 183
  Museum of Kangra Art 184
  Namgyal Monastery 183
  Norbulingka Institute 184

Dhauli (Odi) 316
  Peace Pagoda 317
Dholpur (Raj) 212
Dhuandhar Falls (MP) 274
Diamond Harbour (WB) 309
Digboi (Assam) 330
Digha (WB) 310
Dimapur (Nag) 334
disabled travellers 426
Diu island (Guj) 234
Diu town (Guj) 235
diving and snorkelling 410, 411,
  414, **431**
Dixit, Shiela 129
Dolphin's Nose (AP) 360
Dooars (WB) 314
Draksharaman (AP) 360
Drew, Jane 149
driving 420
**Druk Thupten Sangag Choling
  Monastery (WB)** 312
Dudhwa National Park (UP) 160
Duliajan (Assam) 330
Dundlod (Raj) 208
Dwarka (Guj) 232
  Temple of Dvarkadish 232
Dzongri (Sik) 325

E

earthquakes 231
Eastern Ghats 22
East India Company 53, 57, 210,
  245, 291
economy 59, 68, 69, 71, 72, 77, 164
  outsourcing & IT boom 77
  special economic zones 80
electricity 426
Elephant Beach (A & N) 414
elephants 204
elephant safaris 415
Elephant Training Camp (A & N)
  415
Ellora (Mah) 105, 106, 241, 267
  tours 269
embassies and consulates 426
emergency numbers 426
environmental issues 26, 418
  air pollution 130, 234, 236, 265
  conservation 26
  endangered species 165
  illegal logging 345
  in the Kerala backwaters 406
  water pollution 255
  wildlife poaching 25, 26, 27
Eravikulam National Park (Ker) 403
Ernakulam (Ker) 403
etiquette 427
  at religious sites 150
  on beaches 399
Everest, Mount 312

F

Faizabad (UP) 160
Faridkot (Pun) 148
Fatehpur (Raj) 208
  Nadine Le Prince Haveli 208
Fatehpur Sikri (UP) 54, 108, 156
festivals and events 11, **92**, **427**

art biennale (Kochi) 110
Ayappan pilgrimage (Sabarimala) 396
Carnival (Goa) 281
classical music and dance festival (Chennai) 369
dance festival (Khajuraho) 276
Dasara (Mysore) 348
Dussera (Kullu) 180
Festival of the Joyful Heart (Shat Suk Myasiem) (Shillong) 331
Ganesh Chathurthi (Mumbai) 254, 255
Gangasagar Mela (Sagardwip) 310
Garo 100-drum festival (Tura) 331
Hola (Nahan) 186
Hornbill festival (Nag) 335
International Kite Festival (Ahmedabad) 227
kambala (buffalo race) (Kar) 352
Kartik Purnima (Pushkar) 210, 211
Khichri Mela (Gorakhpur) 161
Kumbha Mela 175, 266
Lavi (Rampur) 179
Magh Mela (Allahabad) 161
Maha Kumbh Mela (Allahabad) 162
Mahamastakabhisheka (Sravanabelagola) 350
Maha Shivratri 275
Minjar fair (Chamba) 185
Pandhapur Yatra pilgrimage (Kolhapur) 266
Pong Labsal (Gangtok) 325
Pooram (Thrissur) 404
Purna Kumbha Mela (Allahabad) 161
Ramnagar Ram Lila (Varanasi) 163
Rath Yatra (Puri) 317
Sangamam arts festival (Chennai) 369
Shivrati Fair (Mandi) 185
Urs Mela 210
Vallamkali (Ker) 400
film and television industry 98, 243, 293, 295
MGR Film City (Chennai) 98
Ramoji Film City (Hyderabad) 357
fishing 330
food and drink
alcohol 91
Bombay Duck 249, 252
Chettinad cuisine 382, 384
feni 280
Indian cuisines 87
masala dosa 353
street food 90, 253, 256
tea 311, 328
football 294
Forrest, G.W, 250
Forster, E.M. 272
Fort Aguada (Goa) 282
forts 110
Agra **155**, 156
Ajatasatru (Rajgir) 168
Anandpur Sahib (Pun) 148

Bahu (Jammu town) 187
Barabati (Cuttack) 319
Bathinda (Pun) 148
Bekal (Ker) 405
Bharatpur (Raj) 212
Chittaurgarh (Raj) 217
Daulatabad (Mah) 267
Faridkot (Pun) 148
Fort William (Kolkata) 294
Gandikota (AP) 361
Gingee (TN) 379
Golconda (T) 354, 358
Gwalia (MP) 271
Gwalior (MP) 270
Jaigarh (Amber) 204
Jaisalmer (Raj) 220
Janjira (Mah) 263
Jhansi 157
Junagarh (Bikaner) 209
Kangra (HP) 184
Kausambi (UP) 161
Kesgarh (Anandpur Sahib) 152
Kumbalgarh (Raj) 216
Lal Qila (Delhi) 132, **133**
Meherangarh (Jodhpur) 219
Nahargarh (Jaipur) 204
Penukonda (AP) 361
Purana Qila (Delhi) 131, **137**
Rao Hamir (Raj) 211
Red Fort (Agra) 108
Red Fort (Delhi) 109
Sindhudurg (Mah) 263
Sinhagad (Mah) 265, 267
Siri (Delhi) 141
St Angelo (Kannur) 405
St George (Chennai) 366
Taragarh (Bundi) 213
Tughlaqabad (Delhi) 143
Vellore (TN) 379
Vijaydurg (Mah) 263
Fry, Maxwell 149
Furkating (Assam) 330
further reading 439

G

Gaitor (Raj) 204
Royal Cenotaphs 204
Galta (Raj) 204
Monkey Temple 204
Gandhi, Indira 69, 82, 151, 187
assassination 70
Gandhi, M.K. 31, **62**, 63, 65, 135, 227, 229, 254, 268
assassination 68, 82
birthplace 233
Gandhi, Rahul 72
Gandhi, Rajiv 70
assassination 70
Gandhi, Sanjay 70
Gandhi, Sonia 71
Gangaikondacholapuram (TN) 382
Brihadesvara Temple 382
Ganges, River 21, 145, 154, 162, 173, 174, 289, 302
estuary 310
source of 175
Gangotri (Utt) 175
Gangtok (Sik) 324
Chogyal's Palace 325

Deer Park 325
Hotel Tashi Delek 325
Orchid Sanctuary 325
Research Institute of Tibetology 325
Tibetan Refugee Craft Centre 325
Ganguly, Sourav 294
Ganpathipule (Mah) 263
gardens. See parks and gardens
Garo hill country (Meg) 332
Gaumukh (Utt) 175
Gaur (WB) 308
Gaya (Bih) 168
Visnupada Temple 168
gay and lesbian travellers 427
geography and geology 21
Ghoom (WB) 313
Yiga Cholang Gelugpa Buddhist Temple 313
Ghrusnesvar Temple (Mah) 267
Gill, Robert 259
Gingee Fort (TN) 379
Gir Forest (Guj) 24, 234
Goa 57
transport 280, 282
Godavari River (Mah) 22, 261, 266, 267, 268, 360
Gokarna (Kar) 354
Kooti Theerta tank 354
Mahabaleshwar Temple 354
Golconda Fort (T) 354, 358
golf 179, 295, 302
gompas. See monasteries
Gopalpur-on-Sea (Od) 318
Gorakhpur (UP) 161
Gorkha Janmukti Morcha 311
government. See politics and government
Govind Singh 40
Gowda, H.D. Deve 71
Gramphu (HP) 182
Grand Trunk Road 306
Guindy Deer Park (TN) 371
Gujarat 197, **225**
transport 226
Gujural, Inder Kumar 71
Gulbarga (Kar) 352
Jami Mosque 352
Saiyid Muhammad Husaini Gisu Daras tomb 352
Gulmarg (J & K) 176, 188
Gundu Island (Ker) 403
Gurgaon. See Delhi
Guru Nanak 39, 40
Guru Shikhar (Raj) 218
Guruvayur (Ker) 405
Krishna Temple 405
Guwahati (Assam) 327
Belle Vue Hotel 327
Kamakhya Mandir 329
Navagraha Mandir 327
Raj Bhavan 327
State Museum 327
Sukhlesvar Janardhan Temple 327
Umananda (Peacock Island) 327
Gwalior (MP) 241, 270
Ghaus Muhammad's mausoleum 271
Gwalior Fort 270, 271

Jai Vilas Palace 270
Sarod Ghar museum 271
Sas Bahu temples 270
Sikh gurudwara 270
Teli-ka-Madir 270
Gyaraspur (MP) 274

H

Halebid (Kar) 107, 350
Hoysaleswara Temple 350
Hampi (Kar) 53, 341, 351
handicrafts. See art and crafts
Hanuman 163
Haridwar (Utt) 174
Har-ki-Pauri 175
Harihara I 53
Haryana 69, 146
transport 147
Hassan (Kar) 350
Havelock, General 159
Havelock Island (A & N) 413, 414
Hazare, Ana 73, 78
Hazaribagh National Park (Jha) 320
health and medical care 79, 428
altitude sickness 190
Ayurvedic therapies 398
Hemis (J &K) 192
Hemkund (Utt) 175
hiking. See trekking and hiking
hill stations 9, 125, 178
Almora (Utt) 176
Dalhousie (HP) 185
Darjeeling (WB) 289, 311
Kodaikanal (TN) 390
Mahabalesvar (Mah) 266
Matheran (Mah) 264
Mount Abu (Raj) 217
Mussoorie (Utt) 174
Nainital (Utt) 176
Naukuchiyatal (Utt) 176
Pachmarhi (MP) 274
Panchgani (Mah) 266
Ponmudi (Ker) 397
Ranikhet (Utt) 176
Udhagamandalam (TN) 388
Yercaud (TN) 390
Himachal Pradesh 21, 146, 173, 177
climate 177, 182
Himalayas 21, 311
Hirni waterfall (Jha) 320
history 19
2008 terrorist attacks 72
ancient times 48
British rule 58, 132, 245, 264, 291, 311
Danish presence 306
Delhi Sultanate 52, 131
Dutch presence 58, 307
French presence 307, 379
Gupta Empire (Golden Age) 50, 51
Independence movement 61
Maratha Empire 263
Mauryan Empire 49
modern times 67
Mughal Empire 53, 54, 132, 201
Partition 67, 145

Portuguese presence 57, 245, 279, 307
railways, building of 60
sectarian violence 71, 82
separatist insurrections 70
spice trade 57
Uprising of 1857 60, 125, 157
World War I 63
World War II 65, 334
horse racing 294
horseriding 266
Hospet (Kar) 351
hotels. See accommodation
hot springs
Manikaran (HP) 181
Nubra Valley (J & K) 193
Vashisht (HP) 182
Hugli river (WB) 294, 307
Hugli (WB) 307
Church of Our Lady of Bandel 307
Humayun 104, 132
Hume, Allan Octavian 61
Hundru waterfall (Jha) 320
Huxley, Aldous 251
Hyderabad (AP) 341
British Residency 111
Char Minar mosque 108
Hyderabad-Secunderabad (T) 354
Hyderabad (T)
Bagh-e-Aam gardens 357
Birla Venkatesvara Temple 357
Botanical Gardens 357
Charminar 356
Falaknuma Palace 356
Hussain Sagar Lake 355
Kala Pahad 357
Lad Bazaar 356
Legislative Assembly 357
Mecca Masjid 356
Nehru Zoological Park 357
Old City 355
pearl market 356
Planetarium 357
Qutb Shahi tombs 357
Ramoji Film City 357
Salar Jung Museum 356
Shilparamam Crafts Village 357
State Archaeological Museum 357

I

Imphal (Man) 337
Kwairamband Bazaar 337
Manipur State Museum 337
Indian Institute of Technology (TN) 371
Indian National Congress 61
Indore (MP) 272
Indravati National Park and Tiger Reserve (Cha) 275
Indus river 192
industry 68, 77, 234, 305, 320, 346, 355
motor industry 147
textiles 349
Inland Customs Line 311
insurance 430
internet 430
Itanagar (ArP) 333

J

Jagdalpur (Cha) 275
Jagesvar (Utt) 176
Jahangir, Emperor 55, 104, 154
Jaidev 310
Jaipur (Raj) 201
Central Museum 203
City Palace 202
City Palace Museum 109
Hawa Mahal 203
Jantar Mantar 203
Nahargarh Fort 204
Sawai Man Singh II Museum 202
transport 200
Jaisalmer (Raj) 220
Gadi Sagar Tank 221
Main Chowk 221
Nathmali-ki-Haveli 221
Palace of the Maharawal 221
Patwa Haveli 221
Rani ki Mahal 221
Salim Singh Haveli 221
shopping 221
Jaldapara (WB) 314
Jalori Pass (HP) 181
Jammu and Kashmir 186
transport 186
Jammu town (J & K) 187
Amar Mahal Palace 187
Bahu Fort 187
Dogra Art Gallery 187
Raghunath Temple 187
Ranbireshwar Temple 187
Jamnagar (Guj) 232
Lakhota Palace 232
Jamshedpur (Jha) 320
Janjira (Mah) 263
Jaunpur (UP) 161
Jawalamukhi (HP) 184
Jayaram, Jayalalitha 98, 373
Jhansi (UP) 157
fort 157
Jharkhand 289, 305, 319
transport 307
Jhunjhunu (Raj)
Rani Sati Temple 208
Jinnah, Muhammad Ali 63, 67
Jodhpur (Raj) 218
Meherangarh Fort 219
Umaid Bhavan 111, 219
Jog Falls (Kar) 354
Johna waterfall (Jha) 320
Joshimath (Utt) 175
Narsingh Bhagwan temple 175
Junagadh (Guj) 233

K

Kabir 39
Kabru, Mount 312
Kadmat (Lak) 411
Kailasa Hill (AP) 360
Kala Raksha Trust (Guj) 232
Kalidasa 51
Kalimpong (WB) 314
Tharpa Choling 314
Zangdog Palrifo Brang Monastery 314
Kalpa (HP) 180

Kalpeni (Lak) 410
Kamarpukur (WB) 310
Kanadukathan (TN) 384
Kanchenjunga, Mount (Sik) 21, 312
Kanchipuram (TN) 106, 379
  Ekambaresvara Temple 379
  Kailasanatha Temple 379
Kanger Valley (Cha) 275
Kangra (HP) 184
Kangra Valley (HP) 183
Kanha National Park (MP) 274
Kanheri Caves (Mah) 257
Kanniyakumari (TN) 384
  Wandering Monk Museum 383
Kannur (Ker) 405
  Fort St Angelo 405
  Kanhirode Weavers' Cooperative
    Society 405
  Mopplah Town 405
  Payyambalam beach 405
Kanpur (UP) 158
  All Souls' Memorial Church 158
Kappad (Ker) 405
Karaikkudi (TN) 384
Karla cave temple (Mah) 264
Karnataka 343
  transport 346
Karni Mata 210
Karunagapalli (Ker) 400
Karunanidhi, M. 374
Kashmir 68, 69, 70, 71, 72, 188.
  See also Jammu & Kashmir
Kathiawar Peninsula (Guj) 225
Kausambi (UP) 161
Kavaratti (Lak) 410
Kaveri River 23
Kaza (HP) 183
Kaziranga National Park (Assam)
  330
Kedarnath (Utt) 175
Kendubilwa (WB) 310
Keoladeo Ghana National Park
  (Raj) 28, 212
Kerala 22, 341
  climate 402
  transport 395
Keylong (HP) 182
Khajuraho (MP) 105, 158, 241, 272
  Archaeological Museum 272
Khan, Ajmad Ali 271
Khandagiri (Odi) 316
Khaziranga National Park (Assam)
  26
Khecheopalri Lake (Sik) 324
Khuldabad (Mah) 267
Khuri (Raj) 221
Khushinagar (UP) 161
  Muktabandhana stupa 161
Khusrau, Amir 39
Kinnaur (HP) 179
Kipling, Rudyard 177, 212, 270,
  274, 306
Kochi (Ker) 403, 393
  Jew Town 404
  Matancherry Palace 404
  St Francis's Church 404
Kodaikanal (TN) 390
  Bryant Gardens 390
  Coaker's Walk 390
  Kodai Lake 390

Pillar Rocks 390
Kodungallur (Ker) 404
Kohima (Nag) 334
Kolhapur (Mah) 266
  Kotiteerth temple 266
  Malalaksmi Temple 266
  New Palace 266
  Pandhapur Yatra pilgrimage 266
  Raj Wada 266
Kolis 247
Kolkata Night Riders 295
Kolkata (WB) 289, 289, 306
  Academy of Fine Arts 294
  Armenian Church of Our Lady of
    Nazareth 298
  Ashutosh Museum 299
  Asiatic Society 300
  BBD Bagh (Dalhousie Square)
    297
  Bentinck Street 297
  Birla Academy of Art and Culture
    302
  Birla Industrial and Technological
    Museum 300
  Birla Planetarium 295
  Botanical Gardens 302
  Calcutta Gallery 294
  Calcutta Golf Club 295
  Chinatown 297
  Chowringhee 296
  Eden Gardens 294, 295
  Esplanade 296
  Fort William 294
  Freemason's Hall 300
  Gandhi Statue 295
  ghats 302
  Government House 111
  Gwalior Monument 303
  Haora Bridge 303
  High Court 296
  history 59, 67
  Home for the Destitute and Dying
    (Nirmal Hriday) 301
  India Museum 296
  Indian Coffee House 299
  Jain temple 297
  Jorashankho 298
  Jute Balers Association 297
  Kalighat 301
  Kali Temple 301
  Kolkata Museum 296
  Kolkata Polo Club 294
  Kolkata University 299
  Kumartuli 299
  La Martinière College 300
  Magen David synagogue 297
  Maidan 294
  Marble Palace 299
  Metiaburuz Shi'ite Mosque 302
  Nakhoda Mosque 298
  National Library 301
  Nehru Children's Museum 295
  Netaji Bhavan 300
  Netaji Subhas Road 297
  Nicco Park 303
  Oberoi Grand 296
  Old China Bazaar 297
  Old Mission 299
  Parasnath Mandir 299
  Park Street 300

Pathuriagata 298
Presidency General Hospital 294
Rabindra Bharati University 298
Rabindra Mancha 298
Rabindra Sadan 294
Rabindra Sarovar Lake 302
Racecourse 294
Rajabazar 299
Raj Bhavan 296
Rajya Sabha 296
Ramakrishna Mission Institute of
  Culture 302
restaurants 297
Saheed Minar 295
Salt Lake 303
Science City 303
South City Mall 302
South Park Street Cemetery 300
Sri Aurobindo's Statue 295
St Andrew's Kirk 297
St John's Church 296
Stock Exchange 297
St Paul's Cathedral 295
Strand 294
Swabhumi 303
Tagore's Castle 298
Tiretta Market 297
Tollygunge Club 302
Tolly's Nullah 301
Town Hall 296
transport 293, 297
Victoria Memorial 294
Vidyasagar Setu bridge 303
War Memorial 295
Wet-o-Wild Beach Tropicana 303
Writers' Building 297
Zoological Gardens 301
Kollam (Ker) 399
  British Residency 399
Konark (Odi) 106, 318
  Sun Temple 289, 318
Kondapali (AP) 359
Konkan coast 241, 262, 343, 353
Koraput (Odi) 289, 318
Kotamsar (Cha) 275
Kota (Raj) 214
  City Palace 214
  Maharao Madho Singh Museum
    214
Kottayam (Ker) 401
Kovalam (Ker) 393, 397
Kozhikode (Ker) 405
  Krishna Menon Art Gallery and
    Museum 405
  Pazhassi Raja Museum 405
Krishna 156
Krishna River 22, 261
Kufri (Utt) 176
Kullu (HP) 180
Kullu Valley (HP) 180
Kumarakom Bird Sanctuary (Ker)
  401
Kumari, Mayawati 155, 156
Kumar, Nitish 164
Kumbalgarh Fort (Raj) 216
Kunzam Pass (HP) 182
Kurseong (WB) 312
Kurukshetra (Har) 153
Kutch (Guj) 225, 231
Kuttanad (Ker) 399

L

Ladakh (J & K) 125, 173, 186, 189
Ladakh J & K) 21
Lahaul Valley (HP) 182
Lahori, Ustad Ahmad 170
Lakshadweep Islands 23, 409, 341, 432
  climate 409
  transport 410
Lakshmibai, Rani 157
Langthabal (Man) 337
language 435, 244, 341, 345, 358, 374, 410
Le Corbusier 149
Ledo (ArP) 334
Leh (J & K) 190
  Dzomsa 190, 191
  Ecology Centre 191
  Leh Palace 191
  Old Leh 191
  Soma Gompa 191
  Tsemo Gompa 191
Lepaksi (AP) 107, 361
  Birabhadra Temple 361
  Nandi 361
Lhotse, Mount 312
Likir (J & K) 193
literature 104, 248, 440
  Mahabharata 131
Little Andaman Island (A & N) 415
Loduvra (Raj) 221
Lonavala (Mah) 264
Lothal (Guj) 230
Lucknow (UP) 125, 158
  Alambagh 159
  Bara Imambara 160
  Chowk 160
  Dilkusha 158
  Dr Ambedkar Memorial 159
  Hazratganj 159
  Hussainabad Imambara 160
  Imambara Sibtainabad 159
  Kurshid Manzil 159
  La Martinière College 159
  Residency Compound 159
  Shah Najaf Imambara 159
  Sikandarbargh 159
  Taron Wali Kothi 159
Ludhiana (Pun) 152
Lumbini (Nepal) 161
Lutyens, Sir Edwin 111, 132

M

Machilipatnam (AP) 359
Madarihat (WB) 314
Madhav National Park (MP) 272
Madhya Pradesh 241, 261, 268
  climate 269
  transport 268
Madras. See Chennai
Madras Crocodile Bank (TN) 26
Madras Crocodile Bank Trust and Centre for Herpetology (TN) 371
Madurai (TN) 106, 383
  Gandhi Memorial Museum 383
  Minakshi Sundaresvara Temple 383
  Murugan Temple 383

palace of Tirumalai Nayak 383
Mahabalesvar (Mah) 266
Mahabharata 36, 104
Mahadeo Hills (MP) 269
Mahanadi River 22
Mahaprabhu, Chaitanya 307
Maharashtra 241, 261
  transport 264
Maharishi Mahesh Yogi 175
Mahatma Gandhi Bridge (Bih) 166
Mahatma Gandhi Marine National Park (A & N) 414
Mahavira 41, 161, 167
Mahé (Ker) 405
Maheshwar (MP) 270
Mahmud of Ghazni 52
Majuli island (Assam) 330
Makalu, Mount 312
Malda (WB) 308
Malvan (Mah) 263
Mamallapuram (TN) 105, 375
  Adivaraha Temple 376
  Arjuna's Penance (Descent of the Ganges) 375
  Five Rathas 376
  Krishna Mandapam 376
  Mahisasuramardini Mandapam 376
  Shore Temple 375
  Trimurti Cave 376
  Varaha Mandapam 376
Manali (HP) 125, 173, **181**
  Dhungri Temple 181
Manas National Park (Assam) 330
Mandawa (Raj) 208
Mandi (HP) 185
  Bhutnath Temple 185
  Raj Madhan Temple 185
Mandore (Raj) 220
  Hall of Heroes 220
  Mahavira temple 220
  Osian Temple 220
  Sachiya Mata Temple 220
Mandrem (Goa) 283
Mandu (MP) 241, 272
  Bhangi Gate 272
  Hindola Mahal 273
  Jahaz Mahal 272
  Jama Masjid 273
  Nikanth Temple 273
  Reva Kund 273
Mandvi (Guj) 230
Maner (Bih) 167
  Bari Dargah 167
  Choti Dargah 167
Mangalore (Kar) 353
Manikaran (HP) 181
Manipur 324, 335, 432
Mannar National Marine Park (TN) 391
maps 430
Margao (Goa) 282
  Church of the Holy Spirit 282
  Largo da Igreja 282
  market 283
  Sat Banzam Gor 282
markets and bazaars. See also shopping
  Bara Bazaar (Shillong) 332
  Bengaluru (Kar) 346

Bidar (Kar) 352
Devaraja Market (Mysore) 349
Dilli Haat Food and Crafts Bazaar (Delhi) 140
Jyotiba Phule (Crawford) Market (Mumbai) 253
Kalimpong (WB) 314
Khan Market (Delhi) 139
Kwairamband (Imphal) 337
Lad Bazaar (Hyderabad) 356
Leh (J & K) 191
Lodi Colony Market (Delhi) 139, 140
Margao (Goa) 283
Old China Bazaar (Kolkata) 297
Paharganj Bazaar (Delhi) 132
Palika Bazaar (Delhi) 132
pearl market (Hyderabad) 356
Tiretta (Kolkata) 297
Martand Temple (J & K) 188
martial arts 336, 397
Martin, Claude 159, 300
Masrur (HP) 184
Matheran (Mah) 264
Matho (J & K) 192
Mathura (UP) 104, 156
  Dvarkadhish shrine 157
  Government Museum 104
  Kesava Deo Mandir 157
  museum 157
  Potara Kund 157
  Vishram Ghat 157
Maurya, Chandragupta 49
mausoleums. See tombs
Mawphluang (Meg) 332
Mawsynram (Meg) 332
Mayawati 81
Mayer, Albert 149
media 430
Meghalaya 331
Melghat Wildlife Sanctuary (Mah) 268
Mercury, Freddie 244
Middle Andaman Island (A & N) 415
minerals and mining 22, 320
Minicoy (Lak) 410
Mirik (WB) 312
Mistry, Rohinton 248
Mizoram 324, 337, 432
Modhera (Guj) 230
  Sun Temple 230
Modi, Narendra 82, 226
Moirang (Man) 337
  Thankgjing Temple 337
monasteries 104, 173
  Alchi (J & K) 192, 193
  Druk Thupten Sangag Choling (WB) 312
  Hemis (J & K) 192
  in Ladakh 192
  Jarasandha-ki-Baithak (Rajgir) 168
  Jetavana (Sravasti) 161
  Likir (J & K) 193
  Majuli island (Assam) 330
  Namgyal (Dharamsala) 183
  Phyang (J & K) 192
  Red Hat Ningmapa (Pemayangtse) 325
  Rizong (J & K) 193
  Rumtek (Sik) 325

Sanga Choelling (Sik) 324
Sankar (J & K) 192
Shey Gompa (Shey) 192
Spitok (J & K) 192
Tashiding Ningmapa (Sik) 325
Tawang (ArP) 334
Tharpa Choling (Kalimpong) 314
Tikse (J & K) 192
Zangdog Palrifo Brang
  (Kalimpong) 314
money matters 430
budgeting for your trip 425
money-saving tips 11
Morjim (Goa) 283
Morris, Jan 251
mosques 107
Arhai din ka Jhonpra (Ajmer) 210
Char Minar (Hyderabad) 108
Fatehpuri (Delhi) 134
Imambara (Chinsura) 307
Jama Masjid (Ahmedabad) 227
Jama Masjid (Delhi) 132, 134
Jama Masjid (Mandu) 273
Jama Masjid (Mumbai) 253
Jama Masjid (Srinagar) 188
Jami (Gulbarga) 352
Kodungallur (Ker) 404
Mecca Masjid (Hyderabad) 356
Metiaburuz Shi'ite (Kolkata) 302
Moti Masjid (Delhi) 142
Nakhoda (Kolkata) 298
Pao Mekkam (Assam) 329
Pather Masjid (Srinagar) 188
Patther-ki-Masjid (Patna) 166
Qadmam-i-Rasul (Cuttack) 319
Qutb Minar (Delhi) 52, 107
Quwwat-ul-Islam (Delhi) 142
Shah Hamadan (Srinagar) 188
Sher Shah Masjid (Patna) 166
Sidi Bashir's (Ahmedabad) 229
Sidi Saiyad's (Ahmedabad) 229
Sunehri Masjid (Delhi) 134
Mother Teresa 301
Motihari (Bih) 167
Mount Abu (Raj) 106, 217
Dilwara Jain temples 218
guided walks 217
Mountbatten, Lord Louis 67
Mount Girnar (Guj) 233
Mount Harriet (A & N) 414
Mudumalai (TN) 391
Mukhalingam (AP) 360
Mukurti National Park (TN) 391
Mumbai (Mah) 111, 241, **243**,
  262
Afghan Memorial Church 249
Bandra 256
Banganga Tank 254
Basilica of Mount Mary 256
Bhuleshwar 253
Byculla 255
Chathrapathi Shivaji Terminus
  252
Chhatrapati Shivaji Maharaj Vastu
  Sangrahalaya 109
Chowpatti Beach 253, 255
Churchgate station 252
climate 244, 245
Colaba 244, 247
Dharavi 255

Elephanta Island and Caves 105,
  244, 257
Flora Fountain 252
Fort district 244, 251
Gateway of India 244, 247
General Post Office 252
Haji Ali 255
Horniman Circle 251
Hutatma Chowk 252
Jama Masjid Mosque 253
Jehangir Art Gallery 250
Jyotiba Phule (Crawford) Market
  253
Kala Ghoda 244, 249
Kalbadevi 253
Leopold Café 248
Mahalakshmi Temple 254
Maharaja Chatrapati Sivaji
  Museum 250
maidans 250
Malabar Hill 254
Mangaldas Lane 253
Mani Bhavan 254
Marine Drive 253
Mumba Devi Temple 253
Mumbai University 250
Nariman Point 247, 253
National Centre for the Performing
  Arts 253
Panjarapool animal sanctuary
  253
Portuguese Church areas 245
Royal Asiatic Society Library 251
Salsette 245
Sassoon Docks 249
S Dr Bhau Daji Lad Museum 255
Secretariat 250
shopping 249
slums 255
Slum Tours 257
St Andrew's Church 245
street food 253, 256
St Thomas' Cathedral 252
Taj Mahal Palace and Tower 249
terrorist attacks of 2008 72
tiffin wallahs 251
transport 244, 252
Victoria Terminus 252
Mumtaz Mahal 108, 155
Munnar (Ker) 403
Murshidabad (WB) 308
Hazarduari 308
Murud (Mah) 263
museums and galleries
Academy of Fine Arts (Kolkata)
  294
Anokhi Museum of Hand Printing
  (Amber) 204
Anthropological Museum (Port
  Blair) 413
Archaeological Museum (Bhopal)
  273
archaeological museum
  (Bodhgaya) 169
Archaeological Museum (Delhi)
  138
Archaeological Museum
  (Khajuraho) 272
Archaeological Museum (Thrissur)
  405

Architecture (Chandigarh) 149
art gallery (Thanjavur) 381
Art Museum (Tanjavur) 107
Ashutosh Museum (Kolkata) 299
Bhuri Singh Museum (Chamba)
  184
Birla Academy of Art and Culture
  (Kolkata) 302
Birla Industrial and Technological
  Museum (Kolkata) 300
Birla Museum (Bhopal) 273
Calcutta Gallery (Kolkata) 294
Calico Museum of Textiles
  (Ahmedabad) 229
Central Museum (Jaipur) 203
Chhatrapati Shivaji Maharaj Vastu
  Sangrahalaya (Mumbai) 109
City Palace Museum (Jaipur) 109
Crafts Museum (Delhhi) 139
Dakshina Chitra (Muttukkadu)
  371
Dogra Art Gallery (Jammu town)
  187
Dr Ramnath A Podder Haveli
  Museum (Nawalgarh) 208
Fort St George Museum (Chennai)
  366
Gandhi Darshan (Delhi) 135
Gandhi Memorial Museum
  (Madurai) 383
Gandhi Smarak Sangrahalaya
  (Delhi) 135
Gandhi Smriti (Delhi) 138
Government Museum and Art
  Gallery(Chandigarh) 149
Government Museum (Chennai)
  107
Government Museum (Mathura)
  104
Gurusaday Museum
  (Bratacharingam) 309
Handicrafts Museum
  (Bhubaneshwar) 316
Hazarduari (Murshidabad) 308
India Museum (Kolkata) 296
Indira Gandhi Memorial Museum
  (Delhi) 138
Jawaharlal Nehru Memorial
  Museum (Delhi) 138
Jehangir Art Gallery (Mumbai) 250
Kangra Art (Dharamsala) 184
Kolkata Museum (Kolkata) 296
Krishna Menon Art Gallery and
  Museum (Kozhikode) 405
Lalit Kala Akademi (Delhi) 136
Maharaja Chatrapati Sivaji
  Museum (Mumbai) 250
Maharao Madho Singh Museum
  (Kota) 214
Mani Bhavan (Mumbai) 254
Manipur State Museum (Imphal)
  337
Mathura museum (Mathura) 157
Mizoram State Museum (Aizawl)
  337
Museum of Habitat (AP) 361
Museum of Man (Bhopal) 273
museum of sculpture (Gwalior)
  270
Nagarjunakonda Sagar (AP) 359

Napier Museum of Arts and Crafts (Thiruvananthapuram) 397
National Art Gallery (Chennai) 368
National Gallery of Modern Art (Delhi) 110, 138
National Museum (Delhi) 109, 139
National Rail Museum (Delhi) 139
Nehru Children's Museum (Kolkata) 295
Netaji Bhavan (Kolkata) 300
Nicholas Roerich gallery (Naggar) 181
Odisha State Museum (Bhubaneshwar) 316
Patna Museum (Patna) 165
Pazhassi Raja Museum (Kozhikode) 405
Raja Kelkar Museum (Pune) 265
Rajaraja Museum (Thanjavur) 381
Ramakrishna Mission Institute of Culture (Kolkata) 302
Salar Jung Museum (Hyderabad) 356
Sangeet Natak Akademi (Delhi) 136
Sanskriti Museums (Delhi) 143
Sarod Ghar (Gwalior) 271
Sawai Man Singh II Museum (Jaipur) 202
Science City (Kolkata) 303
S Dr Bhau Daji Lad Museum (Mumbai) 255
Shilpgram (Udaipur) 216
Shri Chitra Art Gallery (Thiruvananthapuram) 397
Shri Sadul Museum (Bikaner) 209
Sri Jayachamarajendra Art Gallery (Mysore) 348
Srisailam (AP) 359
State Archaeological Museum (Hyderabad) 357
State Government Museum (Chennai) 368
State Museum (Guwahati) 327
Sulabh International Museum of Toilets (Delhi) 136
Tibet House Museum (Delhi) 140
Tribal Research Centre (Udhagamandalam) 389
Tribal Research Institute and Museum (Ranchi) 320
Tribal Research Museum (Bhubaneshwar) 316
Tripura Government Museum (Agartala) 333
Wandering Monk Musum (Kanniyakumari) 383
Mussoorie (Utt) 174
Muttukkadu (TN) 371
Dakshina Chitra 371
Mysore (Kar) 348
Chamundi Hill 348
Devaraja Market 349
Karnataka Silk Industries Factory 349
palace 348
Sri Jayachamarajendra Art Gallery 348
St Philomena's Church 348

N

Naddi (HP) 183
Nadia (WB). See Nawadwip (WB)
Nagaland 324, 334, 432
Nagarhole National Park (Kar) 350
Nagarjunakonda Sagar and Dam (AP) 359
Nagercoil (TN) 385
Nagesh Temple (Goa) 285
Naggar (HP) 181
Nicholas Roerich gallery 181
Nagpur (Mah) 268
Nahan (HP) 185
Nainital (Utt) 176
Nalanda (Bih) 167
Sri Mahavihara Arya Bhikshu Sanghasya 167
University of Sri Mahavihara Arya Bhikshu Sanghasya 168
Wat Thai Nalanda 167
Nal Sarovar Bird Sanctuary (Guj) 230
Namboodiripad, E.M.S. 394
Namdapha National Park (ArP) 334
Nameri Sanctuary (Assam) 330
Nanda Devi National Park (Utt) 174
Nanda Devi (Utt) 173
Nandanakanan (Odi) 319
Naramada River (MP) 261
Narayan, J.P. 69
Narkanda (HP) 176, 179
Narmada River (MP) 273, 274
Nasik (Mah) 266
national parks and wildlife sanctuaries 10, 26, 148
Annamalai (TN) 391
Bandhavgarh (MP) 274
Bandipur (Kar) 350
Bannarghatta (Kar) 347
Corbett (Utt) 176
Dampha (Miz) 337
Dudhwa National Park (UP) 160
Eravikulam (Ker) 403
Gir Forest Reserve (Guj) 24
Hazaribagh (Jha) 320
Indravati National Park and Tiger Reserve (Cha) 275
Jaldapara (WB) 314
Kanha (MP) 274
Kaziranga (Assam) 330
Keoladeo Ghana (Raj) 28, 212
Khaziranga (Assam) 26
Kumarakom Bird Sanctuary (Ker) 401
Madhav (MP) 272
Mahatma Gandhi Marine National Park (A & N) 414
Manas (Assam) 330
Mannar National Marine Park (TN) 391
Melghat (Mah) 268
Mukurti (TN) 391
Nagarhole (Kar) 350
Nal Sarovar Bird Sanctuary (Guj) 230
Namdapha (ArP) 334
Nameri Sanctuary (Assam) 330
Nanda Devi (Utt) 174
Navegaon (Mah) 268

Nilgiri Biosphere Reserve (Kar) 349
Palamau (Jha) 320
Periyar Wildlife Sanctuary (Ker) 402
Ranthambore (Raj) 211
Sajankali (WB) 309
Sanjay Gandhi National Park (Mah) 257
Sariska Tiger Reserve (Raj) 27, 206
Sasan Gir Lion Sanctuary (Guj) 234
Simlipal (Odi) 318
Sudhanyakali (WB) 309
Sultanpur Bird Sanctuary (Har) 153
Sunderbans (WB) 22, 289, 308
Tadoba (Mah) 268
Valley of Flowers (Utt) 175
Wild Ass Sanctuary (Guj) 232
National Research Centre on Camel (Raj) 209
Naukuchiyatal (Utt) 176
Navegaon National Park (Mah) 268
Nawadwip (WB) 307
Nawalgarh (Raj) 208
Dr Ramnath A Podder Haveli Museum 208
Nehru, Jawaharlal 67, 148, 187
Neil Island (A & N) 415
Nepal, border with 161, 167, 313
newspapers and magazines 430
Nicobar Islands. See Andaman & Nicobar Islands
nightlife 431
Goa 284
Nilgiri Biosphere Reserve (Kar) 349
Nilgiri Hills 23
Norgay, Tenzing 312
North Andaman Island (A & N) 415
Northeast, The 323
entry permits 324, 335
transport 330
Northern Plains 145
North, The 125
Nowicki, Matthew 149
Nubra Valley (J & K) 193
Nurpur (HP) 185

O

Odisha 289, 305, 314
climate 314
transport 307
oil 330
Old Goa (Goa) 284
Basilica of Bom Jesus 110, 284
Chapel of St Catherine 285
Church of Our Lady of the Rosary 285
Church of St Cajetan 285
Church of St Francis of Assisi 284
Church of the Augustinian Monastery 285
Convent of St Monica 110, 285
Monte Santo 285
Sé (Cathedral of St Catherine) 110, 284

Om Beach (Kar) 354
Omkaresvar (MP) 272, 273
  Mandhata Temple 272
opening hours 431
oracles 192
Orcha (MP) 271
Orissa. *See* Odisha
Orwell, George 167

P

Pachmarhi (MP) 274
Padmanabhapuram (Ker) 397
Padmanabhapuram (TN) 387
Padum (J & K) 193
Paes, Leander 294
Pahalgam (J & K) 188
Pakistan 145
  border with 152, 187
  creation of 67
  relations with 68, 71, 84
palaces
  Agha Khan (Pune) 265
  Amar Mahal (Jammu town) 187
  Bhuj (Guj) 231
  Bundi (Raj) 213
  Chogyal's (Gangtok) 325
  City Palace (Alwar) 205
  City Palace (Jaipur) 202
  City Palace (Kota) 214
  City Palace (Udaipur) 215
  Daria Daulat (Srirangapatnam)
    349
  Daulat Khana (Ajmer) 210
  Deeg (Raj) 206
  Falaknuma (Hyderabad) 356
  Hawa Mahal (Wadhwan) 235
  Hindola Mahal (Mandu) 273
  Jag Mandir (Udaipur) 216
  Jag Niwas (Udaipur) 216
  Jahaz Mahal (Mandu) 272
  Jai Vilas (Gwalior) 270
  Lakhota (Jamnagar) 232
  Lakshmi Vilas (Vadodara) 235
  Lalgarh (Bikaner) 209
  Leh (J & K) 191
  Marble Palace (Kolkata) 299
  Matancherry (Kochi) 404
  Mysore (Kar) 348
  Narsing Dev (Datia) 271
  New (Kolhapur) 266
  Padmanabhapuram (TN) 387
  Palace of the Maharawal
    (Jaisalmer) 221
  Pushbanta (Agartala) 333
  Puttan Malika
    (Thiruvananthapuram) 396
  Raj Bhavan (Kolkata) 296
  Raj Wada (Kolhapur) 266
  Rani ki Mahal (Jaisalmer) 221
  Sajjangarh (Udaipur) 216
  Shanivarvada (Pune) 265
  Shey (J & K) 192
  Stok (J & K) 192
  Thanjavur (TN) 380
  Tipu Sultan's (Bengaluru) 347
  Ujjayanta (Agartala) 333
  Umaid Bhavan (Jodhpur) 219
Palai (Ker) 401
Palakkad Gap (Ker) 404

Palamau National Park (Jha) 320
Palani Hills 23
Palitana (Guj) 235
Palolem (Goa) 284
Panaji (Goa) 281
  Church of the Immaculate
    Conception 281
  Fontainahas 281
  Largo da Igreja 281
  Menezes-Braganza Institute 282
  Secretariat 281
Panchgani (Mah) 266
Panch Ghagh waterfall (Jha) 320
Pandim, Mount 312
Pandua (WB) 308
Pangong Tso (J & K) 193
Panipat (Har) 148
Pao Mekkam mosque (Assam) 329
Paonta Sahib (HP) 185
paragliding 182
Parasnath Hill (Jha) 320
parks and gardens. *See
  also* amusement parks, national
  park and wildlife sanctuaries
  Bagh-e-Aam (Hyderabad) 357
  Botanical Garden
    (Nandanakanan) 319
  Botanical Garden (Shillong) 332
  Botanical Gardens (Hyderabad)
    357
  Botanical Gardens (Kolkata) 302
  Botanical Gardens
    (Udhagamandalam) 389
  Bryant Gardens (Kodaikanal) 390
  Chasma Shahi (Srinagar) 188
  Cubbon Park (Bengaluru) 346
  Deer Park (Gangtok) 325
  Garden of the Five Senses (Delhi)
    143
  Harwan (Srinagar) 188
  Lalbagh Botanical Gardens
    (Bengaluru) 346
  Lloyd Botanical Gardens
    (Darjeeling) 312
  Lodi Gardens (Delhi) 132, 139
  Maidan (Kolkata) 294
  maidans (Mumbai) 250
  Nishat (Srinagar) 188
  Orchid Sanctuary (Gangtok) 325
  Pinjore Gardens (Har) 147
  Qudsia Bagh (Delhi) 133
  Rambagh (Agra) 155
  Rock Garden (Chandigarh) 150
  Rose Garden (Chandigarh) 149
  Shalimar (Srinagar) 188
  Sikandarbargh (Lucknow) 159
  Thread Garden
    (Udhagamandalam) 389
  Venuvana (Rajgir) 168
Parsis 248
Parthasarathi Temple (Ker) 400
Parvati Valley (HP) 181
Patel, Sardar Vallabhai 82
Patiala (Pun) 152
Patna (Bih) 165
  Bankipur 165
  Didarganji Yakshi 165
  Golghar 165
  Gulzaribagh 166
  Haramandirji 166

  High Court 165
  Khuda Baksh Oriental Library 166
  Kumhrar 166
  Maharaja's Palace 165
  Padri-ki-Haveli (St Mary's Church)
    166
  Pataliputra 166
  Patna Museum 165
  Patna Women's College 165
  Patther-ki-Masjid 166
  Qila House 166
  Raj Bhavan 165
  Sher Shah Masjid 166
Pattadakal (Kar) 106, 351
Paunar (Mah) 268
Pelling (Sik) 324
Pemayangtse (Sik) 324, 325
  Red Hat Ningmapa Monastery
    325
people
  Adivasi 34, 269, 275, 289, 319,
    331, 411
  Andamese 412
  Armenians 298, 307
  Chinese 297
  Kolis 247
  Nepalis 324
  Parsis 248, 254
  Tibeto-Burmese 334, 335
  Todas 387, 388
Periyar Wildlife Sanctuary (Ker)
  402
Phalgu River 168
Phalut, Mount 313
photography 427, 431
Phyang (J & K) 192
Pinjore Gardens (Har) 147
Pipli (Odi) 317
Piprahwa (UP) 161
plantlife 29
  hardwood forests 22, 269
  mangrove jungle 309
  of the Southern Ghats 387
  of the Western Ghats 402
  orchids 289, 325
  sandalwood 345
  tropical rainforests 22, 343, 391
Pochampalli (T) 358
Point Calimere (TN) 391
politics and government 64, 155.
  See also economy
  Bahujan Samaj Party 81
  Bengali Party 293
  Bharatiya Janata Party 71
  Communist Party of India 80
  constitution 68
  corruption 69, 70, 71, 73, 78,
    155, 156, 164, 167
  Indian Administrative Service 174
  in Kerala 394
  in Kolkata 293
  in Tamil Nadu 373
  Janata Party 70
  Left Front Party 293
  National Front Party 70
  of Gujarat 226
  Shiv Sena Party 243, 255
  socialism 69
  Trinamool Congress 293
polo 294

Ponmudi (Ker) 397
population
Delhi 129
Karnataka 345
Kolkata (WB) 293
Mumbai (Mah) 244
Uttar Pradesh 153
Porbandar (Guj) 233
Port Blair (A & N) 413
Anthropological Museum 413
Cellular Jail 413
postal and courier services 431
Pragpur (HP) 184
Prasad, Rajendra 82
Premiji, Azim 81
Prinsep, James 232
public holidays 432
Puducherry (TN) 377, 379
Raj Nivas 379
Sacred Heart Church 379
Pune (Mah) 241, 264
Agha Khan Palace 265
Osho International Meditation
Resort 266
Parvati Temple 265
Qamarali Darvesh 265
Raja Kelkar Museum 265
Shanivarvada 265
Shinde Chatri 265
Temple of Patalesvar 265
Punjab 69, 145
climate 22
history 70
transport 147
Puri (Odi) 106, 289, 305, 317
Jagannath Temple 317
Pushkar (Raj) 210
Puttaparthi (AP) 361

R

Radcliffe, Sir Cyril 67
Radhanagar beach (A & N) 415
radio stations 430
Rahman, A.R. 100
rail travel 222, 420
development of 245
international 418
Konkan Railway 263, 280, 353
luxury rail tours 223, 422
rail passes 422
to/from Andhra Pradesh 360
to/from Bihar 164
to/from Chennai (TN) 366
to/from Delhi 130
to/from Goa 280
to/from Gujarat 226
to/from Karnataka 346
to/from Kerala 395
to/from Kolkata (WB) 293
to/from Madhya Pradesh 268
to/from Maharashtra 264
to/from Mumbai (Mah) 244
to/from Punjab & Haryana 147
to/from Rajasthan 202
postal Tamil Nadu 375
to/from Telangana 354
to/from The Northeast 330
to/from Uttarakhand 175
to/from Uttar Pradesh 154

to/from West Bengal, Odisha and
Jharkhand 307
to Khajuraho (MP) 276
rail travel, scenic and heritage
lines 178
Blue Mountain Railway (TN) 389
Darjeeling Himalayan Railway
(WB) 311
Kalka–Simla 177
to Darjeeling (WB) 289
Raipur (Cha) 274
Rajasthan 197, 22
history 201
transport 202
Rajgir (Bih) 167
Ajatasatru Fort 168
Gridhrakuta Hill 168
Jarasandha-ki-Baithak monastery
168
Jivakamhavana 168
Karanda Tank 168
Maddakuchchi 168
Manyar Math 168
Pippla Cave 168
Ratna Giri 168
Saptaparni cave 168
Venuvana 168
Vishva Shanti (World Peace)
Stupa 168
Rajrappa (Jha) 320
Rama 160, 167, 377
Ramachandran, M.G. 98, 367, 373
Ramakrishna 306
birthplace 310
Ramappa Temple (T) 358
Ramayana 37, 104, 160, 163, 266
Rameswaram Island (TN) 377
Ramalingesvara Temple 377
Ramanatasvami Temple 378
Rampur (HP) 179
Ramtek temple (Mah) 268
Ranakpur (Raj) 106
Ranakpur temple complex (Raj)
217
Ranchi (Jha) 320
Eastern Railway Hotel 320
Lutheran Church 320
Shiva Temple 320
St Paul's Anglican Church 320
Tribal Research Institute and
Museum 320
Ranikhet (Utt) 176
Ranns of Kutch (Guj) 22, 197, 231
Ranthambore National Park (Raj)
211
Rao Hamir (Raj) 211
Rao, P.V. Narasimha 70
Ratnagiri (Odi) 317
Ray, Satyajit 293, 295
Razaq, Abdul 362
Rekong Peo (HP) 180
religion 19, 33, 49, 169, 314
Brahmins 32, 49, 373
Buddhism 40, 50, 154, 164, 173,
177, 183, 192
Christianity 51, 280
devotional music 96
Hinduism 33, 35, 83, 156, 160,
161, 162, 173
in Kerala 394

in politics 82
Islam 38, 52, 154
Jainism 41, 50, 164
Kashmiri Pandits 187
mythology 37
Nipponzan Myohoji movement
168
religious tensions 226
Sikhism 38, 39, 166
sun worship 318
Zoroastrian faith 248
Renuka (HP) 186
restaurants 90
restricted areas 179, 409, 411,
432
Rice, Clifford 403
rickshaws and tongas 423
Rishikesh (Utt) 175
Muni-ki-Reti 175
Rizong (J & K) 193
Roerich, Nicholas 181
Roe, Sir Thomas 273
Rohtang Pass (HP) 182
Ross Island (A & N) 414
Ross, Sir Ronald 294
Roy, Arundhati 401, 401
Roy, Jamini 293
Ruantlang (Miz) 337
rugby 294
Calcutta Cup 294
Rumtek Monastery (Sik) 325
Rushikonda (AP) 360

S

Sabarimala (Ker) 396
Sagardwip (WB) 310
Kapil Muni Temple 310
Sai Baba 361
Sai Baba Ashram (Kar) 348
Sajankali sanctuary (WB) 309
salt tax 64, 311
Samode (Raj) 205
Sam (Raj) 221
Sanchi (MP) 103, 273
Sandakphu (WB) 313
Sanga Choelling Monastery (Sik)
324
Sanganer (Raj) 204
Sangla (HP) 180
Sanjay Gandhi National Park
(Mah) 257
Sankar (J & K) 192
Sardar Sarovar dam (MP) 273
Sariska Tiger Reserve (Raj) 27,
206
Sarnath (UP) 163
Dhamekh Stupa 164
Sasan Gir Lion Sanctuary (Guj)
234
Sasaram (Bih) 167
Sher Shah's Mausoleum 167
Saspul (J & K) 193
sati 208
Saurashtra (Guj) 225, 232
Sawai Madhopur (Raj) 211
science and technology 70, 346
Secunderabad. See Hyderabad-
Secunderabad
Sela Pass (ArP) 334

Serampore (WB) 306
  Serampore College 306
  St Olaf's Church 306
Sevagram (Mah) 268
Shah Jahan, Emperor 55, 107,
  109, 129, 132, 133, 155, 154
Shanghvi, Dilip 81
Shanta-Durga Temple (Goa) 285
Shantiniketan (WB) 310
Shatrunjaya Hill (Guj) 235
Shekhavati (Raj) 207
Sher Shah 132
Shey (J & K) 192
  Shey Gompa 192
Shillong (Meg) 331
  Bara Bazaar 332
  Botanical Garden 332
  Pinewood Hotel 332
  Raj Bhavan 332
  Ward Lake 332
Shillong Peak (Meg) 331, 332
Shiva 162, 381
Shivaji Maharaj 263
Shivpuri (MP) 271
Shoja (HP) 181
shopping 432. See also markets
  and bazaars
  crafts 133, 139, 140
  designer fashions 139
  gems and jewellery 202, 356,
    370, 432
  handicrafts 249, 432
  what to buy 432
Shri Naina Devi Temple (HP) 185
Sibsagar (Assam) 329
Sidhudurg Fort (Mah) 263
Sikandra (UP) 156
Sikkim 289, 323, 432
Simhachalam (AP) 360
Simla (HP) 177
  Jakhu Temple 179
  restaurants 180
Simlipal National Park (Odi) 318
Singh, Govind 152, 166
Singh, Maharaja Ranjit 151
Singh, Manmohan 72
Singh, V.P. 70
Sinhagad Fort (Mah) 265, 267
Sinquerim (Goa) 282
Sipra River (MP) 272
Sirhind (Pun) 152
Sirpur (Cha) 274
Sisters of Charity 301
Skinner, James 135
Snake Park (TN) 371
social issues 77
  child labour 79
  discrimination 31, 64, 319
  literacy 78
  poverty 72, 73, 243, 255, 319
  sanitation 79
  wealth gap 78, 81, 345
  women's status 73, 85
society 31, 51
  caste system 31, 155, 164, 248
  family life 33
  funerary rituals 162, 254
  marriage 33, 68
  women's status 68, 394
Solang (HP) 176, 182

Somnath (Guj) 233
Somnathpur (Kar) 349, 350
  Keshava Vishnu Temple 349, 350
Sonamarg (J & K) 189
Sonepur (Bih) 167
Southern Ghats 345, 387
South, The 341
space programme 81
Spiti Valley (HP) 182
Spitok (J & K) 192
sports 130, 294. See also by name
Sravanabelagola (Kar) 350
Sravasti (UP) 161
  Jetavana monastery 161
Sri Aurobindo 379
Sri Aurobindo Ashram (TN) 379
Sri Kalahasti (AP) 361
Sri Mangesh Temple (Goa) 285
Srinagar (J & K) 175, 188
  Chasma Shahi garden 188
  Harwan garden 188
  Hazratbal shrine 188
  Jama Masjid 188
  Nishat garden 188
  Pather Masjid 188
  Shah Hamadan Mosque 188
  Shalimar garden 188
Sri Narayana Guru 398
Sringeri (Kar) 350
Srirangam (TN) 106, 383
  Sriranganathasvami Temple 383
Srirangapatnam (Kar) 349
  Daria Daulat 349
  Gumbaz Mausoleum 349
Srisailam (AP) 359
Stagna (J & K) 192
St Alphonsa of India 401
step wells
  Adalaj Vav (Guj) 230
  Dad Hari-ni-Vav (Guj) 229
  Raniji-ki-Baori (Bundi) 214
St Francis Xavier 284, 285
Stok Palace (J & K) 192
St Thomas 52, 370
Suchindram (TN) 385
Sudhanyakali sanctuary (WB) 309
Sullivan, John 388
Sultanpur Bird Sanctuary (Har)
  153
Sunderbans National Park (WB)
  22, 289, 308
Suraj Kund (Har) 147
Surat (Guj) 236
  British cemetery 236
Surendranager (Guj) 235
**Swami Vivekananda memorial
  (TN)** 385
synagogues
  Magen David (Kolkata) 297
  Pardesi (Kochi) 404

T

Tabo (HP) 183
Tadoba (Mah) 268
Tadpatri (AP) 361
  Ramalingesvara Temple 361
  Venkataramana Temple 361
Tagore, Rabindranath 293, 298,
  306, 310

Taj Heritage Corridor (UP) 155,
  156
Tamil Nadu 23, 365
  climate 366
  transport 375
Tanjavur (TN) 106
  Art Museum 107
Tansen 270, 272
Tapti River (MP) 261
Tarakeshwar Temple (WB) 310
Tarapith (WB) 311
**Tashiding Ningmapa Monastery
  (Sik)** 325
Tata, J.N. 249
Tata, Sir Jamshedji 320
Tawang (ArP) 334
taxis
  car with driver services 420
  Delhi 133
  prepaid taxis 420
technology. See science and
  technology
Telangana 354
  transport 354
Telengana plateau 22
telephones 432
television 100, 430
temples 9, 51
  Adivaraha (Mamallapuram) 376
  Airavatesvara (Darasuram) 382
  Ajanta (Mah) 267
  Akshardham (Delhi) 103, 143
  Amba Mata (Guj) 234
  at Chamba 184
  at Jagesvar (Utt) 176
  at Kangra (HP) 184
  at Khajuraho (MP) 272
  at Sirpur (Cha) 274
  at Vrindavan (UP) 157
  Baha'i Lotus (Delhi) 141
  Bangla Sahib Gurudwara (Delhi)
    133
  Bedsa (Mah) 264
  Benimadhava (Tribeni) 307
  Bhaja (Mah) 264
  Bhojpur (Bhopal) 273
  Bhutnath (Mandi) 185
  Bijli Mahadeva (HP) 180
  Birla Venkatesvara (Hyderabad)
    357
  Brihadesvara
    (Gangaikondacholapuram) 382
  Brihadesvara (Thanjavur) 380
  Channekeshava (Belur) 350
  Chattarpur (Delhhi) 143
  Chennakesavara (Chennai) 369
  Chennammallikesvara (Chennai)
    369
  Chidambaram (TN) 380
  Chottanikkara (Ker) 404
  Dhungri (Manali) 181
  Digambara (Delhi) 134
  Dilwara Jain temples (Mount Abu)
    218
  Durga (Aihole) 351
  Durgiana (Amritsar) 152
  Dvarkadish (Dwarka) 232
  Ekambaresvara (Kanchipuram)
    379
  Ellora (Mah) 267

Ghrusnesvar (Mah) 267
Golden (Amritsar) 70, 109, 147, 150
Hangsesvari (Bansberia) 307
Hanuman Chatti (Yamunotri) 175
Hanumangarhi (Ayodhya) 160
Hanuman Mandir (Delhi) 133
Hoysaleswara (Halebid) 350
ISKCON Sri Radha Krishna Mandir (Bengaluru) 347
Jagannath (Puri) 317
Jagdish (Udaipur) 216
Jain temple (Kolkata) 297
Jakhu (Simla) 179
Jor Bangla (Visnupur) 310
Kailasanatha (Kanchipuram) 379
Kalachand Sri Mandir (Visnupur) 310
Kali Bhavatarini (Dakshinesvar) 306
Kali (Kolkata) 301
Kamakhya Mandir (Guwahati) 329
Kanakadurga (Vijayawada) 359
Kapelesvara Shiva (Chennai) 369
Kapil Muni (Sagardwip) 310
Karla (Mah) 264
Keshava Vishnu (Somnathpur) 349, 350
Konark Sun (Odi) 289
Kotiteerth (Kolhapur) 266
Krishna (Guruvayur) 405
Krishna Paratasaraty (Chennai) 370
Lad Khen (Aihole) 351
Lakshmi Narayan (Bilaspur) 185
Lakshmi Narayan (Delhi) 133
Lingaraj (Bhubaneshwar) 315
Lord Venkatesvara (Tirupati) 361
Madan Gopal (Visnupur) 310
Madan Mohan (Visnupur) 310
Mahabaleshwar (Gokarna) 354
Mahabodhi (Bodhgaya) 169
Mahakalesvar (Ujjain) 272
Mahalakshmi (Mumbai) 254
Mahalaksmi (Kolhapur) 266
Mahavira (Mandore) 220
Mandhata (Omkaresvar) 272
Martand (J & K) 188
Minakshi Sundaresvara (Madurai) 383
Monkey (Galta) 204
monkey (Varanasi) 163
Muktesvara (Bhubaneshwar) 316
Mumba Devi (Mumbai) 253
Murugan (Madurai) 383
Nagesh (Goa) 285
Narsingh Bhagwan (Joshimath) 175
Nasiyan Jain Temple (Ajmer) 210
Navagraha Mandir (Guwahati) 327
Nikanth (Mandu) 273
Nipponzan Myohoji (Rajgir) 168
on Parasnath Hill (Jha) 320
Osian (Mandore) 220
Parasnath Mandir (Kolkata) 299
Parasuramesvar (Bhubaneshwar) 315
Parvati (Pune) 265

Patalesvar (Pune) 265
Radheshyam (Bilaspur) 185
Raghunath (Jammu town) 187
Rajarani (Bhubaneshwar) 316
Raj Madhan (Mandi) 185
Ramalingesvara (Rameswaram Island) 377
Ramalingesvara (Tadpatri) 361
Ramanatasvami (Rameswaram Island) 378
Ramappa (T) 358
Ramtek (Mah) 268
Ranakpur (Raj) 217
Ranbireshwar (Jammu town) 187
Rani Sati (Jhunjhunu) 208
rock-cut temples (Ellora) 258
rock-cut temples (Masrur) 184
Sachiya Mata (Mandore) 220
Sas Bahu (Gwalior) 270
Shanta-Durga (Goa) 285
Shatrunjaya Hill (Guj) 235
Shinde Chatri (Pune) 265
Shiva (Ranchi) 320
Shore (Mamallapuram) 375
Shri Naina Devi (HP) 185
Shyam Rai Mandir (Visnupur) 310
Siddhesvara (Bhubaneshwar) 316
Sisiresvara (Bhubaneshwar) 315
Sispganj Gurudwara (Delhi) 134
Sri Kalahasti (AP) 361
Sri Mangesh (Goa) 285
Sri Padmanabhasvami (Thiruvananthapuram) 396
Sri Ramakrishna (Belur Math) 306
Sriranganathasvami (Srirangam) 383
Sukhlesvar Janardhan (Guwahati) 327
Sun (Konark) 318
Sun (Modhera) 230
Suraj Kund (Har) 147
Tarakeshwar (WB) 310
Teli-ka-Mandir (Gwalior) 270
temple towns (TN) 378
Thankgjing (Moirang) 337
Tiruvannamalai (TN) 379
Trimbakesvar (Trimbakesvar) 267
Tripura Sundari (Udaipur) 333
Uttaresvara (Bhubaneshwar) 315
Vadakkunnatham (Thrissor) 404
Vaital Deul (Bhubaneshwar) 315
Vasudeva (Bansberia) 307
Venkataramana (Tadpatri) 361
Virabhadra (Lepaksi) 361
Vishvanath (Varanasi) 163
Visnupada (Gaya) 168
Wat Thai Nalanda (Nalanda) 167
Yiga Cholang Gelugpa (Ghoom) 313
tennis 294, 302
Tezpur (Assam) 329
Thackeray, Bal 243
Thanjavur (Tanjore) (TN) 380
art gallery 381
Brihadesvara Temple 380
palace 380
Rajaraja Museum 381
Saraswathi Mahal Library 381
Thar Desert (Raj) 22, 197, 200, 221

theatres and performance venues
Cochin Cultural Centre (Kochi) 395
India Habitat Centre (Delhi) 142
India International Centre (Delhi) 142
Indira Gandhi National Centre for the Arts (Delhi) 137
Kamani Auditorium (Delhi) 142
Kathakali Centre (Kochi) 395
Krishna Gana Sabha (Chennai) 369
Music Academy (Chennai) 369
National Centre for the Performing Arts (Mumbai) 253
Rabindra Kala Sangam (Delhi) 136
Rabindra Sadan (Kolkata) 294
Sangeet Natak Akademi (Delhi) 142
Thiruvalluvar, image of (TN) 384
Thiruvananthapuram (Ker) 393, 396
Margi School 396
Napier Museum of Arts and Crafts 397
Puttan Malika Palace 396
Shri Chitra Art Gallery 397
Sri Padmanabhasvami Temple 396
Thrissur (Ker) 404
Archaeological Museum 405
Vadakkunnatham Temple 404
Tibet
border with 179
Tibetan Government in Exile 183
Tiger Hill (WB) 312
Tikse (J & K) 192
time zone 414, 433
Timur (Tamburlaine) 53
tipping 433
Tipu Sultan 349
Tirathgarh Falls (Cha) 275
Tiruchirapalli (TN) 382
Tirunelveli (TN) 385
Tirupati (AP) 361
Lord Venkatesvara Temple 361
Tiruvannamalai (TN) 379
Tiruvarur (TN) 381
Tod, James 215, 220
toilets 433
tombs 107
Ahmed Shah I (Ahmedabad) 227
Aurangzeb (Khuldabad) 267
Bari Dargah (Maner) 167
Bhulbhulaiyan (Delhhi) 142
Bibi ka Maqbara (Aurangabad) 267
Chini ka Rauza (Agra) 155
Choti Dargah (Maner) 167
Dargah Sharif (Ajmer) 210
Ghaus Muhammad's mausoleum (Gwalior) 271
Gol Gumbaz (Bijapur) 108, 352
Gumbaz Mausoleum (Srirangapatnam) 349
Haji Ali (Mumbai) 255
Hauz-i-Shamsi (Delhi) 142
Humayun (Delhi) 108, 140
Ibrahim Rauza (Bijapur) 108, 352

Itimad-ud-Daula (Agra) 155
Jamali Kamali (Delhi) 142
Muhammad Shah (Delhi) 139
Nila Gumbad (Delhi) 140
Qutb Shahi tombs (Hyderabad) 357
Safdarjang (Delhi) 140
Saiyid Muhammad Husaini Gisu
  Daras (Gulbarga) 352
Sheikh Nizamuddin Aulia 140
Sher Shah's Mausoleum
  (Sasaram) 167
Sikandra (UP) 156
Taj Mahal (Agra) 55, 108, 109,
  155, 156
Tansen (Gwalior) 270
tourist information 433
tours
  camel treks 197, 209, 220, 221
Tranquebar (TN) 377
transport 418
trekking and hiking 431
  Himalayas 175, 180, 183, 193
  Karnataka 350
  Kerala 397
  Madhya Pradesh 275
  Sikkim 325
  Tamil Nadu 390
  West Bengal 313
Tribeni (WB) 307
  Benimadhava Temple 307
  Darya Zafar Khan 307
Trimbakesvar (Mah) 266
  Trimbakesvar Temple 267
Tripura 332
Tso Moriri (J & K) 193
Tura (Meg) 332
Tuticorin (TN) 385

U

Udaipur (Raj) 214, 333
  Bagore-ki-Haveli 216
  City Palace 215
  Jagdish Temple 216
  Jag Mandir 216
  Jag Niwas 216
  Sajjangarh 216
  Shilpgram 216
  Tripura Sundari temple 333
Udayagiri (Odi) 316
Udaygir (MP) 274
Udhagamandalam (TN) 388
  Botanical Gardens 389
  Thread Garden 389
  Tribal Research Centre 389
Udupi (Kar) 353
Ujjain (MP) 272
  Mahakalesvar Temple 272
Unesco sites 103
  Airavatesvara Temple (Darasuram)
    382
  Ajanta (Mah) 258
  Blue Mountain Railway (TN) 389
  Brihadesvara Temple
    (Gangaikondacholapuram) 382
  Champaner (Guj) 236
  Darjeeling Himalayan Railway
    (WB) 311
  Hampi (Kar) 351
  Humayun's Tomb (Delhi) 108, 140

Khajuraho (MP) 272
Nanda Devi National Park (Utt)
  174
Qutb Minar Complex (Delhi) 142
Sanchi (MP) 273
Shore Temple (Mamallapuram)
  375
Sunderbans (WB) 308
Taj Mahal (Agra) 55, 108, 109,
  156
Thanjavur (Tanjore) (TN) 380
Uttarakhand 173
Uttar Pradesh 125, 145, **153**

V

Vadodara (Guj) 235
  Lakshmi Vilas Palace 235
Vagator (Goa) 283
Vaishali (Bih) 167
Vajpayee, Atal Bihari 71
Valley of Flowers National Park
  (Utt) 175
Varanasi (UP) 125, 162
  monkey temple 163
  Ramnagar 163
  Sankat Mochan 163
  Vishvanath Temple 163
Varkala (Ker) 399
Varma, Raja Ravi 397
Vasai (Mah) 245
Vashisht (HP) 182
Vedanthangal (TN) 391
Vellore (TN) 379
Vembanad Lake (Ker) 401
Verinag (J & K) 188
Vidisha (MP) 274
Vijayawada (AP) 359
  Kanakadurga Temple 359
Vijaydurg (Mah) 263
Viper Island (A & N) 413
visas and passports 434
Vishakapatnam (AP) 359
Vishnu 168, 175
Visnupur (WB) 310
  Dalmadal 310
  Jor Bangla 310
  Kalachand Sri Mandir 310
  Madan Gopal 310
  Madan Mohan 310
  Rashmancha 310
  Shyam Rai Mandir 310
Vizhinjam (Ker) 398
Vrindavan (UP) 157
Vypeen Island (Ker) 403

W

Wadhwan (Guj) 235
  Hawa Mahal 235
Waltair (AP) 359
Warangal (T) 358
Wardha (Mah) 268
water 434
waterfalls
  Chitrakut (Cha) 275
  Dassam (Jha) 320
  Dhuandhar Falls (MP) 274
  Hirni (Jha) 320
  Hundru (Jha) 320

Jog (Kar) 354
Johna (Jha) 320
Panch Ghagh (Jha) 320
Tirathgarh (Cha) 275
Waynad (Ker) 405
websites 433
weights and measures 434
West Bengal 80, 305
  transport 307
Western Ghats 22, 23, 241, 343,
  394, 402
Wheeler, Mortimer 377
whitewater rafting 431
Wild Ass Sanctuary (Guj) 232
wildlife 24. See also birdlife,
  national parks and wildlife
  sanctuaries
  Asiatic lions 24, 197, 234
  bears 24
  camels 193
  conservation 26
  crocodiles 26, 27, 268, 309
  deer and antelopes 28
  elephants 22, 25, 27, 332, 345
  game tourism 29
  Hullock gibbons 332
  Indian wild ass 232
  leopards 24, 269
  marine life 391, 411
  monkeys 179
  of Tamil Nadu 391
  of the Southern Ghats 387
  Project Elephant 26
  Project Tiger 26, 320
  rhinoceroses 25, 26, 330
  river dolphins 28, 165
  sea turtles 29, 317
  snakes 27
  tigers 24, 25, 27, 197, 206, 211,
    269, 270, 309, 332
Willingdon Island (Ker) 403
winter sports 175, 176, 179, 182,
  189
women travellers 434

Y

Yakshun (Sik) 325
Yamuna, River 161, 173
  source of 175
Yamunotri (Utt) 175
  Hanuman Chatti 175
Yercaud (TN) 390
yoga 386

Z

Zanskar (J & K) 193
zoos
  Darjeeling (WB) 312
  Delhi Zoo 138
  Guindy Deer Park (TN) 371
  Madras Crocodile Bank (TN) 26
  Madras Crocodile Bank Trust and
    Centre for Herpetology (TN) 371
  Nandanakanan (Odi) 319
  Nehru Zoological Park
    (Hyderabad) 357
  Snake Park (TN) 371
  Zoological Gardens (Kolkata) 301

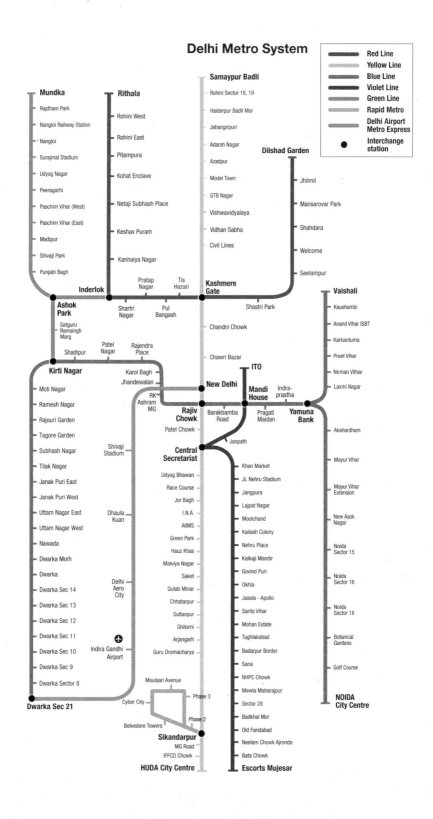

Delhi Metro System

Red Line ████
Yellow Line ████
Blue Line ████
Violet Line ████
Green Line ████
Rapid Metro ████
Delhi Airport Metro Express ████
● **Interchange station**

Mundka
- Rajdhani Park
- Nangloi Railway Station
- Nangloi
- Surajmal Stadium
- Udyog Nagar
- Peeragarhi
- Paschim Vihar (West)
- Paschim Vihar (East)
- Madipur
- Shivaji Park
- Punjabi Bagh

Rithala
- Rohini West
- Rohini East
- Pitampura
- Kohat Enclave
- Netaji Subhash Place
- Keshav Puram
- Kanhaiya Nagar

Samaypur Badli
- Rohini Sector 18, 19
- Haiderpur Badli Mor
- Jahangirpuri
- Adarsh Nagar
- Azadpur
- Model Town
- GTB Nagar
- Vishwavidyalaya
- Vidhan Sabha
- Civil Lines

Dilshad Garden
- Jhilmil
- Mansarovar Park
- Shahdara
- Welcome
- Seelampur

Inderlok
Ashok Park
- Satguru Ramsingh Marg

Pratap Nagar · Tis Hazari
Kashmere Gate

Vaishali
- Kaushambi
- Anand Vihar ISBT
- Karkarduma
- Preet Vihar
- Nirman Vithar
- Laxmi Nagar

Shartri Nagar · Pul Bangash
Shastri Park

- Chandni Chowk

Patel Nagar · Rajendra Place
Shadipur

- Chawri Bazar

Kirti Nagar
- Moti Nagar
- Ramesh Nagar
- Rajouri Garden
- Tagore Garden
- Subhash Nagar
- Tilak Nagar
- Janak Puri East
- Janak Puri West
- Uttam Nagar East
- Uttam Nagar West
- Nawada
- Dwarka Morh
- Dwarka
- Dwarka Sec 14
- Dwarka Sec 13
- Dwarka Sec 12
- Dwarka Sec 11
- Dwarka Sec 10
- Dwarka Sec 9
- Dwarka Sector 8

Dwarka Sec 21

Karol Bagh
Jhandewalan
RK Ashram MG

ITO
New Delhi
Mandi House
Indra-prastha

Rajiv Chowk
Barakhamba Road · Pragati Maidan
Yamuna Bank

Patel Chowk
Janpath

Shivaji Stadium

Central Secretariat
- Udyog Bhawan
- Race Course
- Jor Bagh
- I.N.A.
- AIIMS
- Green Park
- Hauz Khas
- Malviya Nagar
- Saket
- Qutab Minar
- Chhatarpur
- Sultanpur
- Ghitorni
- Arjangarh
- Guru Dromacharya

Dhaula Kuan

Delhi Aero City

✈ Indira Gandhi Airport

- Khan Market
- JL Nehru Stadium
- Jangpura
- Lajpat Nagar
- Moolchand
- Kailash Colony
- Nehru Place
- Kalkaji Mandir
- Govind Puri
- Okhla
- Jasola - Apollo
- Sarita Vihar
- Mohan Estate
- Tughlakabad
- Badarpur Border
- Sarai
- NHPC Chowk
- Mewla Maharajpur
- Sector 28
- Badkhal Mor
- Old Faridabad
- Neelam Chowk Ajronda
- Bata Chowk

Escorts Mujesar

- Akshardham
- Mayur Vihar
- Mayur Vihar Extension
- New Asok Nagar
- Noida Sector 15
- Noida Sector 16
- Noida Sector 18
- Botanical Gardens
- Golf Course

NOIDA City Centre

Moulsari Avenue
Phase 3
Cyber City
Phase 2
Belvedere Towers

Sikandarpur
MG Road
IFFCO Chowk

HUDA City Centre